The Art of Watching Films

The Art of Watching Films

FIFTH EDITION

Joseph M. Boggs
Western Kentucky University

Dennis W. Petrie
Tri-State University

Mayfield Publishing Company
Mountain View, California
London • Toronto

Library of Congress Cataloging-in-Publication Data

Boggs, Joseph M.
The art of watching films / Joseph M. Boggs, Dennis W. Petrie. — 5th ed.
p. cm.
Includes bibliographical references and index.
ISBN 0-7674-0532-3
1. Film criticism. I. Petrie, Dennis W. II. Title.
PN1995.B525 1999
791.43'01'5—dc21 99-22859
CIP

Manufactured in the United States of America
10 9 8 7 6 5 4 3 2 1

Mayfield Publishing Company
1280 Villa Street
Mountain View, CA 94041

Sponsoring editor, Janet M. Beatty; production editor, Melissa Williams Kreischer; manuscript editor, Jennifer Gordon; design manager, Jean Mailander; text designer, Ellen Pettengell; cover designer, Susan Breitbard; art editor, Amy Folden; photo researcher, Brian Pecko; manufacturing manager, Randy Hurst. The text was set in 10.5/13 Janson by Thompson Type and printed on acid-free 45# Somerset Matte by R. R. Donnelley & Sons Company.

For
Elizabeth Petrie Gill
and
Robert D. Briles

Preface

The teaching of film has changed tremendously since the first edition of this book was published in 1978. At that time, film appreciation was generally taught by means of a 16mm projector in the classroom, and the films that students could study were limited to what they could see in local theaters or on network television. Since then, technology and cable revolutions have changed our options. VCRs and laserdisc players have made watching films an incredibly easy, enjoyable, and rewarding experience. And now, new DVD compression technology allows for the dissemination of more kinds of video information than ever before—and all of it is presented on a widely available disc the size of an audio CD with a sharpness that may be twice that of the videocassette. The DVD's greater storage capacity accommodates space for both widescreen and full-screen versions of films, in addition to a full menu of language, dubbing, and subtitling options. The DVD's additional tracks can introduce commentaries by directors, actors, writers, editors, cinematographers, and other film technicians; "making of" documentaries can reveal unique insights into the filmmaking process; direct digital access to individual scenes facilitates examination that is vastly more satisfactory than that afforded by the linear prison of the videocassette format or even the larger size of the laser disc. Now more than ever a movie is ours to study like a book. We can watch it as many times as we like and scrutinize it sequence by sequence, shot by shot, and even frame by frame. The ability to view a single scene over and over can lead to a much deeper understanding of the art of filmmaking than can be acquired by just watching movies from beginning to end in a theater or classroom.

Approach and Organization

The assumption underlying this text is that there is an art to watching films. The development of special skills and the use of certain techniques and technology can sharpen and enhance the film experience. Our aim is not to transform ordinary filmgoers into expert movie critics. Rather, our aim is to help students become more aware of the complexity of film art, more sensitive to its nuances, textures, and rhythms, and more perceptive in "reading" its multilayered blend of image, sound, color, and motion.

The analytical approach that we use is by no means the only valid approach, but it offers one distinct advantage over others: It is teachable. Emotional and intuitive approaches are highly subjective and thus difficult to use in class. Helping students develop their critical thinking skills, in contrast, offers them a rational framework that can support the study of films as diverse as *On the Waterfront*, *The Fugitive*, *The Matrix*, *The Seventh Seal*, and *Pleasantville*.

In its formal organization and intent, *The Art of Watching Films* is as straightforward as possible. Since its subject is primarily narrative film, the text first develops a foundation for understanding theme and story (Chapters 2 and 3) and then moves on to discuss the dramatic and cinematic elements that filmmakers use to "tell" the film story (Chapters 4–11). With an understanding of these basic film elements established, Chapter 12 provides a framework for integrating knowledge of all these elements into an analysis of the whole film. Subsequent chapters (Chapters 13–16) explore major specialized concerns and problems of film analysis.

Our primary goal is to challenge students to sharpen their powers of observation, help them to develop the skills and habits of perceptive watching, and encourage them to discover complex aspects of film art that they might otherwise overlook. We designed this text to complement any film studied, to function as a treasure map to aid students in finding the riches embodied in the real "text" of any film course—the films themselves.

Features

Color An entire chapter on color (Chapter 7), illustrated in color, highlights the element of the film experience that critics often overlook and filmgoers often take for granted. The chapter discusses in some depth the creative function of color in the modern film, providing a basic understanding of filmmakers' uses of color and a starting point from which students can explore complex, subtle, and very human responses to color film.

Video Exercises and Study Questions Two kinds of end-of-chapter assignments give film appreciation a hands-on immediacy. Assuming that most students have at least limited access to a VCR, we have devised video exercises for eight of the chapters of the text. To view the section of film dealt with in each exercise, set the VCR counter at "0000" (or the real-time counter at 0:00:00) at the very end of the studio logo, just as the "movie proper" begins (the "movie proper" includes such things as "Paramount Pictures Presents," opening credits, and the main title). Then fast-forward until the numbers given in the exercise appear.

Designed to engender either class discussion or written response, the study questions help students organize their thoughts and focus their attention on the very heart of a film. The questions also increase students' involvement in the film experience, encouraging them to participate actively in an exciting quest rather than responding passively to the surface details.

Test Examples and Illustrations Detailed examples help students comprehend basic concepts or techniques. Because *The Art of Watching Films* is aimed at beginners, most of the examples are taken from films that are contemporary rather than classic, American rather than international, and commercially successful rather than esoteric. Most examples are also readily available for rental and purchase in videocassette, laserdisc, and DVD formats.

More than 500 images from contemporary and classic films illustrate key points in the text. Extensive, informative captions strengthen the link between the visual and textual examples.

Writing About Film Many instructors ask students to respond in writing to a film—to give formal structure and an essayist's logic to their own critical responses. In Appendix B are guidelines for writing a film analysis and three sample student papers. The first is a lengthy, complete analysis of John Ford's *The Grapes of Wrath*, showing how a student might approach a paper assigned as a major class project. The second is a shorter, simpler paper focusing on important techniques employed in Martin Scorsese's *Taxi Driver*. Both of these illustrate the types of analysis that you can expect students to write by using this text and a video source for multiple viewings. So that students can grasp the interrelationship of the text, film, and finished paper, we have noted in the margins of both papers the pages in *The Art of Watching Films* that helped each student writer. The third student essay is a sharply focused examination of Martin Scorsese's *The Age of Innocence*, without textual annotations.

Controversy The text introduces students to controversial issues that profoundly affect the films we see, such as censorship (Chapter 16), the cinematic liberties taken in fact-based films like *Mississippi Burning*, *Lean on Me*, *JFK*, *Quiz Show*, and *Midnight in the Garden of Good and Evil* (Chapter 13) and colorization (Chapter 7)

New to This Edition

We have effected many changes that we hope will make this edition both more attractive and more teachable:

- **Updated visual and text examples.** Every chapter has been brought up to date with numerous text examples, and almost 100 new photos have been added. Up-to-date topics include computer-generated imaging (CGI) and its contribution to special effects films such as *Contact*, *Independence Day*, and *Dark City*.

- **An expanded discussion of genre films is featured in Chapter 14.** Lengthier treatments of film *noir*, war films, horror movies, science fiction and fantasy films, screwball romantic comedies, and musicals are now included.
- **Detailed discussions of both documentary films and animated feature films now appear in Chapter 15.**
- **A chapter on censorship is included.** At the request of many users of previous editions, we have updated and reintroduced Chapter 16, "Censorship and Other Forces That Shape the American Film."
- **Films for Study lists at the ends of chapters have been greatly increased and now include U.S. release dates.**
- **A new appendix (A)** has been added that discusses the pitfalls and challenges inherent in attempting to examine films primarily through television viewing.
- **A new student paper** has been added to the existing two examples in the appendix on writing about film. "Dramatic Foils in *The Age of Innocence*" appears without annotation so that it can serve as both a model and an exercise in student evaluation.
- **Expanded glossary and bibliography** provide students with more help.

Instructor's Manual

Accompanying the text is a manual written by Kenneth Jurkiewicz, a long-time user of the text at Central Michigan University. It contains a complete set of test items, a list of film and video rental sources, and other resources. The test items are also available as computer files suitable for IBM-compatible and Macintosh computers.

Publisher's Note

After a lengthy and courageous battle with cancer, Joseph M. Boggs, beloved husband, father, baseball and jazz aficionado, teacher, and author, died in early June of 1996—soon after the publication of the fourth edition of The Art of Watching Films. *At Boggs's request, his long-time friend, former student, and colleague Dennis W. Petrie, who had been closely involved with the book since its inception, was invited to guide the creation of this fifth edition.*

Acknowledgments

My good friend Joe Boggs was an energetic, passionate man, with high expectations of both life and art. So when, during the final year of his illness, he kept demanding that I agree to become a kind of designated hitter for his popular film book, I was of two minds: First, I found his unwavering belief in my abilities immensely flattering, but I also considered the task rather daunting. How could I possibly satisfy Joe's hopes for this new edition? In the end, though, I accepted his petition without question. My own love of film and my admiration for Joe were equally boundless; I realized that I must embrace the endeavor, and, as I worked, my appreciation for Joe's accomplishments continued to grow. To Joe Boggs, then, I am most deeply indebted for my experience with this project. As Joe, of course, knew I would, I have greatly enjoyed its challenges, and I pray that he would find the results of my struggles worthy.

There are, however, many others to thank for their kind assistance and encouragement, including my family, friends, colleagues, and students.

Key among these is an esteemed collaborator of Joe Boggs's, his son Michael Boggs, whose wise counsel and creative suggestions, notably in this edition's early stages, were of huge value to me. I am immensely grateful for his generosity.

My work on this book would have been virtually impossible without the enormous help of a few essential friends and colleagues nearby: Thomas P. Tierney, Jane A. Tubergen, Michael Blaz, Ray Condon, and, especially, Sue Van Wagner and Robert D. Briles, who were incredibly selfless in their assistance and supportive indulgence. I am forever in their debt.

Even over vast distances, Sandy Ridlington and Robert C. Petersen were still willing to offer creative input and encouragement at a moment's notice. Jacqueline E. Orsagh cheerfully provided observations and photographs from an insider's seat on a Louis Malle movie set. Elaine and Don Zimmer and Jane and Red Graves fed my cravings for movie memorabilia. Ray Hatton enthralled me with his acute observations about the spiritual aspects of cinema. And Jeanne Braham inspired me through her always gracious and talented example. I offer them all my heartfelt thanks.

In addition, I wish to express my appreciation to Elliott Armstrong, Deborah Blaz, Anne Bowden, Carol Briles, Miriam J. Briles, Miles Hession II, M. Sue Kahle, Glodine B. Petrie, and Roberta Tierney for their abiding thoughtfulness and support.

Among my students, I want particularly to thank Denise Tomlinson for permission to print her essay on *The Age of Innocence*, a new addition to the student papers for study in Appendix B.

At Mayfield Publishing Company, a whole cadre of talented and enthusiastic individuals nourished me with incredible patience and care. Among these, I am especially indebted to Senior Editor Janet M. Beatty, Senior Production Editor Melissa Williams Kreischer, and Jennifer Gordon, who copyedited the manuscript. I also wish to thank Design Manager Jean Mailander, Photo Researcher Brian Pecko, Art Editor Amy Folden, Marketing Manager Joe Hanson, and Marketing Communications Specialist Josh Tepfer.

Finally, I thank my colleagues who served as reviewers for this edition: Richard Booth, Crafton Hills College; R. W. Chapman, Des Moines Area Community College; Mary Jayne Davis, Salt Lake Community College; Richard C. Ekker, Modesto Junior College; John Heidger, St. Louis Community College; Deborah H. Holdstein, Governors State University; Scott L. Jensen, Weber State University; Kenneth Jurkiewicz, Central Michigan University; David Liban, University of Memphis; David J. Popowski, Mankato State University; Joanna E. Rapf, University of Oklahoma; and Donald L. Soucy, New England Institute of Technology.

Dennis W. Petrie

Contents

Preface vii

Chapter 1

Film Analysis 1

The Uniqueness of Film 2

Difficulties of Film Analysis 3

Why Analyze Films? 6

Chapter 2

Thematic Elements 10

Theme and Focus 11

Focus on Plot 11

Focus on Emotional Effect or Mood 11

Focus on Character 13

Focus on Style or Texture 14

Focus on Ideas 14

Identifying the Theme 23

Evaluating the Theme 24

Questions 27

Video Exercises 28

Films for Study 29

Chapter 3

Fictional and Dramatic Elements 31

Film Analysis and Literary Analysis 32

The Elements of a Good Story 32

A Good Story Is Unified in Plot 33

A Good Story Is Credible 33

A Good Story Is Interesting 37

A Good Story Is Both Simple and Complex 38

A Good Story Handles Emotional Material With Restraint 41

The Significance of the Title 42
Dramatic Structure 43
Linear, or Chronological, Structure 44
Nonlinear Structures 45
Endings: Fine-Tuning the Dénouement 46
Conflict 47
Characterization 49
Characterization Through Appearance 50
Characterization Through Dialogue 50
Characterization Through External Action 52
Characterization Through Internal Action 53
Characterization Through Reactions of Other Characters 53
Characterization Through Contrast: Dramatic Foils 54
Characterization Through Caricature and Leitmotif 54
Characterization Through Choice of Name 57
Varieties of Characters 57
Allegory 61
Symbolism 62
Universal and Natural Symbols 62
Creating Symbolic Meanings 63
Symbolic Patterns and Progressions 66
Symbolic Values in Conflict 68
Metaphors 68
Overreading Symbolism 70
Irony 70
Dramatic Irony 70
Irony of Situation 72
Irony of Character 72
Irony of Setting 72
Irony of Tone 72
Cosmic Irony 74
Questions 74
Video Exercises 77
Films for Study 78

Chapter 4

Visual Design 79
Color Versus Black and White 80
Screen Format 81
Film Stock 82

Production Design/Art Direction 85
The Script: The Starting Point 87
Setting and Its Effects 88
Studio Versus Location Shooting 94
Period Pieces 96
Living Spaces and Offices 96
Fantasy Worlds 97
Costume and Makeup Design 98
Lighting 101
The Budget's Effect on the Film's Look 105
Questions 106
Video Exercises 108
Films for Study 108

Chapter 5

Cinematography 110

The Importance of the Image 111
The Cinematic Film 111
Cinematic Points of View 112
Objective Point of View 113
Subjective Point of View 114
Indirect-Subjective Point of View 116
Director's Interpretive Point of View 118
Elements of Cinematic Composition 119
Focusing Attention on the Most Significant Object 121
Keeping the Image in Motion 124
Creating an Illusion of Depth 130
Techniques for Specialized Visual Effects 137
Hand-Held Camera 137
Camera Angles 137
Color, Diffusion, and Soft Focus 140
Special Lenses 140
Slow Motion 141
Fast Motion 145
The Freeze Frame, the Thawed Frame, and Stills 145
Special Lighting Effects 147
Questions 148
Video Exercises 149
Films for Study 150

Chapter 6

Editing and Special Visual Effects 151

Editing 152
Selectivity 153
Coherence, Continuity, and Rhythm 154
Transitions 154
Rhythms, Tempo, and Time Control 162
Expansion and Compression of Time 166
Creative Juxtaposition: Montage 173
Movie Magic: Special Effects in the Modern Film 177
Questions 185
Video Exercises 185
Films for Study 186

Chapter 7

Color 187

Recorded Color 190
Color in the Modern Film 192
Effects of Color on the Viewer 192
Color as a Transitional Device 197
Expressionistic Use of Color 200
Color as Symbol 202
Surrealistic Use of Color 203
Leitmotifs in Color 204
Color to Enhance Mood 205
Comic Book Color 206
Comic Strip Color 207
Painterly Effects in Color 208
Ironic Use of Color 210
Special Color Effects 210
Colorization 212
Color Versus Black and White 213
Questions 217
Video Exercises 218
Films for Study 219

Chapter 8

Sound Effects and Dialogue

Sound Effects and Dialogue 220
Sound and the Modern Film 221
Dialogue 222
Three-Dimensionality in Sound 223
Visible and Invisible Sound 226
Points of View in Sound 228
Special Uses of Sound Effects and Dialogue 230
Sound Effects to Tell an Inner Story 230
Distortion of Sound to Suggest Subjective States 231
The "Personality" of Mechanical Sounds 232
Slow-Motion Sound 233
Ironic Juxtaposition of Sound and Image 234
Placing Unusual Emphasis on Sound 234
Using Sound for Texture, Time, and Temperature 236
Sound as a Plot Device 237
Sound as a Transitional Element 238
Voice-Over Narration 239
Silence as a Sound Effect 243
Rhythmic Qualities of Dialogue and Sound Effects 245
Questions 245
Video Exercises 245
Films for Study 246

Chapter 9

The Musical Score

The Musical Score 247
The Remarkable Affinity of Music and Film 248
The Importance of the Musical Score 248
General Functions of the Musical Score 249
Special Functions of the Musical Score 251
Covering Weaknesses or Defects in the Film 251
Heightening the Dramatic Effect of Dialogue 252
Telling an Inner Story 252
Providing a Sense of Time and Place 253
Evoking Nostalgic Feelings 254
Foreshadowing Events or Building Dramatic Tension 254
Adding Levels of Meaning to the Visual Image 255
Characterization Through Music 255

Triggering Conditioned Responses 257
Traveling Music 258
Providing Important Transitions 259
Accompanying Titles 259
Musical Sounds as Part of the Score 260
Music as Interior Monologue 260
Music as a Base for Choreographed Action 260
Synthesizer Scoring 262
Economy in Film Music 264
Questions 265
Video Exercises 266
Films for Study 267

Chapter 10

Acting 268

The Importance of Acting 269
The Goal of the Actor 269
Becoming the Character 270
Differences Between Film Acting and Stage Acting 272
Types of Actors 279
Impersonators 280
Interpreters and Commentators 280
Personality Actors 280
The Star System 280
Casting 282
Casting Problems 286
The Typecasting Trap 287
Supporting Players 292
Extras and Small Parts 293
Actors as Creative Contributors 297
Subjective Responses to Actors 300
Questions 302
Video Exercises 304
Films for Study 305

Chapter 11

The Director's Style 306

The Concept of Style 308

Subject Matter 309
Cinematography 313
Editing 314
Setting and Set Design 315
Sound and Score 315
Casting and Acting Performances 316
Screenplays and Narrative Structure 317
Evolving Styles and Flexibility 321
Special Edition: The Director's Cut 324
Questions 325
Films for Study 328

Chapter 12

Analysis of the Whole Film 338

Addressing Viewer-Centered Challenges 339
Categorical Rejection 339
Mistaking the Part for the Whole 341
Great Expectations 342
An Excess of Expertise 342
The Influence of External Factors 343
Preconceptions: Reviews and Other Sources 344
The Basic Approach: Watching, Analyzing, and Evaluating the Film 348
Theme and Filmmakers' Intentions 349
The Relationship of the Parts to the Whole 349
The Film's Level of Ambition 350
Objective Evaluation of the Film 350
Subjective Evaluation of the Film 351
Other Approaches to Analysis, Evaluation, and Discussion 351
The Film as Technical Achievement 352
The Film as Showcase for the Actor: The Personality Cult 352
The Film as Product of a Single Creative Mind: The Auteur Approach 353
The Film as Moral, Philosophical, or Social Statement 353
The Film as Emotional or Sensual Experience 354
The Film as Conventionalized Form: The Genre Approach 355
The Film as Political Statement: The Marxist Approach 355
The Film as Gender Statement: The Feminist Approach 356
The Film as Insight to the Mind: The Psychoanalytical Approach 357
The Eclectic Approach 359
Rereading the Reviews 362

Evaluating the Reviewer 362
Developing Personal Criteria 364
Questions 366
Films for Study 368

Chapter 13

Adaptations 369

The Problems of Adaptation 370
Change in Medium 370
Change in Creative Artists 370
Cinematic Potential of the Original Work 373
Problems Created by the Viewer 374
Adaptations of Novels 375
Literary Versus Cinematic Points of View 375
First-Person Point of View: A Special Problem 379
The Problem of Length and Depth 380
Philosophical Reflections 381
Summarizing a Character's Past 383
Cinematic Compression of Time Versus Novelistic Summary 385
Literary Past Tense Versus Cinematic Present Tense 386
Other Factors Influencing Adaptations of Novels 387
Adaptations of Plays 389
Structural Divisions 390
Sense of Space 390
Film Language Versus Stage Language 393
Stage Conventions Versus Cinema Conventions 394
Other Changes 396
From Fact to Film: Reality to Myth 399
Questions 404
Films for Study 406

Chapter 14

Genre Films, Remakes, and Sequels 408

Genre Films 409
Values 410
The Strengths of Genre Films 410
The Formulas 411
Stretching and Breaking the Formulas 417
Other Popular Genres 418

Remakes and Sequels 425
Remakes 429
Sequels 432
Questions 438
Films for Study 440

Chapter 15

Other Film Experiences 446

Foreign Language or International Films 447
Voice Dubbing 447
Subtitles 449
Other Kinds of Foreignness 450
Cultural Prejudice 453
Silent Films 454
Color in Silent Films 454
Language in Silent Films 456
Documentary Films 460
Animated Feature Films 466
Historically Important Films 474
Social Problem Films 476
Questions 477
Films for Study 479

Chapter 16

Censorship and Other Forces That Shape the American Film 482

Does Film Shape or Reflect American Values? 483
The Motion Picture Production Code, 1930–1960 484
Censorship in Transition, 1948–1968 490
The MPAA Rating System 492
Censorship and Films on Television 498
Beyond the Code and Rating System 498
Changing Formulas for the Treatment of Sex, Violence, and Language 501
Questions 503
Films for Study 504

Appendix A

The Art of Watching Movies on TV 505

The TV-Viewing Environment 505
Conventions and Habits of Watching Movies on Television 508
Commercial Breaks 508
The Made-for-Television Film 510
Questions 514

Appendix B

Writing a Film Analysis 515

Sample Student Paper: Analysis of a Complete Film 516
Sample Student Paper: Analysis of Selected Film Elements 524
Sample Student Paper: Analysis for Study 526

Notes 530

Glossary 538

Selected Bibliography and Study Materials 547

Credits 554

Index 555

Chapter 1

Film Analysis

The cinema is a work of art when motion conforms to a perceptible rhythm with pause and pace and where all aspects of the continuous image relate to the whole.

—JOSEF VON STERNBERG, DIRECTOR

The Uniqueness of Film

The tremendous expense involved in producing motion pictures reminds us that film is both an industry and an art form. Each film is the child of a turbulent marriage between businesspeople and artists. Yet despite an ongoing battle between aesthetic and commercial considerations, film is recognized as a unique and powerful art form on a par with painting, sculpture, music, literature, and drama.

As a form of expression, the motion picture is similar to other artistic media, for the basic properties of other media are woven into its own rich fabric. Film employs the compositional elements of the visual arts: line, form, mass, volume, and texture. Like painting and photography, film exploits the subtle interplay of light and shadow. Like sculpture, film manipulates three-dimensional space. But, like pantomime, film focuses on *moving* images, and as in dance, the moving images in film have rhythm. The complex rhythms of film resemble those of music and poetry, and like poetry in particular, film communicates through imagery, metaphor, and symbol. Like the drama, film communicates visually *and* verbally: visually, through action and gesture; verbally, through dialogue. Finally, like the novel, film expands or compresses time and space, traveling back and forth freely within their wide borders.

Despite these similarities, film is unique, set apart from all other media by its quality of free and constant motion. The continuous interplay of sight, sound, and motion allows film to transcend the static limitations of painting and sculpture—in the complexity of its sensual appeal as well as in its ability to communicate simultaneously on several levels. Film even surpasses drama in its unique capacity for revealing various points of view, portraying action, manipulating time, and conveying a boundless sense of space. Unlike the stage play, film can provide a continuous, unbroken flow, which blurs and minimizes transitions without compromising the story's unity. Unlike the novel and the poem, film communicates directly, not through abstract symbols like words on a page but through concrete images and sounds. What's more, film can treat an almost infinite array of subjects:

> It is impossible to conceive of anything which the eye might behold or the ear hear, in actuality or imagination, which could not be represented in the medium of film. From the poles to the equator, from the Grand Canyon to the minutest flaw in a piece of steel, from the whistling flight of a bullet to the slow growth of a flower, from the flicker of thought across an almost impassive face to the frenzied ravings of a madman, there is no point in space, no degree of magnitude or speed of movement within the apprehension of man which is not within reach of the film.[1]

Film is unlimited not only in its choice of subject but also in its approach to that material. A film's mood and treatment can range from the lyric to the epic. In point of view, a film can cover the full spectrum from the purely objective to the intensely subjective; in depth, it can focus on the surface realities and the purely sensual, or it can delve into the intellectual and philosophical. A film can look to the remote past or probe the distant future; it can make a few seconds seem like hours or compress a century into minutes. Film can run the gamut of feeling from the most fragile, tender, and beautiful to the most brutal, violent, and repulsive (Figure 1.1).

Of even greater importance than film's unlimited range in subject matter and treatment, however, is the overwhelming sense of reality it can convey. The continuous stream of sight, sound, and motion creates a here-and-now excitement that immerses the viewer in the cinematic experience. Thus, through film, fantasy assumes the shape and emotional impact of reality. The technological history of film can in fact be viewed as a continual evolution toward greater realism, toward erasing the border between art and nature. The motion picture has progressed step by step from drawings, to photographs, to projected images, to sound, to color, to wide screen, to 3-D. Attempts have even been made to add the sense of smell to the film experience by releasing fragrances throughout the theater. Aldous Huxley's novel *Brave New World* depicted a theater of the future where a complex electrical apparatus at each seat provided tactile images to match the visuals:

> Going to the Feelies this evening, Henry? . . . I hear the new one at the Alhambra is first-rate. There's a love scene on a bearskin rug; they say it's marvellous. Every hair of the bear reproduced. The most amazing tactual effects.[2]

Although Huxley's "Feelies" have not yet become reality, the motion picture has succeeded, through Cinerama and other wide-screen, curved-screen projection, and virtual reality or IMAX techniques, in intensifying our experience to a remarkable degree. In fact, by creating images that are larger than life, films have sometimes been made to seem more real than reality. A cartoon published shortly after the first Cinerama film (*This Is Cinerama*, 1952) was released illustrates the effectiveness of this device. The cartoon pictures a man groping for a seat during the famous roller-coaster sequence. As he moves across a row of seats, a seated spectator, in a panic, grabs his arm and screams hysterically, "Sit down, you fool! You'll have us all killed!" Anyone who has seen *This Is Cinerama* knows the cartoon is no exaggeration.

Difficulties of Film Analysis

The properties that make film the most powerful and realistic of the arts also make analysis difficult. A motion picture moves continuously in time and space. Once frozen, a film is no longer a "motion" picture, and the unique property of the medium is gone. Therefore, film analysis requires us to respond sensitively to the simultaneous and continuous interplay of image, sound, and movement

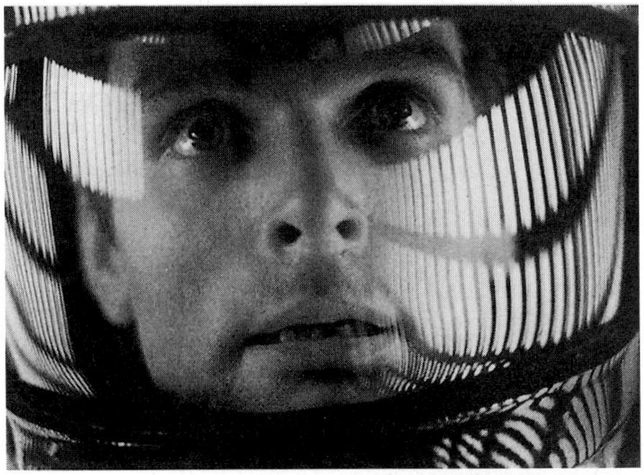

Figure 1.1 The Unlimited Potential of Film Through the technical magic of the medium and the artistic vision of filmmakers, we can experience unique journeys in time, space, and feeling. We can leap backward in time to the Middle Ages and watch a chess match between Death and a knight returning from the Crusades in *The Seventh Seal.* We can vicariously experience a wide spectrum of romance, from the sweet innocence of *Love Finds Andy Hardy* or *Forrest Gump* to the obsessive search for lost love that spans centuries in *Bram Stoker's Dracula.* Or we might follow a family of uprooted tenant farmers from Oklahoma to California in *The Grapes of Wrath,* travel into deep space with a team of astronauts in *2001: A Space Odyssey,* or reach the ocean's bottom with scientists in *Titanic.*

on the screen. This necessity creates the most difficult part of the task: We must somehow remain almost totally immersed in the experience of a film while we maintain a high degree of objectivity and critical detachment. Difficult though it may seem, this skill can be developed, and we must consciously cultivate it if we desire to become truly "cineliterate." Recent innovations in videocassette recorders (VCRs), laserdisc players, and now digital videodisc (DVD) players can help.

The technical nature of the medium also creates difficulties. It would be ideal if we all had some experience in cinematography and film editing. In the absence of such experience, we should become familiar with the basic techniques of film production so that we can recognize them and evaluate their effectiveness. Because a certain amount of technical language or jargon is necessary for the analysis and intelligent discussion of any art form, we must also add a number of important technical terms to our vocabularies.

The most difficult part of our task has already been stated: We must somehow become almost totally immersed in the experience of a film and at the same time maintain a high degree of objectivity and critical detachment. The complex nature of the medium makes it difficult to consider all the elements of a film in a single viewing; too many things happen too quickly on too many levels to allow for a complete analysis. Therefore, if we wish to develop the proper habits of analytical viewing, we should see a film twice whenever possible. In the first viewing we can watch the film in the usual manner, concerning ourselves primarily with plot elements, the total emotional effect, and the central idea or theme. Then, in a second viewing, because we are no longer caught up in the suspense of what happens, we can focus our full attention on the hows and whys of the filmmaker's art. Constant practice of the double-viewing technique should make it possible for us to gradually combine the functions of both viewings into one.

We must also remember that film analysis does not end when the film is over. In a sense, this is when it really begins. Most of the questions posed in this book require the reader to reflect on the film after leaving the theater, and a mental replay of some parts of the film will be necessary for any complete analysis.

Why Analyze Films?

Before we turn to the actual process of film analysis, it may be worthwhile to look into certain fundamental questions that have been raised about the value of analysis in general. Perhaps the most vocal reactions against analysis come from those who see it as a destroyer of beauty, claiming that it kills our love for the object under study. According to this view, it is better to accept all art intuitively, emotionally, and subjectively, so that our response is full, warm, and vibrant, uncluttered by the intellect. This kind of thinking is expressed in Walt Whitman's poem "When I Heard the Learn'd Astronomer":

When I heard the learn'd astronomer;
When the proofs, the figures, were ranged in columns before me;
When I was shown the charts and the diagrams, to add, divide, and measure them,
When I, sitting, heard the astronomer, where he lectured with much applause in
  the lecture-room,
How soon, unaccountable, I became tired and sick;
Till rising and gliding out, I wander'd off by myself,
In the mystical moist night-air, and from time to time,
Look'd up in perfect silence at the stars.

If we were to agree with Whitman, we would throw analysis out the window, judging it to be a cold, intellectual, bloodless, and unfeeling process that destroys the magical, emotional, and mystical aspects of experience. However, Whitman's either/or, black-and-white polarization of poet and astronomer is flawed. It denies the possibility of some middle ground—a synthesis that retains the best qualities of both approaches and embraces as equally valid both the emotional/intuitive and the intellectual/analytical approaches. This book rests on that middle ground. It assumes that the soul of the poet and the intellect of the astronomer can coexist within all of us, enriching and enhancing the film experience. If this is true, analysis need not murder our love of the movies. We can experience beauty, joy, and mystery intellectually as well as intuitively. With the astronomer's telescope, we can experience the poetic beauty of Saturn's rings, the moons of Jupiter, and the Milky Way—mysteries of the universe invisible to the naked eye. Likewise with the tools of analysis, we can discover the deepest reaches of understanding that only the poet within us can fully appreciate. By creating new avenues of awareness, analysis can make our love for movies stronger, more real, more enduring.

Analysis also suffers from the misconception that it not only destroys our love for the object but destroys the object as well. In "The Tables Turned," William Wordsworth compares analysis to the work of a medical student cutting apart a cadaver or a physician performing an autopsy:

Sweet is the lore which Nature brings;
Our meddling intellect
Misshapes the beauteous forms of things
We murder to dissect.

To assume that analysis destroys the beautiful, however, is to assume that physicians who have carefully studied the human body—its bone and muscle structure, its circulatory and nervous systems, and all its many organs—are no longer awed by the miracle of life, warm, vibrant, and pulsing with energy. Film analysis does not work with parts that are dead, nor does it kill. Film analysis takes place only in the mind. Each part being studied pulses with life because analysis sees each part as connected to the lifeline of the whole. And that's the point. The analytical approach enables us to see and understand how each part functions to contribute its vital energy to the pulsing, dynamic whole.

The following quotation from Richard Dyer MacCann's introduction to *Film: A Montage of Theories* might well serve as the basic assumption of this book:

> Arnold Hauser [a famous art critic] contended, and I think rightly, that "all art is a game with and a fight against chaos." The film that simply says life is chaos is a film which has not undertaken the battle of art.[3]

If we accept MacCann's judgment, we can agree that the analytical approach is essential to the art of watching films.

Analysis means breaking up the whole to discover the nature, proportion, function, and interrelationships of the parts. Film analysis, then, presupposes the existence of a unified and rationally structured artistic whole. Therefore, the usefulness of this book is restricted to structured or narrative films—films developed with a definite underlying purpose and unified around a central theme. Limiting our approach to structured films does not necessarily deny the artistic value of unstructured films. Many of the films that experimental or underground filmmakers are producing do communicate effectively on a purely subjective, intuitive, or sensual plane and are meaningful to some degree as experiences. But because many of these films are not structured or unified around a central purpose or theme, they cannot be successfully approached through analysis.

It would be foolish to suggest that a structured film cannot be appreciated or understood at all without analysis. If a film is effective, we should possess an intuitive grasp of its overall meaning. The problem is that this intuitive grasp is generally weak and vague and limits our critical response to hazy generalizations and half-formed opinions. The analytical approach allows us to raise this intuitive grasp to a conscious level, bring it into sharp focus, and thereby reach more valid and definite conclusions about the film's meaning and value. The analytical approach, however, does not reduce film art to rational and manageable proportions. Analysis neither claims nor attempts to explain everything about film. The elusive, flowing stream of images will always escape complete analysis and complete understanding. In fact, no final answers exist about any work of art. A film, like anything else of true aesthetic value, can never be completely captured by analysis.

But the fact that there are no final answers should not prevent us from pursuing some important questions. Our hope is that, through analysis, we can reach a higher level of confusion about films, a level where we are reaching for the most significant aspects of the film art as opposed to the mundane, the practical, and the technical. If analysis enables us to understand some things so that we learn to see them habitually, our minds will be free to concentrate on the most significant questions.

Analysis helps us to lock an experience in our minds so that we may savor it in memory. By looking at a film analytically, we engage ourselves with it intellectually and creatively and thus make it more truly our own. Furthermore, because our critical judgments enter into the process, analysis should fine-tune our tastes. A mediocre film can impress us more than it should at first, but we might like it less after analyzing it. A great film or a very good one will stand up under analysis; our admiration for it will increase the more deeply we look into it.

Analysis offers several clear benefits. It allows us to reach valid and definite conclusions on a film's meaning and value; it helps us to lock the experience of a film into our minds; and it sharpens our critical judgments. But the ultimate purpose of analysis, and its greatest benefit, is that it opens up new channels of awareness and new depths of understanding. It seems logical to assume that the more understanding we have, the more completely we will appreciate art. If the love we have for an art form rests on rational understanding, it will be more solid, more enduring, and of greater value than love based solely on irrational and totally subjective reactions. This is not to claim that analysis will create a love of films where no such love exists. Love of film does not emerge from a book or from any special critical approach. It comes only from that secret, personal union between film and viewer in a darkened room. If that love does not already exist for the viewer, this book and its analytical approach can do little to create it.

But if we truly love films, we will find that analysis is worth the effort, for the understanding it brings will deepen our appreciation. Instead of canceling out the emotional experience of watching the film, analysis will enhance and enrich that experience. As we become more perceptive and look more deeply into the film, new levels of emotional experience will emerge.

Chapter 2

Thematic Elements

Movies are about things—even bad movies are *about* things. *Rambo III* is about something. It has a theme, even if it doesn't want to have a theme. . . . You have to know in some way what you are about to do. Even if that theme gets rerouted or ends up in subtext, somehow there has to be some sense of why you are doing this.

—Paul Schrader, Director and Screenwriter

Theme and Focus

In the context of novels, plays, and poetry, the word *theme* connotes an idea—the central idea, the point, the message, or the statement made by the work as a whole. For film analysis, however, that definition of theme is too narrow. The theme of a film is not necessarily an idea at all.

In the context of film analysis, **theme** refers to the unifying central concern of the film, the special focus that unifies the work. As the director Sidney Lumet has observed,

> What the movie is about will determine how it will be cast, how it will look, how it will be edited, how it will be musically scored, how it will be mixed, how the titles will look, and, with a good studio, how it will be released. What it's about will determine how it is to be made.[1]

A filmmaker may choose to focus on ideas but is just as likely to emphasize one of the four other major elements: (1) plot, (2) emotional effect or mood, (3) character, and (4) style or texture. All five elements are present in *all* films; but in any given film, one is predominant. Keeping in mind this broader concept of theme will help us to analyze films ranging from *Groundhog Day* to *The Piano* or from *The Age of Innocence* to *Pulp Fiction.*

Focus on Plot

In adventure stories and detective stories, the filmmaker focuses on plot—on what happens. The aim of such films is generally to provide escape from the boredom and drabness of everyday life, so the action is exciting and fast paced. Characters, ideas, and emotional effects are subordinate to events, and the final outcome is all-important. Events and the final outcome, however, are important only within the context of the specific story being told; they have little real significance. The theme of such a film can best be captured in a concise summary of the plot (Figure 2.1).

Focus on Emotional Effect or Mood

In a relatively large number of films the director creates a highly specialized mood or emotional effect. In such films, it is possible to identify a single mood or emotion that prevails throughout the film or to view each segment of the film as a step leading to a single powerful emotional effect. Although plot may be very important in such a movie, events are subordinate to the emotional response they produce. Most horror films, the Alfred Hitchcock suspense thrillers, and romantic tone poems such as *A Man and a Woman* can be interpreted as having a mood or emotional effect as their primary focus and unifying element.

Figure 2.1 Focus on Plot *Robocop, Clear and Present Danger, Speed,* and *Independence Day* are fast-paced action films that focus on what happens.

Figure 2.2 Focus on Emotional Effect or Mood A wide variety of emotional effects or moods can serve as a thematic concern in modern films. There are movies to scare us, like *The Shining* (top left), movies to make us cry, like *The Piano* (top right), movies to make us feel romantic, like *City of Angels* (bottom left), and movies to make us laugh, like *There's Something About Mary* (bottom right).

The theme of such films can best be stated by identifying the prevailing mood or emotional effect that the filmmaker has created (Figure 2.2).

In some films, a balanced combination of two emotions may make it difficult to tell which emotion is dominant. *Beverly Hills Cop*, for example, might be classified as a comedy/suspense film, *An American Werewolf in London* as a comedy/horror film. An analysis of such films needs to consider the elements that contribute to each effect and the way the two prevalent emotions play off each other (Figure 2.3).

Focus on Character

Some films, through both action and dialogue, focus on the clear delineation of a single unique character. Although plot is important in such films, what happens is important primarily because it helps us understand the character being developed. The major appeal of these characters lies in the qualities that set them apart from ordinary people. The theme of such films can best be expressed

Figure 2.3 Mixed Emotions Some films do not focus on building a single emotional effect but instead blend two different emotions in the same story, as does *The Full Monty,* with its unique blend of comedy and pathos.

in a brief description of the central character, with emphasis on the unusual aspects of the individual's personality (Figure 2.4).

Focus on Style or Texture

In a relatively small number of films, the director tells the story in such a different way that the film's style or texture becomes its dominant and most memorable aspect, making a stronger impact on our minds and senses than any of the other thematic elements. Such films have a quality that sets them apart—a unique look, feel, rhythm, atmosphere, or tone that echoes in our minds and senses long after we leave the theater. The unique style or texture permeates the film (not just isolated segments), and all the cinematic elements are woven together into one rich tapestry. Such films are often not commercially successful because the mass audience may not be prepared for or comfortable with the unique viewing experience that they provide (Figure 2.5).

Focus on Ideas

In most serious films, the action and characters have a significance beyond the context of the film itself—a significance that helps to clarify some aspect of life,

Figure 2.4 Focus on Character Some films, such as *Sergeant York* (top left), *The Great Santini* (top right), and *Raging Bull* (bottom), focus on the unusual aspects of unique people.

experience, or the human condition. The idea may be communicated directly through a particular incident or stated by a particular character. Most often, however, the idea is presented more subtly, and we are challenged to find an interpretation that we feel best fits the film as a whole. This indirect approach increases the likelihood of varying interpretations, but varying interpretations are not necessarily contradictory. They may be equally valid, complementary statements saying essentially the same things in different terms or approaching the same idea from different angles.

Figure 2.5 Focus on Style or Texture Both *Nashville* and *The English Patient* leave us feeling we have experienced a one-of-a-kind movie.

Figure 2.6 Moral Implications It is doubtful that any young person who has seen *Midnight Express* will ever attempt to smuggle drugs out of Turkey—or any other foreign country. Nor would any viewer of *Welcome to the Dollhouse* long with nostalgia for his or her years in middle school.

Perhaps the first step in identifying the central idea is accurately identifying the abstract subject of the film in a single word or phrase—for example, *jealousy*, *injustice*, *prejudice*. If this is as specific as we can get in determining the theme, we should not despair; some concepts can be stated explicitly but others cannot. At any rate, the identification of the true subject is a valuable first step in film analysis. If possible, however, we should attempt to carry the determination of central idea beyond the mere identification of the subject and see if we can formulate a statement that accurately summarizes the subject that is dramatized in the film and conveyed by all its elements. If such a specific statement of the film's central concern is possible, the film's central idea might fall into one of the following categories.

1. **Moral Statements.** Films that make moral statements are intended primarily to convince us of the wisdom or practicality of a moral principle and thereby persuade us to apply the principle in our own lives. Such principles often take the form of a maxim or proverb such as "The love of money is the root of all evil." Although many modern films have important moral implications, very few are structured around a single moral statement, and we must be careful not to mistake a moral implication for a moral statement or judgment (Figure 2.6).
2. **The Truth of Human Nature.** Quite different from films that focus on unique characters are films that focus on universal or representative characters. Such films move beyond character study into the realm of idea as theme, for such characters take on significance beyond themselves and

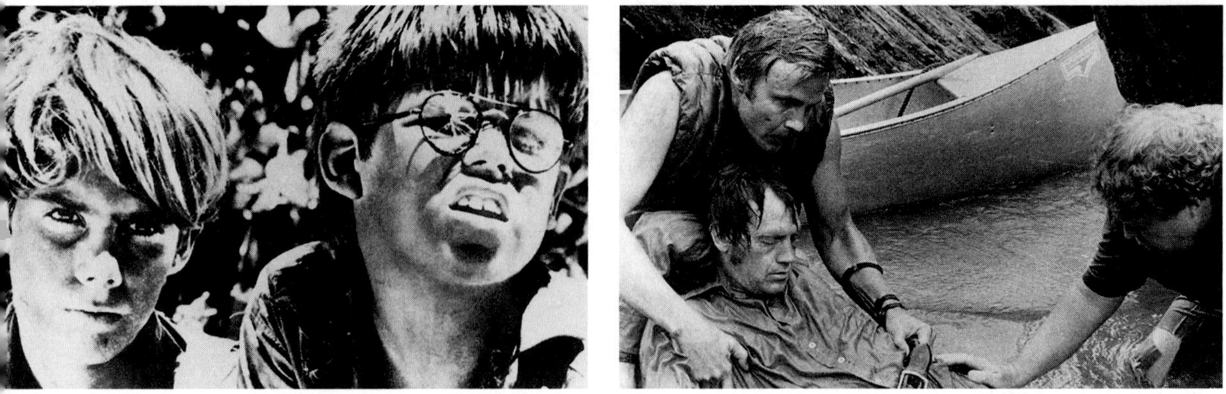

Figure 2.7 The Truth of Human Nature Films like *Lord of the Flies* (1963) and *Deliverance* take a penetrating look at the nature of humankind when the thin veneer of civilization has been removed.

the context of the particular film in which they appear. Because those characters are representative of humanity in general, they serve as cinematic vehicles to illustrate some widely or universally acceptable truth about human nature (Figure 2.7).

3. **Social Problems.** Modern filmmakers are very concerned with social problems and show their concern in films that expose social vices and follies or criticize social institutions. Although the underlying purpose of such films is social reform, they rarely spell out specific methods of reform; usually they concentrate instead on defining the problem and emphasizing its importance. A social problem film may treat its subject in a light, satirical, or comic manner, or it may attack the subject in a savage, harsh, and brutal manner. The social problem film, unlike the human nature film, concerns itself not with criticism of the human race in general or with the universal aspects of human nature but with the special functions of human beings as social animals and with the social institutions and traditions they have created (Figure 2.8).
4. **The Struggle for Human Dignity.** Many serious films portray a basic conflict or tension between two opposing sides of human nature. One is the desire to surrender to animal instincts and wallow in the slime of human weakness, cowardice, brutality, stupidity, and sensuality. The other is the struggle to stand erect, to display courage, sensitivity, intelligence, a spiritual and moral sense, and strong individualism. This conflict is best shown when the central characters are placed in a position of disadvantage, having been dealt a bad hand in some way, so that they must play against tremendous odds. The conflict may be external, with the character struggling against some dehumanizing force, system, institution, or attitude.

Figure 2.8 Social Problem Films Films like *Do the Right Thing* and *Amistad* (racial and ethnic prejudice) and *In the Company of Men* (sexual harassment in the workplace) force us to examine current social problems.

Or the conflict may be internal, with the character struggling for dignity against the human weaknesses present in his or her own personality (Figure 2.9).

A triumphant victory is sometimes, but certainly not always, achieved. However, the struggle itself gives us some respect for the character, win or lose. Boxers are often treated in films with the dignity theme. In *On the Waterfront*, Terry Malloy (Marlon Brando) achieves his dignity by leading the dock workers to rebel against a corrupt union, but Malloy's summary of his boxing career echoes clearly his personal struggle: "I could'a had class . . . I could'a been a contender . . . I could'a been *somebody!* . . . Instead of just a bum, which is what I am." Sylvester Stallone takes the character of Terry Malloy and gives him the chance to be "somebody" in each film of the *Rocky* series. Another example is *Requiem for a Heavyweight*, in which over-the-hill fighter Mountain Rivera (Anthony Quinn) fails to achieve dignity but wins respect for his effort.

5. **The Complexity of Human Relationships.** Some films focus on the problems, frustrations, pleasures, and joys of human relationships: love,

Figure 2.9 The Struggle for Human Dignity In *Nell,* a sheltered recluse (Jodie Foster) who has created her own strange language struggles to maintain her human dignity and sense of identity as she is forced into social interaction.

friendship, marriage, divorce, family interactions, sexuality, and so on. Some show the gradual working out of a problem; others help us gain insight into a problem without providing any clear resolution. Although a great many films of this sort deal with universal problems in the continuing battle of the sexes, we must also be on the lookout for unusual treatments such as *Midnight Cowboy* (a "love" story about two men) and *The Odd Couple* (a "marriage" treatment) (Figure 2.10).

6. **Coming of Age/Loss of Innocence/Growing Awareness.** The major character or characters in such films are usually, but not always, young people going through experiences that force them to become more mature or to gain some new awareness of themselves in relation to the world around them. Such concepts can be treated comically, seriously, tragically,

Figure 2.10 The Complexity of Human Relationships Michael Douglas and Kathleen Turner, in *The War of the Roses* (top left), show that breaking up is hard to do. True love can be a struggle to work out, especially when three brothers are in love with the same woman, as the Julia Ormond and Brad Pitt characters discover in *Legends of the Fall* (top right). Films such as *Boogie Nights* (bottom left), *Chasing Amy* (bottom right), multiply the complexities.

or satirically. The central character of these films is always dynamic—that is, different in some way at the end of the film from what he or she was at the beginning. The changes that occur may be subtle internal changes or drastic changes that significantly alter the character's outward behavior or lifestyle (Figures 2.11, 2.12).

7. **A Moral or Philosophical Riddle.** Sometimes a filmmaker may purposely strive to evoke a variety of subjective interpretations by developing a film around a riddle or puzzling quality. The filmmaker attempts to suggest or mystify instead of communicating clearly and attempts to pose moral or philosophical questions rather than provide answers. The typical

Figure 2.11 Coming of Age In movies like *American Graffiti, Summer of '42, The Thief,* and *Risky Business* (clockwise from top), young people go through experiences that cause them to become more aware or more mature.

Figure 2.12 Compounding the Problems Coming of age is always difficult, but it is almost overwhelming for the characters played by Elizabeth Moss and Fairuza Balk in *Imaginary Crimes.* They must live on the empty promises of their widower con-man father (Harvey Keitel).

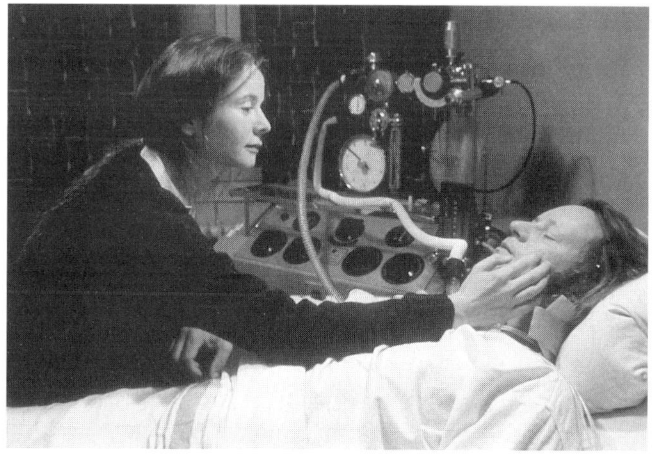

Figure 2.13 A Moral or Philosophical Riddle In *Persona* and *Breaking the Waves,* directors Ingmar Bergman and Lars von Trier suggest multiple meanings that mystify us.

reaction to such films is "What's it all about?" This type of film communicates primarily through symbols or images, so a thorough analysis of these elements will be required for interpretation. After even the most perceptive analysis, a degree of uncertainty will remain. Such films are wide open to subjective interpretation. But the fact that subjective interpretation is required does not mean that the analysis of all film elements can be ignored. Individual interpretation should be supported by an examination of all elements (Figure 2.13).

Identifying the Theme

Identifying the theme of a film is often difficult. The theme is not likely to reveal itself in a flash of light midway through the screening. Although simply watching a film may give us a vague, intuitive grasp of its basic meaning, accurately stating the theme is quite another matter. Often we cannot do so until we leave the theater and begin thinking about or discussing the film. Sometimes, just describing the movie to someone who has not seen it will provide an important clue to the theme, because we tend to describe first the things that made the strongest impression on us.

Identifying the theme can be considered both the beginning and the end of film analysis. After seeing a film, we should make a tentative identification of its theme to provide a starting point for close analysis. The analysis itself should clarify our vision of the film and show all its elements functioning together as a unique whole. However, if our analysis of the individual thematic elements does not support our original view of the film's theme, we should be prepared to reconsider our opinion in light of the new direction that our analysis indicates.

Plot, emotional effect or mood, character, style or texture, and ideas are the central concerns of most films. There are exceptions, however—films that do not focus exclusively on any one element and films that focus on more than one. In our efforts to identify theme, we must also be aware that certain films may possess, in addition to the single unifying central concern that we define as *theme*, other, less important, areas of emphasis called **motifs.** These are images, patterns, or ideas that are repeated throughout the film and are variations or aspects of the major theme. Above all, we should remember that the statement of the theme cannot convey the full impact of the film itself. It merely clarifies our vision of the film as a unified work and enhances our appreciation of its thematic elements as they function together in a unique artistic whole.

Evaluating the Theme

Once we have identified the theme, it is important to make some kind of evaluation of it, especially in a serious film that attempts to do more than simply entertain. For the most part, theme evaluation is a subjective process, and any attempt to provide systematic guidelines for making this kind of value judgment would be prejudicial. A few generalizations, however, are permissible.

One standard commonly applied in theme evaluation is universality. A universal theme is one of lasting interest, one that is meaningful not just to people here and now but to all human beings in all ages. Therefore, a theme with universal appeal may be considered superior to one with an appeal strictly limited in time and place. Four social problem films illustrate this point. Those strictly limited in time and place like *Wild in the Streets* (the generation gap of the 1960s) and *Easy Rider* (a grab bag of 1960s problems) had a powerful impact on young film audiences when they were released but seem ludicrous today (Figure 2.14). However, *On the Waterfront* (union corruption in the 1950s) and *The Grapes of Wrath* (the plight of migrant farm workers in the 1930s) speak to us in loud, clear voices today, despite their age. Migrant farm workers still have problems, and corrupt unions still exist; but those films have universal appeal because of the real and powerful characters portrayed, the heroic struggles waged for human dignity, and the artistry with which both films were made.

There is, of course, no real formula for the classic film, the kind we never grow tired of seeing (Figure 2.15). The classic film has a sense of rightness to it time and time again. Its power does not fade or diminish with the passing years but actually grows because of its universal themes and motifs. *The Grapes of Wrath* is not simply about migrant workers forced to leave the Oklahoma Dust Bowl in the 1930s. It is about the common man, the downtrodden, the underdog, about courageous men and women, about people who endure and their

Figure 2.14 Themes Limited in Time and Place *Wild in the Streets* and *Easy Rider* dealt with problems and issues that seemed very relevant in the late 1960s and early 1970s, but many of their concerns seem ridiculous today.

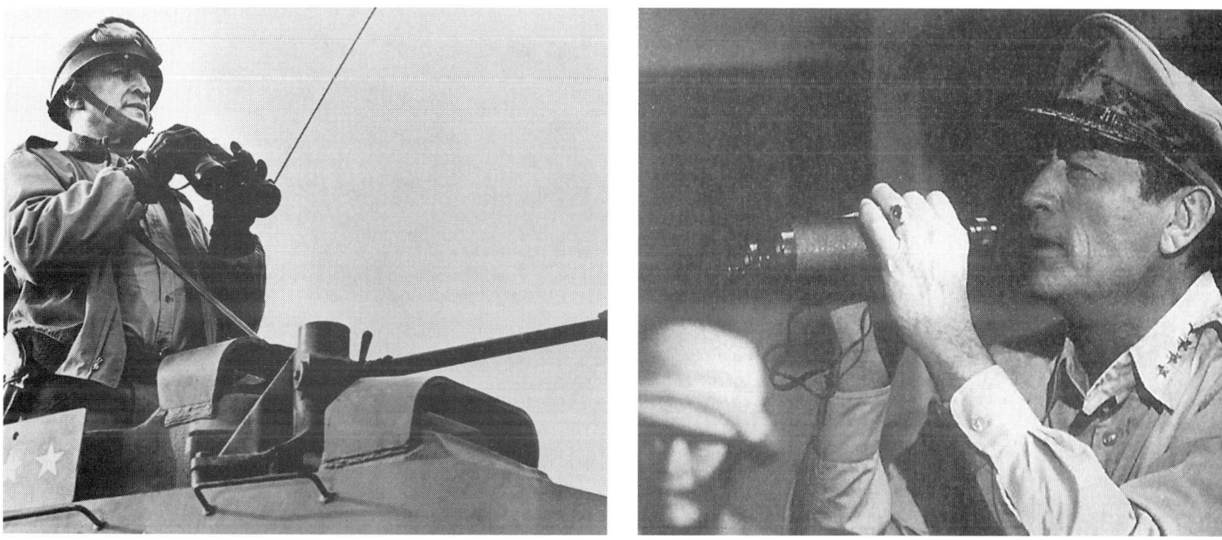

Figure 2.15 What Makes a Classic? *Patton* and *MacArthur* both treat famous generals who have won their place in history. *Patton* (starring George C. Scott) seems destined to become a film classic; *MacArthur* (starring Gregory Peck) is already gathering dust as a footnote in film history.

constant struggle to preserve their dignity. In the same way, *Casablanca* is more than just a story about two people losing and then finding each other in a world too chaotic for romantic dreams. It is a story about a beautiful woman and a mysterious man, about war, responsibility, courage, duty, and most of all, about doing the right thing. Such classics endure because of their strong, universal themes (Figure 2.16).

This does not mean that we place no value on themes that lack universality. Even if a theme's appeal is limited to a specific time and place, it may have some relevance to our own experience. We will naturally consider a theme that says something significant to us superior to one that does not.

We also have the right to expect that a thematic idea be intellectually or philosophically interesting. In other words, if a film attempts to make a significant statement, that statement should be neither boring nor self-evident but should interest or challenge us.

Figure 2.16 Universal Themes Although the specific problems forced upon Rick (Humphrey Bogart) and Ilsa (Ingrid Bergman) by World War II have long since disappeared, *Casablanca* lives on because of strong universal themes that reach beyond the romantic love story at its core.

Questions

On Theme and Focus

What is the film's primary focus: plot, emotional effect or mood, character, style or texture, or ideas? On the basis of your decision, answer one of these questions:

1. If the film's primary concern is plot, summarize the action abstractly in a single sentence or a short paragraph.
2. If the film is structured around a mood or emotional effect, describe the mood or feeling that it attempts to convey.
3. If the film's focus is on a single unique character, describe the unusual aspects of his or her personality.
4. If the film seems to be structured around a unique style or texture, describe the qualities that contribute to the special look or feel of the film.
5. If the film's primary focus is an idea, answer these questions:
   a. What is the true subject of the film? What is it really about in abstract terms? Identify the abstract subject in a single word or phrase.
   b. What comment or statement does the film make about the subject? If possible, formulate a sentence that accurately summarizes the idea dramatized by the film.

On Identifying the Theme

1. Although a director may attempt to do several things with a film, one goal usually stands out as most important. Decide which of the following was the director's *primary* aim, and give reasons for your choice.
   a. providing pure entertainment—that is, temporary escape from the real world
   b. developing a pervasive mood or creating a single, specialized emotional effect
   c. providing a character sketch of a unique, fascinating personality
   d. creating a consistent, unique feel or texture by weaving all of the complex elements of film together into a one-of-a-kind film experience
   e. criticizing society and social institutions and increasing the viewer's awareness of a social problem and the need for reform
   f. providing insights into human nature (demonstrating what human beings in general are like)
   g. creating a moral or philosophical riddle for the viewer to ponder
   h. making a moral implication to influence the viewer's values or behavior
   i. dramatizing one or more characters' struggle for human dignity against tremendous odds
   j. exploring the complex problems and pleasures of human relationships

k. providing insight into a growth experience, the special kinds of situations or conflicts that cause important changes in the character or characters involved

2. Which of the items listed in the previous question seem important enough to qualify as secondary aims?

On Evaluating the Theme

1. Is the film's basic appeal to the intellect, to the funny bone, to the moral sense, or to the aesthetic sense? Is it aimed primarily at the groin (the erotic sense), the viscera (blood and guts), the heart, the yellow streak down the back, or simply the eyes? Support your choice with specific examples from the film.
2. How well does your statement of the film's theme and focus stand up after you have thoroughly analyzed all elements of the film?
3. To what degree is the film's theme universal? Is the theme relevant to your own experience? How?
4. If you think the film makes a significant statement, why is it significant?
5. Decide whether the film's theme is intellectually or philosophically interesting, or self-evident and boring, and defend your decision.
6. Does the film have the potential to become a classic? Will people still be watching it twenty years from today? Why?

Video Exercises

Watch the first 5 minutes of any two of the following films: *To Kill a Mockingbird*, *Summer of '42*, *Midnight Cowboy*, *Shane*, *The Grapes of Wrath*, *Raiders of the Lost Ark*, *The World According to Garp*, and *Patton*. Then answer these questions.

1. From the 5-minute segments you have just seen, can you make intelligent guesses about each film's primary concern?
2. What does the music suggest about the emotional quality of each film? Will the film be happy, sad, or bittersweet? Funny, serious, or a mixture of the two?
3. What do you learn about the characters introduced in the beginning? Which of the characters are point of view characters (characters with whom we identify and through whose eyes we experience the film)? Which of the characters will we end up viewing more objectively, from a distance?

Films for Study

Focus on Plot

Air Force One (1997)
Bound (1996)
Con Air (1997)
The Hunt for Red October (1990)
Independence Day (1996)
Raiders of the Lost Ark (1981)
The Road Warrior (1981)
The Rock (1996)
Titanic (1997)
Tomorrow Never Dies (1997)

Focus on Emotional Effect or Mood

Bang the Drum Slowly (1973)
Bram Stoker's Dracula (1992)
The Bridges of Madison County (1995)
The Piano (1993)
Psycho (1960)
Scream (1996)
The Silence of the Lambs (1991)
Somewhere in Time (1980)

Focus on Character

The Apostle (1997)
Blue Sky (1994)
Central Station (1998)
Coal Miner's Daughter (1980)
Crumb (1994)
Elizabeth (1998)
Georgia (1995)
The Great Santini (1979)
Mrs. Brown (1997)
Nell (1994)
Patton (1970)
Raging Bull (1980)
Sergeant York (1941)
Sling Blade (1996)
Ulee's Gold (1997)
Zorba the Greek (1964)

Focus on Style or Texture

The Age of Innocence (1993)
Big Night (1997)
Brazil (1985)
Days of Heaven (1978)
Dead Man (1996)
The English Patient (1996)
Fargo (1996)
L.A. Confidential (1997)
Last Year at Marienbad (1961)
Like Water for Chocolate (1992)
Lost Highway (1997)
McCabe & Mrs. Miller (1971)
Nashville (1975)
The Pillow Book (1997)
Raising Arizona (1987)
3 Women (1977)
Wild at Heart (1990)

Focus on Human Nature

Deliverance (1972)
Groundhog Day (1993)
In the Company of Men (1997)
Lord of the Flies (1963)
Secrets & Lies (1996)
Shane (1953)

Struggle for Human Dignity

The Full Monty (1997)
The Grapes of Wrath (1940)
Il Postino (The Postman) (1994)
On the Waterfront (1954)
One Flew Over the Cuckoo's Nest (1975)
Requiem for a Heavyweight (1962)
Schindler's List (1993)
Shine (1996)

Complexity of Human Relationships

Boogie Nights (1997)
Chasing Amy (1997)
Jackie Brown (1997)
Midnight Cowboy (1969)
Nobody's Fool (1986)
Primary Colors (1998)
Terms of Endearment (1983)
Three Colors: Blue (1993), *White* (1994), *Red* (1994)
The Truth About Cats & Dogs (1996)
The War of the Roses (1989)
When Harry Met Sally . . . (1989)
The World According to Garp (1989)

Coming of Age/Growing Awareness

Educating Rita (1983)
Empire of the Sun (1987)
Going All the Way (1997)
Good Will Hunting (1997)
A Little Princess (1995)
Manny & Lo (1996)
October Sky (1999)
Ponette (1997)
Sixteen Candles (1984)
Summer of '42 (1971)
The Thief (1998)
To Kill a Mockingbird (1962)

Moral or Philosophical Riddle

Blue Velvet (1986)
Breaking the Waves (1996)
The Game (1997)
Persona (1966)
Pulp Fiction (1994)
The Purple Rose of Cairo (1985)
2001: A Space Odyssey (1968)

Focus on Social Problems

Amistad (1997)
Dead Man Walking (1995)
Falling Down (1993)
Kids (1995)
Margaret's Museum (1997)
Mississippi Burning (1988)
Natural Born Killers (1994)
Norma Rae (1979)
The Rainmaker (1997)
A Time to Kill (1996)
Welcome to the Dollhouse (1996)

Chapter 3

Fictional and Dramatic Elements

I don't want to film a "slice of life" because people can get that at home, in the street, or even in front of the movie theater. They don't have to pay money to see a slice of life. And I avoid out-and-out fantasy because people should be able to identify with the characters. Making a film means, first of all, to tell a story. That story can be an improbable one, but it should never be banal. It must be dramatic and human. What is drama, after all, but life with the dull bits cut out?

—Alfred Hitchcock, Director

Film Analysis and Literary Analysis

Film has properties that set it apart from painting, sculpture, novels, and plays. It is also, in its most popular and powerful form, a storytelling medium that shares many elements with the short story and the novel. And because film presents its stories in dramatic form, it has even more in common with the stage play: Both plays and movies act out or dramatize, show rather than tell, what happens.

Unlike the novel, short story, or play, however, film is not handy to study; it cannot be effectively frozen on the printed page. The novel and short story are relatively easy to study because they are written to be read. The stage play is slightly more difficult to study because it is written to be performed. But plays are printed, and because they rely heavily on the spoken word, imaginative readers can conjure up at least a pale imitation of the experience they might have watching a performance on stage. This cannot be said of the screenplay, for a film depends greatly on visual and other nonverbal elements that are not easily expressed in writing. The screenplay requires so much filling in by our imagination that we cannot really approximate the experience of a film by reading a screenplay, and reading a screenplay is worthwhile only if we have already seen the film. Thus, most screenplays are published not to be read but rather to be remembered.

Still, film should not be ignored because studying it requires extra effort. And the fact that we do not generally read films does not mean we should ignore the principles of literary or dramatic analysis when we see a film. Literature and films do share many elements and communicate many things in similar ways. Perceptive film analysis rests on the principles used in literary analysis, and if we apply what we have learned in the study of literature to our analysis of films, we will be far ahead of those who do not. Therefore, before we turn to the unique elements of film, we need to look into the elements that film shares with any good story.

Dividing film into its various elements for analysis is a somewhat artificial process, for the elements of any art form never exist in isolation. It is impossible, for example, to isolate plot from character: Events influence people, and people influence events; the two are always closely interwoven in any fictional, dramatic, or cinematic work. Nevertheless, the analytical method uses such a fragmenting technique for ease and convenience. But it does so with the assumption that we can study these elements in isolation without losing sight of their interdependence or their relationship to the whole.

The Elements of a Good Story

What makes a good story? Any answer to this question is bound to be subjective; however, some general observations might be made that will apply to a large variety of film narratives.

A Good Story Is Unified in Plot

The structured film is one that has some broad underlying purpose or is unified around a central theme. Regardless of the nature of its theme—whether its focus is on plot, emotional effect, character, style or texture, or idea—the fictional film generally has a plot or storyline that contributes to the development of that theme. Therefore, the plot and the events, conflicts, and characters that constitute it must be carefully selected and arranged so that their relationship to the theme is clear.

A unified plot focuses on a single thread of continuous action, where one event leads to another naturally and logically. Usually a strong cause-and-effect relationship exists between these events, and the outcome is made to seem, if not inevitable, at least probable. In a tightly unified plot, nothing can be transposed or removed without significantly affecting or altering the whole. Thus, every event grows naturally out of the plot, and the conflict must be resolved by elements or agents present in and prepared for in the plot itself.

A unified plot does not introduce out of thin air some kind of chance, coincidental, or miraculous happening, or some powerful superhuman force that swoops down out of nowhere to save the day. Consider, for example, this hypothetical scene from a western. A wagon train is attacked by a band of Indians. Doom seems certain. Suddenly, out of nowhere, appears a company of U.S. cavalry troops who just happen to be passing by on maneuvers, a hundred miles from the fort. Although such chance occurrences happen in real life, we reject them in fiction. The arrival of the cavalry to save the settlers would be acceptable if a reason for it were established earlier in the story (if, for example, a rider had been sent to bring the soldiers).

Although plot unity is a general requirement, exceptions do exist. In a film whose focus is the clear delineation of a unique character, unity of action and cause-and-effect relationships between events are not so important. In fact, such plots may be episodic (that is, composed of events that bear no direct relationship to each other), for the unity in such films emerges from the contribution each event makes to our understanding of the character being developed, rather than from the interrelationships of the events.

A Good Story Is Credible

To become fully involved in a story, we must be convinced that it could be true. A filmmaker can create the illusion of truth in a variety of ways.

1. **Externally Observable Truths: The way things really are.** The most obvious and common kind of truth in a film story is the approximation of life as it is. To borrow Aristotle's phrase, these are stories such as "might occur and have the capability of occurring in accordance with the laws of probability or necessity." This kind of truth is based on overwhelming evidence in the world around us, so it may not always be a pleasant truth.

Figure 3.1 The Way Things Really Are *The Last Picture Show, Driving Miss Daisy,* and *Rain Man* are credible because they conform to what we perceive as real-life experiences.

Human beings are flawed creatures. Married couples don't always live happily ever after, and tragic accidents, serious illnesses, and great misfortunes often befall people who don't seem to deserve them. But we accept such truths because they conform to our own experience of the way life is (Figure 3.1).

2. **Internal Truths of Human Nature: The way things are supposed to be.** Another set of truths seems true because we want or need to believe in them. Some of the greatest film classics do not even pretend to represent the actualities of real life; instead, they offer a fairy-tale or happily-ever-after ending. The good guy always wins, and true love conquers all. But in a very special way, these stories are also believable, or at least can be made to seem so, because they contain what might be called internal truths—

Figure 3.2 The Way Things Are Supposed to Be We also find movies credible that present images of the world as we might like it to be, such as *The Mirror Has Two Faces, Dave,* and *Mr. Smith Goes to Washington.*

beliefs in things that are not really observable but that seem true to us because we want or need them to be. Indeed, the concept of poetic justice (the idea that virtue will be rewarded and evil punished) serves as an example of such an internal truth. We seldom question poetic justice in a story simply because it is the way things are supposed to be. Thus many film stories are convincing because they conform to an inner truth and satisfy a human need to believe. Of course, such truths can ring false to those who do not want or need to believe them (Figure 3.2).

3. **Artistic Semblance of Truth: The way things never were and never will be.** Filmmakers are also capable of creating a special kind of truth. With their artistry, technical skills, and special effects, they can create an imaginary world on the screen that, for the duration of the film, seems totally believable. In such films, truth depends on the early and thoroughly convincing establishment of a strange or fantastic environment, sense of

Figure 3.3 The Way Things Never Were and Never Will Be By using their special brand of artistry, filmmakers can create on the screen an imaginary world that makes us willingly accept incredible settings, characters, and events in such films as *Edward Scissorhands* (top left), *Poltergeist* (top right), *Batman* (bottom left) and *Men in Black* (bottom right).

another time, or unusual characters, so that we are caught up in the film's overall spirit, mood, and atmosphere. If the filmmaker is skillful at creating this semblance of truth, we willingly agree to suspend our disbelief (as Samuel Taylor Coleridge observed), and we leave our skepticism and our rational faculties behind as we enter the film's imaginary world. If the fictional reality is successfully established, we may think to ourselves, "Yes, in such a situation almost anything can happen." By communicating this pervasive and real sense of an unusual situation or environment, filmmakers in effect create a new set of ground rules by which we judge reality. And for the brief period of an hour or two, we can believe thoroughly in the truth of *Rosemary's Baby*, *The Day the Earth Stood Still*, *King Kong*, *Mary Poppins*, *The Wizard of Oz*, or *E.T. The Extra-Terrestrial* (Figure 3.3).

Thus the plausibility of a story depends on at least three separate factors: (1) the objective, external, and observable laws of probability and necessity; (2) the subjective, irrational, and emotional inner truths of human nature; and (3) the semblance of truth created by the filmmaker's convincing art. Although all these kinds of truths may be present in the same film, usually one kind of truth is central to the film's overall structure. The other truths may contribute but play supporting roles.

A Good Story Is Interesting

An important requirement of a good story is that it capture and hold our interest. A story can be interesting in many ways, and few if any stories have equal appeal to all filmgoers, for whether a story is interesting or boring is, to a great extent, a subjective matter. Some of us may be interested only in fast-paced action/adventure films. Others may be bored by anything without a romantic love interest at its center. Still others may be indifferent to any story that lacks deep philosophical significance.

But regardless of what we expect from a motion picture—whether it be the relaxation gained from being entertained or a clue to understanding the universe—we never go to the movies to be bored. Our tolerance for boredom seems very limited: A film may shock us, frustrate us, puzzle us, or even offend us, but it must *never* bore us. Thus, we fully expect the filmmaker to heighten the film's reality by doing away with irrelevant and distracting details. Why should we pay to watch the dull, the monotonous, or the routine when life provides them absolutely free of charge?

Even the Italian neorealist directors, who stress everyday reality in their films and deny the validity of invented stories, argue that their particular brand of everyday reality is not boring because of its complex echoes and implications. As Cesare Zavattini puts it, "Give us whatever 'fact' you like, and we will disembowel it, make it something worth watching."[1] To most of us, the expressions "worth watching" and "interesting" are synonymous.

Suspense To capture and maintain our interest, the filmmaker employs a multitude of devices and techniques, most of which are in some way related to suspense. These elements heighten our interest by exciting our curiosity, usually by foreshadowing or hinting at the outcome. By withholding bits of information that would answer the dramatic questions raised by the story, and by floating some unanswered question just beyond our reach, the filmmaker provides a motive to keep us constantly moving with the story's flow (Figure 3.4).

Action If a story is to be interesting, it must contain some elements of action. Stories are never static; some sort of action or change is essential if a story is to be worth telling. Action, of course, is not limited to physical activities such as

Figure 3.4 Suspense In *Witness* the solution to a brutal murder is locked in the mind of an Amish boy (Lukas Haas), who witnessed the crime. Suspense builds steadily throughout the film as a policeman (Harrison Ford) tries to protect him from corrupt law enforcement agents.

fights, chases, duels, and great battles. It may be internal, psychological, or emotional. In films such as *Star Wars* and *Jurassic Park*, the action is external and physical; in *The Remains of the Day* and *Manhattan*, the action occurs within the minds and the emotions of the characters. Both sorts of films have movement and change. The interest created by the exciting action in *The Road Warrior* is obvious and needs no explanation. But the action within a human being is not so obvious. Nothing very extraordinary happens in *The Remains of the Day*, but what takes place in the hearts and minds of its characters is extremely interesting and exciting (Figures 3.5, 3.6).

Internal action stories require more concentration from the viewer, and they are more difficult to treat cinematically. But they are worthwhile subjects for film and can be as interesting and exciting as films that stress external and physical action.

A Good Story Is Both Simple and Complex

A good film story must be simple enough so that it can be expressed and unified cinematically. Edgar Allan Poe's idea that a short story should be capable of

Figure 3.5 External Action The exciting action in *The Last of the Mohicans* gives us little time for reflection. We are kept on the edge of our chairs throughout and, by film's end, are totally exhausted by the constant, fast-paced tension.

Figure 3.6 Internal Action Although there is little physical action in *The Remains of the Day*, what is happening in the minds and hearts of the Emma Thompson and Anthony Hopkins characters is extremely interesting and exciting.

being read in a single sitting applies to film. Experiencing a film is less tiring than reading a book, and the single sitting for a film may be a maximum of, say, two hours. Beyond that time limit, only the greatest films keep us from becoming restless or inattentive. Thus the story's action or theme must usually be compressed into a unified dramatic structure that requires about two hours to unfold. In most cases, a limited, simple theme, such as that in *Manhattan*, which focuses on a small slice of one person's life, is better suited for the cinema than is a story that spans the ages in search of a timeless theme, as D. W. Griffith attempted in *Intolerance*. Generally, a story should be simple enough to be told in the time period allotted for its telling.

However, within these limits, a good story must also have some complexity, at least enough to sustain our interest. And although a good story may hint at the eventual outcome, it must also provide some surprises or at least be subtle enough to prevent the viewer from predicting the outcome after the first hour. Thus, a good story usually withholds something about its conclusion or significance until the very end.

But new elements introduced into the plot at the very end may make us question the legitimacy of the surprise ending, especially if such elements bring about an almost miraculous conclusion or make too much use of coincidence or chance. A surprise ending can be powerful and legitimate when the plot prepares us for it, even when the plot elements and the chain of cause and effect leading up to the ending escape our conscious attention. The important thing is that the viewer never feel hoodwinked, fooled, or cheated by a surprise ending. The viewer should gain insight by means of the ending. Such insight occurs only when the surprise ending carries out tendencies established earlier in the story. A good plot is complex enough to keep us in doubt but simple enough so that the seeds of the outcome can all be found.

A filmmaker's communication techniques must also be a proper blend of simplicity and complexity. Filmmakers must communicate some things simply, clearly, and directly, so that they are clear to all viewers. But to challenge the minds and eyes of the most perceptive viewers, they must also communicate through implication and suggestion, leaving some things open to interpretation. Some viewers are bored by films that are too complex, that make too much use of implication or suggestion. Other viewers—those who prefer an intellectual challenge—are not interested in films that are too direct and simple. Thus, a filmmaker must please both those who do not appreciate films they cannot easily understand and those who reject films they understand all too easily.

Filmgoers' views of life also influence their attitudes toward a film's complexity or simplicity. Those who see life itself as complex and ambiguous are likely to demand that kind of complexity and ambiguity in the films they see. Such viewers may reject an escapist film because it falsifies the nature of existence by making it seem too easy, too neat, too pat. Other viewers may reject

Figure 3.7 Complexity The levels of confusion created by the constant jumping back and forth between illusion and reality in *The Stunt Man* may stimulate some viewers but may be too complex to provide the relaxing entertainment expected by others.

Figure 3.8 Simplicity The constant tension and unmotivated violence in *Scream* may entertain viewers looking for escapist entertainment but bore others who demand more depth and complexity.

the complex view of life presented in realistic or naturalistic films for the opposite reason—because the film is too full of ambiguities, too complex, or because it does not conform to the inner subjective truth of life—life as they would like it to be (Figures 3.7, 3.8).

A Good Story Handles Emotional Material With Restraint

A strong emotional element or effect is present in almost any story, and film is capable of manipulating our emotions. But this manipulation must be honest and appropriate to the story. Usually we reject as sentimental films that overuse emotional material. Such films might even make us laugh when we're supposed to cry. So a filmmaker must exercise restraint.

Reactions to emotional material depend on the individual viewer. One viewer may consider the film *The Bridges of Madison County* a beautifully touching and poignant experience, whereas another scoffs and calls it "sentimental trash." The difference often lies in the viewers themselves. The first viewer probably responded fully to the film, allowing himself to be manipulated by its emotional effects without considering the filmmaker dishonest. The second viewer probably felt that the film unfairly attempted to manipulate her emotions, and she responded by rejecting it.

When the emotional material in a film is understated, there is little danger of offending. In understatement the filmmaker downplays the emotional material, giving it less emphasis than the situation would seem to call for. In *To Kill a Mockingbird,* Atticus Finch (Gregory Peck) uses a simple phrase to thank the boogeyman, Arthur "Boo" Radley (Robert Duvall), for saving the lives of Scout and Jem: "Thank you, Arthur . . . for my children." The effect of understatement is demonstrated by the tremendous emotional weight carried by the simple phrase "thank you," which we often use for the most trivial favors. The normally insignificant phrase takes on great significance, and we are moved by what is *not* said. The voice-over narration from the same film offers another example of understatement:

> Neighbors bring food with death and flowers with sickness and little things in between. Boo was our neighbor. He gave us two soap dolls, a broken watch and chain, a pair of good luck pennies, and our lives.

A wide variety of elements and techniques influence our emotional response to a film. Both understatement and the overuse of emotional material are reflected in the way the plot is structured, in the dialogue and the acting, and in the visual effects. Elements of a film's visual environment or setting (discussed at length in Chapter 4), and its creation of atmosphere, can also appeal to the viewer's senses and affect his or her emotional reaction. But a filmmaker's approach to presenting emotional material is perhaps most evident in the musical score, which can communicate on a purely emotional level and thus reflects the peaks and valleys of emotional emphasis and understatement (see Chapter 9).

The Significance of the Title

The importance of a suitable title is not overlooked by writers like Neil Simon:

> When looking for a fun title, you're looking for something that's going to grab them. In the titles to my plays that really mean something to me, I try to tell the audience what the play is about, what the character is about. I try to tell the story in the title.

> . . . When I don't have it, I'll work very hard because it's as important to me as writing the first scene, getting the title. I feel comfortable if it sounds right.[2]

In most films, we can understand the full significance of the title only after seeing the film. In many cases, the title has one meaning to a viewer before seeing the film and a completely different, richer, and deeper meaning afterward. Titles are often ironic, expressing an idea exactly the opposite of the meaning intended, and many titles allude to mythology, biblical passages, or other literary works. For example, the title *All the King's Men* is taken from "Humpty Dumpty" and serves to remind us of the nursery rhyme, which provides a nutshell summary of the plot. *All the King's Men* concerns a southern dictator (king) who rises to a position of high power (sat on a wall) but is assassinated (had a great fall). As in the case of Humpty Dumpty, "all the king's men" are unable to put the king together again. On another level, the title literally tells us what the story is about. Willie Stark, the politician, is the primary energy force. However, Jack Burden, Stark's press secretary and right-hand man, is actually the focal character, and the story is very much concerned with the lives of others who work for Stark in one capacity or another. Thus, the story is in a sense about "all the king's men." On yet another plane the title serves to link the fictional character Willie Stark to the real-life politician Huey Long, on whose career the story is loosely based. Long's favorite nickname for himself was "The Kingfisher," from a character on the old "Amos 'n' Andy" radio show, and Long once wrote a song around his campaign slogan, "Every man a king, but no one wears a crown."

Some titles may call attention to a key scene that becomes worthy of careful study when we realize that the title of the film has been taken from it. Although the title seldom names the theme (as it does in *Sense and Sensibility* and *Good Will Hunting*), it is usually an extremely important clue in identifying it. Thus, it is essential to think carefully about the possible meanings of the title after seeing any film.

Dramatic Structure

The art of storytelling as practiced in the short story, novel, play, or film has always depended on a strong dramatic structure—that is, the aesthetic and logical arrangement of parts to achieve the maximum emotional, intellectual, or dramatic impact. Dramatic structure can be linear or nonlinear, depending upon the author's needs and wishes. Both patterns contain the same elements: exposition, complication, climax, and dénouement. They differ only in the arrangement of these elements.

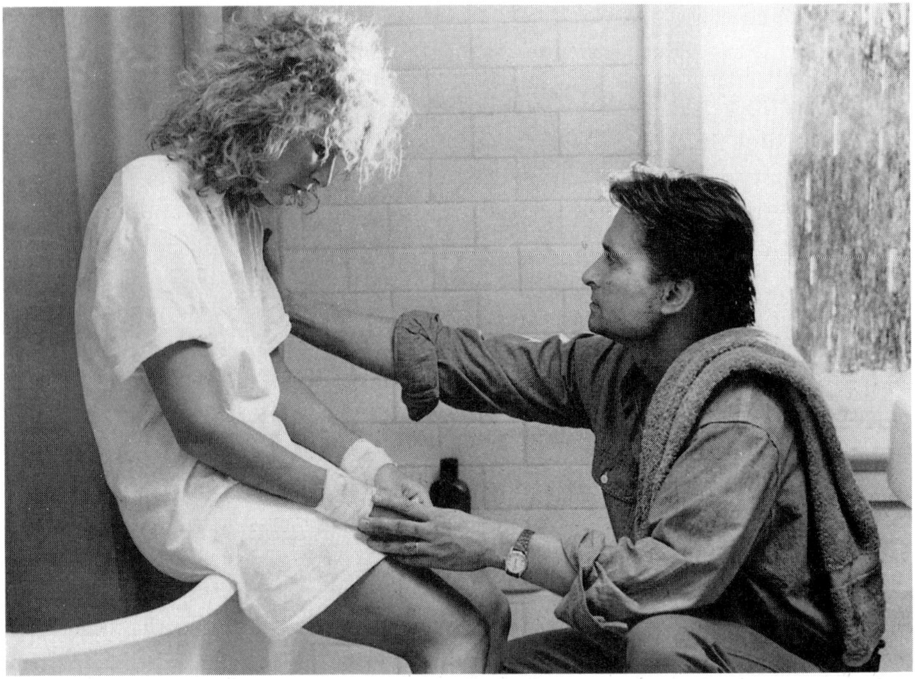

Figure 3.9 Linear Structure In *Fatal Attraction,* the brief fling that leads to Glenn Close's obsessive pursuit of Michael Douglas occurs at the beginning of the film, and the story proceeds in strict chronological order to its violent conclusion.

Linear, or Chronological, Structure

Screenwriter Ernest Lehman describes films having the linear, or chronological, structure in terms of acts:

> In the first act, who are the people, what is the situation of this whole story? Second act is the progression of that situation to a point of high conflict and great problems. And the third act is how the problems and the conflicts are resolved. That's putting it a little patly, but that's the way it ought to be.[3]

The first part of the story, called the **exposition,** introduces the characters, shows some of their interrelationships, and places them within a believable time and place. In the next section, the **complication,** a conflict begins and grows in clarity, intensity, and importance. Because dramatic tension and suspense are created and maintained during the complication, this is usually the longest section. When the complication has reached its point of maximum tension, the two forces in opposition confront each other at a high point of physical or emotional action called the **climax.** At the climax, the conflict is resolved and there follows a brief period of calm, the **dénouement,** in which a state of relative equilibrium returns (Figure 3.9).

Figure 3.10 Nonlinear Structure *Jacknife* begins in the present with its two major characters, played by Robert De Niro and Ed Harris, having difficulties renewing a Vietnam War friendship. The film then flashes back to combat scenes that give us insight into the Harris character's present mental state.

Nonlinear Structures

There are many variations of nonlinear structure, including *in medias res* beginnings and episodic structures, in which the elements are not arranged chronologically. A story that begins ***in medias res*** (a Latin phrase meaning "in the middle of things") opens with an exciting incident that actually happens *after* the complication has developed. This technique, used by Homer to begin the *Iliad* and the *Odyssey*, captures the audience's interest at the outset and creates a state of dramatic tension. The necessary expository information is filled in later as the situation permits, through such means as dialogue (characters talking about the situation or events that led to the complication) or **flashbacks** (filmed sequences that go back in time to provide expository material). In this manner exposition can be built up gradually and spread throughout the film instead of being established at the beginning, before dramatic interest starts to build (Figure 3.10).

Providing exposition is not the only function of flashback. The use of visual flashback gives a filmmaker great flexibility. By using flashback, the filmmaker can present information as he or she desires, when it is most dramatically appropriate and powerful or when it most effectively illuminates the theme. (**Flash-**

forward, a filmed sequence that jumps from the present into the future, has been tried in such films as *Easy Rider*, *They Shoot Horses, Don't They?* and *Love! Valour! Compassion!* It is doubtful whether this device will ever gain widespread acceptance.) As long as coherence is maintained so that the relationship between one scene and another is clear, the director can violate strict chronological order at will.

Sometimes, however, a director may purposely try to confuse the time sequence. In the haunting and mystifying *Last Year at Marienbad*, Alain Resnais seems determined to keep us wondering whether the scene we are watching is taking place in the present (this year) or in the past (last year) or, in fact, whether it really takes place at all. Writer-director Quentin Tarantino has tried some unusual scrambled chronology in his films, including *Reservoir Dogs* and *Pulp Fiction*, presumably to establish a stylistic trademark.

Endings: Fine-Tuning the Dénouement

Movies and plays, unlike short stories and novels, are often field-tested before an audience. Just as plays have tryouts on the road before they open on Broadway, yet-to-be-released films are given sneak previews in carefully selected locations to see how audiences like them. Highly sophisticated test-marketing techniques are employed to determine the final version of many films. Woody Allen, Frank Capra, and Danny DeVito are all strong believers in using sneak previews to test audience response. As DeVito puts it: "It's like asking the audience to be your barometer. It's a very, very informative process. As far as I'm concerned, the audience has the final cut."[4]

Filmmakers are especially interested in the audience's response to the ending, or dénouement, of their films. An unsatisfactory ending often results in poor word-of-mouth (WOM), and poor WOM means poor results at the box office. According to Griffin Dunne, star and coproducer of *After Hours*, "If the last five minutes are disturbing, it has an overriding effect on the first ninety."[5] *After Hours* originally ended with Dunne's character (encased in a plaster cast) being mistaken for a sculpture and "carted away toward an unknown, but surely ugly future." Audience response was negative, and a new ending that was "less stifling" and "more positive" was shot. Both endings were then previewed, and audiences expressed a clear preference for the happier ending.

In the original ending of *Fatal Attraction*, Michael Douglas's fingerprints were found on the knife that Glenn Close used to commit suicide, evidence that sent Douglas to jail for murder. The preview audience, however, had so strongly identified with Douglas and his family that that ending proved totally unsatisfactory and a different ending was shot. Another change that pleased its viewers was altering the original conclusion of *My Best Friend's Wedding*. The preview audiences insisted that the Julia Roberts character end up dancing with her gay friend (Rupert Everett) rather than marrying the less interesting romantic lead (played by Dermot Mulroney).

Figure 3.11 Conflict The mainspring of practically any film is the dramatic tension created by human conflict. In *One Flew Over the Cuckoo's Nest,* mental patient Randall McMurphy (Jack Nicholson) and Nurse Ratched (Louise Fletcher) battle constantly from the moment they meet until McMurphy is lobotomized.

Conflict

In his essay "Why Do We Read Fiction?" Robert Penn Warren observes,

> A story is not merely an image of life, but of life in motion . . . individual characters moving through their particular experiences to some end that we may accept as meaningful. And the experience that is characteristically presented in a story is that of facing a problem, a conflict. To put it bluntly: No conflict, no story.[6]

Conflict is the mainspring of every story, whether it be told on the printed page, on the stage, or on the screen. It is the element that really captures our interest, heightens the intensity of our experience, and quickens our pulses and challenges our minds (Figure 3.11).

Although there may be several conflicts within a story, some kind of major conflict at its core ultimately has the greatest importance to the story as a whole. The major conflict is of great importance to the characters involved, and there is some worthwhile and perhaps lasting goal to be gained by the resolution of that conflict. Because it is highly significant to the characters, and because significant conflicts have important effects on people and events, the major conflict and its resolution almost always bring about an important change, either in the people involved or in their situation.

The major conflict has a high degree of complexity; it is not the sort of problem that can be quickly and easily resolved by an obvious or simple solution. Thus its outcome remains in doubt throughout the greater part of the film. The complexity of the struggle is also influenced by the fact that the forces in conflict are nearly equal in strength, a fact that adds greatly to the dramatic tension and power of the work. In some films, the major conflict and its resolution may contribute greatly to the viewer's experience, for it is the conflict and its resolution (or sometimes its lack of resolution) that clarify or illuminate the nature of human experience.

Some major conflicts are primarily physical, such as a fistfight or a shootout in a western. Others are almost completely psychological, as is often the case in the films of Federico Fellini or Ingmar Bergman. In most films, however, the conflict has both physical and psychological dimensions, and determining where one stops and the other begins is often difficult. It is perhaps simpler and more meaningful to classify major conflicts under the broad headings of external and internal.

In its simplest form, an **external conflict** may consist of a personal and individual struggle between the central character and another character. On this level the conflict is nothing more than a contest of human wills in opposition or seeking similar goals, as might be illustrated by a prizefight, a duel, or two suitors seeking to win the affections of the same woman. Yet these basic and simple human conflicts have a tendency to be more complex than they first appear. Conflicts can seldom be isolated completely from other individuals, society as a whole, or the value systems of the individuals involved. Thus, they often grow into representative struggles between groups of people, different segments of society or social institutions, or different value systems.

Another type of external conflict pits the central character or characters against some nonhuman force or agency, such as fate, the gods, the forces of nature, or the social system. Here the forces the characters face are essentially nonhuman and impersonal. Jefferson Smith's (James Stewart) struggle against the political corruption and graft of the "Taylor machine" in *Mr. Smith Goes to Washington* is an example of an external conflict that pits a single individual against "the system." A more physical type of external conflict occurs in the legend of John Henry, who struggles to prove his worth against the dehumanizing forces of technology.

An **internal conflict** centers on an interior, psychological conflict within the central character. The forces in opposition are simply different aspects of the same personality. For example, in James Thurber's "The Secret Life of

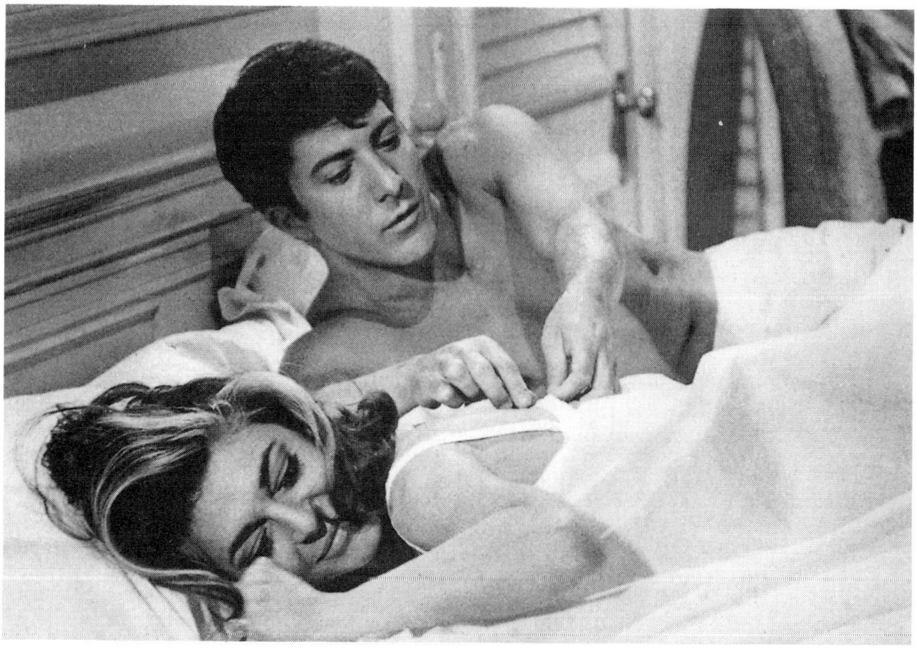

Figure 3.12 Internal Conflict Benjamin Braddock (Dustin Hoffman) gets all the internal conflict he can handle when he is seduced by the wife of his father's law partner in *The Graduate.*

Walter Mitty," we have a conflict between what a man actually is (a small, timid, incompetent creature, henpecked by an overbearing wife) and what he wants to be (a brave and competent hero). By escaping constantly into the world of his daydreams, Mitty reveals himself to be living in a permanent state of conflict between his heroic dreams and the drab reality of his existence. In all such internal conflicts, we see a character squeezed between the two sides of his or her personality, torn between equally strong but conflicting desires, goals, or value systems. In some cases, this inner conflict is resolved and the character grows or develops as a result, but in many cases, like that of Walter Mitty, there is no resolution.

The standard Woody Allen character in films such as *Annie Hall*, *Manhattan*, and *Play It Again, Sam*, is torn by internal conflicts and insecurities. In *Play It Again, Sam*, the central character tries to overcome his self doubts and insecurities by emulating his screen hero, Humphrey Bogart (Figure 3.12).

Characterization

You can only involve an audience with people. You can't involve them with gimmicks, with sunsets, with hand-held cameras, zoom shots, or anything else. They couldn't care less about those things. But you give them something to worry about, some person they can worry about, and care about, and you've got them, you've got them involved.[7]

—Frank Capra, Director

If we are not interested in a film's most human elements—its characters—there is little chance that we will be interested in the film as a whole. To be interesting, characters must seem real, understandable, and worth caring about. For the most part, the characters in a story are believable in the same way that the story is believable. In other words, they conform to the laws of probability and necessity (by reflecting externally observable truths about human nature), they conform to some inner truth (man as we want him to be), or they are made to seem real by the convincing art of the actor.

If characters are truly credible, it is almost impossible to remain completely neutral toward them. We must respond to them in some way: We may admire them for their heroic deeds and their nobility or pity them for their failures. We may love them or identify with them for their ordinary human qualities. We may laugh at them for their ignorance or laugh with them because theirs is a human ignorance that we all share. If our reaction to them is negative, we may detest them for their greed, their cruelty, their selfishness, and their underhanded methods. Or we may scorn them for their cowardice.

Characterization Through Appearance

Because most film actors project certain qualities of character the minute they appear on the screen, characterization in film has a great deal to do with casting. A major aspect of film characterization is revealed visually and instantaneously. Although some actors may be versatile enough to project completely different qualities in different roles, most actors are not. The minute we see most actors on the screen, we make certain assumptions about them because of their facial features, dress, physical build, and mannerisms and the way they move. Our first visual impression may be proven erroneous as the story progresses, but it is certainly an important means of establishing character. Consider the immediate reactions we have to Richard Harris and Robert Duvall when they appear for the first time in *Wrestling Ernest Hemingway* or to Jack Palance as the gunfighter Wilson in *Shane* (Figure 3.13).

Characterization Through Dialogue

Characters in a fictional film naturally reveal a great deal about themselves by what they say. But a great deal is also revealed by how they say it. Their true thoughts, attitudes, and emotions can be revealed in subtle ways through word choice and through the stress, pitch, and pause patterns of their speech. Actors' use of grammar, sentence structure, vocabulary, and particular dialects (if any)

Figure 3.13 Characterization Through Appearance The strange physical appearance, the unusual uniform, and the exaggerated facial expressions immediately characterize the Gyro Captain (Bruce Spence) when we first meet him in *The Road Warrior.* But in *Fargo,* police chief Marge (Frances McDormand), pregnant and wearing a floppy-earmuffed cap, makes an early impression on the viewer that belies her shrewd and swift intelligence.

Figure 3.14 Characterization Through Dialogue The quaint, formal, archaic Quaker dialogue of Mattie (Kim Darby) and the rough-hewn but stilted dialogue of Rooster Cogburn (John Wayne) add an unusual quality to their characters in *True Grit.*

reveals a great deal about their characters' social and economic level, educational background, and mental processes. Therefore, we must develop a keen ear, attuned to the faintest and most subtle nuances of meaning revealed through the human voice—listening carefully not only to what is said but also to how it is said (Figure 3.14).

Characterization Through External Action

Although appearance is an important measure of a character's personality, appearances are often misleading. Perhaps the best reflections of character are a person's actions. It must be assumed, of course, that real characters are more than mere instruments of the plot, that they do what they do for a purpose, out of motives that are consistent with their overall personality. Thus, there should be a clear relationship between a character and his or her actions; the actions should grow naturally out of the character's personality. If the motivation for a character's action is clearly established, the character and the plot become so closely interwoven that they are impossible to separate, and every action that the character takes in some way reflects the quality of his or her particular personality.

Of course, some actions are more important in revealing character than others. Even the most ordinary choice can be revealing, for some kind of choice is involved in almost everything we do. Sometimes the most effective characterization is achieved not by the large actions in the film but by the small, seemingly insignificant ones. For example, a fireman may demonstrate his courage by saving a child from a burning building, yet such an act may be only a performance of duty rather than a reflection of a choice. His essential character might be more clearly defined by risking his life to save a little girl's doll, because such an action would be imposed on him not by his duty as a fireman but by his personal judgment about the value of a doll to a little girl.

Characterization Through Internal Action

There is an inner world of action that normally remains unseen and unheard by even the most careful observer/listener. Yet the dimension of human nature that this world embraces is often essential to a real understanding of a character. Inner action occurs within characters' minds and emotions and consists of secret, unspoken thoughts, daydreams, aspirations, memories, fears, and fantasies. People's hopes, dreams, and aspirations can be as important to an understanding of their character as any real achievement, and their fears and insecurities can be more terrible to them than any real catastrophic failure. Thus, although Walter Mitty is a dull, drab, insignificant creature, scarcely worth caring about when judged purely by his external behavior, he becomes an exciting and interesting personality when we read his mind and see his daydreams.

The most obvious way in which the filmmaker reveals inner reality is by taking us visually or aurally into the mind so that we see or hear the things that the character imagines, remembers, or thinks about. This may be achieved through a sustained interior view or through fleeting glimpses revealed by means of metaphors. In addition to providing glimpses into the inner action by revealing the sounds and sights the character imagines he sees and hears, the filmmaker may employ tight close-ups on an unusually sensitive and expressive face (reaction shots) or may utilize the musical score for essentially the same purpose.

Characterization Through Reactions of Other Characters

The way other characters view a person often serves as an excellent means of characterization. Sometimes, a great deal of information about a character is already provided through such means before the character first appears on the screen. This is the case in the opening scene of *Hud*. In this sequence Lonnie (Brandon DeWilde) is walking along the main street of the little Texas town at around 6:30 in the morning, looking for his uncle, Hud (Paul Newman). As

Lonnie passes a beer joint along the way, the owner is out front, sweeping up the pieces of glass that used to be his large front window. Lonnie notices the broken window and observes, "You must have had quite a brawl in here last night." The owner replies, "I had *Hud* in here last night, that's what I had." The man's emphasis on the name "Hud" and his tone of voice clearly reveal that "Hud" is a synonym for "trouble." A complex and intriguing characterization is provided through the conversations of other characters about Rick (Humphrey Bogart) in *Casablanca* before the character is ever seen on the screen. An effective bit of reactive characterization is also seen in *Shane*, as the gunfighter Wilson (Jack Palance), a personification of pure evil, walks into a saloon, empty except for a mangy dog curled up under a table. As Wilson enters, the dog puts his ears back and his tail between his legs and slinks fearfully out of the room.

Characterization Through Contrast: Dramatic Foils

One of the most effective techniques of characterization is the use of **foils**—contrasting characters whose behavior, attitudes, opinions, lifestyle, physical appearance, and so on are the opposite of those of the main characters. The effect is similar to that achieved by putting black and white together—the black appears blacker and the white appears whiter. The tallest giant and the tiniest midget might be placed side by side at the carnival sideshow, and the filmmaker sometimes uses characters in much the same way. Consider, for example, the effective contrasts in the characters played by Andy Griffith and Don Knotts on the old "Andy Griffith Show." Griffith, as Sheriff Taylor, was tall and a little heavy, and he projected a calm, self-confident, easygoing personality. Knotts, as Deputy Fife, was the exact opposite—short, skinny, and insecure, and a bundle of nerves (Figures 3.15, 3.16).

Characterization Through Caricature and Leitmotif

In order to etch a character quickly and deeply in our minds and memories, actors often exaggerate or distort one or more dominant features or personality traits. This device is called **caricature** (from the technique used in cartooning). In television's "M*A*S*H," the perpetual womanizing of Hawkeye Pierce (Alan Alda) and the eternal naiveté, innocence, and keen hearing of Radar O'Reilly (Gary Burghoff) are examples of caricature, as, in film, are Felix Unger's (Jack Lemmon) obsession with neatness and Oscar Madison's (Walter Matthau) messiness in *The Odd Couple*. A physical feature, such as the way a person moves, may also be caricatured, as seen in Chester's (Dennis Weaver) exaggerated, stiff-legged limp on the old "Gunsmoke" series, or in Grandpa's (Will Geer) half-limp shuffle in "The Waltons." Voice qualities and accents may also function in this way, as illustrated by the backwoods nasal voice employed by Ken Curtis as

Figure 3.15 Dramatic Foils In Peter Ustinov's 1962 film version of *Billy Budd,* Herman Melville's allegory of good and evil, the sweet, naive, and innocent Billy (Terence Stamp) contrasts sharply with the grim, satanic Master of Arms Claggart (Robert Ryan). The striking opposites in their characters are emphasized by their features, facial expressions, clothing, and voice qualities. Stamp is baby-faced; his features are soft and smooth, his expressions sweet, almost effeminate; his eyes are light blue, wide open, innocent. Ryan's face is mature and lined, the jaw and mouth strong and hard set; his expressions are sour and cynical; his eyes are dark, narrow, piercing, malevolent. Billy's fair complexion, blond (almost white) hair, and white shirt contrast with Claggart's dark hair and clothing. Billy's voice is soft, sometimes melodious; Claggart's is deep, unctuous, cold.

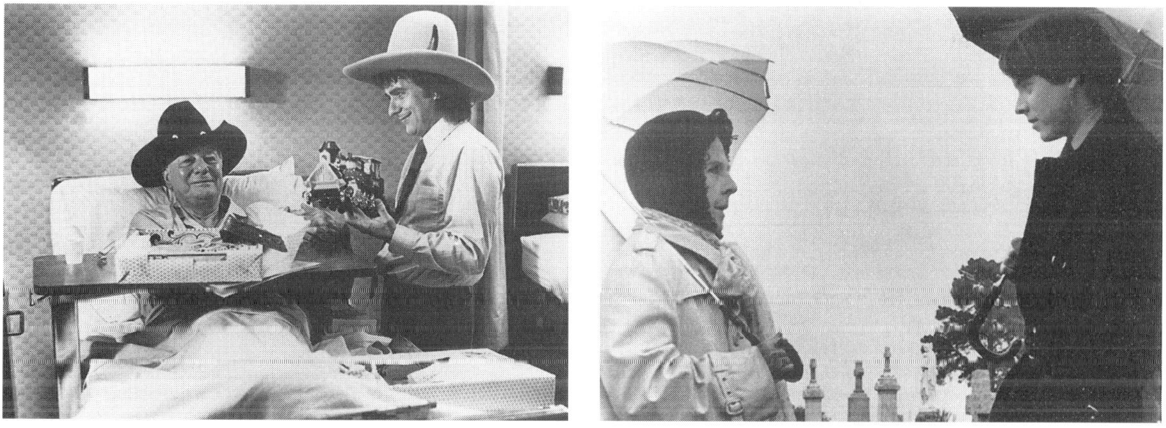

Figure 3.16 Dramatic Foils for Humor Opposite character types are often brought together to intensify the humor. This is the case with the constantly inebriated playboy Arthur Bach (Dudley Moore) and his sober-sided valet, Hobson (John Gielgud), in *Arthur.* It is also the case in the strange love story of Harold (Bud Cort) and Maude (Ruth Gordon) in *Harold and Maude.* As the ad for the movie described them: "Harold's 20 and in love with death . . . Maude's 80 and in love with life."

Festus Haigan on "Gunsmoke" and the New England aristocratic speech of David Ogden Stiers as Major Winchester on "M*A*S*H."

A similar means of characterization, **leitmotif,** is the repetition of a single phrase or idea by a character until it becomes almost a trademark or theme song for that character. Because it essentially exaggerates and emphasizes (through repetition), such a device acts very much like caricature. Examples of leitmotif might be seen in the repeated Fred Astaire dance routines performed by the prosecuting attorney (Ted Danson) in *Body Heat* or in the repetition of the phrase "sports fans" by Colonel Bull Meechum (Robert Duvall) in *The Great Santini*. One of the union henchmen in *On the Waterfront* adds dignity to his yes-man role by constantly using the word *definitely*. Perhaps Charles Dickens rates as the all-time master of both techniques. Recall Uriah Heep from *David Copperfield*, who continually wrings his hands (caricature) and says, "I'm so 'umble" (leitmotif). Modern films such as *Catch-22* still employ such techniques effectively, although not quite as extensively (Figure 3.17).

Figure 3.17 Leitmotif In this scene from *Sudden Impact,* Dirty Harry (Clint Eastwood) tells an armed criminal to "Go ahead, make my day." The phrase made such an impression on audiences that it was frequently repeated and became a trademark for the character.

Characterization Through Choice of Name

One important method of characterization is the use of names possessing appropriate qualities of sound, meaning, or connotation. This technique is known as **name typing.** A screenwriter usually thinks out his characters' names very carefully, as Paul Schrader's choice of name for the Robert De Niro character in *Taxi Driver* illustrates:

> It has to be euphonious, because you want people to repeat the name: to use it in reviews, to use it in copy, a name people want to repeat. And Travis Bickle was succesful in that way; people remembered the name and it appeared in a lot of reviews. . . . A memorable name. Beyond that, you want to have at least one component which is evocative and/or symbolic. Travis is evocative rather than symbolic, Travis/travel. The sense of traveling, never stopping. Then Bickle. Travis is romantic, evocative, and soft—and Bickle is hard, an unpleasant name. And it fits the character.[8]

Because a great deal of thought goes into the choice of names, they should not be taken for granted but should be carefully examined for the connotations they communicate. The connotations of some names, such as Dick Tracy, are rather obvious and clear: Dick is slang for *detective;* Tracy derives from the fact that detectives trace criminals. Other names may have only generalized connotations. Gomer Pyle has a small-town or country-hick ring to it; Cornelius Witherspoon III has an opposite kind of sound. Certain sounds in names have unpleasant connotations. The "sn" sound, for example, evokes unpleasant associations, because a large majority of the words beginning with that sound are unpleasant—*snide*, *sneer*, *sneak*, *snake*, *snail*, *sneeze*, *snatch*, *snout*, and *snort* are a few examples. Thus, a name like Snerd or Snavely has an unpleasant ring automatically. Sometimes a name draws its effect from both its meaning and its sound, such as William Faulkner's Flem (read "phlegm") Snopes. In this vein, because of the connotative power of names, film actors' names are often changed to fit the image they project. John Wayne's real name was Marion Morrison; Cary Grant's was Archibald Leach (Figure 3.18).

Varieties of Characters

Another method for analyzing film characterization utilizes three different types of pairings: stock characters and stereotypes, static versus developing characters, and flat versus round characters.

Stock Characters and Stereotypes It is not essential or even desirable for every character in a film to have a unique or memorable personality. **Stock characters** are minor characters whose actions are completely predictable or typical of their job or profession (such as a bartender in a western). They are in the film simply

Figure 3.18 Name Typing Names in film are often chosen to suggest qualities of the character, as is the case with Travis Bickle (Robert De Niro) in *Taxi Driver.*

because the situation demands their presence. They serve as a natural part of the setting, much as stage properties like a lamp or a chair might function in a play.

Stereotypes, however, are characters of somewhat greater importance to the film. They fit into preconceived patterns of behavior common to or representative of a large number of people, at least a large number of fictional people. Examples of stereotypes are the rich playboy, the western hero's sidekick, the pompous banker, and the old maid aunt. Our preconceived notions of such characters allow the director to economize greatly in treating them.

Static Versus Developing Characters It is often useful to determine whether the most important characters in a film are static or developing characters. **Developing characters** are deeply affected by the action of the plot (internal, external, or both) and undergo some important change in personality, attitude, or outlook on life as a result of the action of the story. The change they undergo is an important, permanent one, not just a whimsical shift in attitude that will change back again tomorrow. The character will somehow never be the same person he or she was when the action of the film began.

The change can be of any type but is significant to the total makeup of the individual undergoing the change. Developing characters become sadder or

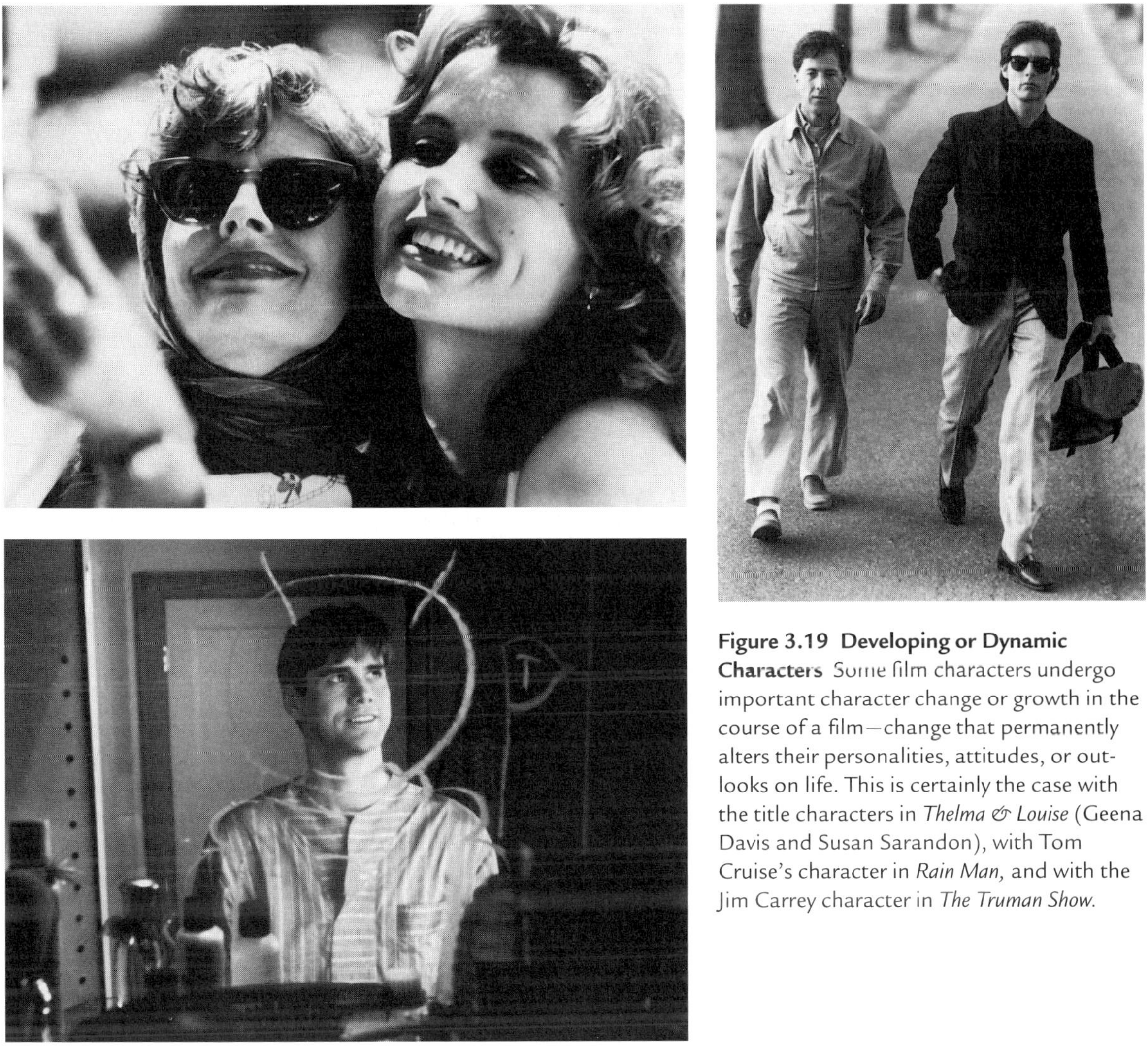

Figure 3.19 Developing or Dynamic Characters Some film characters undergo important character change or growth in the course of a film—change that permanently alters their personalities, attitudes, or outlooks on life. This is certainly the case with the title characters in *Thelma & Louise* (Geena Davis and Susan Sarandon), with Tom Cruise's character in *Rain Man,* and with the Jim Carrey character in *The Truman Show.*

wiser, or happier and more self-confident. They might gain some new awareness of life, become more mature or more responsible, or become more moral or less so. They may become simply more aware and knowing and less innocent or naive. Examples of developing characters include T. S. Garp (Robin Williams) in *The World According to Garp*, Tom Joad (Henry Fonda) in *The Grapes of Wrath*, and Michael Corleone (Al Pacino) in *The Godfather* (Figure 3.19).

Static characters remain essentially the same throughout the film. The action does not have an important effect on their lives (as might generally be the case with the hero of an action/adventure film). Or they are insensitive to the meaning of the action and thus are not capable of growth or change, as is

Figure 3.20 Static Characters Some film characters are not capable of growth or have such strong personalities that they remain unaffected by the important action of the film. This is the case with the title character in *Hud* (Paul Newman) and the Brad Pitt character in *A River Runs Through It*.

the case with the title character in *Hud* (Paul Newman) and, perhaps, with Charles Foster Kane (Orson Welles) in *Citizen Kane* (Figure 3.20).

Screenwriter Robert Towne feels that static characters are almost essential to comedy and developing characters are essential to serious drama:

> One of the things that is almost implicit in comedy is something that is repetitious, static—that is, you pretty much leave a character the way you find him. That's OK in *all* comedy. Repetitive or even compulsive behavior is what *makes* comedy. Archie Bunker is funny because he keeps repeating his prejudices in one form or another, and you expect these things. . . . In dramatic writing the very *essence* is character change. The character at the end is not the same as he was at the beginning. He's changed—psychologically, maybe even physically.[9]

Flat Versus Round Characters Another important distinction is made between flat characters and round characters. **Flat characters** are two-dimensional, predictable characters who lack the complexity and unique qualities associated with psychological depth. They often tend to be representative character types rather than real flesh-and-blood human beings. Unique, individualistic characters who have some degree of complexity and ambiguity and who cannot easily be categorized are called **round characters** or **three-dimensional characters.**

Round characters are not inherently superior to static characters. The terms merely imply how different characters function within the framework of a story. Static characters can be complex and vitally interesting without undergoing any

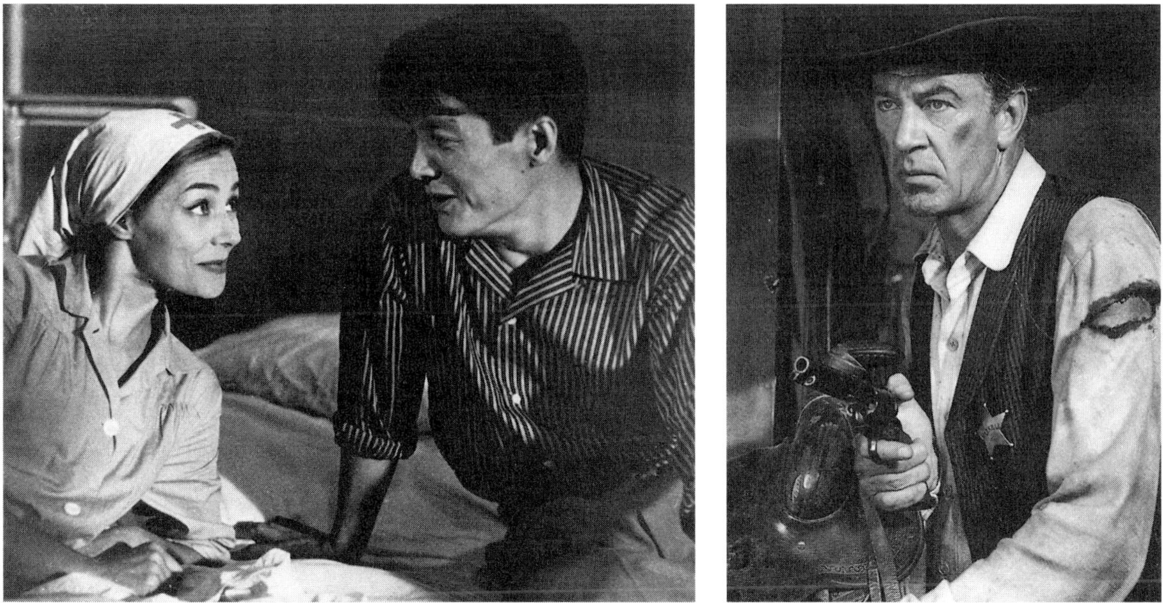

Figure 3.21 Allegory In *Hiroshima, Mon Amour,* director Alain Resnais creates a haunting allegory about love and war, focusing on the need for remembering profound and traumatic experiences. In *High Noon,* Gary Cooper plays a duty-bound lawman who must single-handedly face down revenge-bent desperadoes because the cowardly townspeople have deserted him. The film is generally considered to be an allegory on the McCarthy purge in Hollywood.

character change. In fact, flat characters may function *better* than round characters when attention needs to be directed away from personalities and toward the meaning of the action—for example, in an allegory.

Allegory

A story in which every object, event, and person has an abstract (as opposed to merely concrete) meaning is known as an **allegory.** In allegory, each element is part of an interdependent system that tells a clear, separate, complete didactic story on a purely figurative level.

A major problem with allegory is the difficulty of making both levels of meaning equally interesting. Often, so much importance is placed on the figurative story that we lose interest in the concrete story. Unfortunately, allegorical characters, to be effective as emblems, cannot have many unique and particular characteristics, for the more specific the characters are, the less representative they may be (Figure 3.21). But these difficulties do not necessarily prevent allegory from being effective in cinematic form, as is evidenced by such excellent films as *Woman in the Dunes, Swept Away, Lord of the Flies* (1963), and *The*

Seventh Seal. In both film and literature, however, the most frequently used (and more subtle) method of conveying meaning beyond the literal involves symbolism.

Symbolism

In most general terms, whether in a work of art or in everyday communications, a **symbol** is something that stands for something else. It communicates that something else by triggering, stimulating, or arousing previously associated ideas in the mind of the person perceiving the symbol.

All forms of human communication involve the use of symbols. We understand the meaning of a symbol if we already possess the ideas or concepts associated with or built into the symbol. A traffic light, for example, communicates its message symbolically. When the light turns green or red, we do more than observe with interest the change from one color to another; we respond to the symbolic message it gives. To a cavewoman who has never seen a traffic light, however, the change in color has no symbolic meaning. Therefore, it would be very dangerous for the cavewoman to walk around in the heart of a busy city at rush hour.

Approaching a work of art requires some understanding of the nature, function, and importance of its symbols. Almost anything can take on symbolic meaning in a film. In many stories, the setting has strong symbolic overtones. Characters are often used symbolically, and once characters become symbolic, the conflicts in which they take part become symbolic also. Therefore, it is essential to become aware of the special nature of symbolic communication in film.

In any story form, a symbol is something (a particular object, image, person, sound, event, or place) that stands for, suggests, or triggers a complex of ideas, attitudes, or feelings and thus acquires significance beyond itself. A symbol is a special kind of energized communication unit that functions somewhat like a storage battery. Once a symbol is charged with a set of associations (ideas, attitudes, or feelings), it is capable of storing those associations and communicating them any time it is used.

Universal and Natural Symbols

Filmmakers can use universal symbols, or they can create symbols for a particular film. Universal symbols are precharged—ready-made symbols infused with values and associations that most of the people in a given culture understand. By using objects, images, or persons that automatically evoke complex associations, filmmakers save themselves the job of creating each of the associated attitudes and feelings within the context of each film. They need only use symbols appropriately to make full use of their communication potential. Thus, the

American flag (triggering the complex set of feelings and values that we associate with America) and the cross (evoking a variety of values and feelings associated with Christianity) can be used effectively as symbols for a broad audience. Viewers' reactions will vary according to their attitudes toward the ideas represented, but all people from the same culture will understand the general symbolic message.

Many universal symbols are charged with their meanings externally—through past associations with people, events, places, or ideas—rather than through their own inherent characteristics. For example, there is nothing inherent in the shape of a cross to suggest Christianity; rather, the religious values and ideas attached over the ages to the crucifixion of Christ have given the cross its symbolic meaning.

Some objects, however, have natural or inherent qualities that make them particularly well suited to be symbols. A buzzard is an easily recognized symbol of death. Buzzards are black, a color associated with death, and the habits of the buzzard also make it an effective symbol. A buzzard is a scavenger, a creature that feeds only on dead flesh and will not even come near a living creature. Also important is the buzzard's visibility: By soaring in long, lazy circles over an area where something is dead or dying, the buzzard signals the presence of death. Thus, buzzards communicate the idea of death indirectly but clearly, so an observer need not see the dead object itself to know that death is present. The habits or lifestyles of hawks and doves are equally significant in determining their symbolic meaning.

Creating Symbolic Meanings

In many cases, filmmakers cannot depend on precharged symbols but must create symbols by charging them with meaning derived from the context of the film itself. They do this by loading a concrete object or image with a charge of associations, feelings, and attitudes and then employing it to evoke those associations. In charging an object with symbolic value, storytellers have a dual purpose. First, they want to expand the meaning of the symbolic object in order to communicate meanings, feelings, and ideas. Second, they want to make clear that the object is being treated symbolically. Thus, many of the methods used to charge an object symbolically also serve as clues that the object is taking on symbolic value (Figure 3.22).

There are four principal methods of charging symbols:

1. **Repetition.** Perhaps the most obvious way of charging an object is by drawing attention to it more often than a simple surface object might seem to deserve. Repetition increases the significance and symbolic power of the object at each appearance (Figure 3.23).
2. **Value Placed on an Object by a Character.** An object is charged symbolically when a particular character places value and importance on it. By

Figure 3.22 Charging the Symbol Two symbolic representations of death use completely different qualities to build the symbolic meaning. In *The Seventh Seal,* Ingmar Bergman uses a traditional image to portray death: a grim reaper carrying a scythe, a pale-faced, mysterious man in a black cloak and hood (Bengt Ekerot). In *All That Jazz,* Bob Fosse uses a beautiful, seductive woman (Jessica Lange) dressed in white to express the same idea.

Figure 3.23 Repeated Images of Symbolic Separation In this scene from *Shane,* the farmer's wife, Marian (Jean Arthur), stands inside the house while Shane (Alan Ladd), the ex-gunfighter who is now the farmer's hired hand, stands outside looking in the window. This symbolic separation is repeated visually throughout the film. Shane is always an outsider, present with but not part of the warm family circle or the close-knit group of farmers. On several occasions, Shane is framed through an open doorway, looking in on a warm family scene or sitting off to the side by himself in a meeting of the farmers. The scene shown here has additional levels of meaning: Shane and Marian have a strong but unspoken mutual attraction but keep a wall between themselves out of basic human decency and their mutual love and respect for the farmer (Van Heflin).

showing extraordinary concern for an object (as in the captain's concern for his palm tree in *Mister Roberts*), or by repeatedly mentioning an object or idea in the dialogue, the character indicates that an object or idea has more than ordinary significance. Symbols charged in this way may be of relatively minor importance, functioning only to offer insight into the character. Or they may have major significance to the overall dramatic structure, as illustrated by the famous "Rosebud" symbol in *Citizen Kane*.

3. **Context.** Sometimes an object or image takes on symbolic power simply through its placement in the film, and its symbolic charge is built up through associations created (1) by its relationship to other visual objects in the same frame, (2) by the editorial juxtaposition of one shot with another, or (3) by the object's importance in the film's structure.

   A symbolic image in the film version of Tennessee Williams's play *Suddenly, Last Summer*—the Venus flytrap—may be used to illustrate all three methods of charging an image through context. The Venus flytrap is a large, white-flowered plant whose leaves have two hinged blades. When an insect enters the space between them, the blades close like a mouth, trapping the insect inside. The plant then feeds on the insect. In *Suddenly, Last Summer*, once the nature of the plant and its feeding habits are made clear, the Venus flytrap is used to suggest or represent a major idea—the carnivorousness or cannibalism of the characters.

   The plant's nature is explained by Mrs. Venable (Katharine Hepburn), and the plant occupies a position near her chair so they share the same visual frame. As Mrs. Venable talks about her dead son, Sebastian, we begin to see the relationship between the woman and the plant, for her conversation reveals her to be a cannibal, savagely feeding on and deriving her nourishment from the memory of her son. The same effect could be achieved through editorial juxtaposition—by cutting immediately from a close-up of Mrs. Venable's mouth as she drones on about her son to a close-up of the jaws of her Venus flytrap snapping shut on an unsuspecting insect.

   Even if it were not repeatedly charged within the context of the film, the Venus flytrap could still function as a symbol. Consider, for example, how the image might be used only at the beginning and the end of the film: As the film begins, a close-up of the Venus flytrap serves as a background to the titles. Then, as the titles draw to a close, an insect lands on the flower and is trapped as the jaws close suddenly around it. The plant is not seen again until the film's closing shot, where it appears, seducing another insect into its folds. In this case its position in the film's structure would force us to consider its symbolic function and its meaning to the film as a whole.

4. **Special Visual, Aural, or Musical Emphasis.** Film has unique ways of charging and underscoring symbols and providing clues that an object is to be seen as a symbol. Visual emphasis may be achieved through dominant

colors, lingering close-ups, unusual camera angles, changes from sharp to soft focus, freeze frames, or lighting effects. Similar emphasis can also be achieved through sound effects or use of the musical score. Individual natural sounds or musical refrains can become symbolic in their own right if complex associations are built into them by any of the three methods discussed above.

Although filmmakers want to express their ideas clearly, they may not always want to express them too simply or too clearly. Thus, some symbols may be very simple and clear, and others may be complex and ambiguous. Symbols of the latter type can seldom be interpreted with one clear and certain meaning; there may be no single right answer to what a given symbol means, but several equally valid but different interpretations. This is not to say that a filmmaker using ambiguous symbols is deliberately trying to confuse us. The intention is usually to use complexity to enrich or enhance the work.

Symbolic Patterns and Progressions

Although symbols may function singly without a clear relationship to other symbols, they often interact with other symbols in what might be called *symbolic patterns.* In such a case, the filmmaker expresses the same idea through several symbols instead of relying on only one. The resulting symbolic pattern may have a certain progression, so that the symbols grow in value or power as the film progresses.

An excellent example is the complex pattern of symbols that gradually builds up to the climax of *Suddenly, Last Summer.* The idea of a savage universe inhabited by creatures who devour each other is established by the Venus flytrap and Mrs. Venable. Other symbolic images with the same meaning are used to achieve a pattern of ever increasing dramatic power. The third symbolic image in this pattern appears in Mrs. Venable's description of a sight she and Sebastian witnessed on the Encantadas:[10]

> Over a narrow black beach of the Encantadas as the just-hatched seaturtles scrambled out of the sandpits and started their race to the sea. . . . To escape the flesh-eating birds that made the sky almost as black as the beach! . . . And the sand was all alive, all alive, as the hatched seaturtles made their dash for the sea, while the birds hovered and swooped to attack and hovered and—swooped to attack! They were diving down on the hatched seaturtles, turning them over to expose their soft undersides, tearing the undersides open and rending and eating their flesh. . . .

Having set up three symbols for the same idea (the Venus flytrap, Mrs. Venable, and the birds), the playwright gives us a suggestion of their significance as Mrs. Venable continues her story:

> He spent the whole blazing equatorial day in the crow's nest of the schooner watching this thing on the beach until it was too dark to see it, and when he came down from the rigging he said, "Well, now I've seen Him," and he meant God. . . . He meant that God shows a savage face to people and shouts some fierce things at them, it's all we see or hear of Him. . . .

The next image in the pattern occurs in Catherine's (Elizabeth Taylor) description of Sebastian himself, which adds strong overtones of homosexuality to the already shocking image:

> We were going to blonds, blonds were next on the menu. . . . Cousin Sebastian said he was famished for blonds, he was fed up with the dark ones and was famished for blonds . . . that's how he talked about people, as if they were—items on a menu—"That one's delicious-looking, that one is appetizing," or "That one is not appetizing"—I think because he was nearly half-starved from living on pills and salads. . . .

As the next image in the pattern begins to develop, there is an effort to link the children that constitute this image with the earlier image of the carnivorous birds:

> There were naked children along the beach, a band of frightfully thin and dark naked children that looked like a flock of plucked birds, and they would come darting up to the barbed wire fence as if blown there by the wind, the hot white wind from the sea, all crying out "Pan, pan, pan!" . . . The word for bread, and they made gobbling voices with their little black mouths, stuffing their little black fists to their mouths and making those gobbling noises with frightful grins!

At the film's climax, the image of the carnivorous birds is repeated, but this time on a completely human level, which makes it even more shocking:

> Sebastian started to run and they all screamed at once and seemed to fly in the air, they outran him so quickly. I screamed. I heard Sebastian scream, he screamed just once before this flock of black plucked little birds that pursued him and overtook him halfway up the hill.
>
> I ran down . . . screaming out "Help" all the way, till— . . . Waiters, police, and others—ran out of the buildings and rushed back up the hill with me. When we got back to where my Cousin Sebastian had disappeared in the flock of featherless little black sparrows, he—he was lying naked as they had been naked against a white wall, and this you won't believe, nobody has believed it, nobody would believe it, nobody, nobody on earth could possibly believe it, and I don't blame them!—they had devoured parts of him.
>
> Torn or cut parts of him away with their hands or knives or maybe those jagged tin cans they made music with, they had torn bits of him away and stuffed them into those gobbling fierce little empty mouths of theirs. . . .

This incident takes place in a village whose name is also symbolic: Cabeza de Lobo, which means "Head of the Wolf," another savage and carnivorous image.

Thus, by means of a complex pattern of symbols, the film makes a statement about the human condition. The idea of Earth as a savage jungle where creatures devour each other is made clear by a series of symbols: the Venus flytrap, the turtle-devouring birds, Sebastian's own hungers, and the little human cannibals of Cabeza de Lobo. Williams has arranged these symbols so that they become increasingly vivid, powerful, and shocking as the story unfolds.

Symbolic Values in Conflict

Some conflicts in films are self-contained and have no meaning beyond themselves. Most conflicts, however, tend to take on symbolic qualities so that the individuals or the forces involved represent something beyond themselves. It seems natural for the forces in opposition to align themselves with different generalized concepts or value systems, and even the most ordinary whodunit and typical western at least vaguely imply a conflict between law and order and lawlessness and chaos, or simply between good and evil (Figure 3.24). Other symbolic ideas that might be represented by a film's conflict are civilization versus barbarism, sensual versus spiritual values, change versus tradition, idealism versus pragmatism, and the individual versus society. Almost any conflict can be stated in symbolic or generalized terms. Because comprehension of such symbolic interpretations is often essential to identifying and understanding a film's theme, the major conflict should be analyzed on both the literal and the symbolic levels.

Metaphors

Closely related to symbolism is the filmmaker's use of **visual metaphors.** Whereas a symbol stands for or represents something else, a visual metaphor is a comparison that helps us better understand an image because of its similarity to another image. This comparison is usually achieved through the editorial juxtaposition of two images in two successive shots. An example is a metaphor in Sergei Eisenstein's *Strike:* Shots of workers being pursued and killed are alternated with shots of a butcher slaughtering a bull.

In this example, the secondary image (the butchering) is extrinsic—that is, it has no place within the context of the scene itself but is imposed artificially into the scene by the filmmaker. In a realistic or naturalistic film, **extrinsic metaphors** may seem forced, heavy-handed, or even ludicrous, destroying a sense of reality that may be very important to the film. In contrast, comedy or

Figure 3.24 Symbolic Conflict In *The Road Warrior,* the traditional western conflict between law and order and savagery and chaos is seen in a fresh environment and situation: a post-World War III environment in which gasoline means survival. Like the western genre hero, Max (Mel Gibson) comes out of nowhere and sides with the civilized community against the savages. Max aids the settlers in their escape from the besieged fort; then, with the savages momentarily subdued and the civilized group on its way to found a new settlement, he goes his own way.

fantasy films can use such images freely, as can serious films that stress an interior or subjective viewpoint.

Intrinsic metaphors emerge directly from the context of the scene itself and are more natural and usually more subtle than extrinsic metaphors. *Apocalypse Now* contains an intrinsic metaphor very similar to the extrinsic butchering metaphor in Eisenstein's *Strike*. While Captain Willard (Martin Sheen) is in the temple carrying out his assignment—"terminating Kurtz (Marlon Brando) with extreme prejudice"—the camera cuts to the courtyard, where a giant bull is axed in a gruesome ritual sacrifice.

The dramatic power and communicative effectiveness of any symbol or metaphor depend also on originality and freshness. A tired and worn-out symbol can no longer convey profound meanings, and a metaphor that has become a cliché becomes a hindrance rather than a help. This is problematic in watching older films, for metaphors and symbols that are clichés today might actually have been fresh and original when the film was made.

Overreading Symbolism

However, symbolic interpretation can be carried to ridiculous extremes, as this account by *North by Northwest* screenwriter Ernest Lehman reveals:

> I once saw a French film magazine filled with diagrams of the movements of the characters in *North by Northwest* and how they all had meaning: going from left to right here . . . and scenes with circular movements there. Hitch and I used to laugh sometimes when we read about the symbolism in his pictures, particularly in *Family Plot*. By mistake a propman had two pieces of wood set up so they looked vaguely like a cross, and the car goes downhill and crashes through a field, goes through a fence and knocks over the cross. So some learned New York critic commented: There's Hitchcock's anti-Catholicism coming out once again. When I was at the Cannes Film Festival with *Family Plot*, Karen Black, Bruce Dern and I attended a press conference, and some French journalist had the license plate in the picture all worked out: 885 DJU. He had some *elaborate* explanation for those numbers. When he got through explaining it, I said, "I hate to tell you this, but the reason I used that license plate was that it used to be my own, and I felt it would be legally safe to use." So much for symbolism.[11]

We should always keep in mind that although decoding a film's symbols may lead to rich and profound insights, it can also be carried to the point of absurdity. As Sigmund Freud, the granddaddy of symbolism, once put it: "Sometimes a cigar is just a good smoke."

Irony

Irony, in the most general sense, is a literary, dramatic, and cinematic technique involving the juxtaposition or linking of opposites. By emphasizing sharp and startling contrasts, reversals, and paradoxes, irony adds an intellectual dimension and achieves both comic and tragic effects at the same time. To be clearly understood, irony must be broken down into its various types and explained in terms of the contexts in which it appears.

Dramatic Irony

Dramatic irony derives its effect primarily from a contrast between ignorance and knowledge. The filmmaker provides the audience with information that a character lacks. When the character speaks or acts in ignorance of the true state of affairs, the dramatic irony functions to create two separate meanings for each line of dialogue: (1) the meaning of the line as it is understood by the unenlightened character (a literal or face value meaning) and (2) the meaning of the line to the enlightened audience (an ironic meaning, opposite to the literal meaning).

Figure 3.25 Dramatic Irony In this scene from *Fatal Attraction,* Anne Archer, as Michael Douglas's wife, does not have an inkling that her husband has had a torrid affair with Glenn Close, who has appeared at their apartment pretending to be interested in leasing it. Because we not only know about the affair but also know that Close is capable of extremely bizarre behavior, this relatively ordinary scene is loaded with suspense and intensifies our sympathy for the unsuspecting Archer.

By knowing something that the character does not know, we gain pleasure from being in on the joke or secret. In *Oedipus Rex,* for example, Oedipus does not realize that he has already killed his father and married his mother when he refers to himself as "the child of Good Luck" and "the most fortunate of men." Because *we* are aware of the truth, we hear the line as a painful joke. On a less serious plane is an example from *Superman.* Although *we* know that Clark Kent is really Superman, Lois Lane does not. Therefore, every time Lois accuses Clark of cowardice because he disappears whenever trouble starts, we have to chuckle because of our inside knowledge.

Dramatic irony may function in a purely visual way, either for comic effect or to build suspense, when the camera shows us something that the character on the screen cannot see. For example, a character trying to elude a pursuer in a comic chase may be crawling toward the same corner as his pursuer, but only *we* see and anticipate the coming shock of sudden confrontation. Horror films employ similar scenes to both intensify and prolong suspense. Because of its effectiveness in enriching the emotional and intellectual impact of a story, dramatic irony has been a popular technique in literary and dramatic art since Homer employed it in the *Odyssey;* it remains popular and effective to this day (Figure 3.25).

Irony of Situation

Irony of situation is essentially an irony of plot. It involves a sudden reversal or backfiring of events, so that the end result of a character's actions is exactly the opposite of his or her intentions. Almost the entire plot structure of *Oedipus Rex* involves irony of situation: Every move that Oedipus and Jocasta make to avoid the prophecies actually helps to bring them about. This particular type of irony is often associated with O. Henry. An excellent example is his story "The Ransom of Red Chief," where two hoodlums kidnap a child who is such a demon that they end up having to pay his parents to take the boy back.

Irony of Character

Irony of character occurs when characters embody strong opposites or contradictions or when their actions involve sharp reversals in expected patterns of behavior. Oedipus, for example, is probably the most ironic character ever created, for the opposites built into his character constitute an almost endless list: He is both the detective and the murderer he is seeking; he sees, yet he is blind (in direct contrast to his foil, the blind "seer" Tiresias); he is the great riddle-solver, but he does not know his own identity; he is his mother's husband and his children's brother; and in the end, when he finally "sees," he blinds himself. Superman, in his alter ego as mild-mannered reporter Clark Kent, is another ironic character. The irony is intensified by Lois Lane's thinking him not only mild-mannered but cowardly.

Irony of character may be present when a character violates our stereotyped view of him, as illustrated by this imaginary scene. Two soldiers, played by Woody Allen and John Wayne, are trapped in a foxhole by enemy gunfire. When mortar shells start falling around the foxhole, the John Wayne character panics, buries his head under his arm, and begins sobbing uncontrollably. The Woody Allen character puts his bayonet between his teeth, grabs a grenade in each hand, and charges the machine-gun nest alone.

Irony of Setting

Irony of setting occurs when an event takes place in a setting that is exactly the opposite of the setting we usually expect for such an event—for example, a birth in a graveyard, or the shootout on an Amish farm in *Witness* (Figure 3.26).

Irony of Tone

Because film communicates simultaneously on several different levels, it is well suited for many types of irony, but irony of tone can be especially effective. In essence, irony of tone involves the juxtaposition of opposites in attitudes or

Figure 3.26 Irony of Setting This idyllic lakeside scene (complete with blooming flowers) seems the perfect setting for a tender moment in *Frankenstein,* when the childlike monster finds a young friend who does not fear him. For a few brief moments, they share flowers and happily toss them into the water. Then the monster realizes he has no more flowers to toss and reaches out toward the girl. . . .

feelings. In literature it is exemplified by Erasmus's *The Praise of Folly*. The reader must read between the lines to discover that the work is actually a condemnation of folly. Swift's classic essay "A Modest Proposal" is another example. The author's proposal—put forth in rational, calm, and modest style—is outrageous: The Irish people ought to sell their year-old children to be eaten like suckling pigs by the wealthy English landlords. In film, such irony may be effectively provided through contrasting emotional attitudes communicated simultaneously by the soundtrack and the visual image. Consider, for example, the juxtaposition of an optimistic "What a Wonderful World" that accompanies the bombing sequence in *Good Morning, Vietnam*.

Many different kinds of irony are possible in film because of film's ability to communicate on more than one level at a time. In fact, the multilayered nature can become so complex that its effect is difficult to describe. This is the case in the final scene of *Dr. Strangelove*, which combines three separate contrasting elements: (1) the visuals, composed of multiple shots of atomic mushroom clouds filmed in slow motion; (2) the soundtrack, where Vera Lynn's voice, sticky and sweet, sings "We'll Meet Again Some Sunny Day"; and (3) the significance of the action, which is the end of all life as we know it. The ironic effect is provided by the ingenious touch of the Vera Lynn song, which adds a sweet, haunting quality to the pictorial element, so that we become aware of the almost breathtaking beauty of the mushroom clouds. This ironic combination of beauty and horror creates a powerful effect. Such effects are rare in film, but the filmgoer must be constantly aware of the potential for ironic expression in the musical score, in the juxtaposition of sight and sound, and in transitions of almost any kind.

Cosmic Irony

Although irony is basically a means of expression, the continuous use of ironic techniques might indicate that the filmmaker holds a certain philosophical attitude, or ironic worldview. Because irony pictures every situation as possessing two equal sides, or truths, that cancel each other out or at least work against each other, the overall effect of ironic expression is to show the ridiculous complexity and uncertainty of human experience. Life is seen as a continuous series of paradoxes and contradictions, characterized by ambiguities and discrepancies, and no truth is ever absolute. Such irony implies that life is a game in which the players are aware of the impossibility of winning and the absurdity of the game even while they continue to play. On the positive side, however, irony's ability to make life seem both tragic and comic at the same moment keeps us from taking things too seriously or too literally.

Looked at on a cosmic scale, an ironic worldview implies the existence of some kind of supreme being or creator. Whether this supreme entity be called God, Fate, Destiny, or the Force makes little difference. The implication is that the supreme being manipulates events to deliberately frustrate and mock humankind and is entertained by what is essentially a perpetual cruel joke on the human race.

Although irony usually has a humorous effect, the humor of cosmic irony bites deep. It can bring a laugh but not of the usual kind. It will be not a belly laugh but a sudden outward gasp of air, almost a cough, that catches in the throat between the heart and mind. We laugh perhaps because it hurts too much to cry.

Questions

On Story Elements

How does the film stack up against the five characteristics of a good story?

1. How well is it unified in plot or storyline?
2. What makes the story believable? Pick out specific scenes to illustrate the kinds of truth that are stressed by film:

   a. objective truth, which follows the observable laws of probability and necessity
   b. subjective, irrational, and emotional inner truths of human nature
   c. the semblance of truth created by the filmmaker
3. What makes the film interesting? Where are its high points and its dead spots? What causes you to be bored by the film as a whole or by certain parts?
4. Is the film a proper blend of simplicity and complexity?
   a. How well is the story suited in length to the limits of the medium?
   b. Is the film a simple formula that allows you to predict the outcome at the halfway point, or does it effectively maintain suspense until the very end? If the ending is shocking or surprising, how does it carry out the tendencies of the earlier parts of the story?
   c. Where in the film are implication and suggestion effectively employed? Where is the film simple and direct?
   d. Is the view of life reflected by the story simple or complex? What factors influenced your answer?
5. How honest and sincere is the film in its handling of emotional material? Where are the emotional effects overdone? Where is understatement used?

On the Significance of the Title

1. Why is the title appropriate? What does it mean in terms of the whole film?
2. How many different levels of meaning are expressed in the title? How does each level apply to the film as a whole?
3. If the title is ironic, what opposite meanings or contrasts does it suggest?
4. If you recognize the title as being an allusion, why is the work or passage alluded to an appropriate one?
5. If the title calls your attention to a key scene, why is that scene important?
6. How is the title related to the theme?

On Dramatic Structure

1. Does the film use linear (chronological) or nonlinear structure? If it begins with expository material, does it capture your interest quickly enough, or would a beginning "in the middle of things" be better? At what point in the story could an *in medias res* beginning start?
2. If flashbacks are used, what is their purpose and how effective are they?

On Conflict

1. Identify the major conflict.
2. Is the conflict internal (individual against self), external, or a combination of the two? Is it primarily a physical or a psychological conflict?

3. Express the major conflict in general or abstract terms (for example, brains versus brawn, human being against nature).
4. How is the major conflict related to the theme?

On Characterization

1. Identify the central (most important) character or characters. Which characters are static and which are developing? Which characters are flat and which are round?
2. What methods of characterization are employed and how effective are they?
3. Which of the characters are realistic and which are exaggerated for effect?
4. What about each character's motivation? Which actions grow naturally out of the characters themselves? Where does the filmmaker seem to be manipulating the characters to fit the film's purpose?
5. What facets of the central character's personality are revealed by what he or she chooses or rejects?
6. Which minor characters function to bring out personality traits of the major characters, and what do these minor characters reveal?
7. Pick out bits of dialogue, images, or scenes that you consider especially effective in revealing character, and tell why they are effective.
8. Which characters function as stock characters and stereotypes? How can the presence of each in the film be justified?

On Symbolism

1. What symbols appear in the film, and what do they represent?
2. What universal or natural symbols are employed? How effective are they?
3. Which symbols derive their meaning solely from their context in the film? How are they charged with symbolic value? (In other words, how do you know they are symbols and how do you arrive at their meaning?)
4. How are the special capabilities of film (the image, the soundtrack, and the musical score) employed to charge symbols with their meaning?
5. Which symbols fit into a larger pattern or progression with other symbols in the film?
6. How are the major symbols related to the theme?
7. Is the story structured around its symbolic meanings to the extent that it can be called an allegory?
8. Which symbols' meanings are clear and simple? Which symbols are complex and ambiguous? What gives them this quality?
9. Are visual metaphors employed effectively? Are they primarily extrinsic (imposed artificially on the scene by editing) or intrinsic (a natural part of the setting)?
10. How fresh and original are the film's symbols and metaphors? If they seem clichéd or timeworn, where have you encountered them before?

On Irony

1. What examples of irony can you find in the film?
2. Is irony employed to such a significant degree that the whole film takes on an ironic tone? Is an ironic worldview implied?
3. Do any particular examples of irony achieve comic and tragic effects at the same time?
4. Where in the film is suspense or humor achieved through dramatic irony?
5. How do the ironies contribute to the theme?

Video Exercises

To locate the sequences for these exercises, set the VCR counter at "0000" or, for real-time counters, at "0:00:00" at the very end of the studio logo, just as the "movie proper" begins (the movie proper includes such things as "Paramount Pictures Presents," opening credits, and the main title). Then, to view the section of film dealt with in each exercise, fast-forward until the numbers listed here in brackets appear on the VCR counter.

1. **Treatment of Emotional Material.** Watch the final segments of *Love Story* [4160 to end; 1:28:03 to end] and *Terms of Endearment* [5100 to end; 1:52:42 to end]. Describe the treatment of the emotional materials in each of the stories. Where is understatement used? Which of the two films best mixes its emotions of sorrow with humor? How are special film techniques like music and visual elements employed? Which ending is the most powerful and why?
2. **Title Information.** In addition to the words of the title, the visual design of the title (the way it appears on the screen) also has significance. Look at the main titles and opening credits of *Superman*, *The Grapes of Wrath*, *Citizen Kane*, and *To Kill a Mockingbird*. What is revealed in or suggested by the design of the titles and the way that information is put on the screen? How does the soundtrack or title music reinforce that information?
3. **Dramatic Structure 1.** Watch the first 15 minutes of *The Grapes of Wrath* and *Citizen Kane*, and then answer questions 1 and 2 in "On Dramatic Structure" on page 75.
4. **Dramatic Structure 2.** Directors often structure scenes in unusual ways to achieve dramatic effects. Watch the "Tom Joad's Homecoming" scene from *The Grapes of Wrath* [1620 to 1945; 0:23:04 to 0:28:42], and then answer these questions.
   a. Why do Tom and Casey hang around outside the house when they arrive, instead of going right in?
   b. What happens to Casey during this sequence? Why?
   c. Why do Connie and Rosasharn ride in the back of the truck instead of in the cab with Al?

   d. How are all these things important to the effectiveness of this sequence?
5. **Characterization.** Watch the first 20 minutes of *Casablanca*, paying special attention to every bit of information, both visual and verbal, that relates to the character Rick (Humphrey Bogart). What do we know about Rick at the end of this short segment?
6. **Symbolism**
   a. Watch the first 30 minutes of *The Seventh Seal* and *All That Jazz*. Characters representing Death appear in both films. Focus your attention on these characters, and then answer questions 3, 4, 5, and 6 in "On Symbolism" on page 76.
   b. Watch the first 5 minutes of *Summer of '42*. During the opening voice-over, the camera very clearly charges an object with symbolic value. What is the symbolic object, how is its importance identified, and how does it relate to the film as a whole?
   c. Watch the last sequence in *Patton* [Part II: 4220 to end; 1:06:00 to end]. While a voice-over tells us of the practice of honoring conquering Roman generals, a visual image suggests a symbolic facet of Patton's personality that has been repeated throughout the film. What is the image and what does it suggest?
7. **Irony.** Watch the final sequences of *Dr. Strangelove* [4460 to end; 1:30:00 to end] and the baptismal sequence in *The Godfather* [Cassette 2: 2515 to 2875; 0:39:38 to 0:46:08], and explain how the contrasting elements function together to create an extremely powerful effect. In your discussion, consider the role played by all the various film elements (visual details, dialogue, music, sound effects, editing, and so on).

Films for Study

Affliction (1998)
All the King's Men (1949)
Breaking the Waves (1996)
The Bridges of Madison County (1995)
Catch-22 (1970)
Citizen Kane (1941)
Eyes Wide Shut (1999)
Gods and Monsters (1998)
Hiroshima, Mon Amour (1959)
Hud (1963)
Lord of the Flies (1963)
The Piano (1993)
Pulp Fiction (1994)
The Remains of the Day (1993)
Reservoir Dogs (1992)
The Seventh Seal (1957)
Star Wars: Episode I—The Phantom Menace (1999)
Suddenly, Last Summer (1959)
The Sweet Hereafter (1997)
Swept Away (1975)
The Winter Guest (1997)
Woman in the Dunes (1963)
The World According to Garp (1982)
Wrestling Ernest Hemingway (1993)

Chapter 4

Visual Design

I believe in overall design. . . . Improvisation is for the birds and for the amateurs. You don't improvise a statue or a painting. If you do, it isn't much good. Michelangelo put it best when he said that he does not conceive of anything. He looks at a block of marble and, he says, he looks at it long enough until he sees the shape. From then on, he says, "I just take everything superfluous off and disclose what's in that stone." That to me is a marvelous recipe. You see the whole design, a shape. I'm talking about what to me would be the full flowering of a screen work. It isn't that you can't do it other ways. But the other ways, they're just not the full flowering of the screen potential.

—Rouben Mamoulian, Director

The story, incorporating many of the fictional and dramatic elements discussed in Chapter 3 and shaped into a screenplay format, is the basis and the starting point for any film production. But even a beautifully structured and written screenplay is little more than a bare skeleton for a motion picture. The key members of the production team who together will plan the visual design or look of the film—the director, the cinematographer, the production designer, and the costumer—must analyze that skeleton. Each member of this team focuses on a single goal: creating a master plan for a consistent visual texture or style that is artistically suited to the film story to be told.

To accomplish this goal, the production team needs to answer a number of extremely important questions: Does the story to be filmed demand color, or would black and white be more effective? Do the story and its setting require a wide-screen format, or would the standard screen frame work better? What kind of lighting will best convey the mood or tone of the story? What aspects of the story's setting should be emphasized, and can this emphasis best be accomplished in a studio or on location? What kind of costumes and makeup will best fit the personalities and lifestyles of the characters? Answering these questions requires weighing a variety of complex factors.

Color Versus Black and White

Planning the look of a film begins with considering a question about the most basic element of a movie's style: Should the story be photographed in color or in black and white? Forty years ago, this decision was a critical part of design planning for most movies. Color photography had become more than a novelty, and new film stocks and processing techniques were offering filmmakers opportunities for greater creativity and flexibility. But although color photography was quickly becoming the preference of movie audiences, many directors, cinematographers, and production designers maintained their loyalty to black and white. They felt that black-and-white images kept audiences focused on the characters and the story being told, helping them avoid distraction from gaudy, cluttered backgrounds. Some filmmakers believed that shooting in color was less artistic, because color photography did not require the subtle lighting they used when shooting in black and white. Director John Ford explains his preference for black and white:

> [Color is] much easier than black-and-white for the cameraman. It's a cinch to work in, if you've got any eye at all for color and composition. But black-and-white is pretty tough—you've got to know your job and be very careful to lay your shadows properly and get the perspective right. In color—there it is; but it can go awfully wrong and throw a picture off. There are certain pictures, like *The Quiet Man*, that call for color—not a blatant kind—but a soft, misty color. For a good dramatic story, though, I much prefer to work in black-and-white; you'll probably say I'm old-fashioned, but black-and-white is real photography.[1]

In 1971, director Peter Bogdanovich decided to film *The Last Picture Show* in black and white:

> I didn't want the film to look pretty. I didn't want it to be a nostalgia piece. . . . Color always had tendency to prettify, and I didn't want that. I realized, being a fellow with a memory about movies, that if I were making this film even 15 years ago, this is the kind of film that would have been shot in black-and-white. And since those days were better in terms of filmmaking, and nobody was put under the restriction of being told they had to shoot in color because of television, the great directors who used both color and black-and-white made the right choices. . . . You alternated, you know, depending on the story and not on any kind of economic consideration.[2]

Eventually, the audience demand to see color images—both in the movie theater and on television screens—forced filmmakers to adapt and to develop new techniques that incorporated the subtleties of black-and-white filmmaking with the added richness and depth made possible by the use of color. Most modern filmmakers feel that color cinematography allows them to create more powerful, realistic images and to communicate better with audiences. As members of the design team plan the look of a film, they are likely to consider establishing a **color palette**—a limited number of specific colors used or emphasized throughout the film to subtly communicate various aspects of character and story to the viewer. Color used in this way becomes more than mere decoration for the film; it enhances the movie's dramatic elements. Cinematographer Nestor Almendros says:

> I prefer color. The image carries more information, it reveals more. I am nearsighted, and color helps me see, interpret, "read" an image. As it reached its apogee, black-and-white cinematography ended its cycle and exhausted its practical possibilities. In color photography there is still room for experimentation.[3]

Although the role of black-and-white cinematography in modern film is greatly diminished, black and white is making a small comeback. It is sometimes contrasted with color images for various special effects. Since the late 1970s, however, over 95 percent of all American feature films have been made in color. Thus, filmmakers need to stay current with developments in color photography and keep its impact on viewers in mind as they plan a movie's visual design. (For a detailed examination of the use of color, see Chapter 7.)

Screen Format

Another important element for the design team to consider is screen format—the size and shape of the projected image. The visual boundaries established for the image dictate the photographic composition of the frame and, according to cinematographer Nestor Almendros, help the audience know how to read beyond the obvious information provided on the screen:

> I need the frame with its four sides. I need its limits. In art, there is no artistic transposition without limits. . . . And what counts in two-dimensional art is not only what is seen but what is not seen, and what does not let itself be seen. . . . By means of the camera's viewfinder, the outside world goes through a process of selection and organization. Things become pertinent; thanks to the parameters of the frame, they take shape in relation to vertical and horizontal limits. We at once know what is good and what is bad. Like the microscope, the frame is an analyzing tool.[4]

Essentially, there are two basic shapes for the projected image: standard screen and wide screen. The width of the **standard screen** is 1.33 times its height. The width of the **wide screen** (known by trade names such as **Cinemascope, Panavision,** and Vistavision) varies from 1.85 to 2.55 times its height. The different dimensions and shapes of these screens create different types of compositional problems (Figures 4.1, 4.2).

The wide screen lends itself to a panoramic view of a vast landscape or large numbers of people, as well as to the rapid motion characteristic of westerns, war dramas, historical pageants, and fast-paced action/adventure dramas. The standard screen is more suitable for an intimate love story set in a small apartment, requiring the frequent use of tight close-ups and very little movement of subjects in space. A wide screen can actually distort an image and detract from the film's visual effectiveness if the physical set is too narrow for its field of view. The wide-screen formats such as Cinemascope and Panavision, however, can contribute significantly to the effectiveness of horror or suspense films. A kind of visual tension is created by a slow **panning** or dollying camera that heightens suspense by bringing new visual information into view at the outer edges of the screen, increasing our feeling of vulnerability.

Film Stock

Film stock may have an important effect on the visual image. **Smooth-grain film stock** produces an image that is extremely smooth, or slick. Such film also registers a wide range of subtle differences between light and dark, enabling the director to create fine tones, artistic shadows, and contrasts. Because of the clarity and artistic perfection of these images, they often have a more powerful visual impact than does reality.

Rough-grain film stock produces a rough, grainy-textured image with harsh contrasts between blacks and whites and almost no subtle contrasts. Because newspaper pictures and newsreels have this coarse, rough-grain look, this type of film has become associated with a documentary here-and-now quality, as though reality had to be captured quickly, with little concern for clarity and artistic perfection.

STANDARD SCREEN 1.33:1

The *standard screen* was the dominant screen shape until 1953. The television frame has these dimensions, as do *most* 16mm prints available for rental today. Thus Cinemascope and other wide-screen films have visual information cut off on both sides in 16mm or TV formats.

WIDE SCREEN 1.85:1

The wide screen is also called the *standard American wide screen* to distinguish it from its European counterpart, a slightly narrower format with a 1.66:1 aspect ratio. A popular compromise shape (between the standard screen and the ultrawide formats), the wide-screen image is achieved by masking off the top and bottom of the standard frame.

PANAVISION 2.2:1

Panavision is probably the most popular ultrawide system in use today, perhaps because its slightly narrower format is more flexible from a compositional standpoint than its predecessor, Cinemascope. Both Panavision and Cinemascope employ anamorphic lenses, which "squeeze" a wide image onto standard-frame 35mm film in the camera and then "stretch" the image into a wide-screen format when projected.

CINEMASCOPE 2.55:1

Figure 4.1 Popular Screen Widths Cinemascope can be said to have two aspect ratios. In the 1950s its dimensions were 2.55:1; it has since been narrowed slightly, to 2.35:1, to accommodate an optical soundtrack. When theaters began installing special screens for Cinemascope in the 1950s, many of the screens were curved slightly to enhance the three-dimensional effect. Although popular with the public, the system had many critics, among them director George Stevens, who claimed, "the wide screen is better suited to a boa constrictor than a man." The lines drawn on this shot from *L.A. Confidential* show the amount of side information lost when wide-screen films are reduced to the 16mm or TV format.

Figure 4.2 The Projected Image The four different screen sizes and shapes are illustrated by four different croppings of the same scene from *Scream*.

a. Standard screen 1.33:1

b. Wide screen 1.85:1

c. Panavision 2.2:1

d. Cinemascope 2.55:1

Figure 4.3 Smooth-Grain Film Stock Director Jack Cardiff used smooth-grain black-and-white film stock in *Sons and Lovers* to give an artistically heightened reality to the stark Welsh setting and the tender romance developing between Dean Stockwell and Mary Ure.

Figure 4.4 Rough-Grain Film Stock The look of rough-grain film stock is simulated by this frame enlargement from Barbara Kopple's 1976 coal-strike documentary, *Harlan County, U.S.A.* Rough-grain film stock is sometimes used in feature films in sequences where the director wants to convey a kind of here-and-now immediacy or create a TV news, newsreel, or documentary effect.

A cinematographer may employ both types of stock for different effects. A romantic love scene would probably be shot with smooth-grain film, a riot or a furious battle scene with rough-grain film (Figures 4.3, 4.4).

Production Design/Art Direction*

Once decisions about color versus black and white, screen format, and film stock are made, the awesome task of production design gets under way.

> It's one thing to dress a set to represent Anytown, U.S.A., but a true aptitude for movie magic is needed to rebuild John Steinbeck's *Cannery Row* on a sound stage, make moviegoers feel at home far far away in another galaxy, turn New York City into a maximum security prison, or show how Los Angeles might look with a population of two hundred million in the year 2020.[5]

* There is some confusion about the difference between an art director and a production designer. The titles are synonymous when only one or the other is listed in the credits for a film. When both titles are listed, the production designer has conceived the look or visual texture of the film, and the art director has been responsible for supervising the work required to execute that plan.

Figure 4.5 Award-Winning Design This elaborate design for the fantasy land of Shangri-La in *Lost Horizon* won an Academy Award for Columbia Studios' Stephen Goosen in 1937.

Modern production designers meet those sorts of challenges and finally are being recognized for their critical contributions to the look of modern films. The production designer first makes elaborate and detailed sketches and plans for the set and then supervises, down to the last detail, the construction, painting, furnishings, and decoration until he or she achieves the exact look intended. In every stage of filmmaking the production designer consults with three other people directly responsible for the visual texture of the film: the director, the cinematographer, and the costumer. All three work together closely, seeking each other's opinion, conferring, and coordinating their efforts to achieve a unified visual effect.

In the modern film, this collaboration is often so integrated that art directors are asked to suggest camera angles and lighting in their design—decisions that in the past were left completely to the director and cinematographer. Such requests make very good sense because production design has such a tremendous influence on the look of a film. It affects the cinematographer's choice of lighting, angles, and focus. Many overhead and low-angle shots in *Batman*, for example, are literally dictated by Anton Furst's sets of Gotham City, where they not only enhance the sense of vertical space but also make painted backdrops and miniature models more convincing. Likewise, the director's decisions about many other factors may be subtly altered by the mood created by a finely wrought set, as in *Metropolis*, *Blade Runner*, and *Dark City* (Figure 4.5).

The Script: The Starting Point

As is true at every step in the filmmaking process, the basic blueprint is the script. It is the script that provides the unity of vision for a film. As production designer Paul Sylbert puts it:

> You cannot impose a style on a film. It must grow out of a vision arising from the script and a knowledge of how to form the various scenes into a whole, and it should, like the film itself, have its own movement. Style in film results from every part of it, and those parts must cohere, and they must be directed at some effective result. Design is not self-expression. It is an expressive use of objects, forms, and colors in the service of the script.[6]

Sometimes the script suggests visual metaphors and reinforces the need for a specific color palette, so that a few carefully chosen colors are emphasized to suggest a mood or atmosphere. For example, production designer Patrizia Von Brandenstein saw Mozart and Salieri, the two major characters in *Amadeus*, as being polar opposites, and she incorporated that interpretation into her visual design:

> Salieri wore a lot of red clothing. . . . I thought everything about Salieri was dark, Italianate, full of passion, but from an older time, dark and turgid, heavy like the music—like the fabrics he wore, velvet and wool. . . . Mozart's world was reflective, bright, silvery, pastel, brilliant, tingling like crystal, faceted like his music. It was the music that drove the design.[7]

Paul Sylbert made similar use of visual metaphor in the design of *Hardcore*. He created two totally different environments through the use of two different color palettes:

> *Hardcore* presented two very different worlds. The first is the Calvinism of Grand Rapids, Michigan, and the second is the world of pornography. . . . It goes from Rembrandt to hell in one move. The delft stuff and all that Dutch world in the house in Grand Rapids was great for those uptight people. The contrast between Grand Rapids and the porno world was between Calvinism and hell. You used a wide color palette in designing the porno world. There's a wide range of colors and the whole idea was to have a broad palette. The narrowness of the palette of the Grand Rapids scenes—the brown tones and the blue delft and the wood—was a reflection of the spirit of Calvinism. I kept the palette narrow in Grand Rapids so that once I got into this new world, I was suddenly free to do anything. The idea was to free the palette. I was allowed to go red, white, pink, orange, black, powder blue in the motel rooms and whorehouses. The wildness was a color version of the anarchy that went on in that other world.[8]

The production designer can also help to enhance concepts from the script by controlling the sense of space in a given scene. To emphasize the fearful power of Cardinal Wolsey in *A Man for All Seasons*, designer John Box created a strong sense of claustrophobia to portray Sir Thomas More's meeting with Wolsey (Figure 4.6):

> I was not principally interested in the architecture, but in the atmosphere and the habits of the people of the period. Take that early scene where Wolsey is confronted by Thomas More. Fred Zinneman's intention was to present Wolsey as power and authority. That, to me, meant a feeling of claustrophobia which would accentuate the character and power of Wolsey, and would involve the audience with Thomas More as he was confronted by the great man of the time. So we put Wolsey in a small room to emphasize his largeness. He wears red robes, so we don't want any other colors to lead your eye away from the central figure, so the walls become a darker shade of the same red. There are no corners in the room. The table at which he sits is smaller than it would have been in reality, to accentuate Wolsey's size. We had to have a window because he looks out of it, a table because he is sitting at it, a candle because he needs light. Nothing else was necessary, emphasizing just claustrophobia and the power of the political cleric.[9]

Sometimes a production designer wants to do just the opposite—to create within a limited space the illusion of a large space. Using the technique known as **forced perspective,** the designer physically distorts certain aspects of the set and diminishes the size of objects and people in the background to create the illusion of greater foreground-to-background distance. Charles Rosher, cinematographer of F. W. Murnau's classic silent film *Sunrise,* describes the technique:

> I worked with a wide-focus lens of 35 to 55mm, for the scenes in the big cafe. All the sets had floors that sloped slightly upwards as they receded, and the ceilings had artificial perspectives: the bulbs hanging from them were bigger in the foreground than in the background. We even had dwarfs, men and women, on the terrace. Of course all this produced an amazing sense of depth.[10]

One movie featuring a scene of George Washington at Valley Forge used a large number of midgets as soldiers in the background, and several parts of the set were reduced in size to create a greater illusion of space on a cramped sound stage.

Setting and Its Effects

The **setting** is the time and place in which the film's story takes place. Although the setting may often seem unobtrusive or be taken for granted, it is an essential ingredient in any story and makes an important contribution to the theme or total effect of a film. Because of the complex interrelationships of setting with other story elements—plot, character, theme, conflict, symbolism—the effects of setting on the story being told should be analyzed carefully. And because of its important visual function, it must also be considered a powerful cinematic element in its own right.

Figure 4.6 The Claustrophobic Set In *A Man for All Seasons,* designer John Box emphasized the awesome power of Cardinal Wolsey (Orson Welles) by artistically shrinking the room where his confrontation with Sir Thomas More (Paul Scofield) takes place. Bob Fosse, in directing *Cabaret,* demanded that most of the film be shot in a smoky, confined space to create a feeling of constraint in both his actors and their audience.

In examining the setting as it relates to the story, it is necessary to consider the effect of four factors on the story as a whole:

1. *Temporal factors:* The time period in which the story takes place
2. *Geographic factors:* The physical location and its characteristics, including the type of terrain, climate, population density (its visual and psychological impact), and any other physical factors of the locale that may have an effect on the story's characters and their actions
3. *Social structures and economic factors*
4. *Customs, moral attitudes, and codes of behavior*

Each factor has an important effect on the problems, conflicts, and character of human beings and must be considered as an integral part of any story's plot or theme.

Setting as Determiner of Character The four aspects of setting listed above are important to understanding the naturalistic interpretation of the role of setting. This interpretation is based on the belief that our character, destiny, and fate are all determined by forces outside ourselves, that we may be nothing more than products of our heredity and environment, and that freedom of choice is only an illusion. Thus, by considering the environment a significant shaping force or even a dominant controlling one, this interpretation forces us to consider how environment has made characters what they are—in other words, how characters' nature has been dictated by factors such as their time in history, the particular place on Earth they inhabit, their place in the social and economic structure, and the customs, moral attitudes, and codes of behavior imposed on them by society. These environmental factors may be so pervasive that they serve as something much more important than a backdrop for the film's plot.

In some cases the environment may function as an antagonist in the plot. Protagonists may struggle against environmental forces pressing upon them, seeking to express some freedom of choice or escape from a trap. Thus, the serious consideration of the cruel, indifferent, or at least powerful forces of the environment is often a key to understanding a character and his or her dilemma.

Setting as Reflection of Character The environment in which a person lives may provide the viewer with clues to understanding his or her character. This is especially true for the aspects of their environment over which individuals exercise some control. Houses, for example, may be excellent indicators of character. Their usefulness is illustrated by the following examples of exterior views that might appear in a film's opening establishing shot.

Picture a small, neat, white, green-shuttered cottage with red roses around the doorstep and bright and cheerful curtains at the windows. It is surrounded by a newly whitewashed picket fence. Such a setting has been traditionally used in films to suggest the happy honeymoon couple, full of youth, vigor, and optimism for a bright future.

Figure 4.7 Setting as a Reflection of Character The vicious dark side of Mrs. Venable (Katharine Hepburn) in *Suddenly, Last Summer* is reflected by her taste in art—this grotesque sculpture in her courtyard.

At the other extreme, consider the image evoked by Edgar Allan Poe's description of the Usher house in his classic short story "The Fall of the House of Usher": bleak, gray walls, vacant eyelike windows, crumbling stones, rotten woodwork, and a barely perceptible zigzag crack in the masonry from roof to foundation. This opening picture, a reflection of the Usher family's decadence, becomes even more significant as the story progresses, for Roderick Usher and the house in which he lives are so closely interwoven symbolically and metaphorically that they become one: The house's vacant eyelike windows portray the eyes of Roderick Usher, and the zigzag crack in the masonry is equated with the crack in Usher's mind.

The filmgoer must be aware of interactions between environment and character, whether the setting is serving as a molder of character or merely as its reflection (Figure 4.7).

Setting for Verisimilitude One of the most obvious and natural functions of the setting is to create a semblance of reality that gives the viewer a sense of a real time and a real place and a feeling of being there. Filmmakers recognize the great importance that an authentic setting plays in making a film believable. Thus they may search for months to find a proper setting and then move crew, actors, and equipment thousands of miles to capture an appropriate backdrop for the story they are attempting to film.

To be convincing, the setting chosen should be authentic in even the most minute detail. In a film set in the past, even the slightest anachronism may be jarring. A filmmaker shooting a story about the Civil War must be careful that the skies do not show jet vapor trails or the landscapes do not include high-tension power lines.

Some films capture the unique qualities of the time and place in which they are set so effectively that these factors become the most important elements of the film—more powerful and memorable than the characters or the story line. *McCabe & Mrs. Miller*, *The Fifth Element*, *Blade Runner*, and *The Last Picture Show* are good examples of such films.

Setting for Sheer Visual Impact When doing so is permissible within the limits of a film's theme and purpose, filmmakers choose a setting with a high degree of visual impact. For example, the plot and structure of westerns such as *Shane* and *True Grit* do not demand great scenery, but the filmmakers realized that the beauty of the wide western landscape, with its snowcapped mountains and rainbow-colored rock formations, would be effective as long as it did not violate the overall tone or atmosphere of the films. David Lean is especially successful in choosing settings with a powerful visual impact, as demonstrated in *Dr. Zhivago*, *Ryan's Daughter*, and *Lawrence of Arabia*. The barren Australian desert provides an otherworldly backdrop for the action of *The Road Warrior*. Both *Legends of the Fall*, filmed in western Canada, and *Out of Africa* owe much to the images of the landscapes behind their stories.

Setting to Create Emotional Atmosphere In certain specialized films, setting is important in creating a pervasive mood or emotional atmosphere. This is especially true in horror films and to some extent in the science fiction or fantasy film (such as the *Alien* films and Stanley Kubrick's *The Shining*), in which the unusually charged emotional atmosphere created and maintained by the setting becomes an important factor in achieving a suspension of disbelief by the viewer. Setting may also create a mood of tension and suspense in keeping with the overall tone of the film, in addition to adding credibility to plot and character elements (Figure 4.8).

Setting as Symbol The setting of a film story may take on strong symbolic overtones when it is used to stand for or represent not just a location but some idea associated with the location, as in Agnieszka Holland's version of *The Secret Garden* (1993). Another example of a symbolic environment is the garden setting for *Suddenly, Last Summer*. The garden becomes a symbol for the worldview reflected by the other symbols: Men are carnivorous creatures living in what is essentially a savage jungle in which they devour one another in a constant struggle of fang and claw, obeying only the law of the survival of the fittest. That this worldview is reflected in the setting is illustrated by Tennessee Williams's own description of the set:

Figure 4.8 Setting for Emotional Atmosphere, Characterization, and Visual Impact In sharp contrast to the drab, ordinary, run-down Bates Motel in *Psycho* is the Bates home, located on a hill behind the motel. Its strange, foreboding, haunted quality contributes immensely to the emotional atmosphere of the film. The house also contributes to the characterization of Norman Bates (Tony Perkins), as both reflection and determiner of his character. The starkness of the house, silhouetted against the sky, makes a strong visual impact. Here, Perkins is shown standing next to the house as it appears in *Psycho II*.

> The interior is blended with a fantastic garden which is more like a tropical jungle, or forest, in the prehistoric age of giant fern-forests when living creatures had flippers turning into limbs and scales to skin. The colors of this jungle-garden are violent, especially since it is steaming with heat after rain. There are massive tree-flowers that suggest organs of the body, torn out, still glistening with undried blood; there are harsh cries and sibilant hissings and thrashing sounds in the garden as if it were inhabited by beasts, serpents and birds, all of a savage nature. . . .[11]

Setting as Microcosm A special type of symbolic setting is the type known as a **microcosm,** meaning "the world in little," in which the human activity in a small and limited area is representative of human behavior or the human condition in the world as a whole. In such a setting special care is taken to isolate the characters from all external influences so that the "little world" seems self-contained. The limited group of people, which contains representative human types from various walks of life or levels of society, might be isolated on a desert island, in an airplane, on a stagecoach, or in a western town. The implication of the microcosm often comes very close to being allegorical: The viewer should see strong similarities between what happens in the microcosm and in the world at large, and the film's theme should have universal implications. Screenwriter Paddy Chayefsky has described his *Hospital* as a microcosm-of-society picture. The hospital represents an advanced, highly technical and affluent society that is incapable of running itself. Films such as *Lord of the Flies*, *Ship of Fools*, and *High Noon* can all be seen as microcosms; television's "Gilligan's Island," however, lacks the universal implications of a microcosm, though it possesses many microcosmic qualities.

Studio Versus Location Shooting

In recent years, production designers have been doing much of their work in studios because many directors are returning to the sound stages, preferring to stylize a realistic background rather than to go on location. There are three reasons for this preference. One is that many directors were raised on the studio-made products of the 1930s and 1940s and admired their look and feel so much that they are now trying to create similar styles in their own films. Another reason is the need to compete with made-for-television movies, which are usually filmed on location, have relatively small budgets, and pay less attention to visual texture and production design than do movies made for the big screen. A more impressive look is created for the big screen, where the attention, care, and expenditures necessary for obtaining the desired look can be better appreciated.

Perhaps the single most important reason why directors prefer to shoot a film in a studio is the completely controlled environment. Lighting can be completely controlled in a studio; on location the primary light source, the sun, is constantly moving from east to west. In cities, traffic must usually be controlled in some way, and natural environmental sounds can be bothersome. Prolonged shooting in cities or residential areas can be very disruptive to everyday life, and residents often come to view movie crews with the hostility usually reserved for an army of occupation.

The decision to go on location, however, is usually dictated by the script, and the work of the production designer is just as important on location as in the studio. He or she works closely with the director to choose the places where the film will be shot and then designs and oversees the construction of any sets needed on location. For *Days of Heaven* production designer Jack Fisk worked closely with director Terrence Malick to scout locations. When they finally found the perfect place in Canada (for a story set in Texas), the beauty of the rolling fields of wheat blowing in the wind reminded Fisk of the ocean, so he designed an unusual farmhouse with features that vaguely resembled a ship. To build this set required a battle with the producers, who wanted an ordinary-looking ranch house. Like most other designers, Fisk believes that audiences are disappointed with a truly realistic setting and expect to see a kind of heightened reality, which he attempts to provide.

Figure 4.9 Composite Settings Production designers are often required to create the illusion that two completely different sets in different locations are different parts of a single location. In this scene from *Raiders of the Lost Ark,* Harrison Ford is running away from the huge rolling boulder in a cave interior set in England. A few seconds later in the film, he emerges from the cave into a sunlit exterior in Hawaii.

A more realistic, contemporary story like *The River* calls for a subdued form of heightened reality, so production designer Chuck Rosen was thrilled when a local man told him: "My Lord, Lord almighty, this farm here looks exactly like my granddaddy's farm." To achieve this look on location near Kingsport, Tennessee, was no easy matter. Universal purchased 440 acres of mountain forest specifically for the movie. Sixty of those acres were leveled to create a river-bottom farm, and Rosen designed and constructed a two-story farmhouse, a main barn, an equipment building, and a double corncrib. A dam was built below the farm on the Holsten River, raising the water level by four feet, and a levee was built to keep the farm from flooding. Because filming continued into late November, bright autumn foliage had to be sprayed with green paint for summer scenes. A huge cornfield by the river, however, was planted late and was so well watered that four rows of corn had to be sprayed brown or replaced with dead stalks for the autumn flood scene. Although this was the first "60-acre set" Rosen had ever done, he achieved the main thing he had hoped for: "It looks like it belongs."[12]

Sometimes a script will force production designers to jump back and forth between a controlled studio set and a distant exterior location, creating the illusion that both sets are part of the same neighborhood. In *Raiders of the Lost Ark*, for example, Harrison Ford escapes from a huge rolling boulder in an interior cave set in England and emerges from the cave in Hawaii (Figure 4.9).

Period Pieces

A **period piece** is a film that takes place not in the present but in some earlier period of history. To recreate the look of a period, the production designer must do extensive architectural research. To get a feel for life in the period, the production designer reads books, letters, newspapers, and diaries. *GoodFellas*, which begins in the 1950s and ends in the 1980s, provides an excellent example of all the factors that the production designer has to consider. Kristi Zea, *GoodFellas* production designer, recalls the project:

> The film presented a challenge for both the costumes and the sets, because there was a need for us to quickly reflect certain trends within each of the time periods. Overall, the make-up, hair, and clothing were more sensitive to time passage than the actual locations were. Of course, cars immediately give you a period. The fifties had a sepia-like, subtle color scheme. The cinematographer, Michael Ballhaus, actually changed the film stock to maximize the chromatic look of the sixties. The early seventies was pretty garish, too. Then the eighties were more somber, more kinetic, more drugged out. If you walk on Mulberry Street and peek into one of those social club windows, it could still be in 1952; nothing's changed. In a certain way, even the people have a period look to them. The interior of the cab stand, the house, and everything from the fifties actually had a late forties look to it. They were poor; they wouldn't have brand-new furniture. So to do a clear-cut fifties look for that section of the film wasn't a good idea, because that's not what these people would have had in their houses. We actually picked a late forties look for all of the early scenes. For the sixties scenes we wanted to say sixties. All of these guys had new cars. No one would drive around in a ten-year-old car, so that kept us in a very specific period.[13]

Living Spaces and Offices

To construct sets showing living quarters or offices, designers refer to the script to make decisions that support the story and the characters. Settings are consciously designed as personalized environments that reflect a character and underscore or enhance the mood of each scene (Figure 4.10). Production designer Robert Boyle describes the challenge:

> If the script says this is about a homeless person, you better do it within the parameters of the logic of the homeless. I always start with the economics of the characters. Very often they are not indicated in the script. You read a script. The first thing I ask is how much do these people make, what can they afford, because economics are the basis of our lives. Then I want to know who their friends are. I want to know what their educational background is: Did they go to college, did they drop out of high school, are they from the streets, or are they more earthy, country people? Then there's that whole range of sexual choice: Are they hetero-

Figure 4.10 Settings as Personalized Environments Ironically, sitting amid the luxurious furnishings of her huge old house and surrounded by glamorous photos of herself, it seems as if Norma Desmond (Gloria Swanson) will never be lonely or have any problem with self-esteem in *Sunset Boulevard*. Such is not the case with the Steve Martin character in *The Lonely Guy*.

> sexual or homosexual? You have to know all this before you can sit down with a pencil and start to draw.[14]

If the film is based on a novel, the designer may choose to go to the novel for descriptive details about the setting and the character. A design with this kind of research behind it can help the actor settle into the role and deliver a fuller, more accurate performance.

When designing interior sets that have windows, the production designer will also create a world outside, often using scenic backings that have been photographed. They provide an extra dimension to the film's world in the same way that off-screen environmental sounds do.

Fantasy Worlds

Perhaps the most serious challenge that a production designer faces is the building of a complete fantasy world. For *Blade Runner*, production designer Lawrence G. Paull created a complete futurescape for the year 2020 by using additive architecture—that is, by building protrusions onto existing structures. The structures used were located on the New York street set in the back lot of Burbank Studios. *Blade Runner* also required twenty-five interior sets, including one created inside an industrial refrigerator locker. Through inventive production design and the use of practically every technical trick in the book, Paull created a set that enabled director Ridley Scott to "build layers of texture, so

Figure 4.11 Inventive Production Design Lawrence G. Paull built multiple layers of texture into his set for *Blade Runner* so that director Ridley Scott could pack every square inch of the screen with visual information. The result was a set so powerful that it nearly overwhelms the characters and the story, even in action scenes like this one showing Harrison Ford running across a rooftop.

that visual information is imparted in every square inch of screen" and to convince viewers that they have been transported to another time and another place—in this case a time and place that no one has yet experienced in reality (Figure 4.11).[15]

Costume and Makeup Design

By the time the costume designer is called in, the production designer has already made many decisions about the look of the costume. An integrated or coherent design synchronizes the colors of the set with the patterns and colors of the costumes. After the color palette is determined, many people, with widely differing degrees of control over decisions, enter into the total process of costume design: the director, the production designer, the costumer, and the actor, as well as the hairstylist and the makeup artist. Like production design, costume design begins with the script. Costume designer Edith Head describes the interaction of design team members and performers:

> We are given a script, and we have conferences with the director or producer and with the stars. What we do is create an illusion of changing an actor or actress into someone else. It is a cross between magic and camouflage. In real life, clothing is worn for protection, to look good, or whatever reason you like. In motion pictures, it's to help the actress on the screen give the impression that she is the person in the story. We have three magicians—hairstylist, makeup artist, and clothes designer—and through them we're supposed to kid the public that it really isn't Paul Newman, it's Butch Cassidy. We go through any kind of device we can to break the mold of the actor or actress.[16]

To successfully transform an actor into his or her character requires that the actor feel a comfortable sense of rightness with the clothing. Charlton Heston, for example, makes a point of wearing a costume as much as he can. He wants the costume to feel like clothing, not like a costume. For many actors, the process of internalizing the character to be played really begins when they see themselves in costume.

A skilled costume designer can improve an actor's figure. The use of a little extra fabric can slim the appearance of a woman with a boxy, high-waisted build and create the illusion of a wonderful figure. In each *Die Hard* movie and in *Hudson Hawk*, the on-screen appearance of Bruce Willis, who is short in the leg and long in the body, was improved by costume designer Marilyn Vance. She gave him a longer-legged look by increasing the rise of his trousers (the distance between the crotch and the waist) to reduce the apparent length of his torso.

The degree of a director's involvement with costume design varies. Edith Head, the dean of American costume designers, recalls working with Alfred Hitchcock, George Roy Hill, and Joseph L. Mankiewicz:

> When you work with a director, you immediately have to find out his point of view. . . .
>
> If you ask Hitchcock what he wants, he'll say, "My dear Edith, just read the script." Hitch is the only person who writes a script to such detail that you could go ahead and make the clothes without discussing them. I do sketches for him, though. A Hitchcock script is so completely lucid: "She's in a black coat, she has a black hat, and she's wearing black glasses." That was Karen Black's character in *Family Plot*, the last one we did. A lot of scripts give no clues at all. When you work a great deal with a director you know his likes and dislikes. Hitchcock has a phobia about what he calls "eye-catchers," such as a woman in bright purple or a man in an orange shirt. Unless there is a story reason for a color, we keep muted colors, because he feels they can detract from an important action scene. He uses color like an artist, using soft greens and cool colors for certain moods.
>
> When we did *The Sting* and *Butch Cassidy and the Sundance Kid*, George Roy Hill had done as much research as I had. In fact, he did more on some of it. He is a perfectionist. When you work with him day by day, it's as though he were another designer.

Mankiewicz I never met, because they borrowed me just to do clothes for Bette Davis. He called me and said, "I love your work. Just do what you think is right."[17]

Period films create a tremendous challenge for a costume designer. Extensive research is required to determine the total costume—not just the right clothes but the hats, the hairstyles, the jewelry, and the gloves. Edith Head explains why today's films, in contemporary settings, don't make the same kind of demands:

> Today's pictures are mostly men. There are very few women's pictures, and the women's pictures are mostly character pictures. In the past we made all men handsome and all women sexy and glamorous. Now we just buy them both a pair of blue jeans![18]

Actors often provide valuable input to costuming, especially when they have clear and definite ideas about the characters they are to play. Mary Astor, a star of the 1930s and 1940s, took an active role in designing her character's attire in *Act of Violence:*

> I worked out the way this poor alley cat should look, and insisted firmly (with Zinneman's help) that the one dress in the picture would not be made at the MGM wardrobe, but be found on a rack at the cheapest department store. We made the hem uneven, put a few cigarette burns and some stains on the front. I wore bracelets that rattled and jangled and stiletto-heeled slippers. I had the heels sanded off at the edges to make walking uncomfortable. I wore a fall, a long unbecoming hairpiece that came to my shoulder. And I put on very dark nail polish and chipped it. I used no foundation makeup, just too much lipstick and too much mascara—both "bled," that is, smeared, just a little. Zinney said, "You look just right!" And camera helped with "bad" lighting.[19]

Makeup decisions also help to create the desired look. Makeup can enhance the natural look of an actor or transform an actor into a different version of himself or herself or into a totally different person. The transition may be accomplished through gradual and subtle changes throughout the film, or it may be abrupt. Orson Welles, as Charles Foster Kane, undergoes an effective aging transition in *Citizen Kane*, as does young Kirsten Dunst in *Interview With the Vampire* and *Little Women.* Jack Nicholson takes on a very different face for the role of Jimmy Hoffa in *Hoffa.* Extreme examples of the makeup artist's skill are roles that call for the actor's look to be totally transformed—for example, the role that Roddy McDowell plays in *Planet of the Apes* and John Hurt in the title role in *The Elephant Man*.

Although some actors begin to internalize their roles with costuming, makeup can also be an important step. Sir Laurence Olivier, whose stage experience taught him the skills of makeup, claimed that he couldn't "get" a character until he found the right nose. He typically experimented with several putty noses until satisfied.

Figure 4.12 Costuming, Hairdressing, and Makeup The important contributions of the costume designer, hairdresser, and makeup artist are evident in these pictures from *Sunset Boulevard* and *King Kong*. Gloria Swanson's glittering, metallic top, heavy necklace and bracelet, dark lipstick, and perfectly sculpted coiffure literally shout out glamour and confidence, even boldness. Fay Wray's look, in contrast—her flowing, diaphanous gown, her long, loosely curled hair, and her understated makeup—is a soft whisper of old-fashioned feminine vulnerability (every big ape's dream).

Orson Welles, in his capacity as director of *Citizen Kane*, used makeup for a unique purpose. He knew that his Mercury Theatre actors were totally unknown to movie audiences, so, to make them seem more familiar, he asked his makeup man to create the look of character stereotypes common in popular genre films (Figure 4.12).

Lighting

Does the action of the film take place in the daytime or at night, indoors or outdoors? Is the film set in Transylvania or Las Vegas? The nature of the story and the shooting location have a significant effect on the contribution of lighting to the look of a film.

Ingmar Bergman's films are usually set in Sweden. There, the sun never rises high in the sky, so strong side lighting is dominant. The quality of light in the dry air of the California desert is very different from the quality of light in a tropical rain forest. Such geographic factors must be accepted as givens. Certain aspects of lighting, however, can be artistically controlled, and some of the most critical decisions affecting the film's look concern lighting. In the hands of skilled directors and cinematographers lighting becomes a powerful, almost magical tool. As Todd Rainsberger puts it in his excellent work on James Wong Howe:

Figure 4.13 Low-Key and High-Key Lighting Low-key lighting puts most of the set in shadow and shows the couple with just a few highlights, increasing the intimacy and dramatic intensity of the scene. High-key lighting opens up the frame with light in background areas and balances the lighting throughout the set. Although high-key lighting diminishes the intimacy and dramatic intensity that the scene has with low-key lighting, it provides more complete visual information about the couple and the setting.

> Just as no two artists use the same brush strokes, no two cameramen control light in exactly the same manner. The angle, quality, and intensity of the light can vary in an infinite number of ways. Recording a scene on film is thus not a copy of a single unchanging reality, but the selective recording of a filmic reality which is the unique result of a particular choice of light sources.[20]

By controlling the intensity, direction, and diffusion of the light, a director is able to create the impression of spatial depth, delineate and mold the contours and planes of the subject, convey emotional mood and atmosphere, and create special dramatic effects. The way a scene is lit is an important factor in determining the scene's dramatic effectiveness. Subtle variations in lighting create mood and atmosphere for the action that is to take place. Because lighting should reinforce the mood of each scene, close observation of the lighting throughout a film should reveal the film's overall mood or tone.

Two terms designate different intensities of lighting. **Low-key lighting** puts most of the set in shadow; just a few highlights define the subject. This type of lighting heightens suspense and creates a somber mood; thus, it is used in mystery and horror films. **High-key lighting,** in contrast, results in more light areas than shadows, and subjects are seen in middle grays and highlights, with far less contrast. High-key lighting is suitable for comic and light moods, such as in a musical. Generally speaking, high-contrast scenes, with a wide range of difference between light and dark areas, create more powerful and dramatic images than do scenes that are evenly lit (Figure 4.13).

The direction of the light also plays an important role in creating an effective visual image. The effect created by flat overhead lighting, for ex-

Figure 4.14 Directions of Lighting These pictures illustrate the different effects achieved by overhead lighting (top left), side lighting (top right), back lighting (bottom left), and front lighting (bottom right).

ample, is entirely different from the effect created by strong side lighting from floor level. Back lighting and front lighting also create strikingly different effects (Figure 4.14).

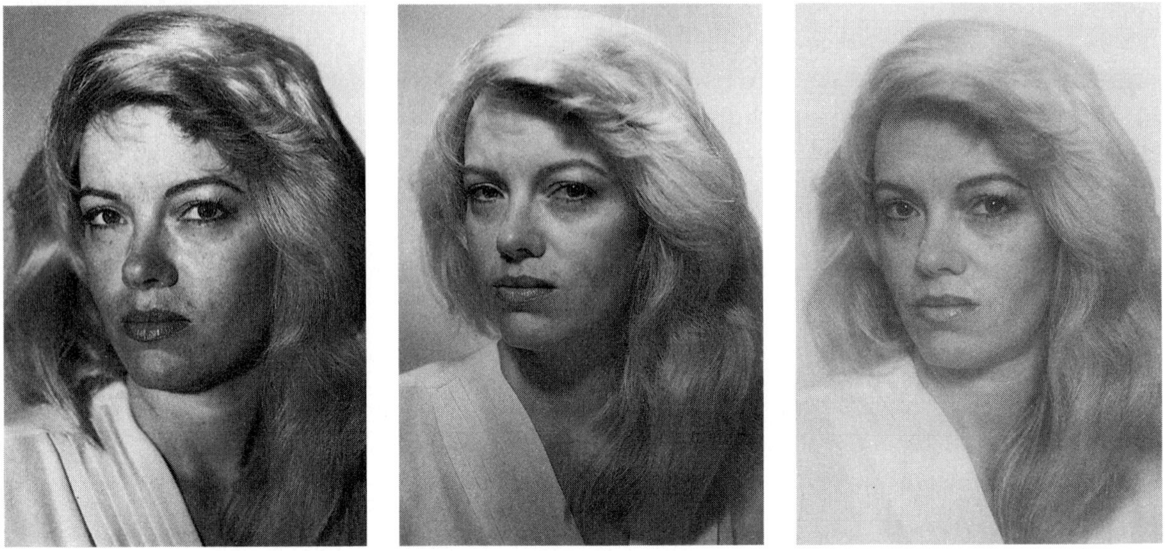

Figure 4.15 Character of Light These pictures illustrate the different effects of changing the character of the light: direct, harsh, or hard lighting; medium and balanced lighting; and soft and diffused lighting.

Whether light is artificial or natural, the director has the means to control what is commonly referred to as the character of the light. The character of light can generally be classified as direct, harsh, or hard; medium and balanced; or soft and diffused (Figure 4.15).

Because the character of light on actors' faces can suggest certain inner qualities, cinematographer James Wong Howe individualized the major characters in *Hud* with lighting designed to fit the personalities the actors were portraying. The lighting for Patricia Neal was strong and undiffused. Paul Newman was generally seen in dark contrasts; Melvyn Douglas was shadow lit; and Brandon DeWilde was brightly lit.

The intensity, direction, and character of light affect the dramatic effectiveness of an image. The director and cinematographer together plan the look they want for the lighting. Then the cinematographer assumes the primary responsibility for the lighting.

Today's filmmakers generally strive for a very natural effect in their lighting. Scenes often look as though the cinematographer used no supplemental light at all. Vilmos Zsigmond, one of the great current cinematographers, describes his philosophy in this way:

> I try to light so that it feels as if it comes from natural sources. That's why I like to have windows in my shots—windows, or candles or lamps. Those are my true light sources. Studying the Old Masters, Rembrandt, Vermeer, de la Tour, I found that

> they painted their best works relying on light effects coming from realistic sources. They even selected their subjects because they loved the light and the people. They were very selective and improved upon nature. They simplified and eliminated multiple shadows to concentrate on the dramatic. That is what a cinematographer does: improves on nature.[21]

Master cinematographer Nestor Almendros also stresses the importance of naturalness: "I use a minimum of artificial light. . . . *Days of Heaven* was shot with very little light. Rather than create an artificial moment, I'd wait for the real one to happen. One great moment is worth waiting for all day."[22] Even when he is working on interiors in a studio for a film like *Kramer vs. Kramer*, Almendros stresses a natural light technique by imagining the sun outside Kramer's apartment, justifying a subject lit from behind by a window or lamp, and making sure that all lighting seems to come from windows and table or floor lamps.

Vilmos Zsigmond was not the first person to seek inspiration from paintings. As early as the 1920s, Cecil B. DeMille and other directors were attempting to use lighting to imitate the effects achieved by painters like Rembrandt. Some forty years later, Franco Zeffirelli achieved painterly effects successfully in his *Taming of the Shrew*. He created the soft, muted color of faded paintings by placing a nylon stocking over the camera lens and lighting his interior scenes in the Rembrandt manner (Figure 4.16).

John Ford and Gregg Toland, his cinematographer, designed *The Grapes of Wrath* to suggest the look of Dorothea Lange's stark black-and-white photographs of the Dust Bowl. Howard Hawks used lighting in *Rio Bravo* to suggest the hard lighting in the western paintings of Frederick Remington. In preparing to shoot *The Verdict*, Sidney Lumet and his cinematographer, Andrzej Bartkowaik, spent an entire day studying a collection of prints of Caravaggio's paintings. They analyzed his treatment of backgrounds, foregrounds, and textured surfaces, paying particular attention to the sources of light. Then they applied what they had learned to *The Verdict*, with what Lumet called "extraordinary" results.

The Budget's Effect on the Film's Look

The visual design elements discussed in this chapter can play important roles in the overall effectiveness of a movie. Many filmmakers, however, do not have a budget that allows them to develop a unified look for their projects. Inventive camera angles, subtle lighting effects, authentic costuming, and detailed settings take time and money to create, and many low-budget films must be made without a distinctive visual style.

Sometimes, a lack of artistic flourish can work to a film's advantage. And sometimes, high-quality screenwriting and powerful acting performances can

Figure 4.16 The Rembrandt Effect In *The Taming of the Shrew,* director Franco Zeffirelli used special lighting and a nylon stocking over the camera lens to soften the focus and mute the colors so that the image has the quality of a Rembrandt painting. The technique is especially effective in interior scenes like this one picturing Elizabeth Taylor as Katherine engaged in a shrewish conversation with her off-screen sister.

be presented more effectively to an audience that is undistracted by flashy visual effects or complicated editing styles. Low-budget films like *Breaking Away*, *Return of the Secaucus Seven*, *sex, lies, and videotape*, and *Clerks* have been executed with great success despite the absence of a distinct visual style.

Questions

On Color Versus Black and White

1. Was the filmmaker's choice of color or black and white correct for this story? What factors do you think influenced this decision? Try to imagine the film as it would appear in the other film type. What would the differences in total effect be? (If the film is in color, try watching the first 10 minutes on a VCR with the television color turned off.)

2. Are any special color effects used to achieve a unique overall look? If so, what was the director trying to achieve with the unusual effect? How successfully is the overall effect carried out?

On Screen Format

1. Was the film originally shot for a standard screen or a wide screen? Does the choice of screen format suit the story being filmed? Try imagining the film in the opposite format: What would be gained or lost?

On Production Design/Art Direction

1. How important is the set or location to the overall look of the film? Is it essentially a realistic or authentic set, or is it stylized to suggest a heightened reality?
2. Was the movie filmed primarily on location or in the studio? What effect does the place of filming have on the style or look of the film?
3. How do the settings serve as personalized environments to enhance or reinforce the actors' performances? To what degree do the settings underscore or enhance the mood or quality of each scene?
4. Is the setting so powerful and dominant that it upstages the actors?
5. If the film is a period piece, a fantasy, or a science fiction story taking place in a future time or on a strange planet, is the set convincing enough to make us believe (during the film) that we are really in another time and place? If so, what factors or details present in the set contribute to its convincing effect? If the set is not completely convincing, why does it fail?
6. Which of the four environmental factors (temporal factors; geographic factors; social structures and economic factors; and customs, moral attitudes, and codes of behavior) play significant roles in the film? Could the same story take place in any environment?
7. Which environmental factors are most important? What effect do these factors have on the plot or the characters?
8. Why did the filmmaker choose this particular location for filming this story?
9. How does the film's setting contribute to the overall emotional atmosphere?
10. What important interrelationships exist between the setting and the characters or between setting and plot?
11. Is the setting symbolic in any way? Does it function as a microcosm?

On Lighting

1. Is the lighting of the film as a whole (a) direct, harsh, and hard; (b) medium and balanced; or (c) soft and diffused? Does high-key or low-key lighting predominate? How do the lighting decisions fit the film's story?

2. Does the lighting throughout seem artificial, coming from places where there are no visible light sources, or does it seem to emanate naturally from sources visible or suggested on-screen?
3. Is the lighting designed to give the film the look of a painting? How effective is this technique, and how well does the painterly style fit the subject matter of the film?
4. How does the lighting contribute to the overall emotional attitude or tone of the film?

On Costume and Makeup Design

1. What details of costuming and makeup help the actors be "in character"? Do these factors also play a role in creating a sense of time and place?
2. Does the makeup for the film's major characters simply enhance the natural look of the actors or significantly transform their appearances? If significant or sometimes subtle changes (such as aging) are required by the script, how effectively are these changes achieved?

Video Exercises

1. Watch *Psycho* (1960), *The Taming of the Shrew*, or *Fanny and Alexander* and describe the unique visual details built into the interior sets for each film. How do the interior sets contribute to a sense of the characters who live there or function as an appropriate backdrop for the action that takes place?
2. Watch the first 10 minutes of any of the following films; then list and describe the important visual details that help establish a sense of time and place in this short time frame: *Casablanca, Shane, The Grapes of Wrath, Summer of '42, To Kill a Mockingbird, Manhattan, Blade Runner,* and *Brazil.* How do basic film elements other than the visual image (music, sound, dialect, and so forth) help contribute to a sense of time and place in these short segments?

Films for Study

The Age of Innocence (1993)
Barry Lyndon (1975)
Batman (1989)
Beloved (1998)
Blade Runner (1982)
Bram Stoker's Dracula (1992)
Brazil (1985)
Casablanca (1942)
A Clockwork Orange (1971)
Days of Heaven (1978)
Dick Tracy (1990)
Fanny and Alexander (1983)
The Grapes of Wrath (1940)
Little Women (1994)
Manhattan (1979)
Moulin Rouge (1952)

Mrs. Dalloway (1998)
The Portrait of a Lady (1996)
Psycho (1960)
Schindler's List (1993)
The Secret Garden (1993)
The Seventh Seal (1957)
Shane (1953)
Summer of '42 (1971)
The Taming of the Shrew (1967)
To Kill a Mockingbird (1962)
The Verdict (1982)
Young Frankenstein (1974)

Chapter 5

Cinematography

The camera is the "eye" of the motion picture. It is not merely a mechanical thing of cogs and wheels and optical glass that records an image on a strip of film. Rather, it is an artistic tool—like a painter's brush, or a sculptor's chisel. In the hands of a craftsman it becomes the instrument through which a dramatic story can be placed on film—so that later on, in darkened theaters all over the world, vast audiences can see the film, react to it, and be entertained.

—HERBERT A. LIGHTMAN, EDITOR OF *AMERICAN CINEMATOGRAPHER*

The Importance of the Image

Film speaks in a language of the senses. Its flowing and sparkling stream of images, its compelling pace and natural rhythms, and its pictorial style are all part of this nonverbal language. So it follows naturally that the aesthetic quality and dramatic power of the image are extremely important to the overall quality of a film. Although the nature and quality of the story, editing, musical score, sound effects, dialogue, and acting can do much to enhance a film's power, even these important elements cannot save a film whose images are mediocre or poorly edited.

As important as the quality of the image may be, however, it must not be considered so important that the purpose of the film as an artistic, unified whole is ignored. A film's photographic effects should not be created for their own sake as independent, beautiful, or powerful images. In the final analysis, they must be justified psychologically and dramatically, as well as aesthetically, as important means to an end, not as ends in themselves. Creating beautiful images for the sake of creating beautiful images violates a film's aesthetic unity and may actually work against the film.

The same principle applies to overly clever or self-conscious camerawork. Technique must not become an end in itself; any special technique must have some underlying purpose related to the purpose of the film as a whole. Every time a director or cinematographer employs an unusual camera angle or a new photographic technique, they should do so for the purpose of communicating (either sensually or intellectually) in the most effective way possible, not simply to show off or try a new trick. A sense of naturalness, a feeling that something had to be done in a certain way, is more praiseworthy than clever camerawork.

Because the visual element is the motion picture's primary and most powerful means of communication, cinematography can completely dominate a film, taking it over by sheer force. But when this occurs, the artistic structure of the film is weakened, the dramatic power of the film fades, and watching the film becomes simply an orgy of the eyeballs. As cinematographer Vilmos Zsigmond puts it:

> I believe photography should never be dominating. The photography in *The Deer Hunter* doesn't look flashy to me; it doesn't overpower the film. It's with the story, never above it. It never tries to tell you how good I am or how good the lighting is. It's on the same level. The performances, the directing, the music, the camerawork are all on the same level. That's what I like about it, and that's what I think photography should be.[1]

The Cinematic Film

A cinematic film takes advantage of all the special properties and qualities that make the film medium unique. The first and most essential of these is the quality of continuous motion. A cinematic film is truly a *motion* picture—a flowing, ever changing stream of images and sounds sparkling with a freshness and vitality all its own, a fluid blend of image, sound, and motion possessed by a restless compulsion to be vibrantly alive, to avoid the quiet, the still, and the static.

The second quality of a cinematic film evolves naturally out of the first. The continuous and simultaneous interplay of image, sound, and motion on the screen sets up varied, complex, and subtle rhythms. Clear, crisp visual and aural rhythms are created by the physical movements or sound of objects on the screen, by the pace of the dialogue, by the natural rhythms of human speech, by the frequency of editorial cuts, by the varying length of shots between cuts, and by the musical score. The pace of the plot also has distinct rhythms. All these serve to intensify the film's unique sense of pulsing life.

A cinematic film also makes maximum use of the great flexibility and freedom of the medium: its freedom from the spoken word and its ability to communicate directly, physically, and concretely through images and sounds; its freedom to spirit us about on a kind of magic carpet ride, to show us action from any vantage point, and to vary our point of view at will; its capability to manipulate time and space, expanding or compressing them at will; and its freedom to make quick and clear transitions in time and space.

Although film is essentially a two-dimensional medium, a cinematic film overcomes this limitation by creating an illusion of depth. It creates the impression that the screen is not a flat surface but a window through which we observe a three-dimensional world.

All these qualities are present in a truly cinematic film. If they are not present in the subject matter, it is up to the director, the cinematographer, and the editor to build them in. Otherwise, the film's dramatic scenes are not communicated in all the fullness of the medium's potential.

Cinematic Points of View

To appreciate fully the workings of the cinematic film, we must be willing to watch in a little different way, focusing not just on *what* we are seeing but also on *how* it is being shown and *why* it is being shown that way. To increase our perception effectively, we must become familiar with the different ways the movie camera sees the action taking place before it—that is, with different **cinematic points of view.*** This first stage in sharpening our watching skills requires constantly considering the following questions for every segment of the film we intend to analyze:

* Because cinematic point of view is largely a matter of camera placement, it is introduced here as part of the discussion of cinematography. To understand the effects of shifting from one point of view to another, see the section on editing in Chapter 6.

- From what position and through what kind of eyes does the camera see the action?
- What effect do the position of the camera and its particular ways of seeing the action have on our response to the action?
- How is our response affected by changes in the point of view?

This last question is extremely important, for it shows us that cinematic point of view need not be consistent (unlike literary point of view, for example). In fact, consistency of viewpoint would be boring in a film and would impede effective communication. Thus we expect a filmmaker to spirit us about from one vantage point to another, but we assume that visual continuity and coherence will be maintained so that we can follow intuitively.

Four points of view are employed in motion pictures:

- objective (camera as sideline observer)
- subjective (camera as participant in the action)
- indirect-subjective
- director's interpretive

Generally, all four can be used in every film to varying degrees, depending on the demands of the dramatic situation and the creative vision and style of the director.

Objective Point of View

The **objective point of view** is illustrated by John Ford's "philosophy of camera." Ford considered the camera to be a window and the audience to be outside the window viewing the people and events within. We are asked to watch the actions as if they were taking place at a distance, and we are not asked to participate. The objective point of view employs a static camera as much as possible in order to produce this window effect, and it concentrates on the actors and the action without drawing attention to the camera. The objective camera suggests an emotional distance between camera and subject; the camera seems simply to be recording, as straightforwardly as possible, the characters and actions of the story. For the most part, the director uses natural, normal, straightforward types of camera positioning and camera angles. The objective camera does not comment on or interpret the action but merely records it, letting it unfold. We see the action from the viewpoint of an impersonal observer. If the camera moves, it does so unobtrusively, calling as little attention to itself as possible.

In most films, continuity and clear communication of the dramatic scene demand that some use be made of the objective point of view. The objective viewpoint forces us to pinpoint subtle but perhaps significant visual details by ourselves (Figure 5.1). Overuse, however, may cause us to lose interest.

Figure 5.1 Objective Viewpoint In this objective shot of a baseball game in progress, we are clearly sideline observers, not really involved in the action.

Subjective Point of View

The **subjective point of view** provides us with the visual viewpoint and emotional intensity felt by a character participating in the action. Alfred Hitchcock, whose philosophy of camera was opposite to that of John Ford, specialized in creating a strong sense of direct involvement by the audience. He employed elaborate camera movement to create visual sequences that bring us into the suspense, literally forcing us to become the characters and experience their emotions. According to Hitchcock, an important tool in creating this kind of subjective involvement is skillful editing and a viewpoint close to the action, as this passage from his essay "Direction" indicates:

> So you gradually build up the psychological situation, piece by piece, using the camera to emphasize first one detail, then another. The point is to draw the audience right into the situation—instead of leaving them to watch it from outside, from a distance. And you can do this only by breaking the action up into details and cutting from one piece to the other, so that each detail is forced in turn on the attention of the audience and reveals its psychological meaning. If you played the whole scene straight through, and simply made a photographic record of it with the camera always in one position, you would lose your power over the audience.

Figure 5.2 Subjective Viewpoint In this subjective shot, the camera puts us in the game, giving us the catcher's view of the action.

> They would watch the scene without becoming really involved in it, and you would have no means of concentrating their attention on those particular visual details which make them feel what the characters are feeling.[2]

When the cinematic point of view is subjective, our experience becomes more intense and more immediate as we become intimately involved in the action. Generally, this viewpoint is maintained by a moving camera, which forces us to see exactly what the character is seeing and in a sense to become the character (Figure 5.2).

It is almost impossible to sustain a purely subjective point of view throughout a film, as was attempted in *Lady in the Lake*. The story of this 1946 film by Robert Montgomery was told entirely through the eyes of its detective hero, and the only time the hero's face was seen was in a mirror. His hands and arms occasionally appeared below eye level, as they would normally be seen from his viewpoint. The difficulty of sustaining such a viewpoint over an entire film is obvious, for clarity of communication and continuity usually demand that a film switch back and forth between the objective and subjective points of view.

The change from objective to subjective point of view is often accomplished in the following manner. An objective shot that shows a character looking at something off-screen (called a **look of outward regard**) cues us to wonder what the character is looking at. The following shot, called an **eye-line shot,** shows us subjectively what the character is seeing. Because the simple logical relationship between the two shots provides a smooth and natural movement from an objective to a subjective point of view, this pattern is common in film.

The alternation of objective and subjective viewpoints, and the tight link between sight and sound, are further illustrated by the following scene:

> **Establishing shot:** Objective camera view from street corner, focusing on a workman using an air hammer in center of street (apparent distance 50 to 75 feet). *Sound:* Loud chatter of air hammer mingled with other street noises.
>
> **Cut to subjective view:** Close-ups of air hammer and violently shaking lower arms and hands of workman, from workman's point of view. *Sound:* Hammer is almost deafening—no other sounds heard.
>
> **Cut back to objective camera:** Heavy truck turns corner beyond workman, bears down on him at top speed. *Sound:* Loud chatter of air hammer, other street noises, rising sound of approaching truck.
>
> **Cut to subjective view:** Close-up of air hammer and workman's hands as seen from his viewpoint. *Sound:* First, only deafening sounds of air hammer, then a rising squeal of brakes mixed with hammer noise.
>
> **Quick cut to a new subjective view:** Front of truck closing quickly on camera from 10 feet away. *Sound:* Squeal of brakes louder, hammer stops, woman's voice screaming, cut short by sickening thud, followed by darkness and momentary silence.
>
> **Cut back to objective viewpoint** (from street corner): Unconscious figure of workman in front of stopped truck. Curious crowd gathering into circle. *Sound:* Mixed jumble of panicked voices, street noises, ambulance siren in distance.

The alternation between the objective and the subjective view provides both a clear understanding of the dramatic flow of events and a strong sense of audience involvement.

Indirect-Subjective Point of View

The **indirect-subjective point of view** does not provide a participant's point of view, but it does bring us close to the action so that we feel intimately involved and our visual experience is intense. Consider a close-up that conveys the emotional reaction of a character. We recognize that we are not the character, yet we are drawn into the feeling that is being conveyed in a subjective way. A close-up of a face contorted in pain makes us feel that pain more vividly than would an objective shot from a greater distance. Another example is the kind of shot

Figure 5.3 Indirect-Subjective Viewpoint Although we do not have any character's point of view, this indirect-subjective shot brings us close to the action and involves us in it as we focus on the tension in the batter's hands as he awaits the pitch. Because we are so close to the batter, we identify with him and feel his tension.

that was common in the old westerns. With the stagecoach under attack by outlaws, the director inserts close-ups of pounding hoofs to capture the furious rhythm and pulsing excitement of the chase, bringing us close to the action and increasing the intensity of our experience. The indirect-subjective point of view gives us the feeling of participating in the action without showing the action through a participant's eyes (Figure 5.3).

The key to the effectiveness of the indirect-subjective viewpoint is this closeness to the action, as Alfred Hitchcock explains:

> So what you are doing is you are taking the audience right close up into the scene, and the montage of the various effects gets the audience involved. That's its purpose. It becomes much more powerful than if you sit back and look. Say you are at a boxing match and you are eight to ten rows back; well, you get a very different effect if you are in the first row, looking up under those ropes. When these two fellows are slugging each other, you get splashed almost.
>
> In *Psycho* once that figure comes in and starts to stab, you're in it. Oh, you're absolutely in it. The distance of the figures, you see.[3]

Figure 5.4 Director's Interpretive Viewpoint By choosing an extremely low-angle view of the batter, the director makes us see him in a special or unusual way, perhaps to give us the pitcher's emotional perspective as he prepares to pitch to a powerful slugger in a close game.

This "distance of the figures" makes the viewer's response to the shower scene in *Psycho* so very different from the response to the equally violent ending of *Bonnie and Clyde*. Indirect-subjective close-up shots of Bonnie and Clyde are used sparingly in the slow-motion dance of death, but the primary viewpoint is objective, and the viewer, like the camera, stands off to the side, out of harm's way. In *Psycho*, the rapid editing between occasional subjective viewpoints and close-up indirect-subjective shots puts the viewer in the shower with Janet Leigh and creates a real sense of *personal* danger.

Director's Interpretive Point of View

The director is always manipulating our viewpoint in subtle ways. The filmmaker chooses not only what to show us but also how we will see it. By photographing a scene from special angles or with special lenses, or in slow or fast motion, and so on, he or she imposes on the image a certain tone, emotional attitude, or style. We are thus forced to react in a certain way to what we see, thereby experiencing the **director's interpretive point of view.** We are *consciously* aware that the director wants us to see the action in some *unusual* way (Figure 5.4).

There are examples of all four points of view in the following typical western sequence showing a stagecoach being attacked by bandits:

Objective point of view: Stagecoach and horses as seen from the side (from a distance of 50 to 75 feet) being pursued by bandits. Shot here could be either from a panning camera in fixed position or from a mobile camera tracking alongside or parallel to the path of the stagecoach.

Subjective point of view: Camera shot from stage driver's point of view, looking out over horses' backs, with arms and hands holding and slapping reins seen below eye level.

Indirect-subjective point of view: Close-up of stage driver's face from side as he turns his head to look back over his shoulder (a look of outward regard). His face registers fear, determination.

Subjective point of view: Camera shot of bandits in hot pursuit of stagecoach, from the point of view of driver looking back over top of stage.

Indirect-subjective point of view: Close-up of face of driver, now turned frontward again, registering strain, jaw set in determination, sweat streaming down face, screaming at horses.

Director's interpretive point of view: Slow-motion close-up of horses' heads in profile, their eyes wild with strain, mouths in agony straining at their bits, flecks of foamy sweat shaking from their necks. (By filming this shot in slow motion, the director in effect comments on the action, telling us how to see it. The slow-motion photography conveys the horses' exhaustion, intensifies the tremendous effort they are putting out, and gives us a sense of the futility of the stage's attempt to escape.)

Although some practice may be required to spot the cinematic viewpoints in a segment of film, it is basically a very simple process. The next stage in the art of watching films, analyzing the different aspects of cinematic composition and fully appreciating the skills of the cinematographer, is a bit more complex.

Elements of Cinematic Composition

Principles of visual composition have been well established since antiquity. Evidenced in painting and still photography, these so-called natural laws focus on three fairly simple visual concepts:

1. Vertical lines suggest strength, authority, and dignity.
2. Diagonal lines crossing the frame suggest action and dynamic movement—the power to overcome obstacles (Figure 5.5).
3. Curved lines denote fluidity and sensuality; compositions that suggest a circular movement evoke feelings of exaltation, euphoria, and joy.

According to Nestor Almendros, a cinematographer must know these principles but must "then forget them, or at least not consciously think about them all the

Figure 5.5 Powerful Composition The strong diagonal lines of the stairway and railings parallel the line of fire to create a dynamic composition in this powerful scene from *The French Connection.*

time."[4] A cinematographer who thinks about them all the time risks losing touch with his or her primary challenge.

Because a cinematic film is a unique medium, the problems in composition that it poses for the director and cinematographer are also unique. Both must keep in mind that every **shot** (a strip of film produced by a single uninterrupted running of the camera) is but a segment, a brief element in a continuous flow of images. And they must create each shot with a view to its contribution to the whole. The difficulty of creating a shot is compounded by the movement of the image itself. The image is in a constant state of flux, and the camera records those movements at a rate of twenty-four frames per second. Every frame in a shot cannot be set up according to the aesthetic principles of composition used in still photography. The cinematographer's choices in each shot are dictated by the nature of the film medium. Every shot must be designed with the goals of *cinematic* composition in mind. These goals are (1) directing attention to the

Figure 5.6 Size and Closeness of the Object In most cases, our attention is naturally drawn to larger, closer objects or faces, such as the man's face in this picture, rather than to smaller, more distant objects or faces.

Figure 5.7 Sharpness of Focus When a larger, closer face in the foreground is in soft focus or blurred, our attention is drawn to a smaller and more distant face in sharp focus. The eye is drawn almost automatically to what it can see best.

object of greatest significance, (2) keeping the image in constant motion, and (3) creating an illusion of depth.

Focusing Attention on the Most Significant Object

Above all, a shot must be so composed that it draws attention into the scene and toward the object of greatest dramatic significance. Only when this is achieved are the film's dramatic ideas conveyed effectively. Several methods of directing attention are open to the filmmaker.

- **Size and Closeness of the Object.** Normally, the eye is directed toward larger, closer objects rather than toward smaller, more distant objects. For example, the image of an actor's face appearing in the foreground (closer to the camera and therefore larger) is more likely to serve as a focal point for our attention than is a face in the background. In a normal situation, then, the size and relative distance of the object from the camera are important factors in determining the greatest area of interest (Figure 5.6).
- **Sharpness of Focus.** The eye is also drawn almost automatically to what it can see best. If a face in the foreground is slightly blurred and a face in the background, though smaller and more distant, is sharp and clear, our eyes are drawn to the background face because it can be seen best. An object in sharp focus can divert our attention from a closer, larger object in soft focus, even if the larger object fills half the screen (Figure 5.7).

Figure 5.8 Background in Motion Although the horse and carriage in the background are moving, they are part of a generalized traffic movement in the street, so our attention remains on the static but dramatically more important interaction between Julie Christie and Alan Bates in this scene from *The Go-Between*.

Figure 5.9 Extreme Close-Up There's no doubt about where our attention is directed in this dramatic close-up of Tony Perkins in *Psycho II*.

- **Movement.** The eye is also drawn to an object in motion, and a moving object can divert our attention from a static one. Thus, a single moving object in an otherwise static scene draws our attention. Conversely, if movement and flow are a general part of the background, moving objects do not divert our attention from static but more dramatically important objects (Figure 5.8).
- **Extreme Close-Ups.** A **close-up** is a shot of a person or object taken at close range. A tight or extreme close-up brings us so close to the object of interest (an actor's face, for example) that we cannot look elsewhere. The face so fills the screen that there is nothing else to see (Figure 5.9).
- **Arrangement of People and Objects.** The director focuses our attention by his or her arrangement of people and objects in relation to each other. Because each arrangement is determined by the nature of the dramatic moment being enacted and the complex interrelationships involved, the director must depend more on an intuitive sense of rightness than on any positioning formulas (Figure 5.10).
- **Foreground Framing.** The director might decide to frame the object of greatest significance with objects or people in the near foreground. To make sure that our attention is not distracted by the framing objects or people, the director generally emphasizes the most important subject with the brightest lighting and sharpest focus (Figures 5.11, 5.12).

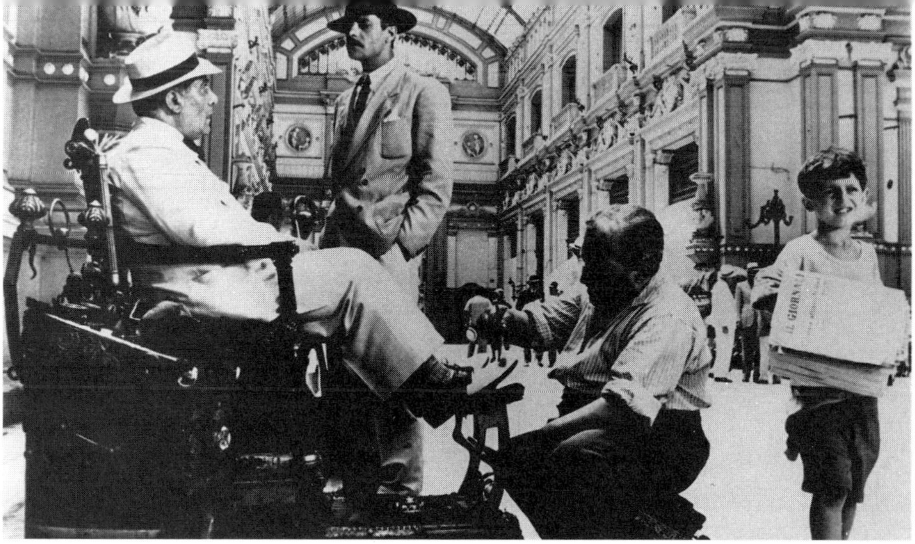

Figure 5.10 Dramatic Arrangement of People and Objects There are no set formulas for positioning characters and objects within the frame. The director must rely on an intuitive sense of rightness in composing each shot to communicate the nature of the dramatic moment and in positioning actors to reveal subtle and complex interrelationships. In this scene from Lina Wertmuller's *Seven Beauties,* we focus our attention on Giancarlo Giannini because of the physical locations of the other characters and because Giannini's position in the center of the architectural frame created by the grand foyer in the background and his standing posture make him dominant.

Figure 5.11 Foreground Framing In *E.T. The Extra-Terrestrial* Peter Coyote and Dee Wallace talking in the foreground set up a frame that calls our attention to the listener, Henry Thomas. Subtle differences in lighting and Thomas's position in the center of the plastic tunnel also direct our attention to him.

Figure 5.12 The Menacing Frame Although Michael Myers's menacing figure dominates the screen, lighting and sharp focus draw attention to his sister Laurie (Jamie Lee Curtis) in this scene from *Halloween H_2O.*

Figure 5.13 High Contrast These pictures from *Gandhi* and *The Usual Suspects* use high contrast in very different ways to focus our attention. In the scene from *Gandhi,* the dark-skinned figure of Gandhi (Ben Kingsley) stands out against the bright sunlight on the parched Indian landscape beyond. In the scene from *The Usual Suspects,* the darkness of the lounge draws our attention to the face of Keyser Soze's henchman (Pete Postlethwaite), who is highlighted only by the chandeliers.

- **Lighting and Color.** Special uses of light and color also help draw the eye to the object of greatest significance. High-contrast areas of light and dark create natural centers of focal interest, as do bright colors present in a subdued or drab background (Figure 5.13).

In composing each shot, the filmmaker continually employs these techniques, either separately or in conjunction with each other, to focus our attention on the object of greatest dramatic significance. The filmmaker guides our thoughts and emotions where he or she wants them to go. Focusing our attention is certainly the most fundamental concern of cinematic composition, but, as we shall see, it is not the only one.

Keeping the Image in Motion

Because the essential characteristic of the cinematic film is continuous motion—a flowing, ever changing stream of images—the director or cinematographer must build this quality of movement and flux into every shot. To create the stream of constantly changing images, the cinematographer employs several techniques.

Fixed-Frame Movement The fixed camera frame approximates the effect of looking through a window. In **fixed-frame movement,** the camera remains in one position, pointing at one spot, as we might look at something with a frozen stare. The director works movement and variety into the shot by moving the subject. This movement can be rapid and frantic (like the physical action of a barroom brawl) or calm and subtle (like the changing facial expression of an actor speaking and gesturing normally).

Several types of movement are possible within the fixed frame. Movement can be *lateral* (from the left to right of the frame), *in depth* (toward or away from the camera), or *diagonal* (a combination of lateral and in-depth movements). Purely lateral movement creates the impression of movement on a flat surface (which the screen is) and therefore calls attention to one of the medium's limitations: its two-dimensionality. So, to create the illusion of three dimensions, the cinematographer favors in-depth movement (toward or away from the camera) and diagonal movement over purely lateral movement.

Panning and Tilting Usually when the camera remains in a fixed physical location, it captures movement by approximating the head and eye movements of a human spectator. The camera's movements incorporate what is essentially a human field of view. With the body stationary, if we turn the head and neck from left to right and add a corresponding sideward glance of the eyes, our field of view takes in an arc slightly wider than 180 degrees. And if we simply move the head and eyes up and down, our eyes span an arc of at least 90 degrees. Most movements of the camera fall within these natural human limitations. A closer look at these camera movements will clarify these limitations.

Panning Moving the camera's line of sight in a horizontal plane, to the left and right, is called **panning.** The most common use of the camera pan is to follow the lateral movement of the subject. In a western, for example, the panning camera may function in this way. The wagon train has been attacked by Indians and has moved into a defensive circle. The camera for this shot is set up in a fixed location looking over the shoulder of one of the settlers as she attempts to pick off circling Indians with a rifle. The circling Indians move from right to left. The camera (and the rifle) move to the right and pick up a subject (target Indian). Then, both camera and rifle swing laterally to left as the subject Indian rides by; when he reaches a center position, the rifle fires and we watch him fall off the horse and roll to the left of the center. Then either the camera pans back to the right to pick up a new target or an editorial cut starts the next shot with the camera picking up a new target Indian (far right), and the pattern is repeated.

Another type of pan is used to change from one subject to another. This might be illustrated by a shootout scene in the middle of the street of a western town. The camera occupies a fixed position on the side of the street, halfway between the dueling gunfighters. After establishing the tense, poised image of the gunman on the right, the camera leaves him and slowly pans left until it focuses on the other man, also tense and poised.

Because the eye normally jumps instantaneously from one object of interest to another, a pan must have a dramatic purpose; otherwise, it will seem unnatural and conspicuous. There are several possible reasons for using a pan. In the gunfight scene, the slow fluid movement of the camera from one man to the other may help expand time, intensifying the suspense and the viewer's anticipation of the first draw. Also, it may reflect the tension in the environment as a whole by registering the fear and suspense on the faces of the onlookers across the street, who become secondary subjects as we see their facial expressions in passing or catch glimpses of them frantically diving for cover. Finally, the pan may simply help to establish the relative distance between the two men. Although this type of pan can be effective, it must be used with restraint, particularly if there is a great deal of **dead screen** (screen area with no dramatically or aesthetically interesting visual information) between the two subjects.

On rare occasions, a complete 360-degree pan may be dramatically effective, especially when the situation calls for a sweeping panoramic view of the entire landscape. Such might be the case in a western where the fort is completely surrounded by Indians. A full 360-degree pan, as in Sidney Lumet's *A Long Day's Journey Into Night,* clearly indicates the impossibility of escape and the hopelessness of the situation. Also, a 360-degree pan might be useful in dramatizing the situation of a character waking up in an unfamiliar and unexpected environment. A person waking up in a jail cell, for instance, would turn his or her body enough to survey the surroundings completely.

Tilting Moving the camera's line of sight in a vertical plane, up and down, is called **tilting.** Tilting approximates the vertical movement of our head and eyes. The following hypothetical sequence illustrates how the tilt is used. The camera occupies a fixed position at the end of an airport runway, focused on a jet airliner taxiing toward the camera. As the plane lifts off, the camera tilts upward to follow the plane's trajectory to a point directly overhead. At this point, although it would be technically possible to create an axis to follow the plane in one continuous shot, the shot stops and a new shot begins with the camera facing in the opposite direction. The second shot picks up the plane still overhead and tilts downward to follow its flight away from the camera. This movement approximates the way we would normally observe the incident if we were standing in the camera's position. As the plane turns right and begins to climb, the camera follows it in a diagonal movement that combines the elements of both panning and tilting. Thus, though the camera is in a fixed location, it is flexible enough to follow the movement of the plane as represented by the following arrows: takeoff to directly overhead ↑, crossover to turn ↘, turn and climb ↗.

In most panning and tilting shots, the movement of the camera approximates the normal *human* way of looking at things. Many shots in every film are photographed in this manner, showing the story unfolding as a person watching the scene might view it.

The Zoom Lens In the techniques described so far, the camera remains in a fixed position. The fixed camera, however—even though it can pan and tilt—lacks

Figure 5.14 Zooming in on the Action These three pictures represent different stages in a continuous shot of a single action using a zoom lens. At the start of the zoom, the cameraman picks up the center fielder as he starts after a fly ball. At this stage, the player's image fills a very small portion of the screen. At the midway point in the zoom, the player's image is magnified—he appears about three times larger. By the time he catches the ball, the zoom lens has continued to increase magnification until his figure almost fills the whole screen.

the fluidity necessary to create a truly cinematic film. The zoom lens offers a solution to this problem. The **zoom lens**—a series of lenses that keep an image in constant focus—allows the camera to appear to glide toward or away from the subject, but without any movement of the camera. Zoom lenses can magnify the subject ten times or more, so that we seem to move closer to the subject although our actual distance from the camera does not change.

To a camera stationed behind home plate in a baseball stadium, the center fielder, some four hundred feet away, appears extremely small, the same size that he would appear to the naked eye. By zooming in on him, the cinematographer is able to keep him in constant focus, and in effect we glide smoothly toward the center fielder until his figure almost fills the screen, as if we were seeing him from a distance of forty feet or less (Figure 5.14). The camera simply magnifies the image, but the effect is one of moving toward the subject. By reversing the process, the cinematographer can achieve the effect of moving away from the subject.

The use of the zoom lens not only allows us to see things more clearly but also gives us a sense of fluid motion in and out of the frame, thereby increasing our interest and involvement. And all of these variations are possible without ever moving the camera.

The Mobile Camera When the camera itself becomes mobile, the possibilities of movement increase tremendously. By freeing the camera from a fixed position, the cinematographer can create a constantly shifting viewpoint, giving us a moving image of a static subject. By mounting the camera on a boom or a crane (itself mounted on a truck or dolly), the cinematographer can move it fluidly alongside, above, in front of, behind, or even under a running horse. The mobile camera can thus fulfill almost any demand for movement created by a story situation.

Film stories are often framed effectively by slow camera movement for beginnings and endings. By moving the camera slowly and fluidly forward to enter a scene, the cinematographer creates a sense of mystery, discovery, and anticipation while bringing us into the heart of the narrative and involving us in the action. The opposite—fluid camera movement away from the scene—is often used to give a powerful sense of ending to a film. It can be especially effective when it pulls away from continuing action, as in the final helicopter camera shot in *Zorba the Greek*, picturing Zorba (Anthony Quinn) and his friend (Alan Bates) dancing on the beach. Our slow exit while the action is in progress gives us the feeling that the dance continues indefinitely.

The mobile camera can also provide the tremendous sense of immediacy and dynamism that French director Abel Gance strove for in his 1927 *Napoleon*. Film historian Kevin Brownlow describes Gance and his film in the *Napoleon* program brochure:

> To him, a tripod was a set of crutches supporting a lame imagination. His aim was to free the camera, to hurl it into the middle of the action, to force the audience from mere spectators into active participants.
>
> Technicians in the German studios were putting the camera on wheels. Gance put it on wings. He strapped it to the back of a horse, for rapid inserts in the chase across Corsica; he suspended it from overhead wires, like a miniature cable-car; he mounted it on a huge pendulum, to achieve the vertigo-inducing storm in the convention.

Two recent developments have greatly increased the potential of the mobile camera. The first of these, the **Steadicam,** is a portable, one-person camera with a built-in gyroscopic device that prevents any sudden jerkiness and provides a smooth, rock-steady image even when the person carrying it is running up a flight of steps or down a rocky mountain path. The second development, the **Skycam,** is a small, computerized, remote-controlled camera that can be mounted on the top of a lightweight magnesium pole or can “fly” on wires at

Figure 5.15 The Packed Screen The most obvious way to keep the screen alive is to pack almost every square inch of its surface with visual information, as in this scene from *Murder on the Orient Express*.

speeds of up to twenty miles an hour and can go practically anywhere that cables can be strung. Helicopter mounts with gyroscopic stabilizers also create spectacular gyrosphere shots.

Editing and Movement The editing process also contributes greatly to the cinematic film's ever changing stream of images. The editing, in fact, often creates the most vibrant visual rhythms in a film, as the editorial cuts and transitions propel us instantaneously from a **long shot** (a shot, taken from some distance, that shows the subject as well as its surroundings) to a close-up, from one camera angle to another, and from one setting to another.

The cinematographer thus uses a wide variety of techniques, either separately or in various combinations, to keep the visual image in constant motion:

- the movement of the subject within the fixed frame
- vertical or horizontal movement of the camera (tilting and panning)
- apparent movement of the viewer toward or away from the objects in the frame (zoom lens)
- completely free movement of the camera and constantly changing viewpoint (mobile camera and editorial cuts)

Dead Screen and Live Screen The director must be concerned with keeping the image alive in another sense. In almost every shot, the director attempts to communicate a significant amount of information in each frame (Figure 5.15). To achieve this **live screen,** each shot must be composed so that the visual frame

Figure 5.16 Background in Motion A director attempts to incorporate some kind of motion into almost every shot and often uses natural background movement to keep the screen alive. This type of background motion, a very subordinate type, does not divert our attention from the primary subject. In this scene from *Suddenly, Last Summer,* a static shot of Elizabeth Taylor is kept alive by filming her against the gently lapping sea waves.

Figure 5.17 Strong Visual Impact in a Static Background The figures of Diane Keaton and Woody Allen occupy a very small portion of the frame in this scene from *Manhattan*. The imposing architecture of the Queensborough Bridge in the background provides an aesthetically pleasing composition and a strong sense of three-dimensionality and underscores the sense of place that is an integral part of the film.

is loaded with cinematic information, and large blank areas (dead screen) are avoided—unless, as in some cases, there is a dramatic purpose for dead screen (Figures 5.16 and 5.17).

Creating an Illusion of Depth

Cinematic composition must be concerned with creating an illusion of depth on what is essentially a two-dimensional screen. To achieve this, the cinematographer employs several different techniques.

1. **Movement of Subject (Fixed Frame).** When using a fixed frame, the director creates the illusion of depth by filming the subject moving toward or away from the camera, either head-on or diagonally. Purely lateral movement, perpendicular to the direction in which the camera is aimed, creates a two-dimensional effect and, to avoid a flat image, should be minimized.
2. **Movement of Camera.** A camera mounted on a truck or dolly may create the illusion of depth by moving toward or away from a relatively static object. As it passes by or goes around objects, we become more aware of

the depth of the image. Because the camera eye actually moves, the objects on both sides of its path constantly change their position relative to one another. The change varies according to the changing angles from which the moving camera views them. Director Allan Dwan describes this illusion:

> To get the real effect of a dolly at any time, you have to pass something. If you're not going past anything, you don't get the effect. You pass buildings or you pass a tree or you pass something, and it's very interesting. We used to notice, years and years ago before any of these effects were tried, or anything like stereoscopic photography was thought about, that if we passed a tree, then the tree became solid and round. If you dolly past a tree, it seems to revolve. It turns around. It isn't flat anymore. But stand still and photograph a tree and it's just a flat tree. But move past it and it rounds right away. Just becomes solid. And we used to get that effect. We'd take certain buildings—buildings with pillars—and get a wonderful effect going past those pillars if we dollied. The pillars seemed to revolve but they got solid because as you went around them you had the feeling that they were of substance and not just flat.[5]

3. **Apparent Camera Movement (Zoom Lens).** By magnifying the image, the zoom lens gives us the sensation of moving closer to or farther from the camera. Not surprisingly, the zoom lens may also be used to create the illusion of depth. But because camera position does not change during zooming, there is no real change in perspective. The objects to the sides do not change their position in relation to one another as they do when the camera moves. For this reason, a zoom lens does not create the illusion of depth quite as effectively as a mobile camera.
4. **Change of Focal Planes (Rack Focus).** Most cameras, including still cameras, are designed to focus on objects at different distances from the lens. Because the eye is ordinarily drawn to what it can see best—that is, to the object in sharpest focus—the cinematographer can create a kind of three-dimensionality by using **rack focus**—in one continuous shot focusing the camera lens, in turn, on objects in different planes of depth (different distances from the camera). If the frame includes three faces, all at different distances from the camera, the cinematographer may first focus on the nearest face and then, while the shot continues, focus on the second face and then on the third, thus, in effect, creating the illusion of depth within the frame (Figure 5.18).
5. **Deep Focus.** In direct contrast to the change in focal planes is **deep focus**—the use of special lenses that allow the camera to focus simultaneously and with equal clarity on objects anywhere from two feet to several hundred feet away. This depth of focus approximates most clearly the ability of the human eye to see a deep range of objects in clear focus (Figure 5.19). The sustained use of this technique has a profound effect on the way the audience views the dramatic action. Writing about cinematographer Gregg Toland's use of deep focus in *Citizen Kane*, Frank Brady explains:

Figure 5.18 Rack Focus—Moving Deeper Into the Frame Because our attention is naturally drawn to what we can see best, the illusion of depth can be created by changing the focus during a continuous shot. These three pictures represent different stages in a single running shot. In the first picture, our attention is drawn to the sharply focused image of the batter. As the shot continues, the camera focuses on the pitcher and then on the shortstop, giving us the feeling that we are being drawn deeper into a three-dimensional frame. (The order could also be reversed, beginning the shot with the shortstop in focus and ending with the batter in focus.)

Figure 5.19 Deep Focus In this picture from *The Right Stuff,* all seven of the actors playing the astronauts are in sharp focus despite their varying distances from the camera.

Figure 5.20 Three-Dimensional Arrangement of People and Objects The characters around Humphrey Bogart are carefully positioned for a three-dimensional effect in this scene from *Casablanca*.

> [Deep focus] permitted the camera to record objects at varying distances in the same shot, in sharp, clear focus, rather than deemphasizing background. By allowing several points of view or interest to occur simultaneously, this deep-focus photography encompassed the same range of vision as the human eye. It permitted the spectator, not the camera, to decide which character or piece of action to concentrate upon. Essentially, this form of cinematography provided the same kind of freedom that a playgoer has while watching a stage play, where the audience is not forced to look at a close-up or a single character, for example, as he must in a film, but can allow his eyes to take in anything—or everything—that is happening on stage. . . . It was an innovative and daring technique, and [director Orson] Welles had Toland shoot as many scenes as possible using the vitality of deep focus.[6]

Because each shot is loaded with rich visual and dramatic information in several planes of depth, the pace of editing is slow when deep focus is used.

6. **Three-Dimensional Arrangement of People and Objects.** Perhaps the most important consideration in creating a three-dimensional image is how to arrange the people and objects to be filmed. If they are placed in separate focal planes, the cinematographer has a truly three-dimensional scene to photograph. Without such an arrangement, there is no real purpose for the various effects and techniques described above (Figure 5.20).
7. **Foreground Framing.** A three-dimensional effect is also achieved when a shot is set up so that the subject is framed by an object or objects in the

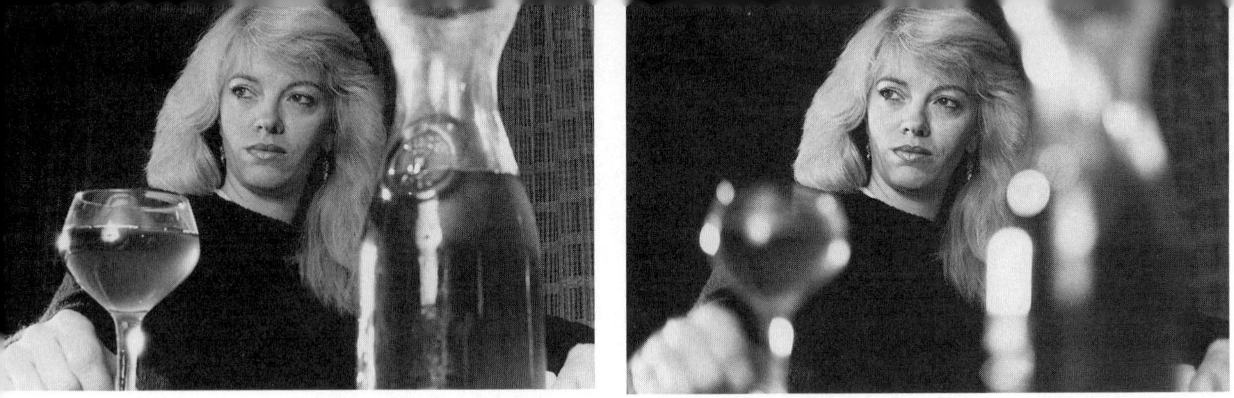

Figure 5.21 Foreground Framing In one shot, the wine glass and carafe in the foreground framing the woman's face are in focus. In the other, they are completely out of focus.

Figure 5.22 Lighting for Depth In the first photo, the flat lighting serves to minimize the sense of depth. When the direction, intensity, and quality of the light are changed, the same scene has greater depth and more dramatic punch.

near foreground. When the object that forms the frame is in focus, a strong sense of three-dimensionality is achieved. When the foreground frame is thrown out of focus, or seen in very soft focus, the three-dimensional effect is weakened somewhat but not lost, and the entire mood or atmosphere of the scene changes (Figure 5.21).

8. **Special Lighting Effects.** By carefully controlling the angle, direction, intensity, and quality of the lighting, the director can further add to the illusion of depth (Figure 5.22). Occasionally, the director may even control the source and direction of the lighting for the purpose of expanding the limits of the frame. By positioning the light source out of camera range—to either side of, or behind, the camera—the filmmaker can cause the shadows of objects outside the frame to fall inside the frame, thus suggest-

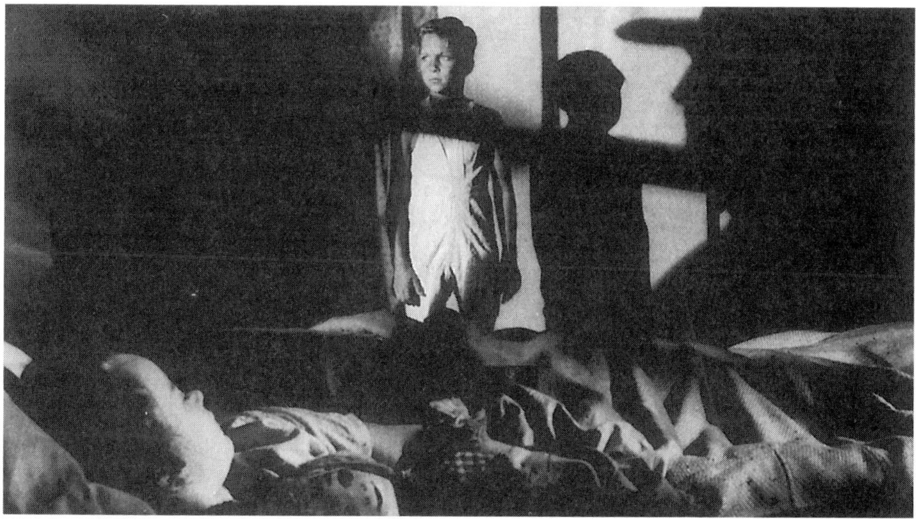

Figure 5.23 Three-Dimensional Shadows In this scene from Charles Laughton's *The Night of the Hunter,* the orphaned boy, John, stands guard over his sleeping sister, Pearl, and looks out the window at the villainous "preacher," Harry Powers (Robert Mitchum). Mitchum sits on a bench in the yard, a gas lamp behind him casting his shadow through the window and onto the room's back wall. If the scene were evenly lit, with no shadows, it would have only two important planes of depth: Pearl, sleeping in the foreground, and John, standing in the background. Although the shadows add only one *real* plane of depth (the wall), our mind's eye is aware of objects or shapes in five different planes: Mitchum seated in the yard, the window frame, Pearl sleeping on the bed, John, and the back wall. Even more important to the scene's dramatic power is the very real sense of Mitchum's presence in the room as his shadow looms over and threatens the shadow of John on the wall.

ing the presence of those objects. When these shadows come from objects behind the camera, they can add greatly to the three-dimensionality of the shot (Figure 5.23).

9. **Use of Reflections.** Directors also make imaginative use of reflections to create a sense of depth and pack additional information into a frame. In *The Grapes of Wrath*, for example, as the Joad truck travels across the Mohave Desert at night, the camera looks out through the windshield at the strange world it is driving through. At the same time, the pale, ghostly reflections of Tom, Al, and Pa are seen on the glass as they talk about what they are seeing. In this way, information that would usually require two shots is compressed into one. The same technique is used in *Hardcore*, where the worried face of the father (George C. Scott) is reflected in the windshield as he tries to track his runaway daughter in a big-city porno district (Figure 5.24). In *Citizen Kane*, just after the protagonist's second wife has left him, a whole bank of mirrors lining both sides of a grand hallway in Xanadu reflect not one but multiple Charles Foster Kanes.

Figure 5.24 Use of Reflection A worried father (George C. Scott) searches for his runaway daughter through a big-city porno district in this scene from *Hardcore*. By showing his reflected image on the car's windshield, director Paul Schrader has not only provided an additional plane of depth but has in effect doubled the information in the frame. We see not only what the father sees but also his reaction to it. In this scene from *Dead Man Walking,* Sister Helen Prejean's (Susan Sarandon) face is reflected on the prison glass that separates her from death row inmate Pat Sonnier (Sean Penn).

As it is used, late in the film, the effect intensifies the essential mystery of personality developed throughout. The film reveals to its journalistic investigators that, externally, the extraordinary Kane is many men in one. The viewer understands that, internally, too, like most humans, Kane is vastly fragmented. The celebrated hall of mirrors sequence at the end of *The Lady From Shanghai* finds Orson Welles using this technique again—this time for sustaining psychological suspense.

The nine effects described in this section have nothing to do with specialized three-dimensional projection systems such as 3-D and Cinerama. But most of them do provide a fairly effective illusion of depth. Despite a revival of 3-D in films like *Jaws 3-D*, *The Spacehunter*, and *Friday the 13th*, *Part 3*, and some new projection techniques, the effect has not been much improved, and the troublesome 3-D glasses are still required. The quality of the films released in 3-D hasn't done much to help sell the product. Lily Tomlin perhaps sums up the problem best:

> *Bwana Devil* in 3-D was modestly billed as "The Miracle of the Age." On the poster it promised, "A Lion in Your Lap! A Lover in Your Arms!". . . What more could one ask for? Well, a better script, perhaps. Is there a rule somewhere that says that for every giant techno-step we take forward we must take one step back and touch base with banality? So often, what we expect to be techno-leaps turn out to be techno-trash.[7]

Techniques for Specialized Visual Effects

Directors and cinematographers employ a variety of cinematic techniques to create specialized visual effects. The effects created by these techniques enhance certain qualities of the action or dramatic situation being filmed.

Hand-Held Camera

Related to the concept of cinematic point of view is the specialized dramatic effect achieved through use of a hand-held camera. The jerky, uneven movement of the camera heightens the sense of reality provided by the subjective viewpoint. In *Alambrista!* Robert Young employed a hand-held camera, making the perspective jump madly to reflect the disassociation his Hispanic hero feels in a foreign country. If the viewpoint is not intended to be subjective, the same technique can give a sequence the feel of a documentary or newsreel. The hand-held camera, jerkiness and all, is especially effective in filming violent action scenes because the random, chaotic camera movement fits in with the spirit of the action. During the past two decades, however, the hand-held camera has been overused in so-called slasher horror films in an attempt to create suspense.

Camera Angles

Cinematographers do more with the camera than simply position it for one of the four basic viewpoints. The angle from which an event or object is photographed is an important factor in cinematic composition. Sometimes cinematographers employ different camera angles to add variety or to create a sense of visual balance between one shot and another. Camera angles also communicate special kinds of dramatic information or emotional attitudes. Because the objective point of view stresses or employs a normal, straightforward view of the action, unusual camera angles are employed primarily to present other points of view, such as the subjective viewpoint of a participant in the action or the interpretive viewpoint of the director.

One type of objective camera angle is particularly worthy of mention. When an extremely high camera angle is combined with slow, fluid camera movement, as though the camera were slowly floating over the scene, the impression is that of a remote, external, detached spectator carefully examining a situation in an objective, almost scientific, manner. This kind of shot is used repeatedly throughout Richard Rush's *The Stunt Man* to establish and maintain the image of the film director, Eli Cross (Peter O'Toole), as a kind of all-powerful, godlike figure (Figure 5.25).

When the camera is placed below eye level, creating a **low-angle shot,** the size and importance of the subject are exaggerated. If a child is the principal figure in a film, low-angle shots of adults may be very much in evidence, as the director attempts to show us the scene from a child's perspective. For example,

Figure 5.25 Extremely High Camera Angle When the mobile camera seems to float slowly high above the action, as in this scene from *Midnight Express,* we become very remote and detached, and our objectivity (like our viewpoint) becomes almost godlike.

in *Night of the Hunter* two children are attempting to escape from the clutches of a Satanic itinerant preacher (Robert Mitchum) who has already murdered their mother. As the children attempt to launch a boat from the bank, Mitchum's figure is seen from a low angle as he crashes through the brush lining the bank and plunges into the water. The terror of the narrow escape is intensified by the low camera angle, which clearly communicates the helplessness of the children and their view of the monstrous Mitchum.

A different effect is achieved in *Lord of the Flies* (1963), where Ralph, pursued to the point of exhaustion by the savage boys on the beach, falls headlong in the sand at the feet of a British naval officer. The low-angle shot of the officer, exaggerating his size and solidity, conveys a sense of dominance, strength, and protectiveness to Ralph.

An effect opposite to that of the low-angle shot is generally achieved by placing the camera *above* eye level, creating a **high-angle shot,** which seems to dwarf the subject and diminish its importance. Consider, for example, a high-angle shot that would show Gulliver's view of the Lilliputians. Writer-director Francis Ford Coppola and cinematographer Bill Butler open *The Conversation*

Figure 5.26 The Effect of Changing Camera Angles In these three pictures, we see the effects created by three different camera angles on the same subject in the same position. The first picture is taken from what might be called a normal angle: The camera is looking directly at the pitcher at about eye level. The second picture is taken with the camera slightly in front of the mound but located five or six feet above the pitcher's head, looking down on him in a high-angle shot. For the third picture, the camera is located on the ground in front of the pitcher, looking up at him in a low-angle shot.

with a high-angle shot of Union Square in San Francisco. The tantalizing, persistent memory of this camera angle continues to color viewers' perception throughout the film—on levels of plot, character, and theme.

The director may employ certain camera angles to suggest the feeling he or she wants to convey about a character at a given moment (Figure 5.26). In *Touch of Evil*, Orson Welles employs a high camera angle to look down on Janet Leigh as she enters a prison cell. The shot emphasizes her despair, her state of mind, and her helplessness. By making us see the character as he sees her, Welles interprets the emotional tenor and atmosphere of the scene for us. In one of the most famous shots in *Citizen Kane*, Gregg Toland utilizes an extremely high camera angle as Kane makes a political speech; the protagonist is, then, shown as a tiny, insignificant figure in the film frame. Most shrewdly, though, Welles places this image in front of a gigantic poster of Kane that creates the opposite effect simultaneously: The politician looms powerfully above the world. Thus, the interior conflicts within Kane's life are presented cinematically.

Color, Diffusion, and Soft Focus

Directors use filters to create a wide range of specialized effects. They may use special filters to darken the blue of the sky, thereby sharpening by contrast the whiteness of the clouds, or they may add a light-colored tone to the whole scene by filming it through a colored filter. For example, in *A Man and a Woman* a love scene was filmed with a red filter, which imparted a romantic warmth.

On rare occasions, a special filter may be used to add a certain quality to a whole film. An example is Franco Zeffirelli's film version of *The Taming of the Shrew*, where a subtle light-diffusing filter (a nylon stocking over the camera lens) was used to soften the focus slightly and subdue the colors in a way that gave the whole film the quality of a Rembrandt painting. This technique, called the **Rembrandt effect,** was designed to give the film a mellow, aged quality, intensifying the sense that the action was taking place in another time period. A similar effect was employed in *McCabe & Mrs. Miller* and *Summer of '42*, but in the latter the quality suggested was not of a historical era but of the hazy images of the narrator's memory. For *Excalibur*, director John Boorman used green gel filters over his arc lamps to give the forest exteriors a lyric vernal glow, emphasizing the green of the moss and the leaves and creating a sense of otherworldliness.

Soft (slightly blurred) **focus** can also help to convey certain subjective states. In *Mr. Smith Goes to Washington*, soft focus is used to reflect a warm, romantic glow (falling in love) that comes over Saunders (Jean Arthur) as Jeff Smith (Jimmy Stewart) describes the natural beauties of the Willet Creek country where he plans to build his boys' camp.

In *The Graduate*, Elaine Robinson (Katharine Ross) is seen out of focus as she learns that the older woman with whom Benjamin had an affair wasn't "just another older woman." The blurred face expresses her state of shock and confusion, and her face comes back into focus only when she fully takes in what Benjamin (Dustin Hoffman) is trying to tell her. A similar technique is used earlier in the film to convey Benjamin's panic. After hearing Mr. Robinson's car pull up, Benjamin races hurriedly from Elaine's bedroom to return to the bar downstairs. As he reaches the foot of the stairs, Benjamin is shown in blurred focus as he dashes down the hall to the bar. He comes back into focus only as he reaches the relative safety of the barstool, just as Mr. Robinson enters the front door.

Special Lenses

Special lenses are often employed to provide subjective distortions of normal reality. Both wide-angle and telephoto lenses distort the depth perspective of an image, but in opposite ways. A **wide-angle lens** exaggerates the perspective, so that the distance between an object in the foreground and one in the back-

Figure 5.27 The Effects of Wide-Angle and Telephoto Lenses These two pictures illustrate the different effects achieved by photographing the same scene with a wide-angle lens and a telephoto lens. The wide-angle shot (left) makes the distance between the man and woman seem much greater, and the frame covers a much wider area in the background. The telephoto shot (right) seems to bring the man and woman closer together and narrows the area of background in the frame.

ground seems much greater than it actually is. A **telephoto lens** compresses depth so that the distance between foreground and background objects seems less than it actually is (Figure 5.27).

The effect of this distortion becomes most apparent when background-to-foreground movement is introduced. In *The Graduate*, for example, the hero is filmed running toward the camera in a frantic race to interrupt the wedding ceremony, and a telephoto distortion makes him appear to gain very little headway despite his efforts, thus emphasizing his frustration and his desperation. Had a wide-angle lens been used in the same way, his speed would have been greatly exaggerated.

A special type of extreme wide-angle lens, called a **fish-eye lens,** bends both horizontal and vertical planes and distorts depth relationships. It is often used to create unusual subjective states such as dreams, fantasies, or intoxication (Figure 5.28).

Slow Motion

If the action on the screen is to seem normal and realistic, film must move through the camera at the same rate at which it will be projected, generally twenty-four frames per second. However, if a scene is filmed at greater-than-normal speed and then projected at normal speed, the action is slowed. This

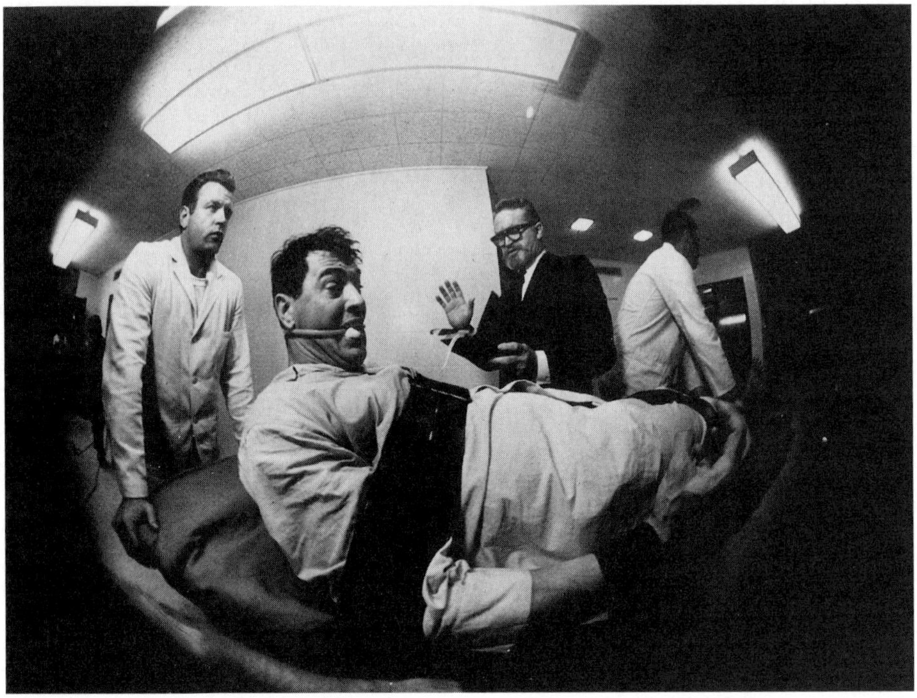

Figure 5.28 Fish-Eye Lens The distortion of a fish-eye lens conveys Rock Hudson's fear and frustration as he is given a new identity in *Seconds*.

technique is called **slow motion.** The use of slow-motion footage creates a variety of effects (Figure 5.29).

1. **To Stretch the Moment to Intensify Its Emotional Quality.** A common goal of slow-motion photography is to concentrate our attention on a relatively brief period of action and intensify whatever emotion we associate with it by stretching out that fragment of time. Ironically, the same footage could be used to make us savor the thrill of victory or suffer the agony of defeat. With the camera located just beyond the finish line, two runners could be photographed in slow motion as they run toward the camera, well ahead of the pack. The winner breaks the tape only a stride ahead of the second-place finisher. If the music swells into a joyous victory theme as the winner breaks the tape and is congratulated at the finish line (still in slow motion), we tend to identify with the winner; we share his joy and savor each handshake and embrace. However, if the same footage is accompanied by slow, discordant music, we tend to identify with the runner-up and share his disappointment as he congratulates the winner and turns to walk away. In *Chariots of Fire* both kinds of moments are

Figure 5.29 Slow-Motion Showcase Practically every sporting event pictured in *Chariots of Fire,* like the race shown here, makes some use of slow-motion cinematography to help us see parts of each event in a special way.

stretched by slow motion, and both victories and defeats are further intensified by slow-motion replays of parts of each race.

In the suicide scene in *Dead Poets Society*, director Peter Weir uses ethereal images, a ghostly slow motion, and an absence of sound as Neil ritualistically prepares himself for death. We do not see him shoot himself or hear the shot. But slow motion has intensified the moment so that we know something horrible is going to happen. Then, as we see the father running in slow motion to find the body, we hope against hope that it hasn't happened, but we know that it has.

Another almost unbearable stretching of the moment occurs in *The Dollmaker*, as Gertie Nevels (Jane Fonda) desperately tries to save her daughter from being run over by a slowly moving train. The slow motion intensifies Gertie's anguish and her helplessness as she runs toward the child but fails to reach her in time.

2. **To Exaggerate Effort, Fatigue, and Frustration.** Slow motion effectively conveys a subjective state by exaggerating a character's physical effort, fatigue, or frustration. Many of us have experienced slow-motion dreams in which our feet become leaden when we're trying to escape danger or catch some fleeting object of desire. So we identify with characters who are putting forth tremendous physical effort or experiencing fatigue

or even general physical frustration. The action, music, and sound all help to trigger the proper feeling; slow-motion sound is particularly effective (see "Slow-Motion Sound" in Chapter 8).

In *Chariots of Fire*, Eric Liddel (the Scotsman) is bumped off the track and falls into the grass infield. His fall and the time-consuming effort of getting to his feet to begin running again are exaggerated by slow motion. A similar effect is created in *Bang the Drum Slowly* as the terminally ill catcher Bruce (Robert De Niro) circles under a high pop-up. Slow-motion photography combined with blurred sound makes a relatively simple act seem tremendously difficult, awkward, and tiring.

3. **To Suggest Superhuman Speed and Power.** The most ironic use of slow motion is to suggest superhuman speed and power. Fast motion would seem the more likely technique to suggest speed; however, the herky-jerky movements created by fast motion are comical and even grotesque. Humans moving in fast motion look like insects. Human beings photographed in slow motion look serious, poetic, larger than life. Slow motion suggesting superhuman capabilities is used effectively in films like *Chariots of Fire* and *Superman* as well as in television's "Six Million Dollar Man" and "The Bionic Woman."
4. **To Emphasize the Grace of Physical Action.** Even when the illusion of superhuman speed and power is not called for, slow motion can be used to impart grace and beauty to almost any human or animal movement, especially rapid movement. In *Bang the Drum Slowly* this poetry-in-motion technique is used to enhance Arthur's (Michael Moriarty) pitching, creating the smooth, graceful, seemingly effortless motion of a Major League pitcher.
5. **To Suggest the Passage of Time.** When a series of slow-motion shots are combined in such a way that each shot slowly dissolves into the next, we get the impression that a relatively long period of time is passing. In *Bang the Drum Slowly*, slow-motion shots of unrelated baseball action are joined, compressing into a few choice seconds on the screen the feeling of a long, slow month or so of a baseball season.
6. **To Create a Sharp Contrast With Normal Motion.** Slow motion can be used to stretch time and build tension before the start of filming at a normal speed. In *Chariots of Fire*, the Olympic runners are pictured in slow motion as they walk into the stadium to prepare for their event. The anticipation of the race is increased as the runners remove outer garments, go through warm-up exercises, dig their starting holes in the dirt track, and settle into their starting positions. Then the tension and nervousness of preparing for the event are released suddenly as the starting gun sounds and the runners explode off their marks in regular film speed. A sharp contrast is created between the tension of waiting and preparing for a big event and the event itself.

Fast Motion

If a scene is filmed at less-than-normal speed and then projected at normal speed, the result is **fast motion.** Fast motion resembles the frantic, jerky movements of the old silent comedies and is usually employed for comic effect or to compress the time of an event. Stanley Kubrick used fast motion for comic effect in a scene from *A Clockwork Orange*. Alex (Malcolm McDowell) picks up two young girls and takes both to his room for a frantic sex romp, which is filmed in fast motion and accompanied musically by the *William Tell* Overture.

An extreme form of fast motion is **time-lapse photography,** which has the effect of greatly compressing time. In time-lapse filming, one frame is exposed at regular intervals that may be thirty minutes or more apart. This technique compresses into a few seconds something that normally takes hours or weeks, such as the blossoming of a flower or the construction of a house. Supported by a kinetic, mesmerizing score by Philip Glass, this camera technique is used to great emotional and thematic effect in the nonnarrative 1983 film *Koyaanisqatsi*.

The Freeze Frame, the Thawed Frame, and Stills

The freeze frame, the thawed frame, and stills provide a sharp contrast to a film's dynamic motion and give the filmmaker powerful ways to convey a sense of ending, a sense of beginning, and transitions. Each technique creates a special emphasis that forces us to think about the significance of what we are seeing. Of course, these techniques, if not used sparingly—for special moments only—quickly lose their impact.

The Freeze Frame A **freeze frame** is an effect achieved in the laboratory after a film is shot. A single frame is reprinted so many times on the film strip that when the film is shown, the motion seems to stop and the image on the screen remains still, as though the projector had stopped or the image had been frozen. The sudden appearance of a freeze frame can be stunning. The frozen image draws our attention because it is so shockingly still.

The most common use of the freeze frame is to mark the end of a powerful dramatic sequence (and serve as a transition to the next) or to serve as the ending of the entire film. At the end of a powerful sequence, a freeze frame jolts us, as though life itself has stopped. Frozen, the image on the screen burns itself into our brain and is locked into our memory in a way that moving images seldom are. At the end of a sequence, a freeze frame is similar to the old tableau effect used on the stage, where the actors freeze in their positions for a brief moment before the curtain falls, creating a powerful image to be remembered during the time that elapses between scenes or acts.

When used as the movie's final image, the freeze frame can be especially strong. With the ending of the movement on the screen comes a sense of

Figure 5.30 The Freeze-Frame Ending Hopelessly outnumbered and totally surrounded by Bolivian soldiers, Butch (Paul Newman) and the Kid (Robert Redford) leave the safety of their barricade and come out shooting. *Butch Cassidy and the Sundance Kid* ends at this point on a freeze frame of the image shown above, as a deafening roar on the soundtrack suggests the fusillade of bullets that takes their lives.

finality. As the motion stops, the freeze frame becomes like a snapshot. We can hold it in our minds and savor its beauty or impact for several seconds before it fades from the screen. It also gives us time to resonate and reflect, to catch up with our emotions, our senses, and our thoughts.

The freeze frame can also be used to convey difficult information with taste, delicacy, and subtlety, either at the film's end or at the end of a scene. In the final scene of *Butch Cassidy and the Sundance Kid*, the images of Butch and the Kid are frozen in their last full moment of vitality as a deafening roar on the soundtrack suggests the fusillade of bullets that takes their lives. As the camera slowly pulls back from their frozen images, we remember them in their last moment of life (Figure 5.30). A similar use occurs in *The World According to Garp*. As Garp's car careens up the dark asphalt toward the driveway accident, the camera zooms quickly in on Walt, then freezes him in a close-up that is accompanied by a moment of silence. As the next scene opens, Walt is missing and the other members of the family are seen recuperating.

Freeze frames can also signal a transition. In *Chariots of Fire* a hurdler is caught and frozen in mid-hurdle. The colored freeze frame fades to black and white, and the camera pulls away to reveal the image to be a picture in a newspaper being read the next day, thus providing a quick time–place transition.

The Thawed Frame A **thawed frame** begins with a frozen image that thaws and comes to life. This technique can be used at the beginning of a scene or of the whole film, or it can serve a transitional function.

At the film's beginning, the frozen image is often a painting or drawing that slowly changes to a photograph and then thaws into life. In *Citizen Kane*, the thawed frame is a transitional device. Kane and one of his friends are seen looking through the front window of a rival newspaper, at a group picture of the paper's staff. The camera moves in for a close-up, so we see only the picture. Then there is a flash of light and the group members start to move, revealing that the flash of light was made by a photographer taking a new group picture of the same people, who now work for Kane.

Stills **Stills** are photographs in which the image itself does not move. A sense of motion occurs as the camera pulls in or backs off from them or moves over them. When several stills are used in sequence, each still usually dissolves slowly into the next, creating the impression of information slowly unfolding or being remembered. In *Summer of '42*, a montage of stills under the credits opens the film, creating the impression of snapshots from the narrator's memory. In *Butch Cassidy and the Sundance Kid*, sepia-tone stills are combined in a "Happy Times in New York City" montage. Another striking example of the use of still photography is in Chris Marker's celebrated short film, *La Jetée*, which served as an inspiration for *Twelve Monkeys*.

Special Lighting Effects

In *The Grapes of Wrath* Gregg Toland employs a light reflected in the pupils of Tom Joad's (Henry Fonda) eyes at his first emotional meeting with Ma Joad (Jane Darwell) after four years in prison. Although the special lighting is done with such subtlety that it is not obvious to the casual viewer, it gives the moment a very special quality. Tom's eyes literally light up as he greets her.

Another special moment of reunion is created by lighting on the eyes of Lara (Julie Christie) in *Doctor Zhivago* when she sees Zhivago (Omar Sharif) in a remote village library after a year of separation. By highlighting her eyes, the cinematographer intensifies the emotional impact of the scene. Either Christie's eyes did not express the emotion fully enough or the change was so subtle that it needed to be pulled out from background details to create the desired effect.

Subtle changes in lighting are also employed in another touching scene from *The Grapes of Wrath*. As Ma Joad burns her souvenirs while preparing to leave for California, she discovers a pair of earrings she wore as a young woman. As she puts them up to her ears, subtle changes in the direction of light, accompanied by some gradual diffusion, make her seem to grow younger before our eyes. Then, as she takes them down again and the memory fades, we see the wrinkling and hard lines reappear as the original lighting returns.

At the conclusion of the superb documentary film *Visions of Light: The Art of Cinematography*, several master cinematographers offer observations about the power and future of cinematic storytelling. Ernest Dickerson, who was the director of photography (DP) on Spike Lee's *Do the Right Thing* and *Malcolm X*, says that "if the director is . . . the author of the performances [and] . . . story of the film, the cinematographer is the author of the use of light in the film and how it contributes to the story." John Bailey, who shot Robert Redford's *Ordinary People* and Paul Schrader's *Mishima*, believes that "today in motion picture technology, we are really at a precipice, a jumping off point into an . . . unknown but possibly very exciting future, in the same way that, in the '50s, when Cinemascope and . . . Cinerama, all these new formats, really shook up the whole way we were looking at films. We have that opportunity now." Finally, Allen Daviau, the cinematographer for Steven Spielberg's *E.T.* and Barry Levinson's *Avalon*, begins to capture the subtlety and mystery of the form: "Someone once said that the lighting, the look of a film, makes the pauses speak as eloquently as the words—that you have moments in films that happen because of what is there visually, how someone is lit or not lit. You put something in the audience's mind visually and they will carry away images as well as the words."[8]

Questions

On the Cinematic Film

1. To what degree is the film cinematic? Cite specific examples from the film to prove that the director succeeds or fails in (a) keeping the image constantly alive and in motion, (b) setting up clear, crisp visual and aural rhythms, (c) creating the illusion of depth, and (d) using the other special properties of the medium.
2. Does the cinematography create clear, powerful, and effective images in a natural way, or does it self-consciously show off the skills and techniques of the cinematographer?

On Cinematic Points of View

Although the director probably employs all four cinematic viewpoints in making the film, one point of view may predominate to such a degree that the film leaves the impression of a single point of view. With this in mind, answer these questions:

1. Do you feel that you were primarily an objective, impersonal observer of the action, or did you have the sense of being a participant in the action? What specific scenes used the objective point of view? In what scenes did you feel like a participant in the action? How were you made to feel like a participant?
2. In what scenes were you aware that the director was employing visual techniques to comment on or interpret the action, forcing you to see the action in a special way? What techniques were used to achieve this? How effective were they?

On Elements of Cinematic Composition

1. Which methods does the director use to draw attention to the object of greatest significance?
2. Does the director succeed in keeping the screen alive by avoiding large areas of dead screen?
3. What are the primary or most memorable techniques used to create the illusion of three-dimensionality?

On Specialized Visual Effects

1. Although a thorough analysis of each visual element is impossible, make a mental note of the pictorial effects that struck you as especially effective, ineffective, or unique, and consider them in light of these questions:
   a. What was the director's aim in creating these images, and what camera tools or techniques were employed in the filming of them?
   b. What made these memorable visual images effective, ineffective, or unique?
   c. Justify each of these impressive visual effects aesthetically in terms of its relationship to the whole film.
2. Are special lighting effects used for brief moments in the film? If so, what are the effects intended, and how successful are they?

Video Exercises

Instructions for locating specific sequences are given on page 77.

1. **Cinematic Qualities.** Watch the first 10 minutes of the following films: *The Grapes of Wrath*, *Citizen Kane*, *The Taming of the Shrew*, *Terms of Endearment*, and *2001: A Space Odyssey*. Evaluate each brief segment in terms of the five questions under "On the Cinematic Film" on page 148. Which film is the most cinematic? Which is the least cinematic? Explain your choices in as much detail as possible.
2. **Deep Focus.** Watch the brief sequence from *Citizen Kane* in which Mr. Thatcher comes to pick up Charles [1380 to 1650; 0:18:25 to 0:22:40].

How is deep focus employed in this sequence, and what is its effect? How does the use of deep focus affect the editing of this sequence? What role does sound play in reinforcing the illusion of a three-dimensional image here?

3. **Slow Motion.** Watch the suicide sequence from *Dead Poets Society* [5000 to 5225; 1:42:28 to 1:47:30], and describe your reaction to it. What unusual things do you notice about the composition and the use of sound? How much and for what purpose is slow motion used in this sequence?
4. **Lighting.** Watch the sequences in *The Grapes of Wrath* in which Muley Graves appears [0750 to 1635; 0:12:15 to 0:23:07], and describe the different kinds of lighting employed in those sequences. What effect is created by each type of lighting used? In which scenes is the lighting most effective?
5. **Cinematic Viewpoints.** Watch the first 5 minutes of *The Grapes of Wrath*, *Casablanca*, and *Citizen Kane*. Try to identify the cinematic viewpoint of each shot in all three segments, and then answer question 1 under "On Cinematic Points of View" on page 148. How does the editing differ in each of these three films?

Films for Study

The Age of Innocence (1993)
Altered States (1980)
Bang the Drum Slowly (1973)
The Big Lebowski (1998)
The Black Stallion (1979)
Blade Runner (1982)
Blood Simple (1984)
Bonnie and Clyde (1967)
Boogie Nights (1997)
Braveheart (1995)
Brazil (1985)
Butch Cassidy and the Sundance Kid (1969)
Casablanca (1942)
Chariots of Fire (1981)
Citizen Kane (1941)
A Clockwork Orange (1971)
The Deer Hunter (1978)
Elizabeth (1998)
The English Patient (1996)
Gandhi (1982)
The Graduate (1967)
The Grapes of Wrath (1940)
Jaws (1975)
Koyaanisqatsi (1983)
Kundun (1997)
The Lady From Shanghai (1948)
McCabe & Mrs. Miller (1971)
Metropolis (1926)
Napoleon (1927)
The Piano (1993)
Psycho (1960)
Raging Bull (1980)
Raiders of the Lost Ark (1981)
Raising Arizona (1987)
The Seventh Seal (1957)
Shakespeare in Love (1998)
A Simple Plan (1998)
Summer of '42 (1971)
Sunrise (1927)
The Taming of the Shrew (1967)
Terms of Endearment (1983)
The Third Man (1949)
2001: A Space Odyssey (1968)
The Usual Suspects (1995)
Witness (1985)
The World According to Garp (1982)

Chapter 6

Editing and Special Visual Effects

A feature-length film generates anywhere from twenty to forty hours of raw footage. When the shooting stops, that unrefined film becomes the movie's raw material, just as the script had been the raw material before. It now must be selected, tightened, paced, embellished, and in some scenes given artificial respiration, until the author's and the director's vision becomes completely translated from the language of the script to the idiom of the movies.

—RALPH ROSENBLUM, FILM EDITOR

Editing

Of utmost importance to any film is the contribution made by the editor, whose function is to assemble the complete film, as if it were a gigantic and complex jigsaw puzzle, from its various component parts and soundtracks. The great Russian director V. I. Pudovkin believed that editing is "the foundation of the film art" and observed that "the expression that the film is 'shot' is entirely false, and should disappear from the language. The film is not *shot*, but built, built up from separate strips of celluloid that are its raw material."[1] Alfred Hitchcock reinforces this viewpoint: "The screen ought to speak its own language, freshly coined, and it can't do that unless it treats an acted scene as a piece of raw material which must be broken up, taken to bits, before it can be woven into an expressive visual pattern."[2]

Because of the importance of the editing process, the editor's role may nearly equal that of the director. Regardless of its quality, the raw material that the director provides may be worthless unless careful judgment is exercised in deciding when each segment will appear and how long it will remain on the screen. This assembly of parts must be done with artistic sensitivity, perception, and aesthetic judgment as well as a true involvement in the subject and a clear understanding of the director's intentions. Therefore, for the most part, the director and the editor must be considered almost equal partners in the construction of a film. In some cases, the editor may be the true structuring genius, the master builder or architect. In fact, the editor may have the clearest vision of the film's unity, and he or she may even make up for a lack of clear vision on the director's part.

Such would seem to be the case with many of Woody Allen's films. According to Ralph Rosenblum, who edited six of them, Allen is obsessed with keeping a strain of seriousness running through practically any film he makes. Much of this seriousness Rosenblum eliminates in the cutting room. *Annie Hall*, for example, was shot as a philosophical film (working title—*Anhedonia*). The focal character was Alvy Singer, Annie was a secondary character, and the mood fell somewhere between *Interiors* and *Manhattan*. In the editing process, Rosenblum refocused the film on the Alvy/Annie relationship by eliminating whole sequences and plot lines, and he helped Allen develop and shoot a new ending to match the new focus. The end result was a film that won Academy Awards for best picture, director, actress, and original screenplay. However, the editor, who changed the whole emphasis and tone of the film from what was originally conceived and shot by the director, was not even nominated. Evan Lottman, editor of *Sophie's Choice*, explains the problem:

> [Editing is] invisible. Seeing the finished product cannot tell you the value of the editing. You don't know whether the material was great and the editor screwed it up, or if it was poor material and he made a wonderful movie out of it. You don't

know whether moments in the movie were created in the editing room or whether they were part of the director's original conception. But if the picture works, the editing works, and nobody's going to call special attention to it.[3]

To appreciate the role that editing plays, we must look at the basic responsibility of the editor: to assemble a complete film that is a unified whole in which each separate shot or sound contributes to the development of the theme and the total effect. To understand the editor's function, it is also important to comprehend the nature of the jigsaw puzzle. The basic unit with which the editor works is the **shot** (a strip of film produced by a single continuous run of the camera). By joining or splicing a series of shots so that they communicate a unified action taking place at one time and place, the editor assembles a **scene.** The editor then links a series of scenes to form a **sequence,** which constitutes a significant part of the film's dramatic structure much in the same way that an act functions in a play. To assemble these parts effectively, the editor must successfully carry out his or her responsibilities in each of the following areas.

Selectivity

The most basic editing function is selecting the best shots from several **takes** (variations of the same shot). The editor chooses the segments that provide the most powerful, effective, or significant visual and sound effects and eliminates inferior, irrelevant, or insignificant material. Of course, we cannot fully appreciate the editor's selectivity because we do not see the footage that ends up on the cutting-room floor. As *Black Rain* editor Tom Rolf describes the process:

> It's imposing my choice over yours, having the arrogance to say this is better than that. It's being a critic. It's an art form you're interpreting. It's a matter of choices and keeping it straight in your head. It's like having an enormous picture puzzle—1,000 pieces will make it look perfect but they give you 100,000. It's going through all the pieces, to try to get the best parts. That's what editing is.[4]

When deciding what to eliminate, the editor considers several different takes of the same piece of action. While the film is being shot, the director begins the selection process by telling the continuity supervisor which takes are good enough to be printed. Soon after each day's shooting, **dailies** (also called *rushes*) are printed and viewed by the director, the cinematographer, and others. After screening the dailies, which are unedited, the director may decide to throw out more shots—shots that contain flaws not spotted during the shooting. By the time the editor finally gets the film, obviously bad footage has been discarded. But there are still difficult and subtle decisions to be made.

For a given five seconds' worth of action, the editor may be working with ten takes of that segment of action and dialogue, filmed with three different cameras from three different angles. If the sound quality is adequate in each shot, the editor chooses a shot to fill that five-second slot in the finished film after considering these factors: the camera technique (clear focus, smooth camera movement, and so on), composition, lighting, acting performance, and best angle to match the previous shot.

If each shot were equal in quality, the decision would be simple: The editor would go with the best angle to match the previous shot. But usually it's not that easy, and some of the editor's decisions amount to difficult compromises. According to *Ben-Hur* editor Ralph Winters:

> A good editor will choose the path which gives him the most amount of material. It depends on the way it was shot. I've had sequences that had three, four, or five angles and we played it all in one angle, because when we looked at the film everyone felt that the scene sustained itself. Any time a scene sustains itself, you want to let it play, because the people in the audience have a chance to relate to whomever they want up on the screen. I can have my eye shift back and forth where it wants instead of being directed by close-ups. If you are playing a two-shot and you can make it better by intercutting close-ups because those performances are better, then you should do it. If you're given a mediocre scene and you have no coverage, that's the way it's going to play.[5]

The best shot in terms of lighting and composition may be the weakest in acting performance and dramatic impact. Or the best acting performance may be poorly composed or have lighting problems or be slightly out of focus.

Coherence, Continuity, and Rhythm

The film editor is responsible for putting the pieces together into a coherent whole. He or she must guide our thoughts, associations, and emotional responses effectively from one image to another, or from one sound to another, so that the interrelationships of separate images and sounds are clear and the transitions between scenes and sequences are smooth. To achieve this goal, the editor must consider the aesthetic, dramatic, and psychological effect of the juxtaposition of image to image, sound to sound, or image to sound, and place each piece of film and soundtrack together accordingly (Figure 6.1).

Transitions

In the past, filmmakers made routine use of several **opticals**—effects created in the lab during the printing of the film—to create smooth and clear transitions between a film's most important divisions, such as between two sequences that take place at a different time or place. These traditional transitional devices include the following:

Figure 6.1 Editing Sequence—Action and Reaction Part of the editor's job is to weave a coherent tapestry of action and reaction, rendering the sequence of events crystal clear while building dramatic effect, tension, and suspense by cutting back and forth between the characters involved in the action and the action itself. Sometimes the editor achieves this effect by cutting the action into minute bits and showing significant character reaction to each bit of action. The complex relationship between action and reaction is clearly illustrated by the final ambush sequence from *Bonnie and Clyde*.

Spooked by the appearance of a number of lawmen in a small Louisiana town, Bonnie and Clyde (Faye Dunaway and Warren Beatty) drive off, much to the relief of their accomplice C. W. Moss (Michael J. Pollard), who watches from a window. Meanwhile, down the road, a trap is being set by C. W.'s father, Malcolm (Dub Taylor). The editor establishes a relationship between Malcolm's "flat tire" and Bonnie and Clyde's trip with a few quick cuts between them. Sighting Malcolm, Clyde pulls over and gets out to help with the tire. Several quick events (an approaching car, a covey of quail suddenly flushed from a nearby bush, and Malcolm's sudden dive under his truck) evoke dramatic reactions from Bonnie and Clyde before the shooting from the nearby bushes begins.

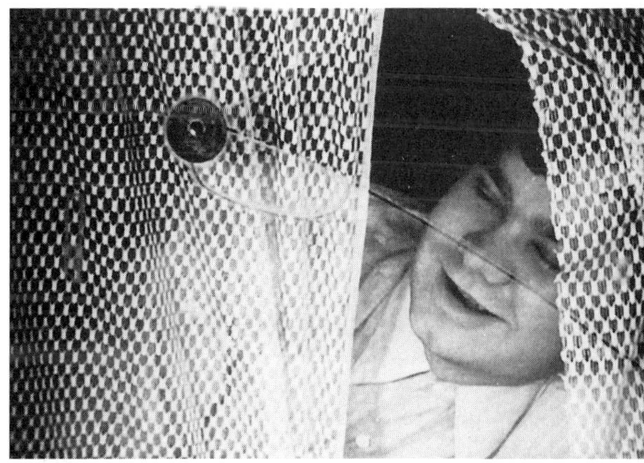

▲ a. ▼ c.

▲ b. ▼ d.

▲ e. ▼ g.

▲ f. ▼ h.

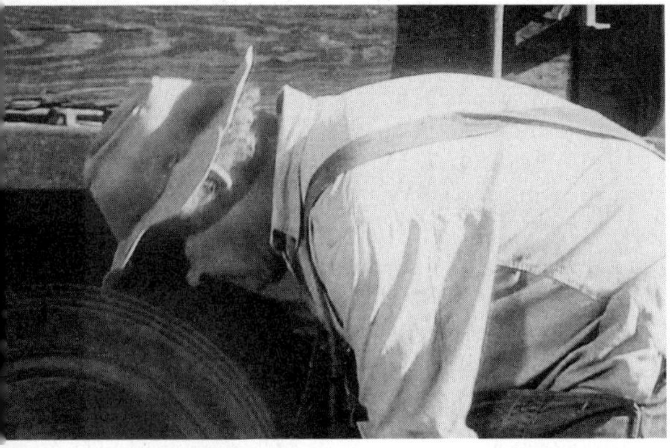

▼ i.

▼ j.

▼ k.

▼ l.

▲ m. ▼ o.

▲ n. ▼ p.

▼ q.

▼ r.

▼ s.

▼ t.

▲ u. ▼ w.

▲ v. ▼ x.

▼ y.

▼ z.

▼ aa.

▼ bb.

▲ cc. ▼ ee.

▲ dd. ▼ ff.

▼ gg.

▼ hh.

▼ ii.

▼ jj.

▲ kk. ▼ mm.

▲ ll. ▼ nn.

▼ oo.

▼ pp.

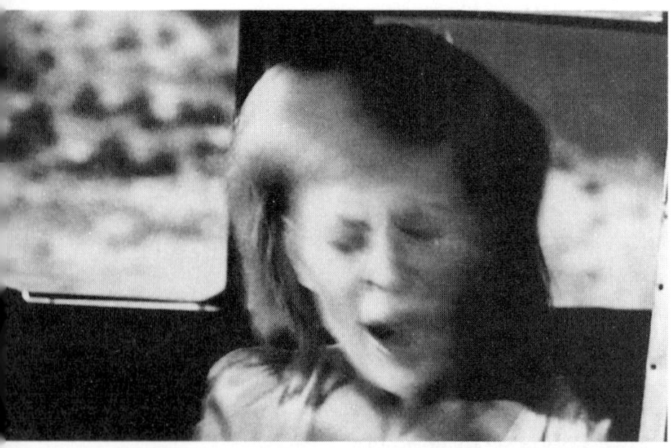

▼ qq.

▼ rr.

- **Wipe.** A new image is separated from the previous image by means of a horizontal, vertical, or diagonal line that moves across the screen to wipe the previous image away.
- **Flip Frame.** The entire frame appears to flip over to reveal a new scene, creating a visual effect very similar to turning a page.
- **Fade-Out/Fade-In.** The last image of one sequence fades momentarily to black, and the first image of the next sequence is gradually illuminated.
- **Dissolve.** The end of one shot gradually merges into the beginning of the next. The effect is produced by superimposing a fade-out onto a fade-in of equal length or imposing one scene over another.

Each of them is most effective in a specific situation or context. Generally speaking, dissolves signal relatively great transitions and are used to make the viewer aware of major scene changes or the passage of time. Flips and wipes are faster and are employed when the time lapse or place change is more logical or natural.

Modern filmmakers have used these devices in films such as *The Sting* and *Pennies From Heaven* to suggest the film style that was typical of the period when the story takes place. But most modern filmmakers do not make extensive use of them and instead rely on a simple cut from one sequence to another without giving any clear transitional signal. This change can be attributed to audiences' visual conditioning by TV commercials to follow quick cuts without confusion. The soundtrack has also taken on some of the transitional functions formerly handled optically.

Regardless of the nature of transitions, whether they are long and obvious (as in a slow dissolve) or short and quick (as in a simple instantaneous cut), the editor is the person who must put them together so that they maintain continuity—so that the flow from one sequence to another or merely from one image to another is logical.

When possible, the editor uses a **form cut** to smooth the visual flow from one shot, scene, or sequence to another. In this type of cut, the shape of an object in one shot is matched to a similarly shaped object in the next shot. Because both objects appear in the same area of the frame, the first image flows smoothly into the second. In Stanley Kubrick's *2001*, a piece of bone flung into the air dissolves into a similarly shaped orbiting object in the following sequence. In Sergei Eisenstein's *Potemkin*, the handle of a sword or dagger in one shot becomes the similarly shaped cross around a priest's neck in the following shot. Although form cuts provide smooth visual transitions, they may also create ironic collisions of sharply contrasting ideas.

Similar to the form cut are cuts that use color or texture to link shots. For example, a glowing sun at the end of one shot may dissolve into a campfire at the beginning of the next. Of course, there are limitations to this type of transition; and when they are overdone, they lose the sense of naturalness that makes them effective.

The editor must also assemble shots to achieve coherence *within* a sequence. For example, many sequences require an **establishing shot** at their beginning to provide a broad picture of the setting so that we get a feel for the environment in which the scene occurs. The editor must decide if an establishing shot is necessary for a clear understanding of the closer and more detailed shots that follow.

Two different editing patterns have become more or less standard in making transitions in time and space. The more traditional pattern, **outside/in editing,** follows a logical sequence and concentrates on orienting us to the new setting. It allows us to move into a new setting from the outside and gradually work our way inside to the details. The logical context of each step is clearly shown so that we always know exactly where we are. We get our bearings with an establishing shot of the whole setting, move into the setting itself, and then focus our attention on the details of that setting.

Inside/out editing does the exact opposite. We are jolted suddenly from a line of action that we completely understand to a close-up detail in a new and unfamiliar place. We don't know where we are or what is happening. Then, in a sequence of related shots, we back off from the detail of the first close-up and gradually find out where we are and what is happening. Thus, we move from a disorienting shot to distant, more general shots that help us understand fully the action in the context of the new scene (Figure 6.2).

Airport '77 begins with a couple of burglars breaking into an airport office at night and stealing information from a file cabinet. While that burglary is in progress, we jump immediately to a close-up of a hand pushing throttle levers forward. In the next shot, we back up to establish that the hand belongs to Jack Lemmon, who is in the pilot seat of a jetliner, and a view through the cockpit glass shows the runway in front of the plane. The next shot takes us one step farther back, and we see that Lemmon is not in a real cockpit at all but in a simulator training cockpit. Thus, the viewer is jolted with a transition first, and the overall location of the scene is established later. The inside/out pattern creates a dynamic, explosive, exciting edit, which adds oomph and suspense to the transition. Kathryn Bigelow, in the virtuoso opening of *Strange Days*, uses a similar editing pattern. The scene introduces the audience to a kinetic and thrilling robbery (photographed using constant subjective point-of-view shots) that seems to end with the camera's—and the viewers'—falling off the top of a tall building. Suddenly, though, it is revealed that this heart-thumping excitement is in fact recorded on a futuristic experiential device worn by the film's protagonist, played by Ralph Fiennes.

Rhythms, Tempo, and Time Control

Many factors work together and separately to create rhythms in a motion picture: the physical objects moving on the screen, the real or apparent movement

Figure 6.2 Editing Sequence—Outside/In and Inside/Out This sequence combines two common patterns of editing. In the first, the outside/in pattern, we get our bearings with an establishing shot of the new setting and then move closer in to focus on the main characters and details of the new environment. This can be accomplished in a variety of ways: The editor may begin with a static distant shot and take us closer and closer by cutting to shots taken from a static camera positioned in progressive stages closer to an object of interest. The same basic effect can also be accomplished with a slow zoom that gradually magnifies the object of interest or by a continuous shot from a mobile camera that physically moves closer to the subject.

In the outside/in portion of this editing sequence, two methods are used. The first three photos represent excerpts from a continuous shot taken from a helicopter. The shot begins with an establishing shot of the Manhattan skyline with the Brooklyn Bridge in the foreground. The camera then swings around the bridge and heads toward the heart of Brooklyn. The sound through this part of the sequence has been subdued: soft, muffled traffic noises. The editor then cuts to a close-up of an elevated train moving diagonally toward the camera. The sound suddenly overwhelms us as the fast-moving train approaches, and we suddenly feel ourselves in the city. The next shot is taken from a camera rotated 180 degrees to pick up the train as it speeds away. The following shot focuses on a detail that has no logical connection to the train: a close-up of a shoe display in a store window. At this point, the outside/in portion of the sequence ends and the inside/out portion begins.

As the strong beat of the *Saturday Night Fever* theme ("Stayin' Alive") starts up, a foot outside the window is placed alongside the displayed shoe. The next shot picks up that foot and its mate walking to the beat down a city sidewalk. Succeeding shots move upward from the feet to show a swinging paint can and the torso and face of the character Tony (John Travolta). Shots in the sequence continue to show Tony's interaction with his environment (turning to look after a pretty girl and finally stopping at a cellar-level pizza joint). To connect our location with the opening outside/in sequence, the editor also includes a quick shot of an elevated train passing during Tony's strut.

▲ a. ▼ c.

▲ b. ▼ d.

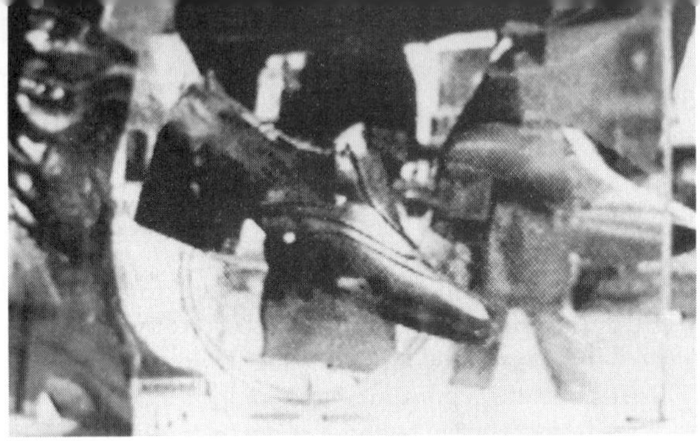

▲ e. ▼ g.

▲ f. ▼ h.

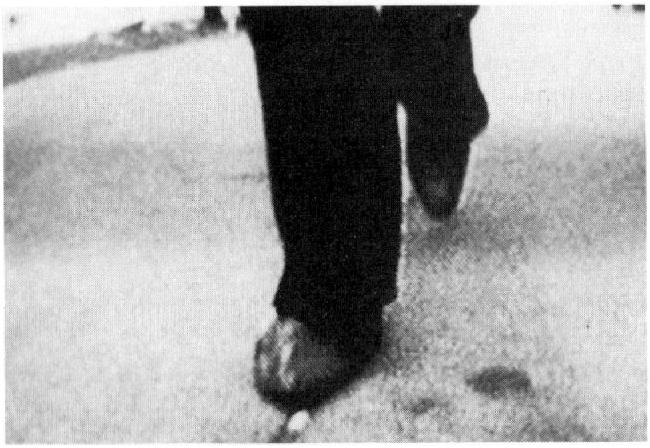

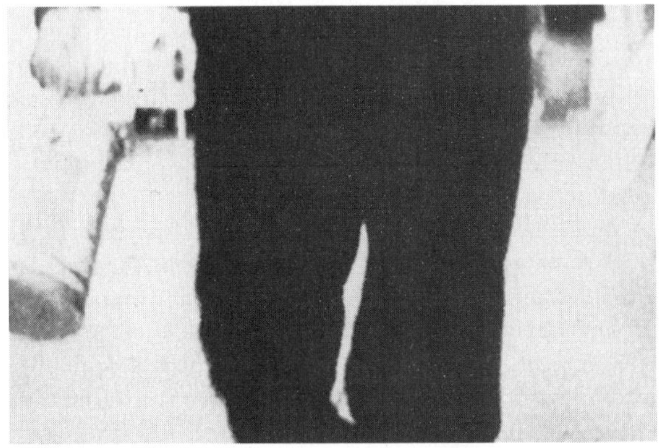

▼ i.

▼ j.

▼ k.

▼ l.

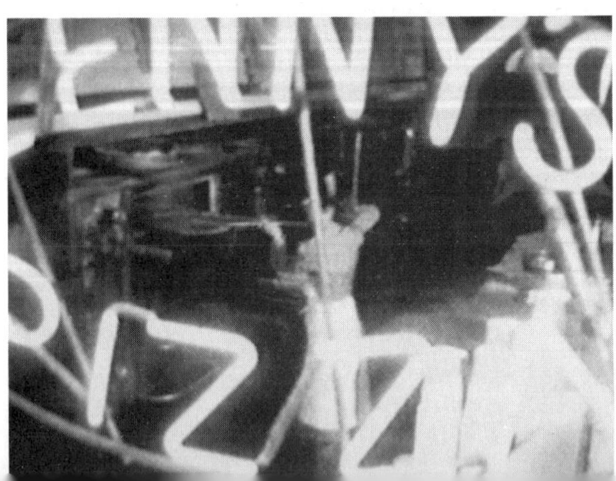

of the camera, the musical score, and the pace of the dialogue and the natural rhythms of human speech, as well as the pace of the plot itself. These factors set up unique rhythms that blend into the whole. But these rhythms are natural, imposed on the film by the nature of its raw material. Perhaps the most dominant tempo of the film, its most compelling rhythm, results from the frequency of editorial cuts and the varying duration of shots between cuts. The rhythm established by cuts is unique because cuts divide a film into a number of separate parts without interrupting its continuity and flow. Editorial cuts impart to a film an externally controllable and unique rhythmic quality.

The rhythm established by editorial cutting is such a natural part of the film medium that we are often unaware of cuts within a scene, yet we respond unconsciously to the tempo they create. One reason we remain unaware is that the cuts often duplicate the manner in which we look at things in real life, glancing quickly from one point of attention to another. Our emotional state is often revealed by how quickly our attention shifts. Thus, slow cutting simulates the impressions of a tranquil observer, and quick cutting simulates the impressions of an excited observer. Our responsiveness to this convention of **glancing rhythms** allows the editor to manipulate us, exciting or calming us almost at will.

Although the editor generally alternates one tempo with another throughout the film, the cutting speed of each scene is determined by the content of that scene, so that its rhythm corresponds to the pace of the action, the speed of the dialogue, and the overall emotional tone. Editor Richard Marks describes the difference between action cutting and dramatic cutting this way:

> [W]ith an action sequence you're cutting on movement. It always gives you justification to cut and create its own rhythms. There's an internal rhythm to a movement. The axiom of action cutting is, never complete an action. Always leave it incomplete so it keeps the forward momentum of the sequence. In dramatic cutting you have to create your own rhythms—how long you stay on a character, how much of a beat you give a character before you cut to someone else, who you play on camera, and who you play off camera. Yet you must try and remain faithful to the internal rhythms of an actor's performance.[6]

The fact that the story, the action, the dialogue, and the visuals all set up different natural rhythms makes editors often think of their jobs in terms of being sensitive to the "music" already playing in the scene. But sometimes that music is unnatural and totally preplanned in story-boarding before the scene is ever shot, as evidenced by Alfred Hitchcock's use of musical imagery to describe yet another editing rhythm: the carefully thought-out juxtaposition of long shot with close-up, creating a dramatic change in image size:

> It is very, very essential that you know ahead of time something of the orchestration: in other words, image size. What I mean by orchestration is, take the close-up, well, that's like in music: the brass sounding brassy, loud sound before

you need it. Sometimes you see film cut such that the close-up comes in early, and by the time you really need it, it has lost its effect because you've used it already.

Now I'll give you an example of where a juxtaposition of the image size is also very important. For example, one of the biggest effects in *Psycho* was where the detective went up the stairs. The picture was designed to create fear in an audience, and in the anticipation of it, it is all there. Here is the shot of the detective, simple shot going up the stairs, he reaches the top stairs, the next cut is the camera as high as it can go, it was on the ceiling, you see the figure run out, raised knife, it comes down, bang, the biggest head you can put on the screen. But that big head has no impact unless the previous shot had been so far away.

So that is just where your orchestration comes in, where you design the set-up. That's why you can't just guess these things on the set.[7]

Expansion and Compression of Time

Director Elia Kazan, making the transition from stage to film, was enthusiastic about cinematic techniques for manipulating time:

> [F]ilm time is different from stage time. One of the most important techniques a film director has is the ability to stretch a moment for emphasis. On a theatre stage, true time goes its normal course; it's the same on stage as it is in the audience. But in a film we have movie time, a false time. Climaxes in life go clickety-click and they're over. When a film director comes to a crucially important moment, he can stretch it, go from one close-up to another, then to people who are dramatically involved or concerned watching the action, so back and forth to everyone connected with what is happening. In this way time is stretched for dramatic emphasis. Other parts of the film can be slipped over swiftly so that they are given no more time on the screen than their dramatic value justifies. Film time then becomes faster than real time. A film director can choose to leap into the "meat" of a scene or from high moment to high moment, leaving out what, in his opinion, is not worth the attention of the audience. Entrances and exits—unless they're freighted with dramatic substance—mean nothing. It doesn't matter how the character got there. He's there! So cut to the heart of the scene.[8]

Skillful editing can greatly expand our normal sense of time, through intercutting a normal action sequence with a series of related details. Take, for example, the brief action of a man walking up a flight of stairs. By simply alternating a full shot of the man walking up the stairs with detailed shots of the man's feet, the editor expands the scene and sense of time of the action. If close-ups of the man's face and his hand gripping the rail are added, our feeling of the time the action takes is expanded even more.

By using **flash cuts,** short machine-gun bursts of images sandwiched together, the editor can compress an hour's action into a few seconds. For example, by choosing representative actions out of the daily routine of a factory worker, the editor can, in a minute or two, suggest an entire eight-hour shift. By overlapping so that the first part of each shot is superimposed over the last part of the preceding shot, the editor can achieve a fluid compression of time.

Another editorial technique used to compress time is the **jump cut,** which eliminates a strip of insignificant or unnecessary action from a continuous shot. For example, a continuous shot in a western follows the movement of the sheriff as he walks slowly across the street, from left to right, from his office to the saloon. To pick up the pace, the editor may cut out the section of film that shows the sheriff crossing the street and jump-cut from the point at which he steps into the street to his arrival at the sidewalk on the other side. A jump cut speeds up the action by not showing a portion of the action.

The term *jump cut* also refers to a disconcerting joining of two shots that do not match in action and continuity. As Ephraim Katz observes in *The Film Encyclopedia*, "Traditionally, such breaks in continuity and smooth transition have been considered intolerable, but some modern filmmakers employ jump cuts freely and deliberately."[9] Indeed, a film's wit can be sharpened considerably by its concerted use of the device. In *Cabaret*, for instance, director Bob Fosse and editor David Bretherton frequently utilize the jump cut for startling effects that are both humorous and affecting. Near the end of the film, Fritz (Fritz Wepper), the young gigolo, confesses to Brian (Michael York) that he is, in fact, a Jew, although he has lied about this element of his identity to the Jewish woman he loves, Natalia Landauer (Marisa Berenson). At the moment of this revelation, he despairs of her ever consenting to marry him. But soon we see Fritz standing at Natalia's front door, exclaiming loudly, "I am a Jew!" And a jump cut takes us immediately to the wedding ceremony.

One of the most effective techniques of editorial cutting is the use of **parallel cuts** (or *intercutting*), quickly alternating back and forth between two actions taking place at separate locations. Parallel cutting creates the impression that the two actions are occurring simultaneously. It can be a powerful suspense-building device. A common use of parallel cuts is seen in "cavalry to the rescue" sequences, where the settlers in their circled wagons are under Indian attack and the U.S. cavalry is on the way. By cutting back and forth from the besieged settlers to the hard-riding cavalry troops, the editor makes the eventual confrontation seem closer and closer and builds suspense. Such modern films as *Cabaret*, *The Godfather*, and *Mrs. Dalloway* use parallel cutting in a brilliant fashion, ironically uniting darkness and jollity, violence and piety, colorful chaos and authoritarian order (Figure 6.3).

An entirely different kind of time compression is achieved by cutting to brief flashbacks or memory images. This technique merges past and present into the same stream and often helps us understand a character. The motivation of Peter Fonda's beekeeper/grandfather character in *Ulee's Gold*, for example, is slowly revealed through such flashbacks.

Figure 6.3 Editing Sequence—The Ironic Montage In this powerful segment from *The Godfather,* Francis Ford Coppola intercuts a sequence showing Michael Corleone (Al Pacino) serving as godfather to the infant son of his sister Connie (Talia Shire) with a montage showing the brutal murders of rival mob leaders ordered by Michael. The soft, golden, spiritual light of the church casts a warm glow over the baptism. The priest intones the ceremony in Latin accompanied by organ music, his voice and the organ droning on as scenes of murder are interspersed with shots from the baptism. The irony of the sequence is intensified by Michael's affirmation (in English) of his belief in God and his pledge, during the most violent moments of the montage, "to renounce Satan and all his works." When the ceremony is completed, Michael immediately orders the murder of Carlo, the father of the just-baptized infant. By juxtaposing these very opposite actions, Coppola ironically underscores Michael's heartlessness as he steps into his new role as the true godfather of the Corleone family.

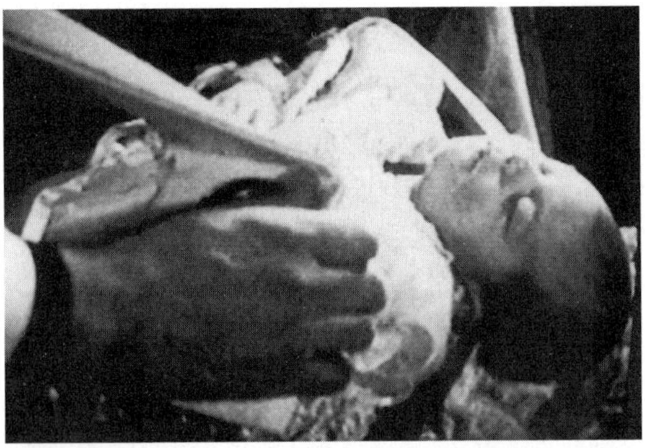

▲ a. ▼ c.

▲ b. ▼ d.

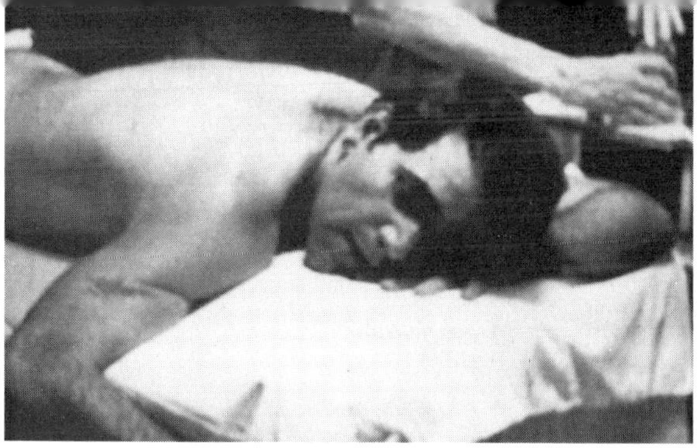

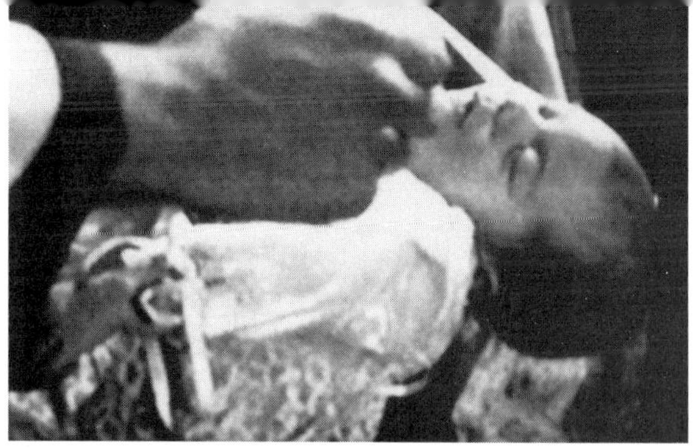

▲ e. ▼ g.

▲ f. ▼ h.

▼ i.

▼ j.

▼ k.

▼ l.

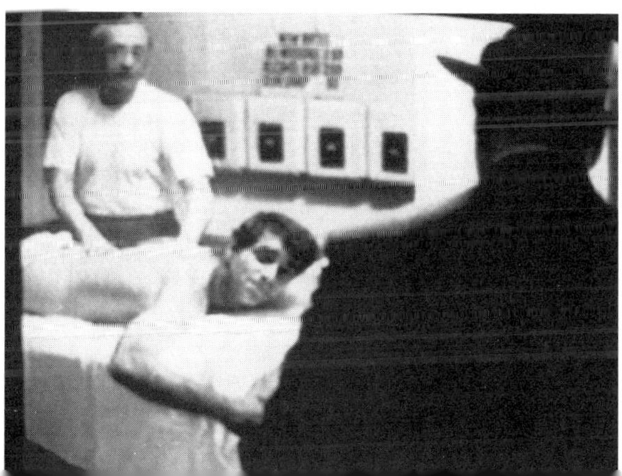

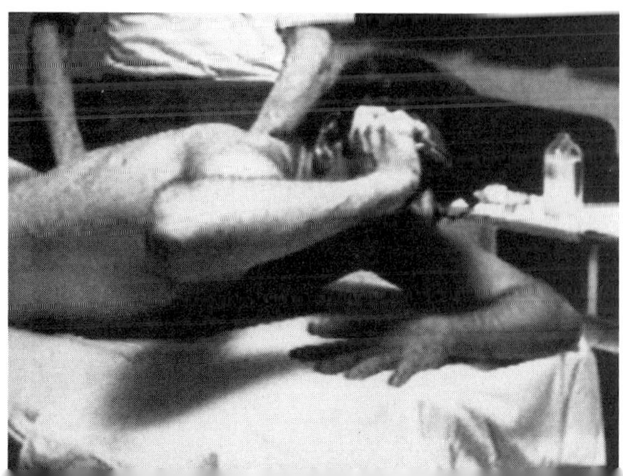

▲ m. ▼ o.

▲ n. ▼ p.

▼ q.

▼ r.

▼ s.

▼ t.

▲ u. ▼ w.

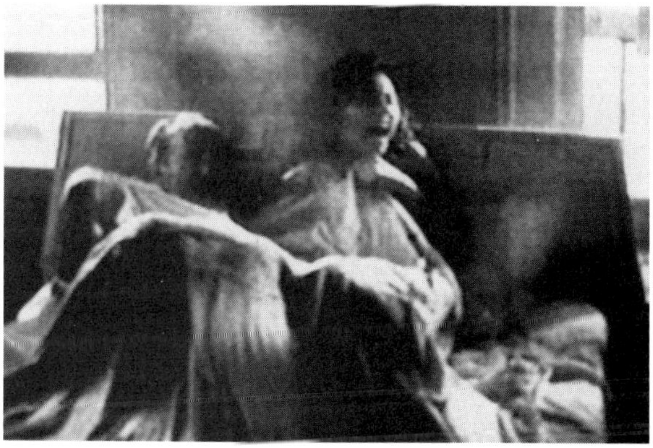

▼ y.

▼ aa.

▲ v. ▼ x.

▼ z.

▼ bb.

▲ cc. ▼ ee.

▲ dd. ▼ ff.

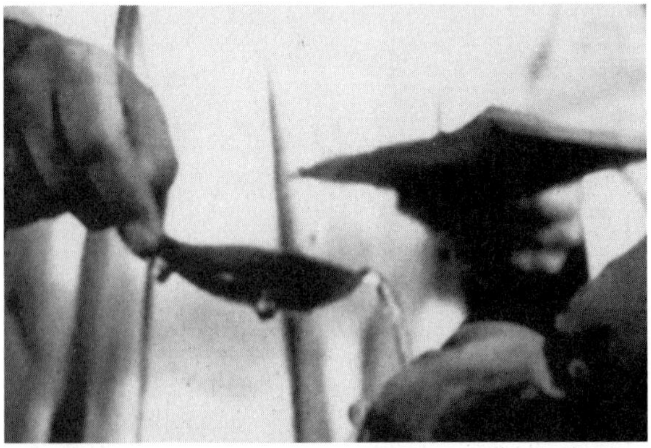

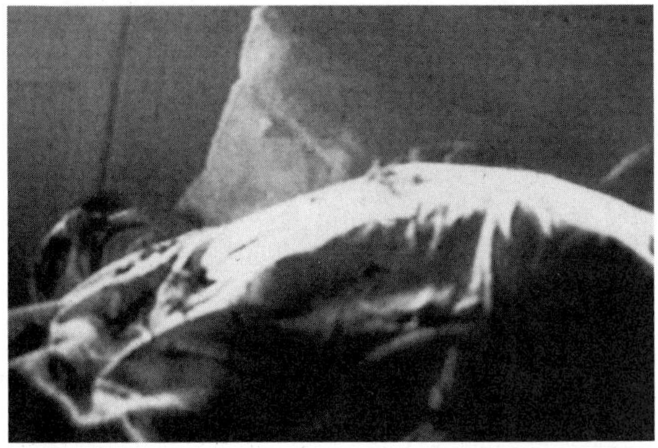

▼ gg.

▼ hh.

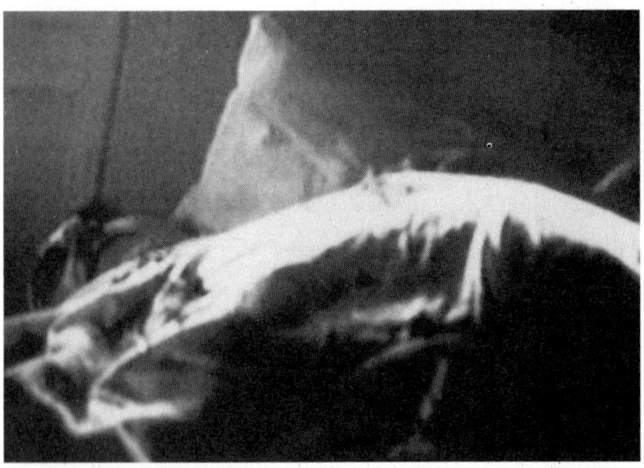

▼ ii.

▼ jj.

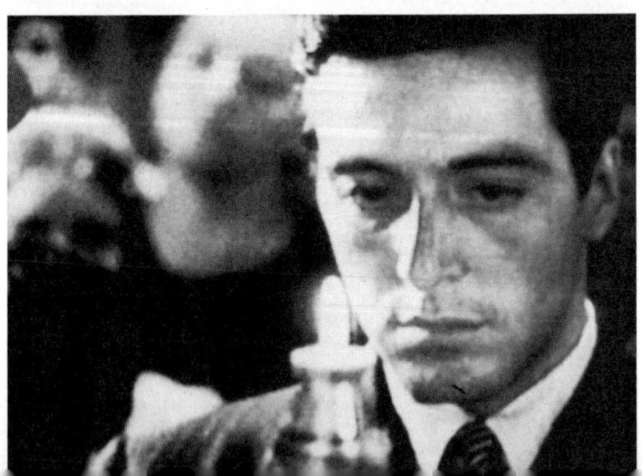

▲ kk.

▲ ll.

▼ mm.

▼ nn.

▼ oo.

▼ pp.

Creative Juxtaposition: Montage

Often the editor is called on to communicate creatively within the film. Through unique juxtapositions of images and sounds, editors can convey a specific tone or attitude. Or they may be called on to create, through visual and aural images, a **montage**—a series of images and sounds that, without any clear, logical, or sequential pattern, form a visual poem in miniature. The unity of a montage derives from complex internal relationships that we understand instantly and intuitively (see Figure 6.3).

In creating a montage, the editor uses visual and aural images as impressionistic shorthand to create a mood, atmosphere, transition in time or place, or a physical or emotional impact. As defined by the great Russian director and film theorist Sergei Eisenstein, a montage is assembled from separate images that provide a "partial representation which in their combination and juxtaposition, shall evoke in the consciousness and feelings of the spectator . . . that same initial general image which originally hovered before the creative artist."[10]

A cinematic montage might be created around images that have universal associations with death and old age. The visual and aural images could be edited as follows:

Shot 1: Close-up of wrinkled faces of aged couple, both in rocking chairs. Their eyes are dim and stare into the distance as the chairs rock slowly back and forth. *Sound:* Creaking of rocking chairs, loud ticking of old grandfather clock.

Shot 2: Slow dissolve to close-up of withered leaves, barely clinging to bare branches, light snow falling, thin layer of snow on the black bare branches. *Sound:* Low moaning wind; grandfather clock continues to tick.

Shot 3: Slow dissolve to seacoast scene. The sun's edge is barely visible on the horizon of the water; then it slips away, leaving a red glow and gradually darkening sky, light visibly fading. *Sound:* Soft rhythm of waves washing up on shore; grandfather clock continues ticking in the background.

Shot 4: Slow dissolve from red glow in sky to a glowing bed of coals in a fireplace. A few feeble fingers of flame flicker and then sputter and die. The glowing coals, as if fanned by a slight breeze, glow brighter and then grow dimmer and dimmer. *Sound:* Continued sound link of ticking grandfather clock.

Shot 5: Return to same scene as shot 1, close-up of wrinkled faces of aged couple rocking in their rocking chairs. *Sound:* Creaking chairs and the continuous tick of grandfather clock; gradual fade to black.

Montage is an especially effective technique when the director desires to compress a great deal of meaning into a very brief segment (for a contrasting approach, see ***mise-en-scène*** in the Glossary). In *The Grapes of Wrath*, John Ford used a montage that might be titled "The Joads' Journey Through Oklahoma" and another that might be called "Invasion of the Big Cats" (tractors). Effective montages appear in *Patton* (the "Winter Night Battle" montage), in *Rocky* (the "Training for the Big Fight" montage), in *Mr. Smith Goes to Washington* (the "Patriotic Washington Tour" montage), in *Waking Ned Devine* (the "Informing the Villagers" montage), and in *Edtv* (the various "Watching Ed on TV Throughout America" montages) (Figure 6.4).

Figure 6.4 Editing Sequence—Invasion of the Big Cats From *The Grapes of Wrath* To dramatize the helplessness of the Okies in this sequence from *The Grapes of Wrath,* John Ford employs a dynamic flashback montage suggesting overwhelming power. To introduce the montage, Tom Joad (Henry Fonda) asks Muley Graves to explain why he is hiding out in the Joad house:

"What happened?"

"They come. . . . They come and pushed me off. They come with the cats."

"The what?"

"The cats. . . . The Caterpillar tractors."

The montage that follows consists of a series of nine quick shots of earth-moving equipment, mostly heavy Caterpillar tractors. Each shot in the montage quickly dissolves into the next, and, as indicated by the arrows on the photos, the lines of force or movement are constantly varied, creating the impression that we are under attack from every direction. Throughout the montage, a constant close-up moving image of a heavy metal tractor tread is superimposed over the tractor images, giving us the feeling that we are being run over by something. The montage ends with a Caterpillar tractor actually rolling over the camera.

As the montage ends, Muley sums up the result of this invasion:

"And for every one of 'em, there was ten . . . fifteen families throwed right out of their homes. A hundred folks. . . . And no place to live but on the road."

▲ a. ▼ c.

▲ b. ▼ d.

▲ e. ▼ g.

▲ f. ▼ h.

▼ i.

▼ j.

▼ k.

▼ l.

Movie Magic: Special Effects in the Modern Film

As admission prices escalated and the lure of television kept more and more people at home for their entertainment, motion pictures began to incorporate elements that television could not provide. One was the special effect, which created visual spectacle on a grand scale and showed audiences things they had never seen before.

Recent advances in technology have made elaborate special effects (f/x) an important part of the modern film. Given proper time and money, there are few things modern special-effects technicians cannot realize on-screen—though truly top-quality visuals can be prohibitively expensive. This capability has opened a new frontier to the filmmakers; it allows them to use the medium to its fullest extent and enables them to really show viewers what they wish to show, instead of just telling them about it. This increased flexibility is also a great asset to the industry. Too often, however, elaborate visual effects do not just serve to enhance the story but become the focus of the film. Certainly, f/x masters Rick Baker and Richard Edlund provide the most striking aspects of *The Nutty Professor* (1996) and *Multiplicity*, respectively. In the former, special makeup effects enable Eddie Murphy to play not only a very fat Sherman Klump but also most of the members of his hilarious family; in the latter, miraculous visual effects permit Michael Keaton to portray three cloned versions of his overworked protagonist. Robert Zemeckis explains in his commentary on the DVD version of his film *Contact* that nearly every shot utilized some form of visual effect, either obvious or unobtrusive.

Special effects have been an integral part of film throughout its history. Such cinema pioneers as Georges Mèliés (*A Trip to the Moon*, 1902), D. W. Griffith (*Intolerance*, 1916), Fritz Lang (*Metropolis*, 1926), and Willis O'Brien (special effects coordinator for Merian C. Cooper's *King Kong*, 1933) originated the most basic techniques such as the now-standard **matte** and **glass shots.** But only recently has technology produced effects so sophisticated that the audience often cannot distinguish between footage of a real object and a special-effect miniature (Figure 6.5). Not all effects are of the flashy laser-blast variety. They range from effects that simply recreate in dramatic form a familiar, historic, or real event to effects that create totally fantastic people, creatures, places, or occurrences that stretch the viewer's imagination. Modern masters such as Douglas Trumbull of the Future General Company and John Dykstra of George Lucas's Industrial Light and Magic wield the tools of technological "motion control"—the **blue-screen process,** optical printers, and **computer-generated digital imaging (CGI)** to create their magic spells.

Miniaturization was used to recreate the sinking of the American naval fleet at Pearl Harbor on December 7, 1941, in *Tora! Tora! Tora!* Special effects, often the backbone of disaster films, simulate the destruction of Los Angeles in *Earthquake!*, the loss by aging of the Genesis planet in *Star Trek III: The Search for Spock*, the exploding of the White House in *Independence Day*, and even the burning of Atlanta in *Gone With the Wind.*

Figure 6.5 Special-Effect Miniature Creating the illusion that a miniature model is a full-sized fighter/bomber is essential to making us believe the incredible speed and other capabilities of these X-Wing fighters in *Star Wars*.

Other effects extend human powers: *Time Bandits*' Evil Wizard casts lightning bolts from his fingertips, *Excalibur*'s Merlin weaves his magic, and Clark Kent defies gravity as Superman (Figure 6.6).

Flying-vehicle effects, a staple of many science fiction films, range from the frenetic outer-space dogfights in *Star Wars*, to the majestic liftoff of the Mothership from *Close Encounters of the Third Kind*, to the spectacular shift to warp speed by *Star Trek*'s Starship *Enterprise*. This optical effect, like the dissolves and wipes described earlier, is created in the printing process. The primary image (such as a spaceship) is superimposed on another image (such as a starfield background), and the two are composited onto one strip of film by an optical printer. Modern optical printers are guided by computer, affording precise matching of a tremendous number of different images.

Movie audiences are so fascinated with strange creatures that the unnatural monsters can be as crude as the early Godzilla (a man in a rubber suit) or as convincing as Alien (likewise, a man in a rubber suit). They may be remote controlled (like the title creature in *E.T. The Extra-Terrestrial*), a sophisticated puppet (like the Jedi master Yoda from *Star Wars*, *The Empire Strikes Back*, *Return of the Jedi*, and *The Phantom Menace*), or stop-motion animated (like the

Figure 6.6 "You'll Believe a Man Can Fly" A real effort was made in *Superman* to make us believe the flying sequences. In this scene, Superman (Christopher Reeve) is taking Lois Lane (Margot Kidder) on a romantic demonstration flight over Metropolis. In *Superman II* and *Superman III,* less attention was paid to the flying effects, and the results were not as convincing.

ape in the original *King Kong*); or they may combine all these techniques and more (like the dragon Vermithrax Pejorative in *Dragonslayer*). They may be subtly inhuman, like certain forms of Count Dracula in *Bram Stoker's Dracula*, or unmistakably monstrous, like the giant snake in *Conan the Barbarian* or *Anaconda* (Figure 6.7). The master of this technique is Ray Harryhausen. Perhaps the most endearing use of such technology so far has been in *Babe*, the 1995 film for children of all ages that combined puppets and computer-generated effects with real animals to create a seamless and believable entertainment.

The mythical concept that some human beings can magically transform themselves into other life forms has enjoyed tremendous popularity over the years. This effect has come far since 1941, when Lon Chaney Jr. became the Wolfman. Subsequent transformations have turned men and women into snakes (*Conan the Barbarian*), black panthers (*Cat People*), reptilian monsters (*The Sword and the Sorcerer*), primates and amorphous superconscious beings (*Altered States*), enormous insects (*The Fly* and *Starship Troopers*), and, of course, werewolves (*The Howling*, *An American Werewolf in London*, and *Wolf*)—all on-

Figure 6.7 Evolving Life Forms Creature effects are becoming more and more sophisticated in modern films, progressing from the rather primitive but effective single-frame animation of the original *King Kong* to the wise and highly expressive puppet face of the Jedi master Yoda from *The Empire Strikes Back* to a combination of animation and remote-controlled movement in and the multiple f/x magic of *Babe*.

screen. Curiously, many of these makeup effects were not makeup in the traditional sense at all but rather were sculpted remote-controlled models (such as the transforming head from *American Werewolf*) (Figure 6.8). So unorthodox were the transformation effects for *The Thing* (1982) that an effort was made to have artist Rob Bottin's work classified as visual effects instead of makeup. The title character in *Bram Stoker's Dracula* becomes a study in the transformation process, taking not just one but several physical forms: bats, wolves, rats, and even an evil, fast-creeping mist.

Gore effects—the simulation of many different kinds of deaths, decapitations, and eviscerations—are at least partly responsible for the upsurge of murder movies in the "hack 'n' slash" horror vein.

Creative production designers work with special-effects teams to create diverse locales such as the glittering crystalline world of Krypton in *Superman*, the drug-induced, hallucinogenic reality of *Altered States*, the interior of the human body in *Fantastic Voyage*, the sparkling high-tech starship bridge of *Star*

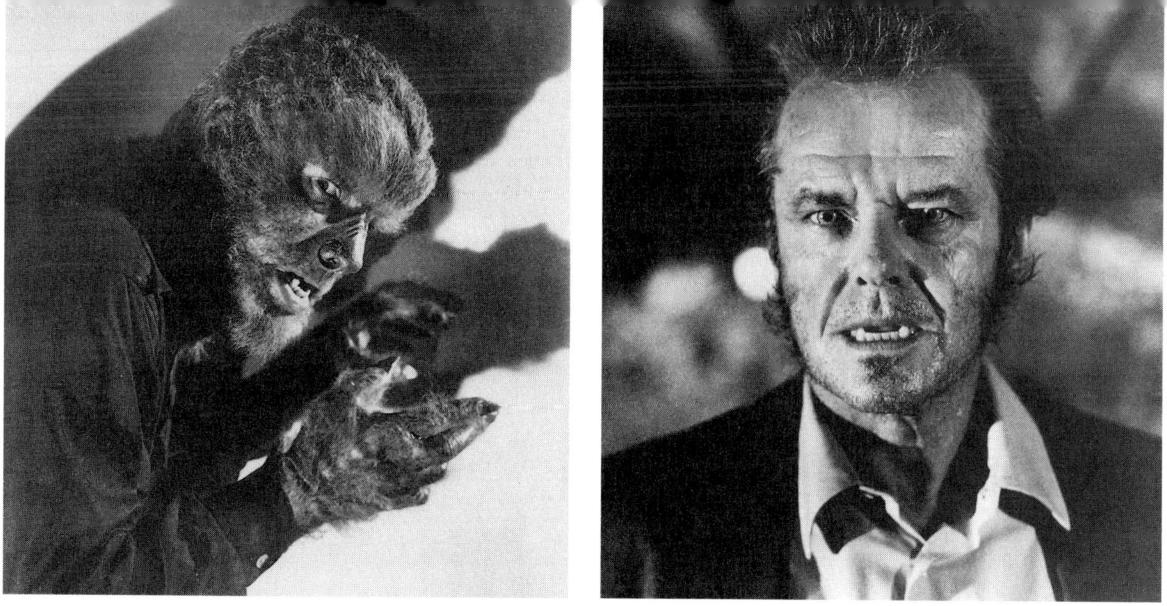

Figure 6.8 Transformation In *The Wolf Man,* Lon Chaney Jr. became the Wolfman at the full moon by having his Wolfman makeup applied in six or seven stages while the camera was turned off, creating the illusion of a slow, miraculous transformation when the film was run continuously. The man-becomes-beast techniques used in such films as *The Howling, An American Werewolf in London,* and *Altered States* are much more complex and employ sculpted, remote-controlled latex models of the actors' heads. Rick Baker's subtle transformation of Jack Nicholson in *Wolf* (1994) allows the director, Mike Nichols, to focus on character rather than plot or merely special effects.

Trek: The Wrath of Khan, and the oppressive, smog-shrouded futurescape of *Blade Runner.*

The effects that are currently available provide filmmakers with a seemingly endless variety of tricks to use, yet many of the effects that seem so amazing and fascinating today will probably seem tame and outdated when they are compared with those in next season's releases. The primary factor in this rapid increase in technology is CGI—computer-generated imaging. In June 1990, when active discussions began about making Michael Crichton's novel *Jurassic Park* into a film, the computer programs that would be needed to animate the dinosaurs didn't exist. They not only exist today, but *Jurassic Park* and its sequel, *The Lost World*, have established a new benchmark for measuring the effectiveness of computer animation in film. The prehistoric creatures move seamlessly through the frame, their motions just as believable and lifelike as those of their human costars. Actually, computer animation is only part of the story, for the special effects often combine several different technologies, as Peter Biskind describes the first Tyrannosaurus rex attack in the first film.

> The scene itself plays like a blur of motion, but in reality, only the top half of the dinosaur was built [as a full-scale puppet], and it was set on top of a flight simulator, which was bolted to the soundstage floor. "It was like a giant shark up on legs,"

Figure 6.9 Novelty Effects A blend of past and present has been achieved in films like *Dead Men Don't Wear Plaid* and *Zelig.*. In *Dead Men,* Steve Martin's image was superimposed over the foreground figure in shots like this one from *Dark Passage,* creating the illusion that Martin and Humphrey Bogart are playing a scene together. In *Zelig,* Woody Allen seems to stand between Calvin Coolidge and Herbert Hoover in newsreel footage (opposite page).

> says [Rick] Carter [production designer], "and perfectly designed to be as threatening as you could ever imagine." The motion was achieved by moving the sets around the dinosaur, and the live action footage was enhanced by a computer. Anytime the entire dinosaur is visible in the frame, computer animation is responsible.[11]

Computer animation was also used to fill the skies over Germany with B-17 bombers in *Memphis Belle.* The unusual and powerful images in *The Abyss* and *Terminator 2: Judgment Day* utilized reflection mapping, a technique that simulates reflections of real-world images on three-dimensional objects that are modeled and rendered on a computer. The results are especially convincing in *Terminator 2,* featuring a superhuman villain with powers of regeneration that previously could be realized only by Looney Tunes animators. A similar technique was used seriously in the computer animation of *The Prince of Egypt* to create crowd scenes.

The real measure of an effect's success has become how well the effect is integrated into the storyline of the film. No longer is it a challenge to make the effect itself believable. In the modern film, the integration of special effects, not the domination of special effects, is the proper measure of success.

The best films use their special effects as little—or as much—as necessary, and no more. *Star Wars* incorporated some 365 individual visual effects, all of which serve to propel the story forward. In contrast, *Time After Time* (1979) uses only a few simple optical effects to send H. G. Wells into the future, but they effectively establish that film's whimsical nature. Tremendous time and money were devoted to the flying sequences of *Superman* (1978) because it was crucial to the film's credibility that the audience believe a man could fly.

In the best films, the visuals create the atmosphere for the story and impel the story forward; they become simply one of many properly integrated elements of the film. *E.T. The Extra-Terrestrial* is filled with dazzling effects from beginning to end; E.T. itself is on-screen for a great portion of the picture. Yet all these dazzling effects do not impair the warm, friendly ambience of the film because they are well integrated.

The potential power of such visuals, however, often tempts filmmakers to overuse them, to let them overwhelm the story. *The Thing* (1982) featured so many transformation sequences that the internal suspense the director was striving for was destroyed, and so much focus was placed on *Blade Runner*'s grimly detailed futurescape that its characters seem lost in it. Francis Ford Coppola's *Bram Stoker's Dracula* provides us with many special effects from the entire sweep of cinema history, causing one critic to complain that "the film throws so much fancy technique at its story that the usually foolproof drama at its core gets drowned in a tide of images."[12]

At the other extreme is Mike Nichols's *Wolf.* Jack Nicholson transforms gradually, first by subtle changes in his personality after being bitten by a wolf, then finally into the animal, with little emphasis on the special effects required.

There is a final role that special effects can play, achieving the novel or nontraditional effect, or gimmick, called for by certain films. Noteworthy novelty effects include the use of clips from classic films to allow Steve Martin to interact with stars like Humphrey Bogart in *Dead Men Don't Wear Plaid* and Woody Allen to interact with Calvin Coolidge and Herbert Hoover in *Zelig* (Figure 6.9). Recent advances in computer-generated imagery have taken this interaction effect one step farther in *Forrest Gump.* The film's chocoholic hero interacts directly with historical figures such as Presidents Kennedy, Johnson, and Nixon, shaking hands with them and engaging in what seem to be two-way conversations.

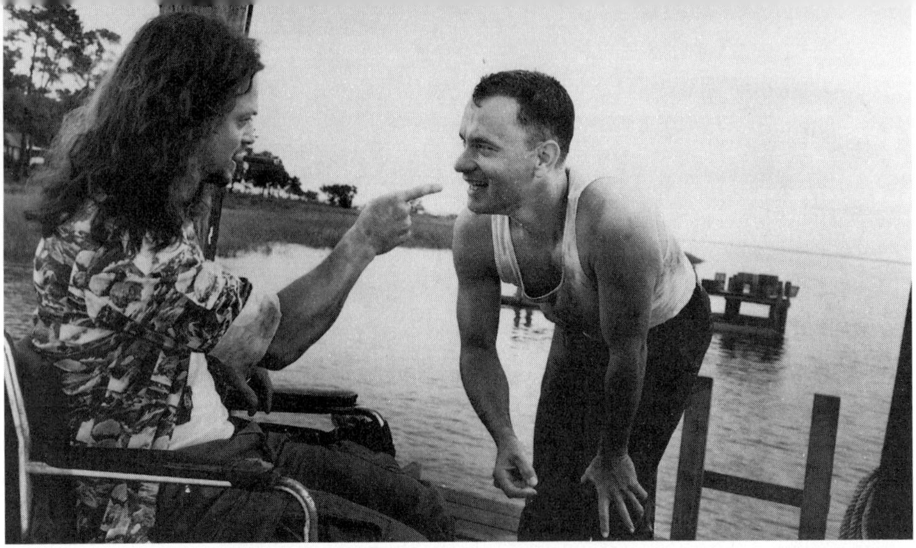

Figure 6.10 Credible F/X In *Forrest Gump,* the protagonist (Tom Hanks) admires and assists his former military boss, Lieutenant Dan (Gary Sinise), who has lost his legs in the Vietnam War. Through the magic of computer imaging, the effect is so convincing that many viewers cannot believe that the actor has not shared his character's medical fate. Successful special visual effects, then, help to ensure that narratives will be credible.

Special visual effects are also used in a serious, thematically integrated fashion in *Forrest Gump.* During the Vietnam conflict, Gump's buddy Lieutenant Dan loses his legs in combat. Through the magic of digital manipulation, special-effects wizards used computers to "erase" the lower limbs of the fully ambulatory actor Gary Sinise; the effect was so realistic that many viewers were amazed. Upon seeing the film, for example, the actress Anne Bancroft said she "was so shocked. I thought [Sinise] had lost his legs. I turned to Mel [Brooks, her husband, the film director] and I said, 'Mel, did he lose his legs?' And Mel said, 'I don't know.' I felt so sorry for that poor man."[13] Such magical movie moments, of course, gladden the hearts of special-effects creators (Figure 6.10).

In the future, according to James Cameron, the director of *The Abyss, Terminator 2, True Lies,* and *Titanic,* actors will be able to perform without boundary, through images stored in computers. Thus, conceivably, Arnold Schwarzenegger "may still be around one thousand years from now," acting in newly "animated" roles. As Joe Dante, director of the *Gremlins* movies, points out, however, a special effect now is "only as good as an actor's reaction to it. So if you have a really great effect and you cut to an actor who doesn't look like he's believing what he's seeing, then your effect is no good." The magic still has plenty of reasons to endure, though. Richard Edlund thinks that "visual effects will continue to expand, and, as long as they continue to satisfy the audience's desire to be put in a place they couldn't otherwise possibly be put, they will continue to be successful."[14]

Questions

On Editing

1. How does the editing effectively guide our thoughts, associations, and emotional responses from one image to another so that smooth continuity and coherence are achieved?
2. Is the editing smooth, natural, and unobtrusive, or is it tricky and self-conscious? How much does the editor communicate through creative juxtapositions—ironic transitions, montages, and the like—and how effective is this communication?
3. What is the effect of editorial cutting and transitions on the pace of the film as a whole?
4. How does the cutting speed (which determines the average duration of each shot) correspond to the emotional tone of the scene involved?
5. What segments of the film seem overly long or boring? Which parts of these segments could be cut without altering the total effect? Where are additional shots necessary to make the film completely coherent?

On Movie Magic: Special Effects in the Modern Film

1. How effective are the special effects employed in the film? Do they dominate the film to the point that the film is just a showcase for the effects, or are they an integrated part of the film?
2. To what degree does the credibility of the entire film depend on the audience believing in its special effects? Do special effects overshadow the major characters so much that they seem secondary to the effects?

Video Exercises

Instructions for locating specific sequences are given on page 77.

1. **Editing.** Watch the famous shower sequence from *Psycho* (1960) [2825 to 2995; 0:46:00 to 0:49:23] and the "final ambush" sequence from *Bonnie and Clyde* [5215 to end; 1:46:00 to end]. In which sequence is your involvement or concern greatest? Why? In which sequence do you feel real physical danger? What causes the difference?

   After Clyde gets out of the car, he and Bonnie do not exchange words, but they do communicate their thoughts and feelings, both to each other and to the audience. What do they say with their faces and body language? (Try to "caption" as many shots as possible.) How does the editing make the meaning of their expressions clear?

   Turn the sound off and watch both sequences again. Which sequence do you think the sound contributes the most to? Why?

What is the purpose of the camera's moving behind the car for the final seconds? Why doesn't the camera remain between the bodies of Bonnie and Clyde so we can view them with Malcolm (Dub Taylor) and the ambush party?

2. **Montage.** Examine each of these examples of montage:
   a. From *The Grapes of Wrath:* "Invasion of the Big Cats" [1170 to 1250; 0:15:28 to 0:16:45] and "The Joads' Journey Through Oklahoma" [2350 to 2435; 0:36:16 to 0:37:53]
   b. From *Patton:* "Winter Night Battle" [Part II: 3480 to 3650; 0:48:38 to 0:50:54]
   c. From *Rocky:* "Training for the Big Fight" [4600 to 4700; 1:30:00 to 1:33:05]
   d. From *Mr. Smith Goes to Washington:* "Patriotic Washington Tour" [1475 to 1680; 0:19:50 to 0:23:07]

   What is the purpose of each montage? How are sound, dialogue, voice-over narration, superimposed images, and music used to help tie the images together?

Films for Study

Editing

The Age of Innocence (1993)
Annie Hall (1977)
Bonnie and Clyde (1967)
Bound (1996)
Cabaret (1972)
Casablanca (1942)
Citizen Kane (1941)
Dressed to Kill (1980)
Edtv (1999)
The Godfather (1972)
The Godfather Part II (1974)
Jaws (1975)
JFK (1991)
Napoleon (1927)
Natural Born Killers (1994)
Prospero's Books (1991)
Psycho (1960)
Raging Bull (1980)
Raiders of the Lost Ark (1981)
The Road Warrior (1981)
The Sting (1973)
Strange Days (1995)
Ulee's Gold (1997)
Waking Ned Devine (1998)

Special Visual Effects

The Abyss (1989)
Altered States (1980)
Apollo 13 (1995)
Babe (1995)
Babe: Pig in the City (1998)
Beetle Juice (1988)
The Borrowers (1997)
Bram Stoker's Dracula (1992)
Contact (1997)
Dark City (1998)
Dead Men Don't Wear Plaid (1982)
The Fifth Element (1997)
Forrest Gump (1994)
Gremlins 2 The New Batch (1990)
Independence Day (1996)
Jurassic Park (1993)
King Kong (1933)
The Matrix (1999)
Star Wars trilogy (Special on—1997)
Star Wars, Episode I: The Phantom Menace (1999)
Superman (1978)
Terminator 2: Judgment Day (1991)
Titanic (1997)
The Truman Show (1998)
2001: A Space Odyssey (1968)
Zelig (1983)

Chapter 7

Color

Color is an integral element of a picture. Its use means much more than the mechanical recording of colors which the camera has heretofore blotted out. Just as music flows from movement to movement, color on the screen . . . flowing from sequence to sequence, is really a kind of music.

—Robert Edmond Jones, Stage Designer/Color Consultant

Color holds a powerful position among the elements of film structure. A kind of universal language, it appeals equally to the illiterate and the sophisticated, to the child and the adult. Its function on the screen is both utilitarian and aesthetic. When made relevant to the picture's subject, color offers an immediate resonance that vivifies mood, delineates character, enhances meaning. When structured to further movement from sequence to sequence, color adds a new richness of film expression that immeasurably deepens the total work.[1]

—LEWIS JACOBS, CRITIC

The added richness and depth that color provides make awareness of color and its effects on the audience essential to perceptive film watching. Although color probably gives us more immediate pleasure than any of the other visual elements, it is also probably more difficult to understand. Human responses to color are not purely visual responses; they are also psychological or even physiological. Some of color's effects on the human mind and body border on the miraculous: Premature babies born with a potentially fatal jaundice do not require a blood transfusion if they are bathed in blue light. Decorating restaurants in red apparently stimulates the appetite and results in increased food consumption. Blue surroundings can significantly lower human blood pressure, pulse, and respiration rates. And violent children relax, become calm, and often fall asleep within minutes when placed in a small room painted bubble-gum pink.

Color attracts and holds our attention; our eyes are more quickly attracted by color than by shape or form. Any reader skimming through a book with color pictures looks at those pictures first and looks at them more often than at pictures in black and white. Advertisers who have run identical ads in full color and in black and white have gotten fifteen times better results from the color ads. Practically every package on the supermarket shelves has at least a touch of red, for red seems to attract attention better than any other color.

Individual responses to color vary, for color is a purely human perception of a visual quality that is distinct from light and shade. Color is simply radiant energy. Colors are properties not of surfaces or objects but of human perceptions. **Color**—the special quality of light reflected from a given surface—is greatly influenced by subjective factors that arise within the brain. Color not only is seen but is felt emotionally by each viewer and is therefore subject to his or her personal interpretation. The word **hue** is a synonym for *color.*

We need to define some other terms. **Value** refers to the proportion of light or dark in a color. White is the lightest value perceptible to the human eye, and black is the darkest perceptible value. *Value* is a comparative concept, for we generally compare a colored surface with the normal value of a color—that is, the value at which we expect to find the color represented on a **color wheel** (Figure 7.1). Anything lighter than the normal value is a **tint;** anything darker is a **shade.** Therefore, pink is a tint of red, and maroon is a shade of red.

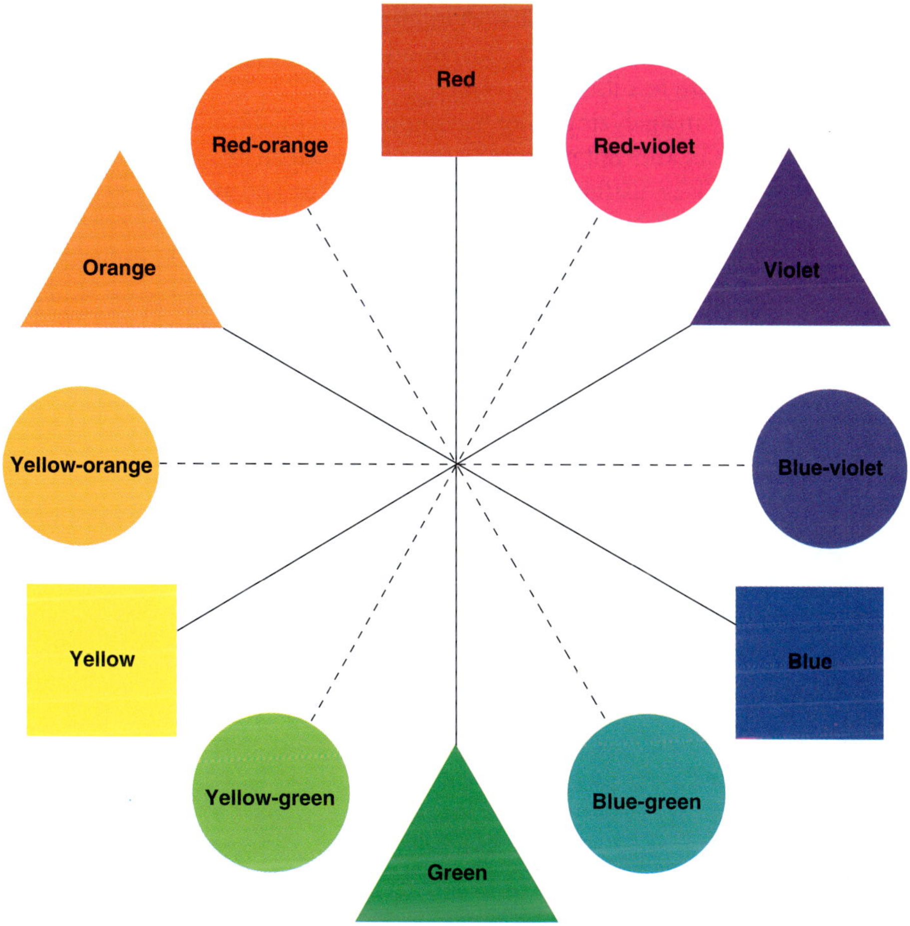

Figure 7.1 An Integrated Color Wheel Artists use this device to help clarify the relationships that exist between the primary and secondary hues. The squares show the three primary colors (red, blue, and yellow), and the triangles show the three secondary colors (violet, green, and orange). These colors are separated by six intermediate colors, appearing in the circles.

Saturation and *intensity* are other important concepts. In a discussion of color, these terms are interchangeable. A **saturated color** is a hue so unadulterated and strong that it is as pure as it can be. White and black are both saturated colors of maximum intensity. Pure white cannot be made any whiter; pure black cannot be made any blacker. A saturated or high-intensity red is a pure red—what we might call fire-engine red. It can't be made any redder. If a saturated red were made darker (or grayer), it would become a *shade* of red and would be lower in intensity. If a saturated red were made lighter (or whiter), it would become a *tint* of red and would be lower in intensity. When a color is lowered in intensity, it is said to be a **desaturated** or **muted color**. The term *muted* is perhaps easier to understand because of its clear association with music: A mute on a trumpet, for example, makes the sound of the instrument less pure and clear, less bright, and less loud.

The difficulty in analyzing color is compounded by the fact that objects are seldom viewed in an atmosphere totally removed from all external optical influences. There is a clear distinction between **local color** and **atmospheric color.** A green leaf pulled off a tree, placed on a white tabletop in a room with white walls and a white floor, and illuminated by a perfectly white light radiates *local* color. A leaf radiates *atmospheric* color when it is viewed on the tree on which it is growing: The leaf appears translucent and yellowish when the sun shines through it; it turns dark green and opaque when a cloud passes over the sun. As the sun sets, the leaf may first appear ruddy and then look almost blue as the sun drops below the horizon. Thus, under normal conditions, we usually see a complex and constantly changing atmospheric color:

> Local color is always submerged in a sea of light and air—in an atmosphere which combines a wide range of color influences. Not only does the sunlight change constantly through the day, but colored objects influence one another. Neighboring colors enhance or subdue one another; colored lights literally pick up reflections from one another; and even the dust particles in the air lend their own color to the objects.[2] (Figure 7.2)

In planning and shooting a modern color film, the director, the cinematographer, the production designer, and the costumer must be constantly aware of such factors if they are to control and manipulate the color to conform to their aesthetic vision.

Recorded Color

The earliest filmmakers experimented with the use of color (see pages 454–456), but the technology needed to capture photographic images in color within the camera was not available until the 1920s. Dr. Herbert Kalmus's two-color Technicolor film was employed for color sequences in blockbusters like *Ben-Hur* (1926) and *Phantom of the Opera* (1925). The process was expensive, costing 30 percent more than a similar black-and-white production, and audiences grew quickly bored or irritated with the poor registry of the colors. Caucasian flesh tones, for example, varied from pink to orange. Several years later, in 1932, the Technicolor Corporation perfected three-color Technicolor film, and color film, still expensive and difficult to work with, gradually came into its own.

The Technicolor Corporation maintained tight controls over the use of its film, requiring that each Technicolor production use its cameramen, consultants, and equipment. Although the Technicolor dyes tended to create pure or saturated colors more strikingly brilliant than colors in the real world the film was recording (Figure 7.3), Technicolor's domination of color cinematography

Figure 7.2 Atmospheric Colors A wide range of color influences come into play in the four pictures shown here. The trees under which Clark Gable and Vivien Leigh are standing cast a faint greenish haze over their faces in *Gone With the Wind*. The roaring blaze of a fire-bombed church casts an orange glow over the faces of Gene Hackman and Willem Dafoe in *Mississippi Burning*. The blue club lights surrounding the dark dance floor in Jackrabbit Slim's cast a blue aura over John Travolta in *Pulp Fiction*. The instrument-panel lights in the spacecraft cast a pinkish glow over the faces of Keir Dullea and Gary Lockwood in *2001: A Space Odyssey*.

Figure 7.3 Brilliant Technicolor The rich, saturated colors of Technicolor, more brilliant than reality and clearly evident in this grand ball scene from *Gone With the Wind,* were chemically and digitally restored for the film's 1998 re-release.

continued until 1952, when the introduction of Eastman Color film made color production simpler and more economical. Since the mid-1970s, Eastman Color has been the preeminent film type. Meanwhile, the Technicolor technology has survived and flourished exclusively in mainland China, where, for example, the filmmaker Zhang Yimou has produced such richly hued films as *Ju Dou* and *Raise the Red Lantern.* Only in the late 1990s, with the growing concern for film preservation, has there been a revival of interest in Technicolor in the United States.

Color in the Modern Film

With the technology under control and readily available, and with a theater and television audience not only accustomed to but demanding movies in color, it is important to understand how color functions in the modern film: how it affects our experience of a film, how it affects us generally, and what, if any, advantages color has over black and white. Since the 1950s, the color film has increased greatly in subtlety and sophistication, and its potential seems almost unlimited.

Effects of Color on the Viewer

To begin, let's consider certain basic assumptions about the effects of color and the way it communicates—things that profoundly affect the creative choices of the director, the cinematographer, the production designer, and the costumer.

Figure 7.4 Seeing Red A saturated red is a great attention-getter, as shown in these striking photographs from *The Mask of Zorro* (top left), *Rocky IV* (top right), *Kundun* (bottom left), and *The Last Emperor* (bottom right).

1. **Color Attracts Attention.** The director has several methods of keeping attention focused on the center of interest. Our eye is drawn to large objects, to the object closest to the camera, to the object in the sharpest focus, to movement, and to close-ups. A dramatic arrangement of people and objects and highlighting the object of greatest interest also attract our attention. Color is another option. By using bright or saturated colors on the object of greatest interest and placing that object against a contrasting background, the director can easily capture the viewer's eye (Figures 7.4, 7.5).

Figure 7.5 A Unique Red The dull-textured red velvet chair in this shot from *A Room With a View* reflects the light in a unique way, projecting a feel of richness and luxury.

2. **Colors Contribute to Three-Dimensionality.** The director can capitalize on another characteristic of color to ensure that attention is attracted to the proper object: Some colors seem to advance toward the foreground, and others seem to recede into the background. Colors such as red, orange, yellow, and lavender are **advancing colors.** When given high intensity and dark value, they seem to advance, making objects appear larger and closer to the camera than they are. Interior decorators and others know that a chair covered in red will seem larger and closer to an observer than the same chair covered in **receding colors** such as beige, green, or pale blue. Taking advantage of the advancing and receding characteristics of color fosters the illusion that the image on the screen is three-dimensional.

   Several other techniques may be used in a color film to create the illusion of different planes of depth. By controlling the lighting and color choices, the director can dramatize or accent the illusion of solidity and form by contrasting darkness against lightness, contrasting pure color against grayed color, contrasting warm color against cool color, and contrasting detail, texture, and microstructure against plainness or filminess.

The problems of creating the illusion of three-dimensionality in black and white are simplified in color, according to production designer Robert Boyle:

> Black and white is a little harder to do than color. The difference is you can separate the planes with color, but with black and white you have to separate the planes with values. The cameraman's job in a black and white film is the difficult one, because you separate the planes with light, particularly when you are trying to indicate depth. Anybody can go out and snap a color shot and the planes will just naturally separate by the intensity of the color, but in black and white you have to do it all with value. You have to assess whether a yellow and a light red are going to be different enough in values to separate the planes. There may be a red room in the foreground and behind that you'll have a light gray, and that will separate the planes and help the cameraman.[3]

3. **Colors Create an Impression or Feeling of Temperature.** Colors convey or at least seem to convey a sense of temperature. The **warm colors** are the colors that advance: red, orange, yellow, and lavender. The **cool colors** are the colors that recede: blues, greens, and beiges. It is likely that warm colors are so designated because of their associations with fire, the sun, and sunsets, and blues and greens are deemed cool because of their associations with water and the shade of trees (Figure 7.6).

   These generalizations, however, are not without certain complications. There are various degrees of color temperature. Red with a touch of blue is cooler than a saturated red. Yellow with a hint of green becomes a cool yellow. A reddish violet seems warm, but a bluish violet is comparatively cool. A blue with a faint purplish tinge suggests warmth, and some greens have enough yellow to seem warm. Filmmakers are aware of these connotations and use them to good effect, as Mark Rydell did in creating the effects of the warm, loving relationship between two women in the house and the bitter cold outside in his film of D. H. Lawrence's *The Fox:*

   > [E]very object in the house, every color, was chosen in warm tones to support the erotic tension in the house and everything in the exterior was in the blue tones to emphasize the cold. Those are the kinds of things that are done that have an unconscious impact on people. . . . I'm very careful to select things like that. I think color has real impact. The choice of colors is seemingly inadvertent—but it's not. Every garment is selected for a particular kind of emotional tone.[4]

4. **Colors Function Together in Different Ways.** Certain combinations of color, or color schemes, produce predictable and consistent visual effects. **Monochromatic harmony** results from a scheme based on variations in the value and intensity of one color. **Complementary harmony** results

Figure 7.6 Warm and Cool Colors In *The Lost Boys,* the vampire (Kiefer Sutherland), dressed in blue and bathed in pale blue light, becomes a cool contrast to the warm yellow candles in the foreground and the warm flesh tones and brightly colored dress of the woman in the far background.

from the use of colors directly opposite each other on the color wheel, such as red and green. Complementary colors react with each other more vividly than do other colors. **Analogous harmony** results from the use of colors adjacent to one another on the color wheel, such as red, red-orange, and orange. Such colors create a soft image with little harsh contrast. **Triad harmony** results from the use of three colors equidistant from one another on the color wheel, such as the primary colors: red, yellow, and blue.

Color-conscious directors generally have a clear vision of the color tone or types of color harmony they want to incorporate into their film, and they convey that vision to the cinematographer, production designer, and costumer during an extensive period of preproduction planning. If special color effects need to be provided by the film laboratory during the printing process, laboratory technicians may also be consulted. Because different types of film stock respond to color in different ways, experts from Eastman Kodak or Technicolor may even be brought into the process.

Figure 7.7 Oz in Reverse In *Blue Velvet,* David Lynch begins his story with an idealized small-town atmosphere portrayed in glowing colors, with brilliant flowers, white picket fences, playing children, and cute dogs. Then the director mutes the color, darkens the image, and takes us on an unforgettable journey into the dark underbelly of vice, evil, and corruption beneath the surface. Shown here is the overly curious Kyle MacLachlan being threatened by Isabella Rossellini.

Color as a Transitional Device

Color has probably been used most often to signal important changes. This can be accomplished by using color in conjunction with black and white or by switching to an obviously different color emphasis or style at the point of transition. Director David Lynch used the latter strategy in *Blue Velvet* (Figure 7.7). The most obvious kind of color transition is the technique used in *The Wizard*

Figure 7.8 Still in Kansas Dorothy (Judy Garland) and Toto sit beneath gathering storm clouds in a dull, drab black-and-white Kansas during the opening segment of *The Wizard of Oz.* **Not in Kansas Anymore** Dorothy (Judy Garland) and the Scarecrow (Ray Bolger) get acquainted on the yellow-brick road in *The Wizard of Oz.*

Figure 7.9 Lively/Scary Color In the early sections of *Pleasantville,* the television town exists only in gradations of gray. The inhabitants of *Pleasantville* find the gradual experience of becoming colorful both frightening and exhilarating.

of Oz, where the dull, drab Kansas of Dorothy's real world suddenly becomes the glowing Technicolor Oz of her dream (Figure 7.8).

Color also provides a transition between two separate worlds in a unique time-travel film, *The Navigator: A Medieval Odyssey*. Produced in New Zealand and directed by Vincent Ward, the film concerns a journey from the Middle Ages to the present through the center of the Earth. The title character, a young visionary from a primitive medieval Christian clan, lives in a gloomy, stark, black-and-white world but dreams or has visions of the modern world in muted color. Through his dreams, he "knows the way" and leads members of his clan through the center of the Earth to deliver a cross to "the other side" (the modern world). As they enter the great vertical cavern that leads to the other world, limited color enters the image transitionally as torches dropping through the pit or carried by the clansmen glow orange without coloring the cavern walls or the faces of the men. Then, as they emerge into the modern world on the outskirts of a large city, we see a night scene with full but very muted color. *Pleasantville*, a seriocomic examination of evolving American life during the past fifty years, also utilizes color as a transitional device. Magically transported to the black and white fantasy world of a 1950s television sitcom, two '90s teenaged siblings gradually become the catalysts for blossoming color in characters who manage to attain a strong personal and social awareness (Figure 7.9).

A transition from present to past is keyed through color in *D.O.A.* (1988), which opens in a *film noir* black and white as Dennis Quaid, dying from a slow-acting but fatal poison, staggers into a police station to tell his story. As the detectives begin taping his testimony, we watch him briefly on a black-and-white TV monitor until the film goes into a dramatic flashback, changing to color as it shows the word *color* printed on a blackboard, with Quaid as a college English professor discussing the use of color as metaphor in literature. The film returns to the *film noir* black and white in the midst of the final, violent climax of the flashback.

A more sophisticated use of color for transition occurs in *Sophie's Choice*. During the concentration camp scenes, the color is muted so much that it almost disappears, thus conveying the grimness of those scenes and setting them apart from the bright and cheerful colors of the present-time sequences.

Martin Scorsese's *Raging Bull* uses color for another unusual transitional effect. The opening credits in color are superimposed over a black-and-white slow-motion image of Robert De Niro (as Jake La Motta) shadowboxing alone in the corner of the ring. With the color titles, Scorsese seems to be saying, "This is a modern film." With the black-and-white image behind the titles, he seems to be saying, "This is a realistic film. I'm not going to idealize or glorify the subject." Then, suddenly, near the middle of the film, Scorsese integrates La Motta home movies, in color, complete with shaky camera movement, fuzzy focus, and all the other standard ills of home movies. There's a wedding scene and a "kids by the pool" scene. The color provides a realistic, compressed interlude of happier days before La Motta returns to his grim career in the ring.

Expressionistic Use of Color

Expressionism is a dramatic or cinematic technique that attempts to present the inner reality of a character. In film, there is usually a distortion or exaggeration of normal perception to let the audience know that it is experiencing a character's innermost feelings (Figure 7.10).

In Michelangelo Antonioni's *Red Desert*, a variety of interesting color effects are achieved. Whereas traditional films express characters' emotions through acting, editing, composition, and sound, Antonioni uses color expressionistically to make us experience the world of the film through the mind and feelings of the central character, Giuliana, the neurotic wife of an engineer. The garish colors of factory vats, pipelines, slag heaps, poisonous yellow smoke, and a huge black ship passing through the gray mist of the harbor (along with an almost deafening roar and clatter of industrial machinery) make us aware that Giuliana is overwhelmed and threatened by industrialization. In her dull, everyday life, the color is desaturated or muted, taking on a dull, gray, nightmarish cast. But

Figure 7.10 Expressionistic Color Color can be used expressionistically to make us experience the world of the film through the mind and feelings of the central character. Early in *What Dreams May Come,* the phantom Chris Nielsen (Robin Williams) tries unsuccessfully to console his widow, Annie (Annabella Sciorra). In this scene, the colors are muted (desaturated) to convey her despair. Later in the film, the two are reunited, and as they frolic in a spectacular oil-painted paradise, the colors become bright and saturated.

when Giuliana tells her young son a story reflecting her own fantasies, the colors suddenly change from dull browns and grays to the brilliant sea greens, the blue skies, and the golden sand and rocks of a fairy-tale island, calling attention to the vast difference between the real world she lives in and her fantasies.

One of the dangers of trying to create internalized or expressionistic effects in color is made clear by two vastly different interpretations of one scene from *Red Desert*, the scene in which Giuliana and Corrado make love in Corrado's hotel room. One critic describes the scene like this:

> Corrado's room is dark brown paneled wood, the color of earth, when Giuliana comes in. After they make love . . . the room appears pink (flesh-colored), almost like a baby's room. Where she had seen Corrado as a strong, masculine figure, he seems to her like a child after her disillusion with him—the color, when Antonioni wants it that way, a correlative of his heroine's sense of things.[5]

Another critic interprets the scene in this manner:

> In a later sequence in the engineer's hotel room, the walls change color from their original hard gray to warm pink because Giuliana feels them pink, with her body next to a warm strong man. He, ironically, neither cares how she feels or how she feels the walls.[6]

Both critics are right about the walls. One wall is dark, paneled wood; the other three are hard gray. The gray walls are the ones that appear pink. But the difference in interpretation here indicates a major difficulty with the expressionistic use of color. We must remember that color is not just seen but is also felt by the individual viewer and is subject to his or her personal interpretation. At least two critics did not experience the pink room of *Red Desert* in the same way.

Color as Symbol

In Ingmar Bergman's *Cries and Whispers*, we see evidence of another problem with communicating clearly with color. In that film, the bedroom of the dying Agnes is literally drowning in saturated reds: red bedspread, red carpet, red walls, red drapes, and even a red dressing screen. Bergman has said that the deep-red sets symbolize his vision of the soul as a red membrane, but individual viewers may be unaware of this symbolism. The red actually is so appealing to the eye that it distracts attention away from the subtle drama that the faces and the dialogue are struggling to convey. Similarly, Peter Greenaway plays with color in his controversial *The Cook, The Thief, His Wife, & Her Lover*. In graphically presenting the erotic passions, jealousies, and angers of its characters, this film first creates brilliantly individuated color schemes for its interior settings (including the various rooms of a large restaurant). Then it changes the colors of the characters' clothing as they walk from room to room. What may be extremely subtle color symbolism for some viewers may be merely confusing for others.

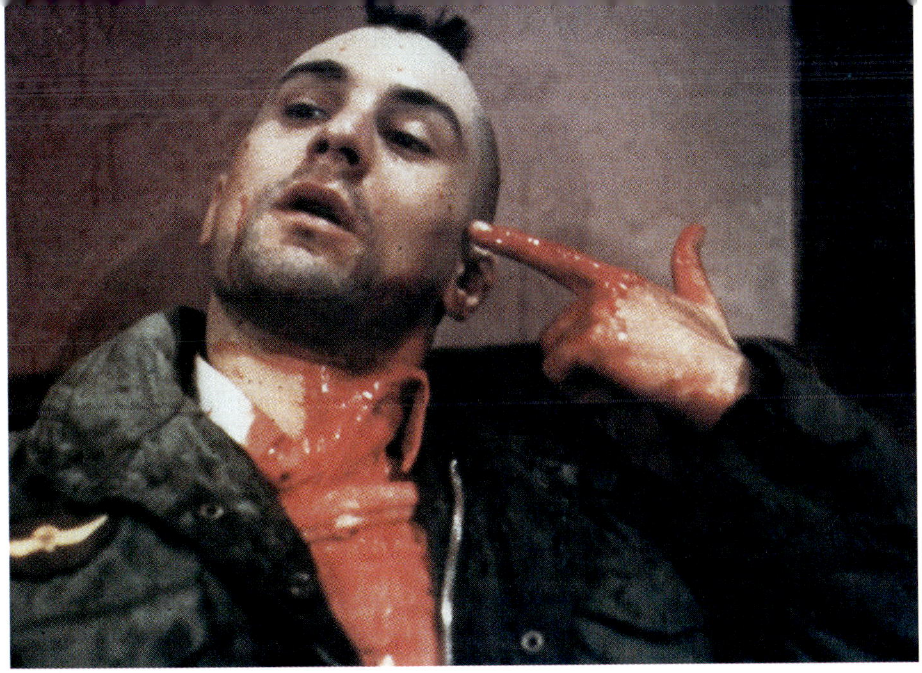

Figure 7.11 Surrealistic Color Robert De Niro appears here as the deranged and suicidal Travis Bickle in the violent climax of *Taxi Driver*.

Surrealistic Use of Color

Surrealism is a dramatic or cinematic technique that uses fantastic imagery in an attempt to portray the workings of the subconscious. Surrealistic images have an oddly dreamlike or unreal quality.

The prolonged slaughter at the end of *Taxi Driver* is separated from the rest of the film with slow-motion visuals and surrealistic color (Figure 7.11). As screenwriter Paul Schrader describes it:

> The movie goes out of whack at that point. The color goes crazy. You no longer hear the sounds of the street. You get into that weird slow motion. *Intentionally* out of whack.[7]

As Travis Bickle (Robert De Niro) shoots the pimp on the doorstep and enters the building, the dominant color becomes a gritty, sleazy yellow in hallways and rooms dimly lit by naked tungsten bulbs. In this surreal dim yellow glow, the film takes on a nightmarish quality: Even the blood, which is literally everywhere, seems gritty and dirty, more real than real. The creative genius behind this extremely powerful effect was neither director Martin Scorsese nor his cinematographer, Michael Chapman, but the Motion Picture Rating Board:

> [A]bsurdly, it made Scorsese overlay the final bloodbath with a chemical tint so that it would look less realistic. The black-red gore turns out to be almost more powerful than the splattering ketchup of the original. Scorsese thinks it is worse.[8]

Figure 7.12 Offensive Colors Jack Nicholson appears in sartorial splendor as the Joker in *Batman*.

Leitmotifs in Color

Directors may employ colors associated with given characters for a kind of trademark effect. Robert Altman used this technique in his hauntingly beautiful *3 Women*. In practically every scene, Millie Lammoreaux (Shelley Duvall) is dressed in yellow or yellow in combination with another color. Pinky Rose (Sissy Spacek) dresses, as her name implies, in pink. Willy Hart (Janice Rule) wears muted colors, mostly purples, blues, and grays, throughout. As the film progresses and Millie and Pinky undergo a Bergmanesque role reversal, Pinky's pinks go to reds as her personality becomes dominant, and Millie's bright yellows are subdued. All retain something close to their basic colors until the film's puzzling end, when all three characters merge together into a monochromatic harmony. Millie has taken over the role of Willy as mother figure and adopted her style of dress and manner; Pinky has reverted to childhood and acts like a ten-year-old girl. But all the colors are now muted tints of gray and blue, as if to suggest that all three characters have lost what little individuality or sense of self they ever had.

The clashing, garish colors of the Joker's costume in *Batman* help to reinforce his personality (Figure 7.12). As if his evil deeds and twisted mind aren't villainous enough, he also offends us with his green hair, bright orange shirt, purple jacket, and bright red lips. The colors of his outfit also serve to set him apart from the very conservative Batman costume: a rich, dark, and very formal blue accented by a touch of yellow. In his Euro-gore classics such as *Suspiria*, Dario Argento also uses color intensely.

Figure 7.13 The Golden Hour Cinematographers love to shoot during "the golden hour," the period just before sunset, when the light has a golden glow and strong side lighting can create a romantic mood, as in these scenes from *A Room With a View* (top left) and *Ever After* (bottom). Natural backlighting can also be used to achieve a kind of halo effect, seen here highlighting the pure and honest "girl next door" (Glenn Close) in *The Natural* (top right).

Color to Enhance Mood

In his beautiful tone poem *A Man and a Woman*, French director Claude Lelouche experimented with a variety of film stocks, switching from full realistic color to monochromatic scenes in sepia and blue gray, created by printing black and white on colored stock. Although the scenes depicting the woman's idealized memories of her dead husband (a movie stuntman) are consistently filmed in Hollywood color, the transitions from color to black and white throughout the rest of the film follow no logical formula. Nevertheless, these color transitions blend in perfect harmony with the musical score to enhance the overall romantic mood of the film. John Woo utilizes subtle colors to build empathy for his protagonists (Figure 7.13).

Figure 7.14 Prevailing Shadows Like that of its comic book model, the look of *Batman* is dominated by dark blue and black shadows.

Comic Book Color

For comic book–based *Batman*, production designer Anton Furst constructed a Gotham that became the single most powerful character in the movie, a personification of contemporary corruption and decay. Vertical towers, domes, and spires reach high into a polluted sky above a base of sewers and claustrophobic alleys, creating a unique architectural style that might best be labeled Deco-Gothic. Sets are angled and lighted for a *film noir* effect and are further distorted by high and low camera angles and harsh side lighting from unseen sources. Deep blue black shadows prevail, and the browns and grays of brick and concrete are muted, totally without warmth (Figure 7.14). Gray smoke and white steam complete the image of pollution and total corruption. Even the occasional bright spot signals corruption, like the brilliant splash of red in a sleazy street girl's outfit or the sickly pulsing pinkish glow of a dirty neon sign. So pervasive is the atmosphere created by the set that one cannot help but agree with sniggering mobster Jack Napier (Jack Nicholson) when he says: "Decent people shouldn't live here. They would be happier someplace else."

Figure 7.15 Comic Strip Colors To achieve a Sunday funnies look for *Dick Tracy,* cinematographer Vittorio Storaro limited himself to seven primary and secondary colors and gave a special color emphasis to each character. Blue, indigo, and violet—colors that Storaro says "belong on the inside of our subconscious"—suggest the dark side of the assembled gangsters in this shot.

Comic Strip Color

Whereas *Batman* was based on a comic book with relatively sophisticated and subtle color treatment, Warren Beatty's *Dick Tracy* was based on a Sunday-paper comic strip in which bold, primary colors prevail. To achieve this look, Beatty and cinematographer Vittorio Storaro decided to shoot the picture in seven primary and secondary colors, controlling the color by using painted backdrops (called *mattes*) behind the live action. The overall effect is unique (Figure 7.15). The primary colors—red, blue, and yellow—almost explode from the screen; wet city streets glow crimson, blue, and purple. As Storaro tells it, each color choice was carefully thought out, especially in developing what he calls a "dramaturgy of color" for the characters:

> Tracy, with his yellow raincoat and yellow hat, represents one side of the color spectrum: light, day, sun. Tess is mainly represented by orange, a warm color. Red is the Kid. They face the opposite side—Big Boy, Breathless, Pruneface—who belong on the inside of our subconscious, which is blue, indigo, violet. So the story of Dick Tracy and Breathless is really an impossible communion between the sun and moon, day and night, good and evil.[9]

Painterly Effects in Color

More and more directors and cinematographers are beginning to think of filming as being similar to painting. In addition to their attempts to achieve **painterly effects** with lighting, a great deal of experimentation is being done to create a kind of palette in color film, so that the actual nature of the color can be mixed to achieve the same kinds of effects that artists achieve with subtle blendings of the colors on the palette. In *What Dreams May Come*, Vincent Ward takes this kind of effect one step further: When the protagonist, Robin Williams, walks through a beautiful Monet-like landscape, he discovers that its colors literally become oil paints.

In *Moulin Rouge* John Huston attempted what he called "a wedding of black and white and color" in an attempt to give the entire film the look of a Toulouse-Lautrec painting. To achieve this look, it was necessary to flatten the color (rendering it in planes of solid hues) and eliminate highlights and the illusion of three-dimensionality created by the lighting of rounded, three-dimensional forms. He achieved this by using a filter that was designed to simulate fog in exterior scenes and by adding smoke to the set so that a flat, monochromatic quality prevailed. As Huston puts it: "It was the first picture that succeeded in dominating the color instead of being dominated by it."[10] Huston further experimented with color in *Reflections in a Golden Eye*, where an amber golden look was given to the whole picture through a laboratory process. Studio heads, however, did not like the golden look and released the film without the effect.

Because painters are often associated with certain periods, filmmakers have often attempted to achieve a sense of time past by using the look of a well-known painter of the period. Franco Zeffirelli created a fairly effective sense of time past by filtering *The Taming of the Shrew* through a nylon stocking, muting colors and softening sharp edges so that the whole film resembles a faded Rembrandt painting. Some scenes in Barry Levinson's *The Natural* had the look of Edward Hopper paintings, and both *Biloxi Blues* and *Radio Days* were bathed with a warm, yellow-brown, nostalgic glow, approximating a Norman Rockwell look (Figure 7.16).

For some cinematographers, the perfect period look would be achieved by capturing on film the sepia-tone look of faded photographs. But as Laszlo Kovacs, cinematographer of *F.I.S.T.*, tells it, the sepia-tone look is difficult to achieve:

> I would have loved if somehow we could have discovered how to do sepia in color. That's the hardest thing to do; I mean, it's easy to go to amber or to yellowish and reddish tones, but sepia is a brown which is not a color. It's a dirt. It's a combination of everything. Somehow it's almost impossible to create that sepia tone, all that faded quality. It's always a problem. You see a period picture, and it looks too new. It should look as if it was really made in the thirties and was pulled out from a drawer, like old faded prints.[11]

Figure 7.16 Painterly Effects In *Biloxi Blues* (top left), Mike Nichols obtained a Norman Rockwell look by applying a warm, yellow-brown nostalgic glow. Many directors, including Franco Zeffirelli in *The Taming of the Shrew* (top right), Shekhar Kapur in *Elizabeth* (bottom left), and John Madden in *Shakespeare in Love* (bottom right), have re-created the look of a faded Rembrandt painting, and captured a sense of time past, by muting rich colors and softening the focus. (Also see Figure 7.10 for Vincent Ward's remarkable French Impressionist-inspired view in *What Dreams May Come.*)

Figure 7.17 Ironic Use of Color A warm spiritual glow from the sanctuary lights and stained-glass windows permeates the climactic baptismal scene as Michael (Al Pacino) and Kay (Diane Keaton) Corleone serve as godparents to their infant nephew in *The Godfather*. The scene is intercut with scenes of brutal killings ordered by Michael as his first step in taking over the family business.

Ironic Use of Color

Directors usually plan to use colors to match the mood of their film, but sometimes they choose color effects that go against the emotional tone of the film (Figure 7.17). John Schlesinger has achieved effective results with both approaches:

> In *Midnight Cowboy*, we wanted a garish street look, with the neon signs resonating—it was grittier, grainier. But with *[Day of the] Locust*, Conrad [cinematographer Conrad Hall] and I wanted a much more golden glow over a fairly dark story.[12]

Color patterns are also used ironically in Woody Allen's *Annie Hall* in the flashbacks to Alvy's neurotic childhood, which are imbued with glowing, warm nostalgic tones.

Special Color Effects

A great many of the uses of color are so subtle that they create the desired effect but escape our conscious notice unless we are looking for them (Figure 7.18).

Figure 7.18 Another Time, Another Place To be believable, fantasy films often require a special look to convince us that such events really happened in another time, another place. To achieve this look in *Babe: Pig in the City,* George Miller commandeered a rainbow of colors and set his tale in an urban landscape that magically synthesized elements of many great cities of the world.

In *Deliverance*, for example, director John Boorman and cinematographer Vilmos Zsigmond found that the colors of the bright green leaves as naturally recorded on the film were too cheerful looking. To remedy this, they combined a black-and-white print with a color print to create a sufficiently dark and foreboding woods.

In Kathryn Bigelow's *Near Dark*, the vampire clan must avoid the sun, which literally roasts them alive, so much of the action of the film takes place at night. Cold colors, especially a muted blue, predominate. In one scene, however, when the vampires are attempting to escape from the sunrise, the unhealthiness of the sun (to them) is shown by coloring it a poisonous yellow green.

Colorization

In recent years, one of the most controversial issues facing the film industry has been **colorization**—the computerized coloring of older black-and-white films for use on television and for sale and rental on videocassette. The battle lines were drawn with actors, directors, and writers on one side and companies such as the Turner Broadcasting System, Color Systems Technology, and CBS/Fox Video on the other. The creative and commercial sides of the film industry divided on the questions of art versus profit, but both sides seemed to feel they had too much to lose to back down from their stands on the divisive issue. Creative forces were concerned with protecting the integrity of their work. Orson Welles inserted a clause in his will in an attempt to protect *Citizen Kane* from colorization. However, on the commercial end, huge financial investments have been made in the coloring process. Adding color to a black-and-white feature can cost from $2,000 to $3,000 per minute and run in excess of $250,000 per feature. And with more than 17,000 black-and-white films in the public domain, colorization could involve the expenditure of millions of dollars.

Proponents of colorization argue that most young adults have grown up in a world dominated by color television and that a large part of today's viewing audience prefers to see color movies rather than black-and-white ones. Proponents have taken polls to prove support for their theory, although opponents of colorization claim those limited polls are not indicative of the wishes of the majority of viewers. The people who actually distribute the films—video retailers and TV and cable programmers—have not yet rendered their verdict on the matter. Although color films on videocassette do seem to sell better than black-and-white ones, some retailers point out that the difference could be related to the age of the black-and-white films rather than to the lack of color.

The real dispute between the creative and commercial interests over colorization appears to center on the issue of ownership versus creative rights. The commercial (copyright) owners of films claim the right to colorize their property. The artists (writers, directors, and actors) involved with those same films claim the right to prevent what they consider desecration of their art. To confuse the matter even further, colorers are insisting that they also are artists and that the coloring process itself is an art form.

This last assertion naturally leads to assessment of the quality of the coloring process. In the case of some films (especially musicals and comedies), fans of colorization claim it adds to their enjoyment. But opponents of colorization say that many of the colorized films have a tinted look and that faces often take on an orange-yellow cast. The major trouble with the colorization process is the rendering of skin tones, especially on the faces of women. In the black-and-white version of *Casablanca*, for example, the lighting makes Ingrid Bergman's face literally glow with a kind of translucent beauty, a beauty dependent on subtle highlights and faint shadows. In the colorized version, all subtlety is lost; the glow is gone; and the actress is left looking as though her face is heavily coated with liquid leg makeup. Gilbert Cates, president of the Director's Guild of America, says colorization "removes shadow and substance. . . . It really is neutering the picture."[13] Even some colorists privately agree that output often takes precedence over quality.

Another aspect of the colorization debate is the artist's intent. Proponents of the coloring process say many directors might have selected color over black and white if it had been available. Opponents like Steven Spielberg say directors chose black and white in a creative attempt to add depth and feeling to the visual image:

> In doing a black and white film, which is an artistic selection, the filmmaker had a choice. Huston was a powerful filmmaker when he made *The Treasure of the Sierra Madre*. He could have gone to the studio and said, "For a few dollars more, make it in color." He chose black and white. The same way the Academy of Motion Picture Arts and Sciences recognized black and white as distinguished from color by honoring black and white with an Oscar as well as color films with an Oscar, up to about twenty years ago. Ansel Adams would look pretty silly—a man who mastered the black and white form—with his black and white plates colored in. And I'm just saying that I'm for this: I'm for showing my children John Huston's movies—as one example—the way John Huston wanted his films to be made, not the way a corporation wanted to remake John Huston's movies. I want the Real McCoy shown to my kids.[14]

Even though colorization began in earnest and seemed to be steadily increasing, the arguments surrounding the process show some signs of abating, largely because the National Film Preservation Board, created by an act of Congress in 1988, is designating twenty-five films a year as national treasures and placing them on the National Film Registry. Copyright owners can still colorize those films, but if they do, they will have to include a statement saying that the films have been altered without the consent of the creators. It is unlikely, however, in view of the extensive financial investment already made in colorization, that the process will ever be eliminated.

Color Versus Black and White

> *I still think that black and white has a role in motion pictures, and not everything should be in color. In fact, unless the color is perfect to the idea, it can come between the beholder and the idea of the picture. One's eye can be deflected by the color. And one's*

thoughts as well. For instance, I cannot possibly see doing Freud *in color or other pictures of a deeply psychological nature. Unless the palette and the values coincide or are part of the idea, why, it's better for it not to be in color.*[15]

—John Huston, Director

In most movies . . . I have restricted myself to a color or two only. Black-and-white is like a tuxedo, always elegant. Color, if you're not careful with it, can be vulgar.[16]

—Nestor Almendros, Cinematographer

Black and white certainly has its own unique "tuxedo elegance," its own aesthetic. It is not simply a poor cousin of color but an entirely separate medium with its own strengths, its own idiosyncrasies, its own unique power to communicate. Whereas a color film can rely on the relationship of colors for effect (with very little need for shadows), black and white must rely on tonal relationships and contrasts produced by controlling light and shade. Black and white produces its strongest impact by emphasizing highlights and shadows.

Perhaps the most important element in the aesthetic of the black-and-white film is that the cinematographer is freed from the reality of color. In black and white, each scene must be reduced to shades of gray, to basic elements of shape, tone, line, and texture, producing an image that is less representational than the same scene in color:

> In contrast to the familiar look of a conventional color photograph, a black-and-white picture carries the viewer immediately into the realm of abstraction. Because it renders colors as light or dark shades of grey, giving its subject new visual identities, black-and-white film is at its best when used to interpret rather than merely record. It is superb at capturing patterns and contrasts, textures and forms, and all manner of tonal relationships, from the most powerful to the most subtle.[17]

Although the theoretical argument about the relative merits of color versus black and white is continuous, on a practical level there is no longer a real struggle. Because a vast television audience awaits almost any decent film, the great majority of films today are made in color to improve their chances for eventual sale to television.

Television has become so saturated with color that advertisers are beginning to use black-and-white commercials to catch the viewer's attention. These commercials either are completely in black and white or begin in black and white and then go to color. The most subtle effect is highlighting a single object in one color and muting everything else to black and white, such as in the ads for Lemon-Fresh Clorox (bright yellow, with lots of bouncing lemons), Nuprin (a tiny yellow tablet), Cherry 7Up (a red liquid), and Gatorade (a green liquid). Steven Spielberg employs a single muted color technique with chilling effect in *Schindler's List* in two brief scenes that emphasize Schindler's humanity. Schindler sits on horseback on a hillside watching Jews being driven from their homes in the Kraków ghetto. A beautiful little girl of five or six (a character not otherwise developed in the film) appears walking alone in the crowd, accented by a pale orange red coat, the only spot of color in the black-and-white action. The camera follows her as she slips into a vacant building, climbs the stairs, and hides under a bed as the sound of marching storm troopers grows louder. We see no more color until about an hour later in the film. With Schindler looking on again, the spot of color reappears briefly as the little girl's body, piled on top of other exhumed bodies, is wheeled by on a pushcart to be incinerated.

The apparently insatiable desire of the TV audience to see absolutely everything in color has drastically reduced the number of black-and-white films being produced. In fact, so few black-and-white films are produced today that when one does come out (like *Manhattan*, *Stardust Memories*, *Celebrity*, or *The Elephant Man*), it is praised for its daring. More than just daring is involved, however. Martin Scorsese presented some convincing arguments in his battle to film *Raging Bull* in black and white:

> Well, they came into my apartment, and I mentioned that I wanted to do the film in black and white. They said, "Black and white?" And I said yes. The reason was that five boxing films were opening: *Rocky II* or *Rocky III*, *The Main Event*, *Matilda, the Boxing Kangaroo*, and two others. They were all in color. I said, "This has got to be different." And besides that, I told them that the color stock fades. I went into the whole business, that I was very upset about the Eastman color stocks fading, the prints fading in five years, the negatives fading in twelve years—things like that. I said, "I just don't want it. I want it to be something very special. On top of that, though, it would also help us with the period look of the film." We had an idea of making the film look like a tabloid, like the *Daily News*, like Weegee photographs. That was the concept, so they talked about that, and said, "Okay, all right." They were listening.[18]

Obviously for some films black and white is simply a more powerful and effective medium than color. Of course, the director's decision to use black and white or color should be determined by the overall spirit or mood of the film. A clear demonstration of the correct use of color and black and white can be seen by comparing Sir Laurence Olivier's productions of *Henry V* (1945) and *Hamlet*. *Henry V* is a heroic, or epic, drama, much of which is set outdoors. It has battlefield action, colorful costuming, and pageantry and is ideally suited for color. The mood of the film is positive; it emphasizes the glorious, heroic character of King Henry V, who emerges victorious. *Hamlet*, in contrast, which Olivier chose to make in black and white, is a tragedy, a somber, serious play of the mind. Most of the settings are interior ones, and some scenes take place at night. The brooding, serious, intellectual quality of the hero himself has a starkness to it, a pensive gloom that, in 1947, could not have been captured nearly as well in color as it was in black and white.

By 1990, however, new technology enabled director Franco Zeffirelli to capture the mood of *Hamlet* and the coldness and starkness of medieval Denmark in color. Throughout Zeffirelli's film, starring Mel Gibson, the colors are desaturated (muted). Browns and grays predominate; often the brightest colors are natural flesh tones. Rich and elaborate regal garments are in pastel blues or heavily muted reds. Even an occasional glint of sunlight showing through narrow castle windows provides no cheer or warmth of color and approximates the effect of low-key lighting in a black-and-white film. Glimpses of green vegetation, blue sky, and the sea are so brief that they do nothing to relieve the gloom.

The overall effect of black and white can be paradoxical, for somehow it often seems more true to life, more realistic, than color—despite the fact that we obviously do not see the world around us in black and white. For example, it is difficult to imagine that Stanley Kubrick's *Dr. Strangelove* in color would have been quite as real as it is in black and white. Perhaps Mike Nichols's *Catch-22* would have been much more powerful in black and white for the same reason. The warmth of the color images in *Catch-22*—a warmth that is difficult to avoid when working with color—fights the cold, bitterly ironic tone that underlies the story. Perhaps its sense of starkness is what makes the black-and-white treatment suitable for such film subjects.

The essentially opposite effects of color and black and white might also be explained in terms of another pair of films, *Shane* and *Hud*, both of which are set in the west. Color is perfectly suited to *Shane*, a romantic western in the epic tradition set in a magnificently huge and beautiful landscape with snowcapped mountains ever present in the background. *Hud*, on the other hand, is a contemporary character study of a heel, set in a drab, barren, and sterile landscape. The film emphasizes the harsh realities and glorifies nothing; this story could find adequate expression only in black and white.

The difference in seriousness and overall tone in Woody Allen's *Annie Hall* (color) and *Manhattan* (black and white) also justifies the choices of different film types for those films. Generally, films that seem to demand color treatment are those with a romantic, idealized, or light, playful, and humorous quality, such as musicals, fantasies, historical pageants, and comedies. Also, films with exceptionally beautiful settings might be better shot in color. Naturalistic, serious, somber stories stressing the harsh realities of life and set in drab, dull, or sordid settings cry out for black and white. There are some that fall into a middle ground and can be treated equally well either way.

As experimentation continues, this difficulty will probably be overcome, for film technology has advanced rapidly in recent years. By using all the technology and know-how now available, modern filmmakers are able to create practically any color effect they want to achieve, whether it's done by special lighting, diffusion filters, or special film in the camera or by processing the film in a certain way in the laboratory. This special color effect must of course be consistent in the film from beginning to end, unless it is used only for a special segment set off from the rest of the film—like a flashback, a dream, or a fantasy.

Regardless of what has been accomplished to this point in developing the potential of the color film, there always seems to be more territory to be explored and new worlds to be discovered. A statement by Robert Edmond Jones in his essay "The Problem of Color" could well apply to the situation today:

> Color on the screen is unlike any other kind of color we have ever seen before. It does not belong to the categories of color in Nature or in painting and it does not obey the rules of black-and-white picture making.
>
> We are dealing not with color that is motionless, static, but with color that moves and changes before our eyes. Color on the screen interests us, not by its harmony but by its progression from harmony to harmony. This movement, this progression of color on the screen is an utterly new visual experience, full of wonder. The color flows from sequence to sequence like a kind of visual music and it affects our emotions precisely as music affects them.
>
> The truth is that a new form of art is about to be born into the world, an art for which there is yet no name but which holds an extraordinary and thrilling promise. Shall we call it visual opera? Color music-drama? No matter. It is enough to say that this new mobile color may quite conceivably turn out to be the art form of tomorrow.[19]

Today, filmmakers and audiences alike are becoming more sensitive to the power of color in film. Various organizations, such as the American Film Institute and the television cable channel American Movie Classics, are making extraordinary efforts to preserve the great films of the past—and especially to recapture their fading colors. Recently, for example, in preparation for yet another re-release of *Gone With the Wind*, this most popular film's Technicolor values were restored primarily through "dye transfer." Martin Scorsese has observed,

> "Color in the film is important because it reflects the drama . . . and a certain style." Scorsese says that *Gone With the Wind*'s improved look even affects the audience on an emotional and psychological level, evoking the spirit of the Old South. [He believes] "it's as important as the production design or the costuming or the direction of the film, to see it in the proper color."[20]

Questions

On Color

1. If possible, watch the most powerful or memorable moments in the film on a VCR with the color on the TV turned off. What is altered in each of the segments viewed in black and white?
2. If the film uses bright, saturated colors, turn the color down on the TV so that the colors are muted. What effect does this have on the film?
3. Is color used expressionistically anywhere in the film so that we experience the world of the film through the mind and feelings of a central character?

4. Are trademark colors used in costuming or set decoration to help us understand the personalities of any of the characters? If so, what do these colors convey about the characters?
5. Are obvious changes in color used as transitional devices in the film? If so, how effective are these transitions?
6. How important is atmospheric color in the film? Do the uses of atmospheric color reflect some purpose on the director's part? If so, what is that purpose?

On Colorization

1. If possible, watch the film in both black and white and color. How does the colorization affect your response to the film?
2. Evaluate the choice of this film for colorization. What is gained? What is lost? Is the mood or tone of the film altered by the color?

Video Exercises

Instructions for locating specific sequences are given on page 77.

1. **Color 1.** Watch the final segment of *Taxi Driver* [4900 to end; 1:38:25 to end], paying close attention to the color. Describe the quality of the color from 4900 to 5165 (1:38:25 to 1:45:40), and compare it with the color quality from 5165 (1:45:40) to the end.
2. **Color 2.** For each of these movies, *Days of Heaven*, *2001: A Space Odyssey*, *Summer of '42*, *Taxi Driver*, and *Joe Versus the Volcano*, first adjust the color and tint controls on your TV so that the image shows only black and white, and then watch the first 10 minutes. Then readjust the TV image to full, balanced color, watch the same 10-minute segment again, and answer the following questions:
   a. How is the overall effect of each segment altered by the addition of color?
   b. What colors seem to be predominant in the film? Are they generally warm or cool colors?
   c. Are the colors bright and pure (saturated) or toned down and muted (desaturated). How is this choice related to the nature of the film and the story being told?
   d. Describe specific moments in each segment where color is used to focus attention on the object of greatest interest, enhance three-dimensionality, or suggest something about a character or his or her environment.
   e. Describe specific moments in each segment where atmospheric color is emphasized. What purpose can you attribute to this emphasis?

Babe: Pig in the City (1998)
Barry Lyndon (1975)
Batman (1989)
Biloxi Blues (1988)
Blue Velvet (1986)
Bram Stoker's Dracula (1992)
Celebrity (1998)
A Clockwork Orange (1971)
The Conversation (1974)
The Cook, The Thief, His Wife, & Her Lover (1989)
Cries and Whispers (1972)
The Day of the Locust (1975)
Days of Heaven (1978)
Deliverance (1972)
Dick Tracy (1990)
Do the Right Thing (1989)
Dr. Strangelove 1964)
Elizabeth (1998)
Elvira Madigan (1967)
The English Patient (1996)
Ever After (1998)
Fargo (1996)
The Fox (1968)
The Godfather (1972)
The Godfather Part II (1974)
Gone With the Wind (1939)
Hamlet (Branagh, 1996)
Hamlet (Olivier, 1948)
Hamlet (Zeffirelli, 1990)
Howards End (1992)
Joe Versus the Volcano (1990)
Ju Dou (1990)
Juliet of the Spirits (1965)
Kundun (1997)
The Last Emperor (1987)
The Lost Boys (1987)
Midnight Cowboy (1969)
The Mask of Zorro (1998)
Mississippi Burning (1998)
Moulin Rouge (1952)
Napoleon (1927)
The Natural (1984)
The Navigator: A Medieval Odyssey (1988)
Near Dark (1987)
New York Stories: Life Lessons (1989)
Oscar and Lucinda (1997)
Pennies From Heaven (1981)
Pleasantville (1998)
Pulp Fiction (1994)
Radio Days (1987)
Raise the Red Lantern (1991)
Red Desert (1964)
The Red Shoes (1948)
Red Sorghum (1987)
Rocky IV (1985)
Ronin (1998)
A Room With a View (1986)
Schindler's List (1993)
Shakespeare in Love (1998)
Singin' in the Rain (1952)
The Taming of the Shrew (1967)
Taxi Driver (1976)
3 Women (1977)
2001: A Space Odyssey (1968)
The Umbrellas of Cherbourg (1964)
What Dreams May Come (1998)
The Wings of the Dove (1997)
The Wizard of Oz (1939)

Chapter 8

Sound Effects and Dialogue

In motion pictures both image and sound must be treated with special care. In my view, a motion picture stands or falls on the effective combination of these two factors. Truly cinematic sound is neither merely accompanying sound (easy and explanatory) nor the natural sounds captured at the time of the simultaneous recording. In other words, cinematic sound is that which does not simply add to, but multiplies, two or three times, the effect of the image.

—Akira Kurosawa, Director

Sound and the Modern Film

Sound plays an increasingly important role in the modern film because its here-and-now reality relies heavily on the three elements that make up the soundtrack: sound effects, dialogue, and the musical score. These elements add levels of meaning and provide sensual and emotional stimuli that increase the range, depth, and intensity of our experience far beyond what can be achieved through visual means alone.

Because we are more *consciously* aware of what we see than of what we hear, we generally accept the soundtrack without much thought, responding intuitively to the information it provides while ignoring the complex techniques employed to create those responses. The intricacy of a finished soundtrack is illustrated by composer-conductor Leonard Bernstein's description of the sound mixer's contribution to a single scene from *On the Waterfront:*

> For instance, he may be told to keep the audience unconsciously aware of the traffic noises of a great city, yet they must also be aware of the sounds of wind and waves coming into a large, almost empty church over those traffic noises. And meantime, the pedaling of a child's bicycle going around the church must punctuate the dialogue of two stray characters who have wandered in. Not a word of that dialogue, of course, can be lost, and the voices, at the same time, must arouse the dim echoes they would have in so cavernous a setting. And at this particular point no one (except the composer) has even begun to think how the musical background can fit in.[1]

Five different layers of sound are at work simultaneously in the brief scene that Bernstein describes, and each one contributes significantly to the total mix. But compared to many scenes in the modern film, the sounds in *On the Waterfront* are simple and traditional. They are not nearly as complex as the soundtrack for *Raging Bull,* considered a landmark in film sound.

The fight scenes in *Raging Bull* were extremely powerful, requiring the layering of as many as fifty sounds to create the final effect. As sound man Frank Warner (working in part as a **foley artist** to add effects during postproduction) tells it:

> It was done in combining sounds. A very basic part of the punch is hitting a side of beef—that's always been used from Day One. That could be your basic beat, but then you can go from there. When a guy is hit and you see it just ripping, tearing the flesh, you can take a knife and stab and you get a real sharp, cutting sound. As the flesh gave away, water would have been added to the punch. The splatter was all done separately.[2]

Unrecognizable animal sounds and abstract bits and pieces of music were also part of the mix. For the high-velocity delivery of punches, Warner blended jet airplane sounds and the "wwwwhhhooooosssh" of arrows slowed down (Figure 8.1).

Figure 8.1 Mixing His Punches Sound man Frank Warner combined as many as fifty different sounds to create the effects of Jake La Motta (Robert De Niro) delivering, landing, and receiving punches in *Raging Bull*.

Filmmakers can also take advantage of digital recording technology to combine and process sounds, creating aural environments that heighten the viewer's emotional response to a scene. For example, sound editor Cecilia Hall combined as many as fifteen different layers of sound—including animal screams and trumpets—to create the fighter jet sounds in *Top Gun*.

The modern soundtrack demands so much of our conscious attention that if we want fully to appreciate a modern film, we should perhaps be prepared as much to hear the film as to see it.

Dialogue

A major part of our attention to sound in the modern film is naturally directed toward understanding the dialogue, for in most films dialogue gives us a great deal of important information. Film dialogue is different from stage dialogue, and we need to be aware of the unique characteristics of film dialogue.

Dialogue in a typical stage play is an extremely important element, and it is essential that the audience hear almost every word. Thus stage actors use a certain measured rhythm, carefully speaking their lines in turn and incorporating brief pauses in the question–response pattern so that the person occupying the worst seat in the house can hear each line clearly. Because film dialogue can be heard distinctly in every theater seat, this limitation does not apply to film, and dialogue can be treated much more realistically in the movies than onstage.

In *Citizen Kane*, for example, Orson Welles employed the overlapping dialogue, fragmented sentences, and interruptions common to everyday conversation without loss of essential information or dramatic power. This was achieved, as it is now in most films, through careful microphone positioning and recording, skillful editing and mixing of the recorded sound, and subtle variations in sound quality (volume, clarity, reverberation, and tonal qualities). Through such means, the modern filmmaker creates the impression of a highly selective ear turned to what it wants or needs to hear. The most important sounds are singled out, emphasized, and made clear; those of less importance are blurred or muted.

Film dialogue can also be delivered at a much more rapid pace than can stage dialogue. Director Frank Capra put this capability to good use in *Mr. Smith Goes to Washington* and *Mr. Deeds Goes to Town*. He used compressed, machine-gun-paced dialogue in phone conversations that get necessary but nondramatic exposition out of the way so he could get down to the serious business of telling his stories.

The old adage that a picture is worth a thousand words is especially true in film. Filmmakers must, first of all, use dialogue with great restraint to avoid repeating what has already been made clear visually. Furthermore, film's dramatic power and cinematic qualities are both diminished if dialogue is used to communicate what could be expressed more powerfully through visual means. In some cases, the most dramatically effective results are achieved through sparse or monosyllabic dialogue, and in a few films, dialogue is dispensed with entirely. This is not to say that dialogue should never dominate the screen. But it should do so only when the dramatic situation demands it. As a general rule, dialogue in film should be subordinate to the visual image and should seldom assume the dominant role of dialogue on the stage.

Three-Dimensionality in Sound

In *Citizen Kane* (1941), which is generally conceded to be the first modern sound film, Orson Welles created a strong impression of three-dimensional sound without the benefit of the multiple soundtracks and speakers required for true stereo. Perhaps more conscious of the importance of sound and its potential for subtleties because of his radio experience, Welles achieved this effect by varying the sound quality (volume, clarity, reverberation, and tonal qualities) of voices and sound effects to reflect their relative distance from the camera. A sense of aural three-dimensionality was achieved to match the three-dimensional image of Gregg Toland's deep-focus cinematography. This three-dimensionality was achieved on one track (monaural sound) by making voices and sounds sound close up or far away—without the left and right separation of stereo (which is achieved by recording on two separate tracks and then using two or more speakers to play back what was recorded).

In 1952, true three-dimensionality of sound was achieved by combining the techniques pioneered by Welles with a six-track stereophonic system—in the triple wide-screen *This Is Cinerama.* A four-track system was introduced to match the Cinemascope image of *The Robe* in 1953. But as the number of wide-screen films being produced declined and the studios and independent producers returned to the standard screen format, the interest in stereophonic sound declined also.

In the mid-1970s, a different attempt was made to achieve spectacular sound effects in theaters with Sensurround. The Sensurround system derived its sound from two closet-size speaker cabinets located at the rear corners of the theater. These powerful speakers were designed to literally shake the entire theater, but the system was used for relatively few films, such as *Earthquake* (1974) and *Midway* (1976). In *Midway,* the rear speakers effectively provided a realistic 360-degree sound environment by using techniques such as the following: The camera, positioned on one side of an aircraft carrier, looks up toward a kamikaze plane diving toward the carrier. The soundtrack in front grows louder until the plane roars right overhead. Then the huge speaker boxes in the rear take over to complete the roar and give us the sounds and shock waves of the explosion on the deck behind us.

At about the same period (1974), the Dolby system was introduced. An audio recording system that reduces background noise and increases frequency range, it has been combined with a system called "surround sound" from Tate Audio Ltd. to produce a multitrack stereophonic system for theaters. **Dolby-Surround Sound** employs an encoding process that achieves a 360-degree sound field and creates the effect of a greater number of separate speakers than are actually required. It has been used with great power and effectiveness in recent films, achieving the effect of hissing snakes all around us in *Raiders of the Lost Ark* and the cheering fight crowd, managers, and trainers in *Raging Bull.*

In *Das Boot,* an incredible sense of a 360-degree sound environment is created both inside the confined quarters of the German U-boat and in the sea around and above it. The quality of each sound is unique: a strumming guitar, a radio, a phonograph, men talking and laughing, clanging horns, engine noises—all seem to come from different sources and give us a sense of being there. *Das Boot* is a film full of listening. The crew first strains to hear the creaking of

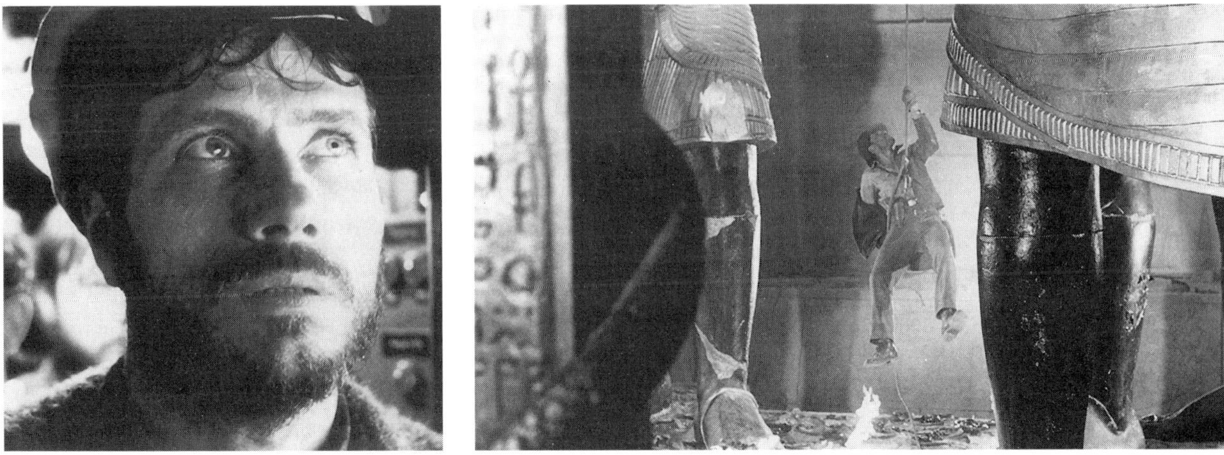

Figure 8.2 Three-Dimensional Sound Thanks to the three-dimensional sound effects in Dolby stereo, destroyers rumble menacingly overhead in *Das Boot* and snakes hiss all around us in *Raiders of the Lost Ark*.

collapsing bulkheads on a ship they sink; then later, with the sub nestled on the bottom in hiding from a destroyer on the surface, the crew grows deathly quiet so as not to give away the sub's position. Their silence emphasizes every noise, which the Dolby stereo locates with pinpoint accuracy. We hear the destroyer's pinging sonar and every turn of its screw as it passes overhead, growing louder and then softer. As the sub sits on the bottom, at a great depth, we hear the rivets straining, then popping, and the sound of water spraying in as parts of the boat fail to withstand the tremendous pressure (Figure 8.2).

Ironically, despite the care lavished on crafting soundtracks these days, many filmgoers never fully experience them. About 60 percent of the theaters in the United States (most of which are older theaters and small suburban theaters) simply have not had the capability to reproduce the quality or the dimensions of the sound recorded in the films they show. Still, according to *Newsweek*, this situation recently has been "improving":

> Six years ago, only a few hundred theaters were equipped to play ear-blasting digital sound. Then "Jurassic Park" was offered to theaters on condition that they upgrade their sound equipment. Today nearly 20,000 can handle state-of-the-art digital. The result has been a kind of free market of noise, with filmmakers competing for sounds grabby enough to match their eye-popping visuals. . . . If we shiver with pleasure when remembering movie sounds from long ago—the newspapers rustling during the breakfast montage in "Citizen Kane," or the recalled waltz music in "Shadow of a Doubt"—it isn't because they were loud, it's because they were pregnant with atmosphere and character.[3]

Visible and Invisible Sound

In the early days of the sound film, the emphasis was placed on recorded sound that was synchronized with the visual image. As the popular term *talking pictures* indicates, the audience of that time was fascinated by the reproduction of the human voice. Although sound effects were employed, they were generally limited to sounds that would naturally and realistically emanate from the images on the screen—that is, to **visible sounds.**

Although the dramatic power of the human voice and the sense of reality conveyed through sound effects certainly contributed new dimensions to the film art, the tight link between sound and image proved very confining, and filmmakers began to experiment with other uses of sound. They soon discovered that **invisible sound,** or sound emanating from sources *not* on the screen, could be used to extend the dimensions of film beyond what is seen and to achieve more powerful dramatic effects as well. Once they realized the unique and dynamic potential of invisible sound, they were able to free sound from its restricted role of simply accompanying the image. Invisible sounds now function in a highly expressive or even symbolic way as independent images, sometimes carrying as much significance as the visual image, and occasionally even more.

This creative use of invisible sound is important to the modern film for a variety of reasons. To begin with, many of the sounds around us in real life are invisible, simply because we find it unnecessary or impossible to look at their sources. Realizing this, filmmakers now employ sound as a separate storytelling element capable of providing information by itself. Sound used in this way complements the image instead of merely duplicating its effects. For example, if we hear the sound of a closing door, we can tell that someone has left the room even if we do not see an accompanying image. Thus the camera is freed from what might be considered routine chores and can focus on the subject of the greatest significance. This is especially important when the emphasis is on reaction instead of action, when the camera leaves the face of the speaker to focus on the face of the listener.

In some cases invisible sound can have a more powerful effect alone than would be possible with an accompanying image. The human mind is equipped with an eye much more powerful than that of the camera. An effective sound image can trigger a response in our imagination much stronger than any visual image. In the horror film, for example, invisible sounds can create a total, terror-charged atmosphere. Story elements that heighten and intensify our emotional response—the clank of chains, muffled footsteps on a creaking stair, a stifled scream, the opening of a creaking door, the howl of a wolf, or even unidentifiable sounds—are much more effective when the sources are *not* seen (Figure 8.3).

As demonstrated by the description of the scene from *On the Waterfront* given at the beginning of this chapter, invisible sounds (such as the sounds of

Figure 8.3 Off-Screen Sound In *M,* an early sound film, an inventive use of off-screen sound builds mystery and suspense as the child killer (Peter Lorre) announces his presence by whistling bits of a classical theme before he appears on the screen.

city traffic, wind and waves, and the child's bicycle) are routinely used to intensify the filmgoer's sense of really being there. And by encircling the viewer with the natural sounds of the scene's immediate environment, the soundtrack suggests a reality beyond the limits of the visual frame. In some films, however, realistic sounds that naturally occur in the story's environment may be distracting for the audience and must be eliminated to maintain the film's focus. Sound editor Skip Lievsay has used this approach in his work on several films for director Spike Lee:

> Quite often with Spike's movies we don't really have nominal city sounds. We don't have a lot of traffic, we do not have any sirens unless you see police cars no crying babies, no screaming, no shouting matches, because as much as they are a part of ordinary life in the city, they're too dramatic, and it's too distracting to have to sort out whether or not dramatically we want to hear those reminders of where we are. The relationship in Spike's movies is more between the people than between the people and their environment. All of his films have very specific scenes that are about the relationship between the people and the environment. In those scenes we use those sounds, but for the rest of the time we try not to use them at all.[4]

In comedy, sound can effectively substitute for the visual image and is usually used to depict comic catastrophes set up and made completely predictable through visual means. For example, in a scene picturing a crazy inventor trying out a homemade flying machine, the picture may show the launching and then let the soundtrack illustrate the predictable crash. A dual purpose is achieved here: Our imaginations intensify the humorous effect of the crash by forming their own picture of it, while the camera focuses on the reactions registered on the faces of the onlookers, which become the focal point of comic interest. Such use of sound also has clear practical benefits, considering the danger to the stuntman and the destruction of expensive properties that go along with showing the crash visually. If sound is used for the crash, the would-be pilot needs only to stagger on-screen, battered and dirty, draped in a few recognizable fragments of the plane.

Thus, sound effects achieve their most original and effective results not through simultaneous use with the visual image but as independent images, enhancing and enriching the picture rather than merely duplicating it.

Points of View in Sound

In a film shot from the **objective point of view** the characters and the action of a scene are perceived as if by a somewhat remote observer who looks calmly on the events without becoming emotionally or physically involved. Camera and microphone perceive the characters externally, from the sidelines, without stepping in to assume the role of participants. The **subjective point of view,** in contrast, is that of one who is intensely involved, either emotionally or physically, in the happenings on the screen. In the completely subjective view, camera and microphone become the eyes and ears of a character in the film; they see and hear exactly what that character sees and hears.

Because maintaining the subjective point of view consistently is difficult if not impossible in film, most directors choose to alternate between the two viewpoints, first establishing each situation clearly from an objective viewpoint, then cutting to a relatively brief subjective shot, and then repeating the same pattern. In each shot, the camera and the microphone *together* create the unified impression of a single viewpoint, so the volume and quality of the sound vary in direct relationship to camera positioning. For example, sounds audible in a subjective close-up may not be audible in an objective long shot, and vice versa. This alternation between the objective and subjective viewpoints, and the tight link between camera and microphone, is further illustrated by the workman-with-air-hammer scene described in Chapter 5:

Establishing shot: Objective camera view from street corner, focusing on a workman using an air hammer in center of street (apparent distance 50 to

75 feet). *Sound:* Loud chatter of air hammer, mingled with other street noises.

Cut to subjective view: Close-ups of air hammer and violently shaking lower arms and hands of workman, from workman's point of view. *Sound:* Hammer is almost deafening—no other sounds heard.

Cut back to objective camera: Heavy truck turns corner beyond workman, bears down on him at top speed. *Sound:* Loud clatter of air hammer, other street noises, rising sound of approaching truck.

Cut to subjective view: Close-up of air hammer and workman's hands as seen from his viewpoint. *Sound:* First only deafening sounds of air hammer, then a rising squeal of brakes mixed with hammer noise.

Quick cut to new subjective view: Front of truck closing quickly on camera from 10 feet away. *Sound:* Squeal of brakes louder, hammer stops, woman's voice screaming, cut short by sickening thud, followed by darkness and momentary silence.

Cut back to objective viewpoint (from street corner): Unconscious figure of workman in front of stopped truck. Curious crowd gathering into circle. *Sound:* Mixed jumble of panicked voices, street noises, ambulance siren in distance.

Sometimes the soundtrack is used to communicate what goes on in a character's mind. When that is the case, the link between camera and microphone is slightly different. The camera usually only suggests the subjective view by picturing the character's face in tight close-up and relies on the soundtrack to make the subjectivity of the viewpoint clear. Just as the image is in close-up, the sound is in close-up, too. In most cases the sound quality is distorted slightly to signal that the sounds being heard are not part of the natural scene but come from inside the character's mind. The camera also serves to make this distinction clear by focusing tightly on the character's eyes. The eyes loom large enough to fill the entire screen and thus become a window of the mind through which we read the character's inner state. The camera in such a sequence can remain in tight close-up while the soundtrack communicates the character's thoughts or sounds and voices from his or her memory. Or the sequence may merely act as a transition to a *visual* flashback. These sequences are frequently filmed in **soft focus** (a slight blurring of focus for effect), another clue to their subjective nature (Figure 8.4). These techniques are especially useful to filmmakers in presenting dreams. In *The Conversation,* when Francis Ford Coppola needs to indicate that the uptight Harry Caul (Gene Hackman) is having a feverish nightmare, the director begins with a tight shot of the character's sleeping face and then returns repeatedly to it as the dream progresses.

Unusual inner emotional states are also represented by the soundtrack through use of variations in volume, reverberation, or other distortions in the

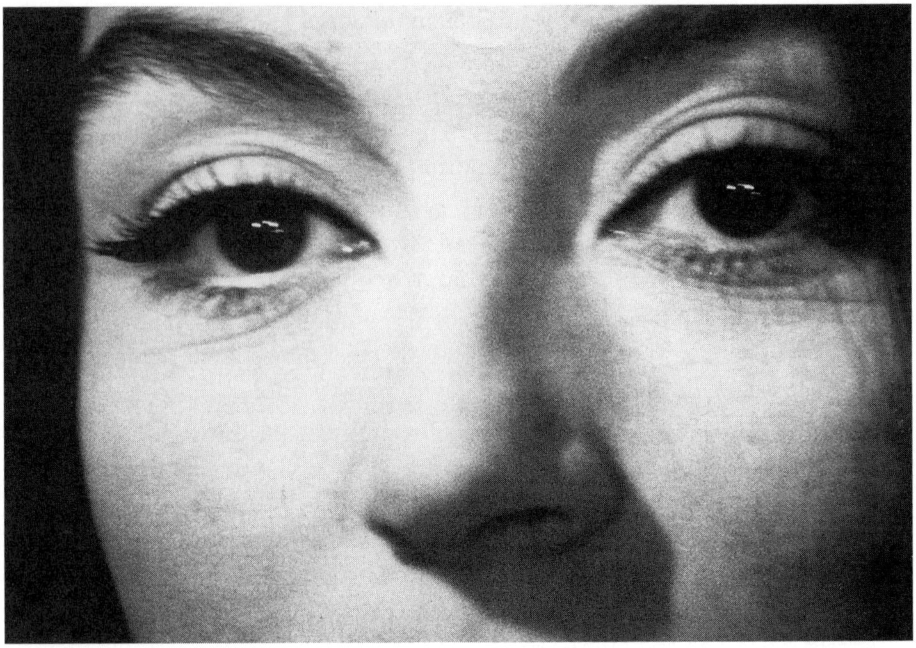

Figure 8.4 The Eyes as a Window of the Mind Director Claude Lelouch moves the camera in for a tight close-up on the eyes of Anouk Aimée as he prepares for a memory voice-over or a visual flashback in *A Man and a Woman.*

voices or natural sounds that the character hears. Physical reactions such as extreme shock, excitement, or even illness are sometimes suggested by drumbeats, which supposedly represent a high pulse rate or a pounding heart. Extreme amplification and distortion of natural sounds are also used to suggest a hysterical state of mind.

Special Uses of Sound Effects and Dialogue

The sound formulas described above have been used over and over again. Innovative filmmakers have used sound effects and dialogue creatively for a variety of specialized purposes.

Sound Effects to Tell an Inner Story

Directors manipulate and distort sound for artistic ends—to put us inside a character so that we can understand what he or she is feeling. In a powerful scene from *On the Waterfront*, Elia Kazan employs the sounds of the waterfront to dramatize the emotions of Terry Malloy (Marlon Brando) and Edie Doyle

(Eva Marie Saint). The priest (Karl Malden) has just convinced Terry to confess to Edie (whom he now loves) that he was involved in setting up the murder of her brother by corrupt union officials. The priest and Terry stand on a hill overlooking the waterfront, and when Edie appears walking toward them on the flats below, Terry hurries down the steep hill to meet her. Almost imperceptibly at first, the rhythmic hammering of a pile driver, which has been a part of the natural sound environment, grows increasingly louder as Terry approaches Edie, thus making us aware of the fear he feels about leveling with her. As he reaches the crucial part of his confession, the steam whistle on a nearby ship shrieks loudly, obscuring his words as we watch his anguished face trying to tell the story we already know. With the deafening shriek of the whistle, we are suddenly inside Edie—feeling the shock, the horror, and the disbelief of what she has just heard, as she covers her ears with her hands to protest a truth she cannot accept. The steam whistle stops just before Terry finishes his story, and as he finishes, Edie stares at him for a moment in disbelief, then turns and runs away from him in panic, her action accompanied by high, wailing violins. The scene's dramatic intensity is literally beyond words—the faces and the internalized sounds alone tell the entire story.

In *All That Jazz*, Bob Fosse takes a totally different approach in his directing of Joe Gideon's "heart-attack warning" scene. At the opening of the scene, everything is normal. Cast members for a new musical are sitting around reading dialogue from a very funny script. The entire cast periodically breaks into laughter. Suddenly, without warning, we no longer hear the laughter—we still see the faces laughing, but the sound is gone. The soundtrack carries only the close-up sounds of Joe Gideon (Roy Scheider). We hear him striking a match, his finger drumming on the table, a labored breathing, his wristwatch ticking, and his shoe grinding out a cigarette on the floor. With all sound external to Gideon cut off (despite constant visual reminders that we should be hearing it) and every close-up sound of Gideon magnified, Fosse has literally grabbed us by the ears, pulled us inside Joe Gideon's circulatory system, and sent a clear message that something's terribly wrong here. After Gideon holds a pencil in both hands behind the chair, snaps it in two, and drops the pieces, the sound returns to normal, the reading ends, and the room is vacated. The next scene shows three of the producers in the back of the cab discussing his symptoms and the fact that he is now in the hospital undergoing tests.

Distortion of Sound to Suggest Subjective States

In *When a Stranger Calls,* Carol Kane, as a teenage babysitter, receives threatening phone calls from a psychopathic killer, who repeatedly asks her, "Why haven't you checked the children?" The police finally trace the call to another phone *within* the house. Before the police can get there, the children are brutally murdered. The killer is captured and imprisoned. Seven years later, Kane is

Figure 8.5 Distortion of Sound The cold, metallic voice of the killer on the phone sets up terrifying echoes of the past for Carol Kane in *When a Stranger Calls.*

married and has two children of her own. On the evening that the killer escapes from prison, Kane's husband takes her out for a special dinner celebrating a job promotion, and they leave their children in the care of a babysitter. As they settle down to their meal in the restaurant, a waiter tells Kane that she has a telephone call at the cashier's desk. She unsuspectingly answers the phone, assuming the babysitter has called with a question. We do hear a question in the receiver—but it's the killer's voice, cold and metallic: "Have you checked the children . . . ildren . . . dren . . . ren?" The familiar but distorted voice echoes louder and louder, blending into her hysterical scream as we are suddenly yanked inside her fear and horror (Figure 8.5).

The "Personality" of Mechanical Sounds

Mechanical sounds can be integrated into the overall tone of a specific scene by giving them personalities. In *The Grapes of Wrath*, John Ford uses the different personalities of two auto horns to underscore the emotions in a scene. As the Joad family stands around the yard welcoming Tom back from prison, Tom's brother Al drives up in the old Joad truck and joins in the happy scene with a bright cheerful *uugga!* from the truck's horn. The celebration continues for a minute or so until it is suddenly interrupted by an ominous, low-pitched, and insultingly loud horn as the convertible driven by the land and cattle company

Figure 8.6 Slow-Motion Sound Unusual effects are achieved by the use of slow-motion sound as members of the James Gang are shot up by townspeople as they try to make their escape after a bank robbery in *The Long Riders.*

representative pulls up. The horn freezes the Joads as it sounds, and they wait meekly for the reminder they know is coming: They must be off the land by the next day.

Slow-Motion Sound

Walter Hill matches slow-motion sound to slow-motion action in the final shootout scene of *The Long Riders*. After robbing a bank in Northfield, Minnesota, the James Gang finds itself trapped. As gang members attempt their getaway, gunmen on top of buildings and behind barricades throw up a wall of bullets. At first, the action is a mixture of normal and slow motion. As outlaws and townsmen are wounded, the action goes into slow motion as they reel or fall, and the sound slows down. These brief, slow scenes are alternated with scenes shown at normal speed. But as the action intensifies and focuses on the outlaws as they are riddled with bullets, the *whole sequence* goes into slow-motion picture and sound. The surreal slowness of the image draws us closer to the gang members, and the slow-motion sound makes us feel their pain as the bullets tear into their flesh. The total effect is eerie, with low whistling sounds, muffled roars, grotesquely slowed horse whinnies, and low-pitch human grunts and groans (Figure 8.6).

Martin Scorsese similarly uses slow-motion sound in *Raging Bull* to portray Jake La Motta's (Robert De Niro) fatigue in a difficult fight and to isolate the effect of a single, crucial blow.

Ironic Juxtaposition of Sound and Image

Usually picture and sound work together to carry a single set of impressions. It is occasionally effective, however, to create ironic contrasts between them. In *The Grapes of Wrath*, the Joads have just stopped along the road to look down on a lush green valley of California orchards, their first look at the land of milk and honey they expected. There are cries of glee, excitement, and amazement, accompanied by birds chirping. The camera cuts to Ma Joad as she appears around the back of the truck. We know that Grandma is dead and that Ma Joad has concealed this from the others until they could reach the promised land of California. The cheerful noises that continue provide an ironic counterpoint to Ma's tired, grief-stricken face, serving to strengthen its impact.

Placing Unusual Emphasis on Sound

A director who wishes to place some unusual emphasis on sound has several options. Two obvious methods involve de-emphasizing the visual image: (1) dropping the image altogether by fading to black or (2) purposely making the image uninteresting or dull by holding a meaningless shot for a long period or by prolonging the use of **dead screen** (screen area in which there is little or no interesting visual information).

In *Reds*, to catch our attention and introduce us to the unusual device of the witnesses (old people who actually knew John Reed and Louise Bryant), director Warren Beatty starts the witnesses' testimony before the images begin. The voices start about halfway through the opening, as we watch white credits unfold over a black screen. At the end of the film, the witnesses continue their interesting and significant comments as the visual image fades and is followed by the ending credits, shown again in white against black.

In *Citizen Kane*, Orson Welles employs the dead-screen technique during one of Susan Alexander Kane's (Dorothy Comingore) opera performances. The camera cuts from the performance and begins a long, slow tilt upward, following a pair of cables up the bare gray walls behind the scenery. Faced with looking at this incredibly boring dead screen, we are forced to listen to the painfully off-key voice. The slow tilt is stretched out by the use of an optical printer just the right amount of time so that we properly appreciate our reward at the end, when the camera finally stops at the two technicians on the catwalk. We gain relief from our pain (and our suspense at where this long journey upward over the dead gray background is leading) as one of the technicians holds his nose to indicate his response to the music we have all been suffering through.

Figure 8.7 Exaggerated Sound Effects The amplified sounds of gunfire and Blanche Barrow's (Estelle Parsons) constant hysterical screaming add greatly to the intensity of action scenes in *Bonnie and Clyde*.

The simplest and most obvious way to emphasize a sound is to increase its volume. In *Bonnie and Clyde*, Arthur Penn underscores the violence by amplifying the roar of the gunfire and the constant shrieking of Blanche Barrow (Estelle Parsons) (Figure 8.7). A similar amplification of sound to underscore violence occurs in *Shane*, where gunshots and the sounds of a fistfight are exaggerated. An effective use of amplified sound occurs in the fight between Shane (Alan Ladd) and Joe Starret (Van Heflin) to see which of them will go to town for a showdown with the Ryker clan. The fight is filmed from an extremely low angle: The combatants are framed under the belly of a panicked horse. As the fighters struggle, the horse prances, and the pounding of each hoof is amplified to match its closeness to the camera. The violence panics other animals, who join in the chorus: A barking dog and a bawling cow trying to break out of her stall join in to accompany the snorts, the whinnies, and the pounding hoofs of the panicked horse. Although the sounds of the fistfight in the background are audible, they are somewhat de-emphasized by the loudness of the closer horse hoofs, but the violence of that fight is actually intensified by the exaggerated sound environment.

Moments of stark terror can also be enhanced through amplified sound. Steven Spielberg had composer John Williams use a sudden loud chord as part of one of the major scare scenes in *Jaws*, as a face suddenly appears through a hole in the bottom of the boat Richard Dreyfuss is examining. As Spielberg describes it:

> That's part of the scare. The chord, of course, comes after the face comes out. First you react to the face, then the chord comes a fraction of a second later. It's very easy to scare people with noise, to lift you from your chair with a loud sound. John Carpenter does it with his films all the time. Billy Friedkin did it in *The Exorcist*, with the bureau drawers opening—it wasn't so scary to hear the drawers opening, but he had the volume turned up all the way, and you jumped out of your seats when you heard it in Dolby Stereo.[5]

Using Sound for Texture, Time, and Temperature

In *McCabe & Mrs. Miller*, Robert Altman experimented with a new approach to dialogue and sound recording. In this and such later films as *Nashville*, *The Player*, and *Short Cuts*, he seems to be moving away from the dramatic enhancement of dialogue and sound and toward a thick, realistic sound texture in which dialogue can become a series of fragmented, blurred, and unseparated utterances, equal to but not dramatically more important than the **ambient sounds** (sounds natural to the scene's environment). By blurring the sharp edges of dialogue and thereby de-emphasizing the words, Altman increases our consciousness of the visual elements and weaves visual and aural elements into a more nearly equal blend, creating a unique texture in the film. The ambient sound is thick, rich, and detailed but not dramatically enhanced. In *McCabe & Mrs. Miller*, the stomping and shuffling of boots against a rough wooden floor are there right along with the mumbled, naturalistic dialogue. Typical of the difference in Altman's approach is a scene in which McCabe (Warren Beatty) and another man pass through a crowded saloon on their way upstairs. Someone is telling a joke at the bar, and we hear fragments of it as they pass through, but as they start up the stairs, their loud footsteps obscure the punch line.

Everything in *McCabe & Mrs. Miller* sounds real: the rain, a chair scraped across a floor, mumbled poker-game dialogue, moaning wind, a jug skidding across the ice, gunshots and their reverberation. Sound is often stacked on sound, voice on voice, but stacked in a new way so that we get a strong sense of being there—in a different place and a different time. The texture is so real that we feel the rain and the cold wind and even smell the smoke.

Sound can also be an important element in **period pieces** (films that take place not in the present but in some earlier period of history). By recording the sounds made by authentic objects from the era, filmmakers can enhance the story's credibility for the audience. Mark Mangini used this technique to add realism to the film *Kafka:*

> I spent two months in Prague recording sound and music for *Kafka*. I spent a lot of time on the set recording everything that moved so that I would have good, clean recordings of every prop. I got great recordings of old typewriters, telephones, horse-and-buggies, etc. There was even a scene that got cut out that introduced a bizarre three-wheeled motorcar that I could never have found here in the states. I recorded many things that I could never have found here, but more to the point I recorded the actual things used in the movie and recorded them in the acoustically appropriate environment as used in the film. I think this kind of recording adds a verisimilitude to the sound track that cannot be gotten in postproduction.[6]

Sound-effects editors can even influence the audience's perception of temperature. The film *Body Heat* is set in Florida, and the heat generated by both the weather and the passion of the main characters is central to the story. When the film was shot, however, Florida's temperatures were low, and a cold wind blew constantly. Sound-effects editors added the sounds of crickets, flapping palm fronds, and wind chimes to create the illusion that the film's action occurred in the intense, humid heat of summer.

Skip Lievsay also used sound to raise the temperature of *Do the Right Thing*, set in New York on the hottest day of summer:

> Certain backgrounds like a breeze in the park, nice birds, and happy things just seemed to us to be too cooling. We went with a dry trafficky sound. We did find if we used a little more top end, it would seem just a little bit hotter. For the sequence where people take showers, I recorded some sound effects, and the hottest one by far was the one that seemed the most like steam; it was a very sizzly sound. The tubby, gurgling sound was much more cooling, so we used the sizzling one instead. The dull traffic we used in the picture made that block seem more remote, almost like it was out in the desert.[7]

Sound as a Plot Device

With recent innovations in sound-recording technology have come two films that build suspense and important plot elements around recorded sound. Much in the same way that Michelangelo Antonioni used photographic techniques to intensify suspense in *Blowup*, Brian De Palma used sound-recording technology to answer a basic dramatic question in *Blow Out:* Was the sound just before a fatal car crash caused by a tire blowing out, or were there really two sounds—a rifle shot immediately followed by the blowout? A similar but more intriguing use of recorded sound occurs in Francis Ford Coppola's *The Conversation*. Gene Hackman plays a private investigator specializing in electronic listening devices. While testing some new equipment, he records a young couple's conversation, the full import of which he learns only after playing and replaying the tape and re-evaluating certain assumptions in light of discovering that the true meaning depends on the subtle emphasis on a single word (Figure 8.8).

Figure 8.8 Sound as a Plot Device A professional electronic eavesdropper (Gene Hackman) is troubled by what he has heard in a recorded conversation between the young couple pictured walking by him in this scene from *The Conversation.* The entire plot of the film hinges on interpreting subtle differences in emphasis during their brief exchange.

Sound as a Transitional Element

Sound is also an extremely important transitional device in films. It can be used to show the relationship between shots, scenes, or sequences, or it can make a change in image from one shot or sequence to another seem more fluid or natural.

A fluid and graceful transition between sequences is achieved through the slight overlapping of sound from one shot into the next. The sound from a shot continues even after the image fades or dissolves into an entirely new image. This overlapping usually represents a passage of time, a change of setting, or both. A similar effect is created by the converse—the sound of an *upcoming* sequence slightly precedes its corresponding image. In many cases, sound may overlap sound; the sound from one image fades under the rising sound of the succeeding image. This device provides a smooth flow of sound from one sequence to another when abrupt changes in sound are not desirable.

Sound links, aural bridges between scenes or sequences (changes in place or time), are created through the use of similar or identical sounds in both sequences. For example, a buzzing alarm clock at the end of one sequence becomes a buzzing telephone switchboard at the start of the next. Sound is thus used as a somewhat artificial link between the two sequences to create a sense of fluid continuity. Sometimes even dialogue links provide transition between two sequences. A question asked by a character at the close of one sequence may be answered by another character at the start of the following sequence, even though the two scenes may be set in different times and places.

Sometimes dialogue transitions are ironic, resulting in a sharp or startling contrast between the scenes being joined. Consider, for example, the effect if one scene's last line of dialogue had a character say: "I don't care what happens! Nothing on the face of the Earth could entice me to go to Paris!" and the next scene opened with the same character walking by the Eiffel Tower. Often, as in *The Graduate* and *Cabaret*, this device is used effectively along with the jump cut.

Dozens of examples of dynamic and unusual uses of sound can be found in *Citizen Kane*. Orson Welles employs a variety of sound links to blend scenes and explosive changes in volume to propel us from one scene to another.

Voice-Over Narration

The filmmaker can also employ sound that has no *direct* relationship to the natural sounds and dialogue involved in the story. A human voice off-screen, called **voice-over narration,** has a variety of functions. It is perhaps most commonly used as an expository device to convey necessary background information or fill in gaps for continuity that cannot be presented dramatically. Some films use voice-over narration only at the beginning to give necessary background, place the action in historical perspective, or provide a sense of authenticity. Others may employ voice-over at the beginning, occasionally in the body of the film for transition or continuity, and at the end.

The flavor of a novelistic first-person point of view is often provided through the use of voice-over. This can be accomplished by setting the story in a frame. A visually introduced narrator tells the story through a series of **flashbacks** (as in *Little Big Man* and *The Glass Menagerie*), or the narrator is never introduced visually but is only the voice of a participant recalling past events. In *To Kill a Mockingbird*, for example, the voice-over narration (by an uncredited Kim Stanley) is obviously by an adult relating childhood recollections, but the narrator is never pictured. The adult narrator of that film, in a soft, Southern voice, provides a sense of time and place, describing the pace and style of life in the town of Macomb. Then, by ending the introductory voice-over with "that summer I was six years old" just as Scout Finch appears on the screen, the narrator slips easily from the adult remembering the past into young Scout's viewpoint and the present tense of the film (Figure 8.9).

The narrator for *Summer of '42* performs a similar function (establishing place, time, and point of view) but comments more philosophically on the significance of the events to Hermie, the point-of-view character. Both *To Kill a Mockingbird* and *Summer of '42* employ great restraint in their use of voice-over

Figure 8.9 Voice-Over Narration—Remembering Effective and restrained use of voice-over narration provides a framework for a journey into the past in *To Kill a Mockingbird* (with an adult narrator speaking as a grown-up Scout Finch) and in *Life Is Beautiful.*

narration, as does *The Age of Innocence* (1993) in its utilization of the voice of Joanne Woodward.

The film versions of some novels must depend on voice-over to tell a story that cannot be told effectively through cinematic means. Such is the case with *The Old Man and the Sea*, where the most important part of the story takes place in the old man's mind, in his reactions to what happens rather than in the events themselves. The voice-over becomes a noncinematic compromise. Spencer Tracy, who plays the old man Santiago, simply reads passages from the novel that communicate the character's thoughts and feelings about the action.

A similar problem occurs in *Cannery Row.* John Huston's rich voice and skillful narration add a certain style and quality to the film, but the narration is forced to carry far too much of the burden. The literary style of the narration and its excessive use combine to make us feel that we're reading a movie.

In *Apocalypse Now,* Martin Sheen's narration, necessary to glue together an otherwise incoherent film, flattens the dramatic impact of the visuals by overinterpreting and overexplaining, by telling us too many things we can see for ourselves. Here the voice-over gets in the way. By telling us too much about "the horror," the film prevents us from discovering it for ourselves (Figure 8.10). As a result, we never really feel that horror. In a similar way, the added voice-over narration in the theatrical version of *Blade Runner* weakens its drama.

Figure 8.10 Voice-Over Narration as Structural Glue Director Francis Ford Coppola tried to use the voice-over provided by Martin Sheen (seen here with Marlon Brando) to plug holes in the script of *Apocalypse Now* but succeeded only in diminishing the film's dramatic punch.

Figure 8.11 Voice-Over Narration as Ironic Counterpoint In the Coen brothers' *Raising Arizona,* the marvelous, idiosyncratic voice of Hi (played by Nicolas Cage) guides us through the action, providing both gently ironic instructions for following the intricate plot and constant entertainment.

The voice-over technique is sometimes employed as an ironic counterpoint, providing a level of meaning that is in direct contrast to the image on the screen. In *Raising Arizona*, Hi (Nicolas Cage) provides a formal and stilted but touchingly unperceptive interpretation of the zany events unfolding before our eyes. As a result, we get a level of rich humor and some absurd glimpses into a totally lovable and good-intentioned criminal mind (Figure 8.11).

In *The Opposite of Sex*, the narrator, DeDee Truitt, wonderfully played by Christina Ricci, is a "trash-talking teenager from Arkansas . . . [who] chats on the soundtrack during and between many of the scenes, pointing out the cliches, warning us about approaching plot conventions and debunking our desire to see

Figure 8.12 Postmodern Film Narration Christina Ricci, as DeDee in *The Opposite of Sex,* narrates the film in voice-over and at the same time comically deconstructs the work, furnishing a wickedly delightful running commentary on its dialogue, plot, symbolism, and characterization as the movie progresses.

Figure 8.13 Narration as an Integral Part of Texture Linda Manz's poetic, ironic narration for Terrence Malick's *Days of Heaven* (1978) functions almost as a part of the musical score (top left). The personality of her voice becomes a dominant factor in the film's unique style and texture. Earlier, in *Badlands* (1973) (top right), Malick had used the same technique. In *The Thin Red Line* (1998), the director continues to utilize the voice-over, but this time with multiple speakers (bottom).

the story unfold in traditional ways." DeDee's unique voice is so strong, in fact, that Roger Ebert concludes his review of the film by observing, "I hate people who talk during movies, but if she were sitting behind me in the theater, saying all of this stuff, I'd want her to keep right on talking"[8] (Figure 8.12).

Perhaps the most powerful voice-over narration in film to date is that provided by Linda Manz for *Days of Heaven.* There is a distinctive style to her narration, a poetic rhythm, a texture that permeates the entire film. The unique vocal quality and verbal essence provide more than just the narrative glue to hold the story's structure together; combined with the strange woman-child philosophical reflections and childish utterings, they are integrated so beautifully that they become a major element of the film's unique style and texture (Figure 8.13).

Forrest Gump also provides a clear verbal essence in its voice-over. To emphasize Gump's slowness, Gump-as-character often repeats what Gump-as-narrator has just said as new scenes are introduced, contributing to the unusual blend of humor and pathos that runs through the film (Figure 8.14).

Generally, voice-over narration can be very effective if used with restraint. It is not, however, a truly cinematic technique, and overusing it can be seriously detrimental to the quality of the film.

Silence as a Sound Effect

In certain situations a short **dead track,** the complete absence of sound, may be as effective as the most powerful sound effect. The ghostly, unnatural quality of film without sound forces us to look intently at the image. The natural rhythms of sound effects, dialogue, and music become as natural to the film as the rhythms of breathing; and when these rhythms stop, we immediately develop a feeling of almost physical tension and suspense, as though we are holding our breath and can't wait to start breathing again. This effect is used to great advantage in conjunction with the freeze frame. The sudden change from vibrant, noisy movement to silent, frozen stillness can stun us for a moment.

The most common use of dead track is simply to increase, by contrast, the impact and shock effect of sudden or unexpected sounds that follow these moments of silence. In *Still of the Night,* psychiatrist Sam Rice (Roy Scheider) is following a woman he believes to be Brooke Reynolds (Meryl Streep) through Central Park. The soundtrack is alive with environmental noises: wind, muffled music, and traffic, all blended into a kind of "big-city-alive-in-the-distance" hum. As Rice walks into an underpass and stops, the soundtrack goes dead, providing a few moments of silence to set up the aural shock of a mugger's switchblade springing from its handle a few inches from his face. The opposite of this, the shock of silence after violent sound, is experienced during the moments of almost dead track that immediately follow the final fusillade in *Bonnie and Clyde.*

Figure 8.14 Repetition for Humor The title character of *Forrest Gump* (Tom Hanks) often repeats what Gump-as-narrator has just said as new scenes get under way, emphasizing the slowness that is both Forrest's problem and his charm (top left). Within dialogue, both dark humor and character are presented through repetition in the speech of Aaron/Roy (Edward Norton) in *Primal Fear* (top right) and Karl (Billy Bob Thornton) in *Sling Blade* (bottom).

Rhythmic Qualities of Dialogue and Sound Effects

Both dialogue and sound effects are important for the rhythmic patterns, or cadences, they create. These rhythmic elements often match the visual rhythms and reflect the mood, emotion, or pace of the action. Thus, the pace of the dialogue and the rhythmic qualities of the sound effects influence the pace of the film as a whole.

Questions

On Sound Effects and Dialogue

1. Where in the film are off-screen or invisible sounds effectively employed to enlarge the boundaries of the visual frame or to create mood and atmosphere?
2. What sound effects in particular contribute to a sense of reality and a feeling of being there?
3. Does the film attempt to provide a sense of three-dimensionality or depth in sound? If a stereophonic soundtrack is used, what does it contribute to the overall effect of the film?
4. Where is sound employed to represent subjective states of mind, and how effective is this use of sound?
5. Where is unusual emphasis placed on sound in the film, and what is the purpose of such emphasis?
6. Is sound used to provide important transitions in the film? Why is sound needed to provide these transitions?
7. If voice-over soundtracks are used for narration or internal monologues (thoughts of a character spoken aloud), can you justify their use, or could the same information have been conveyed through purely dramatic means?

Video Exercises

Instructions for locating specific sequences are given on page 77.

1. **Sound Effects.** Watch the indicated sequences from *On the Waterfront* [3500 to 3610; 1:00:00 to 1:03:22] and *All That Jazz* [3600 to 3740; 1:03:30 to 1:06:33]. Each sequence takes us into the mind and feelings of the characters through clever uses of sound. Describe in detail how each sequence accomplishes its goal, and explain how the two methods differ.
2. **Slow-Motion Sound.** Watch the Northfield, Minnesota, raid sequence from *The Long Riders* [4030 to 4280; 1:15:58 to 1:20:36], and describe the interaction of slow-motion cinematography and slow-motion sound. Some of the slow-motion sounds might be difficult to identify. How is this difficulty overcome?

3. **Sound Links.** *Citizen Kane* is known for its innovative use of sound for transitional purposes. Watch the following segments, and describe the methods by which sound links scenes that take place in different locations and at different points in time: [1650 to 1730; 0:22:48 to 0:24:35] and [3470 to 3525; 0:59:34 to 1:00:52].
4. **Voice-Over Narration.** Watch the first 5 minutes of each of the following films, and describe the essential differences in the narrators and the effects of their voice-over narrations in each film: *Days of Heaven, Taxi Driver, Raising Arizona, Stand by Me*, and *The Opposite of Sex.*

Films for Study

Sound Effects and Dialogue

Affliction (1998)
All That Jazz (1979)
Blow Out (1981)
Body Heat (1981)
Bonnie and Clyde (1967)
Citizen Kane (1941)
The Conversation (1974)
Das Boot (1981)
Do the Right Thing (1989)
The Exorcist (1973)
Jurassic Park (1993)
Kafka (1991)
The Long Riders (1980)
M (1931)
McCabe & Mrs. Miller (1971)
Nashville (1975)
On the Waterfront (1954)
The Player (1992)
Primal Fear (1996)
Raging Bull (1980)
Raiders of the Lost Ark (1981)
Shane (1953)
Short Cuts (1993)
Sling Blade (1996)
Still of the Night (1982)
When a Stranger Calls (1979)

Voice-Over Narration

The Age of Innocence (1993)
Apocalypse Now (1979)
Badlands (1973)
Bram Stoker's Dracula (1992)
Cannery Row (1982)
Days of Heaven (1978)
Dead Men Don't Wear Plaid (1982)
Forrest Gump (1994)
Life Is Beautiful (1998)
Mrs. Dalloway (1998)
The Opposite of Sex (1998)
Radio Days (1987)
Raising Arizona (1987)
A River Runs Through It (1992)
Stand by Me (1986)
Summer of '42 (1971)
Taxi Driver (1976)
The Thin Red Line (1998)
To Kill a Mockingbird (1962)

Chapter 9

The Musical Score

The film composer should have the confidence to use exactly what he needs and no more. He shouldn't use his theatrical license to blow the believability of the picture, and I think that believability is closely connected with understatement. The composer wants to pull the moviegoer's mind into that room that's up on the screen, into that feeling that's up there, and it can take very little to achieve that involvement.

—QUINCY JONES, COMPOSER

The Remarkable Affinity of Music and Film

Music has such a remarkable affinity to film that the addition of the musical score was almost an inevitability. Even in the earliest films, the audience would have felt a very real vacuum of silence because the pulsing vitality provided by the moving image seemed unnatural, almost ghostly, without some form of corresponding sound. In fact, so-called silent films were almost always projected with accompanying live piano, organ, ensemble, or orchestra music. So by the time it became possible to use recorded dialogue and sound effects, music had already proved itself as a highly effective accompaniment for the emotions and rhythms built into the images.

Music has made possible an artistic blending of sight and sound, a fusing of music and movement so effective that composer Dimitri Tiomkin was moved to remark that a good film is "really just ballet with dialogue." Muir Mathieson, in *The Technique of Film Music*, put it this way: "Music, having a form of its own, has ways of doing its appointed task in films with distinction, judged purely as music, and with subtlety, judged as a part of the whole film. It must be accepted not as a decoration or a filler of gaps in the plaster, but a part of the architecture."[1]

Both film and music divide time into rather clearly defined rhythmic patterns; perhaps that provides the most important common bond. There are certain natural rhythms inherent in the physical movements of many objects on the screen. Trees swaying in the breeze, a walking man, a galloping horse, a speeding motorcycle, and a machine capping bottles on an assembly line—all establish natural rhythms that create an almost instinctive need for corresponding rhythmic sounds. Another rhythmic pattern is provided by the pace of the plot, by how quickly or slowly it unfolds. Still another is created by the pace of the dialogue and the natural rhythms of human speech. Tempo is also established by the frequency of editorial cuts and the varying duration of shots between cuts, which gives each sequence a unique rhythmic character. Although editing divides the film into a number of separate parts, the continuity and the fluid form of the medium remain, because the cuts create clear rhythmic patterns but do not break the flow of images and sound.

Because music possesses these same qualities of rhythm and fluid continuity, it can be easily adapted to the film's basic rhythms, to its liquid contours, or shapes. This affinity between music and film has led us to accept them almost as unity, as part of the same package, as though music somehow exists magically alongside every film.

The Importance of the Musical Score

Although we often accept film music without question and sometimes even without noticing it, this does not mean that its contribution to the film experience is insignificant. Music has a tremendous effect on our response, greatly enriching and enhancing our overall reaction to almost any film. It accomplishes this in several ways: by reinforcing or strengthening the emotional content of the image, by stimulating the imagination and the kinetic sense, and by suggesting and expressing emotions that cannot be conveyed by pictorial means alone.

Because it has a direct and very significant effect on our reaction to film, the term *background music*, which is so often applied to the musical score, is a misnomer. Music actually functions as an integral or complementary element. Despite its direct effect on us, however, there is general critical agreement on one point: The role of music in film should be a subordinate one.

Two schools of thought exist on the proper degree of this subordination. The older, traditional view is that the best film music performs its various functions without making us consciously aware of its presence. In other words, if we don't notice the music, it's a good score. Therefore, the music for a good score shouldn't be *too* good, for really good music draws attention to itself and away from the film.

The modern view, by contrast, allows the music, on appropriate occasions, not only to demand our conscious attention but even to dominate the picture, as long as it remains essentially integrated with the visual, dramatic, and rhythmic elements of the film as a whole. At such moments, we may become conscious of how intrinsically beautiful the music is, though we should not be so moved that we lose sight of its appropriateness to the image on the screen.

Both modern and traditional views are therefore in agreement on one essential point: Music that calls too much attention to itself at the expense of the film as a whole is not effective. Regardless of the degree of subordination, a good score will always be a significant structural element, performing its proper functions in a perfectly integrated way, serving as a means to an end rather than an end itself. As composer Quincy Jones puts it:

> For me, some of the best moments in pictures come when the music is tied in so organically with the image, is so much a part of it, that you can't imagine it any other way. The themes in *The Bridge over the River Kwai* and *The Third Man* seem to come out of the tapestry of the films.[2]

General Functions of the Musical Score

The two most general and basic functions of the musical score are to create structural rhythms and to stimulate emotional responses, both of which greatly enhance and reinforce the effect of the image.

The musical score creates a sense of structural rhythm both in the film as a whole and in its individual shots by developing a sense of pace corresponding to the pace of the movement within each shot and to the pace of the editing. In this way, the composer articulates and underscores the basic rhythms of the film.

Figure 9.1 "A Sigh Is Just a Sigh" From its opening credits accompanied by Jimmy Durante's recording of "As Time Goes By," *Sleepless in Seattle* leans heavily on familiar ballads to intensify the romantic mood of individual sequences and the film as a whole.

The film score also serves to complement and enhance the narrative and dramatic structure by stimulating emotional responses that parallel each individual sequence and the film as a whole. Because even the most subtle moods are established, intensified, maintained, and changed through the effective use of film music, the musical score becomes an accurate reflection of the emotional patterns and shapes of the film as a whole (Figure 9.1). This does not mean that a film's structured visual rhythms can be separated from its emotional patterns, for both are closely interwoven into the same fabric. Effective film music therefore usually parallels one and complements the other.

The simplest and oldest method of adding music to film is simply selecting a piece of familiar music (classical, pop, folk, jazz, blues, rock, and so on) that fits the rhythmic, emotional, or dramatic demands of the sequence at hand. An excellent example of the use of familiar music was the choice of the *William Tell* Overture for the old "Lone Ranger" radio show. The classical overture not only provided a perfect rhythmic counterpart to the galloping hoof beats and served as a stimulus to the visual imagination, but also gave the program a seriousness of tone that it would not have possessed otherwise. In similar manner, Stanley Kubrick employed such diverse types of music as *Thus Spake Zarathustra*, *The*

Blue Danube Waltz, and "When Johnny Comes Marching Home" to very effective ends in *2001* and *Dr. Strangelove*.

A perfect match of song with dramatic situation—such as Steven Spielberg's choice of "Smoke Gets in Your Eyes" for the romantic dance in the firefighters' Quonset hut in *Always*—can do much to create a magic moment on film. Many directors, however, prefer to use music specially created and designed for the film—music composed either after the film and its accompanying sound-effects track are completed or while the film is being made—so that composer and director can work together in the same creative atmosphere. Many films, of course, use a combination of familiar and original music.

Film music especially composed for a film can be divided into two types.

1. **Mickey Mousing.** So named because it grew out of animation techniques, **Mickey Mousing** is the exact, calculated dovetailing of music and action. The rhythm of the music precisely matches the natural rhythms of the objects moving on the screen. This synchronization requires a meticulous analysis of the filmed sequence by the composer. Although some sense of emotional tone, mood, or atmosphere can be included in Mickey Mouse scoring, the primary emphasis is on the kinetic (the sense of movement and action) and rhythmic elements of the sequences in which the music is used.
2. **Generalized Score.** A **generalized score** (also known as an *implicit score*) makes no attempt to precisely match music and movement; instead the emphasis is on capturing the overall emotional atmosphere or mood of a sequence or of the film as a whole. Often, this is achieved through recurring rhythmic and emotive variations of a few main motifs or themes. Although basic rhythms in such scores are varied to suggest the rhythmic structure of individual action sequences, their primary function is to convey an emotion that parallels the story.

Special Functions of the Musical Score

In the modern film, music is used to perform many varied and complex functions, some of which are rather specialized. Although it is impossible to list or describe all these functions, some of the most basic ones are worthy of our attention.

Covering Weaknesses or Defects in the Film

A nonstorytelling function of the musical score is to disguise or cover up weaknesses in acting and dialogue. When such defects are evident, the director or composer can use heavy musical backing to make weak acting or banal dialogue appear more dramatically significant than it otherwise would. Television soap operas use organ music for this purpose with great frequency (and little sense of shame). Modern action films are frequently criticized for their disregard of narrative credibility, but, as producer Jerry Bruckheimer (*Con Air*, *Armageddon*) observes, a film can divert the audience's attention from such weaknesses. "Sound," he says, "carries you through moments when the action doesn't. Take away the sound and it's dead."[3] Director Martin Scorsese, in characterizing the score that Elmer Bernstein wrote for *The Age of Innocence*, sees greater complexity in the process generally:

> Film music's kind of a slippery thing. It can take hold of your ear when the rest of the movie eludes your imagination, or just doesn't have the strength to challenge it. It can overwhelm you in a great wash of sound, so dramatic inadequacies don't seem quite so treacherous. It can add punch where the story or the filmmaking craft have abandoned the drama. Or—and this is best—it can give the film another dimension, a separate signature.[4]

Heightening the Dramatic Effect of Dialogue

Music is often employed as a kind of emotional punctuation for the dialogue, expressing the feeling underlying what is said. Generally, the musical accompaniment of dialogue must be extremely subtle and unobtrusive, stealing in and out so quietly that we respond to its effects without conscious awareness of its presence. In Neil Jordan's fascinating *The Butcher Boy*, the opposite is too often true. The film, a darkly comic domestic horror story, utilizes Irish accents so thick that subtitles sometimes seem warranted. Elliott Rosenthal's score for it, though aptly indigenous, is frequently performed so loudly that the listener can barely hear the dialogue, much less understand it easily.

Telling an Inner Story

Music often moves beyond a merely subordinate or complementary role to assume a primary storytelling function, enabling the director to express things that cannot be expressed through verbal or pictorial means. This is especially true when a character's state of mind undergoes extreme and rapid changes that neither words nor action can adequately express.

A good example of the use of music to tell an inner story occurs in *On the Beach*. An American submarine captain (Gregory Peck) takes an Australian woman (Ava Gardner) to a mountain resort for a final fling at trout fishing before the lethal radioactive clouds reach Australia. The American, whose family was killed in the nuclear war, has failed to adapt to the reality of the situation and continues to think and talk of his family as though they were alive, making it impossible for him to accept the love of the Australian. The two are in their room in the lodge, listening to the dissonant, off-key voices of the drunken

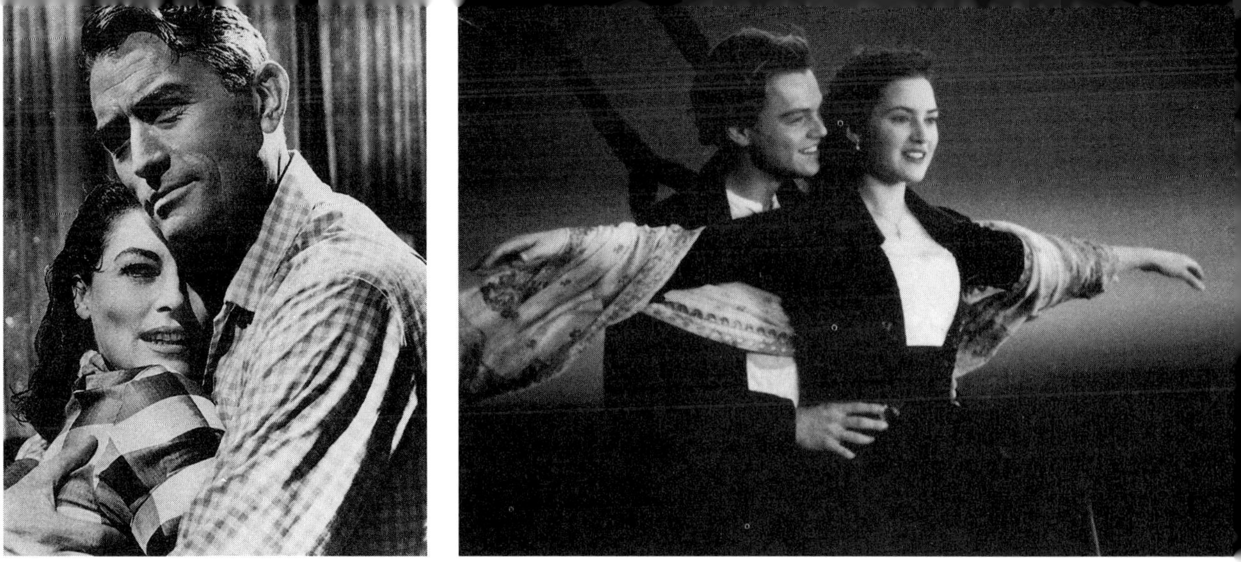

Figure 9.2 Music to Tell an Inner Story An important change in a character's state of mind is conveyed by music in this scene from *On the Beach*. A similar moment occurs in this "instructional" scene between Kate Winslet and Leonardo DiCaprio in *Titanic*.

fishermen downstairs singing "Waltzing Matilda." In an underplayed dramatic scene, Peck finally realizes the futility of his ties with the past and accepts Gardner's love. As they embrace, the loud and drunken voices become soft, sober, and melodious and blend into perfect harmony, reflecting not any actual change in the voices downstairs but the inner story of the change in Peck's state of mind (Figure 9.2). The use of massed voices of choirs to express an inner mystical or spiritual transformation (as in Rachel Portman's score for *Beloved*) is a more obvious example of the same function.

Providing a Sense of Time and Place

Certain pieces of music or even musical styles are associated with specific time periods and locations, and composers can utilize such music to provide the emotional atmosphere that a given setting normally connotes. A sense of scenic spaciousness is conveyed by standard western songs such as "The Call of the Faraway Hills" from *Shane*. Completely different qualities, such as the hustle and bustle of people having a good time and a merry, communal feeling, are conveyed by "town" or "saloon" music. Therefore, when the locale in a western changes from the range to the town or saloon, the visual transition is often preceded slightly by a switch to standard saloon music (player piano accompanied by shouting, laughter, general crowd noises, and an occasional gunshot or two). The music not only tells us that a change of scene is coming but also prepares us mentally for the visual scene before it appears, thereby serving a transitional function.

Music associated with different countries or even different ethnic groups can be used in a similar way. Certain instruments are associated with definite settings or groups of people: the zither, the mandolin, the banjo, the Spanish guitar, and the Hawaiian guitar all have fairly concrete geographical connotations, and these connotations can be varied or even changed completely by the style in which the instruments are played.

The time period of the film is also made realistic through appropriate music and instrumentation, as illustrated by the use of the quaint, old sound of a harpsichord for a period piece and otherworldly or futuristic electronic music for a science fiction film.

Evoking Nostalgic Feelings

When the time frame of a story is within most viewers' memories, recent American films have loaded the soundtrack with popular recordings from the era, thus evoking a strong "remembered flavor" of the time. Such music underscores the past-tense quality of the story for the viewer and, by triggering built-in associations, intensifies and personalizes the viewer's involvement with the story itself.

Nostalgic music is used effectively in such films as *The Last Days of Disco*, *Forrest Gump*, *The Big Chill*, *Coming Home*, *The Last Picture Show*, and *American Graffiti*, which is literally built around such music. In many cases this music is heard coming from some on-screen source such as a radio or record player, but it usually is used as part of the off-screen musical score as well. Such film scores are called "compilation" works.

Foreshadowing Events or Building Dramatic Tension

When a surprising change of mood or an unexpected action is about to occur on the screen, we are almost always prepared for that change by the musical score. By preparing us emotionally for a shocking turn of events, the score does not soften the effect of the shock but actually intensifies it by signaling its approach. In its own way, the music says, "Watch carefully now. Something shocking or unexpected is going to happen," and we respond to the musical signal by becoming more attentive. Even the fact that we know what is going to happen does not relieve the tension thus created, for suspense is as much a matter of when as of what. Music used in this way does not coincide exactly with what is happening on the screen but precedes it, introducing a feeling of tension while the images on the screen retain their calm.

Foreshadowing or tension-building music deliberately plays on our nerves in a variety of ways: by gradually increasing in volume or pitch, switching from a major to a minor key, or introducing percussion instruments and dissonance. The introduction of dissonance into a musical score that has been harmonious to that point automatically creates a sense of nervousness and anxiety. Dissonance in such a situation expresses disorder, chaos, and a breakdown of the normal patterned order of harmony, causing us to become nervous and insecure, exactly the state of mind desired for effective foreshadowing or the building of dramatic tension. For example, the famous breakfast montage from *Citizen Kane*, showing the increasing alienation between Emily and Kane over a period of years, begins with a gentle lilting waltz and ends with a dissonant and harsh variation of the same waltz theme.

Adding Levels of Meaning to the Visual Image

Sometimes music makes us see the visual scene in a fresh, unusual way by combining with the image to create additional levels of meaning. Take, for example, the opening scene in *Dr. Strangelove*, which shows a B-52 bomber refueling in flight. Extremely delicate maneuvering is required to place the refueling boom correctly, trailing like a giant winged hose from the tail of the tanker plane into the fuel-tank opening in the nose of the giant B-52 bomber, which is flying slightly behind and below the tanker. The music accompanying this sequence is the familiar love song "Try a Little Tenderness," played on romantic violins. If we are alert enough to recognize the song and think of its title, the music not only seems very appropriate to the delicate maneuvering required for the refueling operation but could also lead us to see the whole thing as a gentle love scene, a tender sexual coupling of two giant birds. Because this is the opening sequence of the film, the music also helps to establish the satiric tone that runs throughout the film as a whole.

Highly ironic levels of meaning can be achieved by using music that suggests a mood exactly opposite to the mood normally suggested by what is occurring on the screen. This technique is illustrated at the conclusion of *Dr. Strangelove*, in which the sticky-sweet voice of Vera Lynn singing "We'll Meet Again Some Sunny Day" accompanies the image of a nuclear holocaust as it destroys the world.

Characterization Through Music

Music can play a role in characterization. Mickey Mouse scoring may be used to emphasize a peculiar or rhythmic pattern set up by a certain character's physical movement. The score for *Of Human Bondage*, for example, utilizes a "disabled" theme, which rhythmically parallels the main character's limp, thus reinforcing that aspect of his character. Some actors and actresses, such as John Wayne, Robert Mitchum, and Marilyn Monroe, have distinctive walks that exhibit definite rhythmic patterns and can therefore be reinforced musically.

Instrumentation can also be used to aid in characterization in an effect that might be called **Peter-and-the-Wolfing**, scoring in which certain musical instruments and types of music represent and signal the presence of certain characters. Many films of the 1930s and 1940s used this technique, causing the audience to associate the villain with sinister-sounding music in a minor key, the heroine with soft, ethereal violins, and the hero with strong, "honest" music. Although such heavy-handed treatment is not common today, **leitmotifs** (the repetition of a single musical theme or phrase to announce the reappearance of a certain character) were staples of silent-film scores and are still employed to some extent.

Sometimes a character is complex enough to require multiple themes, as composer Jerry Goldsmith discovered while scoring *Patton:*

> [I]t was a challenge to keep the audience aware of the complexity of Patton's personality. We were dealing with three different facets of Patton's imagination. He was a warrior, a man who believed in reincarnation, and a man with stern religious beliefs. [Director] Frank [Schaffner] and I felt it was important for the music to help delineate which facet of his personality was predominant in the various scenes. Like any other art form, music has a structure, and if one wants to make a statement that will evoke emotions and recall a certain idea, it has to be planted at the beginning and developed. At the beginning of the picture I set up the reincarnation theme with the trumpet fanfare, the very first notes of music you hear. When he relived the battle of Carthagenia in his mind you heard these trumpets again, heralding this facet of his personality. The second and most obvious piece of music was the military march, and when he was commanding, this was the predominant theme—the warrior theme. The third was a chorale, which was used in counterpoint to underline his religious character, his discipline, and his determination. When he was the whole man, commanding his troops in victory, the idea was to combine all these musical elements, because he was all of these facets together.[5]

In *Citizen Kane*, composer Bernard Herrmann used two separate leitmotifs for Charles Foster Kane. One, "a vigorous piece of ragtime, sometimes transformed into a hornpipe polka," was used to symbolize the mature Kane's power. The other, "a featherlight and harmonic" theme, symbolized the simpler days of Kane's youth and the more positive aspects of his personality.[6]

A good composer may also use the musical score to add qualities to an actor or actress that that person does not normally have. In the filming of *Cyrano de Bergerac*, for example, Dimitri Tiomkin felt that Mala Powers did not really look French enough for the part of Roxanne. Therefore he Frenchified her by using French-style thematic music whenever she appeared on the screen, thus building up associations in the viewer's mind to achieve the desired effect.

Director Jonathan Demme (*The Silence of the Lambs*, *Philadelphia*) has said that, in choosing music for his films, he tries "to talk about what kind of music the characters might be hearing in their daily life. It's just more true, more subtle, and more fun, too." Like most directors, he prefers to make the choice of a film's composer as early as possible in the process and observes that "editors love to find a piece of music that works with a scene before the scene is cut."[7] For the scoring of *The Truman Show*, Peter Weir (*The Year of Living Dangerously*, *Witness*) ultimately selected German Australian composer Burkhard Dallwitz, but Weir also decided even earlier, through experimenting with a "temp" track, that certain existing pieces by Philip Glass would be included. Weir writes,

> When making a film, I play music constantly during "dailies"—the nightly screenings of the previous day's shooting. I test all kinds of music against the image, searching for the elusive "sound" of the picture.
>
> In the case of *The Truman Show*, since it is the story of a live television program, I was also determining the music that the show's creator, Christof [Ed Harris], would have chosen.
>
> The tracks that seemed to be drawing the most out of the images for me (and presumably Christof) were those of Philip Glass. . . . Complementing these tracks is a score by Burkhard Dallwitz . . . and from the moment he played back his first cue, I knew Christof would have been as delighted with the result as I was.
>
> The use of music in this film is as unusual as the concept of the movie itself. Sometimes the music is Christof's choice, sometimes it's mine![8]

One of the great mavericks of modern cinema, Robert Altman (*M*A*S*H*, *Vincent & Theo*, *The Player*, *Short Cuts*), is celebrated for his willingness to work improvisationally with actors. In *Nashville*, his 1975 epic vision of America, this director carried over his playfulness into the creation of the film's musical score. Altman asked several of the actors playing the film's twenty-four central figures (including Karen Black, Barbara Harris, and Keith Carradine, who won an Oscar for his song "I'm Easy") to compose, *in character*, songs for performance during the narrative's unfolding. Although this film-music experiment had an origin very different from that of the 1972 musical film *Cabaret*, the two works are similar in their strategy: In each case, all songs are restricted to being performed on a "stage." By the early 1970s, the tradition of the great American movie musicals—in which fictional characters suddenly burst into song in reel life—had died. By most accounts, its apex was reached, ironically, in *Singin' in the Rain*, the 1952 comic requiem for the silent-film era.

Triggering Conditioned Responses

The composer takes advantage of the fact that we have been conditioned to associate certain musical stereotypes or musical codes with certain situations. Such codes can be used with great economy and effectiveness. The sudden introduction of a steady tom-tom beat accompanied by a high, wailing, wind instrument ranging through a simple four- or five-tone scale effectively signals the presence of Indians even before they appear. The "cavalry to the rescue" bugle call is equally familiar. Such musical codes cannot be treated in a highly creative way, for to do so would cause them to lose some of their effectiveness

Figure 9.3 Traveling Music In *Breaking Away,* an excerpt from *The Barber of Seville,* a stirring opera by the Italian composer Rossini, provides traveling music for Dave (Dennis Christopher) as he prepares for the big race, and it reinforces the character's obsession with things Italian as well as underscoring the heroic effort involved in his training.

as code devices. Composers do, however, try to make them seem as fresh and original as possible.

Even stereotyped musical codes can create unusual reactions when they are used ironically. In *Little Big Man,* for example, a lively fife and drum "good guys victorious" score accompanies scenes of General Custer's troops as they brutally massacre an Indian tribe. The ironic effect catches us in a tug-of-war between the music and the image. So compelling is the rhythm of the heroic music that we can scarcely resist tapping our toes and swelling with heroic pride while our visual sensibilities are appalled by the unheroic action taking place on the screen.

Traveling Music

Film music is at its best when used to characterize rapid movement. Such music, sometimes called **traveling music,** is often employed almost as a formula or a shorthand code to give the impression of various means of transportation. The formulas are varied to fit the unique quality of the movement being portrayed. Thus, stagecoach music is different from horse-and-buggy music, and both differ essentially from lone-rider music. The old steam engine requires a different type of railroad music than the diesel locomotive (Figure 9.3). On rare occasions, traveling music performs a wide variety of functions, as is illustrated by the use of Flatt and Scruggs's "Foggy Mountain Breakdown" to accompany the famous chase scenes in *Bonnie and Clyde.* The strong, almost frantic sounds of the fast-fingered five-string banjo create a desperate yet happy rhythm that captures precisely the derring-do and spirit of the Barrow Gang, the slapstick comedy, desperation, and blind excitement of the chases themselves, and the nostalgic, good-old-days flavor of the film as a whole.

Providing Important Transitions

Music functions in an important way by providing transitions or bridges between scenes—marking the passage of time, signaling a change of locale, foreshadowing a shift in mood or pace, or transporting us backward in time into a flashback. *Citizen Kane* director Orson Welles and composer Bernard Herrmann both had experience in radio, where musical bridges were virtually mandatory. In *Citizen Welles,* Welles's biographer Frank Brady describes the effect of this experience on the use of music in *Citizen Kane:*

> The most frequent use of music in radio is to provide the transition from scene to scene or situation to situation. Even a single note becomes important in telling the ear that the scene is shifting. In film, the eye usually supplies the transition as the scene is cut or dissolves into the next. Welles and Herrmann both believed that an opportunity to include transitional music, whether it be symbolic or illustrative, to weave parts of the film together or to set it in context, should not be overlooked.
>
> As Welles worked on the script, and as he began to direct specific scenes, he could hear in his mind the suggestion of the music that should be inserted, just as he could hear the additional dialogue or the sound effects that would eventually be added. He sensed where a scene would be more effectively transferred with a musical bridge and where music would conflict with the dialogue. Pencilled notations began to fill his script indicating where music was needed. For instance, as Thompson reads Thatcher's diary and his eye travels over the parchment with old-fashioned handwriting, "I first encountered Mr. Kane in 1871 . . . ," Welles asked Herrmann for a fully melodic transition that would evoke all at once the frivolity and innocence of childhood in the snowbound winter of the Victorian era, and Herrmann responded with a piece of lyrical music that used delicate flutes leading to a blizzard of strings and harps that perfectly captured the guiltlessness and simplicity of a former age. The "snow picture" sequence as it grew to be called, became one of the most charmingly innovative transitions to a flashback ever seen or heard on film.[9]

Accompanying Titles

The music that accompanies the main titles of a film usually serves at least two functions. First, it often articulates rhythmically the title information itself, making it somehow more interesting than it is. If the music consciously captures our attention anywhere in the film, it is during the showing of the titles and credits. Second, music is especially important here, for at this initial stage it usually establishes the general mood or tone of the film. At the opening of *Bonnie and Clyde*, we start to hear a soft, sweet, lyrical Rudy Vallee pop song of the early 1930s, "Deep Night." As the volume rises from a whisper, while still photographs of both real and cinematic characters are projected, the song's melancholy at once soothes us and prepares us for the uncommon violence of the film that follows. This musical element seems to echo a visual one: The tranquil white titles slowly bleed to dark red in a foreshadowing of the movie's later, oft-surprising carnage.

Title music may even introduce story elements through the use of lyrics, as was done in *High Noon* and *Cat Ballou*. Because the opening or establishing scene is generally under way before the credits are completed, it can also dramatically or rhythmically match the visual image behind the credits.

Musical Sounds as Part of the Score

Certain sound effects or noises from nature can be used in subtle ways for their own sake, to create atmosphere in the same way that music does. Crashing waves, rippling streams, bird calls, and moaning winds all possess clear musical qualities, as do many manmade sounds, such as foghorns, auto horns, industrial noises of various kinds, steam whistles, clanging doors, chains, squealing auto brakes, and engine noises. Such sounds can be built up and artistically mixed into an exciting rhythmical sequence that, because of its naturalness, may be even more effective than music in conveying a mood.

Music as Interior Monologue

In the modern film, songs with lyrics that have no clear or direct relationship to the scenes they accompany are increasingly used as part of the soundtrack. In many cases, such songs are used to reveal the private moods, emotions, or thoughts of a central character. This was the case with the lyrics of "The Sounds of Silence" in *The Graduate* and "Everybody's Talkin' at Me" in *Midnight Cowboy*. Such lyrics function on a more or less independent level as a highly subjective and poetic means of communication, capable of expanding the meaning and emotional content of the scenes they accompany.

Music as a Base for Choreographed Action

Usually the director composes, photographs, and edits the images first and adds music later, after the visual elements are already assembled. In a relatively small number of films, however, such as *A Clockwork Orange*, music is used to provide a clear rhythmic framework for the action, which essentially becomes a highly stylized dance performed to the music.

Director John Badham remembers his use of the technique in *Saturday Night Fever:*

> [I]n the opening we took a tape recorder out with us in the street—we already had a demo made by the Bee Gees of "Staying Alive," which was their initial version. But they had promised us they'd always stick to the same tempo in any future versions they did. The tempo was really all I had to have. But I had the rest of the song, too. Every time we shot a shot, that music would be playing, so all the movie that is on screen is in exact tempo to that.
>
> This is not a technique that's peculiar to me; that's the way musicals have been shot for years. In a wonderful picture made by King Vidor, called *Our Daily Bread*, there's about a ten-minute sequence at the end of the film of a community digging an irrigation ditch. Everybody in the town is digging this ditch—and Vidor had music on the set for tempo, so that people with picks, for example, would swing them on counts of one and three—it was a 4/4 tempo. And the people with the shovels were going on the count of two and four. So there was an orchestration of the movement with the music. Consequently the cuts are very rhythmic. It doesn't look as if the music was just plastered over the film, it really blends in, and the two support each other.
>
> In *Saturday Night Fever* the paint can is swinging in the right tempo with the music. Of course, Travolta's feet are going right on the beat. And that makes a big difference for unifying and getting a synergistic action between the sound and the music.[10]

A similar technique is used when the music originates from some on-screen source, such as a radio or record player, and the actor coordinates the rhythms of his movements to it. In *Hopscotch*, Walter Matthau, playing a former CIA agent writing his memoirs, comically structures his typing and related tasks to match the rhythms of a Mozart symphony on the record player.

In *Punchline*, Sally Field and her two daughters redefine the phrase "fast food" as they frantically clean house and throw together a formal dinner for husband John Goodman and two Catholic priests he is bringing home on short notice. The frantic action is choreographed to the accompaniment of "The Sabre Dance" on the stereo. With the meal finally ready, the house cleaned, the table set, and the guests seated, they sit down to begin a quiet dinner soothed by *Pachelbel's Canon* until one of the daughters breaks the mood by telling a shockingly filthy joke.

An extreme example of this technique of "music first" is *The Wall*, Alan Parker's film version of Pink Floyd's 1979 hit album. Pink Floyd's music provides the narrative framework and combines with Parker's images to create a nonstop assault on the senses. Some parts of the film, such as the "Another Brick in the Wall" segment, are choreographed to the music, combining both live action and animation. Although much of the action in *The Wall* is not as completely choreographed as in this section, there are only a few lines of dialogue

Figure 9.4 Choreographed Action The song "Another Brick in the Wall" was recorded on an album released long before the film *Pink Floyd: The Wall* was conceived. The action shown here was choreographed to match the ideas and rhythms of that song.

in the entire film, and the dynamic rhythms of the action and the editing are designed to correspond to, reinforce, or complement the words and music of the Pink Floyd songs (Figure 9.4).

Action that has no essential rhythmic qualities can be edited to music to create an effect very similar to that of choreographed action. The Little League baseball action in *The Bad News Bears* was apparently edited to match the heroic rhythms of orchestral music from the opera *Carmen*, creating the impression of a comic/heroic dance.

The examples just described represent only the most common and obvious uses of music in the modern film. The point to keep in mind is that we must be aware of the various emotions and levels of meaning that music communicates (Figure 9.5).

Synthesizer Scoring

A fairly recent trend is the use of electronic synthesizers for instrumentation on film scores. A synthesizer is essentially a musical computer played on a pianolike keyboard and equipped with various knobs and buttons that permit all sorts of variation in pitch, tone, and decay. It can imitate the sounds of a large variety of

Figure 9.5 Musical Interlude This scene from *Butch Cassidy and the Sundance Kid* was accompanied by the song "Raindrops Keep Fallin' on My Head." The song had nothing whatsoever to do with the film and served only as a musical interlude to separate the film's very different halves.

other instruments while still retaining its own distinct quality. Because of its tremendous flexibility, it is the fastest, most efficient way to score a film. A two-person team—one playing the keyboard, the other controlling the sound qualities—can create a full sound comparable to that provided by a complete orchestra.

Synthesizers have played a part in film scores for some time, at least since *A Clockwork Orange* in 1971, but they have become much more prevalent since *Midnight Express* (1978), which has a complete "synth" score by Giorgio Moroder. Films with synthesizer scores include *Sorcerer*, *Thief*, *American Gigolo*, *Foxes*, *Blade Runner*, *Cat People*, and *Beverly Hills Cop*. The great versatility of synth scoring was most evident in *Chariots of Fire* (1981), a period piece that seemed an unlikely choice for an electronic score. *Chariots* composer Vangelis's challenge was to compose a "score which was contemporary, but still compatible with the time of the film." He met the challenge successfully by mixing synthesizer and a grand piano.[11]

Sometimes it is difficult to know whether to classify electronic scores as music or sound effects. In *Cat People*, for example, the synthesizer often functions as an almost subliminal animal presence behind the image, creating the effect of "listening in on the vital processes of other organisms—of other places, other worlds."[12] Horror movies have been less subtle in their overuse of the tension-building, nervous-pulse sounds, which are repeated over and over without musical development.

Electronic scores are still relatively rare in major films because most top composers still prefer to use an orchestra. Even in the case of *The X-Files*, a 1998 film version of the popular television program, the composer, Mark Snow, chose to "enlarge" with orchestral adaptations his celebrated synthesizer themes from the series.

Economy in Film Music

Generally speaking, economy is a great virtue in film music, both in duration and in instrumentation. The musical score should do no more than is necessary to perform its proper function clearly and simply. However, because of some irresistible temptations to dress up scenes with music whether they need it or not, the normal dramatic film usually ends up with too much music rather than not enough. The Hollywood tendency seems to be toward large orchestras, even though smaller combinations can be more interesting and colorful or even more powerful in their effect on the film as a whole.

The proper amount of music depends on the nature of the picture itself. Some films require a lot of music. Others are so realistic that music would interfere with the desired effect. In many cases the most dramatically effective musical score is that which is used most sparingly. For *All the President's Men*, in 1976, composer David Shire had to be convinced by the director, Alan J. Pakula, that his film needed *any* music written for it. As Shire puts it, "This was a case where a director had a better grasp of what music could do for a film than a composer. That doesn't happen very often." Two years earlier, near the beginning of his career, Shire had shown a similar disinclination for overwriting when he composed the haunting solo piano score for Francis Ford Coppola's *The Conversation*. About that experience, Shire says:

> One of the things that makes scoring films so much fun is the opportunity to constantly write for orchestras of all sizes and shapes, and to write only as much music as a film really needs. The most economical score is often the best one, just as the simplest solution is often the most effective. But it always depends on the picture. If next week I get one that calls for ninety minutes of orchestral scoring, then that's what I'll give it, but *The Conversation* required very little. In that film, about a surveillance expert whose obsessive nature gets him involved with a case that causes him to lose his mind, I used a synthesizer to modulate the texture of the piano cues to give a weird, unsettling effect to underscore the man's dilemma. It's opportunities like this that make film scoring a fascinating business.[13]

Randy Newman, who wrote the scores for *Ragtime*, *The Natural*, and *Toy Story*, is critical of Woody Allen's *Manhattan* score, which he feels is too big for the film. Although he does not object to the full-orchestra treatment during panoramic scenes of the Manhattan skyline, Newman claims that the music often overwhelms the characters and the action with "great genius music by Gershwin and Wagner—and little Woody Allen and other little guys talking on the phone at the same time. It dwarfed them."[14]

The director Sidney Lumet (*Twelve Angry Men*, *The Pawnbroker*, *Murder on the Orient Express*, *Dog Day Afternoon*, *Night Falls on Manhattan*) has observed, "When I haven't been able to find a musical concept that adds to the movie, I haven't used a score. Studios hate the idea of a picture without music. It scares them." Besides, he notes, "talking about music is like talking about colors: the same color can mean different things to different people."[15] Usually, though, we must conclude, an attempt at creating film music is definitely worth the resulting colorful dialogue.

Questions

On General Functions of the Musical Score

1. Where in the film is music used to match exactly the natural rhythms of the moving objects on the screen? At what points in the film does the music simply try to capture the overall emotional mood of a scene?
2. Where does the film employ rhythmic and emotive variations on a single musical theme or motif?
3. Does the musical score remain inconspicuous in the background, or does it occasionally break through to assert itself?
4. If the music does demand our conscious attention, does it still perform a subordinate function in the film as a whole? How?
5. Where in the film is the main purpose of the music to match structural or visual rhythms? Where is the music used to create more generalized emotional patterns?
6. How would the total effect of the film differ if the musical score were removed from the soundtrack?

On Special Functions of the Musical Score

1. Which of the following functions of film music are used in the film, and where are they used?
   a. to cover weaknesses and defects
   b. to heighten the dramatic effect of dialogue
   c. to tell an inner story by expressing a state of mind
   d. to provide a sense of time or place
   e. to evoke remembered experiences or emotions

f. to foreshadow events or build dramatic tension
g. to add levels of meaning to the image
h. to aid characterization
i. to trigger conditioned responses
j. to characterize rapid movement (traveling music)

2. Does the music accompanying the titles serve basically to underscore the rhythmic qualities of the title information or to establish the general mood of the film? If lyrics are sung at this point, how do these lyrics relate to the film as a whole?
3. Where are sound effects or natural noises employed for a kind of rhythmic or musical effect?
4. If lyrics sung within the film provide a kind of interior monologue, what feeling or attitude do they convey?
5. If music is used as a base for choreographed action, how appropriate is the piece selected? How appropriate are its rhythms to the mood and the visual content? How effectively is the choreographed sequence integrated into the film as a whole?
6. Does the score use a full orchestra throughout, a small number of well-chosen instruments, or a synthesizer? How well suited is the instrumentation to the film as a whole? If it is not well chosen, what kind of instrumentation should have been used? How would a different choice of instrumentation change the quality of the film, and why would it be an improvement?
7. Does the amount of music used fit the requirements of the film, or is the musical score overdone or used too economically?
8. How effectively does the score perform its various functions?

Video Exercises

Instructions for locating specific sequences are given on page 77.

Music 1. Watch the indicated sequence from *The World According to Garp* [4265 to 4440; 1:15:12 to 1:18:33], paying special attention to the music. What important story elements does the music in this segment convey? What roles do lyrics, vocal styles, and instrumentation play in this sequence?

Music 2. With the TV sound off, watch the beginning of *The Shining* (1980) through the opening credits with the following musical selections playing on your CD or tape player:

a. "On the Road Again" by Willie Nelson or any instrumental version of "The Orange Blossom Special"
b. "Greensleeves" by Mantovani, "Scarborough Fair" by Simon and Garfunkel, or any familiar Strauss waltz

How does the change in music change the way you respond emotionally and visually to this brief sequence? Now turn the sound up on the TV and watch the sequence again. What is different about the way you see and experience the sequence this time? Describe your responses to each viewing in as much detail as possible.

Music 3. Watch the "Birth of Humanoid Intelligence" sequence from *2001: A Space Odyssey* [0730 to 1115; 0:08:48 to 0:13:58]. Then turn the TV sound off and replay the sequence with six or seven different and greatly varied musical selections from your own record, tape, or CD collection. Which of your musical scores were most effective and why? How do your most effective scores change the meaning or significance of the original?

Music 4. Watch *Sleepless in Seattle* in its entirety, paying special attention to scenes accompanied by music. What thematic strains are repeated frequently during the film? What is their function? How do the popular recorded songs that are used reinforce mood and story elements?

Films for Study

The Age of Innocence (1993)
Amadeus (1984)
American Graffiti (1973)
Apollo 13 (1995)
Batman (1989)
Beloved (1998)
Benny & Joon (1993)
Beverly Hills Cop (1984)
The Big Chill (1983)
Body Heat (1981)
Bonnie and Clyde (1967)
Breaking Away (1979)
Breaking the Waves (1996)
The Bridges of Madison County (1995)
Butch Cassidy and the Sundance Kid (1969)
Cabaret (1972)
Chariots of Fire (1981)
A Clockwork Orange (1971)
The Conversation (1974)
Dances With Wolves (1990)
Dr. Strangelove (1964)
The English Patient (1996)
E.T. The Extra Terrestrial (1982)
The Graduate (1967)
The Grey Fox (1982)
The Harmonists (1999)
Hilary and Jackie (1998)
Jaws (1975)
The Last Picture Show (1971)
Last Tango in Paris (1973)
Living Out Loud (1998)
Little Voice (1998)
The Long Riders (1980)
A Man and a Woman (1966)
My Best Friend's Wedding (1997)
Nashville (1975)
The Natural (1984)
Out of Africa (1985)
The Piano (1993)
Pink Floyd: The Wall (1982)
The Portrait of a Lady (1996)
Saturday Night Fever (1977)
Singin' in the Rain (1952)
Sleepless in Seattle (1993)
Star Wars (1977)
The Sting (1973)
This Boy's Life (1993)
Titanic (1997)
Top Hat (1935)
The Truman Show (1998)
2001: A Space Odyssey (1968)
The World According to Garp (1982)
The X-Files (1998)

Chapter 10

Acting

An audience identifies with the actors of flesh and blood and heartbeat, as no reader or beholder can identify with even the most artful paragraphs in books or the most inspiring paintings. There, says the watcher, but for some small difference in time or costume or inflections or gait, go I. . . . And so, the actor becomes a catalyst; he brings to bright ignition that spark in every human being that longs for the miracle of transformation.

—EDWARD G. ROBINSON, ACTOR

The Importance of Acting

All we are is a very sophisticated recording device whose job is to record an event that has to be created by the actors. No matter how brilliantly you record something, if the event stinks, then you have a brilliant recording of a lousy event. So the crucial element is the actor.[1]

—Mark Rydell, Director

When we consider going to a movie, the first question we usually ask has to do not with the director or the cinematographer but with the actors: Who's in it? This is a natural question, because the art of the actor is so clearly visible. The actor's work commands most of our attention, overshadowing the considerable contributions of the writer, director, cinematographer, editor, and composer of the score. As George Kernodle puts it in *An Invitation to the Theatre:*

> Whether the picture is *Tom Jones, Thunderball, The Sound of Music, Ship of Fools,* or *The Collector,* it is the star that draws the crowds. The audience may be amused, thrilled, or deeply moved by the story, fascinated by new plot devices, property gadgets, and camera angles, charmed by backgrounds that are exotic, or captivated by those that are familiar and real, but it is the people on the screen, and especially the faces, that command the center of attention.[2]

Because we naturally respond to film's most human ingredient, the actor's contribution is extremely important.

Yet despite our tendency to focus attention on the actor, there is general agreement among critics and directors that the actor's role in film should be a subordinate one, one of many important elements contributing to a greater aesthetic whole, the film itself. As Alfred Hitchcock states it, "Film work hasn't much need for the virtuoso actor who gets his effects and climaxes himself, who plays directly to the audience with the force of his talent and personality. The screen actor has got to be much more plastic; he has to submit himself to be used by the director and the camera."[3]

The Goal of the Actor

The ultimate goal of any actor should be to make us believe completely in the reality of the character. If this goal is to be achieved, actors must either develop or be blessed with several talents. First of all, they must be able to project sincerity, truthfulness, and naturalness in such a way that we are never aware that they are acting a part. In a sense, good acting must seem not to be acting at all.

Sometimes actors achieve a certain naturalness through tricks and gimmicks. Knowing that Ratso Rizzo, the character that Dustin Hoffman plays in *Midnight Cowboy*, had a distinct limp, a fellow actor advised Hoffman on how to make the limp consistent: "Once you get the limp right, why don't you put rocks in your shoe? You'll never have to think about limping. It will be there; you won't have to worry about it." Actors use similar tricks to create a trademark for their characters and to keep the characters consistent. But good acting demands much more than tricks and gimmicks. To project the sincerity that a really deep, complex, and demanding role requires, actors must be willing to draw on the deepest and most personal qualities of their inner being. As director Mark Rydell (a former actor himself) says:

> I find that acting is one of the bravest professions of all. An actor has to remain vulnerable. The entire process of learning to act necessitates a kind of peeling away of layers of insulation that we develop from the time we're children, when we were innocent and exposed. The actor has to sandpaper his feelings and his vulnerabilities. He has to be open to assault from circumstances, events, relationships. I suspect that any time you see a great performance, it's because some actor has been courageous enough to allow you to peek at a very personal, private secret of his.[4]

Actors must also possess the intelligence, imagination, sensitivity, and insight into human nature necessary to fully understand the characters they play—their inner thoughts, motivations, and emotions. Furthermore, actors must have the ability to express these things convincingly through voice, body movements, gestures, or facial expressions, so the qualities seem true to the characters portrayed and to the situation in which the characters find themselves. And actors must maintain the illusion of reality in their characters with complete consistency from beginning to end. It is also important for actors to keep their egos under control, so that they can see their roles in proper perspective to the dramatic work as a whole. Veteran Michael Caine offers this definition of the actor's ultimate goal:

> I said before that in my acting I've tried to be a person. At movies, you should not sit there and say this is a poor performance by a poor actor, or that it's a wonderful performance by a wonderful actor. If I'm really doing my job correctly you should sit there and say, "I'm *involved* with this person, and have no idea there's an actor there." So, really, I'm trying to defeat myself the entire time. You should never see the *actor*, never see the wheels going.[5]

Becoming the Character

If an actor's goal is to obscure his or her own personality and to become another person on the screen, the actor must learn to behave reflexively and naturally as this new character. Although there are many subtle variations in the way actors prepare for roles, they generally choose one of two techniques to develop well-rounded, believable characterizations: the inside approach or the outside approach. Actor Edward James Olmos describes the most basic elements of the two approaches:

> The English form of study teaches you to go from the outside in. You do the behavior and it starts to seep inside. The Stanislavski method teaches you to go from the inside out. You begin with the feeling and memory, and those feelings begin to affect your behavior.
>
> In other words, some people will turn around and get a limp and then figure out where the limp came from. Other people have to figure out why they have to limp before they can do the limp.[6]

Cliff Robertson, an Academy Award winner for his performance in *Charly*, believes that he must understand all facets of his character's personality and thought processes. This inside method of preparation allows him to think and respond naturally in the role:

> I worked from the inside—but I'd had seven years of digesting the character. I can't explain it. I still think acting is one of the more mysterious art forms. I'll give you an example: the night before the first day's shooting my wife and I were preparing for bed and she said, "How're you going to play him?" That sort of stopped me. I said, "What do you mean by that?" She said, "*Physically*—how will you play him?" I said, "I don't know." She looked at me and said, "You've had this property for seven years—you've been to all these workshops, and you can't tell me how you see him?" I said, "No, at this minute I can't tell you." I went to work the next morning and [Director] Ralph [Nelson] asked me if I wanted a run-through, and I said, "No, crank 'em up." That's what is called "going with the instrument," I guess—I just went with it. But I had had seven years of osmosis—normally an actor doesn't have that privilege. So when you have that kind of background you *can* go with the instrument.
>
> Normally, when I have, say, two months to think about a role, I'll cut it up in eighteen pieces and examine each piece of the character, all sides, look at it, then put it back together and look at it again. Then cut it up again, give the pieces different positions, so that I literally know the character so well that should the director ask me—and as a director I ask this—"Given a certain set of circumstances, what would this character do?" I would expect the actor to say, "Oh, this character would do this and that, but not the other thing." I feel you should know a character that well.[7]

Joanne Woodward, honored for her work in *Rachel, Rachel* and *The Effect of Gamma Rays on Man-in-the-Moon Marigolds*, describes her outside approach to character development:

> I'm afraid I work backward—especially for someone trained as I have been. Mine is an odd way to work; I work from the outside in. I always have to know what a

> character looks like because to me, having studied with Martha Graham, so much that goes on inside is reflected outside; it has to do with the way you move. So I generally start with the way a character moves. I'm not very intellectual, so I can't go to find very specific things until I find them, as Paul [Newman, her husband] would say, viscerally. I took Rachel's movements from my child, Nell. She's very pigeon-toed, so I just took the way Nell looks and grew it up. And somehow, when you move like that—all sorts of things happen to you inside.[8]

In his book about acting for film, the Oscar-winning actor Michael Caine has observed:

> When becoming a character, you have to steal. Steal whatever you see. You can even steal from other actors' characterizations; but if you do, only steal from the best. If you see Vivien Leigh do something, or Marlon Brando or Robert De Niro or Meryl Streep do something that fits your character, steal it. Because what you're seeing them do, they stole.
>
> The best movie actors become their characters to such an extent that the product isn't viewed by an audience as a performance. It's a strange situation, but in film a person is a person, not an actor; and yet you need an actor to play the person. . . .
>
> You've got to base your character, not on some actor-ish memory of what reality is because, finally, the actor is in charge of the effect he wants. Woody Allen can play a tragic scene about a brain tumor and make the audience laugh. Another actor can fall on a banana skin and make the audience cry. But the audience . . . must see a real person standing there, somebody just like them.[9]

No matter what their methods of preparation, actors who attempt to submerge their own personalities and become a character deserve respect for their efforts, according to director Elia Kazan:

> The beautiful and the terrible thing about actors is that when they work they are completely exposed; you have to appreciate that if you direct them. They are being critically observed not only for their emotions, their technique, and their intelligence, but for their legs, their breasts, their carriage, their double chins, and so on. Their whole being is opened to scrutiny. . . . How can you feel anything but gratitude for creatures so vulnerable and so naked?[10]

Differences Between Film Acting and Stage Acting

Acting for motion pictures and acting for the stage have in common the goals, traits, and skills described above, yet there are important differences in the acting techniques required for the two media. The primary difference results from the relative distance between the performer and the spectator. When acting in the theater, actors must always be sure that every member of the audience can see and hear them distinctly. Thus, stage actors must constantly project the voice, make gestures that are obvious and clear, and generally move and speak so they can be clearly heard and seen by the most remote observer. This is no problem in a small, intimate theater, but the larger the theater and the more distant the spectator in the last row, the farther the actor's voice must be projected and the broader the gestures must be. As actors make these adjustments, the depth and reality of the performance suffer, because louder tones and wider gestures lead to generalized form and stylization. The finer, subtler shades of intonation are lost as the distance between actor and audience increases.

The problem of reaching a remote spectator does not exist in films, for the viewer is in the best possible location for hearing and seeing the actor. Because of the mobility of the recording microphone, a film actor may speak softly, or even whisper, with full confidence that the audience will hear every word and perceive every subtle tone of voice. The same holds true for facial expression, gesture, and body movement, for in close-ups even the subtlest facial expressions are clearly visible to the most remote spectator. The mobility of the camera further assures the actor that the audience will view the scene from the most effective angle. Thus film acting can be, and in fact must be, more subtle and restrained than stage acting.

Henry Fonda learned this lesson when director Victor Fleming accused him of "mugging" while filming a scene for Fonda's first movie, *The Farmer Takes a Wife*. Fonda had played the role on Broadway, and Fleming explained the problem to him in terms he clearly understood: "You're playing the farmer the way you did in the theater. You're playing to the back row of the orchestra and the rear row of the balcony. That's stage technique." The understated Fonda style, using as little facial mobility as possible, began at that moment and served the actor well in almost a hundred films:

> I just pulled it right back to reality because that lens and that microphone are doing all the projection you need. No sense in using too much voice, and you don't need any more expression on your face than you'd use in everyday life.[11]

Actor Robert Shaw put it this way: "Here's the difference: On stage, you have to dominate the audience. You don't have to *think* the way you do when you're in the movies. Stage acting is the art of *domination*. Movie acting is the art of *seduction*."[12]

This is not to say that film acting is less difficult than stage acting. The film actor must be extremely careful in every gesture and word, for the camera and microphone are unforgiving and cruelly revealing, especially in close-ups. Because complete sincerity, naturalness, and restraint are all-important, a single false move or phony gesture or a line delivered without conviction, with too much conviction, or out of character will shatter the illusion of reality. Thus, the most successful film actors either possess or can project, with seeming ease and naturalness, a truly genuine personality, and they somehow appear to be completely themselves without self-consciousness or a sense of strain. This rare quality generally seems to depend as much on natural talent as on disciplined study and training.

Another difficulty faces film actors because they perform their roles in discontinuous bits and pieces, rather than in a continuous flow with one scene following the next, as in theater. Only later, in the cutting room, are the fragments assembled in proper sequence. For this reason, assuming the proper frame of mind, mood, and acting style for each segment of the film becomes a problem. For example, actors required to speak in a dialect far removed from their own natural speech patterns may have difficulty capturing the dialect exactly as they did in a scene filmed two weeks earlier, a problem they would not have in a continuous stage performance. But a clear advantage also arises from this difference. The performance of the film actor can be made more nearly perfect than can that of the stage actor, for the film editor and director can choose the best and most convincing performance from several takes of the same sequence. That way, the film becomes a continuous series of best performances.

Another disadvantage in film acting is that the actors have no direct link with the audience as stage actors do and therefore must act for an imagined audience. Film actors cannot draw on audience reaction for inspiration. Whatever inspiration they receive must come from the director, the crew, and the fact that their work will have more permanence than that of the stage actor.

Film is also for the most part a more physical medium than theater—that is, film actors must use more nonverbal communication than stage actors have to use. Julian Fast discusses this aspect of film acting in his book *Body Language:* "Good actors must all be experts in the use of body language. A process of elimination guarantees that only those with an excellent command of the grammar and vocabulary get to be successful."[13] According to critic Jack Kroll, "Actors who have a genius for this sleight of body are surrogates for the rest of us who are trapped in our own selves. To create a new human being is to re-create the very idea of humanity, to refresh that idea for us who grow stale in our mortality" (Figure 10.1).[14]

The grammar and vocabulary of body language include a vast array of nonverbal communication techniques, but the motion picture is perhaps unique in its emphasis on the eloquence of the human face. Although the face and facial expressions play a part in other storytelling media, such as novels and plays, in film the face becomes a medium of communication in its own right. Magnified on the screen, the human face with its infinite variety of expressions can convey depth and subtlety of emotion that cannot be approached through purely rational or verbal means (Figure 10.2). As Hungarian film critic and theorist Béla Balázs so aptly states, "What happens on the face and in facial expressions is a spiritual experience which is rendered immediately visible without the intermediary of words"[15] (Figure 10.3).

Figure 10.1 Different Approaches Body language speaks volumes about the characters and their relationships in these scenes picturing Jack Nicholson and Shirley MacLaine in *Terms of Endearment* (above left), Mary Murphy and Marlon Brando in *The Wild One* (above right), and Nicholson and Helen Hunt in *As Good As It Gets* (right).

Figure 10.2 The Actor's Face In *The Caine Mutiny*, Humphrey Bogart's face clearly reveals the inner thoughts and feelings of Captain Queeg. In the first picture, the seeds of paranoia have been planted. Bogart's eyes are anxious and worried, and his jaw is a little slack, suggesting Queeg's bewilderment as his self-control slips away. In the second picture, during the storm sequence, all control is gone. Queeg's psychotic state is revealed in the stark terror in the eyes; his jaw is slack, and his face is that of a terrified, cornered animal.

Figure 10.3 Sustained Expression In *Sling Blade,* Billy Bob Thornton convincingly portrays a mentally challenged character by maintaining a simple look throughout the film.

The human face is a marvelously complex structure, capable of transmitting a wide range of emotions through slight changes in mouth, eyes, eyelids, eyebrows, and forehead. This expressiveness helps to explain another important difference between film acting and stage acting: the film's emphasis on reacting rather than acting. The **reaction shot** achieves its considerable dramatic impact through a close-up of the character most affected by the dialogue or action. The actor's face, within the brief moment that it is on the screen, must register clearly yet subtly and without the aid of dialogue the appropriate emotional reaction (Figure 10.4). Some of the most powerful moments in film are built around such "facial acting." Michael Caine elaborates:

> [I]n a movie, you cannot get away with just doing a star performance—moving and talking all the time. People become bored with you. You have to show reactions. On stage a cardboard tree is a cardboard tree, and you suspend reaction. In a movie a tree is a real tree, it loses its leaves and gets covered with snow. And that applies to everybody in a movie. Nothing is in isolation as it is in a theater—and you have to play according to the reactions of someone else to what you're doing. One of the things I'm known for in movies is not acting but *reacting.*[16]

The stage actor's facial reactions, in contrast, are seldom if ever quite so important to a play's dramatic power.

But even in reaction shots the film actor is often assisted by the nature of the medium, for in film much of the powerful and expressive quality of the human face is created by the context in which it appears, and the meanings of many expressions are determined by skillful editing. Thus, the actor's face may not be so beautifully expressive as the visual context makes it appear. This phenomenon was demonstrated in an experiment conducted in the early 1920s by the young Russian painter Lev Kuleshov and film director V. I. Pudovkin:

> We took from some film or other several close-ups of the well-known Russian actor Mosjukhin. We chose close-ups which were static and which did not express any feeling at all—quiet close-ups. We joined these close-ups, which were all similar, with other bits of film in three different combinations. In the first combination the close-up of Mosjukhin was immediately followed by a shot of soup standing on a table. It was obvious and certain that Mosjukhin was looking at this soup. In the second combination the face of Mosjukhin was joined to shots showing a coffin in which lay a dead woman. In the third the close-up was followed by a shot of a little girl playing with a funny toy bear. When we showed the three combinations to an audience which had not been let into the secret, the result was terrific. The public

Figure 10.4 The Reaction Shot
Emma Thompson, as Elinor in *Sense and Sensibility,* uses subtle facial acting in shots that react to Kate Winslet as her sister Marianne.

> raved about the acting of the artist. They pointed out the heavy pensiveness of the mood over the forgotten soup, were touched and moved by the deep sorrow with which he looked on the dead woman, and admired the light, happy smile with which he surveyed the girl at play. But we knew in all three cases the face was exactly the same.[17]

This experiment is not cited to prove that film acting is only an illusion created by editing. But it does show that we are eager to respond to faces, whether or not those faces are really projecting what we think we see.

Film actors must also be able to communicate more with bodily movements and gestures than stage actors. Because the stage actor's chief instrument of expression is the voice, his or her movements are mainly an accompaniment to or an extension of what is said. In film, however, physical movement and gesture may communicate effectively without dialogue. The magnification of the human image on the screen enables the actor to communicate with extremely subtle movements. A slight shrug of the shoulders, the nervous trembling of a hand viewed in close-up, or the visible tensing of the muscles and tendons in the neck may be much more important than anything said.

A classic example of the power of body language in film acting is Jack Palance's portrayal of the gunfighter Wilson in *Shane,* a role he parodies in both *City Slickers* films. Palance plays Wilson as the personification of evil. Every movement, every gesture is slow, deliberate, yet tense, so we get the feeling that Wilson is a rattlesnake, moving slowly and sensuously but always ready to strike in a split second. When Wilson slowly performs the ritual of putting on his black leather gloves in order to practice his profession, Palance makes us sense with horror Wilson's cold, cruel indifference to human life.

Film acting also differs from stage acting in that it requires two kinds of acting. One is the kind required for the action/adventure film. We can refer to it as **action acting.** This type of acting requires a great deal in the way of reactions, body language, physical exertion, and special skills, but it does not draw on the deepest resources of the actor's intelligence and feelings. In contrast, **dramatic acting** calls for sustained, intense dialogue with another person and requires an emotional and psychological depth seldom called for in action acting. Action acting is the art of doing. Dramatic acting involves feeling, thinking, and communicating emotions and thoughts. Action acting is on the surface, with little nuance. Dramatic acting is beneath the surface and full of subtlety. Each type of acting requires its own particular gift or talent.

Some actors can do both, but most are better suited for one or the other and are usually cast accordingly (Figure 10.5). Arnold Schwarzenegger, for example, is essentially an action actor, and Robert De Niro is a dramatic actor. As director Sergio Leone, who has directed both, describes them:

> It's difficult to compare Eastwood and De Niro—if you think about it, they don't even belong to the same profession. Robert De Niro throws himself into this or

Figure 10.5 Action and Dramatic Acting Although he has ventured into comedy with some success in *Twins* and *Junior,* Arnold Schwarzenegger, shown here in *True Lies,* is essentially an action actor. Robert De Niro, pictured here as the villainous ex-con from *Cape Fear,* is clearly one of the finest dramatic actors of our day.

> that role, putting on a personality the way someone else might put on his coat, naturally and with elegance, while Clint Eastwood throws himself into a suit of armor and lowers the visor with a rusty clang. It's exactly that lowered visor which composes his character.
>
> . . . Look at him carefully. Eastwood moves like a sleepwalker between the explosions and hails of bullets and he is always the same—a block of granite. Bobby first of all, is an actor. Clint first of all, is a star. Bobby suffers, Clint yawns.[18]

Although Eastwood has carved some deeper lines into his "block of granite" with recent work like *Unforgiven*, *In the Line of Fire*, and *The Bridges of Madison County*, Leone's description remains valid today.

Although film acting and stage acting have the same basic goals, film acting utilizes fundamentally different techniques to achieve them.

Types of Actors

Besides classifying actors as action and dramatic actors, we can consider how the roles they play relate to their own personalities. In *A Primer for Playgoers*, Edward A. Wright and Lenthiel H. Downs identify three types of actors: impersonators, interpreters and commentators, and personality actors.[19]

Impersonators

Impersonators are actors who have the talent to leave their real personality behind and to assume the personality of a character with whom they may have few characteristics in common. Such actors can completely submerge themselves in a role, altering their personal, physical, and vocal characteristics to such a degree that they seem to become the character. We lose sight of the impersonator's real identity. The roles such actors can perform are almost unlimited.

Interpreters and Commentators

Interpreters and commentators play characters closely resembling themselves in personality and physical appearance, and they interpret these parts dramatically without wholly losing their own identity. Although they may slightly alter themselves to fit the role, they do not attempt to radically change their individual personality traits, physical characteristics, or voice qualities. They choose instead to color or interpret the role by filtering it through their own best qualities, modifying it to fit their own inherent abilities. The end result is an effective compromise between actor and role, between the real and the assumed identity. The compromise adds a unique creative dimension to the character being portrayed, for in their delivery of the lines these actors reveal something of their own thoughts and feelings about the character, but they do so without ever falling out of character. Thus, these actors may simultaneously comment on and interpret the role. Although the range of roles such actors can play is not as wide as that open to impersonators, it is still relatively broad. If they are cast wisely within this range, they can bring something new and fresh to each role they play, in addition to their own best and most attractive qualities.

Personality Actors

Actors whose primary talent is to be themselves and nothing more are **personality actors.** They project the essential qualities of sincerity, truthfulness, and naturalness, and they generally possess some dynamic and magnetic mass appeal because of a striking appearance, a physical or vocal idiosyncrasy, or some other special quality strongly communicated to us on film. These actors, however popular, are incapable of assuming any variety in the roles they play, for they cannot project sincerity and naturalness when they attempt to move outside their own basic personality. Thus, either they must fit exactly the roles in which they are cast, or the roles must be tailored to fit their personality.

The Star System

In the past many personality actors and some interpreter and commentator actors were exploited in what became known as the **star system,** an approach to filmmaking based on the assumption that the average moviegoer is interested more in personalities than in great stories or, for that matter, in film art. The stars were, of course, actors with great mass appeal. The big studios did everything in their power to preserve the qualities of the stars that appealed to the public, and they created films around the image of the star personality. Often a star's presence in a film was the main guarantee of financial success, and such films became nothing more than a suitable package in which to display and market the attractive wares of the actors, who had only to project the charm of their personalities.

For some directors, the star system offered certain clear advantages. John Ford and Frank Capra, for example, used the star system as a myth-making apparatus, building their films around such stars as John Wayne, Barbara Stanwyck, Jean Arthur, Henry Fonda, James Stewart, and Gary Cooper. These actors projected fairly consistent personalities and embraced a constant set of values in each film they did. They came into each new Ford or Capra film trailing clouds of associations and reverberating strong echoes of earlier parts. By surrounding these stars with their stock company of topnotch secondary actors—also in predictable roles echoing earlier parts—Ford and Capra were, in a sense, using pre-established symbols for the values they wanted their characters to represent, and the mythic worlds of their films could rest on the shoulders of actors who already had mythic dimensions.

The fact that so many stars trailed these clouds of associations influenced Steven Spielberg's casting of *Jaws:*

> I didn't pursue that idea of getting stars, because I think it's really important when you're watching a movie that you don't sit there and say, "Oh, look who's in this picture. What was his last picture, wasn't that a good one? Didn't you just love her in such and such . . . ?" I'm not saying I'll never work with a Robert Redford or a Paul Newman or a Burt Reynolds—I would certainly love to. I'm saying that for certain special types of movies, where half the struggle is verisimilitude, if Burt Reynolds had played Richard Dreyfuss's part, there would have been too much imagery of Burt in other movies, with fast cars, attractive women, and blazing action. In my opinion it takes ten to fifteen minutes for the memory to overcome the record of one's past. I had two producers who really gave me my head. Anything I wanted to do was fine with them. They agreed that we should not go after the half-million-dollar players, but should get good people who would be good actors in the right part and would be semianonymous.[20]

There was some general agreement with Spielberg's thinking throughout the industry. During the 1960s and 1970s producers began to turn to lesser-known actors who had the range and flexibility to play a variety of roles and who, of course, demanded less money than established stars. Blockbuster hits such as *2001, The Graduate, Taxi Driver*, and *Jaws* were successful without the presence of top box-office stars. A new era began with a small galaxy of gifted actors who promised not the repetition of tested and tried personalities but the guarantee of high-level performances in fresh and exciting roles (people like

Dustin Hoffman, Robert De Niro, Jodie Foster, Meryl Streep, Robert Duvall, and Glenn Close).

Much of the success of this new galaxy depends on the actors' skill in choosing the films in which they appear. No longer under studio contract and forced to accept roles assigned by studio moguls, the modern star is often part of a deal package that may include a director and screenwriter who are all clients of the same agent. In many respects, the talent agency has usurped some of the power of the big studios in determining what films are made and who stars in them—and enormous salaries are once again in vogue.

Although the star system has changed greatly over the last thirty or forty years, it is certainly not dead. The personality cults that spring up periodically around charismatic actors provide ample evidence to the contrary. We will always be attracted to familiar faces and personalities, for we seem to have a psychological need for the familiar, the predictable, and the comfortable. In addition, as Sidney Lumet suggests,

> There's a mysterious alchemy between star and audience. Sometimes it's based on the physical beauty or sex appeal of the star. But I don't believe that it's ever just one thing. Surely there were other women as attractive as Marilyn Monroe or men as handsome as Cary Grant (though not many). Al Pacino tries to suit his look to the characters—a beard here, long hair there—but somehow it's the way his eyes express an enormous rage, even in tender moments, that enthralls me and everyone else. I think that every star evokes a sense of danger, something unmanageable. Perhaps each person in the audience feels that he or she is the one who can manage, tame, satisfy the bigger-than-life quality that a star has. Clint Eastwood isn't really the same as you or me, is he? Or Michelle Pfeiffer, or Sean Connery, or you name them. I don't really know what makes a star. But the persona that jumps out at you is certainly a most important element.[21]

Casting

> *Sometimes the best thing I can do is cast the movie well. If you cast well then half the battle is already won, because even if the actor doesn't listen to anything you say, you're at least responsible for half of his performance. You reached into a crowded world and pulled a man, a woman, or a child from thin air and plugged them into your vision.*[22]
>
> —Steven Spielberg, Director

Acting skills aside, the casting of actors in roles that are right for them is an extremely important consideration. If their physical characteristics, facial features, voice qualities, or the total personality they naturally project is not suited to the character, their performance will probably not be convincing. Alec Guin-

Figure 10.6 Casting Problems Because Sophia Loren is three inches taller than Alan Ladd, she is photographed standing a step below him in this scene from *Boy on a Dolphin.* When the story is a comedy, however, the romantic lead can be shorter than his leading lady, as is apparent in this scene with Woody Allen and Mira Sorvino in *Mighty Aphrodite*.

ness or Peter Sellers, despite their great ability as impersonators, could not have effectively played the roles assigned to John Wayne, for example, nor could Burt Lancaster have been very effective in roles played by Woody Allen.

Less extreme problems in casting can be solved by sheer genius or camera tricks. For example, in the film *Boy on a Dolphin*, Alan Ladd, who measured 5 feet 6 inches, was cast opposite Sophia Loren, who towered over him at 5 feet 9 inches. But in a scene that showed them walking side by side, Ladd seemed at least as tall as or slightly taller than Loren. What the camera didn't show was that Loren was actually walking in a shallow trench especially dug for the purpose. When the male lead is to be something other than the traditional macho hero, relative size does not seem so important (Figure 10.6). No effort was made to conceal that Dudley Moore is shorter than both Mary Tyler Moore in *Six Weeks* and Elizabeth McGovern in *Lovesick*. And in the film version of *Who's Afraid of Virginia Woolf?* the character named Honey (Sandy Dennis) is repeatedly referred to as "slim-hipped" despite visual evidence to the contrary. The discrepancy is obscured by Dennis's acting; she projects a psychological type of slim-hippedness that is more convincing than the physical semblance of it.

It is also extremely important that the cast of any film be viewed as a team, not as a hodgepodge of separate individuals, for each actor appears on the screen not alone but in interaction with the other actors. Therefore some thought has to be given to the way they will look on the screen with each other. When casting two male leads such as Robert Redford and Paul Newman, for example, the casting director makes sure that they have certain contrasting features so that they stand out clearly from each other. Actors of the same sex are cast with

Figure 10.7 Ensemble Acting In films such as *Reality Bites,* four or more actors are cast in roles of almost equal importance, and none of them actually dominates the film enough to be considered in the starring role. Shown here are Ethan Hawke, Winona Ryder, Janeane Garofalo, and Steve Zahn.

the idea of contrasting their coloring, builds, heights, and voice qualities. If such differences are not apparent, they can be created through such artificial means as costuming, hairstyle, and facial hair (clean-shaven, mustaches, or beards).

The actors must also project, either naturally or through their skill as actors, significantly different personality traits so that they can effectively play off each other as separate and distinct personalities. This is especially important in **ensemble acting,** a performance by a group of actors whose roles are of equal importance; no member of the group has a starring role or dominates the others. Many modern films, such as *The Big Chill, The Right Stuff, Reality Bites, sex, lies, & videotape,* and *Chasing Amy,* feature ensemble acting (Figure 10.7).

One of the most difficult jobs in casting is finding combinations of actors with chemistry between them—preferably a chemistry so powerful that the audience wants to see them together again in another film. Most important in Hollywood productions is what is known as the he/she chemistry (Figure 10.8). Spencer Tracy was paired with a bevy of actresses (Lana Turner, Hedy Lamarr, Jean Harlow, and Deborah Kerr) before he was cast with Katharine Hepburn to form a winning team that could be repeated for success after success. The James Stewart/June Allyson combination also proved very successful. The Woody Allen/Diane Keaton team worked well (perhaps better than the Woody Allen/Mia Farrow combination). The simple truth, however, is that real he/she chem-

Figure 10.8 He/She Chemistry Studios are constantly searching for the perfect couple, so that they can be played opposite each other in film after film. So far, few modern teams have enjoyed the success experienced by Katharine Hepburn and Spencer Tracy (top left), James Stewart and June Allyson (top right), or Richard Burton and Elizabeth Taylor (bottom).

istry is very rare, and no combinations in recent years have been strong enough to endure.

Physical characteristics and natural personality traits are especially important when actors are to be cast in roles where members of the audience are likely to have clear mental images of the character before they see the movie, as in films about familiar historical figures or films based on popular novels. We often have a difficult time believing in actors who violate our preconceived notions of such characters, and even outstanding performances seldom overcome this handicap.

Financial considerations also play an important part in casting. A well-known actor may be the perfect choice for a starring role but may be too high priced for a film with a limited budget. Or an actor may have commitments that prevent her or him from taking the part. Thus, casting becomes a matter of selecting the best available talent within the limits of the film's budget and shooting schedule.

For actors who have an established and loyal following, producers may take a chance and cast them in a role at odds with their established image, hoping that they will automatically draw their special fans. Thus, Mary Tyler Moore was cast as the mother in *Ordinary People*, Robin Williams in *The World According to Garp* and *Dead Poets Society*, Steve Martin in *Pennies From Heaven* and *Parenthood*, and Jim Carrey in *The Truman Show*.

Billy Wilder's methods of casting are perhaps unique because Wilder writes many of the stories he directs, but he does provide an excellent example of the importance of casting. Instead of selecting a cast to fit an existing story, Wilder often starts with a story idea alone and then proceeds to select and sign up his cast. Only after the actors he wants agree to do the film does the actual writing of the script begin. As Wilder himself put it, "What good is it to have a magnificent dramatic concept for which you must have Sir Laurence Olivier and Audrey Hepburn if they're not available?"[23]

Casting Problems

Casting a feature film is often a more difficult matter than just visualizing the right actor for the part and signing him or her to a contract. German director Werner Herzog's experiences with casting *Fitzcarraldo* are certainly not typical, but they do illustrate a variety of problems that can occur on almost any production. Jack Nicholson had originally expressed interest in playing the lead, but then lost interest. Later, Warren Oates agreed to play the title role. However, Oates, who had never signed a contract, backed out four weeks before shooting was to begin because he didn't relish spending three months in a remote jungle location. After a two-month delay, with Jason Robards replacing Oates, and Mick Jagger in a supporting role, shooting finally got under way. Six weeks later Robards came down with amoebic dysentery and flew home. Shortly after that, Mick Jagger had to drop out to honor other commitments. Unable to find a suitable replacement for Jagger, Herzog wrote his character out of the script. Production was then suspended for two months while the director searched for a new leading man. Although Klaus Kinski was not an ideal choice because he could not project the warmth and charm of the obsessed Irishman, Herzog hired him for the part because further delay would certainly have killed the project.

Fate seems to play a hand in casting, for actors often become stars in roles that were turned down by others. Robert Redford got the part of the Sundance Kid only after Marlon Brando, Steve McQueen, and Warren Beatty had turned it down. During a very brief period, Montgomery Clift turned down four roles that virtually made stars of the actors who finally played the parts: the William Holden role in *Sunset Boulevard*, the James Dean role in *East of Eden*, the Paul

Figure 10.9 The Starless Cast Occasionally, a film can be a big hit even when all of the actors are relatively unknown. This was the case with Andie MacDowell and James Spader in *sex, lies, & videotape*.

Newman role in *Somebody Up There Likes Me*, and the Marlon Brando role in *On the Waterfront*. Gene Hackman was offered the part of the father in *Ordinary People* and wanted to do it, but he could not work out the kind of financial deal he wanted. Richard Dreyfuss was originally set to play Joe Gideon in *All That Jazz*, but he was afraid of the dancing the role would require and was used to working with directors who allowed the actor more freedom than Bob Fosse allowed. So the role went to Roy Scheider.

Although the names on the marquee are usually important factors in the success of a film, there are exceptions (Figure 10.9). *Midnight Express* is one. The film did not have any name stars, and the director, Alan Parker, had made only one film, so his name was not a household word either. Yet the film succeeded because its great intensity and excellent performances from relatively unknown actors stimulated audience interest.

The Typecasting Trap

Typecasting consigns an actor to a narrow range of almost identical roles. It is a natural result of two situations. First, the studios have a great deal of money invested in every film they do. Thus, they naturally want to cast an actor in the same kind of role that was successful before, in the hope of repeating the earlier success (Figure 10.10). Second, if an actor repeats a similar role two or three times, the qualities that the actor projected in the role may take on mythic proportions, and the actor may become a figure on which moviegoers hang their fantasies. If this happens, the moviegoing audience not only expects, but

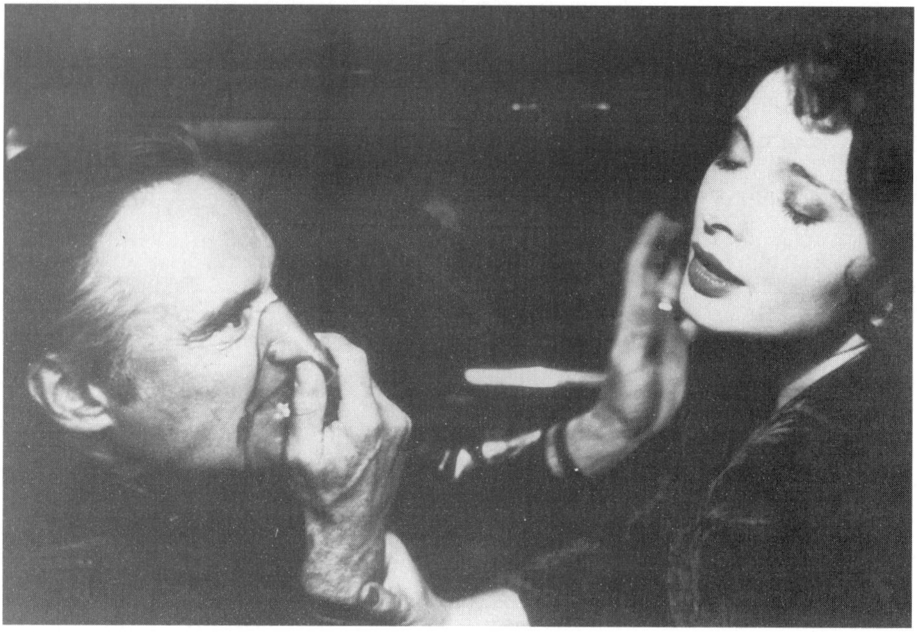

Figure 10.10 Typecasting Dennis Hopper has had such success playing druggies, alcoholics, and psychotic characters that it is difficult to picture him in a normal role. Here, as the drug-crazed sadist Frank in *Blue Velvet,* he simultaneously sucks on his inhaler and brutalizes Isabella Rossellini.

demands, that the role be repeated again and again, with only slight variations. To the fans, anything else is a betrayal, a personal affront to those who have developed what to them is a very personal relationship with a fictional character on the silver screen.

There is a real danger that an actor who is too convincing in an early role will be typecast for the rest of his or her career. For example, Sissy Spacek has projected a fairly consistent screen image: a young, innocent, intelligent, sensitive, but somewhat unsophisticated small-town or country girl. She played Loretta Lynn so convincingly in *Coal Miner's Daughter* that people actually believe that Sissy Spacek *is* that character, "just plain folks," in real life. The fact is that Sissy Spacek is an extremely versatile actress capable of playing practically any part, probably even the sophisticated city-girl roles formerly played by Audrey Hepburn.

Robert De Niro created such a strong impression with his Georgia farmboy Bruce in *Bang the Drum Slowly* that people were saying how sad it was that he had such a strong Georgia accent, for he'd be limited to roles that called for that kind of a character. De Niro, now well known for his meticulous research, had taken a tape recorder to Georgia to study the speech patterns of the residents so he could capture the dialect of the character he was cast to play. By carefully choosing his roles, De Niro has completely broken the typecasting trap. He has shown not only that he can play a variety of roles but that he can alter himself both mentally and physically to project entirely different qualities in each part he plays. In *Bang the Drum Slowly*, playing the second-rate big-league catcher with Hodgkin's disease, he projects a kind of fragile quality, a small man among giants. In *The Deer Hunter*, he stands tall and strong, a quiet, confident leader among men. In *Raging Bull*, he changes his image within the film itself, playing a young, trim, perfectly conditioned fighter (Jake La Motta) in the beginning and then ballooning his weight sixty pounds to play the middle-aged La Motta at the film's end. His transformations are so perfectly executed and his character is so completely transformed that we lose sight of the fact that we're seeing the same actor in all three roles. Dustin Hoffman too has this rare ability, as seen in his portrayal of extremely different characters in *The Graduate*, *Midnight Cowboy*, *Tootsie*, *Rain Man*, and *Billy Bathgate*, as does Ralph Fiennes in *Schindler's List*, *Quiz Show*, *The English Patient*, and *Oscar and Lucinda* (Figure 10.11).

Many young actors are wary of falling into the typecasting trap and plan their careers accordingly, doing everything possible to avoid the dangers. Gary Busey, who like De Niro has altered his weight and his appearance greatly in some of the roles he's played, expresses his philosophy this way: "My idea is to look for roles that make right-angle turns from one film to the next. I try to bring a freshness and spontaneity to each part and scene I play."[24]

As far as casting is concerned, there are often disadvantages for the male actor who is too handsome or the female actor who is exceptionally beautiful, because the strength of their attractiveness cuts down somewhat on the number of roles they can play. Actor Paul Newman says his ability to choose roles is limited by the expectations of the audience:

> I think it's a combination of things. When I first started working in films, I think the audience allowed me greater leeway to experiment. For instance, I don't know that they would accept me as Rocky Graziano today. It's too bad, because there's no sense stretching yourself as an actor to go into a film if you know that by your very presence in that film you will destroy the picture, literally, that the image that audiences have created for you will work against whatever you bring to the film.[25]

There is a limited group of fine leading actors who might be called "the ordinary people," actors who have everyday kinds of faces. Such actors do not have the star quality to become fantasy objects or matinee idols, but their special gift of blandness frees them to become actors of great range and flexibility. Chameleonlike, they can blend into any surroundings, and they seem convincing and natural in almost any part they choose to play. Actors such as Gene Hackman, Robert Duvall, Jane Alexander, Ben Kingsley, and Mary Steenburgen have perhaps a wider range of roles open to them simply because they are not

Figure 10.11 The Actor as Chameleon Without the aid of makeup, Ralph Fiennes transforms himself from the brutal SS officer Amon Goeth in *Schindler's List* (top left) into the naive and seemingly innocent Charles Van Doren in *Quiz Show* (top right). Likewise, Denzel Washington moves convincingly from the conscientious military officer in *Courage Under Fire* (bottom left) to the struggling convict of *He Got Game* (pictured here with Ray Allen, who plays his son) (bottom right).

stereotypically glamorous Hollywood stars (Figure 10.12). Although they are very attractive in their own ways, an everyman or everywoman quality to their appearance prevents them from becoming typecast. Gene Hackman, who never worries about the fact that he is seldom recognized in public, doesn't really want to be a star: "I like to be thought of as an actor. It could be conceived as some

Figure 10.12 Ordinary People The extraordinary talent concealed behind these rather ordinary faces helps give Gene Hackman, Ben Kingsley, Mary Steenburgen, Robert Duvall, and Jane Alexander (clockwise, from top) greater flexibility than the more glamorous stars in the roles they play.

kind of a cop-out, I guess. But I'm afraid that if I start to become a star, I'll lose contact with the normal guys I play best."[26]

Supporting Players

The casting process does not begin and end with the selection of stars for the leading roles. Almost as important as the leading players in any production are the supporting players. Although they may not provide the box-office draw of the big names, the supporting players may be even less interchangeable from movie to movie than the major stars. For example, George Raft was originally chosen to play Sam Spade in *The Maltese Falcon*, and it is fairly easy to imagine him in the role. But could anyone other than Peter Lorre play the part of Joel Cairo?

Supporting players do exactly that—*support* the major roles. The major stars play off them, as friends, adversaries, employers, employees, leaders, or even **foils** (contrasting characters that serve to clearly define the personality of the main character). Supporting players make the stars shine brighter, sharper, and more clearly, providing a sounding board that both helps to bring out all the dimensions of the star's character and makes the most important facets stand out in bold relief.

But supporting players often do much more. Sometimes they create characters that are brilliant in their own right. Although their glow may be less radiant than that of the star players they support, the supporting players often create, usually with (but often without) the star, some of the most memorable moments in film. Consider the contributions of Gene Hackman, Estelle Parsons, Dub Taylor, Gene Wilder, and Michael J. Pollard to *Bonnie and Clyde*, Butterfly McQueen to *Gone With the Wind*, Thomas Mitchell to *Mr. Smith Goes to Washington* and *Stagecoach*, Sterling Hayden and Slim Pickens to *Dr. Strangelove*, Ben Johnson to *The Last Picture Show*, Strother Martin to *True Grit*, *Butch Cassidy and the Sundance Kid*, and *Cool Hand Luke*, Thelma Ritter to practically anything, Lucille Benson to *Slaughterhouse Five* and *Silver Streak*, Paul Dooley to *Popeye* (as Wimpy) and to *Breaking Away* (as the father), Scatman Crothers to *Silver Streak*, *The Shining*, and *One Flew Over the Cuckoo's Nest*, John Goodman to *Everybody's All-American*, *Sea of Love*, and *Always*, Martin Landau to *Tucker*, *Crimes and Misdemeanors*, and *Ed Wood*, and Steve Buscemi to *Fargo* and many other independent films. These great performances highlight how important a contribution supporting actors make to the overall quality of any film (Figure 10.13).

With the possible exception of Macaulay Culkin (*Home Alone*, 1990), the modern film has not had child stars of the magnitude of Shirley Temple, Judy Garland, or Mickey Rooney. Children still make important contributions in supporting roles and often steal the show from the starring actors. Most of these young actors seem to have a gift for projecting the naturalness and sincerity so essential for film acting. Remarkable performances by child actors in films like

Figure 10.13 Supporting Players By interacting with the stars playing leading roles and each other, supporting players help define the most important aspects of the stars' character and in the process may create some of the most memorable moments in film. Pictured here are Thelma Ritter ministering to James Stewart in *Rear Window* (top left), Strother Martin being "taken" by George C. Scott in *The Flim Flam Man* (top right), Martin Landau in *Ed Wood* (bottom left), and Steve Buscemi and Peter Stormare in *Fargo* (bottom right).

E.T. The Extra-Terrestrial, *Sleepless in Seattle*, *The Black Stallion*, *Witness*, *Cinema Paradiso*, *Once Upon a Time in America*, *Forrest Gump*, *The Piano*, *Jerry Maguire*, *Ponette*, and *The Butcher Boy* indicate the quality that can be achieved with careful casting (Figures 10.14, 10.15).

Extras and Small Parts

The casting of extras is another important consideration, for extras are often called on to perform some very important scenes. If they are not reacting properly, if their faces do not show what is being called for by the scene they are in,

Figure 10.14 The Tender Years The charm of *Forrest Gump* owes much to convincing performances by Michael Conner Humphreys as young Forrest and Hanna R. Hall as young Jenny. Perhaps the most impressive achievement in Neil Jordan's *The Butcher Boy* is twelve-year-old Eamonn Owens's extraordinary portrayal of Francie Brady, the title character.

Figure 10.15 Growing Up Great care is taken in casting children to portray the young versions of characters who will mature during a film's story. This illustration shows the superb casting of children for *Once Upon a Time in America*. Left to right, Scott Schutzman is the young Noodles (Robert De Niro). Jennifer Connelly is the young Deborah (Elizabeth McGovern). Rust Jacobs is the young Max (James Woods).

the scene may be ruined. Extras are, in a sense, actors in their own right, not just background for the story. For that reason studios hire casting directors to hire extras to fit the film's requirements. Often this job is done on the actual shooting location. The extras casting director goes to the location in advance of the crew and spends a great deal of time finding the right faces, backgrounds, and personalities to fit the story.

Figure 10.16 Extras Director Edward Zwick chose a handful of outstanding actors like Morgan Freeman and Denzel Washington and backed them up with an entire regiment of carefully picked extras for *Glory,* the epic tale of the first Black soldiers to see combat in the Civil War.

Jody Hummer, location casting director for *The River,* starring Mel Gibson, needed two different sets of extras for that film. One group consisted of farmers, who were to assemble at an auction of a farm that had to be sold. Many of the farm extras in the scene had been through such an auction themselves and responded with great sadness and even tears, and their sincerity showed on the screen. A second set of extras was needed to play a group of drifters hired by the film's villain to break down the levee protecting the riverside farms from flooding. For the drifters, Hummer assembled a group of rough-looking unemployed men who looked desperate enough to take any kind of a job.

In the casting of extras, each face must be right, matching our preconceived notions of what a farmer looks like, what a truck driver looks like, or what a drifter looks like. Each extra should fit the type but look different from every other individual in the group. An impression is thus created of a representative sampling of the particular group (Figure 10.16).

Extras are not always cast only on the basis of appearance, because their part may require a special skill. Even in the brief moment they are on-screen, they must do their assigned tasks with naturalness, a lack of self-consciousness, and a competence that shows. Bob Fosse demanded absolute realism in his films.

If a scene called for waiters to serve drinks, instead of actors he used real waiters because they knew the proper way to put a glass down on a table.

Movies are actually a series of brief moments woven into a whole by the editing process. Great movies are therefore movies that achieve as many great moments as possible, and those great moments in many cases are created not by the stars but by the supporting players or the extras. If we are so dazzled by the performance of the stars that we fail to be fully conscious of the rich moments provided by the supporting actors, bit players, and extras, we miss an important part of the film experience. In Zeffirelli's *The Taming of the Shrew*, for example, the screen is packed with fascinating faces, from the major supporting roles to the briefest appearance by an extra. In a well-cast movie there are no weak links. Each member of the cast contributes significantly to the film, whether he or she is on the screen for five seconds, five minutes, or two hours.

Actors as Creative Contributors

Alfred Hitchcock supposedly felt that actors should be treated like cattle, and he came to production with a complete, detailed plan for every shot. Other directors, like Elia Kazan, came to view actors as collaborators in the development of a film. This attitude is best illustrated in Kazan's retelling of the events leading to the famous "I coulda been a contender" scene in *On the Waterfront:*

> I've been highly praised for the direction of this scene, but the truth is I didn't direct it. By the time [cinematographer] Boris [Kaufman] and I had figured out what to do with the set, the morning was gone and Brando was leaving at four; there was nothing to do except put the actors in their places—who on which side of the seat? did it matter?—and photograph them. By that time in the schedule, Brando and Steiger knew who they were and what the scene was about—they knew all that better than I did by then—so I didn't say anything to them.
>
> But of course the extraordinary element in that scene and in the whole picture was Brando, and what was extraordinary about his performance, I feel, is the contrast of the tough-guy front and the extreme delicacy and gentle cast of his behavior. What other actor, when his brother draws a pistol to force him to do something shameful, would put his hand on the gun and push it away with the gentleness of a caress? Who else could read "Oh, Charlie!" in a tone of reproach that is so loving and so melancholy and suggests that terrific depth of pain? I didn't direct that; Marlon showed me, as he often did, how the scene should be performed. I could never have told him how to do that scene as well as he did it.[27] (Figure 10.17)

The modern trend is more and more toward allowing actors a significant role in determining the nature of their characters and giving them a great deal of input into the total creative process. After directing Susan Sarandon in *The*

Figure 10.17 Crediting the Actor Director Elia Kazan credits Marlon Brando for directing himself in this memorable scene (with Rod Steiger) from *On the Waterfront.*

Tempest, director Paul Mazursky paid tribute to her value as a collaborator: "In working on *Tempest*, Susan helped make the character more dimensional than the one I wrote. She had a lot of good criticisms, and I did some rewriting because of her input. . . . Susan would often say to me, 'There's something wrong here; I really think this is a cliché.' She was usually right." Sarandon enjoys a lively give-and-take with her directors, preferring to act in films where "whatever comes into your head you can express. I don't think I've ever worked on a film where I haven't also worked on rewriting the script—except maybe *The Front Page.* Billy Wilder has a very set idea of a film, and everything has to be done to the letter, to the comma."[28]

Dustin Hoffman, who is credited by director Mike Nichols with making several significant contributions to his character in *The Graduate*, believes that the relationship between the actor and the director should be "a real partnership, not the classically imagined situation where a supposedly 'solid, objective' director simply 'handles' a 'neurotic, subjective' actor." As Hoffman explains it:

> I think that some directors are closed minded about what an actor can contribute. You'll hear directors say sometimes "Yes. I got a performance out of that actor: I had to push him. I had to push him further than he thought he could go." Well, there are probably a lot of uncredited occasions where actors have pushed directors into areas that they haven't gone into before, and I think there have been more than a few occasions where a picture is better because of the actor who is in it.

> They will say, "The actor is subjective—only cares about his own part." Not so. An actor is as capable of considering "the whole" as the director, and often does. Sure we care about our own parts, but we have a responsibility to the entire film also, and I don't think many of us ignore that responsibility.[29]

Hoffman's problems with director Sydney Pollack on *Tootsie* have been well documented. In his struggle with Pollack over who had final control over *Tootsie*, Hoffman, who conceived the idea for the film and wanted to produce it, finally worked out a bargain with the director, giving Pollack the ultimate power of **final cut** (final edited version). But Hoffman maintained script and cast approval as well as the right to go into the cutting room, watch the film being edited, and disagree and show alternatives before the final cut was made.

Actress Emma Thompson (who won an Academy Award for her acting in *Howards End*) wrote the Oscar-winning screenplay for the film adaptation of *Sense and Sensibility*, but this fact did not make her major performance in the Ang Lee–directed movie any easier, apparently. In the production diary that she published along with her screenplay, Thompson gives her reader an excellent sense of the day-to-day pressures with which a working actor (even one who happens to be a star) must cope. Near the end of the shoot, when she is called upon to do a demanding emotional scene, Thompson records her intimate observations about the whole process:

> Interesting and difficult scene this—getting the level of Elinor's [her character's] explosion just right. The level of control. I rely entirely on Ang—I can't quite get outside it. Pleased so far and hope I can hit it again this p.m. Barely able to eat, stomach knotted. We shoot largely out of sequence, of course—so I've already done the loss of control in the last scene, which I tried to make as involuntary as possible. A case of the diaphragm taking over. I remembered going to the bank shortly after my father died to try and sort through his papers. I was feeling perfectly calm and sat in the office talking to the manager when suddenly my diaphragm lurched into action and I was unable to do anything but sob helplessly. Walked home, shoulders heaving, thinking, This is weird, because I couldn't stop, there was no possibility of controlling it. It's never happened before or since and was as though the emotion was quite disconnected from actual thought. That was what I wanted to duplicate for the scene when Elinor finds out Edward [the man she loves] isn't married [as she had thought]. *This* moment, though, is much more one of anger—which I've always found very difficult. It's a hotness that's hard to simulate, a sharp heat. She's furious with Marianne [Elinor's younger sister] but hates feeling the anger and doesn't know quite what to do with it. Like watching someone trying to bottle a genie. In the event I play it several different ways so that during the editing Ang has plenty of choices. He won't know what the right note is until he sees it in context. This is the real bugger with film—sometimes you cannot tell where to pitch an emotion and the only safe course is to offer up as many alternatives as possible.[30]

Perhaps the most extreme example of an actor's influence on the overall direction of a film is that of Jon Voight's creative input in *Coming Home.* After two days of shooting, director Hal Ashby, recognizing the impact of Voight's interpretation of his character, threw out the first script. From that point on, the script was written as they shot. Ashby described the process:

> I would talk with the actors the night before and say, "Here's what I think we ought to do tomorrow," and give the reasons why I thought we should do it. And they'd all come in with their lines, and they were great. They were terrific. And that all was guided by Jon's character—I threw out a screenplay because of where he was. That man received incredible amounts of resistance—down to everybody, including Jane Fonda, wanting him to play it more macho.

And all of this creative input came from the actor for whom Ashby had to fight United Artists to cast. When told by Ashby that he wanted Voight in the cast, producer Mike Medavoy simply said, "No way. Absolutely. The man has no sex appeal." He then proceeded with "a whole big line of reasons not to cast Jon Voight in the role."[31] Voight won an Academy Award for the part.

Subjective Responses to Actors

Our response to actors is very subjective and personal, and often our views are diametrically opposed to those of our friends or our favorite critics. Critics themselves disagree violently in their personal response to acting performances. Meryl Streep, an actor to whom people respond in various ways, summarized this problem herself:

> Once a year I come out in a film and go around and listen to people or read people who tell me what they think of me. It's a revelation. I have too many mannerisms . . . or not enough mannerisms . . . to become a real movie star. Someone says I don't put enough of my own character into my roles.[32]

Those who think she has too many mannerisms apparently see them as acting gimmicks, techniques that make the viewer aware she is acting. Others accept the mannerisms (her nervous tics or twitches) as perfectly natural for the character and accept her as the perfect embodiment of the personality of the character she is playing. Whether Streep's acting style works or not may be a matter of casting. Her mannerisms seemed to fit perfectly in *Still of the Night,* where the audience suspected her all along of being a murderer. The nervous mannerisms made us suspect that the *character* she played was acting as she tried to deceive Roy Scheider (playing a psychiatrist). But *Time* critic Richard Schickel objected to her technique in *Silkwood:*

Figure 10.18 What Stars Project Most real stars project essential qualities of their personalities on the screen. Lily Tomlin describes Warren Beatty's essential image as follows: "Warren has this lovable, slightly perplexed look, like he's worried about something. . . . You don't know if he's lost his girl or his car keys and it doesn't matter because whatever is bothering him bothers you. He has this kind of automatic audience rapport. Also, he's got this subjective almost talking-to-himself speech style that makes you feel like you're overhearing something very private. His voice is breathy, sexy."[33] Beatty is seen here in *Reds* (left) and in his title role in *Bulworth* (right).

> She is an actress of calculated effects, which work well when she is playing self-consciously intelligent women. But interpreting a character who abandoned three children, shares a house with a rather shiftless boyfriend and a lesbian, and shows her contempt for authority by flashing a bare breast at its representative, she seems at once forced and pulled back.[34]

Although some actors seem to create a wide range of responses, most stars project some essential image, some profound quality of their personality that comes through on the screen in every role they play (Figure 10.18). These are basic qualities that cannot be changed, and intelligent casting will never ask this kind of star to move outside his or her essential being. Director Sidney Lumet made this point in discussing the special essence of Montgomery Clift:

> One of the things that was so extraordinary about Monty Clift as an actor—and he was certainly one of the great ones—was that he had a quality that had nothing to do with his talent as an actor. He had a vulnerability, an openness, an almost masochistic receptivity to pain that was terrifying. . . . When you cast Monty, you would have been foolish to put him in something where that quality wasn't what you were going for.[35] (Figure 10.19)

Figure 10.19 Special Qualities Montgomery Clift, shown here in his unforgettable portrayal of the strong-willed bugler Robert E. Lee Pruitt in *From Here to Eternity,* projected an unusual sense of vulnerability and "an almost masochistic receptivity to pain that was terrifying."

Questions

On Acting

1. Which actors did you feel were correctly cast in their parts? Which actors were not cast wisely? Why?
2. How well were the physical characteristics, facial features, and voice qualities of the actors suited to the characters they were attempting to portray?
3. If a performance was unconvincing, was it unconvincing because the actor was miscast, or did he or she simply deliver an incompetent performance?
   a. If faulty casting seems to be the problem, what actor would you choose for the part if you were directing the film?
   b. If the actor proved incompetent in the part, what were the primary reasons for his or her failure?
4. What kind of acting is required of the actors in the starring roles—action acting or dramatic acting? Are the actors well suited to the type of acting demanded by the roles they play? If not, why not? Where are their weaknesses or limitations most evident? If they are well suited, in what scenes is their special type of acting skill most apparent?
5. Drawing on your knowledge of their past performances, classify the actors in the major roles as impersonators, interpreters, or personalities.

6. Try to determine whether the following actors are impersonators, interpreters, or personalities: Woody Allen, Fred Astaire, Dan Aykroyd, Lauren Bacall, Kevin Bacon, Anne Bancroft, Alec Baldwin, Kim Basinger, Angela Bassett, Kathy Bates, Warren Beatty, Ingrid Bergman, Halle Berry, Juliette Binoche, Humphrey Bogart, Kenneth Branagh, Marlon Brando, Jeff Bridges, Sandra Bullock, Richard Burton, James Caan, Nicolas Cage, James Cagney, Michael Caine, Jim Carrey, Charlie Chaplin, Julie Christie, Montgomery Clift, Glenn Close, Claudette Colbert, Sean Connery, Gary Cooper, Kevin Costner, Joan Crawford, Tom Cruise, John Cusack, Willem Dafoe, Bette Davis, Geena Davis, Sammy Davis, Doris Day, Daniel Day-Lewis, James Dean, Catherine Deneuve, Robert De Niro, Johnny Depp, Laura Dern, Leonardo DiCaprio, Marlene Dietrich, Kirk Douglas, Michael Douglas, Robert Downey Jr., Richard Dreyfuss, Faye Dunaway, Robert Duvall, Clint Eastwood, Mia Farrow, Sally Field, Ralph Fiennes, Peter Finch, Laurence Fishburne, Errol Flynn, Henry Fonda, Jane Fonda, Harrison Ford, Jodie Foster, Morgan Freeman, Clark Gable, Greta Garbo, Judy Garland, James Garner, Greer Garson, Richard Gere, Mel Gibson, John Gielgud, Lillian Gish, Danny Glover, Whoopi Goldberg, Cary Grant, Hugh Grant, Alec Guinness, Gene Hackman, Tom Hanks, Ed Harris, Goldie Hawn, Audrey Hepburn, Katharine Hepburn, Barbara Hershey, Charlton Heston, Dustin Hoffman, William Holden, Anthony Hopkins, Rock Hudson, Holly Hunter, John Hurt, William Hurt, Glenda Jackson, Samuel L. Jackson, James Earl Jones, Tommy Lee Jones, Buster Keaton, Diane Keaton, Michael Keaton, Harvey Keitel, Gene Kelly, Deborah Kerr, Nicole Kidman, Kevin Kline, Burt Lancaster, Jessica Lange, Charles Laughton, Vivien Leigh, Jack Lemmon, Sophia Loren, Andie MacDowell, Shirley MacLaine, John Malkovich, Steve Martin, James Mason, Marcello Mastroianni, Walter Matthau, Matthew McConaughey, Steve McQueen, Liza Minnelli, Robert Mitchum, Marilyn Monroe, Demi Moore, Eddie Murphy, Bill Murray, Liam Neeson, Paul Newman, Jack Nicholson, David Niven, Nick Nolte, Chuck Norris, Kim Novak, Gary Oldman, Laurence Olivier, Peter O'Toole, Al Pacino, Gregory Peck, Sean Penn, Anthony Perkins, Michelle Pfeiffer, Brad Pitt, Sidney Poitier, William Powell, Richard Pryor, Dennis Quaid, Anthony Quinn, Robert Redford, Vanessa Redgrave, Christopher Reeve, Burt Reynolds, Tim Robbins, Julia Roberts, Edward G. Robinson, Ginger Rogers, Kurt Russell, Rosalind Russell, Meg Ryan, Winona Ryder, Susan Sarandon, Roy Scheider, Arnold Schwarzenegger, George C. Scott, Peter Sellers, Robert Shaw, Christian Slater, Wesley Snipes, Sissy Spacek, Kevin Spacey, James Spader, Sylvester Stallone, Barbara Stanwyck, Mary Steenburgen, Rod Steiger, James Stewart, Sharon Stone, Meryl Streep, Barbra Streisand, Donald Sutherland, Jessica Tandy, Elizabeth Taylor, Kristin Scott Thomas, Emma Thompson, Spencer Tracy, John Travolta, Kathleen Turner, Lana Turner,

Jon Voight, Denzel Washington, John Wayne, Sigourney Weaver, Raquel Welch, Orson Welles, Robin Williams, Bruce Willis, Debra Winger, Natalie Wood, James Woods, Joanne Woodward.

Justify your decision in categorizing each actor by describing the degree of similarities or differences in his or her roles in at least three movies. Which of the actors are most difficult to categorize and why?

7. Consider the following questions with respect to each of the starring actors:
   a. Does the actor seem to depend more on the charm of his or her own personality, or does he or she attempt to become the character?
   b. Is the actor consistently believable in the portrayal of the character, or does he or she occasionally fall out of character?
   c. If the actor seems unnatural in the part, is it because he or she tends to be overdramatic or wooden and mechanical? Is this unnaturalness more apparent in the way the actor delivers the lines or in the actor's physical actions?
8. In which specific scenes is the acting especially effective or ineffective? Why?
9. In which scenes are the actors' facial expressions used in reaction shots? What reaction shots are particularly effective?
10. How strong is the cast of supporting actors, and what does each contribute to the film? How does each help bring out different aspects of the star's personality? Do the supporting players create memorable moments or steal the show in spots? If so, where in the film do such moments occur?
11. What contributions do the small parts and extras make to the film? Are the faces and bodies well chosen to fit our preconceived notions of what they should look like? Are their "working tasks," if any, performed with confidence and naturalness?
12. Taking as your model Lily Tomlin's description of what Warren Beatty projects (see the caption to Figure 10.18), describe the qualities projected by any of your favorites listed in question 6.

Video Exercises

Instructions for locating specific sequences are given on page 77.

1. Watch the "Scar Competition" scene from *Jaws* [4655 to 5020; 1:26:03 to 1:32:53]. What do the following factors contribute to the power of this sequence: character interaction, voice qualities, reaction shots, camerawork, and lighting?
2. Watch the "Group Captain Mandrake Tries to Call the White House" sequence from *Dr. Strangelove* [3820 to 3980; 1:08:48 to 1:12:32]. Identify specific factors in the performances of Peter Sellers and Keenan Wynn that contribute to the effectiveness and believability of this scene.

3. Watch the "Ma Joad Burns the Souvenirs" sequence from *The Grapes of Wrath* [1965 to 2080; 0:29:14 to 0:31:08]. Carefully note each item Ma Joad examines; then watch her reaction and describe what her face reveals about her feelings connected with that item. Turn the sound off and watch the sequence again. Is the sequence more powerful with or without the music? Why? What role does the lighting play in this sequence?

Films for Study

Adam's Rib (1949)
The African Queen (1951)
The Apostle (1997)
As Good As It Gets (1997)
Becket (1964)
The Butcher Boy (1998)
The Caine Mutiny (1954)
Cinema Paradiso (1988)
City Lights (1931)
Courage Under Fire (1996)
A Cry in the Dark (1988)
Driving Miss Daisy (1989)
The Elephant Man (1980)
Fargo (1996)
From Here to Eternity (1953)
The General (1927)
The Grapes of Wrath (1940)
The Great Santini (1979)
He Got Game (1998)
High Art (1998)
Hilary and Jackie (1998)
Hoosiers (1986)
Jerry Maguire (1996)
La Strada (1954)
Midnight Cowboy (1969)
Modern Times (1936)
My Left Foot (1989)
Nell (1994)
Nobody's Fool (1994)
On the Waterfront (1954)
Out of Africa (1985)
The Piano (1993)
Quiz Show (1994)
Rachel, Rachel (1968)
Raging Bull (1980)
Rain Man (1988)
Reality Bites (1994)
Schindler's List (1993)
Sense and Sensibility (1995)
Seven Beauties (1976)
Sling Blade (1996)
A Soldier's Daughter Never Cries (1998)
A Streetcar Named Desire (1951)
Taxi Driver (1976)
Tender Mercies (1983)
The Trip to Bountiful (1985)
Who's Afraid of Virginia Woolf? (1966)

Chapter 11

The Director's Style

Actually, *everything* a director puts up on the screen is revelatory. Don't you really know all about John Ford from his films? Or Hitchcock, or Howard Hawks? If I reveal a character on the screen, I am necessarily also revealing myself, whether it's Treplev in *The Seagull* or Sean Connery in *The Hill.* I think I have an idea of what my work is about, but I'm not interested in articulating it in words.

—Sidney Lumet, Director

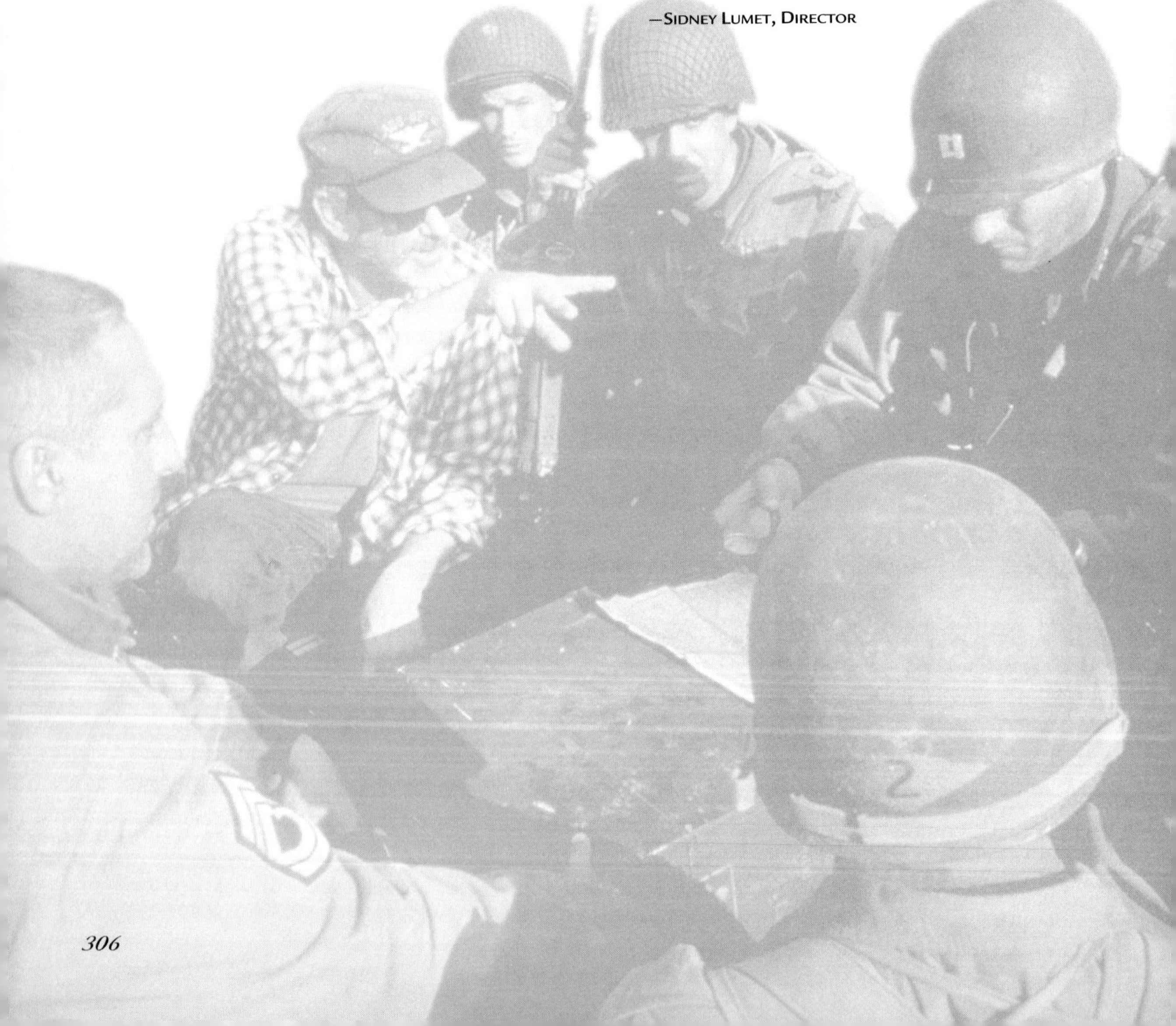

In his recent book of interviews, *Who the Devil Made It*, Peter Bogdanovich, accomplished filmmaker (*The Last Picture Show, What's Up, Doc?, Paper Moon, Mask*) and writer about films and their creators, tries at the outset to define the role of the movie director:

> In 1915, when President Wilson was asked for his reaction to [film pioneer D. W.] Griffith's new picture—*The Birth of a Nation* was the first film ever shown at the White House—the president is recorded as having said: "It is like writing history with lightning." This was a particularly apt description for more than one reason: lightning not only has enormous powers, it is accidental. When I once repeated to Welles Mr. [John] Ford's comment about "most of the good things in pictures" happening "by accident," Orson leapt on it right away. "Yes!" he said. "You could almost say that a director is a man who *presides* over accidents."[1]

Welles's "almost" is very important here, because he was well aware that every director needs as many good helpers as he or she can possibly manage in taking full advantage of these "accidents." Director Sidney Lumet, in *Making Movies*, provides an illustration of this wisdom:

> On my second picture, *Stage Struck*, a scene between Henry Fonda and Christopher Plummer took place in Central Park. I had shot most of the scene by lunchtime. We broke for an hour, knowing that we had just a few shots to do after lunch to finish the sequence. During lunch, snow started to fall. When we came back, the park was already covered in white. The snow was so beautiful, I wanted to redo the whole scene. Franz Planner, the cameraman, said it was impossible because we'd be out of light by four o'clock. I quickly restaged the scene, giving Plummer a new entrance so that I could see the snow-covered park; then I placed them on a bench, shot a master and two close-ups. The lens was wide open by the last take, but we got it all. Because the actors were prepared, because the crew knew what it was doing, we just swung with the weather and wound up with a better scene. Preparation allows the "lucky accident" that we're always hoping for to happen. It has happened many times since: in a scene between Sean Connery and Vanessa Redgrave in the real Istanbul for *Murder on the Orient Express;* in a scene between Paul Newman and Charlotte Rampling in *The Verdict;* and in many scenes with Al Pacino and various bank employees in *Dog Day Afternoon.* Because everyone knew what he or she was doing, practically all of the improvisation wound up in the finished movie.[2]

A motion picture, then, is always a cooperative effort, a joint creative interaction of many artists and technicians working on diverse elements, all of which contribute to the finished film. Because of the technical and physical complexity of filmmaking and the large number of people involved, it might seem misleading to talk of any single individual's style. The director, however, generally serves as the unifying force and makes the majority of the creative decisions, so it is perhaps proper to equate the film's style with the director's style.

The actual amount of control that directors have varies widely. At one extreme is the director who functions primarily as a hireling of a big studio. The studio buys a story or an idea, hires a scriptwriter to translate it into film language, and then assigns the script to a director who more or less mechanically supervises the shooting of the film. At the other extreme is the concept of the director as *auteur*, or author, of the film. An ***auteur*** is a complete filmmaker. He or she conceives the idea for the story, writes the script or the screenplay, and then carefully supervises every step in the filmmaking process, from selecting the cast and finding a suitable setting down to editing the final cut. The Swedish director Ingmar Bergman and the American director Orson Welles are viewed by many as the ultimate auteurs.

Most directors fall into the gray area between those two extremes, for the degree of studio involvement or control and the director's dependence on other creative personalities can vary considerably. But regardless of the actual degree of control, the director has the greatest opportunity to impart a personal artistic vision, philosophy, technique, and attitude into the film as a whole, thereby dictating or determining its style. In analyzing or evaluating a director's style, therefore, we assume that the director has exercised aesthetic control over at least the majority of complex elements that make up a finished film.

A meaningful assessment of any director's style requires the careful study of at least three of his or her films, concentrating on those special qualities of the work that set the individual apart from all other directors. The study of six or more films may be necessary to characterize the style of directors who go through a long evolutionary period of stylistic experimentation before they arrive at anything consistent enough to be called a style.

The Concept of Style

A director's style is the manner in which the director's personality is expressed through the language of the medium. A director's style is reflected in almost every decision the director makes. Every element or combination of elements may reveal a unique creative personality that shapes, molds, and filters the film through intellect, sensibility, and imagination. If we assume that all directors strive to communicate clearly with the audience, then we can further assume that directors want to manipulate our responses to correspond with their own, so that we can share that vision. Thus, almost everything directors do in making a film is a part of their style, because in almost every decision they are in some subtle way interpreting or commenting on the action, revealing their own attitudes, and injecting their own personality indelibly into the film.

Before examining the separate elements that reveal style in film, it is worthwhile to make some observations about the film as a whole. In this general analysis, we might consider whether the film is

intellectual and rational	*or*	emotional and sensual
calm and quiet	*or*	fast-paced and exciting
polished and smooth	*or*	rough and crude-cut
cool and objective	*or*	warm and subjective
ordinary and trite	*or*	fresh and original
tightly structured, direct, and concise	*or*	loosely structured and rambling
truthful and realistic	*or*	romantic and idealized
simple and straightforward	*or*	complex and indirect
grave, serious, tragic, and heavy	*or*	light, comical, and humorous
restrained and understated	*or*	exaggerated
optimistic and hopeful	*or*	bitter and cynical
logical and orderly	*or*	irrational and chaotic

An accurate assessment of these values is a good first step toward an analysis of the director's style. A complete analysis must examine his or her treatment of subject matter, cinematography, editing, and other individual film elements.

Subject Matter

Perhaps no other element reveals more about a director's style than the choice of subject matter. For a director who is truly an *auteur*—a person who conceives the idea for a film and then writes the script or supervises the writing to conform to his or her own vision—the subject is an essential aspect of style. Directors who are not *auteurs* but are free to choose the stories they want to film also express their style by their choice of subject matter. Even studio assignments may reveal a director's style if they call for the director to make a film that is similar to films that he or she has already made.

An examination of subject matter might begin with a search for common themes running through all the films under study. One director may be concerned primarily with social problems, another with men's and women's relationship to God, and yet another with the struggle between good and evil. Directors' choices of subject matter may be related to their tendency to create similar emotional effects or moods in everything they do. Alfred Hitchcock, for example, is clearly identified with the terror/suspense film, in which the mood becomes a kind of theme (Figure 11.1). Some directors specialize in a genre such as the western, historical pageant, or comedy. Others specialize in adapting novels or plays to film.

A director's personal background may be a significant influence on the kind of stories he or she is drawn to. Martin Scorsese, for example, grew up in New York City and often uses his old neighborhood and his old haunts as his setting and seems to focus on types of characters he has known. Scorsese is a very personal filmmaker. Steven Spielberg, in contrast, was a child of the suburbs and is more inclined toward fantasy bigger-than-life stories and characters. Spielberg describes the different subjects that appeal to him and Scorsese:

> [W]e all do different things. I could never make *Raging Bull.* I don't think Marty could have made, let's say, *Close Encounters*, in the same way. He'd have made a wonderful and interesting *Close Encounters.* I don't think I would have made a wonderful or interesting *Raging Bull!* Marty likes primal life, he likes the primal scream. He's the best director of the primal scene in film history. The primal scream scares the stuff out of me, and I've been avoiding it all my life. And so I make movies that are a little bit above life, or below life, but not real life! Beyond real life. And those are the kinds of films that have always attracted me.[3]

That both directors are capable of tackling new subject matter, however, is clearly evidenced by their more recent achievements: Spielberg's brutally real-

Figure 11.1 Master of Suspense Because he supposedly felt that actors should be treated like cattle and came to production with a detailed plan for every shot, Alfred Hitchcock gained a reputation as an *auteur* director. Hitchcock, however, did not write the screenplays for the major American films he directed—although he worked closely with his writers.

Figure 11.2 Tackling New Subjects Steven Spielberg, known for his fantasy films, took a dramatic turn in choice of subject matter with *Schindler's List,* and, later, he continued his journey into realism by directing *Saving Private Ryan,* starring Tom Hanks (shown here). Between these two films, he directed Morgan Freeman and Anthony Hopkins in *Amistad,* about the consequences of a slave ship revolt.

istic docudrama on Jewish persecution during World War II, *Schindler's List* (Figure 11.2), and Scorsese's richly textured study of the manners and mores of upper-crust New York society in the 1870s, *The Age of Innocence*—not to mention his exploration of the mystical traditions and tragic recent history of Tibet in *Kundun.*

The types of conflicts that directors choose to deal with constitute an important thematic thread. Some directors lean toward a serious examination of subtle philosophical problems concerning the complexities of human nature, the universe, or God. Others favor simple stories of ordinary people facing the ordinary problems of life. Still others prefer to treat physical conflict such as occurs in action/adventure films.

The subjects that a director chooses may also show some consistency with respect to the concepts of time and space. Some directors prefer a story in which the action takes place in a very short time period—a week or less. Others prefer historical panoramas spanning a century or more. Spatial concepts may be equally diverse. Some directors specialize in epic films, with casts of thousands and a broad, sweeping landscape as a canvas. Others restrict themselves to a limited physical setting and keep the number of actors in the cast to a bare minimum. Screenwriters like to know who is going to direct the script they are writing, so they can tailor the script to fit that particular director's strengths and limitations. As William Goldman tells it:

> You absolutely tailor toward a director's strength. You absolutely do. If you were writing an Alfred Hitchcock picture, you knew you didn't want to give him scope. He couldn't shoot scope. And if you have David Lean, you don't give David Lean a scene in a room. You give David Lean scope and he can *shoot* it. He's willing to, and he has the skill and brilliance to shoot it. Hitchcock, no. And I use those examples of two extraordinary directors that do different things. Directors *do* different things well.[4]

In some cases, study of a director's typical subject matter may reveal a unified worldview, a consistent philosophical statement on the nature of man and the universe. Even the use of **irony**—the juxtaposition of opposites—can take on philosophical implications reflecting the director's worldview if he or she uses it enough (see the section on irony in Chapter 3). Most directors, however, aren't consciously striving to express or develop a unified worldview, possibly because doing so would stifle their creativity. But that doesn't mean that philosophical patterns don't emerge, as Sydney Pollack explains:

> As I've gotten older and done more films, it's something I read more and more often about my own work. I would constantly read articles—at first they were only from Europe, but now they tend to be written in America, too—that would say, for instance, all my films are "circular." And I kept saying, what the hell is "circular"? Then I started looking at my films, and, by God, they are circular. But what does that mean? I don't know what it means. Then the articles began to say Pollack's films are all concerned with culture clashes, or they're all concerned with destiny, or so and so. And I think all those things are true, and that's fair to say and I'm fascinated to hear about this. But this is not something I set out consciously to do.
>
> When you direct a picture you may be concentrating on a particular task at hand, which taps all sorts of areas in your unconscious that you're not aware of. Those areas seep into the work itself. If I took a love scene from any one of my pictures, or anybody else's, and set it up as a hypothetical experiment and had, let's say, Frankenheimer direct it, myself, Coppola, Mark Rydell—five or six or ten directors—you would get that many different love scenes. The same scene, same actors. You'd get a lyrical love scene, an erotic love scene, a tender love scene, a cynical love scene, a sophisticated love scene. Not in what they say, but in the actual handling of the actors—how do you place them, are they standing or seated, what's the lighting? Is it all in one shot and does the camera keep moving around them? Is it staccato and in cuts? Is the camera focusing only on eyes, or is it details of hands and skin? Now, in the doing of that, you take a kind of lie-detector test; you can't lie, something of who you are and what you believe in gets in there.[5]

Figure 11.3 The Ultimate *Auteurs* Swedish director Ingmar Bergman, shown here with his cinematographer Sven Nykvist, is generally considered the ultimate *auteur* because his work over the years has projected a strong personal artistic vision. In America, Orson Welles (seen here shooting *Citizen Kane* with his cameraman Gregg Toland, sitting at right) sometimes played this role.

Cinematography

The cinematographer oversees the camerawork and plays a significant role in the conceptualizing and treatment of the visual elements. But how can we accurately assess the cinematographer's contribution to the director's style? We weren't present on the set, and we lack important inside information. We cannot really know how much of the visual style of *The Birth of a Nation* was the work of Billy Bitzer, how much imagery in *Citizen Kane* was conceived by Gregg Toland, or how much of *The Seventh Seal* resulted from the creative vision of Gunnar Fischer. Because directors usually choose the cinematographer they want, we can assume their selections are based on a compatibility of visual philosophies, and for simplicity's sake we usually attribute the film's visual style to the director (Figure 11.3).

In analyzing visual style, we must first consider the composition. Some directors use composition formally and dramatically; others prefer an informal or low-key effect. One director may favor a certain type of arrangement of people and objects in the frame; another may place special emphasis on one particular type of camera angle. Important differences may also be noted in "philosophies of camera." For example, some directors stress the **objective camera** (a camera that views the action as a remote spectator); others lean toward the **subjective camera** (a camera that views the scene from the visual or emotional point of view of a participant). Other marks of cinematic style include the consistent use of certain devices—such as unusual camera angles, slow or fast motion, colored or light-diffusing filters, or distorting lenses—to interpret the visual scene in some unique way.

Lighting also expresses directorial style. Some directors prefer to work with low-key lighting, which creates stark contrasts between light and dark areas and leaves large portions of the set in shadow. Others favor high-key lighting, which is more even and contains many subtle shades of gray. Even the character of the lighting contributes greatly to the director's visual style, because a director may favor harsh, balanced, or diffused lighting throughout a series of films.

Treatment of color may also be an element of cinematic style. Some directors use sharp, clear images dominated by bright, highly contrasting hues. Some favor soft, muted, pastel shades and dim or even blurred tones.

Camera movement also reveals a director's style. The possibilities range from favoring the static camera, which moves as little as possible, to favoring the fixed camera, which creates a sense of movement through panning and tilting. Another choice is the "poetic" mobile camera, whose slow, liquid, almost floating movements are achieved by mounting the camera on a dolly or boom crane. And although one director may favor the freedom and spontaneity of the jerky handheld camera, another may make great use of the zoom lens to simulate movement into and out of the frame. The type of camera movement that directors favor is an important stylistic element, for it affects a film's sense of pace and rhythm and greatly affects the film's overall impression.

Some directors are especially concerned with achieving three-dimensionality in their images, and the techniques they use to achieve this effect become an integral part of their visual style.

Editing

Editing is an important stylistic element because it affects the overall rhythm or pace of the film. The most obvious element of editorial style is the length of the average shot in the film. Generally the longer the time between editorial cuts, the slower is the pace of the film.

Editorial cuts that make time/place transitions may take on a unique rhythmic character. One director may favor a soft, fluid transition, such as a slow dissolve, where another would simply cut immediately from one sequence to the next, relying on the soundtrack or the visual context to make the transition clear. David Lynch believes that a subtle balance between slow and fast pacing is essential:

> I think that pacing is extremely important. . . . It shouldn't be boring, but fast pacing doesn't make interesting or good. It may jar you, but it's the feeling of the story that you want and it wants to be told in a certain way and pull you. And a certain slowness, not boring, but a certain slowness contrasted with something fast is very

> important. It's like music. If music was all just fast it would be a bummer. But symphonies and stuff are built on slow and fast and high and low, and it thrills your soul. And film is the same way.[6]

When editorial juxtapositions are used creatively, the director's style may be seen in the relationships between shots. Directors may stress an intellectual relationship between two shots by using ironic or metaphorical juxtapositions, or they may emphasize visual continuity by cutting to similar forms, colors, or textures. They might choose to emphasize aural relationships by linking two shots solely through the soundtrack or the musical score.

Other special tricks of editing, such as the use of parallel cutting, fragmented flash cutting, and dialogue overlaps, are also indicators of style. Editing may also be characterized by whether it calls attention to itself. One director may lean toward editing that is clever, self-conscious, and tricky, whereas another may favor editing that is smooth, natural, and unobtrusive. The use of montages and the nature of the images used also help to characterize editing style.

Setting and Set Design

Closely related to the choice of subject matter is the choice of setting and the degree to which it is emphasized. The visual emphasis placed on the setting may be an important aspect of the director's style. One director may favor settings that are stark, barren, or drab; another may choose settings of great natural beauty. Some may use setting to help us understand character or as a powerful tool to build atmosphere or mood; others may simply allow setting to slide by as a backdrop to the action, giving it no particular emphasis at all.

By choosing to photograph certain details in the setting, the director may stress either the sordid and the brutal or the ideal and the romantic. This type of emphasis may be an important aspect of the director's style, for it may indicate an overall worldview. Other factors of setting that may reflect the director's style are which social and economic classes the director focuses on, whether the settings are rural or urban, and whether the director favors contemporary, historical past, or futuristic time periods. Also, when elaborate or unusual sets have been constructed especially for a film, the director's taste is often apparent in the set design.

Sound and Score

Directors make use of the soundtrack and the musical score in unique and individual ways. Whereas one may simply match natural sounds to the corresponding action, another may consider sound almost as important as the image and use off-screen sound imaginatively to create a sense of total environment.

Yet another director may use sound in an impressionistic or even symbolic manner; still another might stress the rhythmic and even musical properties of natural sounds and use them instead of a musical score.

With respect to screen dialogue, some directors want every word to be clearly and distinctly heard, and they record with this aim in mind. Others allow—even encourage—overlapping lines and frequent interruptions because of the realism these effects produce.

Loudness or softness of the soundtrack as a whole may also reflect something of a director's style. One director may employ silence as a sound effect, whereas another may feel a need to fill every second with some kind of sound. Similarly, some may use a minimum of dialogue, whereas others fill the soundtrack with dialogue and depend on it to carry the major burdens of the film's communication.

Directors also may vary greatly in their utilization of the musical score. One director may be completely dependent on music to create and sustain mood; another may use it sparingly. One may use music to communicate on several levels of meaning, whereas another may use music only when it reinforces the rhythms of the action. Whereas one director may desire the music to be understated or even completely inconspicuous, so we are not even aware of the score, another may employ strong, emotional music that occasionally overpowers the visual elements. Some favor music scored expressly for the film; others employ a variety of familiar music as it fits their purpose. Instrumentation and size of orchestra are also elements of style. Some directors prefer a full symphony sound; others find a few instruments or even a single instrument more effective.

Casting and Acting Performances

Most directors have a hand in selecting the actors they work with, and it must be taken for granted that they can have a strong influence on individual acting performances. In the choice of actors, one director may take the safe, sure way by casting established stars in roles very similar to roles they have played before. Another may prefer to try relatively unknown actors who do not already have an established image. Another may like to cast an established star in a role entirely different from anything he or she has played before. Some directors never work with the same actor twice; others employ the same stable of actors in almost every film they make. Working frequently with the same actors can greatly increase a director's efficiency. Knowing the strengths and weaknesses of the cast and having already established rapport with them, the director can concentrate on getting high-level performances. The downside of such familiarity is the danger that the director and cast will slip into comfortable patterns and repeat themselves in films that seem too much alike.

In their choice of actors, directors may also reveal an emphasis on certain qualities. A director can have a remarkable feel for faces and choose stars and even bit players who have faces with extremely strong visual character—that is, faces that may not be beautiful or handsome but are strikingly powerful on the screen. Or a director may prefer to work with only the "beautiful people." One director may seem to stress the actors' voice qualities, and another may consider the total body or the physical presence of the actor more important.

The director may have a tremendous influence on the acting style of the cast, although the extent of this influence may be difficult to determine even in a study of several films. Almost every aspect of an actor's performance can be influenced by the director—the subtlety of the facial expressions, the quality of the voice and physical gestures, and the psychological depth of the interpretation of the role. Thus, an actor who has a tendency to overplay for one director may show more subtlety and restraint with another. Whether a director has the ability to influence the acting style of each actor under his or her direction is, of course, impossible to detect, but in some cases the director's influence may be obvious. When asked about his technique for rehearsing actors, Orson Welles replied,

> It depends on the actors. I think a director oughtn't to have a method he imposes on actors. I think the *actors* impose the method by their personalities, characteristics, and everything else. There are some actors who are unhappy and insecure unless you come on very strong, very firm, and give them an enormous amount of information. And others who are much better in a party, where you just kind of slip free information into their minds while nobody's looking. . . . One tries to ["sense the different actors"]. I think that separates the boys from the men in directors. There *are* fine directors who are so much themselves that the actors have to toe the line and follow them. But I've always thought . . . that the job of the director is slightly overrated, overinflated, and I think the director must think of himself as the servant of the actors and the story—even when he wrote the story. Really, the big thing is what the actors are going to do—not that the actors are going to do what *you* want. It's to find out what they're going to do and bring it out of them. And I think you have to feel it sincerely—not just pretend that's what you think; you must mean it. I think you have to make an actor believe that he's better than he is. That's the biggest job. . . . There are so many ways of doing it, and it's dictated by the material itself and by the actor. It's so much a question of personality and mood.[7]

Screenplays and Narrative Structure

The way a director chooses to tell the story—the narrative structure—is also an important element of style. A director may choose to build a simple, straightforward, chronological sequence of events, as in *Shane* or *High Noon*, or a complex elliptical structure, jumping back and forth in time, as in *Slaughterhouse Five* or *Pulp Fiction* or *Citizen Kane*. A director may choose to tell a story objectively, putting the camera and the viewer in the vantage point of a sideline observer, bringing the action just close enough so that we get all the necessary information without identifying with any single character. Or a director may tell the story from the viewpoint of a single character and manipulate us so that we essentially experience the story as that character perceives it. Although the camera does not limit itself to subjective shots, we emotionally and intellectually identify with the **point-of-view character** and see the story through his or her eyes. A director may structure the film so that we get multiple viewpoints, seeing the same action repeated as it is perceived from the different viewpoints of several characters. Along the way, there may be side trips into the characters' minds, into fantasies or memories as in *Midnight Cowboy*, *The World According to Garp*, *Annie Hall*, and *Out of Sight* (1998).

Sometimes there may be some confusion about whether what we are seeing is reality or illusion. The dividing line between those two may be clear or blurred. Time may be compressed in montages or clever transitions that jump huge segments of time. Changing time frames may be made clear with newsreel inserts, TV news segments, or popular music on radio, phonograph, or tape or CD players.

Unusual techniques, like the witnesses in *Reds*, may be inserted into the narrative to provide both background information and varying viewpoints. Voice-over narration may be provided from the point-of-view character to set up a frame at beginning or end and to fill in gaps in the filmed narrative. Or voice-over narration may be employed not just to help structure the film but to provide style and humor (as in *Forrest Gump*) or the sense of an author telling the story (as in *Cannery Row*).

Beginnings may be slow and leisurely; the director may prefer to establish characters and exposition before conflict develops. Or he or she may prefer exciting, dynamic *in medias res* beginnings, where conflict is already developing when the film opens. Some directors may prefer endings in which the tying up of all loose ends provides a sense of completeness. Others may prefer endings without a clear-cut resolution—endings that leave questions unanswered and give us something to puzzle about long after the film is over. Some directors prefer upbeat endings—that is, endings on a heroic note, with strong, uplifting music. Some prefer downbeat endings that offer little or no hope. There are spectacular endings, quiet endings, happy endings, and sad endings. Some directors may use trick endings, withholding information from the audience until the end and devising strange and unusual plot twists to produce endings for which we're not prepared.

Some directors create a tight structure so that every single action and every word of dialogue advance the plot. Others prefer a rambling, loosely structured plot with side trips that may be interesting but actually have little or nothing to do with stream of the action. Some structures let the audience in on the secrets but keep the characters guessing, creating a sense of dramatic irony. Other structures withhold information from the audience and create suspense with mystery. Repeated patterns of character are often used. The entire film may end with the resolution of one problem and establish the fact that the character has taken on another similar problem at the end, so that we get a sense that the character has not really learned anything from the experience but will continue going about his or her crazy business (as in *Breaking Away*).

Directors also differ in the way they handle films with multiple narrative levels. Complex plots, with several lines of action occurring simultaneously at different locations, can be broken into fragments jumping quickly back and forth from one developing story to another. Or each stream of action can be developed rather completely before switching to another stream of narrative.

One director may prefer a lazy, slow-paced, gradual unfolding of character or information, focusing on each single detail. Another director may prefer compressed, machine-gun dialogue and quick images to get exposition out of the way as quickly as possible and introduce characters quickly so that he or she can use more time later to focus on the most dramatic scenes.

What actually carries the narrative forward may also vary greatly from one director to the next. Some may provide dialogue for the most important bits of story and action, and others may prefer to tell the story in strictly visual terms with a bare minimum of dialogue. Some narrative structures use traditional formulas for beginnings and endings, emphasizing set patterns like the hero arriving at the beginning and leaving at the end. Others use a structure in which the characters of the story are already present in the beginning, and at the end the camera leaves them to continue their lives. We leave and they stay, but we leave with a strong sense that their story goes on, their lives continue.

The sense of what makes a story and how to tell it, of course, is often determined by the screenwriter, but it should be remembered that many directors simply view the screenplay as a rough outline for a movie and impose their own feel for narrative structure on it, expressing themselves creatively in their fashioning of the film's overall shape and form.

For decades in the Hollywood system of making movies the greatest power typically resided with the producers, who called all the shots, at least in a financial sense. Near midcentury, as the studio system was broken down by antimonopoly legislation and the popularity of television, among other influences, the seat of power shifted: Directors came to have more clout, initiating and sustaining projects. Only late in the twentieth century have screenwriters truly begun to be recognized, through sometimes spectacular remuneration, for their contributions. Frequently, now, writers boldly challenge how directors handle their scripts. But in discussing screenwriters' power, director Sidney Lumet (Figure 11.4) appears to seek a certain balance:

> Movie-making works very much like an orchestra: the addition of various harmonies can change, enlarge, and clarify the nature of the theme. In that sense, a director is "writing" when he makes a picture. But I think it's important to keep the words specific. Writing is writing. Sometimes the writer includes directions in

Figure 11.4 Respected Interpreter Sidney Lumet, shown here directing *The Fugitive Kind,* is widely admired not only for the quality of his diverse films but also for his ability to write about the movie industry, as in his popular book *Making Movies.*

> the script. He gives long descriptions of characters or of physical settings. Close-ups, long shots, and other camera directions may be written into the script. I read these carefully, because they are reflections of the writer's intention. I may follow them literally or find a completely different way of expressing the same intention. Writing is about structure and words. But the process I've been describing—of the sum being greater than the parts—that's shaped by the director.[8]

As we observed in Chapter 3, the struggle between director and writer is essentially the very basic conflict between kinds of language—literary versus cinematic.

But Lumet is also emphasizing the film director's necessary talent for seeing the big picture. In observing director Ang Lee's work on her film *Sense and Sensibility*, screenwriter-actor Emma Thompson says that "he's very interesting on the flow of energy in a film. Always thinks of everything in its widest context." And later, in keeping a daily chronicle of her thoughts, actions, and emotions while making the film, she notes,

> We seem to feel our way into the shots. Ang's style of leadership is somehow to draw us all to him silently and wait for things to happen. He has the shape of shots in his head always and will stand for silent minutes on end thinking through the flow of the scenes to see if what we're doing will fit his vision. I find it very inspiring but it's quite different to being told what to do. More collaborative.[9]

Figure 11.5 Coppola, Allen, and Scorsese—Three *Auteurs* for the Price of One An excellent opportunity to study directing style is provided by *New York Stories*, a feature-length anthology of three comedies: *Oedipus Wrecks* (directed by Woody Allen, center), *Life With Zoe* (Francis Ford Coppola, left), and *Life Lessons* (Martin Scorsese, right).

Evolving Styles and Flexibility

Some directors do not arrive at a static mature style but continue to evolve and experiment throughout their careers. Several prominent directors are examples of constant experimentation and artistic growth. Robert Altman is perhaps one of the most experimental of the present time. A certain freedom of form and an emphasis on texture permeate everything he does, but the films Altman has directed have little in common in subject matter, worldview, or even visual style: *M*A*S*H; Buffalo Bill and the Indians; Nashville; 3 Women; A Wedding; McCabe & Mrs. Miller; Popeye; Come Back to the Five and Dime, Jimmy Dean, Jimmy Dean; Vincent & Theo; The Player; Short Cuts; Ready to Wear;* and *Cookie's Fortune.*

Woody Allen has also experimented with a wide variety of styles. Although his most successful films have focused on the familiar Allen persona (*Take the Money and Run, Bananas, Sleeper,* and *Annie Hall*), experimentation and artistic growth are evident in *Interiors, Manhattan, Stardust Memories, Zelig, Hannah and Her Sisters, Crimes and Misdemeanors, Husbands and Wives, Manhattan Murder Mystery, Bullets Over Broadway, Mighty Aphrodite, Deconstructing Harry,* and *Celebrity.*

Francis Ford Coppola, Mike Nichols, Alan Parker, Martin Scorsese, and Stanley Kubrick are also experimental directors who do films with entirely different kinds of subject matter and narrative structure (Figure 11.5). As the careers of such innovators progress, the films that they direct may become more formal or less formal, more serious or less serious. A filmmaker who directs a comedic farce after having directed a serious drama has not taken a stylistic step backward. Growth results from taking on a new kind of challenge, tackling an

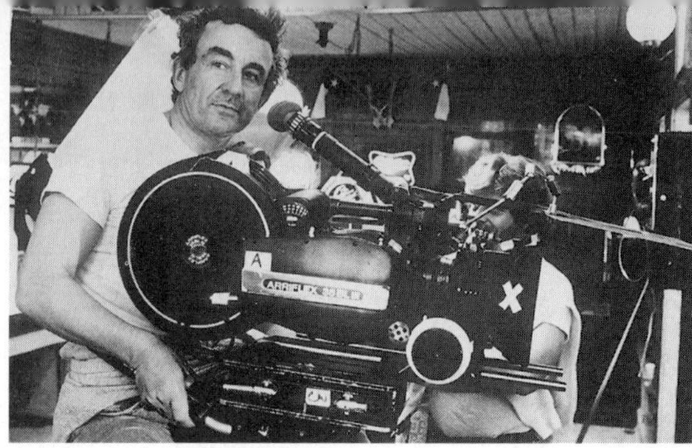

Figure 11.6 Cultural Perceptiveness Among directors whose first language was not English, these three have shown extraordinary perception in making films about American and British cultures: Ang Lee (*Sense and Sensibility, The Ice Storm*), from Taiwan (top left); Louis Malle (*Pretty Baby, Atlantic City, Alamo Bay*), from France (top right); and Milos Forman (*Taking Off, One Flew Over the Cuckoo's Nest, Hair, The People Vs. Larry Flynt*), from Czechoslovakia (bottom).

entirely new genre, or perhaps even bringing new styles to bear on a familiar genre. Or a director may simply break out of genre films altogether.

Innovative directors are often Hollywood outsiders who maintain a high degree of independence, perhaps because they also write and produce (Figure 11.6). Or they are filmmakers who have achieved such financial success that they can afford a gamble or two and put their own money into their experiments. Such experiments, however, often are not well received by the public. Audiences were so enamored of the familiar Woody Allen persona that they were unable to accept the Bergmanesque *Interiors*, for which Allen served as director only and attempted to make a serious and profound art movie. Audiences did accept the serious art of *Manhattan*, mainly because it featured the familiar Allen persona and its humor did not take it too far from the popular *Annie Hall*. It is perhaps much easier for a director like Alan Parker to avoid the trap of audience expectations, because all of the films he has directed have been radically different kinds of stories with very different styles.

Directors must guard against typecasting as carefully as actors do—for practically the same reasons: (1) the expectations of moviegoers who feel betrayed if a director does not continue to deliver the same kind of popular fare that they associate with his or her name and (2) conservative thinking by studios, production companies, and financial backers that are unwilling to gamble huge amounts of money on a director who wants to stretch his or her creative wings (Figure 11.7). Getting financing for a director to do the tried-and-true for

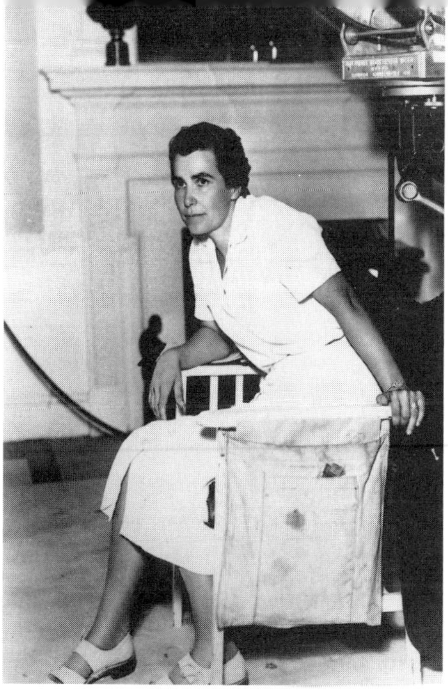

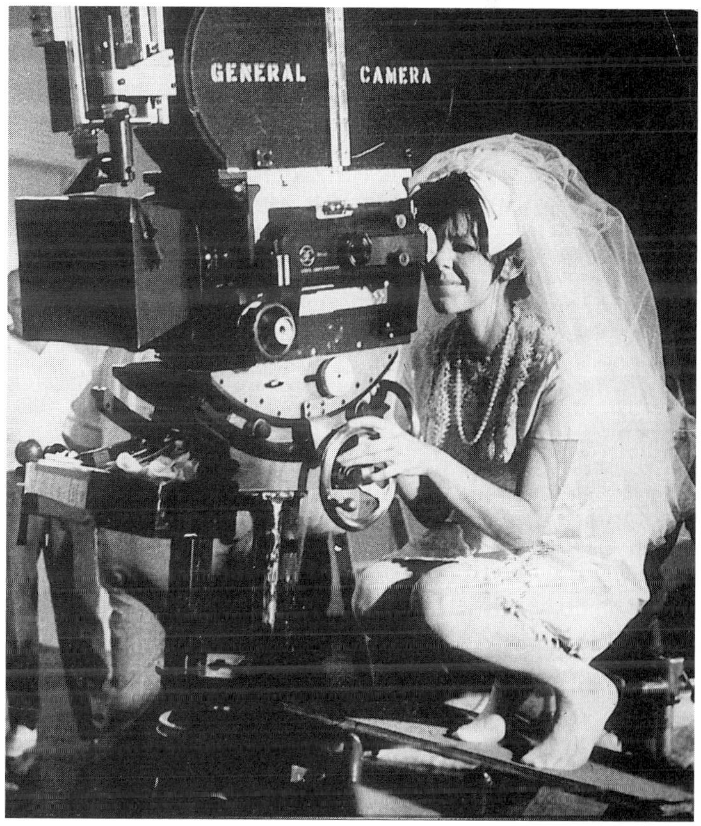

Figure 11.7 Stretching Her Creative Wings Of all filmmaking categories, feature directing, the almost-exclusive domain of men for many decades, was perhaps the hardest for women to enter. These three women, though, were American pioneers: Dorothy Arzner (top left), who directed her first film in 1927 and later became the first female member of the Directors Guild of America; Ida Lupino (top right), who moved beyond acting into directing and producing in the early 1950s with such hits as *The Hitch-Hiker* (1953); and Elaine May (bottom), who forged a path for women directors in comedy and satire with *The Heartbreak Kid* (1972). Now, worldwide, more and more films are being made by directors who happen to be women. Among the most active and accomplished are these directors: Allison Anders, Jane Campion, Lisa Cholodenko, Martha Coolidge, Julie Dash, Claire Denis, Marleen Goris, Lee Grant, Amy Heckerling, Agnieszka Holland, Diane Keaton, Diane Kurys, Penny Marshall, Mira Nair, Nancy Savoca, Penelope Spheeris, Barbra Streisand, Betty Thomas, Agnes Varda, Claudia Weill, and Lina Wertmuller.

which he or she has a proven track record is much easier than finding investors willing to risk money on a more speculative project. One wonders not only whether even Alfred Hitchcock could have succeeded with a film like *Interiors*, or with any other film that did not contain the suspense element that audiences grew to expect from him in film after film after film, but also whether Hitchcock would have been allowed to direct it.

Special Edition: The Director's Cut

A studio or releasing company may be persuaded to re-release a film in a special director's edition if the film does extremely well at the box office or if the director has a lot of clout because of the reception accorded his or her entire body of work. Some directors are frustrated when their film is first released because the studio insisted that they shorten the work to about two hours to conform to standard theater showing schedules. The re-released film, or **director's cut,** includes footage that the director felt should never have been dropped. Director's cuts of David Lean's *Lawrence of Arabia*, Francis Ford Coppola's *Apocalypse Now*, Sergio Leone's *Once Upon a Time in America*, Oliver Stone's *JFK*, and James Cameron's *The Abyss*, for example, have been released. Perhaps the most drastically changed film was Ridley Scott's *Blade Runner*, re-released with some additional footage (including a dream of a unicorn) and a new soundtrack but without the voice-over narration that accompanied the original version.

Steven Spielberg's rationale for his "Special Edition" of *Close Encounters of the Third Kind* and his description of the changes provide some interesting insights into the process:

> I . . . cut part of Richard Dreyfuss's crazy "gardening" in the backyard— . . . because I always felt the second act was the weakest area of my movie, and I tried very, very hard to fix the second act after the first sneak preview—but I simply didn't have the time, because my sneak was very late and the movie was already committed to hundreds of theaters across the nation. There was just no time—it was a work-in-progress that I literally had to abandon. And, despite the phenomenal success of the film, I had no satisfaction, as a filmmaker; that was not the movie I had set out to make. So when the film was a big hit, I went back to Columbia and said, "Now I want to make the movie the way I would have if I'd had those few extra months. I need another million dollars to shoot some added footage." Those added scenes were in the original script, by the way, not just scenes I concocted for the Special Edition, but they were scenes that became expendable when the budget became inordinate. The scenes . . . that were deleted were compromises that I believe thoroughly balance the second act, creating more of a rhythmic parallel between the François Truffaut story and the Richard Dreyfuss story. Almost every

other scene is a juxtaposition between the domestic suburban story and the government cover-up story.[10]

Spielberg contradicts himself in two separate interviews on the addition of the scenes inside the mother ship. In 1982, he told Judith Crist that those scenes were something he himself was curious about so he had the set built. In a 1990 interview with Gene Siskel, he claimed that the studio would not have given him another million dollars without some kind of "real hook to be able to justify re-releasing the film." Whatever the reason for including those scenes, Spielberg never thought they worked and says he would cut them if he had a *Special* Special Edition.

Regardless of one's reaction to Steven Spielberg's indecision, we obviously must consider it in the context of the enormous financial burdens of modern filmmaking. It seems as if every person in Los Angeles is writing a screenplay, and every successful actor and screenwriter has ambitions to direct. Few are hired, however. In the title of his recent book, Hollywood journalist Billy Frolick satirizes this phenomenon: *What I Really Want to Do Is DIRECT.* Frolick's subtitle is *Seven Film School Graduates Go to Hollywood*, and he emphasizes in his commentary the serendipity, the accidental nature, of not only directing, but the act of getting to direct a film. As part of his conclusion, he writes:

> In a 1994 *New Yorker* interview, [the influential film critic] Pauline Kael was asked what kind of person it takes to become a movie director.
>
> "Let's be brutal," Kael answered. "It takes a person who can raise the money to make a movie."
>
> Kael's response *was* brutal—brutally accurate. However, funding features no longer means raising millions of dollars. In the past four years *Clerks, Crumb, El Mariachi, The Brothers McMullen*, and many other acclaimed movies costing well under $100,000 have heralded a golden age of guerrilla narrative and documentary filmmaking. This generation's credo may well be, "Forget the car for graduation, Mom and Dad—finance my directorial debut."
>
> Sadly, though, as instant auteurs emerge regularly from the independent scene, opportunities at the studio level continue to shrink. [Such inspiring films as] *Taxi Driver, Badlands,* [and] *Scarecrow* . . . would have slim chances of being produced today.[11]

Questions

On the Director's Style

1. After viewing several films by a single director, what kinds of general observations can you make about his or her style? Which of the adjectives listed below describe his or her style?

a. intellectual and rational *or* emotional and sensual
b. calm and quiet *or* fast-paced and exciting
c. polished and smooth *or* rough and crude-cut
d. cool and objective *or* warm and subjective
e. ordinary and trite *or* fresh and original
f. tightly structured, direct, and concise *or* loosely structured and rambling
g. truthful and realistic *or* romantic and idealized
h. simple and straightforward *or* complex and indirect
i. grave, serious, tragic, and heavy *or* light, comical, and humorous
j. restrained and understated *or* exaggerated
k. optimistic and hopeful *or* bitter and cynical
l. logical and orderly *or* irrational and chaotic

2. What common thematic threads are reflected in the director's choice of subject matter? How is this thematic similarity revealed in the nature of the conflicts the director deals with?
3. In the films you have seen, what consistencies do you find in the director's treatment of space and time?
4. Is a consistent philosophical view of the nature of man and the universe found in all the films studied? If so, describe the director's worldview.
5. How is the director's style revealed by composition and lighting, philosophy of camera, camera movement, and methods of achieving three-dimensionality?
6. How does the director use special visual techniques (such as unusual camera angles, fast motion, slow motion, and distorting lenses) to interpret or comment on the action, and how do these techniques reflect overall style?
7. How is the director's style reflected in the different aspects of the editing in the films, such as the rhythm and pacing of editorial cuts, the nature of transitions, montages, and other creative juxtapositions? How does the style of editing relate to other elements of the director's visual style, such as the philosophy of camera or how the point of view is emphasized?
8. How consistent is the director in using and emphasizing setting? What kind of details of the natural setting does the director emphasize, and how do these details relate to his or her overall style? Is there any similarity in the director's approach to entirely different kinds of settings? How do the sets constructed especially for the film reflect the director's taste?
9. In what ways are the director's use of sound effects, dialogue, and music unique? How are these elements of style related to the image?
10. What consistencies can be seen in the director's choice of actors and in the performances they give under his or her direction? How does the choice of actors and acting styles fit in with the style in other areas?
11. What consistencies do you find in the director's narrative structure?

12. If the director seems to be constantly evolving instead of settling into a fixed style, what directions or tendencies do you see in that evolution? What stylistic elements can you find in all his or her films?

The pictures on pages 330 through 337 represent films by four different directors: Stanley Kubrick, Steven Spielberg, Federico Fellini, and Alfred Hitchcock. Although it is very difficult (perhaps impossible) to capture a director's visual style in a limited number of still pictures, the pictures reproduced here contain strong stylistic elements. Study the following figures—Figure 11.8 (Kubrick), Figure 11.9 (Spielberg), Figure 11.10 (Fellini), and Figure 11.11 (Hitchcock), and try to answer the questions that follow about each director.

13. What does each set of pictures reveal about the director's visual style as reflected by such elements as composition and lighting, philosophy of camera or point of view, use of setting, methods of achieving three-dimensionality, and choice of actors?
14. The pictures represent four films by each director. Study the pictures *from each film*, and see what you can deduce about the nature of the film.
    a. What do the pictures reveal about the general subject matter of the film or the kind of cinematic theme being treated?
    b. Characterize as clearly as possible the mood or emotional quality suggested by the stills from each film.
    c. If you are familiar with other films by the same director, how do these thematic concerns and emotional qualities relate to those other films?
15. Considering all the stills from each director, indicate whether each director is
    a. intellectual and rational *or* emotional and sensual
    b. naturalistic and realistic *or* romantic, idealized, and surreal
    c. simple, obvious, and straightforward *or* complex, subtle, and indirect
    d. heavy, serious, and tragic *or* light, comical, and humorous
16. Which directors represent *extremes* of each of the descriptive sets listed in question 15?
17. The films of which director seem most formal and structured in composition? The films of which director seem most informal and natural in composition?
18. Which director seems to be trying to involve us emotionally in the action or dramatic situation portrayed in the stills? How does he attempt to achieve this effect? Which director's viewpoint seems most objective and detached, and why do the pictures have that effect?
19. Which director relies most on lighting for special effects, and what effects does he achieve?
20. Which director places the most emphasis on setting to create special effects or moods?

21. What general observations, based on your answers to all the preceding questions, can you make about each director's style?

Films for Study

Woody Allen

Sleeper (1973)
Annie Hall (1977)
Manhattan (1979)
Stardust Memories (1980)
Zelig (1983)
The Purple Rose of Cairo (1985)
Hannah and Her Sisters (1986)
Crimes and Misdemeanors (1989)
Everyone Says I Love You (1996)
Deconstructing Harry (1997)
Celebrity (1998)

Robert Altman

*M*A*S*H* (1970)
Nashville (1975)
3 Women (1977)
Popeye (1980)
Vincent & Theo (1990)
The Player (1992)
Short Cuts (1993)
Kansas City (1996)
Cookie's Fortune (1999)

Ingmar Bergman

Smiles of a Summer Night (1955)
Wild Strawberries (1957)
The Seventh Seal (1957)
Through a Glass Darkly (1961)
Persona (1966)
Cries and Whispers (1972)
The Magic Flute (1974)
Autumn Sonata (1978)
Fanny and Alexander (1983)

Jane Campion

Sweetie (1989)
An Angel at My Table (1990)
The Piano (1993)
The Portrait of a Lady (1996)
Holy Smoke (1999)

Frank Capra

It Happened One Night (1934)
Mr. Deeds Goes to Town (1936)
Lost Horizon (1937)
Mr. Smith Goes to Washington (1939)
Meet John Doe (1941)
It's a Wonderful Life (1946)

Joel Coen

Blood Simple (1984)
Raising Arizona (1987)
Miller's Crossing (1990)
Barton Fink (1991)
The Hudsucker Proxy (1994)
Fargo (1996)
The Big Lebowski (1998)

Francis Ford Coppola

The Rain People (1969)
The Godfather (1972)
The Conversation (1974)
The Godfather Part II (1974)
Apocalypse Now (1979)
Rumble Fish (1983)
Tucker (1988)
The Godfather Part III (1990)
Bram Stoker's Dracula (1992)
The Rainmaker (1997)

Federico Fellini

I Vitelloni (1953)
La Strada (1954)
La Dolce Vita (1960)
8½ (1963)
Juliet of the Spirits (1965)
Fellini Satyricon (1970)
Amacord (1974)

George Roy Hill

Butch Cassidy and the Sundance Kid (1969)
Slaughterhouse-Five (1972)
The Sting (1973)
The World According to Garp (1982)

Alfred Hitchcock

Rear Window (1954)
The Trouble With Harry (1955)
Vertigo (1958)
North by Northwest (1959)
Psycho (1960)
The Birds (1963)

Agnieszka Holland

Europa Europa (1991)
Olivier Olivier (1992)
The Secret Garden (1993)
Total Eclipse (1995)
Washington Square (1997)

Stanley Kubrick

Lolita (1962)
Dr. Strangelove (1964)
2001: A Space Odyssey (1968)

A Clockwork Orange (1971)
Barry Lyndon (1975)
The Shining (1980)
Full Metal Jacket (1987)
Eyes Wide Shut (1999)

Akira Kurosawa

Rashomon (1950)
The Seven Samurai (1954)
Throne of Blood (1957)
Yojimbo (1961)
Kagemusha (1980)
Ran (1985)
Akira Kurosawa's Dreams (1990)

Spike Lee

She's Gotta Have It (1986)
Do the Right Thing (1989)
Mo' Better Blues (1990)
Malcolm X (1992)
Clockers (1995)
Get on the Bus (1996)
He Got Game (1998)
Summer of Sam (1999)

Louis Malle

Murmur of the Heart (1971)
Lacombe, Lucien (1974)
Atlantic City (1980)
My Dinner With Andre (1981)
Au Revoir, Les Enfants (1987)
Vanya on 42nd Street (1994)

Alan Parker

Bugsy Malone (1976)
Midnight Express (1978)
Pink Floyd: The Wall (1982)
Mississippi Burning (1988)
The Commitments (1991)
Evita (1996)

John Sayles

Return of the Secaucus Seven (1980)
Lianna (1983)
The Brother From Another Planet (1984)
Matewan (1987)
Eight Men Out (1988)
The Secret of Roan Inish (1994)
Lone Star (1996)
Men With Guns (1998)
Limbo (1999)

Martin Scorsese

Mean Streets (1973)
Taxi Driver (1976)
Raging Bull (1980)
The King of Comedy (1983)
The Last Temptation of Christ (1988)
GoodFellas (1990)
The Age of Innocence (1993)
Casino (1995)
Kundun (1997)

Steven Spielberg

The Sugarland Express (1974)
Jaws (1975)
Close Encounters of the Third Kind (1977)
Raiders of the Lost Ark (1981)
E.T. The ExtraTerrestrial (1982)
The Color Purple (1985)
Jurassic Park (1993)
Schindler's List (1993)
Amistad (1997)
Saving Private Ryan (1998)

Lina Wertmuller

Love and Anarchy (1973)
Swept Away . . . (1975)
Seven Beauties (1976)
Ciao, Professore! (1992)

Zhang Yimou

Red Sorghum (1987)
Ju Dou (1989)
Raise the Red Lantern (1991)
The Story of Qiu Ju (1992)
To Live (1994)

FIGURE 11.8 STANLEY KUBRICK

a. *A Clockwork Orange*

b. *Barry Lyndon*

c. *The Shining*

d. *Dr. Strangelove*

FIGURE 11.9 STEVEN SPIELBERG

a. *The Color Purple*

b. *Close Encounters of the Third Kind*

c. *E.T. The Extra-Terrestrial*

d. *Schindler's List*

FIGURE 11.10 FEDERICO FELLINI

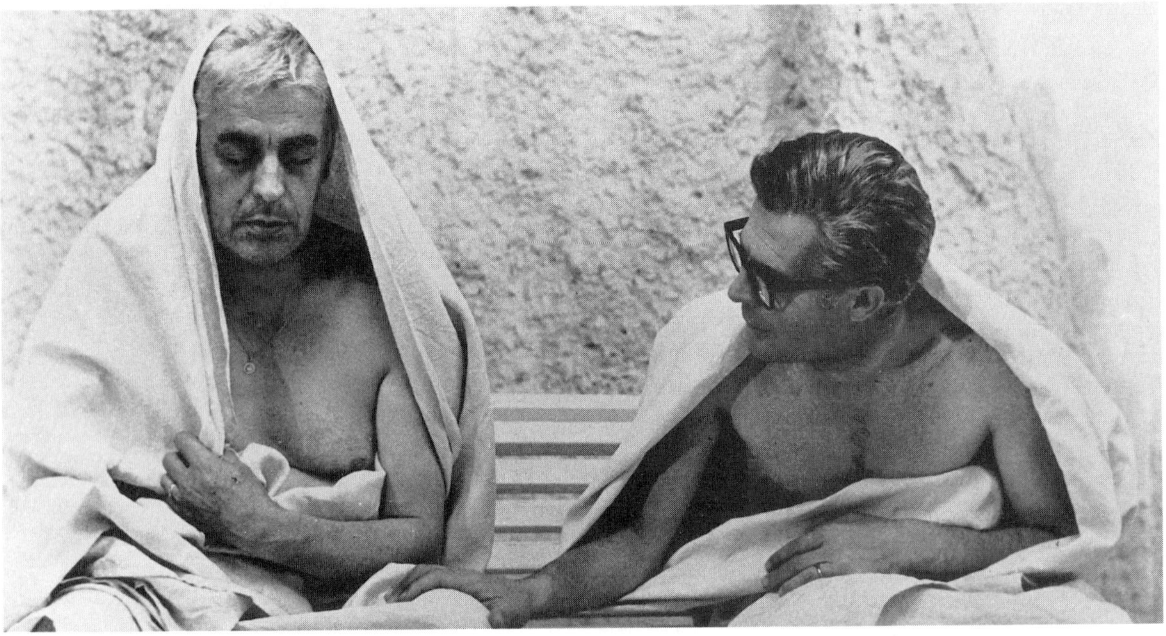

a. *8½*

b. *La Dolce Vita*

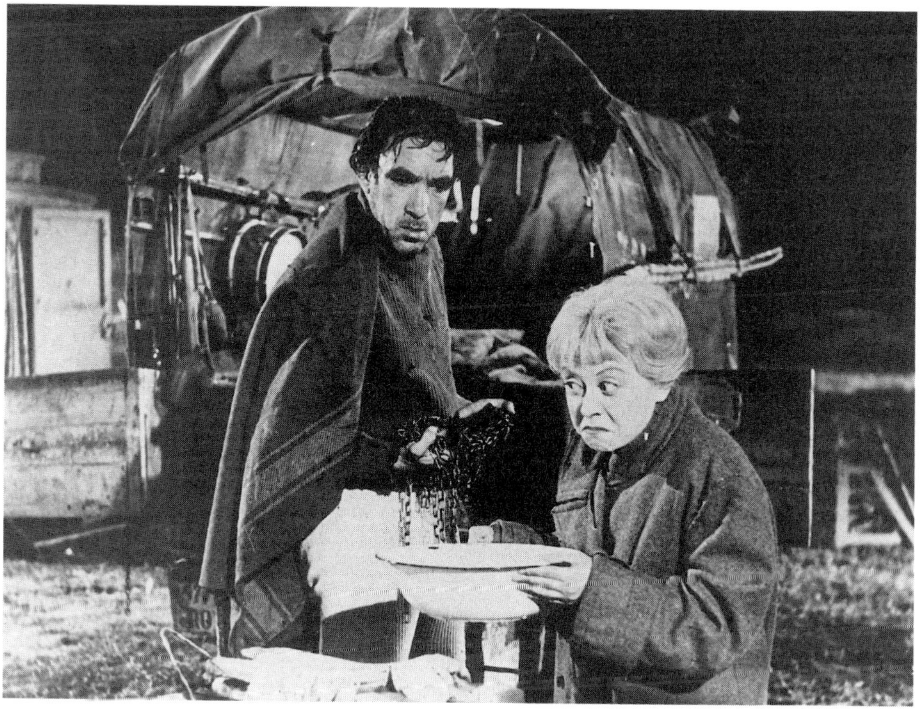

c. *La Strada*

d. *Amarcord*

FIGURE 11.11 ALFRED HITCHCOCK

a. *North by Northwest*

b. *Psycho*

c. *Rear Window*

d. *Vertigo*

Chapter 12

Analysis of the Whole Film

You don't compose a film on the set. You put a pre-designed composition on film. It is wrong to liken a director to an author. He is more like an architect, if he is creative. An architect conceives his plans from given premises—the purpose of the building, its size, its terrain. If he is clever, he can do something within these limitations.

—John Ford, Director

In the previous chapters, we broke the film down into its separate parts. Now we attempt to put the separate parts together, to relate them to one another, and to consider their contribution to the film as a whole. Before we begin to reassemble the pieces, however, we need to consider the whole process involved in the art of watching films. In most cases, the process begins long before we actually see the film.

Addressing Viewer-Centered Challenges

Before we begin our analysis, we need to consider obstacles to objectivity and maximum enjoyment that we ourselves create through our prejudices and misconceptions and by the particular circumstances in which we watch the film. Each of us reacts in a unique and complex way to internal and external forces that are beyond the filmmaker's control. Although these forces lie outside the film itself, they can have a negative effect on how we experience a film. Awareness of these problems should help us overcome them or at least minimize their effect.

Categorical Rejection

One of the most difficult prejudices to overcome is that which leads us to approach certain categories of films with a grim determination to dislike them. Although it is natural to prefer some types of films to others, most of us can appreciate or enjoy some aspects of almost any film. We should keep in mind that some films will not fit our preconceived notions. For example, a person who dislikes gangster movies might stay away from *Bonnie and Clyde;* another, who dislikes war movies, might shun *Patton;* and a third, who dislikes westerns, might ignore *Blazing Saddles*. All would lose a memorable film experience, for those three films are more than simple formula pieces.

Even professional critics may be inclined to reject films categorically. However, they must see all kinds of films and are often pleasantly surprised, as critic Rex Reed was by *Patton* and *M*A*S*H:*

> When Hollywood goes to war, it usually drops nothing but bombs. The movies rarely use the theater of war as a theater of ideas; most war films are, in fact, only mere excuses for various studio technical departments to flex their muscles with the latest developments in scar tissue, heavy machinery, and explosions. It was with more than a fair degree of sound loathing, therefore, that I approached the screenings of both *Patton* and *M*A*S*H*. Two new 20th Century Fox war flicks, I moaned, from the studio that bored us all to death with *The Longest Day?* Now I'm eating crow. They are both extraordinarily fine pictures that do more to raise the artistic level of the war-movie genre in the direction of serious filmmaking than anything I've seen in quite some time.[1] (Figure 12.1)

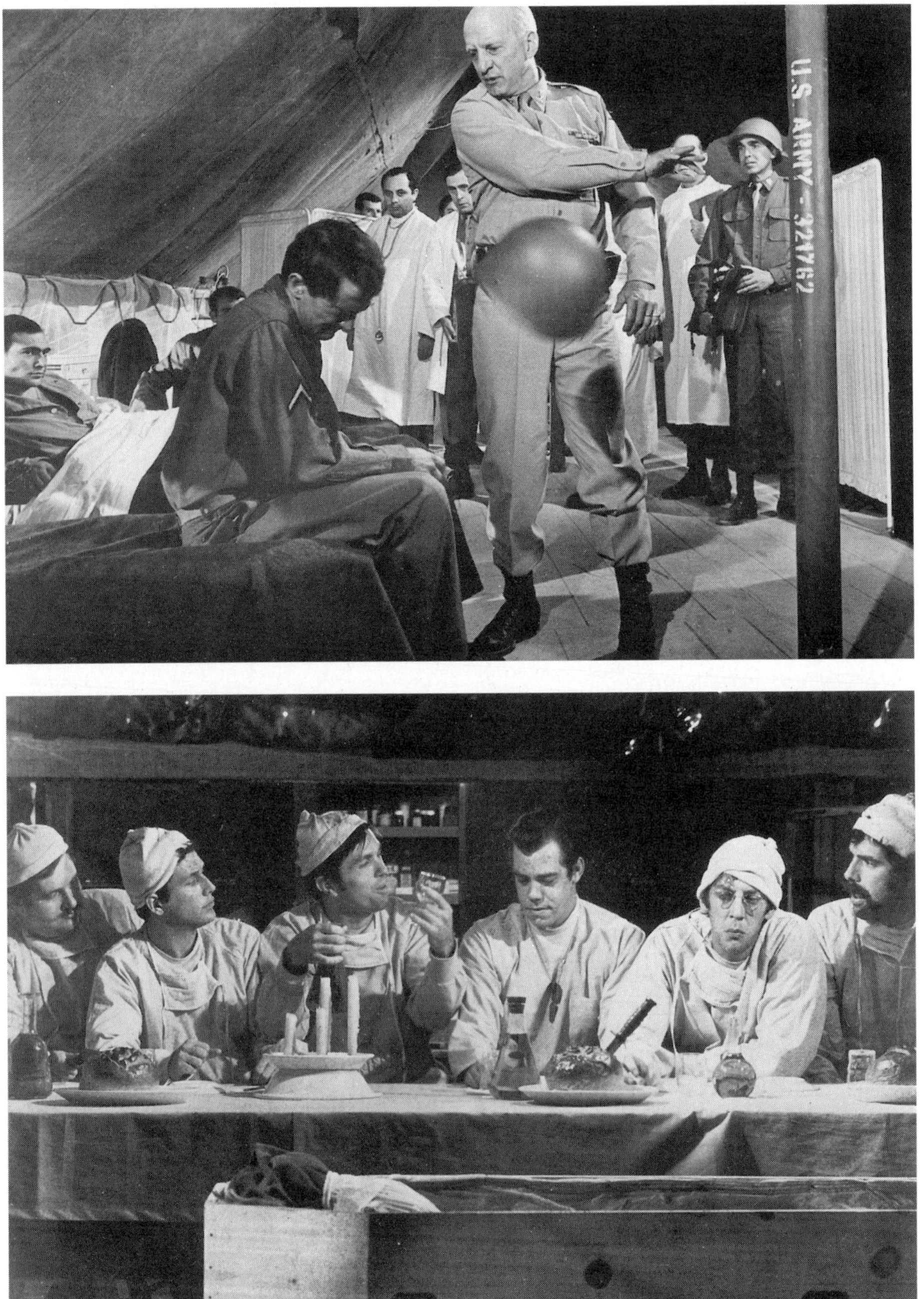

Figure 12.1 Beyond Genre Not every film set against a backdrop of war is a formula war film, as evidenced by the brilliant character study of General George S. Patton in *Patton,* starring George C. Scott as Patton, and the zany black comedy *M*A*S*H,* with Donald Sutherland as Hawkeye Pierce.

Perhaps even narrower in their outlook are filmgoers who have inflexible preconceptions about what movies are supposed to be. This type of categorical rejection is illustrated by two extreme examples. At one extreme are filmgoers who say, "I just want to be entertained," and are offended by a film that is grim and depressing. These same filmgoers may want and even expect a stage play to be grim and depressing but feel that a motion picture should provide light entertainment. At the other extreme—and equally narrow in outlook—are viewers who expect every film to make a deep, serious, profound, and highly artistic statement about the human condition. Such viewers are often disappointed if a film is *not* grim and depressing. A film that is not grim and depressing is likely to be entertaining, but in their opinion entertainment is not the proper function of the motion picture.

Closely related to those who reject films categorically are those who set up their own rigid ground rules and ignore the intentions and artistic aims of the director. This kind of narrowness is apparent in *Time*'s review of *Bonnie and Clyde*. The reviewer condemned the film just because it was not a historically accurate portrayal of the career of Bonnie and Clyde. In making such a judgment, he simply ignored the intentions of the director, Arthur Penn, and judged the film according to his own narrow critical notions. (In *Newsweek*, on August 21, 1967, Joseph Morgenstern first denounced *Bonnie and Clyde* and then one week later reversed his critical opinion of the film.)

Others may reject films for equally ridiculous minor reasons. Some may stay away from black-and-white films because of their preference for color. Others may shun foreign-language films because they have difficulty reading subtitles or because they are bothered by dubbing that is not perfectly synchronized with mouth movement.

Mistaking the Part for the Whole

Almost as detrimental as categorical rejection is the blindness caused by overresponding to individual elements rather than to the film as a whole. An extreme example of this prejudice is offered by viewers who are infected with a near-fatal case of actor worship or antipathy: "I just love all Mel Gibson pictures!" or "I can't stand Julia Roberts movies!" Such extreme reactions are common among viewers who fail to see the actor as subordinate to the film.

Less extreme examples of this blindness include overresponse to certain film elements. The two ingredients most likely to cause this kind of reaction are sex and violence. Some films exploit these ingredients and overemphasize them to the point of the ridiculous, but this is not always the case. Some films demand the use of nudity or violence to tell honestly the story they have to tell. Thus, a perceptive filmgoer does not condemn the use of sex or violence per se, without considering the film as a whole, and neither rejects nor praises a film simply because of its treatment of sex or violence. For example, the violent ending of

Bonnie and Clyde did not, by itself, determine the overall quality of that film. And films such as *Reds* and *The World According to Garp* actually require some emphasis on sexual encounters to tell their stories.

Filmgoers may also overrespond to such elements as the musical score or the visual beauties of the natural landscape. In *Dr. Zhivago*, for example, the song "Lara's Theme" and the beautiful ice palace made vivid and lasting impressions and perhaps convinced many viewers that the film was better than it actually was.

Great Expectations

Another subjective factor that influences film evaluation is expecting too much from a film. A film may have received a lot of publicity for winning awards from the Academy of Motion Picture Arts and Sciences, the New York Film Critics, or the Cannes Film Festival. But even if the film has not won any awards, we may be aware that it has generally won widespread critical acclaim. We may also base our high expectations on the past performances or achievements of the film's actors or its director—or simply on their reputations if we have not seen their work before. Perhaps the most difficult factor to ignore is the word-of-mouth raves of our friends. The result is that our expectations are so high that the film can't possibly measure up, and our disappointment causes a negative reaction to a film that we would have liked immensely if we had never heard of it until we saw it.

Expectations may also run too high if we are particularly fond of a novel that is later adapted to film. Film can never completely reproduce the experience of a novel, and the more we like a novel, the more likely we are to be disappointed with the film version.

Memory even plays tricks and influences our reactions to a film that may have been a favorite many years ago. With the passage of time, we sometimes build the remembered experience up in our minds to the point that the actual film, when viewed again, seems rather drab. Although self-indulgent nostalgia and glorification of the past are natural, we might simply try to see the wisdom of the person who, when told that "*Gone With the Wind* just isn't as good as it used to be," replied, "It never was."

An Excess of Expertise

Although filmmakers go to great lengths to make their films as realistic in every detail as possible and usually hire technical advisers to help with special problems, a relatively small number of us simply know too much for our own good. If we possess special technical skills or inside knowledge, we are often unable to enjoy the film because of minor technical errors to which most viewers are completely oblivious. Take, for example, a concert violinist viewing a film about a great violinist. The actor playing the part has been trained to finger the violin well enough to convince the average viewer, but the concert violinist sees at a glance how awkward or inept the actor's fingering actually is. In such cases, the expert viewer, instead of fretting about the lack of total realism, should try to enjoy other aspects of the film.

The Influence of External Factors

Our response to any film is determined to a large extent by external factors that have nothing to do with our personal prejudices or with the film itself. We can control some of these factors to a degree, but others lie completely beyond our power. Our mood, mental attitude, and physical condition affect our responses to a film. If we are tired or sleepy, have eaten too much, or have had a few drinks, we may lack the concentration required to understand or appreciate the film. If we have had to stand in a ticket line for an extended period, we may develop a grim set to our jaws and a "This better be worth it!" attitude, a prejudice that no film can overcome.

Once inside the theater, other external factors come into play. We may find ourselves in uncomfortable seats, located directly behind the world's tallest man and directly in front of the world's loudest popcorn-box rattlers. A poor soundtrack may make the dialogue difficult to hear, and a scratchy print may take something away from the visual effect. Waiting for the nearsighted projectionist to focus the image may also be taxing. For the most part, however, the moviegoer has an advantage over the film student, who must often watch films in hard classroom seats located in the worst acoustical environment imaginable. In either case we have little choice but to try to make the best of the situation.

Another factor that cannot be overlooked is the reaction we have to the audience around us. A crying baby or a talkative group nearby can keep us from becoming totally immersed in the experience. On the other hand, the reactions of the audience may have certain positive effects that intensify our pleasure in the film. This is especially true with comedy; laughter is contagious, and we enjoy laughing more in a group than we do alone. Imagine the difference between seeing such a picture as *Forrest Gump* in an almost empty theater and seeing it in a theater packed with a highly responsive audience. This herd instinct may also work to some degree with fear and pathos. However, overreaction by members of the audience may have adverse effects. Someone who laughs too hard at things that really aren't funny may make some viewers self-conscious about their own responses, and loud sobbing or sniffling may cause others to resort to laughter.

When watching films on television, we lose the positive effects of the theater audience and face different types of external obstacles (see Appendix A). Complete immersion in films broadcast by network television is impossible. Even if the drastically reduced size of the image and the frequent commercial interruptions can be tolerated, there are generally enough normal household distractions to make viewing films on television somewhat less than satisfactory.

Because some theaters and many cable TV channels still show double features, we might consider how one feature may affect our response to the other. Although theater managers and TV program planners usually schedule two films of the same type in their double features (two horror films, two comedies, and so on), studies have shown that such programming weakens the effect of the second feature. The less alike the two films are, the stronger our reaction will be to the second feature. In other words, ideally a light comedy and a horror show should be shown on the same bill so that we have not only a fresh but also a contrasting emotional reaction to the second feature. If both films are of the same type, the first feature drains us of whatever emotional response is called for, and our response to the second feature is weakened.

The art of watching films, therefore, calls for increased awareness that our responses are uniquely individual and complex and that we react to internal and external forces completely beyond the filmmaker's control. We should attempt to minimize the effect of such factors whenever possible, for they interfere with our analysis and enjoyment as well.

Preconceptions: Reviews and Other Sources

How much should we know about a film before we see it? There is no simple answer to this question. Sometimes we have little control over how much we know about a movie before we see it, but some general guidelines on how to prepare for seeing a film might be helpful.

To begin with, we don't usually go to see a film that we know absolutely nothing about, for several sources exist from which we pick up general ideas about and attitudes toward each film. If we handle this information properly and do not let it overinfluence us, it can enhance our viewing experience. But if we allow these influences to dominate our thinking, the richness of our experience may be diminished.

An easy way to gain some knowledge about a film before seeing it is to read reviews. In addition to helping us decide what films we want to see, reviews provide several kinds of information and opinions. One of the most valuable functions of a review is to provide factual information. A review tells the name of the film, identifies the director and the actors in leading roles, gives a summary of its subject matter and its plot, and tells whether it's in color or black and white. Most reviews also mention or single out the elements in the film that are most significant and most worthy of attention. They may also help us place the film in context by relating it to similar films past or present or by relating it to other films by the same director. The review may even analyze the film, breaking it into its parts and examining the nature, proportions, functions, and interrelationship of these parts. A review almost always includes some kind of value judgment, some negative or positive opinions on the film's overall worth or merit.

We must watch very carefully how we read reviews before seeing the film. We should be interested primarily in a single question: *Is the film likely to be interesting and enjoyable enough to be worth seeing?* To answer this question, all we need to do is read several reviews in a very superficial way, looking for the basic information that all reviews provide. At this point, we should generally ignore or forget the other ideas, opinions, analyses, interpretations, and subjective reactions presented in the reviews. Most importantly, we should not look too deeply into any single critic's evaluation or subjective reactions to the film. To do so may seriously hamper or limit our own response, so that we see the same things the critic saw but nothing more. Taking a critic's opinion too seriously not only restricts our personal and subjective response but often destroys the independence of our judgment of the film's worth and weakens our critical perception. Thus we should prepare ourselves for seeing a film by reading some reviews before we go, but we should not overprepare so that our personal response to the film is overly influenced by the opinions of others.

Imagine how our view of *Bonnie and Clyde* would be distorted and limited if we paid serious attention to *Time*'s review of that film and restricted ourselves to seeing what the reviewer saw:

> Producer Beatty and Director Arthur Penn have elected to tell their tale of bullets and blood in a strange and purposeless mingling of fact and claptrap that totters uneasily on the brink of burlesque. Like Bonnie and Clyde themselves, the film rides off in all directions, and ends up full of holes. . . .
>
> Faye Dunaway's Sunday-social prettiness is at variance with any known information about Bonnie Parker. The other gang members struggle to little avail against a script that gives their characters no discernible shape. . . .
>
> The real fault with *Bonnie and Clyde* is its sheer, tasteless aimlessness. Director Penn has marshalled an impressive framework of documentation: a flotilla of old cars, a scene played in a movie theater while *Gold Diggers of 1933* runs off on the screen, a string of dusty, fly-bitten Southwestern roads, houses and farms. (One booboo: the use of post-1934 dollar bills.) But repeated bursts of country-style music punctuating the bandits' grisly adventures and a sentimental interlude with Bonnie's old Maw photographed through a hazy filter, aims at irony and misses by a mile. And this, if you please, was the U.S. entry in this year's Montreal Film Festival.[2]

Viewers who followed this reviewer's lead could end up focusing their attention on the historical inaccuracies and miss the real experience of the film. Too much emphasis on the trees (or the post-1934 dollar bills) may cause us to miss the entire forest (Figure 12.2).

A similar phenomenon occurs in John McCarten's *New Yorker* review of *Shane*. The critic becomes so upset about the fact that Shane sides with the

Figure 12.2 From Real to Reel The film version of *Bonnie and Clyde*, starring Faye Dunaway and Warren Beatty (left), glamorized the images of Bonnie Parker and Clyde Barrow, the real characters on whom the film was based (right).

homesteaders that he builds his review around his defense of the cattlemen, mentioning them three different times in the review and thus neglecting more important elements in the film:

> High among Hollywood's articles of faith . . . is the doctrine that the gentlemen running cattle in the Old West were somehow criminal because they objected to having their grazing land invaded by homesteaders, bean patches, and Monday workers. I was moved to reflect on these beliefs, all of which strike me as cockeyed. . . .
>
> Stevens (the director) deals with the entirely orthodox notion that the homesteaders in Wyoming were given a highly unfair shake by the cattlemen. I'm not at all sure he really believes this, however, because he takes so much pleasure in filming the cattlemen's noble, unfenced demesne. . . .

My original feeling about the glorification of homesteaders and the vilification of their betters on the range still holds, however tenuously. It is certainly an odd thing when pictures about the cow country do their best to eliminate their principal ingredient.[3]

When reading reviews, we must remember that criticism is a highly subjective process, and if we take any single review or series of reviews too seriously before seeing a film, we will restrict our ability to judge the film independently. Also, if we rely too much on the reviews, we may completely lose faith in our own judgment and end up in a tug-of-war between critical opinions. Consider the dilemma we might face if we took all the reviews of *Bonnie and Clyde* seriously before seeing the film. *Time* summarized the critical views on *Bonnie and Clyde* as follows:

> *Bonnie and Clyde* also stirred up a battle among movie critics that seemed to be almost as violent as the film itself. Bosley Crowther of the *New York Times* was so offended by it that he reviewed it—negatively—three times. "This blending of farce with brutal killings is as pointless as it is lacking in taste," he wrote. *Time*'s review made the mistake of comparing the fictional and the real Bonnie and Clyde, a totally irrelevant exercise. *Newsweek* panned the film, but the following week returned to praise it.
>
> The *New Yorker* ran a respectful appreciation by Guest Critic Penelope Gilliatt, followed nine weeks later with an ecstatic 9,000 word analysis by another guest critic, Pauline Kael. In Chicago, the *Tribune*'s reviewer sided with the nay-sayers. He called it "stomach churning"; the *American* said it was "unappetizing." But the *Daily News* acclaimed it as one of the most significant motion pictures of the decade; the *Sun Times* said it was "astonishingly beautiful." It seemed as if two different Bonnie and Clydes were slipping into town simultaneously.[4]

Reviews, of course, are not the only source of information and attitudes about films. The great amount of publicity released on almost every film can also influence our reactions. Television talk shows frequently feature interviews with actors or directors of recently released films. A great deal of important information is also picked up from the grapevine, the word-of-mouth reviews by friends who have seen the movie. Screenwriter William Goldman believes that reviews are not nearly as influential as word-of-mouth:

> I don't think it matters remotely how bad they said *Poseidon Adventure* was (they all said it was terrible). I think the reason people go to—quote—"big films" is that they hear they're fun or they hear they're good. I think reviewers are crucial to a foreign film. I think they are crucial to a small film, although Vincent Canby didn't write a worse review than the one he wrote for *Rocky*. It didn't matter very much, did it? Word of mouth is important. Everybody would *rather* have good reviews. Nobody likes to be criticized in print. But it's still word of mouth. I mean, why didn't people go to see *Nashville?* Because they heard it was dull, and they were

> right—it was dull. Very, very slow and tedious and pointless and arbitrary. But it got the reviews of the decade. In essence, reviews are mostly cosmetic for a major American film. They may help to form, in a crazy way, word of mouth. But I don't know of anybody who's ever said, "I'm going to see this movie because John Simon said it was wonderful."[5]

We should certainly consider reviews, publicity, and word-of-mouth before seeing a film, but we should take none of it too seriously.

Although it is almost impossible to do, and often highly impractical even when it is possible, seeing a movie "cold"—without knowing anything at all about it—can be highly desirable. Without any kind of information about the film, we can watch it completely free from others' opinions and judge it purely on its own merits. But given the increased price of movies, few of us can simply walk into a theater on impulse, saying, "I think I'll take in a movie." If we get a chance to see a film this way, it is usually when the theater schedules an unannounced sneak preview of a newly released film along with something we want to see anyway.

The Basic Approach: Watching, Analyzing, and Evaluating the Film

When we enter the theater to watch the film, we need to keep certain things in mind. We cannot freeze the film for analysis—only in its continuous flowing form is it truly a motion picture. Therefore, we must concentrate most of our attention on responding sensitively to what is happening on the screen—the simultaneous interplay of image, sound, and motion. Yet at the same time, in the back of our minds, we must be storing up impressions of another sort, asking ourselves How? Why? and How effective is it? about everything we see and hear. We must make an effort to become immersed in the reality of the film, while at the same time maintaining some degree of objectivity and critical detachment.

If we can see the film twice, our analysis will be a much easier task. The complexity of the medium makes it difficult to consider all the elements of a film in a single viewing; too many things happen on too many levels to allow for a complete analysis. Therefore, we should try to see the film twice whenever possible. In the first viewing, we can concern ourselves primarily with plot elements, the total emotional effect, and the central idea or theme. Ideally, after the first viewing, we will have some time to reflect on and clarify the film's purpose and theme. Then, in the second viewing, because we are no longer caught up in the suspense of what happens, we can focus our full attention on the hows and whys of the filmmaker's art. The more practice we have in the double-viewing technique, the easier it will become for us to combine the functions of both viewings into one.

It is sometimes possible in film classes to view the entire film and then screen selected segments that illustrate the function and interrelationship of the different elements to the film as a whole. Then the film can be viewed again in its entirety so that the parts can be seen in the continuous stream of the whole. Use of a VCR or laserdisc or DVD player makes the process even simpler. This practice can be very helpful in developing the habits and skills needed for film analysis. Double-viewing not only helps with our analysis but, in the case of exceptional films, also increases our appreciation. For example, critic Dwight Macdonald wrote, in regard to Fellini's *8½*, "The second time I saw *8½*, two weeks after the first, I took more notes than I had the first time, so many beauties and subtleties and puzzles I had overlooked."[6]

Regardless of which option we have, single-viewing, double-viewing, or breaking the film into segments, we can use basically the same procedure in approaching the film for analysis.

Theme and Filmmakers' Intentions

The first step in analysis should be to get a fairly clear idea of the film's **theme**—unifying central concern—and to identify the filmmakers' (quite often the director's) intentions. Is the element that unifies the work its plot, a single unique character, the creation of an emotional mood or effect, or the creation of a certain style or texture? Or is the film designed to convey an idea or make a statement? Once we have identified the central concern, we can move on to a clearer and more specific statement of theme. What we really want to know is this: *What is the director's purpose or primary aim in making the film? What is the true subject of the film; and what kind of statement, if any, does the film make about that subject?*

The Relationship of the Parts to the Whole

Once we have tentatively identified the film's theme and the director's intentions and have stated the theme as concisely and precisely as possible, we should move on to see how well our decisions stand up under a complete analysis of all film elements. After we have tried to answer all the applicable and relevant questions relating to each separate element, we are prepared to relate each element to the whole. The basic question is this: *How do all the separate elements of the film relate to and contribute to the theme, central purpose, or total effect?* Answering this question involves at least some consideration of all the elements in the film, although the contribution of some is much greater than the contribution of others. Every element should be considered at this point: story, dramatic structure, symbolism, characterization, conflict, setting, title, irony, cinematography, editing, film type and size, sound effects, dialogue, the musical score, the acting, and the film's overall style.

If we can see clear and logical relationships between each element and the theme or purpose, then we may assume that our decision about the film's theme is valid. If we cannot see these clear relationships, we may need to reassess our initial understanding of the theme and modify it to fit the patterns and interrelationships we see among the individual film elements.

Once our analysis at this level is complete and we have satisfied ourselves that we understand the film as a unified work of art, ordered and structured around a central purpose of some kind, we are almost ready to move on to an evaluation process. Once we feel that we understand the director's intentions and have a pretty clear idea of how he or she went about carrying them out, we are free to make some kind of judgment about whether the director succeeded or failed, about the extent to which he or she achieved the original intentions.

The Film's Level of Ambition

Before beginning an objective evaluation, we must consider the film's level of ambition—a factor that is closely related to the director's intentions. It is grossly unfair to judge a film that seeks only to entertain as though it were intended as the ultimate in serious cinematic art. Thus we must adjust our expectations to what the film aims to do. Renata Adler describes the need for this adjustment:

> If a movie stars Doris Day, or if it is directed by John Wayne, the reviewer tries to put himself in a Day or Wayne sympathetic frame of mind and argue, on other grounds, that the film is better Day or lesser Wayne, but once the ingredients are fairly named, the reader knows and is freed to his taste. The same with Luis Buñuel—and comparable situations with great directors do arise—the critical inventory part gets complicated.
>
> I think it is absolutely essential in a review to establish the level of ambition that a film is at, to match it, if possible with the level of your own, and then to adjust your tone of voice. There is no point in admiring an Elvis Presley film in the same tone as a George C. Scott—or in treating simple lapses of competence with the same indignation one has for what seem to be failures of taste and integrity.[7]

This is not to say that we should give up our own standards or ground rules. But we should try to judge the film in terms of what the director was trying to do and the level at which he or she was trying to communicate, before we apply our own yardsticks of evaluation. Therefore, before we make any kind of objective evaluation, we must consider this question: *What is the film's level of ambition?*

Objective Evaluation of the Film

Once we have clearly established the theme, the director's intentions, and the level of ambition and have seen how the elements function together to contribute to the theme, we are ready to begin our objective evaluation. The overall question to consider is simply this: *Given the director's intentions and the film's level of ambition, how well does the film succeed in what it tries to do?* After considering this question, we must review our earlier assessment of the effectiveness of all individual film elements to determine the effect each element has on our answer. Once we have done this, we can proceed to the next question: *Why does the film succeed or fail?*

In attempting to answer this question, we should be as specific as possible, determining not only Why? but Where? We should look into individual elements for strengths and weaknesses, deciding which parts or elements contribute the most to the film's success or failure: *Which elements or parts make the strongest contribution to the theme and why? Which elements or parts fail to function effectively in carrying out the director's intentions? Why do they fail?* We must be careful to weigh each strength and weakness in terms of its overall effect on the film, avoiding petty nitpicking such as concentrating on slight technical flaws.

Because we are making an objective evaluation, we should be prepared to defend each decision with a logical argument based on or supportable by our analysis as a whole. We must explain *why* something works well or *why* a given scene fails to achieve its potential. Every part of this evaluation should be as logical and rational as possible, and we should be able to defend each judgment with a just argument based on a viable framework of critical standards.

Subjective Evaluation of the Film

Up to this point, we have been using a systematic and reasonable critical method. But we have done so with the full awareness that we cannot reduce art to reason or make it as simple as 2 + 2 = 4. Our reaction to films is much more complex than this, for we are human beings, not computers, and we know that much of art is intuitive, emotional, and personal. Thus, our reaction to it will include strong feelings, prejudices, and biases. It will be colored by our life experiences, by our moral and social conditioning, by our degree of sophistication, by our age, by the time and place in which we live, and by every unique aspect of our personality.

Having completed our objective analysis and evaluation, we are ready to allow ourselves the luxury of leaving the rationally ordered framework to describe the nature and intensity of our own response to the film: *What is our personal reaction to the film? What are our personal reasons for liking or disliking it?*

Other Approaches to Analysis, Evaluation, and Discussion

Once we have completed our personal and subjective evaluation, we may want to approach the film from several rather specialized angles or critical perspectives. These exercises in criticism might be especially meaningful as guidelines for classroom discussion. Each approach has its own focus, bias, perspective, and intentions, and each looks for something a little different in the film.

The Film as Technical Achievement

If we have sufficient understanding of the film medium and the techniques of filmmaking, we may want to focus on the technical devices that the filmmaker uses and the importance of these techniques to the film's overall impact. In evaluating the film in this manner, we are more concerned with *how* the director communicates than with *what* he or she communicates or *why*. By these standards, the most nearly perfect film is the one that best utilizes the potential of the medium. Films such as *Citizen Kane* and *2001: A Space Odyssey* both rate very high in this respect. Here are some questions that we should consider with this kind of focus in mind:

- How well does the film utilize the full potential of the medium?
- What inventive techniques are employed, and how impressive are the effects they create?
- Judged as a whole, is the film technically superior or inferior?
- Technically speaking, what are the film's strongest points and what are its weakest?

The Film as Showcase for the Actor: The Personality Cult

If our primary interest is in actors, acting performances, and screen personalities, we may want to focus on the performances of the major actors in the film, especially the established stars or film personalities. Taking this approach, we assume that the leading actor has the most important effect on the quality of the film, that he or she carries the film because of his or her acting skill or personality. Judged through this framework, the best film is one in which the basic personality, acting style, or personal idiosyncrasies of the leading actor in the cast are best projected. In this approach, then, we look on the film as a showcase for the actor's talent and think of it as a Dustin Hoffman, Meryl Streep, Jack Nicholson, Humphrey Bogart, or Katharine Hepburn movie. To give this approach validity, we must be familiar with a number of other films starring the same actor so that we can evaluate the performance in comparison with the roles played by the actor in the past. To evaluate a film through this approach, we might consider these questions:

- How well are the actor's special personality traits or acting skills suited to his or her character and to the action of the film?
- Does this role seem tailored to fit the actor's personality and skills, or does the actor bend his or her personality to fit the role?

- How powerful is the actor's performance in this film compared with his or her performance in other starring roles?
- What similarities or significant differences do you see in the character the actor plays in this film and the characters he or she played in other films?
- Compared with past performances, how difficult and demanding is this particular role for the actor?

The Film as Product of a Single Creative Mind: The Auteur *Approach*

In this approach we focus on the style, technique, and philosophy of the film's dominant creative personality—the director, the *auteur*, the complete filmmaker whose genius, style, and creative personality are reflected in every aspect of the film. Because all truly great directors impose their personalities on every aspect of their films, the film in this approach is viewed not as an objective work of art but as a reflection of the artistic vision or style of the person who made it. A good movie, according to *auteur* theory, is one whose every element bears the director's trademark—the story, the casting, the cinematography, the lighting, the music, the sound effects, the editing, and so on. And the film itself must be judged not alone but as part of the director's whole canon. In using this approach to evaluate a film, we should consider these questions:

- Judging from this film and other films by the same director, how would you describe the directorial style?
- How does each element of this film reflect the director's artistic vision, style, and overall philosophy of film or even his or her philosophy of life itself?
- What similarities does this film have to other films by the same director? How is it significantly different?
- Where in the film do we get the strongest impressions of the director's personality, of his or her unique creativity shaping the material?
- What is the special quality of this film as compared with other works in the director's canon? As compared with those other films, how well does this film reflect the philosophy, personality, and artistic vision of the person who made it?
- Does this film suggest growth in some new direction away from the other films? If so, describe the new direction.

The Film as Moral, Philosophical, or Social Statement

In this approach, often called the *humanistic approach*, we focus attention on the statement the film makes, because the best films are built around a statement that teaches us something. In this kind of evaluation, we must determine whether the acting and the characters have significance or meaning beyond the context of the film itself—moral, philosophical, or social significance that helps us gain a clearer understanding of some aspect of life, human nature, or the human condition. We judge the film as an expression of an idea that has intellectual, moral, social, or cultural importance and the ability to influence our lives for the better. Acting, cinematography, lighting, editing, sound, and so on are all judged in terms of how effectively they contribute to the communication of the film's message, and the overall value of the film depends on the significance of its theme. We might consider these questions when using the humanistic approach to evaluate a film:

- What statement does the film make, and how significant is the truth we learn from it?
- How effectively do the different film elements communicate the film's message?
- How does the film attempt to influence our lives for the better? What beliefs and actions does it attempt to change?
- Is the message stated by the film universal, or is it restricted to our own time and place?
- How relevant is the theme to our own experience?

The Film as Emotional or Sensual Experience

In this approach, which is the opposite of the more intellectual humanistic approach, we judge a film by the reality and intensity of its impact on the viewer. The stronger the emotional or sensual experience provided by the film, the better the film is. Generally, with this approach the preference is for films that stress fast-paced action, excitement, and adventure. Because a strong physical or visceral response is desired, a film is judged favorably if it is simply hard hitting and direct, like a punch in the jaw.

Those who favor this approach show an anti-intellectual bias. They want no message in their films, no significance beyond the immediate experience. They prefer pure action, excitement, and the simple, direct, unpretentious telling of a story. If the experience provided by the film is extremely realistic, vivid, and intense, the film is considered good. In evaluating a film by these standards, we might consider these questions:

- How powerful or intense is the film as an emotional or sensual experience?
- Where in the film are we completely wrapped up and involved in its reality? Where is the film weakest in emotional and sensual intensity?
- What role does each of the film elements play in creating a hard-hitting emotional and sensual response?

The Film as Conventionalized Form: The Genre Approach

A **genre film** is a film based on a formula that has become familiar because it is used so often. Audiences who watch genre films (discussed in detail in Chapter 14)—westerns are one example—know what sorts of characters, settings, plots, and so on to expect. In the genre approach, we judge a film according to how it fits into a body of formula films having essentially the same setting, characters, conflict, resolution, and values. We begin our analysis and evaluation by determining in what ways the film conforms to the standard formula of the genre it represents, as well as how it deviates from the formula.

Because we probably have seen a great many films of this genre before viewing the film under present study, we have clear expectations. As we watch the film, we will be disappointed if our expectations are not fulfilled. At the same time, we should look for variations and innovations that make this film different from others in the genre, for we will be disappointed if the film offers no variety or innovation. A good genre film not only fulfills our expectations by following the traditional patterns and providing complete and totally satisfying resolutions, but provides enough variations to satisfy our demand for novelty. Because genre films are made for a truly mass audience and reinforce the values and myths sacred to that audience, we might also consider how well the film reflects and reinforces basic American beliefs. We might consider these questions in evaluating a genre film:

- What are the basic requirements of the formula for this particular genre, and how well does this film fit the formula?
- Does the film fit the formula in such a way that all our expectations for films of this type are fulfilled?
- What variations and innovations on the standard formula are present in the film? Are these variations fresh enough to satisfy our need for novelty? What variations make the film stand out from other films of the same genre?
- What basic American beliefs, values, and myths are reflected and reinforced by the film? Are these beliefs, myths, and values outdated, or are they still relevant?

The Film as Political Statement: The Marxist Approach

Film may reflect a variety of political stances. One perspective that has been significant might be called Marxist. For some analysts the work of Karl Marx has become an important filter through which to view cinema. Marxist criticism is based on the premise that film—as well as literature and other forms of artistic expression—is a passive product of the economic aspects of a culture and that all movies are ultimately statements about the struggle for power between economic classes. The Marxist approach may include consideration of racial issues, because minority groups are often forced into lower socioeconomic classes by the dominant racial and economic group. To evaluate a film from the Marxist perspective, we might consider these questions:

- What is the socioeconomic level of the main character? Do statements in the script indicate the answer, or do the film's costumes and setting imply the answer?
- How do members of the various social classes interact?
- Is any sort of pattern evident in the types of actors cast in supporting and bit parts? For example, is there a relationship between the race and class of the characters and where they fall on the good guy/bad guy scale?
- Are ambition and the acquisition of wealth and material goods (climbing the social ladder) important to the characters? Does the film present ambition positively or negatively? What factors are important in determining success or failure?
- Does the film seem to celebrate a traditional value system, or does it question the mainstream view?

The Film as Gender Statement: The Feminist Approach

To focus, in any manner, on gender in films is to view them through another kind of political filter. In fact, one might argue that virtually any controversial group (especially minority group) may be at the thematic center of the political approach to movies. Critical reactions—both popular and professional—to modern films have demonstrated the possibilities. Quentin Tarantino's use and treatment of African Americans in *Jackie Brown* (not to mention *Pulp Fiction*), for instance, has raised the ire of Spike Lee. Evangelical Christians have questioned some of the central characterizations in Robert Duvall's *The Apostle*. The elderly, and others, have wondered about the iconic value of Hume Cronyn's aged character in *Marvin's Room. What's Eating Gilbert Grape*, some observers have maintained, risked offending the obese. Long before political correctness, critics noted that Natalie Wood was not Hispanic and asked why she dared pretend to be so in *West Side Story. Rain Man*, *Forrest Gump*, and *Sling Blade* have all elicited charges of possible exploitation of blessedly "different" people. More recently, evolving gay, lesbian, queer, and bisexual criticism has scrutinized such films as *The Object of My Affection* and *The Opposite of Sex* for their political gender statements (or lack thereof).

Similarly, and perhaps more broadly, the feminist approach rests on the assumption that art not only reflects but influences the attitudes of a culture. Feminist film critics attempt to show audiences how traditional cinematic language and symbolism reflect a masculine ideology. They encourage proportionate representation of women in film and urge that female characters not be relegated to traditional, stereotyped roles. Feminist analysis also considers the gender of directors and screenwriters and how it affects the presentation of the material. To evaluate a film from the feminist perspective, we might consider these questions:

- Are the main characters male or female? Was the decision about their gender made by the filmmakers based on the requirements of the story, or do the role assignments reflect gender-based stereotypes?
- How are women portrayed in the film? Are they passive, victimized, or ornamental, or are they active, assertive, and important to the development of the story?
- Who made the film? Do you think the gender of the filmmakers influenced their treatment and presentation of the story?
- Did the film seem to advocate any specific political ideas about the rights and equality of women (workplace discrimination, harassment, abortion rights, and so on)? Were these issues central to the story, or did their inclusion seem halfhearted?

The Film as Insight to the Mind: The Psychoanalytical Approach

Freudian Criticism Advocates for the interpretation of film from a Freudian perspective believe that a movie is an expression of the filmmaker's psyche and that a film's meaning lies beneath the obvious images on the screen. Knowing how the unconscious mind of a neurotic disguises secret thoughts in dream stories or bizarre actions, Freudian critics believe that directors (and screenwriters) rely heavily on symbols and purposely cloak or mystify events and ideas in images that require interpretation for true understanding. They tend to view a film as a kind of fantasy, dream, or daydream, and they use psychoanalysis to provide insights into the mind of the *auteur* who produced it. Recently, there has been a shift away from the analysis of the film's creator and toward the analysis of the film's audience—on the way the film appeals to *our* neuroses by tapping into *our* unconscious, repressed wishes, fantasies, and dreams. When examining the film from a Freudian perspective, one might consider these questions:

- What particular qualities of the film suggest that its true meaning lies beneath the surface and requires psychological analysis to unravel? Where in the film does the director seem to cloak and mystify events and ideas?
- Do you find any of the basic concepts usually associated with Freud suggested or symbolized in this film: the Oedipus complex, the ego, the id, the superego, the libido, unconscious desires, or sexual repression? What insights do they provide into the director's psyche?
- What other symbols do you find in the film, and what is your interpretation of them? What do they reveal about the director's psyche?
- Which of the symbols discussed in the previous two questions strike responsive chords in you personally? Do you think your responses to these

symbols and images are unique to your personality, or are they universal audience responses? If your responses were unique, what kinds of insights or self-discovery resulted from them?

Jungian Criticism The Jungian critic begins with some important basic assumptions. The first of these is that all human beings share a deep psychological bond, a collective unconscious, a kind of shadowy imprinting of universal images, patterns, and life experiences known as archetypes. These archetypes exist beneath the surface and are discernible only in fragments that surface as archetypal images, or shadows. One goal of the Jungian critic is to get a sense of the underlying archetypes suggested by the surface archetypal images evident in a film's characters, plot, and iconography. Jung also believed that all stories and legends are variations or aspects of a central myth, a monomyth, that undergirds all archetypal images and suggests their relationship to an archetype. This all-encompassing myth is the quest, in which the hero struggles to become an independent, self-reliant being. To accomplish this, the hero must free himself from the Great Mother (apparently an image for any kind of entangling or debilitating dependency). When he becomes independent and self-sufficient, he is rewarded by union with his feminine ideal, the anima. Therefore, another goal of the Jungian critic is to analyze the film's characters and their actions in relationship to the monomyth. The following questions might be considered by the Jungian approach:

- Do any of the characters seem familiar beyond ordinary stereotyping? Do they possess universal qualities to such a degree that they might be the surface shadows of archetypes? What aspects or qualities of the characters seem strikingly familiar or universal? What archetypes might these qualities suggest?
- Examine the possible relationships of the story's characters, conflicts, and resolutions to the quest monomyth. Do we have a male hero struggling for freedom from some kind of dependency? Is there a character or concept in the film that could be related to the Great Mother image? Does the hero become a separate, self-sufficient being? Does the resolution of the film's story include the hero's union with his ideal feminine other?
- What other films can you think of which reflect the general universal patterns of the quest monomyth? In what important ways do the universal patterns in these films differ from those in the film under analysis?
- Back off mentally from the specific characters, conflicts, actions, and images of the film, and try to view them as abstractions: broad, general patterns and concepts. Does generalizing and abstracting story elements in this way make the film's images seem more clearly archetypal?

The Eclectic Approach

To analyze every film from the narrow critical framework drawn from one or another of the approaches discussed so far would severely hamper our evaluation. To be fair, we must consider the director's intentions and choose an approach that complements them. Consider the result, for example, of applying the humanistic approach to a James Bond film or an Alfred Hitchcock film.

Vincent Canby's *New York Times* review of Hitchcock's *Frenzy* demonstrates the difficulty of judging a Hitchcock film from a humanistic frame of reference:

> Alfred Hitchcock is enough to make one despair. After 50 years of directing films, he's still not perfect. He refuses to be serious, at least in any easily recognizable way that might win him the Jean Hersholt Award, or even an Oscar for directorial excellence. Take, for example, his new film, "Frenzy," a suspense melodrama about a homicidal maniac, known as the Necktie Killer, who is terrorizing London, and the wrong man who is chased, arrested and convicted for the crimes. What does it tell us about the Human Condition, Love, the Third World, God, Structural Politics, Environmental Violence, Justice, Conscience, Aspects of Underdevelopment, Discrimination, Radical Stupor, Religious Ecstasy or Conservative Commitment? Practically nothing.
>
> It is immensely entertaining, yet it's possible to direct at "Frenzy" the same charges that have been directed at some of his best films in the past, meaning that it's "not significant," that "what it has to say about people and human nature is superficial and glib," that it "does nothing but give out a good time," that it's "wonderful while you're in the theater and impossible to remember 24 hours later."[8]

Because Hitchcock is a strong personality and a strong director who imposes his own stylistic trademark on every film he makes, his films can be profitably discussed from the *auteur* viewpoint (although he did not write his major American films) and, perhaps more appropriately, can be analyzed as emotional or sensual experiences. Because he stresses the subordinate role of the actor to the film, the personality cult approach is worthless, and, as Vincent Canby's remarks indicate, the humanistic approach leads nowhere. The most valid approach is the one that best matches the director's intentions.

But one approach to film evaluation seems more valid than any of the others described so far. The eclectic approach acknowledges that all approaches have some validity, and it selects the aspects of each approach that are appropriate and useful (Figure 12.3). In an eclectic evaluation, we might begin by asking whether the film is good and then try to support our opinion with answers to several of these questions:

- How technically sound and sophisticated is the film, and how well does it utilize the full potential of the medium?

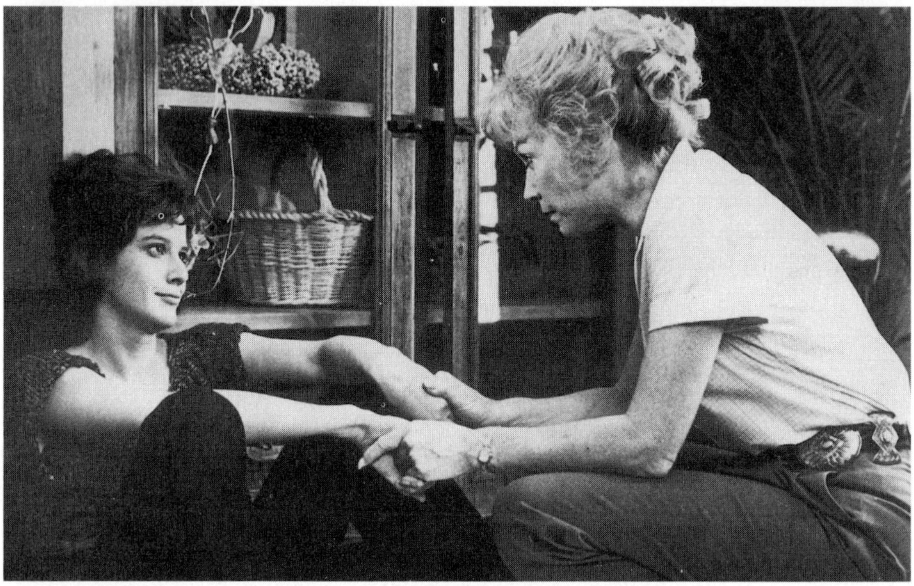

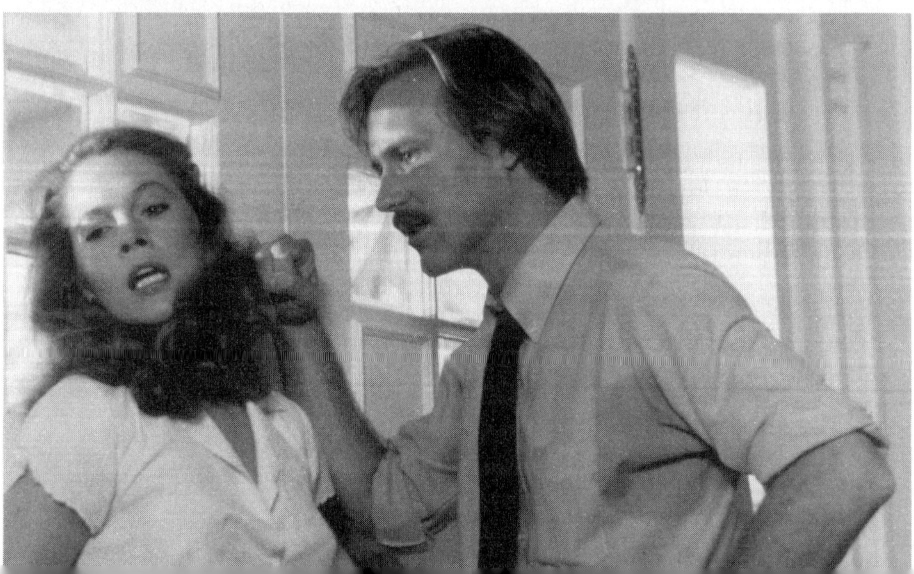

Figure 12.3 Eclectic Critical Possibilities Although an eclectic critical stance is usually the fairest of them all, some films do seem to cry out, first, for more specifically focused analysis. For example, *Persona* invites the *auteur* approach (opposite, top), *Terms of Endearment,* the emotional approach (opposite, middle); *Body Heat,* the genre approach (opposite, bottom); *Dead Man Walking,* the moral or philosophical approach (top); *Blue Sky,* the psychoanalytical approach (bottom left); and *The Crying Game,* the gender approach (bottom right).

- How powerful is the star's performance?
- How well does the film reflect the philosophy, personality, and artistic vision of the director?
- How worthwhile or significant is the statement made by the film, and how powerfully is it made?
- How effective is the film as an emotional or sensual experience?
- How well does the film conform to the patterns of its genre, and what variations or innovations does it introduce into that format?

Rereading the Reviews

We have seen the film, analyzed it, and interpreted it for ourselves. We have formed our own opinions about its worth and have noted our own personal and subjective reactions to it. Now we are ready to return to the reviews. At this point, we should read the review in an entirely different way from that in which we read it before seeing the film. Now we can read all parts of the review in depth, entering into a mental dialogue (perhaps even an argument) with the reviewer as we compare our mental notes and opinions on the film with the written review.

We may agree with the critic on many points and disagree completely on others. Reader and critic may analyze or interpret the film in the same way and yet reach opposite conclusions about its worth. In essence, what results here is a learning experience. Two separate minds—ours and the critic's—come together on the same work, seeking agreement perhaps but also relishing argument. Although we should be open-minded and try to see the critic's point of view and understand his or her analysis, interpretation, or evaluation, we must be independent enough not to be subservient.

Evaluating the Reviewer

We might evaluate the reviewers we read, determining how well we think they have carried out their duties. The key function of the reviewer is to lead us toward a better understanding or a keener appreciation of specific films and of the medium in general. After rereading the review in depth, we might first ask ourselves how well the reviewer succeeds in carrying out this function. In other words: *Does the critic succeed in helping us understand more about the film than we could see for ourselves? Does he or she make the film medium itself seem exciting, so that we want to experience its art more deeply and intensely?*

After answering these basic questions, we can move on to a thorough evaluation of the review by considering these questions:

- In what parts of the review is the critic merely providing factual information, things that cannot possibly be argued with? How thorough is this information, and how clear an idea does it give of the nature of the film?
- In what parts of the review does the critic serve as an objective interpreter or guide by pointing out film elements that are worthy of special attention, by explaining the director's intentions, by placing the film in context, or by describing the techniques employed? Does the critic try to analyze or interpret the film objectively?
- In what part of the review does the critic make relatively objective value judgments about the film's worth? How does the critic support judgments with critical ground rules? Does the critic make these critical ground rules clear? Does the critic provide a logical, convincing argument in support of the evaluation, or does he or she judge the film dogmatically?
- Where in the review does the critic reveal his or her subjectivity, prejudices, and biases? How much does the critic reveal about his or her own personality in this part of the review? How valuable are these subjective parts of the review in stimulating interest in the film or providing material for mental dialogue or argument? What critical weaknesses, limitations, or narrow attitudes are reflected in this review? Does the critic bother to warn us about his or her prejudices?
- Which critical method or approach does the critic emphasize? Does he or she place emphasis on how the film was made (film as technical achievement), on who stars in the film (film as showcase for the actor), on who made the film (the *auteur* approach), on what the film says (the humanistic approach), on the reality and intensity of the experience of the film (the film as an emotional or sensual experience), or on how well the film conforms to or introduces variations on a conventionalized form (the genre approach)? Does the critic focus on political or economic issues (the Marxist approach), or on issues of gender (the feminist approach), or on symbolic interpretation (the psychoanalytical approach)?
- Does the critic carefully consider the director's intentions and the level of ambition of the film and then select an approach to adjust for these expectations? If not, how does this shortcoming affect the review?

So that we are not overly influenced by critics' opinions, we need to develop the discipline of independent thinking, which requires confidence in our skills of observation and analysis and some degree of faith in our own critical judgment. This discipline is extremely important as we develop the confidence to know what we like and the ability to explain why we like it.

Above all, we must develop enough confidence in our own taste, our own insight, our own perception, and our own sensitivity so that, although we may be influenced by critics' opinions or arguments, we are never intimidated by them. We must continually question and weigh every opinion the critics state, and we may question their intelligence, emotional balance, judgment, and even their humanity. For the fact is that, despite the critics' valuable services, criticism remains a secondary and subjective art. No work of criticism has ever provided the last word on film, and none should be accepted as such.

Developing Personal Criteria

To achieve confidence in our critical abilities, it might be helpful to develop some personal criteria for film evaluation. The difficulty of this task is illustrated by the fact that few professional critics have a hard-and-fast set of rules by which they judge films. Dwight Macdonald discusses the difficulty of defining general principles in the introduction to his collected reviews, *On Movies:*

> I know something about cinema after forty years, and being a congenital critic, I know what I like and why. But I can't explain the *why* except in terms of the specific work under consideration, on which I'm copious enough. The general theory, the larger view, the gestalt—these have always eluded me. Whether this gap in my critical armor be called an idiosyncrasy or, less charitably, a personal failing, it has always been most definitely there.
>
> But people, especially undergraduates hot for certainty, keep asking me what rules, principles or standard I judge movies by—a fair question to which I can never think of an answer. Years ago, some forgotten but evidently sharp stimulus spurred me to put some guidelines down on paper. The result, hitherto unprinted for reasons which will become clear, was:
>
> 1. Are the characters consistent, and in fact, are there characters at all?
> 2. Is it true to life?
> 3. Is the photography cliché, or is it adapted to the particular film and therefore original?
> 4. Do the parts go together; do they add up to something; is there a rhythm established so that there is a form, shape, climax, building up tension and exploding it?
> 5. Is there a mind behind it; is there a feeling that a single intelligence has imposed its own view on the material?
>
> The last two questions rough out some vague sort of meaning, and the third is sound, if truistic. But I can't account for the first two being here at all, let alone in the lead-off place. Many films I admire are not "true to life" unless that stretchable term is strained beyond normal usage: *Broken Blossoms, Children of Paradise, Zero de Conduite, Caligari, On Approval,* Eisenstein's *Ivan the Terrible.* And some have no "characters" at all, consistent or no: *Potemkin, Arsenal, October, Intolerance, Marienbad, Orpheus, Olympia.* The comedies of Keaton, Chaplin, Lubitsch, the Marx Brothers and W. C. Fields occupy a middle ground. They have "consistent" characters all right, and they are also "true to life." But the consistency is always ex-

> treme and sometimes positively compulsive and obsessed (W. C., Groucho, Buster), and the truth is abstract. In short, they are so highly stylized (cf. "the Lubitsch touch") that they are constantly floating up from *terra firma* into the empyrean of art, right before my astonished and delighted eyes. . . .
>
> Getting back to general principles, I can think offhand (the only way I seem able to think about general principles) of two ways to judge the quality of a movie. They are rules of thumb, but they work—for me anyway:
>
> A. Did it change the way you look at things?
> B. Did you find more (or less) in it the second, third, *N*th time?
>
> (Also, how did it stand up over the years, after one or more "periods" of cinematic history?)
>
> Both rules are *post facto* and so, while they may be helpful to critics and audiences, they aren't of the slightest use to those who make movies. This is as it should be.[9]

Although Macdonald has little faith in *rigid* principles or guidelines, guidelines of some sort seem necessary for a foundation from which to watch, analyze, interpret, and evaluate films. The basic problem with ground rules, however, is that they tend to be inflexible and fail to expand or contract to fit the work being evaluated. What is needed is a general but flexible set of guidelines or critical principles that apply to most films but provide for exceptions. A groundbreaking film that conforms to none of the basic guidelines, even though it is a great film, may come along. Flexible critical guidelines, which see absolute consistency of approach as neither necessary nor desirable, will let us evaluate such a film. Because we are constantly experiencing new types of films, our guidelines must be constantly changing and growing to meet our needs.

In developing personal criteria for film evaluation, we (like Macdonald) might begin by trying to formulate a series of questions to ask about each movie that we see. Or we might simply try to list the qualities we think are essential to any good movie. Whichever course we choose, the task is not easy, but just making the effort should add to our understanding of why some movies are better than others. Even if we do come up with a set of guidelines that we consider adequate, we should resist the temptation to carve them into stone. The cinema is a dynamic, evolving art form, always capable of providing us with new films that won't fit the old rules. And it is equally important that we keep our minds and eyes open for discovering new things in old films.

Perhaps most important of all, we must keep our hearts open to films of all sorts so that we can continue to respond to movies emotionally, intuitively, and subjectively. Watching films is an art, not a science. The analytical approach should complement or deepen our emotional and intuitive responses, not replace or destroy them. Used properly, the analytical approach will add rich, new levels of awareness to our normal emotional and intuitive responses and help us become more proficient in the art of watching films.

Questions

On Addressing Viewer-Centered Challenges

1. Do you have any strong prejudices against this particular type of film? If so, how did these prejudices affect your responses to the film? Does this film have any special qualities that set it apart from other films of the same type?
2. How much do your personal and highly subjective responses to the following aspects of the film affect your judgment: actors in the film, treatment of sexual material, and scenes involving violence? Can you justify the sex and violence in the film aesthetically, or are these scenes included strictly to increase box-office appeal?
3. What were your expectations before seeing the film? How did these expectations influence your reaction to the film?
4. Do you have some specialized knowledge about any subject dealt with by the film? If so, how does it affect your reaction to the film as a whole?
5. Was your mood, mental attitude, or physical condition while seeing the movie less than ideal? If so, how was your reaction to the film affected?
6. If the physical environment in which you watched the film was less than ideal, how did this influence your judgment?

On the Basic Approach: Watching, Analyzing, and Evaluating the Film

1. What is the director's purpose or primary aim in making the film?
2. What is the true subject of the film, and what kind of statement, if any, does the film make about that subject?
3. How do all the separate elements of the film relate to and contribute to the theme, central purpose, or total effect?
4. What is the film's level of ambition?
5. Given the director's intentions and the film's level of ambition, how well does the film succeed in what it tries to do? Why does it succeed or fail?
6. Which elements or parts make the strongest contribution to the theme and why? Which elements or parts fail to function effectively in carrying out the director's intentions? Why do they fail?
7. What were your *personal* reactions to the film? What are your *personal* reasons for liking or disliking it?

On Evaluating the Reviewer

1. Of what film reviewers in the popular press (newspapers and magazines, local and beyond) are you aware? Do you read their work regularly? If not, choose one critic whose writing is available to you and read carefully at least five of his or her reviews. Can you discern a pattern of central expectations upon which this reviewer's observations are based? Attempt to record them succinctly.

2. Choose two of the nationally known film critics listed below. Then, make a comparative study of their work by locating, through research, each reviewer's opinions of three of your favorite movies. Use the questions on page 363 to guide your evaluations. Some influential film reviewers: Pauline Kael (formerly of *The New Yorker*, now retired), Janet Maslin (*The New York Times*), Stanley Kauffmann (*The New Republic*), Roger Ebert (*Chicago Sun-Times*), Gene Siskel (formerly of *Chicago Tribune*, now deceased), Richard Schickel (*Time*), Richard Corliss (*Time*), David Ansen (*Newsweek*), David Denby (*New York* and *The New Yorker*), Sheila Benson (*Los Angeles Times*), Kenneth Turan (*Los Angeles Times*), Joseph Morgenstern (*The Wall Street Journal*), and Peter Travers (*Rolling Stone*).

On Developing Personal Criteria

1. Try to construct a set of from five to ten questions that you think you should answer when judging the merits of a film, or list from five to ten qualities that you think are essential to a good movie.
2. If you fall short on the preceding question or lack confidence in the validity of the qualities you've listed as essential, try another approach: List your ten all-time favorite films. Then answer these questions about your list, and see what your answers reveal about your personal criteria for film evaluation:
    a. Consider each film on your list carefully, and decide what three or four things you liked best about it. Then decide which of these played the most important role in making you like or respect the film.
    b. How many of the films on your list share the qualities that most appeal to you? Which films seem to be most similar in the characteristics you like best?
    c. Do the qualities you pick show an emphasis on any single critical approach, or are your tastes eclectic? To decide this, answer the following:
        (1) How many of the films on your list do you respect primarily for their technique?
        (2) Do several of the films on your list feature the same actor?
        (3) How many of your favorite films are done by the same director?
        (4) Which of the films on your list make a significant statement of some kind?
        (5) Which of the films have a powerful, intense, and very real emotional or sensual effect?
        (6) Which of the films on your list could be classified as genre or formula films, and how many of them belong to the same genre?
        (7) Which films deal with basic conflicts between the "haves" and "have nots"?
        (8) Which films show women breaking out of traditional, stereotypical roles?

(9) Which of the films on your list rely heavily on complex symbols that require interpretation?

d. What do your answers to questions (1) through (9) reveal about your personal preferences? Do your tastes seem restricted?

e. How does your list of favorite films measure up against your first attempt to establish personal criteria for evaluation? How can your standards be changed, perhaps added to, in order to better match your list of film favorites?

Films for Study

All That Jazz (1979)
Angels and Insects (1995)
The Apostle (1997)
Babe (1995)
Being There (1979)
Beloved (1998)
Blue Sky (1994)
Body Heat (1981)
Bonnie and Clyde (1967)
Breaker Morant (1979)
Breaking Away (1979)
The Bridge on the River Kwai (1957)
Cabaret (1972)
Casablanca (1942)
Casino (1995)
Catch-22 (1970)
Cinema Paradiso (1988)
Citizen Kane (1941)
A Civil Action (1998)
A Clockwork Orange (1971)
The Conversation (1974)
The Crying Game (1992)
Dead Man Walking (1995)
The Deer Hunter (1978)
Do the Right Thing (1989)
Down in the Delta (1998)
Dr. Strangelove (1964)
Election (1999)
The Elephant Man (1980)
Elizabeth (1998)
The English Patient (1996)
The Godfather (1972)
The Godfather Part II (1974)
Gods and Monsters (1998)
The Graduate (1967)
The Grapes of Wrath (1940)
The Hanging Garden (1997)
Hurlyburly (1998)
Jackie Brown (1997)
Like Water for Chocolate (1992)
Love and Death on Long Island (1998)
Marvin's Room (1996)
Matilda (1996)
On the Waterfront (1954)
Ordinary People (1980)
Out of Africa (1985)
Patton (1970)
Persona (1966)
The Piano (1993)
Pulp Fiction (1994)
Pushing Tin (1999)
Red (1994)
Reds (1981)
Secrets & Lies (1996)
The Seventh Seal (1957)
Shakespeare in Love (1998)
A Simple Plan (1998)
Still Crazy (1998)
The Stunt Man (1980)
Taxi Driver (1976)
Terms of Endearment (1983)
The Thin Red Line (1998)
The Truman Show (1998)
A Walk on the Moon (1999)
Woman in the Dunes (1964)
The World According to Garp (1982)

Chapter 13

Adaptations

The Maltese Falcon was produced three times before I did it, never with very much success, so I decided on a radical procedure: to follow the book rather than depart from it. This was practically an unheard of thing to do with any picture taken from a novel, and marks the beginning of a great epoch in picture making.

—JOHN HUSTON, DIRECTOR

The Problems of Adaptation

One of the most difficult problems of film analysis arises when we see a film adaptation of a play we have seen or a novel we have read, for we generally approach such films with unreasonable expectations. We expect the film to duplicate the experience we had when we saw the play or read the novel. That is, of course, impossible. Because we have already experienced the story and are familiar with the characters and events, the adaptation is bound to lack some of the freshness of the original. But many factors other than familiarity should be considered if we are to approach an adaptation with the proper frame of mind. To know what we can reasonably expect from films based on a play or a novel requires insight into the kinds of changes that adaptation will bring, as well as an understanding of the relative strengths and weaknesses of the media involved.

Change in Medium

The medium in which a story is told has a definite effect on the story itself. Each medium has its strengths and limitations, and any adaptation from one medium to another must take these factors into account and adjust the subject matter accordingly. If we are to judge a film adaptation fairly, we should recognize that although a novel, a play, or a film can tell the same story, each medium is a work of art in its own right, and, despite some properties that all three share, each medium has its own distinctive techniques, conventions, consciousness, and viewpoint. We do not expect an oil painting to have the same effect as a statue or a tapestry depicting the same subject, and we should not expect the film adaptation of a novel or a play to have the same effect as the novel or play.

Change in Creative Artists

In our analysis we certainly must consider the influence that any change in creative talents has on a work of art. No two creative minds are alike, and when the reins are passed from one creative hand to another the end product changes. Some kind of creative shift occurs in almost any kind of adaptation. Even when a novelist or playwright adapts his or her own work for the screen, changes (sometimes rather drastic) are sure to be made. Some of those changes may be required by the new medium. For example, the average novel contains more material than a film could ever hope to include, so the screenwriter or director must choose what to leave in and what to take out. Because the novel cannot be translated intact, its emphasis may have to be changed, even if the novelist is writing the screenplay. For example, Jerzy Kosinski wrote both the novella *Being There* and the screenplay for Hal Ashby's film adaptation of it. But, as John Updike has observed, the film is probably better *as a film* than the novella is *as a*

Figure 13.1 Objection Sustained Fifties novelist J. D. Salinger became a fascinating fictional character in H. P. Kinsella's fantasy novel, *Shoeless Joe*. Salinger, however, objected to his name being used for the character, so when the film version (*Field of Dreams*) came out, the character had become a Black novelist/civil rights fighter from the sixties played by James Earl Jones.

work of fiction.[1] Sometimes, problems arise that are totally beyond the screenwriter's or director's control, as in the case of *Field of Dreams* (Figure 13.1). The most significant changes, however, come about because the novelist or playwright must surrender some artistic control to the director and the actors (Figure 13.2).

To expect an exact carry-over from one medium to another when different creative artists are involved seems especially irrational when we consider our attitudes toward different versions of the same vehicle within the same medium. For example, we fully expect the same play staged or filmed by different directors and with different actors to differ in emphasis and interpretation. Consider Sir Laurence Olivier's *Hamlet*, Nicol Williamson's *Hamlet*, Richard Chamberlain's *Hamlet* (made for television), Mel Gibson's *Hamlet*, and Kenneth Branagh's *Hamlet*. All are different and all are praised for being different, for we expect and perhaps even demand that they be different. As filmgoers, we must develop an equally tolerant attitude toward all film adaptations and freely grant the new creative talent some artistic license.

Figure 13.2 Passing the Torch Novelist John Irving (right) discusses a point about his best-selling novel *The World According to Garp* with screenwriter Steve Tesich, who wrote the film version.

Of course, there are limits to which artistic license can justifiably be carried. If a work is changed so much that it is almost unrecognizable, it should probably not bear the same title as the original—as was the case for John Irving's novel *A Prayer for Owen Meany*, whose title was changed to *Simon Birch* for the film adaptation. It has been said, perhaps with justification, that Hollywood frequently distorts the meaning of a novel so thoroughly that nothing is left but the title. Two brief examples may illustrate the validity of that statement.

John Ford, when asked about his indebtedness to the novel in making *The Informer*, supposedly replied, "I never read the book." In a similar vein, playwright Edward Albee was once asked whether he was pleased with the screen adaptation of *Who's Afraid of Virginia Woolf?* He replied ironically that, although it omitted some things he felt were important, he was rather pleased with the adaptation, especially in light of the fact that a friend had called him to pass on the rumor that the filmmakers were seeking someone to cast in the role of George and Martha's nonexistent son. (Screenwriter Ernest Lehman's first draft included a real son who had committed suicide, but director Mike Nichols would not accept that radical change.)

Cinematic Potential of the Original Work

Renata Adler has observed, "Not every written thing aspires to be a movie." And, indeed, some plays and novels are more adaptable to the film medium than others. The style in which a novel is written, for example, certainly affects its adaptability to film. Randall Stewart and Dorothy Bethurum point out important differences in the novelistic styles of Ernest Hemingway and Henry James:

> It is interesting to observe that two such influential prose writers as Hemingway and Henry James should be at the opposite poles of style: one (Hemingway) giving us the rhythms of speech, the other (James) literary convolutions found only on the printed page, one (Hemingway) elemental and sensuous, the other (James) complex and infinitely qualifying. Each style is admirably fitted for the purpose for which it is intended. James is concerned primarily with the intellectual analysis of experience. Hemingway's aim is the sensuous and emotional rendering of experience.[2]

Because of the differences in their style, a Hemingway novel is more easily adapted to the screen than is a novel by Henry James (although several of James's works have become films, including *The Turn of the Screw*, several times; *Daisy Miller*, notoriously by Peter Bogdanovich, starring Cybill Shepherd, in 1974; and, most recently, *The Portrait of a Lady*, *Washington Square*, and *The Wings of the Dove*). The last point made by Stewart and Bethurum is especially important: Hemingway's sensuous and emotional rendering of experience is cinematic; James's intellectual analysis of experience is not. The difference in the two writers' styles and their adaptability to the screen can be observed in the following samples of their work:

> Mrs. Gereth had said she would go with the rest to church, but suddenly it seemed to her that she would not be able to wait till church-time for relief: breakfast, at Waterbath, was a punctual meal, and she had still nearly an hour on her hands. Knowing the church to be near, she prepared in her room for the little rural walk, and on her way down again, passing through corridors and observing imbecilities of decoration, the aesthetic misery of the big commodious house, she felt a return of the tide of last night's irritation, a renewal of everything she could secretly suffer from ugliness and stupidity. Why did she consent to such contacts, why did she so rashly expose herself? She had had, heaven knew, her reasons, but the whole experience was to be sharper than she had feared. To get away from it and out into the air, into the presence of sky and trees, flowers and birds was a necessity of every nerve. The flowers of Waterbath would probably go wrong in color and the nightingales sing out of tune; but she remembered to have heard the place described as possessing those advantages that are usually spoken of as natural. There were advantages enough it clearly didn't possess. It was hard for her to believe that a woman could look presentable who had been kept awake for hours by the wall-paper in her room; yet none the less, as in her fresh widow's weeds she rustled

across the hall, she was, as usual, the only person in the house incapable of wearing in her preparation the horrible stamp of the exceptional smartness that would be conspicuous in a grocer's wife. She would rather have perished than to have looked *endimanchée*.

—Opening paragraph from *The Spoils of Poynton* by Henry James

Nick stood up. He was all right. He looked up the track at the lights of the caboose going out of sight around the curve. There was water on both sides of the track, then tamarack swamp.

He felt of his knee. The pants were torn and skin was barked. His hands were scraped and there were sand and cinders driven up under his nails. He went over to the edge of the track down the little slope to the water and washed his hands. He washed them carefully in the cold water, getting the dirt out from the nails. He squatted down and bathed his knee.[3]

—First two paragraphs of "The Battler" by Ernest Hemingway

Although the problems of adapting a play to the screen are not generally as great as those presented by the James novel, playwrights also have styles that affect the ease with which their plays can be adapted to film. Tennessee Williams, for example, is a more cinematic playwright than Edward Albee. Williams's verbal imagery is more concrete and sensual than Albee's, and his plays contain speeches—such as the one describing Sebastian's death in *Suddenly, Last Summer*—that lend themselves to visual flashbacks.

Problems Created by the Viewer

When we see a film adaptation of a favorite play or novel, we as viewers create many problems that work against our enjoyment of the film. First, our own experience of the play or novel is itself a creative process. Locked vividly in our minds are strong visual images and impressive bits of dialogue from the play or novel. We may even remember the inflections with which the actors delivered the lines in a play. Because we experienced these images or bits of dialogue first, they become the standard by which we measure all later efforts.

What's more, we are not aware of the degree of our selectivity. Because remembering is a selective process, it is also a creative act. Unconsciously and a bit unfairly perhaps, we demand that the adaptation single out for emphasis, or at least treat, all of the things that are important to us—that is, everything our memory has selected from the original. We do not always mind if things are left out, as long as they are not our favorite things. In a sense, we have the same reaction to many film adaptations that we might have toward a friend whom we haven't seen for a long time and who has changed greatly over the intervening years. Mentally prepared to meet an old friend, we meet a stranger and take the changes as a personal affront, as though the friend has no right to undergo them without our knowledge or permission.

Adaptations of Novels

The general problems just discussed influence our reactions to film adaptations of both novels and plays. A more complete understanding requires a deeper examination of the specific challenges posed by each medium. To grasp better the difficulties of translating a novel into film, we must look at certain characteristics of novels.

Literary Versus Cinematic Points of View

Point of view is an important factor in any work of fiction. The point of view controls and dictates the form and shape of a literary work and determines its emphasis, tone, strengths, and limitations. A change in point of view is almost as important in a work of fiction as a change from one medium to another, for **literary point of view** determines to a large degree what the novelist can and cannot do. To appreciate the difficulties the filmmaker faces in translating a novel into film requires some familiarity with five literary viewpoints.

1. **First-Person Point of View.** A character who has participated in or observed the action of the story gives us an eyewitness or firsthand account of what happened and his or her responses to it.

> Yes sir. Flem Snopes has filled the whole country full of spotted horses. You can hear folks running them all day and all night, whooping and hollering, and the horses running back and forth across them little wooden bridges ever now and then kind of like thunder. Here I was this morning pretty near halfway to town, with a team ambling along and me setting in the buckboard about half asleep, when all of a sudden something come swurging up outen the bushes and jumped the road clean, without touching hoof to it. It flew right over my team big as a billboard and flying through the air like a hawk. It taken me thirty minutes to stop my team and untangle the harness and the buckboard and hitch them up again.[4]
>
> —Opening paragraph of "Spotted Horses," by William Faulkner

2. **Third-Person Omniscient Narrator Point of View.** An all-seeing, all-knowing narrator, capable of reading the thoughts of all the characters and capable of being several places at once if need be, tells the story.

> There was a woman who was beautiful, who started with all the advantages, yet she had no luck. She married for love, and the love turned to dust. She had bonny children, yet she felt they had been thrust upon her, and she could not love them. They looked at her coldly, as if they were finding fault with her. And hurriedly she felt she must cover up some fault in herself. Yet what it was that she must cover up she never knew. Nevertheless, when her children were present, she always felt the center of her heart go hard. This troubled her, and in her manner she was all the more gentle and anxious for her children, as if she loved them very much. Only she could not feel love, no, not for anybody. Everybody else said of her: "She is such a

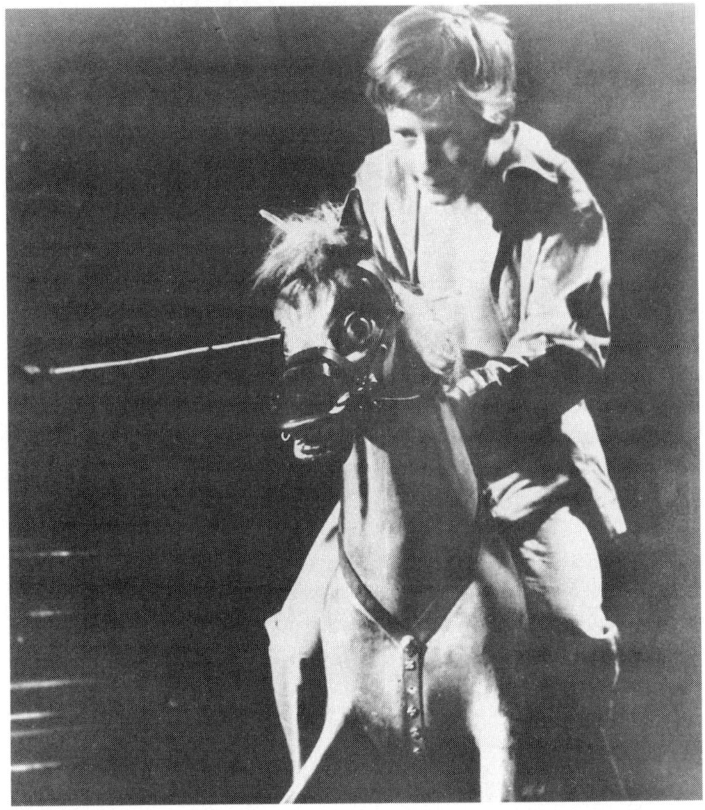

Figure 13.3 Short Story Into Film John Howard Davies rides his rocking horse into a mystical trance where the winners of horse races are revealed to him in the film version of D. H. Lawrence's story "The Rocking-Horse Winner."

good mother. She adores her children." Only she herself, and her children themselves, knew it was not so. They read it in each other's eyes.

There was a boy and two little girls. They lived in a pleasant house, with a garden, and they had discreet servants, and felt themselves superior to anyone in the neighborhood.

Although they lived in style, they felt always an anxiety in the house. There was never enough money.[5] (Figure 13.3)

—Opening paragraphs of "The Rocking-Horse Winner," by D. H. Lawrence

3. **Third-Person Limited Point of View.** The narrator is omniscient except for the fact that his or her powers of mind reading are limited to or at least focused on a single character. This character's thoughts are extremely important to the novel, for he or she becomes the central intelligence through which we view the action.

Although Bertha Young was thirty she still had moments like this when she wanted to run instead of walk, to take dancing steps on and off the pavement, to bowl a hoop, to throw something up in the air and catch it again, or to stand still and laugh at nothing—at nothing, simply.

What can you do if you are thirty and, turning the corner of your own street, you are overcome, suddenly, by a feeling of bliss—absolute bliss!—as though you'd suddenly swallowed a bright piece of that late afternoon sun and it burned in your bosom, sending out a little shower of sparks into every particle, into every finger and toe? . . .

Oh, is there no way you can express it without being "drunk and disorderly"? How idiotic civilization is! Why be given a body if you have to keep it shut up in a case like a rare, rare fiddle?[6]

—Opening paragraphs of "Bliss" by Katherine Mansfield

4. **Dramatic or Objective Point of View.** We are not conscious of a narrator, for the author does not comment on the action but simply describes the scene, telling us what happens and what the characters say, so we get a feeling of being there, observing the scene as we would in a play. This is also known as the *concealed*, or *effaced, narrator point of view*.

The door of Henry's lunchroom opened and two men came in. They sat down at the counter.

"What's yours?" George asked them.

"I don't know," one of the men said. "What do you want to eat, Al?"

"I don't know," said Al. "I don't know what I want to eat."

Outside it was getting dark. The street light came on outside the window. The two men at the counter read the menu. From the other end of the counter Nick Adams watched them. He had been talking to George when they came in.

"I'll have a roast pork tenderloin with apple sauce and mashed potatoes," the first man said.

"It isn't ready yet."

"What the hell do you put it on the card for?"

"That's the dinner," George explained. "You can get that at six o'clock."

George looked at the clock on the wall behind the counter. "It's five o'clock."

"The clock says twenty minutes past five," the second man said.

"It's twenty minutes fast."

"Oh, to hell with the clock," the first man said. "What have you got to eat?"[7]

—Opening paragraphs of "The Killers," by Ernest Hemingway

5. **Stream of Consciousness or Interior Monologue.** This seems to be a combination of third-person and first-person narrative, although the participant in the action is not consciously narrating the story. What we get instead is a unique kind of inner view, as though a microphone and a movie camera in the fictional character's mind were recording for us every thought, image, and impression that passes through the character's brain, without the conscious acts of organization, selectivity, or narration.

Stay mad. My shirt was getting wet and my hair. Across the roof hearing the roof loud now I could see Natalie going through the garden among the rain. Get wet I hope you catch

> *pneumonia go on home Cowface. I jumped hard as I could into the hog-wallow the mud yellowed up to my waist stinking I kept on plunging until I fell down and rolled over in it.* "Hear them in swimming, sister? I wouldn't mind doing that myself." If I had time. When I have time. I could hear my watch. *Mud was warmer than the rain it smelled awful. She had her back turned I went around in front of her. You know what I was doing? She turned her back I went around in front of her the rain creeping into the mud flatting her bodice through her dress it smelled horrible. I was hugging her that's what I was doing. She turned her back I went around in front of her. I was hugging her I tell you. I don't give a damn what you were doing . . .*[8]
>
> —From *The Sound and the Fury* by William Faulkner

Of the five points of view possible in a novel, three require the narrator to look inside a character's mind to see what he or she is thinking. Omniscient, third-person limited, and stream of consciousness all stress the thoughts, concepts, or reflections of a character—elements that are difficult to depict cinematically. These three literary points of view have no natural cinematic equivalents. George Bluestone discusses this problem in *Novels Into Film:*

> The rendition of mental states—memory, dream, imagination—cannot be as adequately represented by film as by language. . . . The film, by arranging external signs for our visual perception, or by presenting us with dialogue, can lead us to *infer* thought. But it cannot show us thought directly. It can show us characters thinking, feeling, and speaking, but it cannot show us their thoughts and feelings. A film is not thought; it is perceived.[9]

Another problem arises from the fact that three of the literary viewpoints—first person, omniscient, and third person limited—make us aware of a narrator, of someone telling a story. The sense of a narrator, or a novelistic point of view, can be imposed (or superimposed) on a film through voice-over narration added to the soundtrack. But this is not a natural cinematic element, and it is rarely completely successful in duplicating or even suggesting literary viewpoints. In film we usually simply see the story unfold. Thus, the dramatic point of view is the only literary viewpoint that can be directly translated into cinema. Few if any novels, however, are written from the strict dramatic point of view, because it requires so much of the reader's concentration; the reader must read between the lines for significance or meaning. This viewpoint is usually restricted to short stories.

The usual solution to such problems of viewpoint is to ignore the novel's point of view, ignore the prose passages stressing thought or reflection, and simply duplicate the most dramatic scenes. However, the prose passages and the point of view often constitute much of the novel's essence. This means that filmmakers cannot always capture a novel's essence cinematically. The following examples of specific problems of adapting a novel into film should help illustrate the point.

First-Person Point of View: A Special Problem

The first-person point of view has no true cinematic equivalent. The completely consistent use of the **subjective camera** (a camera that records everything from the point of view of a participant in the action) does not work effectively in film. Even if it did, the cinematic subjective point of view is not really equivalent to the literary first-person viewpoint. The subjective camera lets us feel that we are involved in the action, seeing it through a participant's eyes. But the literary first-person point of view does not equate reader with participant. Instead, the narrator and the reader are two separate entities. The reader listens while the first-person narrator tells the story.

In novels with a first-person point of view, such as Mark Twain's *Huckleberry Finn* and J. D. Salinger's *The Catcher in the Rye*, the reader has an intimate relationship with the narrator, who tells the story as a participant in the action. The writer speaks directly to the reader and forms emotional ties with him or her. The reader feels that he or she knows the narrator, that they are intimate friends. This bond between narrator and reader is much closer than any tie that a remote, unseen director—who shows the story through pictures—might strive to create with a viewer. The intimacy of the warm, comfortable relationship between a first-person narrator and reader can rarely be achieved in film, even with the help of voice-over narration.

Furthermore, the unique personality of the narrator is often extremely important in the first-person novel. Much of this personality, however, may be impossible to show in action or dialogue, for it is the aspect of personality revealed by the way the narrator tells a story, not the way the narrator looks, acts, or speaks in dialogue, that comes across in the novel. This quality, which would certainly be missing from the film, might be called the *narrator's essence*, a quality of personality that gives a certain flair or flavor to the narrative style and that, though essential to the tone of the book, cannot really be translated into film.

Consider, for example, the verbal flow of Holden Caulfield's first-person narration from *The Catcher in the Rye:*

> Where I want to start telling is the day I left Pencey Prep. Pencey Prep is this school that's in Agerstown, Pennsylvania. You probably heard of it. You've probably seen the ads, anyway. They advertise in about a thousand magazines, always showing some hotshot guy on a horse jumping over a fence. Like as if all you ever did at Pencey was play polo all the time. I never once saw a horse anywhere near the place. And underneath the guy on the horse's picture, it always says: "Since 1888 we have been molding boys into splendid, clear-thinking young men." Strictly for the birds. They don't do any damn more molding at Pencey than they do at any other school. And I didn't know anybody there that was splendid and clear thinking at all. Maybe two guys. If that many. And they probably came to Pencey that way.[10]

Because of the unique personality of the narrator, the first-person point of view affects the tenor of the novel not as a way of seeing but as a way of telling, a verbal essence that sets the tone and style for the whole novel. Thus, it is virtually impossible to imagine a film version of *The Catcher in the Rye* without a great deal of voice-over narration running throughout the film. Although such approaches have been tried in film (one example is Henry Miller's *Tropic of Cancer*, which also has a distinctly flavorful first-person narrative style), for the most part such extensive use of voice-over is not very effective in films.

One fairly successful attempt in which the flavor of the first-person narrator was suggested by the voice-over narration was *To Kill a Mockingbird*. The voice-over, however, was used with restraint, so that the feeling of unnaturalness that often results when someone tells us a story while we are watching it unfold was avoided. And the personality of the narrator here was not as unique as Holden Caulfield's in *The Catcher in the Rye* or that of Miller's narrator in *Tropic of Cancer*, so the burden of style and tone did not rest so much on the narrator's verbal essence. Especially in films that come from original scripts rather than novels, voice-over narration is best used *only* as a method for conveying style and the tone of personality (as in the case of *Taxi Driver*, *Days of Heaven*, and *The Opposite of Sex;* see Chapter 8).

The Problem of Length and Depth

Because of the rather severe limitations imposed on the length of a film and on the amount of material it can successfully treat, a film is forced to suggest pictorially a great many things that a novel can explore in more depth. Novelist/screenwriter William Goldman sums up the problem this way:

> When people say, "Is it like the book?" the answer is, "There has never in the history of the world been a movie that's really been like the book." Everybody says how faithful *Gone with the Wind* was. Well, *Gone with the Wind* was a three-and-a-half-hour movie, which means you are talking about maybe a two-hundred-page screenplay of a nine-hundred-page novel in which the novel has, say, five hundred words per page; and the screenplay has maybe forty, maybe sixty, depending on what's on the screen, maybe one hundred and fifty words per page. But you're taking a little, teeny slice; you're just extracting little, teeny *essences* of scenes. All you can ever be in an adaptation is faithful in spirit.[11]

At best, the film version can capture a small fraction of the novel's depth. It is doubtful that it can ever capture much of what lies beneath the surface. The filmmaker, nevertheless, must attempt to suggest the hidden material. The film-maker's task is eased a bit if he or she can assume that viewers have read the novel. But we still must accept the fact that some dimensions of the novel are inaccessible to film.

A long novel creates an interesting dilemma: Should the filmmaker be satisfied with doing only part of the novel, dramatizing a single action that can be thoroughly treated within cinematic limits? Or should the filmmaker attempt to capture a sense of the whole novel by hitting the high points and leaving the gaps unfilled? If the latter strategy is attempted, complex time and character relationships may wind up being implied rather than clearly stated. Usually the filmmaker must limit not only the depth to which a character can be explored but also the actual number of characters treated. This limitation may give rise to the creation of composite characters, embodying the plot functions of two or more characters from the novel in one film character. Furthermore, in adapting a long novel to film, complex and important subplots might have to be eliminated. Generally, then, the shorter the novel, the better are the chances for effective adaptation to the screen. Many short stories have been translated into film with little or no expansion. (To many readers/viewers, John Huston's adaptation of James Joyce's "The Dead" seems exemplary. Even with short stories, though, the sense of loss in film adaptation can be great, as the short story–to–film video series *The American Short Story* repeatedly demonstrates.) Occasionally, a very popular but superficial novel will become the source for a much more substantial film, such as *The Bridges of Madison County*.

Philosophical Reflections

Often, the most striking passages in a novel are those in which we sense an inner movement of the author's mind toward some truth of life and are aware that our own mind is being stretched by his or her contemplation and reflection. Such passages do not stress external action but rather lead to an internal questioning of the meaning and significance of events, taking the reader on a kind of cerebral excursion into a gray world where the camera cannot go (Figure 13.4). The following passage from Robert Penn Warren's novel *All the King's Men*, for example, could not be effectively treated in film:

> Two hours later, I was in my car and Burden's Landing was behind me, and the bay, and windshield wipers were making their busy little gasp and click like something inside you which had better not stop. For it was raining again. The drops swung and swayed down out of the dark into my headlights like a bead portiere of bright metal beads which the car kept shouldering through.
>
> There is nothing more alone than being in a car at night in the rain. I was in the car. And I was glad of it. Between one point on the map and another point on the map, there was the being alone in the car in the rain. They say you are not you except in terms of relation to other people. If there weren't any other people there wouldn't be any you, and not being you or anything, you can really lie back and get some rest. It is a vacation from being you. There is only the flow of the motor under your foot spinning that frail thread of sound out of its metal gut like a

Figure 13.4 ***All the King's Men*—Change of Focus** Because Robert Penn Warren's powerful novel centers on a first-person narrator addicted to philosophical reflection, Robert Rossen's film version shifts its focus to the man of action, politician Willie Stark (Broderick Crawford).

> spider, that filament, that nexus, which isn't really there, between the you which you have just left in one place and the you which you will be when you get to the other place.
>
> You ought to invite those two you's to the same party some time. Or you might have a family reunion for all the you's with barbecue under the trees. It would be amusing to know what they would say to each other.
>
> But meanwhile, there isn't either one of them, and I am in the car in the rain at night.[12]

Because *All the King's Men* is full of such passages, this one could not be singled out for treatment in voice-over narration. It is also highly improbable that the dramatic scene described here (the narrator, Jack Burden, driving alone in the rain at night) could suggest his thoughts even to a viewer who had read the novel.

When a visual image in a novel is more closely related to a philosophical passage and serves as a trigger to a reflection, there is a greater probability that the filmmaker will be able to suggest the significance of the image to those who have read the novel, but even this is by no means certain. The first of the following two passages from *All the King's Men* gives us a rather clear visual image and could be effectively treated on film. The second is primarily the narrator's reflection on the significance of the visual image and could at best be only suggested in a film:

> In a settlement named Don Jon, New Mexico, I talked to a man propped against the shady side of the filling station, enjoying the only patch of shade in a hundred miles due east. He was an old fellow, seventy-five if a day, with a face like sun-brittled leather and pale-blue eyes under the brim of a felt hat which had once been black. The only thing remarkable about him was the fact that while you looked into the sun-brittled leather of the face, which seemed as stiff and devitalized as the hide on a mummy's jaw, you would suddenly see a twitch in the left cheek, up toward the pale-blue eye. You would think he was going to wink, but he wasn't going to wink. The twitch was simply an independent phenomenon, unrelated to the face or to what was behind the face or to anything in the whole tissue of phenomena which is the world we are lost in. It was remarkable, in that face, the twitch which lived that little life all its own. I squatted by his side, where he sat on a bundle of rags from which the handle of a tin skillet protruded, and listened to him talk. But the words were not alive. What was alive was the twitch, of which he was no longer aware. . . .
>
> We rode across Texas to Shreveport, Louisiana, where he left me to try for north Arkansas. I did not ask him if he had learned the truth in California. His face had learned it anyway, and wore the final wisdom under the left eye. The face knew that the twitch was the live thing. Was all. But, having left that otherwise unremarkable man, it occurred to me, as I reflected upon the thing which made him remarkable, that if the twitch was all, what was it that could know that twitch was all? Did the leg of the dead frog in the laboratory know that the twitch was all when you put the electric current through it? Did the man's face know about the twitch, and how it was all? Ah, I decided, that is the mystery. That is the secret knowledge. That is what you have to go to California to have a mystic vision to find out. That the twitch can know that the twitch is all. Then, having found that out, in the mystic vision, you feel clean and free. You are at one with the Great Twitch.[13]

Summarizing a Character's Past

In the novel, when a character first appears, the novelist often provides us with a quick thumbnail sketch of his or her past, as illustrated by the summary of the origins and past history of Billy, the deaf-mute boy from Larry McMurtry's novel, *The Last Picture Show:*

> While the boys worked Sam stood by the stove and warmed his aching feet. He wished Sonny weren't so reckless economically, but there was nothing he could do about it. Billy was less of a problem partly because he was so dumb. Billy's real father was an old railroad man who had worked in Thalia for a short time just

Figure 13.5 Character Without a Past Sam Bottoms as Billy, the deaf-mute boy in *The Last Picture Show.*

> before the war: his mother was a deaf and dumb girl who had no people except an aunt. The old man cornered the girl in the balcony of the picture show one night and begat Billy. The sheriff saw to it that the old man married the girl, but she died when Billy was born and he was raised by the family of Mexicans who helped the old man keep the railroad track repaired. After the war the hauling petered out and the track was taken up. The old man left and got a job bumping cars on a stock-yards track in Oklahoma, leaving Billy with the Mexicans. They hung around for several more years, piling prickly pear and grubbing mesquite, but then a man from Plainview talked them into moving out there to pick cotton. They snuck off one morning and left Billy sitting on the curb in front of the picture show.
>
> From then on, Sam the Lion took care of him. Billy learned to sweep, and he kept all three of Sam's places swept out: in return he got his keep and also, every single night, he got to watch the picture show. He always sat in the balcony, his broom at his side: for years he saw every show that came to Thalia and so far as anyone knew, he liked them all. He was never known to leave while the screen was lit.[14]

McMurtry summarizes a character's whole background in two brief paragraphs. In the film version, no background on Billy is provided whatsoever (Figure 13.5). Such information could not be worked into the film's dialogue without bringing in an outsider, some character who didn't know Billy, to ask about his past. But having characters spend a great deal of time talking about the back-rounds of other characters does not make for good cinema—it becomes too static, too talky. The only alternative is to dramatize such paragraphs visually. But this type of material not only lacks the importance to justify such treatment but would have to be forced into the main plot structure in a very unnatural manner. The kind of background information that the novelist gives in the passages above is simply not suited to a natural cinematic style, and the background of many film characters therefore remains a mystery. Because novels can and do provide this kind of information, they possess a depth in characterization that films usually lack. However, "backstory" material is provided cinematically in the film versions of *They Shoot Horses, Don't They?* and *Midnight Cowboy*.

Cinematic Compression of Time Versus Novelistic Summary

Cinematic techniques are capable of conveying the impression that time is passing; even relatively long periods of time can be suggested by a well-made transition or even a montage. But film is severely limited by its inability to summarize what happens in that span of time. This kind of summary does not always lend itself to images and dialogue. In *All the King's Men,* Robert Penn Warren summarizes seventeen years of a woman's life as follows:

> As for the way Anne Stanton went meanwhile, the story is short. After two years at the refined female college in Virginia, she came home. Adam by this time was in medical school up East. Anne spent a year going to parties in the city, and got engaged. But nothing came of it. After awhile there was another engagement, but something happened again. By this time Governor Stanton was nearly an invalid, and Adam was studying abroad. Anne quit going to parties, except for an occasional party at the Landing in the summer. She stayed at home with her father, giving him his medicine, patting his pillow, assisting the nurse, reading to him hour by hour, holding his hand in the summer twilights or in the winter evenings when the house shook to the blasts off the sea. It took him seven years to die. After the governor had died in the big tester bed with a lot of expensive medical talent leaning over him, Anne Stanton lived in the house fronting the sea, with only the company of Aunt Sophonisba, a feeble, grumbling, garrulous, and incompetent old colored woman, who combined benevolence and vengeful tyranny in the ambiguous way known only to old colored women who have spent their lives in affectionate service, in prying, in wheedling, and chicanery, in short-lived rebelliousness and long irony, and in second-hand clothes. Then Aunt Sophonisba died, too, and Adam came back from abroad, loaded with academic distinctions and fanatically devoted to his work. Shortly after his return, Anne moved to the city to be near him. By this time she was pushing thirty.
>
> She lived alone in a small apartment in the city. Occasionally she had lunch with some woman who had been a friend of her girlhood but who now inhabited another world. Occasionally she went to a party, at the house of one of the women or at the country club. She became engaged for a third time, this time to a man seventeen or eighteen years older than she, a widower with several children, a

> substantial lawyer, a pillar of society. He was a good man. He was still vigorous and rather handsome. He even had a sense of humor. But she did not marry him. More and more, as the years passed, she devoted herself to sporadic reading—biography (Daniel Boone or Marie Antoinette), what is called "good fiction," books on social betterment—and to work without pay for a settlement house and an orphanage. She kept her looks very well and continued, in a rather severe way, to pay attention to her dress. There were moments now when her laugh sounded a little hollow and brittle, the laughter of nerves, not of mirth or good spirits. Occasionally in a conversation she seemed to lose track and fall into self-absorption, to start up overwhelmed by embarrassment and unspoken remorse. Occasionally, too, she practiced the gesture of lifting her hands to her brow, one on each side, the fingers just touching the skin or lifting back the hair, the gesture of a delicate distraction. She was pushing thirty-five. But she could still be good company.[15]

That summary, comprising only two pages of a 602-page novel, could make an entire film by itself if treated in detail. Some of what happens to Anne Stanton could be suggested by a transitional montage, but no cinematic shorthand is capable of really filling in or summarizing a seventeen-year period the way the novelist can. Film is capable of making clear transitions from one time period to another and suggesting the passage of time, but it is not so effective at filling in the events that take place between the two periods.

Literary Past Tense Versus Cinematic Present Tense

Regardless of the point of view, most novels are written in the past tense, giving the reader a definite sense that the events happened in the past and are now being remembered and recounted. For the novelist there is a distinct advantage to using the past tense. It gives a clear impression that the novelist has had time to think about the events, measure their importance, reflect on their meaning, and understand their relationship to one another.

In contrast, even though a film may be set in the past or take us into the past by way of flashback, a film unfolds before our eyes, creating a strong sense of present time, of a here-and-now experience. The events in a film are not things that once happened and are now being remembered and recalled—they are happening right now as we watch. Various techniques have been employed to overcome this limitation. Special filters have been used to create a sense of a past time, as with the Rembrandt effect in *The Taming of the Shrew*, the hazy and rather faded memory images from *Summer of '42*, or the sepia-tone snapshot stills in *Butch Cassidy and the Sundance Kid* and *Bonnie and Clyde*. In *To Kill a Mockingbird*, voice-over narration is used to capture the past tense, the sense of experience remembered: A narrator's voice, obviously that of an adult, recalls childhood experiences (Figure 13.6).

Another important distinction is the amount of time a reader spends in experiencing a novel versus the amount of time a viewer spends in watching a

Figure 13.6 Cinematic Past Tense In *Little Big Man,* Dustin Hoffman was made up to look 121 years old to portray Jack Crabb, the sole survivor of Custer's Last Stand. As the film begins, the old man is being interviewed by a historian. As Crabb recounts his adventures, the film flashes back to scenes from his youth like this one, in which Faye Dunaway is bathing the young Crabb.

film. If the novel is long, readers may linger in its world for days or even weeks. They can control the pace and stretch the experience out as much as they like; they can even reread passages that interest them. And readers can take time out from the reading process, stopping or freezing the novel's flow to reflect on the writer's ideas at a certain point. In film, however, the pace is predetermined. The visual flow, the sparkling stream of images moves on. Beautiful images, significant truths, strong lines of dialogue cannot be replayed. Thus, the very quickness with which a film sweeps by—its quality of cinematic restlessness—distinguishes it from the novel. (Of course, segments of a film can be replayed on a VCR, laser disc, or DVD player, but breaking the visual flow significantly alters the viewing experience.)

Other Factors Influencing Adaptations of Novels

Commercial considerations also play an important role in determining whether a novel is made into a film. A unique commercial relationship exists between film and novel. A best-selling novel may virtually assure a profit for the producer making a film version, whether the novel has real cinematic potential or not, because of the public's familiarity with the novel. In turn, a screen version that is a box-office success will increase sales of the book. A first-class film adaptation of an unknown novel may even make such a novel a bestseller.

The popularity of a novel may influence the filmmaker in the adaptation. If filmmakers know that a large percentage of their audience will be familiar with the book, they can make creative decisions based on this assumption. Ideally, film adaptations of such novels should be fairly true to the novel. Creative tampering with the basic plot should be kept to a minimum, and the most important characters should be left unchanged and carefully cast. Most importantly perhaps, the director should attempt to capture the overall emotional spirit or tone of the literary work. If creative and selective choices reflect a true understanding and appreciation of the novel, the filmmaker can remind viewers who have read the book of the rich emotional and philosophical material beneath the surface and make them feel its presence. Occasionally an outstanding film, such as *The World According to Garp*, may even be able to communicate or at least suggest to those who haven't read the novel the meaning that lies beneath the surface.

Some filmmakers seem to assume that very few filmgoers will know the novel. These filmmakers disregard the basic spirit of the novel in adapting it to film, thus destroying the film completely for those familiar with the book. In such cases, the film must be judged as a completely distinct work of art. This type of film, a very loose adaptation, actually may be better suited to the medium than is the close adaptation. Ironically, a loose adaptation may seem a better film to those who are not familiar with the novel than to those who have read and loved it. Thus, a viewer who read the book before seeing the film may have a distinct advantage when the film depends on the viewer's knowledge of the book. But when the filmmaker so deviates from the essence of the novel as to create an entirely different work, reading the novel before seeing the film is a real disadvantage for the viewer. Already familiar with the novel, the filmgoer will not be able to judge the film as a film without preconceived notions.

It is sometimes advantageous, then, to see the film before reading the book. The film may aid our visual imagination, and we may later read the novel with relatively clear-cut ideas of how the characters look and sound. And certainly if the film is less successful in its own language than its novel source, then such a choice may be wise. For instance, one should probably experience Clint Eastwood's movie version of *Midnight in the Garden of Good and Evil* before reading the immensely popular nonfiction novel upon which it is based. On the other hand, seeing a film first may restrict much of our imaginative participation in reading the book; our brains lock in the screen's particular images of the book's characters forever.

Adaptations of Plays

The similarity between the film adaptation of a play and the play itself is likely to be greater than the similarity between the film adaptation of a novel and the novel itself. The problems of length and point of view are minimized. The actual running time for a play (not including time between acts or scenes) is seldom longer than three hours. Although some cutting for the film version generally occurs and some selectivity and change may be apparent to viewers who saw the play on the stage, these changes are usually not drastic.

Differences in point of view result from the fact that theatergoers are bound to a single point of view because they must stay in their seats and watch the stage. In contrast, the film version, like a novel, can spirit viewers back and forth from one of the four cinematic viewpoints (see pages 112–119) to another so that they see the action from a variety of physical positions. Through the use of close-ups, the filmmaker can give us a sense of physical and emotional closeness and of being involved in the action. Elia Kazan describes the power of the close-up during his transition from stage to film directing:

> [T]he camera is not only a recording device but a penetrating instrument. It looks *into* a face, not *at* a face. Can this kind of effect be achieved on stage? Not nearly! A camera can even be a microscope. Linger, enlarge, analyze, study. It is a very subtle instrument, can make any face heavier, leaner, drawn, flushed, pale, jolly, depraved, saintly. . . . The close-up underlines the emotional content. There is no technique on stage to match it except an exaggerated hot light or bringing an actor downstage and turning him or her straight out to the audience.
>
> . . . But above all it keeps the story's progress clear. We see in close-up that a person is undecided: the "tight shot" shows the indecision on the person's face, we can read it as clearly as if it were spelled out in words—but with all the values of ambivalence. Then we see the decision being made and the new course of action taken. Except for that close-up, the change of intent or direction would be inexplicable. Because of it, the progression of the story, the "inner line," is kept clear.[16]

This kind of closeness can sometimes be achieved in the small or intimate theater, but the point of view and the physical distance between theatergoer and actors remain essentially the same throughout the play.

In both media the director is able to comment on or interpret the action for the audience, but the film director probably has more options and techniques available for expressing subjective and interpretive views. Stage directors must rely primarily on lighting for these effects; screen directors have at their command additional techniques such as fast motion, slow motion, distorting lenses, changes from sharp to soft focus, and music. Some carry-over exists between the two media, however, for some stage productions simulate certain cinematic effects. For example, a flashing strobe light on actors in motion gives the effect of the fast, jerky motion of the early silent comedies and is used by stage directors to create this effect.

Structural Divisions

Unlike films, plays have clear-cut structural divisions—acts or scenes—that influence the positioning of peaks of dramatic power and intensity. The end of an act may build to a roaring emotional peak, setting up a strong dramatic echo to carry over into the next act. Film has **sequences,** which roughly correspond to acts in plays, but one continuous sequence flows smoothly into the next. Sometimes there are similarities even here, however, for the **freeze frame** gives a sequence a sense of ending much as the conclusion of an act might do. The cinematic device also approximates the effect of the **tableau,** a technique in which actors onstage held dramatic postures for a few seconds before the curtain fell in order to etch the scene deeply in the audience's memory.

Such structural divisions may in some cases work well in both media, but sometimes the end of a stage act builds up to a pitch that is too high for a cinema sequence, where its power would seem unnatural or out of place. Perceptive critics spot such problems. Renata Adler described them in her review of *The Lion in Winter:* "The film is far too faithful to the play. It divides neatly into acts, has a long sag in the middle, is weakest in its climaxes."[17] Neil Simon, who adapts his own plays for the screen, describes the difference this way:

> The curtain doesn't come down; and there are no particular breaks—but it does have a rhythm of its own. You set up the problem, which is the first act; the second act is the complication of the problem; and the third act is the working out of the problem. So it has to have a certain harmony to it, like a piece of music; but I don't have to look for a curtain line in a screenplay as I would with a play.[18]

Sense of Space

The change most certain to occur in a film adaptation of a play is the breaking out of the tight confining physical bonds and limitations imposed by the stage setting. Some kind of movement in space is almost essential to film, and to keep the image moving, the filmmaker usually expands the concepts of visual space involved (Figure 13.7). He or she may find some excuse to get the action moved outdoors for a while at least or may decide to introduce as much camera movement and as many editorial cuts between different viewpoints as possible to keep the image alive.

In *The Sound of Music* screenwriter Ernest Lehman found himself with a special problem. The "Do, Re, Mi" song had been performed on the stage in its entirety in the living-room set and ran a total of 11½ minutes. Knowing that a sequence of this length confined in a room would create a claustrophobic effect,

Figure 13.7 Film as a Restless Medium Goldie Hawn takes the blind Edward Albert (shown here with Michael Warren) on a brief shopping trip to get away from the apartment. In the stage version of *Butterflies Are Free,* the apartment provided the only setting.

Lehman wrote it as a montage sequence, cutting to various locations with the children in different costumes as the song progressed. The impression thus created was that the sequence covered a period of weeks. This solution also made it more convincing that Maria had established a better relationship with the children. Some of the children had obviously grown to like her during the montage. An additional bonus was that director Robert Wise was able to use some of the beautiful scenery around Salzburg.

In the film version of *Who's Afraid of Virginia Woolf?* Mike Nichols moved the camera about constantly, dollying it down hallways and around corners for cinematic effect. He also extended space by adding the scene in the roadhouse, which required a wild car ride to get there and back (in the play, this scene was confined to the living-room set). The film of *Long Day's Journey Into Night* did not go to such extremes, but it employed camera movement and editing to keep the image alive in what was a very confining set—down to the final set-up. Sidney Lumet observes that, in the playwright's work,

> [t]he characters are on a downward spiral of epic, tragic proportions. To me, *Long Day's Journey* defies definition. One of the nicest things that ever happened to me happened on that picture: the last shot. The last shot of the movie is of Katharine Hepburn, Ralph Richardson, Jason Robards, and Dean Stockwell sitting around a table. Each is lost in his or her own addictive fantasy, the men from booze, Mary Tyrone from morphine. A distant lighthouse sweeps its beam across the room

Figure 13.8 Characters on a Powder Keg The tightly confined set of *Who's Afraid of Virginia Woolf?* makes the psychological conflicts especially explosive.

> every forty-five seconds. The camera pulls back slowly, and the walls of the room gradually disappear. Soon the characters are sitting in a black limbo, getting tinier and tinier as the light sweeps across them. Fade out. After he saw the movie, Jason told me that he had read a letter of Eugene O'Neill's in which he describes his image of his family "sitting in blackness, around the table-top of the world." I hadn't read that letter. My heart leapt with happiness. That's what happens when you let the material tell you what it's about. But the material had better be great.[19]

Such changes may alter a play's total effect significantly. Narrowly confined, restricted movement in a play may serve a powerful dramatic end. By keeping the physical action and movement static, by narrowing the physical boundaries in which the characters operate and bottling up the dramatic scene, the director is often able to intensify the conflict. Dramatic tension created by psychological conflicts and developed through verbal means often seems more potentially explosive when its physical setting is narrow and confined (Figure 13.8). In the stage version of *Virginia Woolf* the guests, Nick and Honey, are virtual prisoners in the home of George and Martha. The narrow confines of the set stress their trapped feeling. Although the trip to the roadhouse in the film version adds a cinematic quality, it also relaxes the tension of confinement to some degree.

Film is simply better and more naturally suited to action and movement, the kind provided by physical conflicts on an epic scale. The restless need for motion built into the film medium makes it difficult to cope with static, confined dramatic tension. Film builds its tension best through rhythmic physical action and especially by physical movement toward resolution. A typical example of cinematic tension and its emphasis on movement occurs in *Shane*. The tension is established through violent conflict in a prolonged fistfight between Shane (Alan Ladd) and Joe Starret (Van Heflin) to see who will ride into town for the big showdown. The movement and rhythm of Shane's ride to town further build tension cinematically.

Film is also better equipped to portray physical conflict than the stage. Camera angles, sound effects, and the ability to draw the viewer into close emotional involvement make a fistfight on film much more real than it could ever appear onstage.

Film Language Versus Stage Language

> *In the theatre, words are eighty to eighty-five percent of the importance of what is happening to you for your comprehension. In film, words are about twenty percent. It's a different figure, but it's almost an opposite ratio. For the words are only a little bit of embroidery, a little bit of lacework.*[20]
>
> —Nicholas Ray, Director

Film dialogue differs from stage dialogue. Generally, film dialogue is simpler than that used on the stage. Because the visual image carries so much more weight in film than on the stage, much that might require dialogue on the stage is shown pictorially in film. Filmmakers generally prefer to advance the action by showing what happens rather than by having someone—a character or narrator—tell what happens. Because of the additional burden carried by the visual elements, film dialogue may be simpler, more casual, and less poetic. Language that is too refined, too elaborate, and too poetic is generally out of place and unnatural in film. Poetic dialogue is much better suited to the stage. If film is to speak poetically, it must do so not with words but with its primary element—the image.

To some degree, differences in dialogue may be related to other differences in the media. For example, the more physical space is expanded, the more dominant action and movement become, and the less natural poetic dialogue becomes. Consider what Renata Adler said of Zeffirelli's *Romeo and Juliet:* "The prose suffers a bit, sounding more like *West Side Story* than perhaps it ought to. In the classic speeches, one begins to worry about diction and wish the modern world would recede and let Shakespeare play through."[21] Here Adler fails to

Figure 13.9 Cinematic Shakespeare Olivia Hussey as Juliet and Leonard Whiting as Romeo in a scene from Franco Zeffirelli's version of *Romeo and Juliet* (left). Kenneth Branagh (shown with Derek Jacoby and Julie Christie) in his uncut *Hamlet* (1996).

take into account the basic difference between film language and stage language. Stage language—ornate, complex, refined, and poetic—carries the major burden of communication in a Shakespeare play. But in Zeffirelli's *Romeo and Juliet* (and *The Taming of the Shrew*), we see a new Shakespeare, a more cinematic Shakespeare than had ever been produced before, created by a director who understands his medium well enough to recognize its limitations and utilize its strengths without holding the usual worshipful attitude toward the language of another medium. Zeffirelli's *Romeo and Juliet* is a visual, cinematic experience rather than a verbal and dramatic one; the director captures the spirit and essence of Shakespeare's play without using the entire text. The result is what Zeffirelli intended: good cinema, not pure Shakespeare (Figure 13.9). Kenneth Branagh accomplishes similar feats in his *Henry V* (1989) and *Much Ado About Nothing* (1993); in his unabridged *Hamlet* (1996) Branagh appears intent upon settling for no less than both the fully cinematic and the literary.

Stage Conventions Versus Cinema Conventions

Certain conventions that are perfectly acceptable on the stage cannot always be reproduced cinematically. Among these is the Shakespearean soliloquy. In Sir Laurence Olivier's adaptation of *Hamlet*, for example, the "Frailty, thy name is woman" soliloquy is filmed in the following manner: Through some parts of the speech, Hamlet's face is pictured in tight close-up without lip movement while Olivier's voice speaks the lines on the soundtrack as an interior monologue. At times, Hamlet's lips move, perhaps to show the intensity of his thought. Whatever the intention, the Shakespearean soliloquy, with its ornate, poetic language and structure, does not translate effectively as a cinematic interior monologue, and it seems equally artificial if done as it would be on the stage (Figure 13.10). Theatergoers accept, even expect, such artificiality. Generally, however, viewers of movies have been programmed to think of film as a more realistic medium.

Another stage convention that cannot always be translated in cinematic or visual terms is retrospective narrative, the recounting of past events in stage dialogue. Under some conditions, such material is ideally suited for the cinematic flashback, but not in all cases. In Universal's 1968 version of *Oedipus the King*, for example, the official story of the murder of King Laius—that he was killed by a band of robbers—is recounted and accompanied by a flashback showing the murder as described. The problem is that we know that Oedipus himself

Figure 13.10 Stage Convention Into Film Sir Laurence Olivier tried several variations on the Shakespearean convention in the "Frailty, thy name is woman" soliloquy in his 1948 *Hamlet* but failed to create a natural cinematic equivalent.

killed Laius and his escorts single-handedly. Our difficulty with the flashback is that it pictures an event that did not really happen. When we see the scene in flashback, therefore, we are confused. We see a false version of the event take place before our eyes, but it has a semblance of truth that the *telling* of an event does not necessarily have. For this reason, the cinematic flashback does not work well with past events that are not recounted accurately or truthfully in dialogue. The fact that a later flashback may show the event as it actually happened does little to overcome the fact that the untrue flashback is not natural to the cinema.

There is also the problem of whether to leave space for laughter in the screen version of a comedy. On the stage, the actors can simply wait for laughter to subside before resuming. But Neil Simon says that laughter is too unpredictable to leave space for it in the screenplay:

> Well, you can't really. First of all, you don't know when it's going to come. If you have ten people in the movie theater that day—as opposed to a thousand—and if you leave the space, that gap is going to seem like an hour because you won't get that kind of laughter. What I try to do is cover it with some sort of business. If you think something is a really big funny moment, it's always safe to cover it with something visual and not come in with another line right on top of it.[22]

Surrealistic and expressionistic stage sets also cause difficulties in translation to film. To some degree, they can be represented or suggested through the use of special camera techniques, such as unusual camera angles and distorting lenses. But for the most part we expect the physical setting and background in film to be realistic. For example, today we would probably reject as noncinematic the kind of distorted, expressionistic set used in *The Cabinet of Dr. Caligari*, made in 1919. If *Caligari* were remade, it would probably achieve its strange effects solely through the use of special filters and distorting lenses (Figure 13.11). Again, whereas the stage audience expects the stage set or some part of it to suggest or represent reality without being real, the modern film audience is conditioned to expect real settings and will accept no substitute. This observation is equally true of other aspects of stagecraft as they are translated into film. For example, when Peter Shaffer's *Equus*, a play about a disturbed stable boy who mutilates the eyes of horses, was produced on the stage, it utilized actors dressed in stylized wire armatures to represent its horses. But in Sidney Lumet's film version, real horses were thought necessary, and the effect of the violence shifted radically from mainly symbolic to horrifically realistic (Figure 13.12).

Other Changes

Other types of change can be expected in an adaptation of a play. Even if the original stage actors of a successful play are available, the screen version may not feature them, either because some of the stage actors will not be convincing

Figure 13.11 Expressionistic Distortion of the Set Robert Wiene's *The Cabinet of Dr. Caligari* (1919).

Figure 13.12 Real Horses In the film *Equus*, a stable boy (Peter Firth) is accused of blinding the horses in his care. Here, the animals are very real; in the original stage production on which the film is based, the horses were stylized and representational, formed of wire frames upon actors' bodies, and their effect on the audience was radically different.

Figure 13.13 Poetic Justice Sweet little Rhoda (Patty McCormack), shown here charming her mother (Nancy Kelly) in a scene from the film version of *The Bad Seed,* died at the end of the film but survived in the play.

in front of the camera or because a bigger name is needed as a box-office attraction. Thus, Audrey Hepburn was hired to play Eliza Doolittle in the film *My Fair Lady*, rather than the less-celebrated Julie Andrews (who, ironically, earned an Oscar within the year for her title role in *Mary Poppins*). Kathy Bates, when she was known mainly as an excellent stage actor, lost a central role in *'Night, Mother* to Sissy Spacek for the same reason and, later, a role in *Frankie and Johnny* to Michelle Pfeiffer for slightly different ones. At the time of Pfeiffer's casting much was made in the press about the cruel employment contrast between the brilliant but "stout" brunette stage actress and the miscast slender blonde movie star. Of course, Bates soon settled that score with an Oscar of her own for film acting in *Misery*.

In the past, the big-city theater audience was assumed to be more sophisticated than the nationwide movie audience, and changes to the play were made with this difference in mind. An effort was usually made to simplify the play in the film version, and harsh language was censored to some degree. Endings were even changed to conform to the expectations of the mass audience. The stage version of *The Bad Seed* (1956), for example, ends chillingly with little Rhoda, the beautiful but evil child-murderer who has killed at least three people, alive and well, still charming her naive and unsuspecting father. In the ending of the film version, Rhoda is struck by lightning; in this way the demands of the mass audience for poetic justice are satisfied. Such changes, of course, are less frequent since the Motion Picture Rating System went into effect in the late 1960s. A modern version of *The Bad Seed* would probably keep Rhoda alive for a possible sequel (Figure 13.13).

From Fact to Film: Reality to Myth

My own feeling is that this never happened. . . . But once our movie comes out, it'll become an accepted part of the legend.

—ADAM FIELDS, producer of the Jerry Lee Lewis biofilm *Great Balls of Fire,* referring to the piano-torching scene

Controversies about the factual or fictional nature of four films showcase another problem for the filmgoer, a problem similar in some ways to those presented by adaptations of novels or plays. Whether Jerry Lee Lewis really torched a piano, as portrayed in *Great Balls of Fire*, is not an earthshaking question. But when events of recent history of a magnitude sufficient to be memorable to many people are twisted and distorted or ignored by filmmakers, the issue of factual accuracy versus creative license raises some genuine concern.

The mixture of fictional materials with a factual background has always brought some confusion to filmgoers. As we noted in Chapter 11, President Woodrow Wilson was so impressed with D. W. Griffith's *The Birth of a Nation* that he called it "history writ with lightning." Although Griffith's story focused on the Civil War and its aftermath in the South during Reconstruction, he based his film on a sentimental and highly racist novel, *The Clansman*, and did not even attempt to pass it off as factual. Yet some of the devices he used to establish the setting for certain scenes gave the film an aura of authenticity. For example, a still frame sets up a tableau of the South Carolina state legislature in session with the following detailed caption:

> The negro party in control of the State House of Representatives, Columbia, South Carolina. 101 blacks against 23 whites.—An historical facsimile of the actual photographed scene.

Alan Parker's *Mississippi Burning* takes its title from the official FBI file on the case that it portrays. *Time* critic Richard Corliss described the problem raised by Parker's approach to the subject:

> *Mississippi Burning* is a fiction based on fact; it invents characters and bends the real-life plot; it colors in the silhouette of events with its own fanciful strokes and highlights. In focusing on the agents, Parker and screenwriter Chris Gerolmo italicize the gumshoe heroism of white officials while downplaying the roles of black and white visionaries who risked, and sometimes lost, their lives to help fashion a free America.
>
> At issue is the freedom of a filmmaker—or any artist—to twist the facts as they are recalled, to shape the truth as it is perceived. May a movie libel the historical past? And has *Mississippi Burning* done so? Artistic liberty vs. social responsibility: the stakes are high. The memories are indelible. The battle lines are drawn."[23]

David Halberstam, a reporter covering the civil rights conflicts in Mississippi at the time of the events portrayed in the film, responded to the film in this way:

> Parker seems to reflect the true arrogance of Hollywood when confronted with events that are factual—saying, in effect, "My talent is more important than your reality." I am not completely naive: I know that there is no pure truth; I know that Hollywood is more a city of fantasy than of reality; and I know that in the translation to the screen of what is thought of as a factual story there is a considerable amount of flexibility—if not poetic license, certainly cinematic license—and that the real test is not so much exact truth as essential truth. But in the making of the film there is a carelessness, a lack of accountability, that is simply unacceptable. I realize that the true artist, novelist, or movie director can create his own universe and invent his own events and the people to fill it. I have no problem with that. There is a Mississippi that Parker is welcome to create. But he did not invent his own incident. He chose to base his story on a true event. . . . Because of that there are real parameters Parker must deal with. It is no longer his Mississippi; it is instead the Mississippi of those three young men and all the other young men and women who were so remarkably brave that summer.
>
> The film bears almost no relation to the way things actually happened.[24]

Halberstam goes on to analyze, in some detail, how the film exaggerated, distorted, and simply made up many aspects of its story.

Although Parker did not announce that the story was true at the beginning of the film, he did end the film with a series of freeze-frame epilogues on each of the principal villains, and the actual names and the actual results of the trial certainly create the illusion that we have been watching a true story unfold (Figure 13.14).

Similar charges of excessive cinematic license have been made against John G. Avildsen, the director of *Lean on Me*, a stirring story of Black principal Joe Clark's heroic and successful effort to turn an undisciplined and drug-ridden New Jersey high school into an effective educational institution. According to the critics, the real Eastside High School went downhill during the seven years of Clark's principalship. The percentage of Eastside students that went on to college dropped from 35 to 22 percent. Students' grades did not improve as radically as suggested in the film, and the dramatic moment of the test scores being delivered to Clark on the courthouse steps was pure cinematic license.

When Robert Redford directed *Quiz Show*, he was "accused of hedging the truth to improve the story of the movie and boost box office receipts." The film's critics charged that

> both the [real] game show and "Quiz Show" seem to dodge the truth and create clear heroes and villains for popularity's sake. . . .
>
> From invented dialogue to fabricated court transactions, "Quiz Show" often takes broad dramatic license. Because the film uses the names of real people (some still living) and has been positioned by its makers as a righteous statement on ethics and morality, the "Quiz Show" deviations raise provocative questions about Hollywood's conscience—or its lack of one.

Figure 13.14 Distortions of Reality Because *Mississippi Burning* (top left) dealt with an actual event in American history, critics and reporters familiar with the events portrayed felt that director Alan Parker abused his cinematic license, primarily by overstating the role of two fictional FBI agents (Gene Hackman and Willem Dafoe). Similar charges were leveled against John G. Avildsen for exaggerating the accomplishments of Black principal Joe Clark (Morgan Freeman) in *Lean on Me* (top right), and against Robert Redford for oversimplifying the story of a sore loser (John Turturro, in glasses) during the TV scandals in *Quiz Show* (bottom)

Figure 13.15 Historical Accuracy With the exception of some too-modern exploding cannon balls, *Glory* has been praised as one of the most historically accurate Civil War films. Denzel Washington, pictured here, won an Academy Award as best supporting actor in that film. Likewise, *Saving Private Ryan,* starring Tom Hanks and Matt Damon, was considered to be meticulous in its depiction of the visual details of World War II.

> "If Robert Redford had taken this movie and had changed the names, then I would have no argument," says Don Enright, whose father, Dan, produced "Twenty-One" and is vilified in "Quiz Show."
>
> "But as this movie sits, it is now a half-truth, and a half-truth is the blackest of lies, because it's based on fact and it's impossible to fight."[25]

The real problem with films like *Mississippi Burning* (which even David Halberstam praised as a film), *Lean on Me,* and *Quiz Show* is that the viewers have no way of knowing how the factual material has been handled or distorted (Figure 13.15). The confusion can be cleared up with the simple addition of a disclaimer. If films can protect themselves by declaring that the events and characters depicted are completely fictitious, they should perhaps be required to inform viewers of how fact and fiction are blended. A disclaimer shown before both episodes of the ABC miniseries *Small Sacrifices* (starring Farrah Fawcett) provides a clear solution to the problem (the story was based on the true story of a mother convicted of shooting her three children):

> The following dramatization is based on the book *Small Sacrifices* by Ann Rule. It contains composite changes, name changes and the resequencing of events. Some dramatic license has been taken in the resequencing of events.

Another approach is the disclaimer appearing before the opening credits for *Walking Tall:*

> A motion picture suggested by certain events in the life of Buford Pusser, Sheriff of McNary County, Tennessee . . . a living legend.

Even though the parallels between *Citizen Kane* and the life of William Randolph Hearst are obvious, *Kane* keeps enough distance from the Hearst story to qualify as a fictionalized biography: The names are changed; the mistress is an opera singer, not an actress; and so on. The RKO legal department, however, was concerned enough to insert the following disclaimer at the film's beginning:

> This is not the story of any man be he living or dead. This is the story of the power and strength which impels the lives of many great men seen through the eyes of little men.

When Orson Welles learned of the statement, he was furious about its content (possibly because he had not written it) and replaced it with his own version:

> *Citizen Kane* is an examination of the personal character of a public man, a portrait according to the testimony of the intimates of his life. These, and Kane himself, are wholly fictitious.

Later the disclaimer was dropped.

Hoffa, which plays fast and loose with the disappearance of Jimmy Hoffa because nobody really knows what ultimately happened to the former Teamster boss, includes an almost illegible disclaimer at the end of the credits. The holes in the factual record were important in Jack Nicholson's performance:

> It's not a biography, it's a portrait, and there is a difference. Because no one really knows what happened to Hoffa, it gives you license to do a lot of guessing with other things too. I had a certain amount of license in my job as an actor to have an inside interpretation of the guy.[26]

It may be a bit more difficult to take liberties with the accepted facts about a personality with Mount Rushmore status, as the Merchant-Ivory team found with their release of *Jefferson in Paris.*

Oliver Stone's *JFK* has seemed to many to be the most arrogant of the fact-to-film efforts in recent years, largely because of the docudrama techniques used (newsreel footage, excerpts from the famous Zapruder film showing the assassination of the president, and familiar real names of those involved in later investigations), a clear antigovernment bias, a far-fetched conspiracy theory, and the lack of any kind of disclaimer. (Later, Stone's *Nixon* created a similar controversy.) *Executive Action*, a 1973 conspiracy film focusing on the many inconsistencies in the official explanation of the events in Dallas, used a beginning-of-the-film disclaimer that would have made *JFK* more acceptable:

> Although much of this film is fiction, much of it is also based on documented historical fact. Did the conspiracy we described actually exist? We do not know. We merely suggest that it could have existed.

Otherwise, however, *JFK* is much superior in its filmmaking to *Executive Action*, which is rated in Leonard Maltin's indispensable *Movie & Video Guide* as a "BOMB."[27]

Questions

On Adaptations of Novels

After reading the novel, but before seeing the film, consider these questions concerning the novel.

1. How well is the novel suited for adaptation to the screen? What natural cinematic possibilities does it have?
2. Judged as a whole, does the novel come closer to stressing a sensuous and emotional rendering of experience (as in the Hemingway excerpts) or an intellectual analysis of experience (as in the James excerpt)?
3. How essential is the author's verbal style to the spirit or essence of the novel? Could this verbal style be effectively translated into a pictorial style?
4. What is the novel's point of view? What will necessarily be lost by translating the story into film?
5. If the novel is written from the first-person point of view (as told by a participant in the action), how much of the spirit of the novel is expressed through the narrator's unique narrative style—that is, the particular flair or flavor built into his or her *way of telling* the story rather than the story itself? Could this verbal style be suggested through a minimum of voice-over narration on the soundtrack, so that the device would not seem unnatural? Is the feeling of a warm, intimate relationship between reader and narrator established by the novel, as though the story is being told by a very close friend? How could this feeling be captured by the film?
6. Is the novel's length suited to a close adaptation, or must the novel be drastically cut to fit the usual film format? Which choice would seem most logical for the filmmaker in adapting the novel:
   a. Should he or she try to capture a sense of the novel's wholeness by hitting the high points without trying to fill in all the gaps? What high points do you think must be dramatized?

b. Should the filmmaker limit himself or herself to a thorough dramatization of just part of the novel? What part of the novel could be thoroughly dramatized to make a complete film? What part of the story or what subplots should be left out of the film version?

7. How much of the novel's essence depends on the rendition of mental states: memories, dreams, or philosophical reflections? How effectively can the film version be expected to express or at least suggest these things?
8. How much detail does the author provide on the origins and past history of the characters? How much of this material can be conveyed cinematically?
9. What is the total time period covered by the novel? Can the time period covered be adequately compressed into a normal-length film?

After seeing the film version, reconsider your answers to the questions listed above, and also answer the following.

10. Is the film version a close or a loose adaptation of the novel? If it is a loose adaptation, is the departure from the novel due to the problems caused by changing from one medium to another or by the change in creative personnel?
11. Does the film version successfully capture the spirit or essence of the novel? If not, why does it fail?
12. What are the major differences between the novel and the film, and how can you explain the reasons for these differences?
13. Does the film version successfully suggest meanings that lie beneath the surface and remind you of their presence in the novel? In which scenes is this accomplished?
14. Did reading the novel enhance the experience of seeing the film, or did it take away from it? Why?
15. How well do the actors in the film fit your preconceived notions of the characters in the novel? Which actors exactly fit your mental image of the characters? How do the actors who don't seem properly cast vary from your mental image? Can you justify, from the director's point of view, the casting of these actors who don't seem to fit the characters in the novel?

On Adaptations of Plays

1. How does the film version differ from the play in its concept of physical space? How does this difference affect the overall spirit or tone of the film version?
2. How cinematic is the film version? How does it use special camera and editing techniques to keep the visual flow of images in motion and to avoid the static quality of a filmed stage play?
3. What events that are only described in dialogue during the play does the filmmaker show happening? How effective are these added scenes?

4. Are the play's structural divisions (into acts and scenes) still apparent in the film, or does the film successfully blend these divided parts into a unified cinematic whole?
5. What stage conventions employed in the play are not translatable into cinematic equivalents? What difficulties and changes does this bring about?
6. How does the acting style of the film differ from that of the play? What factors account for these differences?
7. What basic differences can be observed in the dialogue in the two versions? Are individual speeches generally longer in the play or in the film? In which version is the poetic quality of the language more apparent?
8. What other important changes have been made in the film version? Can you justify these in terms of change in medium, change in creative personnel, or differences in moral attitudes and sophistication of the intended audience?

From Fact to Film

1. How does the film story differ from the true story or historical event on which it is based?
2. Can these changes be justified for dramatic purposes?
3. Do the changes significantly distort the essence of the story and the characters involved? How?
4. Was any disclaimer provided to warn viewers that the film was not completely factual? Was there any reason for viewers to believe they were watching a completely factual story?

Films for Study

Novels Into Films

The Accidental Tourist (1988) (Anne Tyler)
Affliction (1998) (Russell Banks)
The Age of Innocence (1993) (Edith Wharton)
All the King's Men (1949) (Robert Penn Warren)
Being There (1979) (Jerzy Kosinski)
Billy Budd (1962) (Herman Melville)
The Bridges of Madison County (1995) (Robert James Waller)
The Color Purple (1985) (Alice Walker)
The English Patient (1996) (Michael Ondaatje)
Ethan Frome (1993) (Edith Wharton)
Field of Dreams (1989) (novel is *Shoeless Joe* by W. P. Kinsella)
The Godfather (1972) (Mario Puzo)
The Graduate (1967) (Charles Webb)
The Grapes of Wrath (1940) (John Steinbeck)
The Great Gatsby (1974) (F. Scott Fitzgerald)
The Heart Is a Lonely Hunter (1968) (Carson McCullers)
The Horse Whisperer (1998) (Nicholas Evans)
Howards End (1992) (E. M. Forster)
The Joy Luck Club (1993) (Amy Tan)
Jurassic Park (1993) (Michael Crichton)
The Last Picture Show (1971) (Larry McMurtry)
Like Water for Chocolate (1992) (Laura Esquivel)
Lord of the Flies (1963) (William Golding)
Midnight Cowboy (1969) (James Leo Herlihy)
Moby Dick (1956) (Herman Melville)
Mrs. Dalloway (1998) Virginia Woolf)
The Natural (1984) (Bernard Malamud)
The Night of the Hunter (1955) (Davis Grubb)

The Object of My Affection (1998) (Stephen McCauley)
The Old Man and the Sea (1958) (Ernest Hemingway)
One Flew Over the Cuckoo's Nest (1975) (Ken Kesey)
Ordinary People (1980) (Judith Guest)
Orlando (1993) (Virginia Woolf)
The Ox-Bow Incident (1943) (Walter Van Tilburg Clark)
Primary Colors (1998) (Anonymous [Joe Klein])
Rachel, Rachel (1968) (novel is *A Jest of God* by Margaret Laurence)
Raintree County (1957) (Ross Lockridge)
The Remains of the Day (1993) (Kazuo Ishiguro)
A Room With a View (1986) (E. M. Forster)
Simon Birch (1998) (novel is *A Prayer for Owen Meany* by John Irving)
The Sweet Hereafter (1997) (Russell Banks)
Terms of Endearment (1983) (Larry McMurtry)
They Shoot Horses, Don't They? (1969) (Horace McCoy)
To Kill a Mockingbird (1962) (Harper Lee)
The Wings of the Dove (1997) (Henry James)
The Witches of Eastwick (1987) (John Updike)
The World According to Garp (1982) (John Irving)

Plays Into Films

The Bad Seed (1956) (Maxwell Anderson)
Butterflies Are Free (1972) (Leonard Gershe)
The Children's Hour (1961) (Lillian Hellman)
Crimes of the Heart (1986) (Beth Henley)
Driving Miss Daisy (1989) (Alfred Uhry)
Equus (1977) (Peter Shaffer)
Hamlet (1948, 1969, 1990, 1996) (William Shakespeare)
I Never Sang for My Father (1970) (Robert Anderson)
Long Day's Journey Into Night (1962) (Eugene O'Neill)
Love! Valour! Compassion! (1997) (Terrence McNally)
A Man for All Seasons (1966) (Robert Bolt)
Mister Roberts (1955) (Thomas Heggen and Joshua Logan)
'Night, Mother (1986) (Marsha Norman)
A Raisin in the Sun (1961) (Lorraine Hansberry)
Romeo and Juliet (1936, 1954, 1968, 1996) (William Shakespeare)
A Soldier's Story (1984) (Charles Fuller)
Steel Magnolias (1989) (Robert Harling)
A Streetcar Named Desire (1951) (Tennessee Williams)
Suddenly, Last Summer (1959) (Tennessee Williams)
The Taming of the Shrew (1967) (William Shakespeare)
A Thousand Clowns (1965) (Herb Gardner)
Who's Afraid of Virginia Woolf? (1966) (Edward Albee)

Fact-Based Films

The Accused (1988)
Blaze (1989)
Bonnie and Clyde (1967)
Born on the Fourth of July (1989) (Ron Kovic)
A Cry in the Dark (1988)
The Elephant Man (1980)
Glory (1989)
Gods and Monsters (1998)
Hoffa (1992)
In Cold Blood (1967) (Truman Capote)
In the Name of the Father (1993)
Jefferson in Paris (1995)
JFK (1991)
Lean on Me (1989)
Midnight in the Garden of Good and Evil (1997) (John Berendt)
Mississippi Burning (1988)
Patton (1970)
Quiz Show (1994)
Raging Bull (1980)
Schindler's List (1993) (Thomas Keneally)
Sergeant York (1941)
Silkwood (1983)
Tombstone (1993)
Walking Tall (1973)

Chapter 14

Genre Films, Remakes, and Sequels

No doubt the producer tries to control the audience. But it is evident that in the end the audience controls the producer; for it is the audience that decides which films, stars, directors, themes, genres will endure. The audience is far from passive. It seizes from the movies what it needs for its own purposes of tutelage and fantasy.

—ARTHUR M. SCHLESINGER, JR., HISTORIAN

Genre Films

The term **genre film** very often refers to film stories that have been repeated again and again with only slight variations. They follow the same basic pattern or formula and include the same basic ingredients. Setting, characters, plot (conflict and resolution), images, cinematic techniques, and conventions are practically interchangeable from one film to another in the same genre—much as the parts for Henry Ford's Model T were interchangeable from one car to another.

This definition of *genre* focuses exclusively upon the formula film, but the term is also used broadly to refer to films dealing with a common subject matter or style. For example, Rex Reed said in his review of *Patton* and *M*A*S*H* that those films "raise the artistic level of the war-movie genre."[1] As the critic Stephen Schiff wrote in *Film Comment* in 1982,

> There was a time when the development of genre was relatively predictable. When moviegoing was an American habit, genre films begat genre films. If a movie did well at the box office, the studios churned out more of the same. In fact, the more commercial a national cinema became, the more diverse and profound its genres, which is why the American film industry has produced such an embarrassment of riches. . . . Genre used to be integral to the studio system. . . . For a fine director like Howard Hawks . . . , directing a genre film was probably like being a blues musician who could wring sublimity out of three chords and a standard 4/4 groove. The director of a Western had certain costumes and settings, character types, and even themes to play with, for those were what the audience expected to see. It was a tiny arena, and a real artist could load a great deal into it.[2]

Schiff continued, "People went to a genre movie because of its movieness, because they knew it would make them feel happy or sad or just plain entertained in a way that only a certain kind of movie could."[3] And, in noting how moviemaking was changing radically in the past few years, he bemoaned the loss of "simple pleasures." Schiff concluded that "directors of the Auteur Age no longer worked *within* the old genres, they worked *on* them."[4] By 1994, in providing the "Preface" for a collection of reviews of genre films, Schiff observed a kind of resurgence of some genres, with the westerns *Dances With Wolves* (1990) and *Unforgiven* (1992) having won best picture Oscars, for example. And he seemed mildly puzzled by the "recombinant genres" phenomenon (the "most boggling of all, perhaps [being] . . . the Teenage Mutant Ninja Turtle films: chopsocky-cartoon-animal-monster-boys'-book-sci-fi-beauty-and-the-beast-buddy fantasies").[5] More recently, writers have remarked upon the difficulty of defining *genre*—in part because of this overlap present in many less exotic films.

In addition, we are now led to conclude that there is

> . . . less of a difference between genre films and other forms of cinema at least in terms of the basic processes of communication and reading. All communicative

forms, including all films, are underpinned by systems—arguably modelled on language—against which they acquire their significance and meaning.[6]

It is not difficult to understand how genre films came into being or why they have enjoyed such success. The repetition of basic formulas resulted from the unique interaction between the studio system and the mass popular audience. Because of the expense of film production, the studios wanted to produce films that would draw a large audience, so that they could realize a substantial profit. The reaction of the mass audience flocking to westerns, gangster movies, *film noir*, war stories, horror pictures, science fiction or fantasy films, screwball romantic comedies, and musicals, for instance, let the studios know what people wanted (and expected), and the studios responded to the great success of these films by repeating the formulas.

As the success of the genre films inspired frequent repetition of the basic formulas, their popularity presented the studios and the directors assigned to direct them with an interesting challenge. So that the public would not become bored, they were forced to introduce variations and refinements while keeping enough of the formula intact to ensure success (much as the original Beetle by Volkswagen was refined every year or two without significantly altering the essential values or familiar look of the beloved "basic Bug").

Values

The audience for which these assembly-line films were produced was in every sense of the word a "mass" audience, including all layers of society and, in the mid-to-late 1940s, numbering nearly 90 million viewers per week. Thus, genre films constituted a fairly unsophisticated art form designed for a large number of unsophisticated people. The popularity of these films was at least partly due to their ability to reinforce basic American beliefs, values, and myths.

The Motion Picture Production Code, which was enforced from the early 1930s until around 1960, encouraged all American films to reflect and reinforce middle-class American institutions, values, and morality. The sincerity of the genre films, however, seems to indicate that, for the most part, the studio heads and directors probably shared those values. In any case, the audience obviously took great pleasure in seeing their values threatened and then triumphant, for the triumph reinforced people's belief in the strength and validity of their values and made them feel secure in Truth, Justice, and the American Way. Genre films fulfilled their expectations with easy, complete, and totally satisfying resolutions.

The Strengths of Genre Films

For the director, there were certain advantages to working within a given genre. Because the characters, the plot, and the conventions were already established, they provided the director with a kind of cinematic shorthand that greatly simplified the task of storytelling. Because formula stories were easy for the audience to understand, they were easy for the director to put on film. The best directors, however, did not simply copy the conventions and string together a predictable pattern of stock situations and images. Accepting the limitations and formal requirements of the genre as a challenge, directors such as John Ford provided creative variations, refinements, and complexities that imprinted each film they directed with a rich and distinctive personal style.

The genre film simplifies film watching as well as filmmaking. We don't have to study the characters in a western. Because of the conventions of appearance, dress, manners, and typecasting, we recognize the hero, sidekick, villain, and female lead, etc., on sight and know they will not violate our expectations of their conventional roles. Our familiarity with the genre makes watching not only easier but in some ways more enjoyable. Because we know and are familiar with all the conventions, we gain pleasure from recognizing each character, each image, each stock situation. The fact that the formula and conventions are established and repeated intensifies another kind of pleasure. Settled into a familiar, comfortable formula, with our basic expectations satisfied, we become more keenly aware of and responsive to the creative variations, refinements, and complexities that make the film seem fresh and original, and by exceeding our expectations each innovation becomes an exciting surprise.

The Formulas

Although each genre has its own formula, it is perhaps easier to recognize a genre film than it is to delineate clearly all the elements of its formula. The basic formula may seem simple when viewed from the distance of memory, but observation reveals that the variations are almost infinite. The six basic elements of a genre formula are setting, characters, conflict, resolution, values reaffirmed, and conventions. The following discussion attempts to crystallize the formula elements of westerns and gangster movies—and to suggest how these genres and the others mentioned above (*film noir*, war stories, horror pictures, sci-fi or fantasy films, screwball romantic comedies, and musicals) have changed over the past few decades.

The Western Formula The action takes place in the American West or Southwest, west of the Mississippi River, usually at the edge of the frontier, where civilization encroaches on the free, savage, untamed land beyond. The time span is usually between 1865 and 1900.

The western hero is a rugged individualist, a natural man of the frontier, often a mysterious loner. Somewhat aloof and very much his own man, he acts in accordance with his personal code, not in response to community pressures or for personal gain: "A man's got to do what a man's got to do." His personal code emphasizes human dignity, courage, justice, fair play, equality (the rights

Figure 14.1 The Western Hero One of the most durable of American heroic types is the western or cowboy hero. He represented essentially the same code and values in hundreds of films over a span of four decades. Bob Steele, a typical western hero of the 1940s, is pictured here (left). Contrast this heroic type with that played by Kevin Costner (shown here with Graham Greene) in *Dances With Wolves* (right).

of the underdog), and respect for women. Intelligent and resourceful, he is also kind, honest, firm, and consistent in his dealings with others, never devious, cruel, or petty. Even-tempered and peaceable by nature, he does not seek violent solutions but responds with violent action when the situation demands it. Extraordinarily quick *and* accurate with pistol or rifle, he is also adept at horsemanship and barroom brawling and is quietly confident of his own abilities. He can act as a capable leader or alone, as the situation requires. As a loner, he stands apart from the community but believes in and fights to preserve its values. His lack of community ties (he usually has no job, no ranch or possessions, no wife or family) gives him the freedom and flexibility for full-time heroics. As a lawman or cavalry officer, however, his independence diminishes. Peace makes him restless. With order restored, he moves on to discover another troubled community (Figure 14.1).

Four basic types of heroine seem to prevail (the first two are ranchers' daughters). First, if the ranch is big and the father wealthy, she may be a Southern lady of the *Gone With the Wind* school. Second, if the ranch is smaller and the father struggling, she may be the tomboy type, beautiful but tough and independent. The third type is the schoolmarm, who is a product of Eastern refinement, intelligent but helpless. Finally, there is the dance-hall girl, who is worldly wise, with a tough exterior but a heart of gold.

Two categories of villain seem to prevail. The first includes savages and outlaws (the uncivilized elements of the untamed frontier) who bully, threaten,

Figure 14.2 The Western Villain One typical western villain operates under the guise of respectability. His dress is impeccable (maybe *too* impeccable). But if there's any doubt, check the mustache and the steely-eyed glare. Sometimes in modern westerns, though, as with Gene Hackman's sheriff in *Unforgiven,* great ambiguity resides in such characters.

and generally terrorize the respectable elements of the frontier community, trying to take what they want by force: rustling cattle, robbing banks or stages, or attacking stagecoaches, wagon trains, forts, or ranches. Stereotypically, Native Americans often fall in this first category. Real motives for their hostility are seldom developed. They are viewed not as individuals but en masse as innately savage and cruel. Sometimes they are led by crazed chieftains seeking vengeance for past crimes against their tribe, or they are manipulated by renegade Whites to facilitate their own evil purposes.

Villains in the second category work under the guise of respectability: crooked bankers, saloon owners, and sheriffs, or wealthy ranchers, all motivated by greed for wealth or lust for power. Slick, devious, and underhanded in their methods, they may hire or manipulate savages and outlaws to bring about their goals (Figure 14.2).

In some cases the villain, in addition to his present crimes, has harmed the hero in the past. As a result, the desire for vengeance is intense and personal.

A hero who does not ride alone is likely to be accompanied by a sidekick, an initiate hero, or both. The *sidekick* is usually a comic character who is a foil for the serious, rugged hero. The sidekick is usually older than the hero. The *initiate hero* is younger. Clean cut, handsome, and a bit naive, the initiate hero is a kind of son figure, anxious for maturity but still a bit green. Loyal and courageous, he tries to follow the hero's example and live up to his code.

Society (town, civilized ranches, wagon trains, stagecoaches, or forts) is threatened from within by corruption and greed or faces external threats from uncivilized forces (outlaws or savages).

Led by the hero, the decent citizens root out the corrupt villains within the community or succeed in fighting off the outlaws or savages attacking the society from without. Villains not killed in the gunfights are frightened off or imprisoned. With the society in decent, just, and capable hands, the hero is free to move on.

Justice prevails, civilization conquers savagery, and good triumphs over evil. Law and order are restored or established, and progress toward a better life on the frontier may resume.

The conventions of the western are so familiar that they need little description. There is a clear and simple definition of character types by conventions of costume and grooming. The hero wears a white or light-colored hat, the villain a black hat. Heroes are clean-cut and clean-shaven. Mustaches are reserved for villains. Sidekicks and villains may have beards, but sidekicks' beards are gray and rustic, and villains' beards are black and impeccably groomed. To detail further the differences in dress and appearance is unnecessary. We recognize the basic roles of the actors when we first see them.

The hero's guns are unique, custom-made: pearl handles, filed sights, hair triggers. All other weapons are standard factory-produced guns.

In addition to conventions of dress, appearance, and weapons, there are conventions of action. Most westerns have one or more of the following: a climactic shootout between the hero and villain in the town's only street (Figure 14.3) or among the rocks of a canyon, a prolonged chase on horseback (usually accompanied by shooting), a knock-down drag-out barroom brawl (with a scared bartender periodically ducking behind the bar), and a cavalry-to-the-rescue scene.

Although a love interest may develop between hero and heroine, and the attraction may be apparent, it never reaches fruition and the hero moves on at the end. To create tension and direct attention to the love interest, the heroine often misunderstands the hero's motives or his actions until the final climax, when he regains her trust and respect before good-byes are said.

At least one convention is structural. Many westerns begin with the hero riding into view from the left side of the screen and end with him riding off in the opposite direction, usually into a fading sunset.

The Gangster Film Formula The gangster film usually takes place in the concrete jungle, among the endless streets and crowded buildings of a decaying older part of the modern city. Much of the action occurs at night, and rain is often used to add atmosphere. In the rural-bandit gangster film, the action takes place in a rural setting with small depressed towns, roadhouses, and filling stations.

Figure 14.3 Western Convention—The Main Street Shootout Scenes like this were part of almost every formula western, and the convention survived in adult westerns like *Lawman* (1971).

The gangster hero is a brutal, aggressive, lone-wolf type. He is cocky and ambitious, the self-made man who fought his way up from nothing and graduated from the school of hard knocks (Figure 14.4).

The gangster's henchmen gain courage from their association with his power. They are generally ignorant and nonverbal. Usually there are at least three: a confession specialist ("I can make him talk, boss"), a henchman as blindly loyal as the family dog, and a henchman who is not only disloyal but too ambitious for his own good.

Women are sexual ornaments, symbols of the hero's status. They are cheap, mindless, and greedy, totally fascinated by the hero's cruelty and power. Sometimes a decent, intelligent woman associates with the hero early in the film but soon discovers his true nature and abandons him. The gangster's mother and sister are civilized and social women with traditional values; the mother is respected, the sister protected.

The gun moll is more intelligent and independent than the sexual ornaments. Treated as a companion instead of a plaything, she's tough and cynical enough to function as the hero's partner in crime.

Figure 14.4 The Gangster Hero Both Paul Muni (right), in 1932, and Al Pacino (left), in 1983, played the protagonist of *Scarface,* each fitting practically every definition of the gangster hero formula. But during the sixty years between the original and remake, the story's language changed radically.

On the most abstract level, the basic conflict is the anarchy of the gangsters versus the social order. Because the police represent the social order, the conflict also involves cops versus robbers. There is usually a conflict of robbers versus robbers, with the struggle involving leadership of the gang or a territorial-rights gang war against a rival mob. An internal conflict within the hero is also probable, with his latent good or social instincts struggling for expression against his essentially cruel and selfish nature.

The hero achieves success temporarily but eventually meets his deserved end. Although he may be given a chance for reform and redemption, the criminal side of his nature is too strong to be denied. He often dies in the gutter, in a cowardly, weak manner. His dignity and strength are gone—everything we admired about him is destroyed. The other gang members are either killed or jailed, and the social order is restored.

Justice prevails, good conquers evil, or evil destroys itself. Crime does not pay, and the weeds of crime bear bitter fruit. Civilized values of human decency, honesty, and respect for law and order are reaffirmed.

Standard gangster dress is required. The hero is overdressed, usually in double-breasted, pin-striped suits, camel-hair coats, luxurious bathrobes, smoking jackets, and so on. When engaged "in business," all gangsters wear overcoats and broad-brimmed hats, with hat brims turned down in front and coat collars turned up. Women wear gaudy jewelry, cheap-looking makeup, low-cut dresses, and expensive coats.

Machine guns, pistols, and bombs are standard weapons. Machine guns are often carried in violin cases. At least one chase scene, with passengers in each

Figure 14.5 Gangster Film Convention—Erasing the Competition A typical gangland killing, with lots of blazing guns (including a submachine gun), takes place in Sergio Leone's *Once Upon a Time in America.*

car exchanging gunfire, is required (Figure 14.5). Whiskey and cigars are necessary props for every interior scene. Speakeasies and posh nightclubs are common sites for conducting business.

Montage sequences are frequently used for violent action. They feature fast editing, compression of time, and explosive sound effects (machine-gun fire or bombings).

Stretching and Breaking the Formulas

Genre films were viable over a fairly long period of time and offered directors enough flexibility to create many interesting innovations on the standard formulas. But changes in social values, the advent of television, and a changing movie audience made some of the conventions much too limiting. Thus, movies like *Shane* and *High Noon* introduced complex new elements, and the western began to break away from the traditional formula. And the gangster film evolved from *Little Caesar* to *Bonnie and Clyde* to *Reservoir Dogs* in its transformation.

Two elements are probably more important than any of the others in keeping the formula viable: the personal code of the hero and the values reaffirmed at the end of the film. When the hero's code is significantly altered and the basic social values are no longer reaffirmed, the formula vanishes. The western and the gangster film formulas depend on good triumphing over evil, on law and order conquering chaos, on civilization overcoming savagery, and on justice prevailing. When these concepts are brought into question, when shades of gray replace clear distinctions between black and white, when the complexities of reality replace the simplicity of myth, the formula is destroyed. In like manner, if the western hero becomes an antihero and is cruel, petty, and overly vengeful, the old formula is gone because our expectations for the hero are not satisfied (Figure 14.6).

However, if these changes reflect changes within the society and its value system, and new heroic codes are established, a new formula may rise from the ashes of the old, and this new formula will be repeated as long as the new values and heroic codes prevail. But it will be a very different kind of formula, a different genre.

Other Popular Genres

Film Noir Although the *film noir* genre flourished in the American 1940s and 1950s and then seemed to die out, the form has continued in the hearty *noir* resonances of many movies in more recent decades. Foster Hirsch, one of the genre's earliest and most ardent admirers, has attempted a comprehensive definition of the type:

> *Film noir* is a descriptive term for the American crime film. . . . From stylized versions of the city at night to documentary-like reports of the city at mid-day, from the investigations of the wry, cynical sleuth to the "innocent" man momentarily and fatally tempted by luxury, to the desperate flailing of the confirmed and inveterate criminal, the genre covers a heterogeneous terrain. In range of theme and in visual style, it is both varied and complex, and in level of achievement it is consistently high. *Film noir* is one of the most challenging cycles in the history of American films.[7]

Eddie Muller, another observer, defines it more poetically: "*Film noirs* were distress flares launched onto America's movie screens by artists working the night shift at the Dream Factory."[8]

Lovers of *film noir* have embraced the resurgence of its popularity in the neo-*noir* movies of the '60s, '70s, '80s, and '90s (see "Films for Study" at the end of the chapter), but they appear unable to agree about their relative merits. For example, some fans of Lawrence Kasdan's impressive debut film, *Body Heat* (1981), claimed that it surpassed its models—such classics of the genre as Billy Wilder's *Double Indemnity* (1944) and Jacques Tourneur's *Out of the Past* (1947). Since the mid-1970s, critics have maintained that Roman Polanski and Robert Towne's *Chinatown* opened new territory for the genre.[9] But others claimed that these newer films were merely perverse, pale copies. In 1997 this same kind of disagreement arose about the value of Curtis Hanson's *L.A. Confidential* (Figure 14.7). Although a majority of the critics praised the Oscar-winning film, James

Figure 14.6 Genre-Based Satire Most of the humor in recent parodies of film genres is based on our familiarity with formula plots, conventions, and characters. Films like *Blazing Saddles* (western) (top left), *Airplane!* (disaster) (bottom right), *Dead Men Don't Wear Plaid* (hard-boiled detective) (bottom left), and *The Naked Gun* (police) (top right) first build on our habitual expectations for their genre and then violate them. Because each of these films incorporates the plot, characters, and conventions of dozens of films, they can be helpful in studying the genres they satirize.

Naremore, in his *More Than Night: Film* Noir *in its Contexts*, calls it "a big-budget, highly publicized, and critically overrated feature that begins in darkly satiric fashion and then segues into crowd-pleasing melodrama."[10]

The noted American director and screenwriter Paul Schrader has observed that "for a long time film noir, with its emphasis on corruption and despair, was considered an aberration of the American character. The western, with its moral

Figure 14.7 ***Femmes Noirs Fatales*** Frequently in classic *film noir* of the 1940s, women proved extremely dangerous to the gullible men who desired them. In Billy Wilder's *Double Indemnity,* Barbara Stanwyck duped Fred MacMurray (top left), just as Jane Greer, in Jacques Tourneur's *Out of the Past,* attempted to outtalk and manipulate Robert Mitchum (top right). In the neo-*noir* films of the 1970s, '80s, and '90s, women characters (such as Kathleen Turner's Matty in Lawrence Kasdan's *Body Heat,* bottom left) could remain just as coldly calculated as their earlier sisters or they could finally show evidence of possessing warm, golden hearts (Kim Basinger's Lynn Bracken, shown here with Guy Pearce, in Curtis Hanson's *L.A. Confidential,* bottom right).

Figure 14.8 The Appeal of War Because the film medium inherently glorifies its subject matter, viewers must constantly scrutinize their motives for watching all war pictures, regardless of how different they may appear in their similar narratives. Compare the group-directed military epic *The Longest Day* (1962) with Steven Spielberg's 1998 *Saving Private Ryan.* Does each condemn battle or subtly celebrate it?

primitivism, and the gangster film, with its Horatio Alger values, were considered more American than the film noir."[11] Meanwhile, the movie that Schrader called "film noir's epitaph," Orson Welles's *Touch of Evil,* starring Charlton Heston, Janet Leigh, and Welles himself, was triumphantly re-released in 1998 in a re-edited version based on a long memo that the director wrote after his studio refused him final cut.[12] *Film noir,* then, is the genre that will not die.

War Films Dying and refusing to die are staples of another resurgent genre, the war movie. Many filmmakers—including Richard Rush in *The Stunt Man* and, most famously, perhaps, François Truffaut—have observed that it is probably impossible to make a genuine antiwar film. For the medium, with its glittering, large-screen images, is ever glorifying its subject. But, during a time when both Steven Spielberg's *Saving Private Ryan* and Terrence Malick's *The Thin Red Line* (the former a closely observed account of the D-Day Invasion of Normandy, the latter a long lyric poem based on the James Jones novel set in Guadalcanal) were released within a six-month period, directors obviously continue to fight the good fight, cinematically. Although Spielberg's somber effort was rewarded with both box-office and critical acclaim, more cynical critics insisted that "*Saving Private Ryan* isn't . . . any different from most other Hollywood war movies," including, one must assume, both gung ho military films and earnest portrayals such as *The Longest Day* and international classics such as Jean Renoir's *Grand Illusion* (Figure 14.8).[13] War may still be hell, but movie war is, still and always, profitable for the cinematic troops. In consuming war films, then, we must be eternally aware of the complexity of our reasons for watching.

Horror Films "The presiding irony of horror," Anthony Lane writes in *The New Yorker*,

> . . . is that while no genre offers more imaginative license, few of the directors—or, indeed, the novelists—who turn to it have more than a thimbleful of imagination in the first place. (They have a sweet tooth for the fantastic and the glutinous, which is hardly the same thing.) When visionaries and obsessives deign to frighten us, on the other hand, the results can be spectacular: look at Murnau's "Nosferatu," Dreyer's "Vampyr," or Karloff's "Frankenstein" pictures (which redefined horror as a species of warped romance).[14]

Lane's dissatisfaction with the genre, however, does not appear to stem from the frequent charge that such "romantic" horror films as John Carpenter's *Halloween* turned viewers away from classic movies like *Frankenstein* and *The Wolf Man* and opened the floodgates for teen-aged terror in so-called slasher horror films. In fact, Lane believes "Carpenter's achievement was to suggest that there was nothing exotic about horror; that it is more inbred than outlandish; and that it was best considered as the evil twin of what one might call the lyrical conservatism of American movies"[15] (Figure 14.9).

And far beyond the domain of mere slasher flicks are the later films of director Wes Craven (for example, *The People Under the Stairs*, *Scream*, and *Scream 2*), who adds what is, for some viewers, a delightfully self-conscious wit to the mayhem. However, consciousness, self or otherwise, is not truly part of the classic horror genre formula.

Science Fiction and Fantasy Films Cultural critic Bruce Kawin has analyzed the way that "particular genre forms appeal psychologically to their audiences." He "defines the audience's experience with horror and science fiction in terms of myths and dreams" and observes that "one goes to the horror film in order to have a nightmare . . . a dream whose undercurrent of anxiety both presents and masks the desire to fulfill and be punished for certain conventionally unacceptable impulses." Kawin distinguishes between science fiction films and horror films by maintaining that these "appeal to different mental activities: 'Science fiction appeals to consciousness, horror to the unconscious.'"[16]

J. P. Telotte, in *Replications: A Robotic History of the Science Fiction Film*, adds, "Certainly, the contemporary science fiction film invites us to catalogue our culture's major anxieties" (including race, gender, and sexuality, as evident in such films as *Blade Runner* and *Aliens*). But Telotte also concludes that "the genre has obviously staked out as its special territory the latest possibilities of artifice . . . through the very latest of technological developments of the cinema. . . . And yet artifice finally seems to be less its end than its method, like our films, simply a most effective way we have developed for gauging the human."[17] Perhaps, then, we should not be surprised to find in such recent and radically different science fiction films as Alex Proyas's expensive, luxurious *Dark City*

Figure 14.9 Scared Unconscious The horror film genre relishes the almost unbearable psychological tension generated by such memorable characters as maniacal Norman Bates (Anthony Perkins) in Alfred Hitchcock's *Psycho,* ferocious Hannibal Lechter (Anthony Hopkins) in Jonathan Demme's *The Silence of the Lambs,* and the amiable-but-dooomed Casey Becker (Drew Barrymore) in the telephonic opening sequence of Wes Craven's *Scream.*

Figure 14.10 Sci-Fi Consciousness Steven Spielberg's *Close Encounters of the Third Kind* (1977) seemed remarkable in part because of its friendly aliens. But other science fiction films before and since—including Robert Wise's *The Day the Earth Stood Still* (1951, with Michael Rennie) (top left), Spielberg's *E. T. The Extra-Terrestrial* (1982, featuring Henry Thomas) (top right), and Robert Zemeckis's *Contact* (1997, starring Jodie Foster) (bottom)—have also posited benevolent beings from other realms.

and Darren Aronofsky's cheaply made and stark-looking *Pi* multiple visual and thematic patterns of the spiral, signifying the chain of human life (Figure 14.10).

Screwball Comedies Iconic spirals can have more than one frame of reference, of course. The image is a staple, too, in the classic romantic comedies of the 1930s and 1940s called screwball. According to Ed Sikov, one of the most authoritative and wittiest writers about the genre, "Screwball comedies play with a funny contradiction: they tantalize us with sumptuous romantic ideals even while they horrify us with the farce lurking underneath."[18] The exact nature of this "horror" may differ greatly between early classic "couple" comedies such as *Nothing Sacred* and *It Happened One Night*, on the one hand, and modern romantic farces such as *My Best Friend's Wedding* and (in the genre's most extreme mix of conservatism and outrageousness) *There's Something About Mary*, on the other. But these films contain an underlying sameness (and universality) that is, finally, humanly comforting (as well as hilarious) (Figure 14.11).

Film Musicals The film historian and theorist Rick Altman has called the American film musical "the most complex art form ever devised."[19] Yet, another critic, Jane Feuer, points out that

> twenty-five years ago most film buffs would have scoffed at the idea that serious books could be written about John Wayne bang-bang Westerns and Rock Hudson kiss-kiss weepies. It was only when Hollywood genre films began to be seen from the perspective of their ideological and cultural meanings (rather than as star vehicles or "pure entertainment") that Westerns, melodramas and *films noirs* became accessible to critical inquiry. Yet the genre most of us think of as quintessentially Hollywood was the only one not fertilized by the new interest in film as ideology. Westerns might now be seen as a conflict between chaos and civilization, but Fred Astaire remains ineffable.[20]

But Feuer insists that "the musical is Hollywood writ large" and, like Altman, believes that it is worthy of our attention.

For his analysis, Altman classifies film musicals into three categories: the fairy tale musical, the show musical, and the folk musical. The first type includes such titles as *Top Hat*, *The Wizard of Oz*, Disney's *Cinderella*, *An American in Paris*, *Hair*, and *Annie*. Illustrations of the show musical type begin with cinema's first talkie, *The Jazz Singer* (1927), encompass what many call the epitome of the form, *Singin' in the Rain*, and extend to the dark visions of Bob Fosse's *Cabaret* and *All That Jazz*. The third type, the folk musical, includes *Rose Marie*, *Meet Me in St. Louis*, *Show Boat*, *Oklahoma!*, *Porgy and Bess*, *West Side Story*, *Woodstock*, *Nashville*, and *Yentl* (Figure 14.12).[21]

Remakes and Sequels

Remakes and sequels are nothing new in the motion picture industry, as this picture caption from Kevin Brownlow's *Hollywood: The Pioneers* tells us:

> Violence was discouraged by the Hays Office, but this scene had strong precedents. Fannie Ward had been branded in *The Cheat* (1915), Pola Negri in the 1922

Figure 14.11 Wacky Couples Romantic screwball comedies originated in the 1930s with such now-classic hilarious duos as Carole Lombard and William Powell (shown here in Gregory La Cava's *My Man Godfrey,* 1936) (bottom) and Katharine Hepburn and Cary Grant (in Howard Hawks's *Bringing Up Baby,* 1938) (top right). Although the genre's comedy has either evolved or disintegrated (depending upon one's perspective) into the raucous ribaldry of the Farrelly Brothers' *There's Something About Mary* (1998, with Cameron Diaz and Ben Stiller) (top left), the form has still retained its "old-fashioned" romantic focus.

Figure 14.12 Film Musical Types—Sugar-Coated or Bitter Many viewers believe that the traditional film musical genre reached its apex in *Singin' in the Rain* (1952, starring Gene Kelly) (top left), whose comedy and romance sweetly and joyfully recaptured the silent movie days of the late 1920s, when movie sound was just beginning to make a noise in Hollywood During recent decades the genre has mainly been dormant, moribund, or considerably transformed in its formula. Two remarkable examples of later musical film experimentation, though, are Bob Fosse's brilliantly cynical *Cabaret* (1972, starring Liza Minnelli) (top right) and Herbert Ross and Dennis Potter's riveting, flawed, bleak *Pennies From Heaven* (1981, with Jessica Harper, Bernadette Peters, and Steve Martin) (bottom)—both set in the early 1930s.

remake, Barbara Castleton in *The Branding Iron* (1920) and now Aileen Pringle in the remake of that, *Body and Soul.*[22]

Although remakes and sequels occur throughout film history, there have been periods of peak production. The industry's most recent obsession with redoing the tried and true began during the early 1970s and has intensified since. Although it may seem strange for Hollywood to rely on remakes and sequels in a period when the number of feature films being released each year is declining drastically, there is solid support for this kind of filmmaking.

The primary reason for Hollywood's reliance on remakes and sequels has to do with increases in the cost of producing motion pictures. As movies become more expensive to make, the gamble becomes much greater. Running a movie studio may be compared to running an aircraft factory that continually builds new models with new configurations, with untested control and power systems, and with $10 million to $200 million invested in each plane. When finished, each plane taxis to the runway, develops tremendous speed, and tries to get off the ground. There is no turning back. If it flies, it flies; but if it crashes, most of the investment is lost. Aircraft executives operating such a business would be very careful with the planes they designed, and the equivalent of a great many remakes and sequels would be turned out.

Of course the aircraft industry doesn't really operate this way. New models are tested for long periods, with very little risk. Miniatures can be tested in a wind tunnel and then flown before the full-size prototype takes to the air. Some reliable constants also provide security: The laws of physics and aerodynamics do not change; they are constant and predictable.

In the motion picture industry, there is no way to test miniature versions of a film in a wind tunnel. A film's success (its ability to fly) is based not on predictable constants like the laws of physics and aerodynamics but on the unpredictable and whimsical laws of human likes and dislikes. Remakes and sequels bring at least a degree of predictability to the marketplace.

Most remakes and sequels are based on movies that, if they are not film classics, have proved by their continuing popularity that they really don't need to be remade at all and usually don't beg for a sequel. Therefore, the studios that remake films are guaranteeing themselves a strange combination of success and failure. Just out of curiosity, the mass audience will go to see remakes of movies they know and love. The urge to make a critical judgment about the remake of any well-known film is almost irresistible—it is probably one of the few laws of human behavior that the studios can predict and trust. The better the original and the more popular it is, the greater is the number of people who can be counted on to see the remake or sequel. Thus, remakes and sequels guarantee a financial return. They also, however, guarantee a kind of failure, for the better the original, the higher are the expectations of the audience for the remake or sequel, which almost always fails to meet those expectations. (A natural human law governs audience response to remakes and sequels: The higher expectations are, the greater the disappointment.) Although there are rare exceptions, remakes and sequels generally lack the freshness and creative dynamics of the original, so the disappointment is usually justified.

Taking for granted that the prime motivation for producing remakes and sequels is profit and the improved odds of betting on a proven winner, we should also admit that there are valid reasons for producing remakes and sequels, and there is a creative challenge involved. Directors of remakes have been clear about that point: They want to make creative changes in new versions—they never attempt to make a Xerox copy. These creative changes take different forms and are justified in different ways. A startling exception to this observation came in 1998, when director Gus Van Sant (*Drugstore Cowboy, My Own Private Idaho, To Die For, Good Will Hunting*) created a poorly received remake of Alfred Hitchcock's *Psycho*. He first made the announcement that he would utilize the same script and shooting schedule as for the 1960 film. Then he insisted that the characters would be adjusted slightly to fit the film's modern audience. Finally, he shot in color and pronounced his movie "an anti-remake film," adding, "I don't have much faith in Hollywood's ability to do remakes. There's a remake curse." Still, after making his movie, he indicated that he'd "be interested in redoing 'Psycho' again."[23]

Remakes

Paul Schrader, director for the 1982 remake of *Cat People* (1942), looks on most remakes with contempt:

> The whole remake trend is an indication of cowardice, obviously. Remakes, sequels, parodies are what I call "back born" movies. They come off something else. With the cost of movies being such, everybody's trying to protect their jobs. For an executive to redo *Animal House* or *Jaws* is clearly a much safer decision.[24]

A reasonably long period of time usually elapses between different versions of the same film, so one of the most frequently used justifications for remaking a film is to update it. Filmmakers have their own ways of explaining what their goal is in updating a film. In their view, they are usually improving the original work by giving it a more contemporary quality or providing a new sensibility for modern audiences. A movie can be updated in a variety of ways:

- **Important changes in style—updating to reflect social change, cinematic styles, lifestyles, or popular tastes:** *Heaven Can Wait* (1978)—a remake of *Here Comes Mr. Jordan* (1941); *A Star Is Born* (1954/1976)—new music, new lifestyle, a whole new ambience for an old story; *The Wizard of Oz/The Wiz* (1939/1978)—modern music and a black cast, a filmed version of a Broadway show; *The Getaway* (1972/1994)—new star couple.

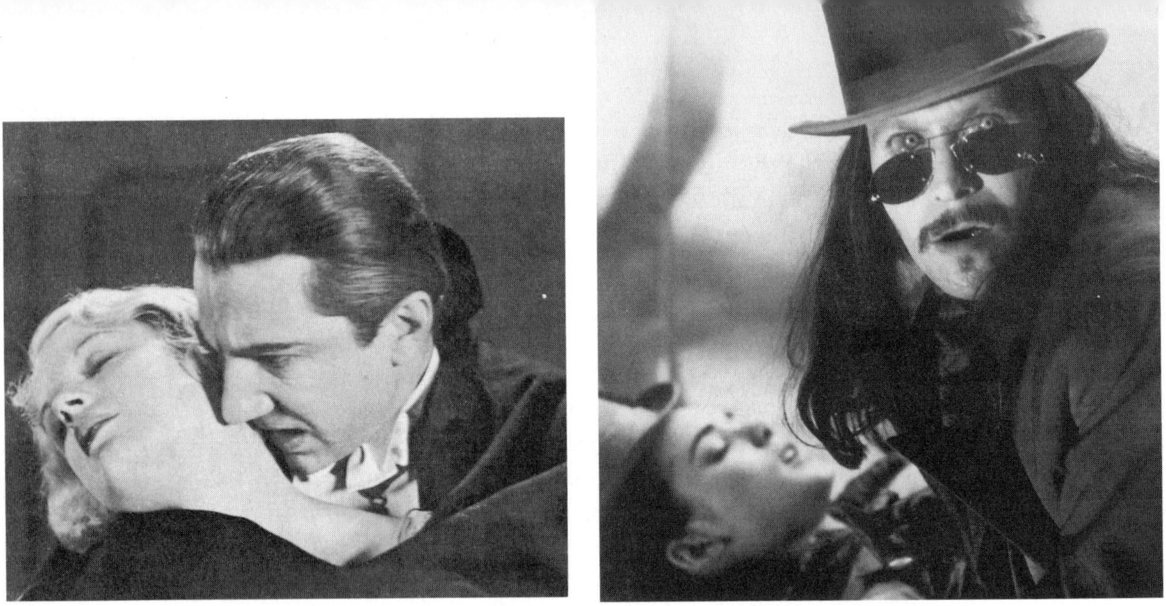

Figure 14.13 Popular Subject The human vampire legend has inspired a large number of films since German director F. W. Murnau's 1922 film version of the Dracula story, *Nosferatu*. Pictured here are Bela Lugosi and Helen Chandler in Tod Browning's 1931 *Dracula* (left) and Winona Ryder and Gary Oldman in Francis Ford Coppola's 1992 *Bram Stoker's Dracula* (right).

- **Changes in film technology—updating to take advantage of new potential in the art form:** *Stagecoach* (1939/1966)—color, wide screen, stereophonic sound; *Ben-Hur* (1926/1959)—color, wide screen, stereophonic sound (1926 version was silent); *King Kong* (1933/1976)—color, wide screen, stereophonic sound, sophisticated animation techniques; *The Thing* (1951/1982)—color, wide screen, stereophonic sound, special effects; *A Guy Named Joe/Always* (1943/1989)—color, wide screen, stereophonic sound; *Dracula/Bram Stoker's Dracula* (1931/1992)—color, wide screen, stereophonic sound, special effects (Figure 14.13); *Frankenstein/Mary Shelley's Frankenstein* (1931/1994)—color, wide screen, stereophonic sound (Figure 14.14).
- **Changes in censorship:** *The Postman Always Rings Twice* (1946/1981)—explicit treatment of steamy passions; *The Blue Lagoon* (1949/1980)—emphasis on sexual awakening of young couple; *Cape Fear* (1962/1991).
- **New paranoias:** *Invasion of the Body Snatchers* (1956/1978)—from subconscious fears of communist takeover in the original to fears of Moonie takeover in the remake.
- **The musical version:** A type of remake that usually provides a greater challenge and greater creative freedom for the filmmaker is the translation of the film into a musical version, where words and music must be integrated into the dramatic framework of the original. Examples: *Oliver Twist* (1948) to *Oliver!* (1968); *A Star Is Born* (1937 drama to 1954 musical); *The Philadelphia Story* (1940) to *High Society* (1956); *Lost Horizon* (1937 drama

Figure 14.14 Technological Updating Advances in film wizardry often explain why films are remade. The addition of color and greatly improved special visual effects, for example, primarily led to the original (1949) *Mighty Joe Young*'s being newly imagined almost fifty years later.

to 1973 musical); *Anna and the King of Siam* (1946 drama) to *The King and I* (1956 musical); and *Pygmalion* (1938 drama) to *My Fair Lady* (1964 musical).

- **Change in format—the TV version:** Television movies have gotten into the remake business, with the following contributions: *Of Mice and Men* (1939/1981), *The Diary of Anne Frank*, *All Quiet on the Western Front*, *From Here to Eternity*, *In Cold Blood*, *The Shining*, *Rear Window*, and *David and Lisa*.
- **Remakes of international films:** The creative challenge of transplanting a film from one culture to another has produced some interesting results. *The Seven Samurai* (Japan, 1954) became *The Magnificent Seven* (USA, 1960). *Smiles of a Summer Night* (Sweden, 1955) became first a Broadway show and later the film *A Little Night Music* (USA, 1978). *Breathless* (France, 1959) was remade in the United States in 1983. The 1983 *Breathless* changes the setting from Paris to Los Angeles and reverses the nationalities of the principal characters. *The Return of Martin Guerre* (France, 1982) became *Sommersby* (USA, France, 1993). *The Vanishing* (France, Netherlands, 1988) was remade in the United States in 1993.

Finally, the critic Leo Braudy has noted that

> the remake resides at the intersection of the genetic and the generic codes. In even the most debased version, it is a meditation on the continuing historical relevance (economic, cultural, psychological) of a particular narrative. A remake is thus always concerned with what its makers and (they hope) its audiences consider to be unfinished cultural business.[25]

Sequels

People love sequels—they wait for them, read about them, and usually see them more than once. But in a town where executives make a habit of looking over their shoulders, selling something already regarded as a sure hit creates a tremendous burden. Movies are not necessarily better the second time around.[26]

—Betsy Sharkey, Entertainment Writer

Remakes generally allow the original to age for a while (sometimes long enough for a whole new generation or two to come along who may not know the original). Sequels have the best chance of success when they follow the original quickly, so that they can capitalize on the original's success. Audiences attend sequels for the same reason they go to remakes. If they enjoyed the original, they go seeking more of the same, and they are curious to see how well the sequel stands up to the original. The motivation for shooting sequels is similar to that for shooting remakes—profit. But the thinking is a little different. With the remake it's a case of "Play it again, Sam. They liked it once; let's make it again." With the sequel, it's a matter of "We've got a good thing going; let's get all the mileage out of it we can" (Figure 14.15).

There are relatively few good reasons for making a sequel other than to realize the profit potential. Nevertheless, there are some very natural sequels—made simply because there was more story to tell—and these sequels can match the original in quality if the story is continued. First-class sequels have been made of *The Godfather* (*The Godfather Part II*) and of *The French Connection* (*The French Connection II*). Most sequels, however, do not have the natural relationship to their original that these two do.

Because sequels don't try to tell the same story but can build on characters already established in the original, they give the filmmakers much more room for creative freedom than remakes do. As long as they pick up some characters from the original, maintain a certain degree of consistency in the treatment of those characters, and retain something of the style of the original, sequels can take off in almost any direction they want to go. A good example of flexibility in sequels can be seen in the sequels to James Whale's original *Frankenstein* (1931). It was followed by *Bride of Frankenstein* (1935), in which Whale introduced odd baroque elements and black humor, and by a kind of combo-sequel, *Frankenstein Meets the Wolf Man* (1943). The parody/sequel *Young Frankenstein* (1974) combines elements of both of the original Frankenstein films and succeeds largely because it lovingly recaptures the style of the original (Figure 14.16).

Much more important than the potential within the original story for a sequel is the audience's response to the original characters. If it becomes clear that a large film audience is fascinated with the cast of the original and would

Figure 14.15 Maximum Mileage The success of the blockbuster hit *Butch Cassidy and the Sundance Kid* (top left) spawned a prequel and two sequels. The prequel, *Butch and Sundance: The Early Days* (1979), featured William Katt and Tom Berenger (top right), chosen because they looked like younger versions of Redford and Newman. The sequels were both TV movies: *Mrs. Sundance* (1974), starring Elizabeth Montgomery as survivor Etta Place; and *Wanted: The Sundance Woman* (1976), starring Katherine Ross (the original Etta) and later retitled *Mrs. Sundance Rides Again* (bottom).

love to see those actors together again, we can be reasonably sure that a sequel will soon be in the making. On any film where the profit potential looks good enough to inspire a sequel, studio contracts will obligate actors to do the sequel. The continuity provided by keeping the actors of the original in the sequel is tremendously important to box-office appeal. Roy Scheider, Lorraine Gary, and Murray Hamilton, for example, served as important links between *Jaws* and *Jaws 2*.

Figure 14.16 Parody/Sequel One of the most successful film parodies in recent times is Mel Brooks's *Young Frankenstein.* Through striking black-and-white cinematography and attention to details of setting and atmosphere, the film captures the style so well that it pays homage to the original.

But *Jaws 2* also provides an example of how important the behind-the-camera people are to making a successful sequel. When the writers, directors, and editors who participated in the original do not participate in the sequel, the film can suffer considerably, often losing the spirit, style, and impact of the original (Figure 14.17). Therefore, the most successful sequels (or series of sequels) result when the whole winning team (actors, director, writers, editor, producers, and so on) stays pretty much intact throughout (Figure 14.18). The phenomenal success of the *Rocky* series is probably due to the continuing participation of most of the original *Rocky* team, but even that success probably won't last much beyond *Rocky V.*

Similar in some ways to the *Rocky* and *Superman* sequels, but very different from the ordinary exploitation-of-a-smash-hit sequel, is the character series. The character series can be developed from a series of novels featuring the same character or characters (Tarzan, James Bond, and Sherlock Holmes), or it can be developed around a character or combination of characters appearing in a single film. If a character or combination of characters has tremendous audience appeal, a series of films may be structured around the character or characters—for example, Abbott and Costello, Crosby and Hope (the "Road" series), Peter

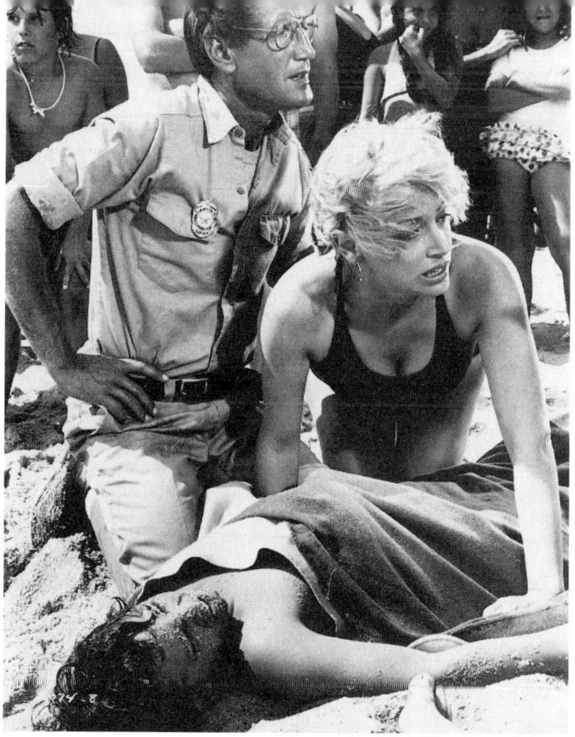

Figure 14.17 Continuity in the Sequel Roy Scheider and Lorraine Gary (seen here in a scene from the original *Jaws*) provided some continuity by appearing in *Jaws 2,* but changes in directing, editing, and writing produced a second-rate sequel. *Jaws 3-D* was a dismal attempt to revive 3-D.

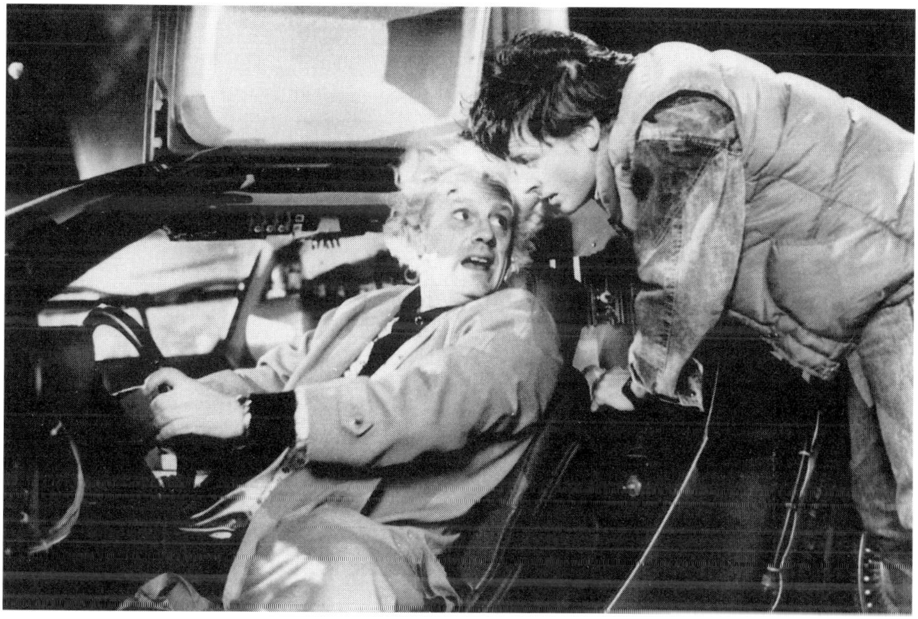

Figure 14.18 Continuity in the Sequel II For the sequels to *Back to the Future*, the producers signed director Robert Zemeckis and actors Michael J. Fox, Christopher Lloyd, and Lea Thompson. To carry the continuity one step further and increase cost efficiency, they filmed *II* and *III* at the same time.

Figure 14.19 Long-Running Character Series Chief Inspector Jacques Clouseau, the character played by Peter Sellers in the Pink Panther series, enjoyed a long and prosperous life, even after the great comic actor's death. When Sellers died after completing five Pink Panther films, director Blake Edwards put together a sixth, *The Trail of the Pink Panther,* made up of outtakes (unused footage) from the earlier films woven into a new story featuring some of the series actors.

Figure 14.20 New Character The addition of Indiana's father (Sean Connery) to the cast of *Indiana Jones and the Last Crusade* provided a delightful interplay between the characters that became the highlight of the whole film.

Sellers as Inspector Clouseau (the "Pink Panther" series, Figure 14.19), and Percy Kilbride and Marjorie Main as Pa and Ma Kettle. *Raiders of the Lost Ark, Indiana Jones and the Temple of Doom*, and *Indiana Jones and the Last Crusade* show that American audiences are still responsive to character series (Figure 14.20). The recent Batman series (*Batman*, *Batman Returns*, *Batman Forever*, and *Batman & Robin*) seemingly changed focus from the hero to fascinating villains, even to the point of trading actors playing the caped crusader (George Clooney for Val Kilmer for Michael Keaton) in midstream (Figure 14.21).

In a character series, continuation of the actors from one film to the next is essential, but so is good writing built around consistency of character. The overall style of the series should be consistent so that the expectations of the audience are satisfied, guaranteeing their return to the next film in the series. The need of the audience for the predictable, for seeing familiar faces in familiar kinds of story formats, has been almost completely satisfied by weekly situation comedies and dramatic series on television.

In rare cases, a series of films are designed as parts of a preconceived larger whole. Although each film can stand on its own as a unified work, each is linked by characters, setting, and events to a larger whole. George Lucas's *Star Wars*

Figure 14.21 Focus on the Villains The Catwoman (Michelle Pfeiffer) and the Penguin (Danny DeVito) are such colorful characters that they almost overshadow the hero in *Batman Returns* (top left). Similarly, in two more recent sequels, the bad guys played by Tommy Lee Jones and Jim Carrey (as Two-Face and The Riddler in *Batman Forever*) (top right) and Arnold Schwarzenegger and Uma Thurman (as Mr. Freeze and Poison Ivy in *Batman & Robin*) also steal the show (bottom).

(1977), *The Empire Strikes Back* (1980), and *Return of the Jedi* (1983) were designed as a trilogy, and now *The Phantom Menace* (1999) has begun another trilogy, set in an earlier time. Titles suggest that *Young Tom Edison* (1940) and *Edison, the Man* (1940) were designed to dovetail for a full Edison biography. Although the profit motive might also be involved in such plans, the writing and dramatic power should be superior to the "Hey! That one made money! Let's whip out another and another!" kind of afterthought, which often seems to impel Hollywood sequels (as in the case of much in the *Planet of the Apes* series).

Questions

On Genre Films

1. Use the formulas for the western and gangster films as a starting point for the study of a series of three or four films in either genre. How do the films being studied fit the formula? Is the formula valid, or do elements appear in each film that are not part of the formula? Do you find elements in the formula that do not occur in the films studied? Adjust the formula so that it fits all the films under study, then test the adjusted formula against two more films from the genre. As a part of the testing, try transferring the parts of one film to another. What characters are interchangeable? What subtle differences exist between one character and another? Which corresponding characters could be exchanged without significantly altering the plot?
2. Using the formulas for the gangster film and the western (or your adjusted versions) as models, study at least three films from any of the following genres and create your own formula for that genre: the *film noir*, the screwball comedy, the disaster film, the boy-meets-girl musical. Then test your formula against two or three more films. Also test the films in the genre to see if parts are interchangeable.
3. Study three films by the same director in one genre, along with at least two films in the same genre by different directors. Are three different directorial styles apparent, or are the styles indistinguishable? Consider the three films by the same director in chronological order. Does the director incorporate personal stylistic trademarks into each of the films? What are those trademarks, and what makes them stand out?
4. What innovations or refinements on the formula does the director provide? Does the director introduce innovations and further refinements as he or she moves from one film to another? Are the innovations and refinements that the director introduces superficial and cosmetic, or are they significant enough to stretch the genre, creating a strain or tension against the outer boundaries of the formula? Does the director seem to learn something new with each film and build on that in the next? Do we see changes in the director's personal vision or worldview from one film to another? How are those changes reflected? (For example, does the director seem to grow more serious or less serious, more pessimistic or more optimistic?)
5. Compare and contrast the styles of two directors working within the same genre. Examine at least two films by each director, and decide how their styles create important differences within the same genre. (For example, how is a Frank Capra screwball comedy different from a Preston Sturges screwball comedy?)

On Remakes

1. Was the remake really necessary? Why is the older version outdated? Why do modern audiences need the story retold? What aspects of the original film are inaccessible to modern audiences? Are these inaccessible aspects so important as to make the film incomprehensible to contemporary filmgoers or are they relatively insignificant?
2. What important changes were made in the remake? Why were they made? Which changes are improvements over the original and which are only changes for the sake of novelty?
3. Which is the better film? Does the remake have the freshness and the creative dynamic of the original? Were you disappointed in the remake? Why or why not?
4. How is the remake like the original? Is an effort made through casting, cinematic style, and so on to capture the spirit and flavor of the original? Do these efforts succeed?
5. If the remake is a musical version, how well are the spirit and story of the original captured in the words and music of the songs? What major changes in plot or setting had to be made in the musical version? How are the characters changed?
6. What advantages does the remake have over the original in terms of freedom from censorship and new technology in the medium? How does it make use of these advantages?
7. If the remake involves a foreign original, how does a change of setting, language, or cultural values affect the remake?

On Sequels

1. Does the sequel grow naturally out of the original? In other words, was there enough story left over from the original to make a natural sequel?
2. How many important members of the original cast and of the behind-the-scenes team were involved in the sequel? If some characters had to be recast, how did that change affect the quality of the sequel?
3. Does the sequel build on the original in such a way that it seems incomplete unless you've seen the original, or is it complete enough to stand on its own as a separate, unified work?
4. Does the sequel capture the flavor and spirit of the original in story and visual style? Is it equal in quality to the original in every aspect? Where does it surpass the original and where is it weaker?
5. If the sequel becomes a character series, what are the qualities of the characters that make them wear well? Why do we want to see them again and again? Are the writers able to keep their characters consistent in film after film? How consistent are the other stylistic elements from one film to another?

Films for Study

Westerns—and Antiwesterns

Blazing Saddles (parody, 1974)
Cimarron (1931)
Dances With Wolves (1990)
Fort Apache (1948)
Heaven's Gate (1980)
High Noon (1952)
Little Big Man (1970)
The Long Riders (1980)
Lust in the Dust (parody, 1985)
McCabe & Mrs. Miller (1971)
My Darling Clementine (1946)
Once Upon a Time in the West (1968)
Red River (1948)
Ride the High Country (1962)
Rio Bravo (1959)
Rustler's Rhapsody (parody, 1985)
The Searchers (1956)
Shane (1953)
She Wore a Yellow Ribbon (1949)
Stagecoach (1939; remade in 1966)
Tumbleweeds (1925)
Unforgiven (1992)
The Wild Bunch (1969)

Gangster Films

The Asphalt Jungle (1950)
Badlands (1973)
The Big Heat (1953)
Bonnie and Clyde (1967)
Bugsy (1991)
The Godfather (1972; sequels: *Part II*, 1974, and *Part III*, 1990)
GoodFellas (1990)
Kalifornia (1993)
Key Largo (1948)
Kiss of Death (1947)
Little Caesar (1930)
The Maltese Falcon (1941)
Mean Streets (1973)
Menace II Society (1993)
Miller's Crossing (1990)
Natural Born Killers (1994)
Prizzi's Honor (1985)
The Public Enemy (1931)
Pulp Fiction (1994)
Reservoir Dogs (1992)
Scarface (1932; remade in 1983)
The Untouchables (1987)
The Usual Suspects (1995)
White Heat (1949)

Film Noir *and Neo*-Noir

The Big Clock (1948; remade as *No Way Out* in 1987)
The Big Lebowski (1998)
The Big Sleep (1946)
Blood Simple (1984)
Body Heat (1981)
Chinatown (1974; sequel: *The Two Jakes*, 1990)
Dead Again (1991)
Dead Men Don't Wear Plaid (parody, 1982)
Detour (1945; remade in 1992)
Devil in a Blue Dress (1995)
D.O.A. (1950; remade in 1988)
Double Indemnity (1944)
Gilda (1946)
The Grifters (1990)
The Killers (1946)
A Kiss Before Dying (1956; remade in 1991)
Kiss Me Deadly (1955)
L.A. Confidential (1997)
The Lady From Shanghai (1948)
The Last Seduction (1994)
Laura (1944)
Murder, My Sweet (1944; remade in 1975 as *Farewell, My Lovely*)
The Naked City (1948)
The Naked Kiss (1964)
Night and the City (1950; remade in 1992)
One False Move (1992)
Out of the Past (1947; remade in 1984 as *Against All Odds*)
Pickup on South Street (1953)
The Postman Always Rings Twice (1946; remade in 1981)
Se7en (1995)
Sunset Boulevard (1950)
They Live by Night (1949)
To Have and Have Not (1944)
Touch of Evil (1958; re-edited from Orson Welles's notes in 1998)

War Films

All Quiet on the Western Front (1930)
Apocalypse Now (1979)
Battleground (1949)
The Bridge on the River Kwai (1957)
Casualties of War (1989)
Das Boot (1981-German)
The Deer Hunter (1978)
The Dirty Dozen (1967)
The Eagle Has Landed (1977)
Europa Europa (1991)
Full Metal Jacket (1987)
Grand Illusion (1937-French)
Is Paris Burning? (1966)
The Longest Day (1962)
*M*A*S*H* (1970)
Paths of Glory (1957)
Patton (1970)
Platoon (1986)
Saving Private Ryan (1998)
Stalag 17 (1953)
The Story of G.I. Joe (1945)
They Were Expendable (1945)
The Thin Red Line (1998; remake of 1964 film)
The Victors (1963)

Horror Films

Alien (1979; sequels: *Aliens*, 1986, *Alien*³, 1992, and *Alien Resurrection*, 1997)
The Birds (1963)
The Cabinet of Dr. Caligari (1919-German)
Carrie (1976)
Cat People (1942; remade in 1982)
Dead Ringers (1988)
Dr. Jekyll and Mr. Hyde (1932; remade in 1941)
Eraserhead (1978)
The Exorcist (1973; followed by two sequels)
The Fly (1958; remade in 1986)
Frankenstein (1931; sequels include *Bride of Frankenstein*, 1935; remakes: *Mary Shelley's Frankenstein*, 1994, the parody/sequel *Young Frankenstein*, 1974, and *The Bride*, 1985)
Freaks (1932)
Friday the 13th (1980; multiple sequels)
Halloween (1978; numerous sequels, including *Halloween H2O*, 1998)
The Innocents (1961)
The Lair of the White Worm (1988)
The Mummy (1932) (remade in 1999)
Naked Lunch (1991)
A Nightmare on Elm Street (1984; many sequels)
Night of the Living Dead (1968; remade in 1990; sequels: *Dawn of the Dead*, 1978, *Day of the Dead*, 1985)
Nosferatu (1922; remakes include *Dracula*, 1931, *Nosferatu, 1979, and Bram Stoker's Dracula*, 1992)
Psycho (1960; several sequels; remade in 1998)
Scanners (1981)
Scream (1996; sequel: *Scream 2*, 1997)
The Shining (1980/1997 for TV)
The Silence of the Lambs (1991)
Suspiria (1977-Italian)
The Wolf Man (1941)

Science Fiction and Fantasy Films

Alphaville (1965-French)
Blade Runner (1982)
Brazil (1985)
The Brother From Another Planet (1984)
Close Encounters of the Third Kind (1977)
Contact (1997)

Dark City (1998)
The Day the Earth Stood Still (1951)
Dune (1984)
E.T. The Extra-Terrestrial (1982)
eXistenZ (1999)
Fahrenheit 451 (1966)
Fantastic Voyage (1966)
The Fifth Element (1997)
Highlander (1986; sequels in 1991 and 1994)
The Incredible Shrinking Man (1957; sequel/parody: *The Incredible Shrinking Woman*, 1981)
Invasion of the Body Snatchers (1956; remade in 1978 and in 1994 as *Body Snatchers*)
The Invisible Man (1933; numerous sequels, including *Memoirs of an Invisible Man* in 1992)
Island of Lost Souls (1933; remade in 1977 and 1996 as *The Island of Dr. Moreau*)
La Jetée (1962 short; inspired *Twelve Monkeys*, 1995)
The Man Who Fell to Earth (1976)
The Matrix (1999)
Metropolis (1926)
Pi (1998)
Planet of the Apes (1968; four sequels)
Seconds (1966)
Soylent Green (1973)
Star Trek—The Motion Picture (1979; followed by several sequels)
Star Wars (1977; sequels in 1980, *The Empire Strikes Back*, and 1983, *Return of the Jedi;* first prequel in 1999, *Episode I: The Phantom Menace*)
The Terminator (1984; sequel: *Terminator 2: Judgment Day*, 1991)
Them! (1954)
The Thing (1951; remade in 1982)
THX 1138 (1971)
A Trip to the Moon (1902, Mèliés short)
2001: A Space Odyssey (1968; sequel: *2010*, 1984)

Romantic Screwball Comedies

Adam's Rib (1949)
The Awful Truth (1937)
Ball of Fire (1941)
Bringing Up Baby (1938; remade in 1972 as *What's Up, Doc?*)
Easy Living (1937)
His Girl Friday (1940; remake of *The Front Page*, 1931; remade in 1974 and, as *Switching Channels*, in 1988)
Holiday (1938)
It Happened One Night (1934)
The Lady Eve (1941)
Mr. Deeds Goes to Town (1936)
My Best Friend's Wedding (1997)
My Man Godfrey (1936)
Nothing Sacred (1937)
The Palm Beach Story (1942)
The Philadelphia Story (1940; remade as *High Society*, 1956)
There's Something About Mary (1998)
The Thin Man (1934; plus a series of sequels)
Tin Cup (1996)
Topper (1937; sequels)
Twentieth Century (1934)
Unfaithfully Yours (1948; remade in 1984)
You Can't Take It With You (1938)

Musicals

All That Jazz (1979)
An American in Paris (1951)
Cabaret (1972)
Carousel (1956)
Curly Top (1935)
Everyone Says I Love You (1996)
Fame (1980)
Fiddler on the Roof (1971)
Footloose (1984)
42nd Street (1933)
Funny Girl (1968; sequel: *Funny Lady*, 1975)
Gold Diggers of 1933 (1933; also 1935 and 1937)
Grease (1978)
Guys and Dolls (1955)
Hair (1979)
A Hard Day's Night (1964)
Jailhouse Rock (1957)
The Jazz Singer (1927; remade in 1953 and 1980)
The King and I (1956; remake of *Anna and the King of Siam*, 1946)
Love Me or Leave Me (1955)
Mary Poppins (1964)
Meet Me in St. Louis (1944)
The Music Man (1962)
My Fair Lady (1964)
Nashville (1975)
New York, New York (1977)
Oklahoma! (1955)
Oliver! (1968; remake of *Oliver Twist*, 1948)
One Hundred Men and a Girl (1937)
Pal Joey (1957)
Pennies From Heaven (1981; remake of a British TV series)
Pinocchio (1940)
Road to Singapore (1940; first in a series)
The Rocky Horror Picture Show (1975)
Rose-Marie (1936; remade in 1954)
School Daze (1988)
Singin' in the Rain (1952)
The Sound of Music (1965)
A Star Is Born (1954; a remake of a 1937 drama; remade in 1976)
Swing Time (1936)
Top Hat (1935)
The Umbrellas of Cherbourg (1964-French)
Victor/Victoria (1982; a remake of a 1936 drama and a 1933 German film)
West Side Story (1961)
The Wizard of Oz (1939; remade in 1978 as *The Wiz*)
Yentl (1983)

Other Remakes

Ben-Hur (1926/1959)
Breathless (1959-French/1983)
Cape Fear (1962/1991)
Clueless (1995/*Emma*, 1996)
Cousin, Cousine (1975-French/*Cousins*, 1989)
Dangerous Liaisons (1960-French/1988/*Valmont*, 1989/*Cruel Intentions*, 1999)
David and Lisa (1962/1998 for TV)
Death Takes a Holiday (1934/*Meet Joe Black*, 1998)
Doctor Dolittle (1967/1998)
Down and Out in Beverly Hills (1986/*Boudu Saved From Drowning*, 1932-French)
Father of the Bride (1950; sequel: *Father's Little Dividend*, 1951/1991; sequel: *Father of the Bride Part II*, 1995)

The Getaway (1972/1994)
Gloria (1980/1999)
Godzilla (1954-Japanese/1998—plus many mutations)
Great Expectations (1934/1946/1974/1998)
A Guy Named Joe (1943/*Always*, 1989)
Hamlet (includes versions in 1948, 1969, 1990, and 1996)
In Cold Blood (1967/1996 for TV)
Jaws (1975/*Jaws 2*, 1978/*Jaws 3-D*, 1983/*Jaws the Revenge*, 1987)
King Kong (1933/1976)
La Cage aux Folles (1978-French-Italian—plus two sequels/*The Birdcage*, 1996)
La Femme Nikita (1990-French-Italian/*Point of No Return*, 1993)
Little Women (1933/1949/1978 for TV/1994)
Lolita (1962/1997)
Lord of the Flies (1963/1990)
Love Affair (1939/*An Affair to Remember*, 1957/*Love Affair*, 1994)
The Man Who Knew Too Much (1934-British/1956, both directed by Alfred Hitchcock)
A Midsummer Night's Dream (1935/1968/1999)
Mighty Joe Young (1949/1998)
Moby Dick (1930/1956/1998 for TV)
Of Mice and Men (1939/1992)
Oscar Wilde (1960/*The Trials of Oscar Wilde*, 1960/*Wilde*, 1998—all British; not genuine remakes because they evolved independently from many of the same source materials)
Ransom (1956/1996)
Rear Window (1954/1998 for TV)
The Return of Martin Guerre (1982-French/*Sommersby*, 1993)
Romeo and Juliet (1936/1954/1966/1968; *William Shakespeare's Romeo & Juliet*, 1996)
The Seven Samurai (1954-Japanese/*The Magnificent Seven*, 1960)
The Shop Around the Corner (1940/*In the Good Old Summertime*, 1949/*You've Got Mail*, 1998)
The Taming of the Shrew (1929/1967/*10 Things I Hate About You*, 1999)
To Be or Not To Be (1942/1983)
The Vanishing (1988-French-Dutch/1993—both directed by George Sluizer)
Wings of Desire (1988-West German-French; sequel: *Faraway, So Close!*, 1993/*City of Angels*, 1998)

Other Sequels

Babe (1995-Australian/*Babe: Pig in the City*, 1998-Australian)
Back to the Future (1985/*Part II*, 1989/*Part III*, 1990)
Batman (1989/*Batman Returns*, 1992/*Batman Forever*, 1995/*Batman & Robin*, 1997)
Beethoven (1992/*Beethoven's 2nd*, 1993)
Die Hard (1988/*Die Hard 2*, 1990/*Die Hard With a Vengeance*, 1995)
The French Connection (1971/*The French Connection II*, 1975)
Here Comes Mr. Jordan (1941/*Heaven Can Wait*, 1978)
Home Alone (1990/*Home Alone 2: Lost in New York*, 1992/*Home Alone 3*, 1997)
Jean de Florette (1986-French; sequel: *Manon of the Spring*, 1986)
The Last Picture Show (1971/*Texasville*, 1990)

Lethal Weapon (1987/*Lethal Weapon 2*, 1989/*Lethal Weapon 3*, 1992/*Lethal Weapon 4*, 1998)
My Father's Glory (1990-French; sequel: *My Mother's Castle*, 1990)
Raiders of the Lost Ark (1981/*Indiana Jones and the Temple of Doom*, 1984/*Indiana Jones and the Last Crusade*, 1989)
Rocky (1976/*II*, 1979/*III*, 1982/*IV*, 1985/*V*, 1990)
Smiles of a Summer Night (1955-Swedish/inspired *A Little Night Music*, 1978, and *A Midsummer Night's Sex Comedy*, 1982)
Superman (1978/*II*, 1980/*III*, 1983/*IV*, 1987)

Chapter 15

Other Film Experiences

The silent film is free of the isolating walls of language differences. If we look at and understand each other's faces and gestures, we not only understand, we also learn to feel each other's emotions. The gesture is not only the outward projection of emotion, it is also its initiator.

—BÉLA BALÁZS, FILM THEORIST

Most of us have grown up with movies, both in the theater and on television. We are so familiar with genre films, remakes, and sequels that we experience them as easily as drawing a breath. They are part of our natural environment. But sometimes we are not very comfortable with foreign language, silent, documentary, and feature-length animated films, because they seem to be products of other cultures, other lifestyles, other sensibilities, or other generations. The "strangeness" of these kinds of films can pose formidable obstacles to appreciation and understanding. In addition, in our culture we often have difficulty dealing with feature films whose main significance is historical and with those focusing on social problems. However, if we make a conscious effort to overcome these obstacles, we will be amply rewarded by the worlds of experience that await in these special films.

Foreign Language or International Films

The most difficult problem in analyzing foreign language or international films is the language barrier itself. Although the image carries the major burden of communication in film, the spoken word still plays an important role. Therefore, some method must be used to help us understand the dialogue. There are two basic methods of translating dialogue in foreign language films: voice dubbing and the use of subtitles.

Voice Dubbing

In the case of a French film, for example, that also plays in America, the **voice dubbing** works as follows: The actors speak the lines of dialogue in their native language (French), and this dialogue is recorded and becomes a part of the soundtrack for the French version. For the American market, the dialogue soundtrack in French is replaced by an English soundtrack—voices in English are recorded to correspond to the mouth and lip movements of the French actors. To match image with soundtrack, the translator carefully selects English words that phonetically approximate the French words being spoken, so that the image of the French actor and the words spoken in English seem synchronized. The precision of voice-dubbing technology enables us to watch the film in the usual way, and, because the actors seem to be speaking English, the film does not seem so foreign. Nevertheless, the disadvantages and limitations of voice dubbing are numerous.

Perhaps the primary flaw is the effect that results from separating actors from their voices: The acting often seems stiff and wooden. Renata Adler, a strong opponent of voice dubbing, states, "The process is hopeless, destroying any illusion of life, and leaving the actor somewhere between a mouthing fish and a blubbering grotesque."[1]

Another problem is that perfectly accurate lip synchronization is never possible. For example, although the French phrase *mon amour* might closely approximate the lip movements of a translation such as *my dearest*, the French word *oui* does not come close to the lip movements of the English word *yes*. Even if perfect lip synchronization were possible, another formidable obstacle would remain: Each language has its own emotional character, rhythmic patterns, and accompanying facial expressions and gestures, all of which seem unnatural when another language is dubbed in. French facial expressions simply do not correspond to English words. Schools of acting are certainly influenced by the nature of the language spoken, especially by its general emotional character. Consider, for example, the stereotypical difference between the Italian acting style, with its emphasis on elaboration and broad gestures, and the Swedish style, which is much more restrained. Thus, because of the impossibility of perfect synchronization and the differences in national emotional temperaments reflected in acting styles, dubbing can never really capture the illusion of reality. A certain artificial quality often permeates the film and becomes a gnawing irritation to the viewer.

Furthermore, the process of voice dubbing eliminates the natural power, character, and unique emotional quality of the original language, the very sound of which, understandable or not, may be essential to the spirit of the film. The sense of reality that is lost in voice dubbing returns when the original language is spoken, for the international film in its own language has a resonance and an authenticity that is impossible to achieve through dubbing.

When the dubbed voices are not carefully chosen to fit the actors and the general tone of the film, the illusion of reality suffers even more. For example, in the Russian film *War and Peace*, the dubbing, according to Renata Adler, makes the inhabitants of Moscow sound as if they came from Texas. In such situations, a certain degree of authenticity might be saved by having the dubbed voices speak English with a Russian accent.

All too often the artificial quality of dubbed international films is due not to the change of language or the casting of voices but to the poor quality of the dubbing techniques. Sometimes there seems to be a general lack of concern with the dramatic performance of the dubbed voices. The dubbed lines usually have little dramatic emphasis; they possess no natural variations in pitch and stress; the rhythms are all wrong. The lines are often read in a lifeless monotone, providing little more than the basic information of the line without vocal subtleties. (However, from an American perspective, at least, such poor dubbing would probably be an improvement over the current practice in the Polish film industry. There, in a method very popular with audiences, predominantly male readers—for all voices—merely narrate movies in a flat, dispassionate manner.)

Wifemistress (a 1977 Italian film directed by Marco Vicario, starring Marcello Mastroianni and Laura Antonelli) is a classic study in how a reasonably good film can be ruined by poor dubbing. On the positive side, the actors are obviously mouthing English words, for the lip synchronization is extremely well matched. But any sense of credibility ends there. The fact that the actors can successfully mouth English words does not mean that they can voice English with the proper inflection. Thus, dubbing is used. The dubbed dialogue is obviously close-miked in a studio, and the English-speaking actors are very close to a microphone, so close that they have to speak softly to keep from distorting their voices as they are recorded. As a result, each speech gives the impression of being whispered. There is no attempt to achieve any sense of depth. Each voice is recorded at the same volume level regardless of the actor's distance from the camera. And there is no ambient sound during conversations, even when the actors talking are in a room almost full of other people. In some cases, the music is overdone in an attempt to kill off some of this ghostly silence. Although the dubbed voices are well cast (Mastroianni speaks for himself), the acting sounds like reading; the dialogue is flat, listless, and completely lacking in dramatic punch.

In contrast to the problems of *Wifemistress* is the excellent dubbing of *Das Boot* (the much longer director's cut is now also widely available with subtitles). The natural rhythms, cadence, and pitch of human voices really talking to each other give the dialogue dynamic life even without completely accurate synchronization with lip movement, and three-dimensional ambient sound conveys enough exciting information to make us forget that the film is dubbed.

Subtitles

When voice dubbing is not employed, foreign language films make use of subtitles. A concise English translation of the dialogue appears in printed form at the bottom of the screen while the dialogue is being spoken. Reading this translation gives us a fairly clear idea of what is being said by the actors as they speak in their native language.

The use of subtitles has several advantages over the use of voice dubbing. Perhaps most importantly, it does not interfere with the illusion of reality to the same degree as dubbing, even though the appearance of writing at the bottom of the screen is not completely natural to the film medium. But because the actors are not separated from their voices, their performances seem more real and human, as well as more powerful. Furthermore, by retaining the voices of the actors speaking in their native language, the subtitled film keeps the power, character, and unique emotional quality of the culture that produced it. The importance of this last point cannot be overestimated. To quote Renata Adler on the subject once more:

> One of the essential powers and beauties of the cinema is that it is truly international, that it makes language accessible in a highly special way. Only in movies can one hear foreign languages spoken and—by the written word in sub-titles—participate as closely as one ever will in a culture that is otherwise closed to one.[2]

Subtitles interfere less with the viewer's overall aesthetic experience of the film, less with the film's cultural integrity, and therefore less with its essential reality. Because much of the film's reality comes through to us intuitively even in a language we cannot understand, it is more important that the voice–image link remain intact than that we clearly understand every word of dialogue.

This is not to say that the use of subtitles does not have its disadvantages. One of the most obvious is that our attention is divided between watching the image and reading the subtitles. If we read slowly or if the editing is fast paced, we may miss important parts of the visual image and lose a sense of the film's continuity. Furthermore, most subtitles are so concise that they are oversimplified and incomplete. They are designed to convey only the most basic level of meaning and do not even attempt to capture the full flavor and quality of the dialogue in the original language.

Another problem often arises from the fact that subtitles are printed in white. The white letters appear on the bottom of the screen, and if the image behind the subtitles is white or light in color, the subtitles become completely illegible. This was the case in parts of *Tora, Tora, Tora!*, where the white subtitles often appeared against the white uniforms of the Japanese naval officers, and in Jean Renoir's great French film *The Rules of the Game*, where white subtitles were obliterated against light-colored costumes and landscapes. Currently, in fact, more and more international films are released in America (especially in their video versions) with easy-to-read yellow-highlighted subtitles.

Despite the disadvantages, the use of subtitles is still perhaps the best solution to the language barrier, especially in a slow-paced film that is edited in such a way that the dialogue can be read before the image changes. In a fast-paced film, where editorial cuts occurring at a very high frequency demand full attention to the image, voice dubbing may be the only answer. Luckily, our new video technology has now made it possible for us to choose either or both of these alternatives: Many laser discs and most DVDs offer menus from which viewers may choose to experience an international film in its own language, or via dubbing (often, into more than one language), or through subtitles (also into multiple languages).

Other Kinds of Foreignness

The language problem is not the only obstacle to understanding and appreciating international films. Other important cultural differences may limit or distract our response. A story about a Russian attempt to use *The Grapes of Wrath* as a propaganda tool against the United States in the late 1940s indicates that cultural differences have a profound effect on how a film is received. Russian officials viewing *The Grapes of Wrath* had seen in it an example of the exploitation of migrant workers by the capitalistic ranch owners. The officials started showing the film to Russian peasants in order to demonstrate how terrible life

Figure 15.1 Cultural Differences An American audience might have difficulty understanding the symbolic importance of class distinctions in a French film like *Grand Illusion* (top left) or an Italian film such as *Swept Away . . .* (top right). European audiences might have an equally difficult time fully understanding American films like *Bob & Carol & Ted & Alice* (bottom left) and *The Ice Storm* (bottom right).

in America was and to convince them of the evils of capitalism. The idea backfired when the peasants responded not with contempt for the capitalists but with envy for the Joads, who owned a truck and had the freedom to travel across the country.

When considering the difficulty of viewing films from another country, we might think of the problems a citizen of another country unfamiliar with the United States might have in understanding fine nuances in films like *Easy Rider* (hippie/drug culture of the 1960s), *Bob & Carol & Ted & Alice* (sexual revolution of the 1960s), or *The Ice Storm* (faddish lifestyle of 1970s New England) (Figure 15.1). Similarly, American audiences might have difficulty making sense of *Swept Away . . .*, an Italian film directed by Lina Wertmuller.

Swept Away . . . is a film narrative operating on several different levels. On a very basic level, it is an allegory about the never-ending battle between the sexes. The principal characters, a deckhand (Giancarlo Giannini) and a yacht owner's wife (Mariangela Melato), are shipwrecked on an island. The couple are opposites in a variety of ways. He is dark haired and dark skinned; she is fair skinned and blonde. He is a southern Italian and lower class; she is a northern Italian and upper class. Politically, she is a capitalist; he is a social democrat. As the male/female battle is waged, a very Italian class and political struggle is also being waged, with levels of meaning beyond the understanding of the average American viewer. Although we can catch the broad outlines of these symbolic levels, the fine nuances and subtleties are lost to us. This is not to say that we cannot enjoy the film, but we must face the fact that we are not really seeing quite the same film that a native Italian would see. The battle of the sexes and the love story it evolves into are universal and clearly understood. The north/south conflict and the political/class struggle are much less clear to an American, in the same way that an Italian would have difficulty understanding our basic myths of North/South differences, political parties, Black/White social problems, our particular American concept of social status, or American democracy.

Other cultural differences might cause us to misunderstand a movie because of its foreignness. If we fail to understand important customs, moral attitudes, or codes of behavior common to the culture producing the film, we certainly lose something. Sometimes an understanding of politics or economics is essential to full understanding; sometimes knowledge of the country's history may play a part. There may be subtle class distinctions or religious values that we must first understand.

Also, we must be aware of cultural symbols that are revealed in unusual clothes, hairstyle, or some other detail that makes a character seem different from the other characters. In *Wifemistress*, for example, a young woman stands out by sporting a very short haircut. She marries a naive young man who expects his wife to be a virgin and kills himself when he discovers she isn't. Does the haircut identify her with a certain lifestyle, as a modern, sexually liberated woman? (The picture is set in the pre-automobile days in Italy, probably in the late nineteenth or early twentieth century.) Many such clues to character may pass us by because we fail to understand the symbolic importance of seemingly insignificant differences.

Another factor that influences our responses is editing rhythm. The editing rhythms of international films differ from those of American films. Whether these filmic differences reflect the different pace of life in other countries would certainly make an interesting study. But, whatever the cause, there are differences. Italian films, for example, average about fifteen seconds per running shot, whereas American films average about five seconds per shot. This difference makes Italian films seem strange to American viewers, and there is danger that American viewers will be bored by the film without knowing why. In addition, a typical (sometimes stereotypical) observation about differences is that American films tend to be plot based whereas European films are usually character based.

The musical scores to many international films, especially Italian and French, seem overdone to Americans, a kind of musical overkill, and the music often seems dated, like American music of an earlier era. Swedish and Danish films use little or no music, which also takes some getting used to. In some cases, the music may be present to trigger responses that are particular to that culture, to which we simply have not been conditioned to respond.

Cultural Prejudice

"If you think this picture's no good, I'll put on a beard and say it was made in Germany. Then you'll call it art." So read a subtitle from Will Rogers's *The Ropin' Fool*, made in 1922. The statement reflects another problem in the analysis of the foreign language film. Because of a long-standing American sense of cultural inferiority, we are much too prone to bow down before almost anything European. Thus, in the 1950s, many European films that were not above the standards of the American grade B movies were lavishly praised by American critics and film buffs simply because they were made in France, Germany, or Italy. This is not to say that there were not some great films produced by these countries during that period, but a tendency existed to praise them all. At the same time, many American filmgoers turned a somewhat jaundiced eye toward the films produced in their own country. Any film made in Europe was automatically considered a highly serious and artistic statement, and the American film was generally ignored or dismissed as slick commercial trash.

The shoe also fits the other foot, for Europeans often appreciate certain aspects of American films that Americans cannot see or appreciate. For example, French critics were much more lavish in their praise of *Bonnie and Clyde* than were American critics. Jerry Lewis (as a director, especially) is also appreciated more by the French than by Americans. This phenomenon cannot easily be explained, but it is perhaps related to several factors. First, the language barrier may cause the audience to read things between the subtitles. At any rate, a more subjective and creative viewing is required when meanings are suggested rather than spelled out clearly. Also, a foreign director's cinematic style may have greater power and fascination because of its strangeness to viewers, who are not moved in the same way by the home-grown varieties they have become accustomed to. Surely this concept helps to explain, in part, the immense popularity in America of such exotic talent as the Spanish director Pedro Almodóvar (*Women on the Verge of a Nervous Breakdown*).

Because a film gives us a reflection of the culture and society that produced it, the overly positive reaction to an international film may actually be caused by the same kind of desire that makes us want to travel. Often we simply want a change of scene, a brief escape from the ordinary and the familiar, or we are curious about other people in faraway places, about their similarities to us and their differences. And sometimes we are simply fascinated by the different flavor, essence, or spirit of another country, by its dominant lifestyle. All of these factors play a part in our reaction to the foreign language film and serve to make our analysis and evaluation subjective.

Silent Films

Silent films present several problems for film analysis. First of all, we seldom have the opportunity to see silent films as they were intended to be seen; instead, we see copies that are dead, decayed, and corrupted, with much of their original brightness and impact lost forever.

Furthermore, many silent films are shown today without the musical accompaniment that normally was provided for the audiences of the silent era. Sometimes a complete score was distributed along with the film and played by a large orchestra, as was the case with *The Birth of a Nation* (1915). Usually, a single piano or organ player simply improvised as the film was shown. Such music filled a definite vacuum, and the silent film without it has a ghostly kind of incompleteness. Thus, many of the silent film's best moments lose their impact because their rhythmic qualities and emotional moods are not underscored as was intended.

Color in Silent Films

Modern audiences are also unaware of another lost quality of the silent film: its use of color. Since the beginning of motion picture history filmmakers and exhibitors have experimented with the use of color. Color was even used in magic-lantern slide shows by hand-painting the slides to be projected. When making that projected picture move finally became possible, it was only natural that attempts were made to color the image as well.

It soon became obvious that efforts to hand-color the large number of frames required for even a ten-minute film were tedious, painstaking, and expensive. In *Potemkin* (1925), the revolutionary battleship flag was photographed as white because it was intended to be painted red by hand. In fact, in the official print of the film, the flag was colored in red ink, individually in every frame in which it appears, by the hand of the director, Sergei Eisenstein. This limited use of color in an otherwise black-and-white film focused the audience's attention on the symbol of the entire revolution, the color red. Over five decades later, director Steven Spielberg created a similar effect in *Schindler's List*—but for a very different reason (see Chapter 7).

A much more important use of applied color during the era of silent films was **tinting,** coloring the film stock before the image was printed on it. Tinting created a two-color effect: black and whatever color the film had been tinted. Codes or formulas for the use of tinting quickly developed. One of the most common was the use of blue-tinted stock for night scenes. The film stock of the time was too slow to allow the filmmaker to shoot scenes at night or to get a clear image by underexposing daylight footage (later called day-for-night shooting). Thus, the blue tinting allowed the filmmaker to indicate that a scene was taking place at night but to film the scene in natural daylight. Because modern copies of the old silent films do not reproduce the tinting, we sometimes fail to catch the difference between a day and a night scene.

There were also other tinting codes and conventions. Some kind of logic usually dictated the tinting: Colors were chosen to suggest either a dominant color in the natural scene or a dominant mood or atmospheric effect. Thus, blue might be used to indicate night, but it could also be used to suggest a melancholy mood. Red could be used for a fire scene, but it could also suggest the bloodshed or violent emotion of a battle or the passion of romantic love. Exteriors might be tinted in bright yellow to suggest sunshine or in green to suggest lush forests, fields, or seascapes. Interiors could be tinted in sepia, which captured the essence of a room lit by gas lamps, oil lanterns, or a fireplace.

Pioneer director D. W. Griffith, often called the father of American film, used many of the tinting conventions in *Intolerance* (1916), but because nearly two thousand feet of the three-and-a-half-hour release print have been permanently lost, it is difficult to fully understand his use of color in the epic. However, we can get a clear idea of the effectiveness of tinted stock from Kevin Brownlow's restoration of Abel Gance's *Napoleon* (1927), which is available on videotape. In *Napoleon*, Gance did not stick with a rigid formula. Although he consistently used amber yellow for interiors and blue for night exteriors, he used both sepia and black and white for day exteriors. For separate battle scenes he employed both amber yellow and red.

Perhaps the most sophisticated use of color in the silent era was in the film that is often called the high point of Griffith's career, *Broken Blossoms* (1919). It is also possibly the first case of a film director attempting to capture an impressionistic painterly effect on film. Inspired by a series of watercolors of London's Chinatown by English artist George Baker, Griffith wanted to capture a dreamlike ambiance to match those paintings. Hendrik Sartov, Griffith's assistant cameraman, used his special skills in mood lighting and soft focus to create a highly impressionistic film out of "brooding London fogs, smoke-filled opium dens, and the petal-like delicacy of [a] boy's rooms."[3] The watercolor effect was achieved by tinting the entire film in soft pastels. Although Griffith's experimentation was the most artistic, the practice of tinting was by no means uncommon. By the 1920s, over 80 percent of all American features were tinted in some fashion by means of chemical baths.

Another technique of applying color to film was **toning**, adding dyes to the film emulsion itself so that the lines and tones of the image were colored. The combining of the toning process with tinted film stock yielded a two-color image. For example, by using purple toning on a pink stock, the filmmaker could create a purple sea against a pink sunset. Green toning on yellow stock could suggest a green meadow or a forest against a sunny yellow sky.

Tinting and toning produced a silent cinema much more expressive than we are able to experience today: Only a few films remain to represent a whole era of experimentation. There are copies of Edwin S. Porter's *The Great Train Robbery* (1903) that have hand-colored costumes, explosions, and gunfire, and some copies of *Intolerance* and Henry King's *Tol'able David* (1921) remain with sequences tinted in orange, green, or blue. Only Brownlow's restoration of Gance's *Napoleon* is readily available on videotape. Of films that were both tinted and toned, only random stills remain, and no copies of Eisenstein's red flag in *Potemkin* or Erich von Stroheim's *Greed* (1925) with the "golden touch" exist.

Language in Silent Films

Although the absence of music certainly creates a problem in appreciation, an even greater drawback is that we are not tuned in to silent films as a unique means of expression. Used to the levels of communication conveyed by the sound film, and conditioned to half-watch everything by the ever-present television, we have lost our ability to concentrate on purely visual elements. If we are to fully appreciate the silent film, we must master a new set of watching skills and become more sensitive and responsive to the language of the silent film, especially its most expressive vehicles: the human face and body.

By the last years of the silent film, the slightest body movement, gesture, or facial expression could express the deepest of passions or the tragedy of a human soul. The actors of the last silent films were able to speak clearly and distinctly to their audience, not through the voice but through a pantomime of eyes, mouth, hands, and body movement. This highly developed art of pantomime gave the silent film a means of expression that was self-sufficient and capable of conveying narrative visually, with a minimum of subtitles (Figure 15.2). Especially adept at this art were the three most celebrated film comedians of the silent period: Charlie Chaplin (*The Gold Rush*, 1925; *City Lights*, 1931), Buster Keaton (*Sherlock, Jr.*, 1924; *The General*, 1927), and Harold Lloyd (*Safety Last*, 1923).

The mass audience of the silent era mastered the art of reading faces, gestures, and body movements, but we must work hard to learn it. We are exposed to it in the modern film in reaction shots, but they are generally of short duration and often lack the subtlety of the greatest silent films. At its best, the language of the silent film could express ideas that words cannot express, as Béla Balázs passionately points out:

Figure 15.2 The Price of Perfection Without Words In this scene from *City Lights* (1931), a blind flower girl believes the tramp to be a tycoon, sells him a flower for his last coin, and keeps the change. Director/actor Charlie Chaplin had a problem figuring out why the blind girl would assume the tramp was a rich man. He finally solved it by having the tramp wander through heavy traffic and then walk onto the sidewalk through the back doors of a limousine parked at the curb. The blind girl, hearing the heavy door close, assumed that the "tycoon" was getting out of an expensive car. To achieve the exact effect he wanted, Chaplin shot 342 takes of this scene.

> The gestures of visual man are not intended to convey concepts which can be expressed in words, but such inner experience, such non-rational emotions which would still remain unexpressed when everything that can be told has been told. Such emotions lie in the deepest levels of the soul and cannot be approached by words that are mere reflections of concepts: just as our musical experiences cannot be expressed in rationalized concepts, what appears on the face and in facial expression is a spiritual experience which is rendered immediately visible without the intermediary of words.[4]

If we are to respond properly to silent films, we must become aware of the subtlety and the power of the silent-film language—a language capable of both silent soliloquy (a single face "speaking" the subtlest shades of meaning) and mute dialogue (a conversation that takes place through facial expressions and gestures). The silent-film language can, through the close-up, reveal not only what is visibly written on the face but also something appearing between the lines, and it is sometimes even capable of capturing contradictory expressions simultaneously on the same face.

The language of silent films is not restricted to the face. The hands, the arms, the legs, and the torso of the actor are also powerful instruments of expression. The language of the expressive face and body is perhaps more individual and personal than the language of words. As each actor in the sound film has distinct voice qualities that are unique to his or her means of verbal expression, each actor in the silent film had a personal style of facial and physical expression of emotion.

One of the most powerful means of expression involving the whole body is the actor's walk. In the silent film, because the walk is usually a natural and unconscious expression of emotion, it became an important aspect of each actor's unique screen personality or style. When used consciously for expression, it could convey such varying emotions as dignity, strong resolution, self-consciousness, modesty, and shame.

Because silent films are the product of another age, they must be judged, at least to some extent, as reflections of the society and culture of that day. Although these films adequately express the sensibility of their own times, anything old-fashioned usually strikes us as comic at first, until we become accustomed to the older fashion or style. Then the strangeness recedes into the background, allowing us to see the universal elements.

Full appreciation of the earliest silent films is often made difficult by the broad and exaggerated gesturing and grimacing of the actors, who were using the melodramatic techniques of the stage acting of that day. These unnatural and forced gestures and expressions seem ridiculous when seen in close-up. As the art of film acting evolved, actors realized the necessity for restraint in gesture and subtlety of expression, but a great many otherwise memorable films remain seriously handicapped by the older acting style (Figure 15.3).

Anyone who thinks the silent film was a primitive and crude art form compared to the modern sound film needs only to study two of the masterpieces of the late silent era: *Sunrise*, the hauntingly beautiful melodrama directed by F. W. Murnau, and *Napoleon*, French director Abel Gance's great epic (recently restored and shown in four-hour and five-hour-and-thirteen-minute versions). Both films were made in 1927 but seem modern in every respect. Both have dynamic, polished visual styles capable of communicating nuances of meaning without titles. Both are extremely sophisticated in acting styles, editing, composition, lighting, use of montages, creating the illusion of three-dimensionality, camera movement, superimposed images, and special effects. In fact, watching silent films of this caliber almost makes one wonder if the movies should ever have learned to talk.

All things considered, silent films have much to offer if we are willing to learn their special language and understand their own unique sophistication. We can observe a different kind of acting skill and see its evolution from overblown exaggeration to the restraint and subtlety of a polished art. We can learn to appreciate the effectiveness of narrative told clearly and quickly through purely pictorial means or with a minimum of subtitles. Alfred Hitchcock was especially impressed with the pictorial simplicity of silent film, which he considered the secret of its universal appeal:

Figure 15.3 Exaggerated Gestures and Expression In this scene from *The Wind* (1928—the last great year of silent films), Lillian Gish's gesture reflects the melodramatic and overblown stage acting style of the day.

> Go back to Chaplin. He once made a short film called *The Pilgrim.* The opening shot was the outside of a prison gate. A guard came out and posted a wanted notice. Next cut: a very tall, thin man coming out of a river, having had a swim. He finds that his clothes are missing and have been replaced with a convict's uniform. Next cut: a railroad station, and there coming towards the camera dressed as a parson with the pants too long is Chaplin.
>
> Now, there are three pieces of film, and look at the amount of story they told. These are the things that I think are so essential, especially when you send your film into a foreign country, Japan, Italy, or wherever. If you send a film which, as I have mentioned elsewhere, is "photographs of people talking" all the way through, and that gets to a foreign country with subtitles underneath, the poor audience will spend the entire evening reading. They won't have time to look at the pictures.[5]

The absence of dialogue can make us more sensitive to the film's visual rhythmic qualities. And, finally, we can learn to appreciate an art form that rose above the formidable barriers of language differences, for the silent film's greatest power is that it speaks a universal language.

Documentary Films

Documentary films constitute another special cinematic experience. Today, when we consider the documentary form, we acknowledge that it is both elemental *and* unique. In fact, even the earliest films emanated from what we could call the documentary urge of their creators, who wished, quite simply, to document life. But modern documentary films, as a type, have been the most underfinanced, underpublicized, underreviewed, and underattended of all movies widely available for viewing.

Certainly, the video revolution has helped to improve this situation. The critically acclaimed *Hoop Dreams* (1994), directed by Steve James, for example, has been seen on videotape or laserdisc by millions of enthusiastic viewers—regardless of whether they are fans of high school basketball (Figure 15.4).

Still, documentary films remain second only to foreign language films in their ability to alienate potential audiences merely through announcing themselves by name. It is basically an orphan genre in the eyes of the public; this is especially ironic in light of how immensely popular nonfiction works of literary art, such as biographies, have become in the United States since the 1960s. In recent decades, *The New York Times Book Review* has dealt with this popularity by splitting its bestseller list into fiction and nonfiction categories. The ever popular lists of top-grossing films, though, have not had to deal with a comparable problem because general viewers continue to avoid nonfictional works, in part, because they perceive them to be less enjoyable than fiction films. Likewise, in the annual Academy Awards competition, filmmakers themselves further minimize the documentary film's popularity and significance by their sometimes careless and irresponsible treatment of the selection process. Such movie bias is unfortunate, because the documentary film has the capability of achieving greatness. When it is working at its optimal level, the film type cannot only gather, articulate, and preserve "reality" but also be superbly entertaining.

If, though, as the British writer Desmond MacCarthy has famously declared, every biographer is "an artist under oath"[6] to observe and respect historical facts, then the filmmaker, by virtue of his or her innately powerful picture-making ability, must be even more aware of the documentarist's responsibility. Thus, too, the watcher of documentary films naturally comes to the screen with a different set of expectations than does the casual viewer of fictional movie narratives. In other words, more is demanded of the documentary form at the same time that its art is generally ignored.

The term *documentary* may itself be misleading, for it belies the complexity that potentially resides in the form. Since it was coined by the English filmmaker John Grierson in the 1930s to describe a type of film that focused on

Figure 15.4 Documentary Appeal *Hoop Dreams* (1994), one of the most popular documentary films of all time, records the lives of high school basketball players dreaming of making pro teams.

social realities, the word has broadened its connotations to include an emphasis on its aesthetic aspects. The most celebrated early practitioner of the art, Robert Flaherty, in such films as *Nanook of the North* (1922) and *Moana* (1925) (about Eskimo and Polynesian life, respectively), examined alien cultures from a sociological perspective. But Flaherty came to understand that moving pictures, even documentary ones, do not merely record objective reality. Like nonfiction literature, nonfiction film *inevitably* presents the subjective vision of its maker as well. Grierson, too, finally admitted clearly the genre's need to break free of the boundaries of didacticism, the need to teach a lesson, observing,

> The documentary idea, after all, demands no more than that the affairs of our time shall be brought to the screen in any fashion which strikes the imagination and makes observation a little richer than it was. At one level the vision may be journalistic; at another it may rise to poetry and drama. At another level, again, its artistic quality may lie in the mere lucidity of its exposition.[7]

Modern documentary makers have often reinterpreted "the affairs of our time," and they have, simultaneously, extended the traditional expeditions into alien cultures. Even the title of a recent, well-received documentary, for example, begins to illustrate not only this expansion but also a further reason for potential audience rejection of documentaries generally: *Sick: The Life & Death of Bob Flanagan, Supermasochist* (1997) presents an intimate examination of a physically ill man who loved pain and embraced it consciously and existentially. The film both repulses and fascinates, perhaps in equal measure. Also like much tamer documentaries, however, it reveals "true" psychological extremes that most fiction film narratives can merely attempt to imitate.

Erik Barnouw, in *Documentary: A History of the Non-Fiction Film*, maintains that "true documentarists have a passion for what they *find* in images and sounds—which always seems to them more meaningful than anything they can invent."[8] Barnouw defines the roles of the documentarist as those of prophet, explorer, chronicler, painter, and catalyst (among others), suggesting that the method by which such an artist decides to utilize these discovered "images and sounds" varies enormously. Although there are, in fact, many possibilities for the treatment of documentary evidence, two techniques exemplify the opposite ends of the spectrum: Either the filmmaker can present a clearly articulated thesis about the documentary's subjects, or the filmmaker can assiduously avoid all such insistence.

The first type, the thesis documentarist, is perhaps most graphically illustrated by the creator of propaganda. For instance, Leni Riefenstahl, the official filmmaker for Adolf Hitler, made movies on a grand scale, including *Triumph of the Will* (1935), documenting Hitler's rallies in Nuremberg in 1934, and *Olympia* (1936), recording at great length and in magnificent style the 1936 Berlin Olympics. At least in their original versions, these films attempted to leave no doubt in the viewer's mind about the worthiness of the Third Reich. Although much critical controversy exists about the true effects of such propaganda, the intentions of these two films are self-evident. Nevertheless, Riefenstahl herself, although sometimes admitting a certain naiveté, has steadfastly maintained that her interests were purely artistic, not political. Interestingly, she most vociferously asserts her innocence in a film—Ray Muller's *The Wonderful, Horrible Life of Leni Riefenstahl* (1993)—that is, in turn, an example of a thesis documentary.

Other excellent models of this type include Michael Moore's *Roger & Me* (1989), which examines the relationship between General Motors and its former workers in Flint, Michigan, and Barbara Kopple's Oscar-winning *Harlan County, U.S.A.* (1977), which portrays the seemingly eternal union struggles of mine workers in eastern Kentucky. Although Kopple's later *American Dream* (1989), also an Academy Award winner, seems by comparison more complicated in its narrative point of view than *Harlan County, U.S.A.*, it nevertheless demonstrates obviously the pain and losses of all parties involved in a Hormel meat-packing company strike in Minnesota. Roger Ebert writes that, in *American Dream*, "the people . . . are so real they make most movie characters look like inhabitants of the funny page."[9]

The antithetical type of documentary tries very hard to avoid judging its subject, attempting instead simply to describe it. Among its best examples—at least outside the confines of experimental films like *Koyaanisqatsi* (1983)—are the works of Frederick Wiseman. In such documentaries as *Public Housing* (1997), about the Ida B. Wells development in Chicago, and *Titicut Follies* (1967), about the inmates of a mental hospital in Massachusetts, this prolific documentarist has used the **direct cinéma** method of shooting, giving his viewers an objective view and understanding of worlds that they are rarely permitted to enter. Erik Barnouw has noted, however, that

> one of the problems hanging over observer-documentarists was the extent to which the presence of the camera influenced events before it. Some practitioners—[Stephen] Leacock, [Louis] Malle—worried about this. Others—[Arthur] Mayles, Wiseman tended to minimize it. Some filmmakers, notably Jean Rouch, held still another view. Rouch maintained that the presence of the camera made people act in ways truer to their nature than might otherwise be the case.[10]

Michael Apted's remarkable series of films about the developing lives of British children—*7 Plus 7, 21, 28 Up* (1985), culminating, most recently, in *35 Up* (1991)—seems to demonstrate the truth of Rouch's theory, especially in Apted's later interviews. There, he uses a **cinéma vérité** technique, which is supposedly "objective unstaged, non-dramatized, non-narrative," but nevertheless "no less real" than *direct cinéma*.[11] Sometimes, though, his very presence seems to incite action from his subjects, rather than merely to observe and record it.

Most documentary filmmakers use a mixture of these extreme approaches. One of the best-received documentaries in recent years, Terry Zwigoff's *Crumb* (1994), seems, in the manner of its editing, "thesis positive" in its sympathetic approach to famous cartoonist R. Crumb and his eccentric family (Figure 15.5). Yet, finally, the viewer is freely left to make his or her own judgments.

No documentarist, however, surpasses Errol Morris in his insistence upon injecting this venerable genre with a very modernist ambiguity. Beginning with *Gates of Heaven* (1978), which Roger Ebert calls "one of the greatest films ever made,"[12] and working rather slowly through five other carefully constructed non-fiction films, Morris has established himself as the most visible artist documentarist. Watching *Gates of Heaven*, the saga of two California pet cemeteries and their owners and clients, we are certain of its enormous good humor, but we are less sure about what attitudes we are to construct from it. *The Thin Blue Line* (1988) is famous for having been the catalyst that freed a man wrongly convicted of murder, but in its artful reconstructions of the crime and its utilization of an eerie Philip Glass score, among other techniques, the film's intentions are ultimately unclear.

Figure 15.5 A Documentary Mix The eccentric appeal of the underground cartoonist R. Crumb and his strange family is perfectly captured in the documentary film *Crumb* (1994), even though viewers are left to draw their own conclusions about the filmmakers' intentions.

"Constructed" documentaries such as *The Thin Blue Line* have always been useful for the information they present about the past. Two other recent works admirably illustrate the type: *When We Were Kings* (1996) and *Theremin* (1993). The former examines the heavyweight title fight between Muhammad Ali and George Foreman in Zaire, twenty-one years after its original photography; the latter celebrates the inventor of electronic music. *Theremin*, like Morris's *The Thin Blue Line*, also solves a mystery: It finally explains, after decades of uncertainty, the disappearance of its title character, Professor Leon Theremin.

Two other films by Errol Morris contain more mixtures of his characteristic earnestness and humor: *A Brief History of Time* (1992) scrutinizes theoretical physicist Stephen Hawking; and *Fast, Cheap & Out of Control* (1997) is an intense meditation upon the subtly interconnected lives of a lion trainer, a topiary artist, a rodent scientist, and a robot designer. In these works, and in *Vernon, Texas* (1981) and *Dr. Death* (1999) Morris continues to extend his general desire to make the documentary form as complex and fascinating as the fiction feature film.

One method other documentary filmmakers have frequently utilized to add complexity and fascination to their work is to star in their own movies. Sometimes, a double narrative occurs through their examining stories within stories.

In a review of Kevin MacDonald and Mark Cousins's *Imagining Reality: The Faber Book of the Documentary*, Ian Christie observes that

> Al Pacino's recent Shakespearean documentary, *Looking for Richard*, belongs to a distinctive vein of cinematic non-fiction, in which the film-maker appears on-screen and becomes, in effect, the protagonist of a drama—which is the making of the film we are watching.[13]

Christie also mentions other excellent models for this type, including Moore's *Roger & Me* and Orson Welles's *F for Fake* (1974), and, at least in spirit, he might well have added *Hearts of Darkness: A Filmmaker's Apocalypse* (1991) and *Marlene* (1984), even though these two films' show business subjects did not actually direct the works. *Hearts of Darkness*, directed by Fax Bahr and George Hickenlooper (with the valuable assistance of Eleanor Coppola, who had shot documentary footage of her husband in the Philippines), records Francis Ford Coppola's struggle in making *Apocalypse Now*. *Marlene* is actor Maximilian Schell's attempt to let us see (in the sense of "understand") as well as hear the aging Marlene Dietrich, who refused to be photographed for it and would only allow audiotaped interviews. Both films were enriched and also made more problematically complicated by the direct (in Dietrich's case) or subtle (in Coppola's) manipulation of the filmmakers by their subjects.*

In 1998 Barbara Kopple released *Wild Man Blues*, a *cinéma vérité* account of clarinet player Woody Allen's tour of European concerts with his Dixieland jazz band, his sister, and his soon-to-be-wife, whom he introduces facetiously at one point as "the notorious Soon-Yi Previn." Although Allen specifies clearly that he intends the film's audience to be primarily interested in his music, he repeatedly undercuts this stance by providing spontaneous one-liners, which Kopple and her crew eagerly record. In the documentary's final, splendid scene, which takes place back in New York in the apartment of Allen's aged parents, the comedian/filmmaker, through calculated quips, also helps Kopple create a hilarious, incendiary ending for her film (Figure 15.6).

It is noteworthy that most of the accomplished documentaries mentioned above are also *about* filmmakers and the art of cinematic illusion. And it should not surprise us that many directors of fiction films have dreamed of creating documentary works. For example, Nicca Ray, the daughter of Nicholas Ray, who directed *Rebel Without a Cause*, starring James Dean, tells us that her father's fondest hope, late in his life, was to complete a documentary.[14] Other directors who do not seize the opportunity to work in the form in its ill-financed state—who, instead, continue to make fiction films—nevertheless find ways to play out their documentary urge. Clint Eastwood, for instance, injects a documentary

*A magnificent precedent for *Hearts of Darkness* exists in Les Blank's documentary *Burden of Dreams* (1982), which chronicles the director Werner Herzog's obsession with making the film *Fitzcarraldo*, itself an examination of obsessive behavior.

Figure 15.6 ***Wild Man Blues*** Barbara Kopple, a director best known for documenting labor disputes in America (*Harlan County, U.S.A.* and *American Dream*), shifted to show business in 1998 for her energetic record of filmmaker Woody Allen's clarinet-playing tour of Europe.

sensibility into his lesser-known films such as *Bird* (1988), about legendary jazz saxophonist Charlie Parker, and *White Hunter, Black Heart* (1990), a fictionalized version of the filming of John Huston's classic *The African Queen.* Ironically though, Eastwood seems to reject that urge in the opening credits of *Midnight in the Garden of Good and Evil* (1997), where the filmmakers unaccountably change the film's source from "nonfiction book" to "novel."

Perhaps the most famous use of documentary elements in recent fiction film has involved James Cameron's techniques in *Titanic* (1997). In this film, the director's own documentary urge was so intense that he created new diving and photographic equipment—at extraordinary expense for his studio—to achieve textural (if not plot) authenticity by recording and presenting the eighty-five-year-old wreck of his subject.[15] *Titanic,* then, like so many other fiction films, pays the ultimate compliment to the documentary form: Cameron uses the real thing to inform his reel thing.

Animated Feature Films

In the United States, the stereotypic modern audience for animated cartoons has been a theater full of screaming kids. Thus, except when they have been obligated to escort their families, the theory goes, most adults have avoided the form. Despite this popular conception, however, the very best feature-length animated films have seldom been created exclusively for children—even in the golden age of Walt Disney's prime productions. For many decades the magical art and wit of these works have courted and deserved the attention of perceptive viewers of all ages. Many observers would say that, during the last several years of the twentieth century, the art form has been rejuvenated. And now, in all three of the primary types of animation (drawing, stop motion, and computer generated), the central aim of artists is to engage a decidedly adult audience.

Like the puppet shows from which they evolved, animated films have long been seriously embraced by the world of international art. By contrast, American culture has too often relegated them to the trivial category of childish cinematic pleasures. In fact,

> the first animations were also the first moving pictues. Victorian optical toys such as the zoetrope . . . debuted in the 1830's as conversation pieces for parlors . . . [and] . . . normally contained drawings depicting succeeding states of an action that, when viewed in rapid motion, produced an illusion of movement.[16]

Later in the nineteenth century, the illusions produced through these simple drawings of early animation developed into those of still photographs being manipulated swiftly, either mechanically or via projection. As the cinema progressed along more or less realistic lines, though, such animation pioneers as Winsor McCay, a New York newspaper cartoonist best known for his *Gertie the Dinosaur* (1914), began to explore possibilities within the fantasy worlds of animated film. By 1928, when Walt Disney created *Steamboat Willie* (and first introduced the world to a talking Mickey Mouse), animated shorts, shown before feature films, were already being produced in abundance by such artists as Max Fleischer (creator of Betty Boop) and Walter Lantz (Woody Woodpecker). Later the Warner Brothers luminaries Chuck Jones, Tex Avery, and Fritz Freleng (among many others) gave audiences the energetic antics of a whole stable of animated personalities, including Bugs Bunny and Porky Pig.

But it was not until the mid-1930s that Walt Disney became obsessed with the idea of entertaining viewers with animated films that were themselves the main show. Premiering in late 1937, Disney's *Snow White and the Seven Dwarfs* set rigorously high standards that today still guide animation artists. In the Disney studio's watershed year of 1940, both *Pinocchio* and *Fantasia* appeared (Figure 15.7). These now-classic works were followed during the next two decades by a series of popular animated entertainments (including *Dumbo*, *Cinderella*, *Alice in Wonderland*, *Peter Pan*, and *Lady and the Tramp*), whose stories frequently originated in well-known literary narratives. The least-accomplished of these movies appeared to be targeted more progressively at younger audiences.

After Disney's death in 1966, his studio continued to make drawn animated films, but the creative energy lessened, and the company's focus shifted to

Figure 15.7 Animated Models Walt Disney set towering standards for animated films with his first feature, *Snow White and the Seven Dwarfs* (1937), and he continued to ameliorate his art with two masterpieces released in 1940: *Fantasia* and *Pinocchio.*

producing live-action films. Then, for the child in all of us again, Disney animation was given new life (as the word *animation* itself is defined) in 1989 by *The Little Mermaid*, which led an astonishing string of new musical animated features. Two years later, *Beauty and the Beast* emerged from an artistic process that utilized computers to assist in the conventional drawing techniques, and the film won an Academy Award nomination for Best Picture, the first such accolade for an animated feature. Like these two films, the best ones that followed—including *The Lion King* (Figure 15.8), *Aladdin*, and *Mulan*—continued the classic Disney conventions: bold visuals, shrewd scripts, and both thematic universality and surprise that we find in all great films, animated or otherwise. Disney's new version of *Fantasia*, called *Fantasia 2000*, incorporates segments from the 1940 version with newly created ones (and, according to Disney executives, was the first feature film to premier in the giant-screen IMAX theaters). Meanwhile, however, critical judgments about the Disney films overall continue to focus on

Figure 15.8 Disney Redux Although the Walt Disney Studio's feature-length animated films seemed to lessen in both quantity and quality after Disney's death, the company rejuvenated itself during the past decade with the release of several modern classics, including *The Lion King* (1994), which combined traditional drawn animation with computer-assisted artwork.

Pinocchio as the finest cinematic achievement in animation. Writing about the film for his "Great Movies" series, for example, Roger Ebert observes,

> The power of the film is generated, I think, because it is really about something. It isn't just a concocted fable or a silly fairy tale, but a narrative with deep archetypal reverberations. ("Cinderella," "Beauty and the Beast" and "The Lion King" share that quality, and so do the scenes involving Dumbo and his mother.)
>
> Once we've grown up and learned, or ignored, the lessons of the film, why does it continue to have such appeal? It may be because of the grace of the drawing. Later Disney films would have comparable skill, but not the excitement of discovery. Is it possible to sense, through thousands of individual drawings by dozens of different artists, a collective creative epiphany? I think so. Disney's loyal animators had been there in the early days when Mickey Mouse cartoons were patronized by Hollywood as kid stuff from a dinky side-street shop. They must have known they were making something great. Their joy saturates the screen.[17]

Almost from its earliest use, drawn animation encouraged the mixing of live action and artwork. Thus, the intricacies of this technique have, over the years, enabled Gene Kelly to dance on-screen with the jaunty cartoon creature Jerry

Figure 15.9 British Magician A modern master of stop-motion animation is Nick Park, whose short films such as *The Wrong Trousers,* starring Wallace and his dog Gromit, provide dry, unsentimental, but affecting humor.

the mouse (*Anchors Aweigh*, 1945) and, in one of the most complex utilizations to date, Bob Hoskins to interact with a whole universe of toon stars (*Who Framed Roger Rabbit*, 1988). Computers have now facilitated such activity far beyond the imaginations of animation pioneers, however.

Along with drawn animation, a second type of animated film developed on a parallel track: stop-motion animation. During this process, small objects or puppetlike figures are moved repeatedly in minute increments while being photographed. Past masters of the technique have included such legendary special-effects animators (working in live-action fantasy films) as George Pal (*When Worlds Collide*), Willis O'Brien (*King Kong* and the original *Mighty Joe Young*), and Ray Harryhausen (*Mighty Joe Young* and *Clash of the Titans*). Contemporary artists of stop-motion animation who best command our imaginations are the British animator Nick Park and the American Henry Selick.

Park, most celebrated for his Oscar-winning films featuring the character Wallace and his dog Gromit—*A Grand Day Out*, *The Wrong Trousers* (Figure 15.9), *A Close Shave*—has said that he personally gets "turned off" by certain characteristic elements in the new Disney animated musical films: "the sanitized stories and the sickly-sweet characters."[18] And Park himself projects a droll, unsentimental sense of humor through his figures.

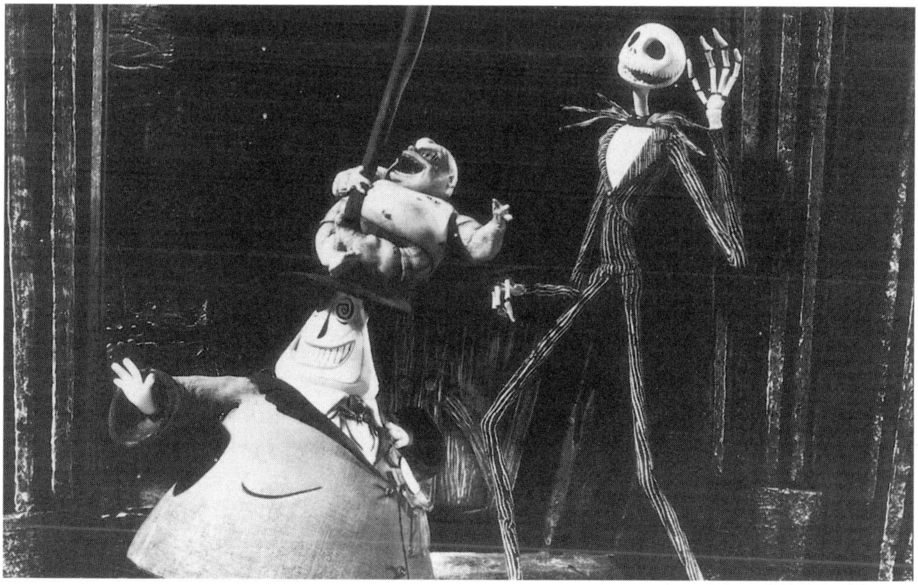

Figure 15.10 American Magician The stop-motion animator Henry Selick, along with the director Tim Burton, his creative partner, has amazed, delighted, and frightened audiences of all ages with *The Nightmare Before Christmas* (pictured) and *James and the Giant Peach.*

Henry Selick directed both Tim Burton's *The Nightmare Before Christmas* (Figure 15.10) and *James and the Giant Peach*—the former a stop-action film that is wholly original and sometimes immensely frightening in its images, the latter an adaptation of Roald Dahl's popular children's book that begins in live action and segues impressively into stop-action animation before returning to live action at its end. *James and the Giant Peach* pulls no punches with its presentation of violence and its treatment of monumental fears (abandonment, for example) that are no less vividly real for adults than for children.

George Miller's charming *Babe* (1995), nominated for a Best Picture Oscar, and its critically acclaimed, poorly released, and little-seen sequel, *Babe: Pig in the City* (1998), both combine live action, puppets (in the form of intricate animatronic devices), and computer animation. Public reaction to the comic violence involving animals in *Pig in the City* has ensured that its small and primary audience will most likely be adults, not children.

Throughout such modern animation features as *Who Framed Roger Rabbit, The Nightmare Before Christmas, James and the Giant Peach*, and *Babe: Pig in the City*, a certain dark, sometimes even macabre, humor abides. A similar "adult" amusement has also become a staple in the third and latest type of animated feature film, which is generated solely by art filtered through computer technology. This process often appears almost to synthesize the smooth movement of drawn images and the plastic surfaces of stop-motion puppets. The first such film, 1995's *Toy Story*, directed by John Lasseter for his Pixar studio, contains

Figure 15.11 Contemporary Animation Pioneer The first wholly computer-generated animated feature, Pixar's *Toy Story* (1995), was directed by John Lasseter and starred Woody, shown here trying to make an important announcement to his comic adversary Buzz Lightyear.

the sort of gentle satire that we have come to expect in children's films (Figure 15.11). But it also presents a sequence in which a child plays with dolls that have been mutilated and reassembled in monstrous new shapes. During 1998, two computer-animated films with remarkably similar subject matter were released: a second work from Lasseter and Pixar (now owned by Disney) called *A Bug's Life;* and *Antz,* from the new Dreamworks studio. Although *A Bug's Life* gives viewers a sweeter, gentler story and, in its visual qualities, seems to be aimed toward children, both it and *Antz* display comic sensibilities that are clearly meant to appeal to adults. The denizens of the insect carnival in *A Bug's Life* (Figure 15.12), for example, are crafty, not merely cute; the hero of *Antz,* voiced by Woody Allen, must surely baffle most small children with his nebulous chat about passionate trysts and psychiatrists.

Finally, if we seek proof that contemporary animated feature films now invite adults to be a major part of their audience, we need only turn to *The Prince of Egypt,* another Dreamworks production (Figure 15.13). Here is a movie that takes as its subject one of the most archetypal narratives of world myth (not to mention Judeo-Christian scripture) and, in addition, envisions its Moses-led characters through immensely stylized and sophisticated visual modes (including elongated El Greco faces). Further, we immediately recognize that the animated feature has grown up when its makers, the Dreamworks team of Steven Spielberg, Jeffrey Katzenberg, and David Geffen, flatly refuse to authorize any miniature toy or product advertising tie-ins with fast food chains. Katzenberg summarized their attitude: "We tried to be uncompromising here—there's nothing cute and adorable in the film. In other words, we didn't make a camel funny."[19]

Figure 15.12 Insect OutTakes John Lasseter's second feature, *A Bug's Life,* was released in 1998 by Disney. Its success in theaters in early 1999 led to its becoming the "world's first DVD created directly from the digital source." Although the film is thus available in a sharp, clear wide-screen version, its Pixar animators were also able to improve the pan-and-scan version by using computer technology to manipulate images to fit the full television screen. Among the cleverest delights of the DVD (clearly addressed to adult viewers) are two sets of hilarious "outtakes" that theater audiences were able to experience only by paying admission to two separate releases of the movie.

Figure 15.13 Animation Royalty After rushing its insect-inspired feature *Antz* into release ahead of its competitor's *A Bug's Life,* Dreamworks also produced *The Prince of Egypt,* "a grand experiment . . . of feature animation" that, according to many observers, heralded a bold, new, grown-up era in the art form.

Film reviewer Richard Corliss has described *The Prince of Egypt* as "a grand experiment, a crusade to expand the frustratingly narrow boundaries of feature animation."[20] And Roger Ebert welcomes the film as revolutionary in its aim, scope, and artistic achievements:

> "The Prince of Egypt" is one of the best looking animated films ever made. It employs computer-generated animation as an aid to traditional techniques, rather than as a substitute for them, and we sense the touch of human artists in the vision behind the Egyptian monuments, the lonely desert vistas, the thrill of the chariot race, and personalities of the characters. This is a film that shows animation growing up and embracing more complex themes, instead of chaining itself in the category of children's entertainment.[21]

Historically Important Films

Another serious problem facing the modern viewer is the analysis and evaluation of historically important films. This type of film, which proves to be significant in the years following its release because of the innovations in cinematic technique or style that it introduces, must not be approached with the same expectations we have of the modern film. In many cases, historically important films are effective neither aesthetically nor as an immediate sensual experience. Such films must be viewed and evaluated in terms of their historical context.

To place the historically significant film in the proper perspective, we should consider it from at least two different viewpoints. First, we should be familiar with films produced prior to the film being viewed, so that we can see it in relationship to what was done before. In this way we will be able to appreciate the innovations in style or cinematic technique that the film introduced and understand the significance of the film's contribution to the development of the medium. Next, we should compare it to the modern film, to determine which of its innovations in style or technique have been assimilated by contemporary filmmakers.

It is in comparison to the modern film that historically important films suffer most, for they are likely to seem timeworn and full of cinematic clichés. Ironically, often the more timeworn and out-of-date a film of this type seems, the more significant it is historically, for such an effect generally means that the film's innovations have become standard practice.

Some historically important films, even those that are most frequently imitated, somehow retain their original power and freshness. When such films prove themselves to be great in their own right and appeal equally to viewers in any time period, they are known not only as historic groundbreakers or milestones but as classics, the power of which no amount of imitation can really destroy.

Sometimes we may encounter a false classic, a film that retains its appeal over a fairly long period of time and then loses it because other works in the

Figure 15.14 Historic Native American Cinema *Smoke Signals,* a dramatic comedy written by poet and fiction writer Sherman Alexie and directed by Chris Eyre, became, in 1998, the first feature film created exclusively by Native American artists.

medium suddenly surpass it. According to Dwight Macdonald, this is what happened to Jean Cocteau's *The Blood of a Poet* (1930): "It suddenly showed its age, looking mannered rather than stylized, more affected than affecting, terribly thin in content and slow in movement."[22]

A very different type of historical significance may be seen in films that are so unusual that the innovations they introduce are never really imitated or assimilated. Such a film is *The Cabinet of Dr. Caligari* (1919), which Macdonald calls "a unique anti-movie that came close to perfection by breaking all the rules."[23] Such a film may be interesting to study because of its one-of-a-kindness or because of the rebellious spirit that produced it, but its value as part of any evolutionary study of the medium is limited, for it is a steppingstone to nowhere.

Finally, some films are immediately historically important, not necessarily because of their stylistic innovations, but in light of their breaking new ground for subjects, themes, and minority representation. In this category, then, fall such diverse American works as the African American filmmaker Oscar Micheaux's *Body and Soul* (1925), starring Paul Robeson, and the first "all Native American" film production, Sherman Alexie and Chris Eyre's *Smoke Signals* (1998) (Figure 15.14).

Figure 15.15 Energetic Ennui In Danny Boyle's social problem film *Trainspotting,* Ewan McGregor and his mates dive with dirty vigor into the drug-infested underground of Edinburgh, Scotland.

Social Problem Films

Social problem films are perhaps even more difficult to evaluate than films of historical importance. The problem presented by both, however, is essentially the same—becoming outdated or timeworn. The aging of the social problem film can occur very rapidly; the film can become not only dated but completely irrelevant in just a few years. This happens when the problem attacked by the film is eliminated or corrected. In a sense the social problem film can enjoy a long life only by failing in its purpose, for its impact is generally lost as soon as the problem portrayed no longer exists. This is especially true of a film that treats a narrow, topical, and very contemporary problem. The more general the problem, the more widespread its effects, and the more resistant it is to reform, the longer is the life span of the social problem film directed against it. As long as the social problem exists, the film has relevance. Thus, a film such as *The Snake Pit* (1948), starring Olivia de Havilland, will retain much of its impact as long as our society continues to stigmatize mental illness and its treatment. And, in the face of continued drug and alcohol abuse within our culture, Otto Preminger's *The Man With the Golden Arm* (1955) and Billy Wilder's *The Lost Weekend* (1945), though dated, continue to disturb and shock us despite more recent and graphic takes on the problems, including *Trainspotting* (1996), *Permanent Midnight* (1998), and *Leaving Las Vegas* (1995) (Figure 15.15).

Once in a while, if a social problem film is artistically done, it becomes more than a mere vehicle to encourage social reform, and it may outlive the problem it attacks. Strong, memorable characters and a good story give social problem films durability even after the specific problem dealt with no longer has relevance. In its specific references, of course, John Ford's magnificent adaptation of John Steinbeck's *The Grapes of Wrath* (1940) is a perfect example of such a film.

Questions

On Foreign Language or International Films

1. Which method is used to translate the dialogue into English—subtitles or voice dubbing? Was this the best way to solve the language problem for this particular film? Why or why not?
2. If subtitles are used, how well do they seem to capture the essence of what the actors are saying? Are the subtitles ever difficult to read because of light-colored backgrounds? Is the film's pace slow enough to allow for both reading the subtitles and following the image?
3. If voice dubbing is used, how closely do the English words spoken on the soundtrack correspond to the mouth and lip movements of the foreign actors? Do you get used to the fact that the voices are dubbed, or is the dubbing a constant irritation? How well suited are the voice qualities and accents on the soundtrack to the actors with whom they are matched? Does the overall emotional quality of the English translation match the facial expressions and gestures of the foreign actors?
4. How good is the quality of the dubbing technique? Are the voice-actors obviously reading their lines close to a microphone in a studio so that they seem to be whispering in your ear? Does the volume of spoken lines vary according to the distance of the actor from the camera? Is ambient sound present? Is music used as an unnatural filler?
5. How does the foreign director's style differ from American cinematic styles? What effect does this have on your response to the film?
6. How does the film reflect the culture of the country that produced it? How is this culture or lifestyle different from what we know in America? How is it similar? What different aspects of this foreign culture do you find most fascinating, and why?
7. In what ways does the film transcend its foreignness to communicate things that are universal? What aspects of the film are so uniquely foreign that they are beyond your understanding?

On Silent Films

1. Is the acting style melodramatic, with broad and exaggerated gestures and facial expressions, or is it subtle, refined, even understated?
2. What is unique about the acting styles of each of the major actors? Which actors depend most on facial expression, and which ones depend on gestures and body movements?

3. How many different emotions are expressed by actors through their walks? Which actors in the film have unique walks that become part of their acting style and the total personality they project?
4. How effective is the film in telling its story without words? How much does the film need to rely on subtitles to make the action absolutely clear?
5. How sophisticated are the visual techniques used in the film compared to modern techniques? If the film were being made today (still silent), what modern visual techniques could be used to improve it? In what ways is the visual style old-fashioned? How much of this old-fashioned quality is due to technical limitations of the time?

On Documentary Films

1. Has the documentary director apparently attempted to create a thesis type of film? If so, what clearly articulated statement does the film make? Do all elements of the filmmaking clearly support this thesis?
2. Has the *direct cinéma* or the *cinéma vérité* technique of shooting been used? In other words, has the presence of the documenting camera altered reality —or heightened it?
3. If the film obviously tries to avoid presenting a thesis, what methods has the director chosen to ensure "objectivity"? Has factual material been presented chronologically or thematically, without editing or artful rearrangement?
4. Does the documentary film reinforce the stereotypes about this form, or does it seem to suggest, through its example, that the genre can be as vital, entertaining, and complex as fiction films?

On Animated Feature Films

1. What type of animation does the feature employ—drawn, stop motion, or computer generated? Would one of the other types have been more appropriate for conveying the film's subject matter and themes?
2. Watch one of the films listed in "Films for Study" (but not mentioned in the chapter discussion) and then identify its ostensibly intended audience. Is the work mainly aimed at children? If so, what elements would likely tend to alienate adult viewers? If not, what elements make the film primarily interesting to grownups?

On Historically Important Films

1. What innovations in cinematic style or technique did this film introduce? Which of these innovations are still being used in the modern film?
2. Does the film seem crude, timeworn, or full of clichés when compared to the modern film, or is it still fresh and powerful? What specific elements or qualities in the film lead you to your answer?

3. What is the film's contribution to the overall development of the motion picture? What would the modern film be like if the innovations introduced by this film had never been made? How have the innovations introduced by this film been polished and refined in the modern film?

On Social Problem Films

1. Does the social problem attacked by the film have a universal and timeless quality, affecting all people in all time periods, or is it restricted to a relatively narrow time and place?
2. Is the film powerful enough in terms of a strong storyline, enduring characters, good acting, artistic cinematography, and so on, to outlive the social problem it is attacking? In other words, how much of the film's impact is caused by its relevance to a current problem and its timing in attacking the problem?
3. If the immediate social problems on which the film focuses were permanently corrected tomorrow, what relevance would the film have to the average viewer twenty years from now?

Films for Study

Foreign Language or International Films

Belle de Jour (1967-France/Italy)
Belle Epoque (1992-Spain)
The Bicycle Thief (1947-Italy)
Children of Paradise (1945-France)
Cinema Paradiso (1988-Italy/France)
The Conformist (1971-Italy/France/West Germany)
Das Boot (1981-West Germany)
8½ (1963-Italy)
The Garden of the Finzi-Continis (1971-Italy)
Grand Illusion (1937-France)
Hiroshima, Mon Amour (1959-France/Japan)
La Dolce Vita (1960-Italy)
La Strada (1954-Italy)
Last Year at Marienbad (1961-France/Italy)
Life Is Beautiful (1998-Italy)
Like Water for Chocolate (1992-Mexico)
Persona (1966-Sweden)
Raise the Red Lantern (1991-China/Taiwan/Hong Kong)
Rashomon (1950-Japan)
Red (1994-Switzerland/France/Poland)
Rules of the Game (1939-France)
Seven Beauties (1976-Italy)
The Seventh Seal (1957-Sweden)
Swept Away . . . (1975-Italy)
The Thief (1997-Russia)
Two Women (1960-Italy)
The Wedding Banquet (1993-U.S./Taiwan)
Wild Reeds (1994-France)
Woman in the Dunes (1964-Japan)

Silent Films

The Birth of a Nation (1915)
Broken Blossoms (1919)
City Lights (1931)
The General (1927)
The Gold Rush (1925)
Greed (1925)
Intolerance (1916)
The Last Laugh (1924-Germany)
Modern Times (1936)
Napoleon (1927-France)
Nosferatu (1922-Germany)
Safety Last (1923)
Sherlock, Jr. (1924)
Sunrise (1927)
The Wind (1928)

Documentary Films

American Dream (1989)
Anne Frank Remembered (1995-Britain)
Best Boy (1979)
A Brief History of Time (1992-U.S./Britain)
Brother's Keeper (1992)
Burden of Dreams (1992)
The Celluloid Closet (1995)
Common Threads (1989)
Cousin Bobby (1991)
Crumb (1994)
Fast, Cheap & Out of Control (1997)
Frank and Ollie (1995)
Gates of Heaven (1978)
Harlan County, U.S.A. (1977)
Hearts of Darkness (1991)
Hoop Dreams (1994)
Koyaanisqatsi (1983)
Let's Get Lost (1989)
The Line King (1996)
Looking for Richard (1996)
Marlene (1984-Germany)
Mr. Death: The Rise and Fall of Fred A. Leuchter, Jr. (1999)
Olympia (1936-Germany)
Public Housing (1997)
Roger & Me (1989)
Sherman's March (1986)
Streetwise (1984)
Theremin (1993)
The Thin Blue Line (1988)
35 Up (1991-Britain)
Titicut Follies (1967)
Triumph of the Will (1935-Germany)
Vernon, Texas (1981)
When We Were Kings (1996)
Wild Man Blues (1998)
Woodstock (1970)

Animated Feature Films

The Adventures of Mark Twain (1985)
Akira (1988-Japan)
Aladdin (1992)
Alice in Wonderland (1951)
An American Tale (1986)
Anastasia (1997)
Anchors Aweigh (1945)
Antz (1998)
Babe (1995-Australia)
Babe: Pig in the City (1998-Australia)
Beauty and the Beast (1991)
Beavis and Butt-head Do America (1996)
A Bug's Life (1998)
Cinderella (1950)
Clash of the Titans (1981)
A Close Shave (1995)
Dumbo (1941)
The Emperor's Nightingale (1948-Czechoslovakia)
Fantasia (1940) and *Fantasia 2000* (1999)
Fritz the Cat (1972)
A Grand Day Out (1989)
The Hunchback of Notre Dame (1996)
James and the Giant Peach (1996)
King Kong (1933)
Lady and the Tramp (1955)
The Lion King (1994)
The Little Mermaid (1989)
Mighty Joe Young (1998)
Mulan (1998)
The Nightmare Before Christmas (1993)
Peter Pan (1953)
Pinocchio (1940)
The Prince of Egypt (1998)
The Rugrats Movie (1998)
The Secret of NIMH (1982)
Snow White and the Seven Dwarfs (1937)
Space Jam (1996)
Tarzan (1999)
Toy Story (1995)
When Worlds Collide (1951)
Who Framed Roger Rabbit (1988)
The Wrong Trousers (1993)

Historically Important Films

Ben-Hur (1926)
Body and Soul (1925)
Broken Blossoms (1919)
The Cabinet of Dr. Caligari (1919-Germany)
The Great Train Robbery (1903)
The Jazz Singer (1927)
Napoleon (1927-France)
Potemkin (1925-Russia)
Smoke Signals (1998)
A Trip to the Moon (1902-France)
Tumbleweeds (1925)

Social Problem Films

Amistad (1997)
Boyz N the Hood (1991)
Citizen Ruth (1996)
Dangerous Beauty (1998)
Dead Man Walking (1995)
Do the Right Thing (1989)
Falling Down (1993)
Get Real (1999)
The Grapes of Wrath (1940)
Guess Who's Coming to Dinner? (1967)
Happiness (1998)
The Ice Storm (1997)
In the Company of Men (1997)
In the Heat of the Night (1967)
Kids (1995)
Leaving Las Vegas (1995)
The Lost Weekend (1945)
Malcolm X (1992)
Manny and Lo (1996)
The Man With the Golden Arm (1955)
Margaret's Museum (1995-Canada)
Menace II Society (1993)
Mississippi Burning (1988)
Natural Born Killers (1994)
Norma Rae (1979)
On the Waterfront (1954)
A Patch of Blue (1965)
Permanent Midnight (1998)
Philadelphia (1993)
The Rainmaker (1997)
Rosewood (1997)
Sling Blade (1996)
The Snake Pit (1948)
A Time to Kill (1996)
Trainspotting (1996-Britain)
Welcome to the Dollhouse (1996)
Wild in the Streets (1968)
Your Friends & Neighbors (1998)

Chapter 16

Censorship and Other Forces That Shape the American Film

Though ignored by theorists, the moral power of art is so evident as to have made it the center of a vociferous, protracted quarrel from Classical Greece to the present. The movies simply stepped into the middle of a centuries-old row when, as soon as they appeared on the scene, censors and critics attacked them for distracting people from their proper moral development by stirring up their lower depths.

—W. R. Robinson, Critic

Does Film Shape or Reflect American Values?

Since 1922, the American film has never been free of some form of censorship or control. Therefore, a complete understanding of many American films requires an analysis of the social and economic pressures that have affected the final products seen on the screen.

No art form exists in a vacuum. The more popular an art is, and the wider its appeal to all segments of the population, the more closely it is tied to the social values, mores, and institutions of its audience. As both an extremely popular medium and an industry involving great financial risk and profit potential, the American film naturally must be responsive to social and economic pressures.

So film is not an independent entity but an integrated part of the social fabric, for its very survival depends on maintaining and continuing its popularity. To achieve real popularity, a movie must, first, be believable. Its action must take place in an environment that has credibility, and its story must reflect the common truths of the society in which it is made. This is not to say that a film must reflect reality as the way things actually are within the society. The truth it portrays may mirror people's hopes, dreams, fears, and inner needs. When real life does not fulfill these needs, people are primed to respond sympathetically to an artistic expression of them in film.

Film does not create *new* truths for society. It cannot reshape a society that is not ready for change. But this fact does not mean that film is not a powerful instrument of social change. The motion picture's power as a social force comes from its ability to pick up, amplify, and spread to society as a whole currents that already exist among segments of the population. Film also speeds popular acceptance of social change. The dramatically powerful presentation of new ways of thinking and behaving on screens twenty feet high in thousands of movie theaters across the country gives those new ways a significant seal of approval.

It is because of film's potential for legitimizing new standards of behavior—and for inspiring imitation of that behavior, especially by young members of its audience—that most systems of censorship or control have originated. In fact, the way systems of censorship develop usually follows a pattern that goes something like this. A traumatic event disrupts the stability of the social structure (some past examples: World War I, the Depression, World War II, the Vietnam War, the women's movement, the sexual revolution, the drug revolution, the civil rights movement). This event causes a significant shift in moral values and codes of behavior within certain segments of the population. Such changes create pressure for the entertainment media to reflect the truth of the new attitudes and standards of behavior. But a conservative element within the society vigorously resists the changes and demands that films be controlled or censored to prevent the spread of the shocking behavior and ensure that movies

Figure 16.1 The Changing Face of Censorship Producer/director Howard Hughes filmed *The Outlaw* in 1941 and released it in 1943. The Motion Picture Association of America withdrew its seal of approval in 1946 because Hughes had made use of unacceptable advertising copy, and local community pressure caused many theaters to cancel its showing. Although the Doc Holliday/Billy the Kid story featured starlet Jane Russell showing more cleavage and passion than the code allowed, the film would receive a ho-hum PG rating if released today.

reflect the truths of society as the conservative element believes they *should be*. Most censorship within the film industry reflects an uneasy compromise between advocates of change and supporters of the status quo (Figure 16.1).

The Motion Picture Production Code, 1930–1960

In the decades following World War I, Hollywood films began reflecting a change in moral standards. Sex, seduction, divorce, drinking, and drug use—new symbols of the sophisticated life—all became standard film fare. In 1922 public outrage against this change led a frightened film industry to organize the Motion Picture Producers and Distributors of America, Inc. They hired Postmaster General Will B. Hays to front the organization, which became known as the Hays Office. Hays and his staff first reacted to state and local censorship by codifying the most frequent objections to film content and advising member companies on what to avoid. By 1930, the organization (now known as the MPAA—Motion Picture Association of America) had published an official Motion Picture Production Code and set up a Production Code Administration to enforce its rulings.

Members of the MPAA agreed not to release or distribute a film without a certificate of approval. In addition, they were required to submit copies of all scripts under production, and each completed film had to be submitted for viewing by the Production Code board before it was sent to the laboratory for printing. A $25,000 penalty for producing, distributing, or exhibiting any film without the seal encouraged member companies to comply with the agreement. Through voluntary compliance, this industry-imposed regulation served to control the moral standards of the American film for the next three decades.

Although the code had strong ties with the Catholic Church, its practical rules did not reflect any single theology. Translated into simplest terms, the code and its rules were designed to require motion pictures to reflect, respect, and promote the institutions and moral values of the American middle class.

Excerpts of the code are reprinted in Box 1. Evident throughout the document is a belief in the powerful influence that movies can exert on the moral standards of an audience. Most of the code deals with the dangers of film as a corrupting influence, but film is also shown to have tremendous potential for good:

> If motion pictures consistently *hold up for admiration high types of characters* and present stories that will affect lives for the better, they can become the most powerful natural forces for the improvement of mankind.

The writers of the code believed that if the motion picture's creative energies were correctly channeled (through conformity to the code), film would become a supermedium—fighting for truth, justice, and the American way.

The fact that film is a mass medium available to children as well as adults was a major concern. In fact, the code can best be understood by relating it to the industry's concern with the "twelve-year-old mind." It was this young, highly impressionable age group—in the process of forming its values and its moral sense and picking its role models—that the code was determined to protect.

It may be difficult for modern film students to take the code seriously. However, an in-depth study of any complex realistic or naturalistic novel of the period and the film based on that novel will illustrate the effect of the code on such adaptations. The profound influence of the code on the American film product can also be seen by studying a relatively small number of American films produced between 1934 and 1966.

One of the clearest examples of the Motion Picture Production Code's control over the medium is the case of *On the Waterfront* (1954). As actor Rod Steiger tells it:

> I remember a magazine review of *On the Waterfront* that called Brando's fight at the end of the picture a March to Calvary and analyzed the entire film in terms of how [director Elia] Kazan had been influenced by the life of Christ. Actually, the scene didn't appear in the original ending of the picture. It was to have concluded with a shot of the dead boy floating down the river. But the Hays Office had called up and said, "Wait a minute. We have a rule: crime cannot triumph in films." Okay, they had a point. A lot of young people were going to see the picture. So in the middle

BOX 1

Excerpts From the Motion Picture Production Code*

Reasons Supporting Preamble of Code

1. Theatrical motion pictures . . . are primarily to be regarded as ENTERTAINMENT. . . .
   The MORAL IMPORTANCE of entertainment is something which has been universally recognized. It enters intimately into the lives of men and women and affects them closely; it occupies their minds and affections during leisure hours; and ultimately touches the whole of their lives. A man may be judged by his standard of entertainment as easily as by the standard of his work. . . .
   Correct entertainment raises the whole standard of a nation.
   Wrong entertainment lowers the whole living conditions and moral ideals of a race.

   Note, for example, the healthy reactions to healthful sports, like baseball, golf; the unhealthy reactions to sports like cockfighting, bullfighting, bear baiting, etc.
   Note, too, the effect on ancient nations of gladiatorial combats, the obscene plays of Roman times, etc.
2. Motion pictures are very important as ART.
   Though a new art, possibly a combination art, it has the same object as the other arts, the presentation of human thought, emotion, and experience, in terms of an appeal to the soul through the senses.
   Here, as in entertainment,
   Art *enters intimately* into the lives of human beings.
   Art can be *morally good*, lifting men to higher levels. This has been done through good music, great painting, authentic fiction, poetry, drama. . . .
   It has often been argued that art in itself is unmoral, neither good nor bad. This is perhaps true of the THING which is music, painting, poetry, etc. But the thing is the PRODUCT of some person's mind, and the intention of that mind was either good or bad. . . . Besides, the thing has its EFFECT upon those who come into contact with it. . . . In the case of the motion pictures, this effect may be particularly emphasized because no art has so quick and so widespread an appeal to the masses. . . .
3. The motion picture . . . has special MORAL OBLIGATIONS.
   A. Most arts appeal to the mature. This art appeals at once *to every class*. . . .

B. By reason of the mobility of a film and the ease of picture distribution . . . this art *reaches places* unpenetrated by other forms of art.
C. Because of these two facts, it is difficult to produce films intended for only certain classes of people. . . . Films, unlike books and music, can with difficulty be confined to certain selected groups.
D. The latitude given to film material cannot . . . be as wide as the latitude given to *book material*. . . .
   a. A book describes; a film vividly presents. One presents on a cold page; the other by apparently living people.
   b. A book reaches the mind through words merely; a film reaches the eyes and ears through the reproduction of actual events.
   c. The reaction of a reader to a book depends largely on the keenness of the reader's imagination; the reaction to a film depends on the vividness of presentation. . . .
E. Everything possible in a *play* is not possible in a film:
   a. Because of the *larger audience of the film*, and its consequential mixed character. Psychologically, the larger the audience, the lower the moral mass resistance to suggestion.
   b. Because through light, enlargement of character, presentation, scenic emphasis, etc., the screen story is *brought closer* to the audience. . . .
   c. The enthusiasm for . . . *actors* and *actresses*, developed beyond anything of the sort in history, makes the audience largely sympathetic toward the characters they portray and the stories in which they figure. Hence the audience is more ready to confuse actor and actress and the characters they portray. . . .

Particular Applications: Crimes Against the Law

The technique of murder must be presented in a way that will not inspire imitation. . . .
Revenge in modern times shall not be justified. . . .
Methods of crime should not be explicitly presented. . . .
The illegal drug traffic must not be portrayed in such a way as to stimulate curiosity concerning the use of, or traffic in, such drugs; nor shall scenes be approved which show the use of illegal drugs, or their effects. . . .
The use of liquor . . . when not required by the plot . . . will not be shown. . . .
There must be no display, at any time, of machine guns, submachine guns, or other weapons generally classified as illegal weapons in the hands of gangsters . . . and there are to be no off-stage sounds of the repercussions

of these guns. There must be no new, unique or trick methods shown for concealing guns. . . .

Pictures dealing with criminal activities, in which minors participate, or to which minors are related, shall not be approved if they incite demoralizing imitation. . . .

Particular Applications: Sex, Costume, and Dance

Sex

The sanctity of the institution of marriage and the home shall be upheld. Pictures shall not infer that low forms of sex relationship are the accepted or common thing. . . . Out of regard for the sanctity of marriage and the home, the *triangle*, that is, the love of a third party for one already married, needs careful handling. The treatment should not throw sympathy against marriage as an institution. . . . Excessive and lustful kissing, lustful embraces, suggestive postures and gestures are not to be shown . . . passion should be treated in such a manner as not to stimulate the lower and baser emotions. . . . Many scenes cannot be presented without arousing dangerous emotions on the part of the immature, the young or the *criminal classes*. . . .

Costume

The fact that the nude or semi-nude body may be *beautiful* does not make its use in the films moral. For, in addition to its beauty, the effect of the nude or semi-nude body on the normal individual must be taken into consideration.

Nudity or semi-nudity used simply to put a *"punch"* into a picture comes under the head of immoral actions. . . . Nudity can never be permitted as being *necessary for the plot*. . . .

Transparent or *translucent materials* and silhouettes are frequently more suggestive than actual exposure. . . .

Dance

Dancing in general is recognized as an *art* and as a *beautiful* form of expressing human emotions. . . . But dances which suggest or represent sexual actions, whether performed solo or with two or more; dances intended to excite the emotional reaction of an audience; dances with movement of the breasts, excessive body movement while the feet are stationary, violate decency and are wrong.

Particular Applications . . . Profanity

No approval by the Production Code Administration shall be given to the use of words and phrases . . . including, but not limited to, the following:

Alley cat (applied to a woman); bat (applied to a woman); broad (applied to a woman); Bronx cheer (the sound); chippie; cocotte; God, Lord, Jesus, Christ (unless used reverently); cripes; fanny; fairy (in a vulgar sense); finger (the); fire, cries of; Gawd, goose (in a vulgar sense); "hold your hat" or "hats"; hot (applied to a woman); "in your hat"; louse, lousy; Madam (relating to prostitution); nance; nerts; nuts (except when meaning crazy); pansy; razzberry (the sound); slut (applied to a woman); S.O.B.; son-of-a; tart; toilet gags; tom cat (applied to a man); traveling salesman and farmer's daughter jokes; whore; damn, hell (excepting when the use of said last two words shall be essential and required for portrayal, in proper historical context, of any scene or dialogue based upon historical fact or folklore, or for the presentation in proper literary context of a Biblical, or other religious quotation, or a quotation from a literary work provided that no such use shall be permitted which is intrinsically objectionable or offends good taste). . . .

Particular Applications: Miscellaneous

Religion

No film or episode may throw *ridicule* on any religious faith. . . .

Locations

The treatment of bedrooms must be governed by good taste. . . .

National Feelings

The use of the flag shall be consistently respectful. . . .

*Editor's Note: To simplify the reader's task, some parts of the code have been rearranged so that all materials relating to a given topic appear together. As originally presented, the code consisted of two parts. The first part began with the section "Preamble," which was followed, in sequence, by the sections "General Principles" and "Particular Applications." The second part consisted of "Reasons Supporting" or "Reasons Underlying" each of the "Particular Applications." Here, the sections have been rearranged so that the supports or reasons appear beneath the particular application to which each pertains.

of making the film, Kazan had to improvise a new ending. March to Calvary? We were just trying to get out of a hole.[1]

Without the code, *On the Waterfront* would have been quite a different movie. In his spinoff novel *Waterfront*, published a year after the film was released, screenwriter Budd Schulberg returned to his original ending, which gave the story what one critic called the "substance impossible in a movie." After testifying against Johnny Friendly at the Crime Commission Hearings, Terry Malloy sees Friendly on a street corner and attacks him verbally. But there is no terrible beating at the hands of Friendly's men by the dockside tool shed, no courageous, painful walk by Terry leading the men up to the loading dock. Friendly simply gives his henchmen "the slightest nods to ride it out" because "Johnny had already passed down the execution order. 'He's got to go.'"

> Three weeks later the remains of a human being were found in a barrel of lime that had been tossed on one of the multi-acre junk heaps in the Jersey swamps. The coroner's report after the inquest attributed death to twenty-seven stab wounds, apparently inflicted with an icepick. No next of kin came forward. The lime-mutilated corpse was never identified. But the boys along River Street, pro mob and anti, knew they had seen the last of a pretty tough kid.[2]

The power of the Production Code Administration diminished slowly from 1952, when Otto Preminger released *The Moon Is Blue* without a seal of approval (but *with* box-office success), until 1966, when Jack Valenti was named president of the Motion Picture Association of America. At that time, machinery for developing a new method of control was set into motion, resulting in the MPAA Rating System of 1968.

Censorship in Transition, 1948–1968

The Production Code Administration controlled the American film product with an iron hand until 1948, when an important Supreme Court antitrust decision (*U.S.* v. *Paramount Pictures*) ruled that the major production companies could no longer own large theater chains. As a result, thousands of theaters across the country were no longer obligated to show any film, regardless of its quality, just because the parent company had produced it, and the major studios lost control of a large captive audience. The Supreme Court decision also opened the door for independently produced movies to be distributed without a code seal.

As early as 1949, Samuel Goldwyn recognized that the industry would have a monumental fight on its hands "to keep people patronizing our theaters in preference to sitting at home and watching a program of entertainment" on television.[3] By 1954, movie attendance had dropped to half of what it had been

Figure 16.2 Provocative Foreign Films The code-bound American films of the 1950s and early 1960s seemed bland and antiseptic when compared to powerful imports like *Hiroshima, Mon Amour* (1959-France/Japan) and *La Dolce Vita* (1960-Italy).

in 1946. When this decline in attendance continued in spite of the industry's technical innovations such as Cinemascope, Cinerama, 3-D, and stereophonic sound, filmmakers recognized that they would have to handle more mature subjects than were being treated on television if they hoped to lure audiences back into the theaters.

Changes were made in the code to allow more flexibility. In 1956, the code was amended to allow themes of miscegenation, prostitution, and narcotics. In 1961 discreet treatments of homosexuality and other sexual deviations were permitted.

In the 1950s and early 1960s, a number of powerful foreign films shown in large cities were having an important influence on American audiences. Strong, provocative films like *The Seventh Seal*, *The Virgin Spring*, *The Lovers*, *La Dolce Vita*, and *Hiroshima, Mon Amour* made code-approved American products seem bland, antiseptic, and dull by comparison. American filmmakers were inspired to take some chances and push for more artistic freedom (Figure 16.2).

By the mid-1960s the industry had begun to accept the idea that not all movies should be made for one mass audience. *Lolita* (1962) was given a seal despite its theme of a middle-aged man's obsessive love for an adolescent. *The Pawnbroker* (1965) was approved despite two nude scenes (Figure 16.3). *Who's Afraid of Virginia Woolf?* (1966) won a seal despite clear violations in theme and language, and *Alfie* (1966) was cleared despite its frank treatment of sex and abortion. With the approval of the last two films, the Production Code Administration made a significant move toward the present rating system. Warner Brothers agreed to restrict attendance to *Who's Afraid of Virginia Woolf?* to

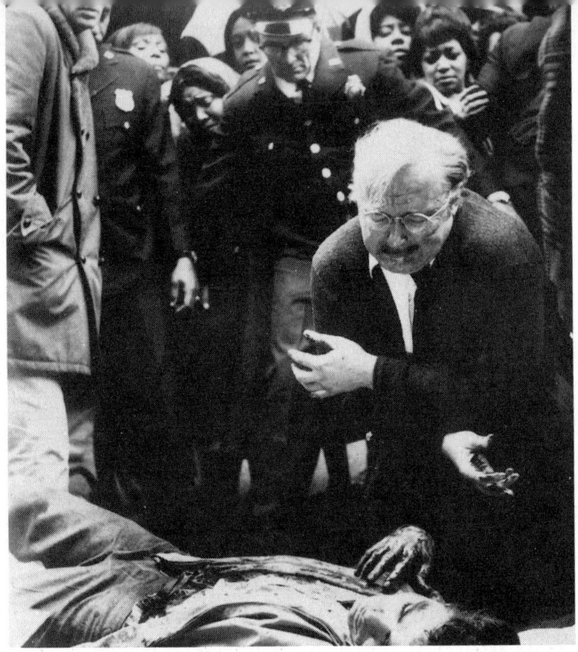

Figure 16.3 American Breakthrough Rod Steiger gave a touching performance as a middle-aged man haunted by memories of his experiences in a Nazi concentration camp in *The Pawnbroker* (1965). The film was granted a MPAA seal of approval despite two nude scenes, both crucial to understanding the story.

adults eighteen and over, and Paramount agreed to advertise *Alfie* as "recommended for mature audiences."

In 1966, the code was simplified, and the Code Administration divided approved films into two categories. The first category included films that presented no problems for the mass audience. The second category was labeled "Suggested for Mature Audiences." The label was advisory only; there were no enforced restrictions.

Two important court decisions in April 1968 forced the industry to provide a clearer system of classification. In *Ginsburg* v. *New York* the court ruled that material protected by the Constitution for adults could still be considered obscene for minors. In *Interstate* v. *Dallas* the court invalidated a city classification ordinance because its standards of classification were vague, but the court indicated that more tightly drawn standards of classification could be constitutional. To prevent state and local classification boards from springing up in response to this ruling, the film industry hurriedly tightened its own classification system and announced the MPAA Movie Rating System to the public six months after the *Dallas* decision. That rating system, with slight modifications, remains in effect today.

The MPAA Rating System

The new rating system was announced to the public on October 7, 1968, and went into effect on November 1. Like the Motion Picture Production Code, which it was designed to replace, the MPAA Rating System is a form of self-

Figure 16.4 A Profoundly Significant G A common misconception about the MPAA Rating System is that G always signifies a children's film. Although it often does, an occasional "profoundly significant film" like *A Man for All Seasons* (with Paul Scofield as Sir Thomas More and Orson Welles as Cardinal Wolsey) fits the "General Audiences" classification.

regulation put into operation to guard against government, state, and local control. By 1966 it was clear that American society had outgrown the moral standards that governed the 1930 code, and honest, realistic films could no longer be produced in conformance with its prohibitions. The new system was conceived as a system of classification rather than as censorship, and each film rated by the Rating System board was (and still is) classified in terms of its suitability for children (Figure 16.4). The board does not prohibit or ban the production or distribution of any motion picture. Its responsibility is limited to the classification of films, to labeling each film clearly so that theater managers can control the audience for each picture in accordance with its classification.

Since November 1968, practically every motion picture exhibited in the United States has carried a rating. Slight modifications have been made in the wording and symbols to clarify misunderstood points, but the rating system in use today is essentially the same one introduced in 1968. As it now stands, the MPAA Rating System classifies films in the manner described in Box 2.

Perhaps the simplest explanation of the MPAA Rating System (and a fairly accurate one) was found in an old joke: "In a G- or PG-rated movie, the guy in

BOX 2

Motion Picture Association of America Voluntary Movie Rating System

G	GENERAL AUDIENCES	All ages admitted.
PG	PARENTAL GUIDANCE SUGGESTED	Some material may not be suitable for children.
PG-13	PARENTS STRONGLY CAUTIONED	Some material may be inappropriate for children under 13.
R	RESTRICTED	Under 17 requires accompanying parent or adult guardian.
NC-17	NO ONE 17 AND UNDER ADMITTED	

SOURCE: *http://www.mpaa.org/movieratings/content.htm*

the white hat gets the girl. In an R-rated movie, the guy in the black hat gets the girl. In an X-rated movie everybody gets the girl."*

A brochure published when the rating system was introduced in 1968 included a list of eleven Standards for Production, but that list provides no help whatsoever in determining how films are actually classified. The biggest problem was the confusion the system caused parents of children sixteen or under. Most of the confusion was spawned by the PG category, those films that anybody could see with "parental guidance suggested." Although television had certainly made the modern child a more sophisticated viewer than his or her pretelevision counterpart, there is a great difference between the maturity of an eight-year-old and that of a sixteen-year-old. Many parents were not sure what to expect in a PG movie and whether to allow their eight-year-old or twelve-year-old to go alone on a Saturday afternoon to see one.

An attempt to solve this problem was first made in 1972, when the industry added this caution to its PG rating: "Some material may not be suitable for preteenagers." Although some pressure was applied to encourage the MPAA to follow the example of the European systems, which distinguish between children (up to twelve) and teenagers (thirteen to sixteen), there was no move to do so until the summer of 1984.

When *Indiana Jones and the Temple of Doom* and *Gremlins* came out in June 1984, there was an immediate negative reaction from critics and parents alike to

*The joke accurately reflects the stigma attached to the X rating, which had become synonymous with pornography. TV stations and newspapers would not advertise X-rated films; most theaters wouldn't show them. In the fall of 1990, the MPAA moved to counteract that stigma by changing the X designation to NC-17 (no children under 17 admitted). The change was brought about by industry pressure to give serious "adults only" films such as *Henry & June* a fair chance in the marketplace.

Figure 16.5 Too Intense for Young Children Steven Spielberg's *Indiana Jones and the Temple of Doom* and Joe Dante's *Gremlins* drew so much criticism for the intensity of their violence that the industry instituted a new PG-13 rating for such films.

the amount and intensity of violence portrayed in both films. A new rating called PG-13 (to cover the gray area between the PG and the R ratings) was instituted on July 1, 1984. Its purpose is to warn parents to use extra caution in allowing young children to attend such films (Figure 16.5).

Because theater owners do not want to enforce a second restrictive rating, PG-13 puts the burden of control squarely on parents, a philosophy very much in tune with the MPAA's stated policies since 1968. Despite the confusion over the PG rating, nationwide surveys prior to 1980 indicated that the public was reasonably well satisfied with the MPAA rating system—three out of five parents approved of it. And the PG-13 rating seems to be eliminating the gray area between the PG and R ratings.

Behind the scenes, the power that the board exercises over the film industry still constitutes a form of censorship, for the board continues to interfere with the creative process. The rating that a film is given exercises a tremendous influence on a film's potential for commercial success. An R rating reduces the potential audience for a film by 20 percent, and an NC-17 rating eliminates 50 percent of the potential audience. To guard against the automatic elimination of potential audience, studio contracts with producers and directors specify that an NC-17 rating must be avoided or that a film must be granted a G or PG rating before it shall "be deemed to have been delivered."[4] Such contracts obligate the producer to make whatever changes are necessary to obtain a desirable rating. If the producer cannot secure an acceptable rating, the studio has two options. It can refuse to accept delivery of the picture (and presumably refuse to pay the producer or director for his or her efforts), or it may accept the film and exercise the right to make "such changes, alterations, or deletions . . . as may be necessary or desirable"[5] for achieving an acceptable rating. Thus the producer and director lose creative control if they do not secure the specified rating *before* the film is delivered to the studio.

To prevent the loss of creative control at this late stage of production, producers and directors often submit scripts to the MPAA Code and Rating Administration for approval ahead of time, so that rating problems can be solved before shooting begins. The Code and Rating Administration, in advising what changes have to be made, enters into the filmmaking process itself by editing both scripts and finished films. Although the pressures bringing about this censorship are economic rather than social, they are nevertheless very real and constitute a form of censorship not totally unlike that of the 1930 Motion Picture Production Code.

A filmmaker who has not secured a satisfactory rating does have the option of appealing the Code and Rating Administration's decision. The MPAA Code and Rating Appeals Board meets in New York; it is separate from the Code and Rating Administration. When a film's rating is appealed, the appeals board screens the film; then before voting, it hears arguments from both the company challenging the rating and the Code and Rating Administration. Ratings are rarely reversed. During the first three years of the MPAA Rating System, only ten of thirty-one appeals were successful. Between 1974 and 1980, around 2,500 films were rated, and only seven appeals were successful.

Perhaps the most successful appeal yet heard by the board involved David Lean's *Ryan's Daughter*, an MGM film. When the film received an R rating, the studio threatened to pull out of the MPAA and claimed that an R rating would so limit the audience for this expensive ($10 million) film that the studio's very life was at stake. Under this considerable pressure from a great and historic motion picture institution, the board changed its rating of *Ryan's Daughter* to a PG so they would not have the demise of a major studio on their conscience. Paramount was in serious financial trouble also when it made a similar appeal for *Paint Your Wagon*, but the board twice refused its appeal for a G rating.

The ratings for other important films have been changed. *Midnight Cowboy*, rated X when it came out in 1969, was re-rated to an R with only the omission of several seconds of violence. Likewise, *A Clockwork Orange*, initially rated X, became an R after a few seconds of violent action were cut (but the film cannot legally be exhibited in England). *Saturday Night Fever*, originally shown as an R, was edited to remove objectionable language and redistributed as a PG to take advantage of its appeal to the "under-seventeen" crowd. *Last Tango in Paris*, released in theaters as an X, has been cut and re-released for cable television as an R but without the impact of the original.

More recently, Steven Spielberg's appeal to change the R rating on *Poltergeist* to a PG was granted, and *Lone Wolf McQuade*, which received an R rating for violence, received a PG from the board after actor Chuck Norris appealed that the violence in *McQuade* "was of a stylized nature similar to that in John Wayne westerns" (Figure 16.6). Brian De Palma fought long and hard and cut some violent scenes to prevent his *Scarface* from getting an X rating. And in July

Figure 16.6 Rating Appeals The MPAA Code and Rating Appeals Board approved appeals for new ratings on *Poltergeist, Scarface,* and *Lone Wolf McQuade. McQuade's* star, Chuck Norris, successfully argued that the film's violence was of a stylized nature comparable to that of John Wayne westerns.

of 1998 De Palma waged a similar struggle with the ratings board to receive a PG-13, rather than an R, rating for *Snake Eyes,* starring Nicolas Cage, because he was contractually obligated to deliver a film with the lower rating to Paramount Studios.

In its effort to adjust to changing parental attitudes in our society, the rating board has in recent years become harder on violence and softer on nudity and sensuality. In the words of Richard D. Heffner, chairman of the Classification and Rating Administration since 1974:

> A moment of nudity that automatically drew an R years back may be PG-rated today, while violence is often rated R now that was not restricted before. It's a result of what we perceive to be changing parental attitudes toward these subjects.[6]

As long as the rating board remains responsive to such shifts in parental attitudes, it will continue to function as the effective instrument of industry control it was designed to be. However, some filmmakers and studios have learned to take full advantage of the constantly changing makeup of the board. Independent director and writer Neil LaBute, whose R-rated first film *In the Company of Men* created much controversy among viewers and critics, received an NC-17 rating for his second feature, *Your Friends & Neighbors.* Most unhappy with this label, LaBute says, he and his financial backers just "waited out that group, and a new one came through and we got an R. The new system is to go early and wait out the tenure of that group and try again."[7]

Censorship and Films on Television

Censorship has caused problems for many feature films shown on television. In the past, objectionable segments were simply cut out so they would not be seen by the television audience. Some experiments have been made with shooting two versions of the same film: one for the theater market, which can restrict its audience through the movie rating code, and a precensored version for the television market, which cannot restrict its audience. The television version of a film may differ radically from the theater version in its treatment of sexual material, nudity, coarseness of language, and violence. Plot changes may be so extensive that the two versions have little in common.

Today such extreme changes are not common, but when a feature film with definite network potential is in production, "cover shots" are often filmed to substitute for shots that are sexually explicit or contain strong language. In this way, a mild version of the film can be created for network TV. The original R-rated version of *Saturday Night Fever*, for example, that was re-edited in 1979 and given a PG rating, was not only rerun in theaters but also shown on TV.

When the networks feel that parents should exercise special care in allowing young children to watch certain films, special warnings are provided concerning language or mature subject matter, along with one of the new television ratings symbols, such as "TVMA." But as a general rule, no film appears on network television until it is edited to at least a PG level (Figure 16.7). The real problem occurs when network greed overcomes good sense and an R-rated movie that does not lend itself to PG editing is scheduled. By the time *Serpico* had been edited to eliminate coarse language, the raw thrust of the movie was gone, and the plot was almost incoherent (Figure 16.8). The ribald *Animal House* was totally fragmented by the necessary butchering, which left eleven minutes of its running time on the cutting-room floor (Figure 16.9).

Beyond the Code and Rating System

The motion picture industry has attempted to enforce codes and ratings to offset demands for some form of censorship, but certain segments of society do not always agree that the codes and ratings fulfill their intent. Films that touch on religious matters often seem to generate the most impassioned criticism by the viewing audience. Religious leaders and their supporters have at times managed to impose an unofficial censorship through their condemnation of a particular film. An example of this type of censorship is the 1988 reaction to Martin Scorsese's *The Last Temptation of Christ* (Figure 16.10).

The movie, which presents a less-than-perfect Christ, enraged Christian fundamentalists, who protested and boycotted theaters that planned to show the

Figure 16.7 From G to Network—A Few Choice Words In *True Grit,* just before taking the reins in his teeth for his headlong charge toward Lucky Ned Pepper (Robert Duvall) and his gang, Rooster Cogburn (John Wayne) yells a challenge containing an unkind reference to the villainous Pepper's mother. An early 1970s showing on NBC bleeped the epithet—a 1995 showing on TNT left it in.

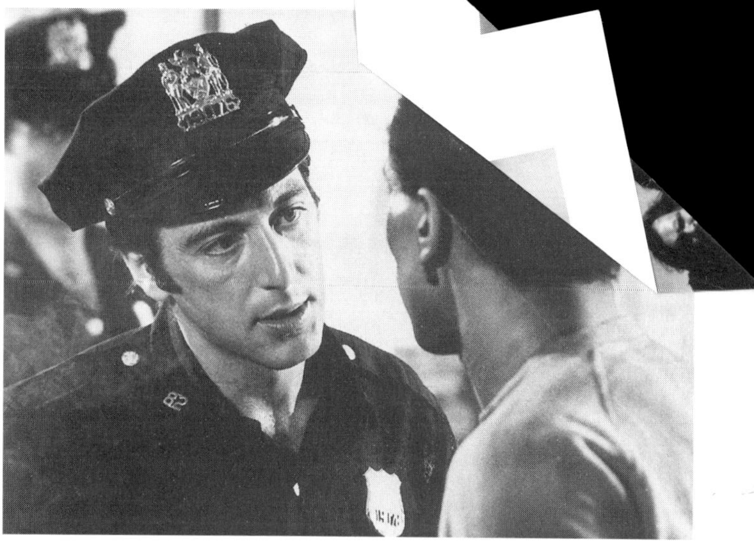

Figure 16.8 From R to Network—A Great Many Choice Words The script of *Serpico,* starring Al Pacino as an honest policeman in a corrupt system, was so loaded with four-letter words that the cutting necessary for network television completely destroyed the grim, realistic power of the original.

Figure 16.9 Censoring Sex and Ribald Humor The eleven minutes cut from *Animal House* for its network TV showing practically destroyed the film's ribald humor and left its plot almost incoherent.

Figure 16.10 Unofficial Censorship Martin Scorsese's *The Last Temptation of Christ* (1988) (with Willem Dafoe as Jesus, right) offended fundamentalist religious groups across the country because it portrayed a very human Jesus struggling with temptation. Nicholas Ray's *King of Kings* (1961) (starring Jeffrey Hunter, left) presented a more traditional picture of Jesus, and no feathers were ruffled.

film. As a result of those protests, many theaters pulled the film from their schedules. Several states in the Bible Belt had no commercial showings of the film. In their violent antipathy to the film, many protesters charged the Jewish leadership of Universal Pictures with plotting an attack on Christianity and called for a boycott of all Universal productions. The release of the film to video retailers across the country was done quietly without the advertising hoopla that usually surrounds new releases. Although many retailers purchased the videocassette version for subsequent rental and resale, they kept it under the counter in an attempt to forestall public outcry in their communities.

Although the Scorsese film did not receive any formal or codified form of censorship, its reception is an example of the unofficial censorship that operates in the United States. An unwritten code applies to films that offend the moral sensibilities of the population or at least segments of the population. In many areas, community leaders and theater owners often agree not to show NC-17-rated films or other controversial motion pictures, to avoid protests or more official types of censorship.

Protests have occurred in recent years, though. Charles Lyons, in an essay titled "The Paradox of Protest," has written that both freedom from censorship and "rules" are necessary for a balanced "cultural climate":

> Debates over film censorship from 1980 to 1992 reflected a culture in conflict over sex, race, family values, and homosexuality. They also demonstrated that political struggles were being fought in a cultural arena. Similar conflicts within society and art have existed throughout history. . . . Among the groups that have protested against movies—antipornography feminists, Asian Americans, and gays and lesbians on the left, and religious groups on the right—the only ones to achieve censorship . . . were associated with the new Christian right.

Lyons later observes, however,

> After Asian Americans and homosexual groups protested against *Year of the Dragon* and *Basic Instinct*, respectively, these constituencies found Hollywood more willing to listen to them. . . . While groups may wave placards and chant against any movie they choose, it is evident that protests can produce unanticipated effects. Some protests, such as those from the religious right, result in recognizable acts of censorship; others, such as those from left groups, create an environment that legitimizes suppression and encourages self-censorship.[8]

Changing Formulas for the Treatment of Sex, Violence, and Language

Contrary to popular belief, the motion picture did not invent violence, sex, or even rough language. Fiction and drama were making use of such materials long before the first movie was shot. Each art form, with or without a formal code of censorship, has its own standards of what's acceptable and what's not at any given time. Standards of acceptability reflect what might be called the fashion of the day. They give rise to formulas for realism, which are determined much as the proper length for hemlines is determined—by what everyone else is doing. Thus, to a degree, violence, sex, and rough language appear in movies not just for their shock value but because their appearance is fashionable. If it were not, we would be offended by what we see and would stop going to movies altogether.

Formulas for realism do change. When a breakthrough film becomes a popular success, it sets new fashions and imitators begin to treat it as a standard. Consider, for example, how the formula for realism has evolved in the treatment of death by gunshot. In *Birth of a Nation*, men shot during the Civil War battles typically threw their arms skyward and fell sideways to the ground. By the 1940s, a cowboy shot in a grade B western clutched one hand to his chest (usually where cowboys were wounded) and crumpled forward. In the 1950s, *Shane* established a new style when the impact of the bullet from villain Jack Palance's gun knocked his victim ten feet backward into a mud puddle. In the

Figure 16.11 Subjective Damnation Sometimes subject matter alone (pedophilia, for instance), not mainly treatment, damns a film to censorship—either active or passive—or faint praise. Two exemplary cases: Todd Solondz's *Happiness* (starring Dylan Baker as a father/psychiatrist/child abuser) and Adrian Lyne's new version of Vladimir Nabokov's novel *Lolita,* starring Jeremy Irons as Humbert Humbert and Dominique Swain as the young object of his obsession (pictured here).

1960s, *Bonnie and Clyde* introduced the slow-motion dance of death, with bullets exploding holes through clothing. When a sensational new effect is introduced in a milestone film like *Bonnie and Clyde*, audiences feel cheated if the same sense of heightened reality is not achieved in the films they see after it.

Similar changes can be traced in the way sexual intimacy is suggested, from *Tarzan, the Ape Man* (1932) to *Last Tango in Paris* (1973) to *Titanic* (1997); and in the way rough language is treated, from *Gone With the Wind* (1939) to *Scarface* (1983) to *Your Friends & Neighbors* (1998). Still, there are clearly limits to modern American culture's apparent permissiveness regarding cinema. Todd Solondz's controversial *Happiness* (1998), which includes a father who is a child molester, was released without an MPAA rating (as Solondz had anticipated). And Adrian Lyne's $50 million remake of Stanley Kubrick's *Lolita* (1997) never obtained general theatrical release in the United States—settling instead, ironically, for screenings on cable television's Showtime, which suggests in advertisements for itself that only Showtime has the fearlessness to be both gritty and good in American movie entertainment (Figure 16.11).

Questions

On Censorship

1. Study three or more films with censorable subject matter made under the Motion Picture Production Code (prior to 1950), and answer these questions:
   a. Where in these films do you find obvious examples of code-caused suppression and restraint?
   b. How would these films be different if they were being made today? Which film (or films) could be significantly improved by being made today with a PG or R rating? How or why would they be improved?
   c. Do the films studied seem too mild mannered to have much impact, or do they effectively suggest such things as violence and sexuality in ways acceptable to the code?
   d. Do these films seem to go out of their way to promote traditional American values? Are American values or institutions questioned in any of these films? If so, how and where are such questions dramatized, and how are such problems resolved?
2. Examine three or more films with censorable subject matter made during the transitional period (1948–1968) and consider the questions above. What evidence do you find of the code's being stretched or disregarded? How do the films of the transitional period differ from those made before 1950?
3. Examine a film made under the Motion Picture Production Code and compare it with its remake produced under the MPAA Rating System. Possible choices include *Scarface*, 1932/1983; *The Postman Always Rings Twice*, 1946/1981; *Here Comes Mr. Jordan*, 1941, remade as *Heaven Can Wait*, 1978; and *Godzilla*, 1954/1998. To what degree are these films different because of the difference in censorship restrictions? Where are the differences most obvious, and how is the overall effect of the film changed by the differences? Which of the two is the better film? Why?
4. Examine four current films presently playing at your local theaters or on video: a film rated G, a film rated PG, a film rated PG-13, and a film rated R. What distinguishes a G film from a PG film, what separates a PG from a PG-13, and what differentiates a PG-13 from an R?
5. Make an attempt to trace the evolution of the MPAA Rating System's classification decisions by comparing films rated PG and R at four-year intervals. Use films released in 1972, 1976, 1980, and 1984. Can you discern any patterns of change affecting where the dividing line is drawn? If so, what do these patterns indicate?
6. Examine several films from each decade from the 1930s to the present, and try to describe the fashion of the age in terms of each decade's formulas for sexual intimacy, the dance of death, and rough language. What other changing patterns or fashions are apparent in the films you viewed?

Films for Study

Alfie (1966-Britain)
American Pie (1999)
Bad Lieutenant (1992)
Basic Instinct (1992)
The Basketball Diaries (1995)
The Birth of a Nation (1915)
Bonnie and Clyde (1967)
Breaking the Waves (1996-Denmark)
A Clockwork Orange (1971)
The Cook, The Thief, His Wife & Her Lover (1989-France/Holland)
Crash (1996-Canada)
Dead Ringers (1988-Canada)
The Deer Hunter (1978)
Dogma (1999)
8mm (1999)
Eyes Wide Shut (1999)
The Godfather (1972)
Gremlins (1984)
Happiness (1998)
Henry & June (1990)
Hiroshima, Mon Amour (1959-France/Japan)
If . . . (1968-Britain)
Indiana Jones and the Temple of Doom (1984)
In the Company of Men (1997)
Kids (1995)
La Dolce Vita (1960-Italy)
Last Tango in Paris (1973-France/Italy)
The Last Temptation of Christ (1988)
Lolita (1962-Britain)
Lolita (1997)
The Lover (1992-France)
The Lovers (1958-France)
Love! Valour! Compassion! (1997)
Midnight Cowboy (1969)
The Moon Is Blue (1953)
Murmur of the Heart (1971-France/Germany/Italy)
National Lampoon's Animal House (1978)
Natural Born Killers (1994)
On the Waterfront (1954)
The Outlaw (1943)
The Pawnbroker (1965)
The Piano (1993-New Zealand/France)
The Pillow Book (1996-Britain/Holland/France)
Pretty Baby (1978)
The Program (1993)
Pulp Fiction (1994)
Raging Bull (1980)
Saturday Night Fever (1977)
Scarface (1983)
Serpico (1973)
Se7en (1995)
The Seventh Seal (1957-Sweden)
Short Cuts (1993)
The Silence of the Lambs (1991)
Snake Eyes (1998)
South Park: Bigger, Longer, and Uncut (1999)
Spanking the Monkey (1994)
Taxi Driver (1976)
There's Something About Mary (1998)
The Untouchables (1987)
The Virgin Spring (1960-Sweden)
Who's Afraid of Virginia Woolf? (1966)
The Wild Bunch (1969)
Year of the Dragon (1985)
Your Friends & Neighbors (1998)

Appendix A

The Art of Watching Movies on TV

The influence is undeniable and even surpasses that of cinema, if only because television reaches a broader audience. In one evening more people saw the televised appearance of *The Bridge on the River Kwai* than had paid admission to the film during the several years of its theatrical run. The appearance on TV of feature films leads many to discuss televised drama and cinema as though the two forms were somehow interchangeable.

—RICHARD E. PECK, CRITIC

The TV-Viewing Environment

A number of factors prevent us from fully experiencing a theatrical film shown on the average home television set. Consider the simple factor of size. An image approximately 20 feet high on the average movie screen is reduced to a maximum height of 1½ feet on the typical home TV. That's an important difference. Watching a movie on television, we must give the movie maximum concentration just to follow the story. It is nearly impossible to become physically involved in the action as you would in a theater. For example, a viewer who is susceptible to carsickness may get a little queasy during the car chase in *Bullitt* or the roller-coaster ride through the underground tunnel in *Indiana Jones and the Temple of Doom*. But the same visceral sensation—that we are actually behind the wheel of a speeding automobile or careening out of control in a mining car—is nearly always lacking when we're watching that little box across the room. The events occurring on television seem remote, locked in the safety of a 19-inch screen, unable to threaten us, to pull us to the edge of our easy chairs. In the theater, the image is larger than life; on television, the image is life size or smaller. The reduction reduces the intensity of our experience and decreases our involvement. It may also sacrifice clarity. For example, in a typical long shot, a lone human figure projected life size may take up a relatively small space on the theater screen. When this image is reduced to the size of the average television image, the actor may be unrecognizable.

Not only is the size of the image reduced. In many cases, the basic shape of the composition is altered as well—for example, when a film in a wide-screen format is squeezed onto the TV screen. So that essential information is not lost when wide-screen formats are adapted to television, a special editing process is used. A scanning device determines when the most significant information in each frame is so far to the left or right of center as to be outside the perimeter of the narrower television picture. TV producers then adjust accordingly by centering this peripheral information in the transmitted TV image. Of course, the cinematographer's art suffers from this process—known as **panning and scanning**—because the visual composition is compromised when part of the image is sliced off. Combined with the reduced size of the image, panning and scanning can sometimes interfere with clear communication of the story, especially in situations where we must keep a clear picture of the actor's relationship to the setting. Often we lose our bearings because the setting in which the action is occurring is not properly revealed in the reduced and narrowed image.

Directors are shooting more and more movies with the films' video futures in mind. *Amadeus*, for example, was filmed in Panavision, the popular wide-screen format that has an image a little more than twice as wide as it is high. But director Milos Forman made compromises in his composition so that *Amadeus* would fit the television format without panning and scanning. Cinematographers achieve this compromise composition by putting marks in their camera viewfinders to frame an image that works for both the theater and the video formats.

However, there is no complete solution for the standard TV set. Even with the narrowest screen format, the standard size that the television's screen shape approximates, information is always cropped around the borders (as we observed in Chapter 4). This cropping adds to the difficulty of reading the subtitles of foreign language films on television. Reading white letters on light backgrounds can be difficult even in the theater. But on television, letters or words are cut off at the bottom or sides of the screen, and the reduced sharpness of the image makes reading subtitles next to impossible. For these reasons, voice dubbing is often the best means for presenting foreign language films on television.

Television compromises a film's sound even more than its image. A modern movie theater equipped with multiple speakers can surround viewers with sound, immerse them in an encompassing aural environment. In *Das Boot*, the rumble of a destroyer passing back and forth over a submerged U-boat moves all over the theater as the sound increases and decreases in volume and shifts from speaker to speaker. Most common television sets, even the largest ones, have a single small speaker (5 inches maximum), and some don't even have a tone control. However, television manufacturers are improving sound quality, and the major television networks and many cable systems are transmitting movies in stereo. Television uses FM for sound, so the quality of sound broadcast by TV stations can equal that of the best FM radio stations. But even when television stations do broadcast better-quality sound, the tinny speakers of the average TV set are incapable of picking it up.

Most of the problems discussed above, however, may be solved very soon. The wonderful world of watching movies on television, we are being told by the developers of the Information Superhighway, is about to undergo drastic and possibly miraculous changes. Film critic Roger Ebert spelled out some of these possibilities in 1990:

> Now it appears that video is poised to wage a final showdown with its older and more aristocratic relative. High-definition television will replace standard broadcast signals within a few years, providing home pictures of much improved clarity and brilliance. I saw high def demonstrated in December 1990 at the Hawaii Film Festival, where technicians from Sony of Japan presented films shot in the format. The picture was impressive. Ordinary TV has a sharp falling-off at either end of the gray scale, but high def provided darker darks and lighter whites and—most important—more subtle gray tones. The colors were truer, too, and bright reds and oranges didn't bloom the way they do on conventional sets.

> . . . The average American household ten years from now will be able to look at a television picture that will be of almost movie quality, on a screen that is limited only by the size of the room. The average American family—not the wealthy people—will be looking at a picture that's eight to ten feet wide, and it may come in through satellite: pay for view.[1]

Ebert's vision of our media future still seems ahead of actual accomplishments, though. The high-definition TV (HDTV) technology, for example, has as yet far overshot the standards and delivery technology. Although the first high-definition television set (a "Panasonic 56-inch-on-the-diagonal, cinema-style wide-screen PT-56WXF90—at only $5,499") was released commercially in San Diego in August 1998, no television networks were tentatively scheduling digital programs in the format until many months later.[2] Even beyond this lengthy delay, of course, there still looms a fairly long transitional period of expensive first-generation products. And because the development of any new system is consumer driven, the actual time frame for implementation is difficult to predict.

The basic HDTV format will indeed be *wide* screen. But when movies that were shot to be projected onto a standard screen are televised, the *sides* of the televised image will be letterboxed. Several years ago, in an attempt to get the jump on the new format, RCA, Panasonic, and JVC all created and produced wide-screen-format televisions—at elevated prices that really tested the market. These sets, however, were not equipped to receive HDTV (in part because of controversies involving broadcast standards), and they have not been very popular commercially.

Super sound systems are already in widespread use. Hi-fi VCRs, laserdisc players, DVD players, and Dolby Pro Logic systems are capable of providing home theater surround-sound with strategically placed multiple speakers.

When present cable wiring is replaced by fiber optics, local cable systems will, in theory, be capable of carrying 500 channels. With this technology in place comes the possibility of video movies on demand, a large variety of current hits stagger-started at fifteen-minute intervals. Several satellite systems—DIRECTV from the Hughes Electronics Corporation and the RCA DSS (Digital Satellite System), for example—are already in operation, offering CD-quality sound, a sharp digital picture, and over 150 channels of customized programming (hit movies are scheduled to start every thirty minutes).

Regardless of the potential for improvement created by the new technology, we still must face the fact that the TV-viewing environment in most households reduces the quality of the viewing experience. A movie theater is dimmed to a level designed to focus the viewer's attention on the screen. Even the soft lights of the exit signs are situated far enough from the screen so as to not distract the viewer. In the home, apartment, or dorm room, however, it's "lights up" while the movie is running. Our attention is drawn to the screen only because it contrasts with its surroundings: The screen is brighter and more colorful, and of course the moving image has a life of its own. But there are many clearly visible distractions throughout the room, and our attention is not focused on the television set in the same way it is focused on the movie screen. In the movie theater there is simply nowhere else to look.

In addition to the visual distractions, there are a multitude of aural distractions. Few households control (or mute) external sounds, so we are constantly distracted by the noises of daily living: horns, sirens, automobile engines, lawn mowers, barking dogs, ringing telephones, airplanes, heating and cooling systems, a roommate practicing the tuba. Thanks to insulation, the modern movie theater muffles or completely eliminates extraneous sounds. Of course, it's possible to concentrate enough on the TV sound to hear through the distractions, but the effort does diminish the movie's magic. In a theater, sound and image wash over you, immerse you, massage you. You needn't direct your attention. Seeing a movie in a theater is like diving into heavy surf with the tide coming in; seeing a movie on television is like taking a sponge bath out of a gallon pail. There's a vast difference in the experience. As actor Richard Dreyfuss describes it:

> I'm saying that this is why film has a power over us. When we sit in a darkened room and symbolically hold hands with one another and say, "Give me this experience"—we are investing religiosity to that experience. So, of course, if there's a painful one or a powerful one—we will be swept up with it. If it's painful, we're not going to deal with it. But if it's on TV, who cares? Because TV has no impact, it is simply part of the furniture sitting next to the potted palm or the refrigerator. It has no impact on a primal level.[3]

Conventions and Habits of Watching Movies on Television

Because of television's constant presence in our lives, we have a distinct tendency to watch television too much. We often give it only half of our attention; but we have it on as background to whatever else we're doing, as a kind of visual Muzak. In a sense, watching movies on television is too convenient, something we take for granted. We frequently watch movies on TV because we are in a room with a television set. We use television for company because we are used to having it on, not because we are really interested in watching what is on. It's warm, it's alive, it's comfortable—pretty much like the family dog. And we pay it about the same kind of attention. The movie-watching habits described in the following confession by Roger Director in *The Movies* magazine are unfortunately more the rule than the exception:

> I don't watch movies at home so I can pretend I'm at the Bijou. I rarely watch a movie all the way through on my TV. I watch it in stitched-together stops and starts depending on what is in the refrigerator, who is on the phone, and my maniacal penchant for speeding breathlessly around the dial. I may watch one scene in a movie repeated on cable a dozen times, another scene once. A one-hour-fifty-minute movie I may spend six hours and forty-three minutes watching, spread out over two months. If I have seen *Raggedy Man* eighteen times, I have seen it once—almost.
>
> Sometimes when watching TV I even find time to read. Lately, in bizarre concordance with my multiple viewings of John Carpenter's *The Thing*, I have been reading Rousseau's *Confessions*. It's a good book. Better than *The Thing*.[4]

Director Martin Scorsese confesses to similar bad habits in his TV watching:

> In a funny way television itself is a different thing. I have it on all the time and every now and then I look at an image. If I'm really going to look at a film on television, I'm going to sit down, turn the lights out and look at a picture. Look at a film, a motion picture. Maybe the images have become like junk images, in a way, like junk mail. And that's unfortunate.[5]

Commercial Breaks

One basic reason that we "half watch" television—especially feature movies on network television—is the distraction of commercial breaks. There is absolutely no way to enjoy on network television a theatrical movie as it was intended to be seen. The film was designed to be shown without interruption. It has a continuous flow, a kind of organic rhythm of its own: a gradual building of tension in some spots, relief from tension in others. There is a pace to the editing, to the dialogue, to the way the story unfolds, to the revelations about the characters, and to the building surges of conflict. The interaction of these rhythms contributes significantly to the overall feel of the film. The director, editor, and composer weave the film's rhythm, shapes, and contours into a single unified and flowing fabric. When the film is cut into eight or more fragments by commercial breaks, its sense of rising and falling tensions, its surging life pulse, and its distinctive wholeness are irretrievably lost.

This is not to say that we cannot follow the plot, for we can. And we can remember the characters as we left them before the break. But after a long commercial break it is difficult to settle back into the rhythm, into the feel or spirit of the film. On television we see the film in segments that average around fifteen minutes in length. The first segment usually is longer to hook the audience; most of the segments are shorter. After a commercial break, there's barely enough time to readjust our rhythms back to the film before four to six more commercials interrupt.

Because TV producers do not give us a chance to get fully involved with the movie anyway, there's no reason for them to give us time to resonate at the end. In the split second before the ending credits would have started to roll in a theater presentation, we're taken instead to a commercial (or two or three). The credits, which would have given us a little time to reflect, are finally run (if they are run at all) under the network promo for next week's movie in the same time slot.

Some movies suffer less than others from this kind of treatment. But none gain by it, and some are practically destroyed. Made-for-TV movies are interrupted by commercials in much the same manner as theatrical films, but they have one distinct advantage. Made-for-TV movies are scripted with network broadcast in mind, and the networks provide scriptwriters with suggested times for commercial breaks so that they can structure the script accordingly. Because they know that a commercial break must come within a relatively narrow time span, the writers can make slight adjustments to accommodate those breaks, usually by structuring a natural break close to the suggested times and by rewriting the last few lines of dialogue before a break to help end a scene.

There does seem to be an increased sensitivity by the networks about the scheduling of commercial breaks. In its first network showing, for instance, *Schindler's List*, because of the nature of its subject matter and themes, was presented without commercial interruptions. Some feature films are permitted to run over the rigid two-hour prime-time slot, so there is probably less butchering of films on network television now than in the past. Sometimes, long films are broken in half and the halves are shown on successive nights or a week apart in the same time slot. This is certainly not the best way to get a feeling for the whole, but it is preferable to mindless butchering that simply cuts out segments to make a film fit its scheduled period.

When such cutting occurs, the original creators of the film—the director and the editor—have no control over what is removed. Thus, the cutting is seldom done with much concern about its effect on the artistic structure of the film as a whole, and what the viewer sees on television may be a badly butchered shell of the film the director intended (Figure A.1). Otto Preminger, John Huston, Steven Spielberg, Woody Allen, and other directors have complained publicly about the distortion of their art by such butchering, and some have threatened legal action against the networks and video distributors. As a result, we have all

Figure A.1 Cutting Beyond the Bone A last-minute scheduling conflict with a Bob Hope Special led NBC to cut the running length of *This Man Stands Alone,* starring Lou Gossett Jr. as a courageous sheriff, from two hours to ninety minutes, including commercials. The plot, then, was incoherent in this abbreviated debut of the made-for-television film.

become familiar with the television and videocassette packaging disclaimer, "This film has been modified as follows from its original version: It has been formatted to fit your screen." However, that exhibitors are now required by law to take note of any visual changes they have made in the work does not lessen the detrimental effect of most of these alterations.

The sensitivity of local stations to the impact of scheduling commercials swings from one extreme to the other. Some local stations seem to have no concern for the movie's structure and even interrupt a crucial line of dialogue. Some have been known to let the projector roll during short commercials. And still others utilize compressed-time prints that present the whole work and still leave time for more commercials, but at the cost of providing an almost subliminal speeded-up feeling to the film. A few stations at least recognize the film's natural break points and schedule commercials accordingly. In some cases, the best films on commercial television are actually the late-night movies aired by local stations. Late at night, there may be fewer commercial breaks, and no definite time period is set for ending, so a film can be shown in its entirety. More and more viewers, of course, effectively bypass the problem with a VCR or laserdisc or DVD player and video rentals, and cable movie channels such as HBO, Cinemax, and Showtime are increasingly gaining popularity over network television for viewing feature films. Satellite systems also provide current films on a pay-per-view basis.

The Made-for-Television Film

Several of the problems that affect feature films shown on television are avoided by the increasingly respected made-for-television films. These films are designed for showing on television instead of in theaters and are usually financed and produced at least in part by one of the major networks. In watching such films, we should be able to detect at least four areas of improvement over the regular theater feature.

1. The film should be structured with some regard for the timing of interruptions, so that the film breaks for commercials at dramatically appropriate times. Networks provide scriptwriters with suggested times for commercial breaks. Although scripts are not structured to make each unbroken portion of film equivalent to an act or a scene in a stage play, writers do tailor their scripts so that little endings occur at each scheduled commercial break.
2. Because it is designed and written for a specified time slot (average: two hours), the made-for-television film should exist as an integrated and complete whole, exactly as the director intended it.
3. The problems caused by the small size of the television screen should be solved by the fact that the film is usually conceived, composed, and shot with the size and shape of the television screen in mind. Because television is essentially a close-up medium, the made-for-television movie emphasizes the intimate, personalized information best suited to the small screen. The visual emphasis is on the actors' faces, usually in interior shots, shots in automobiles, and telephone conversations. Because a small personal drama works better on the small screen than the sweep and grandeur of an epic, character is emphasized over action, and conflicts are more psychological than physical. Director John Badham describes the differences as follows:

   > [*Bingo Long*] was my first feature motion picture—as opposed to television—and, as such, I found I was dealing much more with action than with dialogue. In television you become a master at the art of shooting people talking—lots of closeups and variations on closeups, over-the-shoulder shots and things like that—which gets fairly boring to the director after a while. There's a whole different feeling to composing material and shooting things for a bigger screen, where a much wider shot might be just as good as a giant closeup. You can get back a lot farther. A picture like Kubrick's *2001* is almost all long shots; there are very few even medium closeups in that film. Consequently, when you put *2001* on television, it's very hard to get any of the dynamics of it. The technique with actors is identical for feature films and TV—and the requirements of the story are very similar, though, as I said, you may be able to do more action in a movie than in a television show. The good dramatic rules apply in both places.[6]

4. Censorship should be no problem because the made-for-television network film is designed with the mass unrestricted audience in mind. With network supervision all the way, the result is usually a G- or PG-level product. Little vulgarity or nudity is allowed, and the political bite is mild. The networks want enough controversy to be interesting but not enough to be offensive. In borderline cases, parental warnings can be provided (Figure A.2). Despite the networks' middle-of-the-road posture, some made-for-television films have courageously treated sensitive social problems such as incest, AIDS, rape, teenage suicide, homosexuality, Vietnam, drugs, alcoholism, breast cancer, mental retardation, and prostitution (Figure A.3).

In comparing the quality of made-for-TV movies to that of theater features, we should take into account that made-for-TV movies generally are made with much lower budgets. Lower budgets mean faster shooting schedules and lower production quality.

Figure A.2 Cautionary Censorship ABC, perhaps the boldest of the networks, avoids problems with censorship by advising parental discretion in network promos and in beginning sections of made-for-TV movies like *East of Eden.* And, like all networks now, it provides rating labels recently created for television (TVG, TVMA, and so on).

There is also a certain snobbery among dedicated film buffs against the TV movie. Some of it is justified; some is not. In the early days most of these movies were run-of-the-mill exploitation films or star vehicles, and many were pilots for television series. Barry Diller, formerly in charge of ABC's prime-time programming, admits they made "a lot of junky movies" then.[7] Later, however, he pointed with pride to some landmark films, well-written, hard-biting social problem films like *Friendly Fire*. Some made-for-TV products are so well made that they stand up equally well on the large screen, as witnessed by the success of Steven Spielberg's *Duel*. Others—such as *The Burning Bed* (with Farrah Fawcett), *The Dollmaker* (with Jane Fonda), *An Early Frost* (with Aidan Quinn), and many of the entries in the Hallmark Hall of Fame series—might easily have made that leap to the larger screen.

One advantage of the made-for-TV movie is the flexibility it provides. It can be designed to fit time slots of different lengths. Stories can be filmed with a variety of approaches: as a movie-of-the-week, as a novel-for-television, as a docudrama, or as a miniseries. The length can range from ninety minutes to twenty-five hours, broadcast over several weeks. (Although the miniseries format solves many of the problems of adapting a long, complex novel into a film, it also requires a major commitment of time from the viewer.) This flexibility of format, some well-written scripts, the general seriousness of the subject matter treated, and the overall improvement in quality of the made-for-TV product have combined with a decrease

Figure A.3 Controversial Topics Network television has served the public interest with made-for-TV movies like *Something About Amelia*, with Ted Danson and Roxana Zal (top left), a hard-hitting attack on father–daughter incest; *The Day After*, with Jason Robards and Georgann Johnson (top right), a warning of what a nuclear attack on America would be like; and *Roe vs. Wade*, with Holly Hunter as the woman who challenged the nation's abortion laws in the Supreme Court (bottom left). The networks have also exploited the nation's fascination with bizarre crimes by quickly cranking out docudramas like *Honor Thy Father and Mother: The Menendez Killings*. Pictured here as the brothers accused of murdering their parents are Billy Warlock as Lyle and David Beron as Erik (bottom right).

in the number of theater features produced each year to lure some top movie names to television: Joanne Woodward, Marlon Brando, Robert Mitchum, Jane Fonda, Bette Midler, Robert Duvall, and Tommy Lee Jones have all worked in TV movies in recent years.

A hybrid, the made-for-cable movie, has been introduced by Home Box Office, Turner Productions, and Lifetime, among others, and it has become a considerable success in the late 1990s. For style and quality it falls somewhere between the lower-budget made-for-TV movie and the higher-cost theatrical film.

Questions

On Watching Movies on TV

1. To what degree is the film's continuity destroyed by commercial breaks? Which of these breaks occur at appropriate times in terms of the film's dramatic structure, and which breaks weaken the dramatic tension appreciably?
2. If you saw the film in a theater, can you remember portions that were cut out of the television showing? How important were these segments to the spirit or plot of the film? Can you justify these deletions in terms of the new medium or its mass audience? Were these segments cut out because of time limitations or censorship?
3. If the film is a made-for-television film, how successful is it in solving the problems of the theater film on television?
4. How well is the film suited for viewing on the small screen with relatively poor sound quality? In which scenes do you feel you lack the intensity of involvement needed to enjoy the film? In which scenes does the small-screen format work?
5. Was the movie originally made in a wide-screen format? In which scenes is important information cut off? Are you ever unsure of the character's spatial relationship to his or her environment? How is the aesthetic quality of the composition affected?

Appendix B

Writing a Film Analysis

Films are made to be seen and heard, to appeal to our visual and aural senses. Like any art form, however, films are also meant to be felt and understood, to appeal to our emotions and minds. One of the best ways to determine whether a film has succeeded in any or all of these goals is to analyze the elements that make up the whole work.

To write an analysis of a film, you must study the film carefully. Your critical analysis should be derived from your personal encounter with the film, not from published criticism. Access to a videocassette recorder is essential if you are going to perform a critical analysis of any depth. It is not enough to like or dislike the movie; you must determine why it succeeds or fails in reaching out and encompassing the viewer.

The first step is to view the film in its entirety. From this viewing you can get an initial reaction to the many parts of the film that you will have to explore in more depth. When you first view the film, it is best not to try to take notes or separate the parts of the film; you should be familiar with the textbook in order to know what to look for. After you have formulated a thesis and have begun the process of supporting that thesis, you should view the film at least once more in its entirety and two or three times in segments in order to review scenes of major importance.

The thesis statement is the element around which to structure your analysis. Because the theme or focus of the film is basically the thesis of the filmmaker, identification of that theme can often serve as the thesis of the film analysis itself. You can then view the remainder of the film's elements in light of their success or failure to support the film's central focus.

After determining the thesis, you should view the film again with an eye to noting particular elements used by the filmmaker. At this point you can take a more critical and in-depth look at story, dramatic structure, symbolism, characterization, conflict, and other fictional or dramatic elements. It is important to describe in detail scenes or portions of the film where these elements are used and to discuss their contribution to the film's overall success or failure.

Most of the above mentioned steps are crucial to any literary analysis. The next elements to be considered are peculiar to the film medium. In essence, they are the visual and aural elements that form the basic means of communication in a film. The artistic use of the visual and aural qualities and properties of the film medium determines the effectiveness of a motion picture. Although it is impossible to look at every visual and aural element employed in a film, the use of a VCR or laserdisc or DVD player will enable you to pinpoint and examine the filmmaker's use of camera angles and camera movement, focus, framing, lighting, setting, editing, point of view, special effects, dialogue, and music. After exploring these major cinematic elements and describing specific examples of their use, it is necessary to relate all of these examples and elements to the thesis of your analysis. At this point, the use of a smooth and clear transition is vital to the paper's success.

Though basically objective, a critical analysis should include your personal reactions to the film and explain your reasons for liking or disliking it. Even if the film does not meet your expectations, your analysis should explain how successful the film was in reaching its own level of ambition and in achieving its aims. After completing the film analysis, you probably will not change your immediate reaction to the film. But you are likely to have a better understanding and appreciation of that reaction and the effects of the film on viewers in general.

Sample Student Paper: Analysis of a Complete Film

The paper that follows is an example of a critical analysis of an entire film, *The Grapes of Wrath*. Numbers printed in the margins indicate pages of the textbook that serve as the basis for specific paragraphs of the paper. Once again, it is key to note the importance of personal and independent analysis. The author of this paper read the textbook and viewed the film several times but did not rely on published criticism for the ideas and opinions that she expresses.

John Ford's *The Grapes of Wrath*

—Lisa Cornwell

11–28 Throughout its relatively young life, the motion picture industry has produced an enormous number and variety of films that have ranged from glaring examples of artistic ineptitude to hallmarks of cinematic excellence. Although many of these films have proven memorable for both good and bad reasons, only a few have come to be regarded as true "classics." The films in this category for the most part are centered on a universal and timeless concern that in turn helps those films achieve the enduring excellence that qualifies them as classics. One such film is *The Grapes of Wrath*, directed by John Ford and based on the novel by John Steinbeck.

349–350 *The Grapes of Wrath* tells the story of a family uprooted by the combined forces of
11–28 nature and mechanization and forced into a struggle for survival. Although it is set during the Depression of the 1930s, the film does more than describe the plight of Oklahoma farmers. Director John Ford uses the existing social problem as a background for the development of the film's major themes: familial survival and the related struggle for human dignity, especially for the common man or the "have nots" of society. To a lesser degree, Ford also stresses man's affinity for the land and the need for a communal consciousness among society's underdogs, but those are mainly subthemes used to help support the film's central focus on the family and its survival.

11–28 Throughout the film, that focus is constantly reiterated. When Tom tells Ma of his growing anger against the system, Ma replies, "You gotta keep clear, the family's breaking up. You gotta keep clear." And again, when Tom kills the man who murdered Casey, Ma begs him to stay and help keep the family together. She tells Tom, "They was a time when we was on the lan'. They was a boundary to us then . . . we was the family, kinda whole and clear. An' now we ain't clear no more."

Ford's success in conveying his themes in *The Grapes of Wrath* is greatly aided by his **31–43**
mastery of fictional and dramatic elements, and one of the most important of these is a unified and believable story. Ford and screenwriter Nunnally Johnson manage to transport the Joads from Oklahoma to California using a continuous line of action, with each scene leading logically and inescapably to Tom's growing sense of discontent and resolve and the family's eventual strengthening through adversity. Even though the film ends on an optimistic and perhaps overly sentimental note, *The Grapes of Wrath* presents a realistic and believable portrayal of a migrant family. According to the film, there are no easy solutions to the problems faced by the Joads, and indeed, the viewer receives the impression that there may be no solution except acceptance and the determination to survive.

Another facet of the story that adds to its believability is the understated handling of the **43**
emotional material. The relationships of the individual family members, the death scenes, Connie's desertion of the family, Rose of Sharon's increasing melancholia, and other potentially emotional scenes are played down to a point where they become more indicative of the family's growing acceptance of sorrow as just a part of their everyday lives. There is very little demonstrative affection shown even between Ma and Tom, and Ma makes the statement at the end that "we ain't the kissin' kind." That statement, made as she and Tom say goodbye to one another and briefly kiss, has much more emotional impact than it would have if they wildly clung to one another.

The success of the film's story also owes much to a strong dramatic structure. Using a **43–46**
chronological beginning with Tom's return home and the resulting introduction of the main characters and the problems they face, *The Grapes of Wrath* moves with a growing intensity
toward the climax. The film's major conflict between the "haves" and the "have nots" is **47–49**
introduced in the opening minutes of the film as Tom asks the truck driver for a lift. When the truck driver points out the "No Riders" sticker on the window, Tom's answer reveals his view of society's class conflicts when he replies: "Yeah, but a good guy don't pay no attention to what some heel makes him stick on his truck." Conflict builds as the characters, particularly Tom and Casey, see more and more of the injustices around them. When their passion and the forces surrounding them finally collide in the fight scene, that climax leads naturally to the dénouement and Tom's decision to leave. A flashback near the beginning of the film also furthers the dramatic structure as Muley recalls with painful intensity how the big "cats" invaded his farm. This scene effectively foreshadows the pain and struggle in store for the Joads as the film progresses.

Symbolism is another tool used by Ford to add to the dramatic structure. Much of that **62–70**
symbolism is religious in nature and revolves around the failed preacher, Jim Casey. Beginning with his initials, continuing with his described wandering in search of truth, and ending with the final sacrifice of his life, the film more than hints at Casey as a Christ-like figure. He even tells his persecutors just moments before they kill him that they don't know what they are doing. More religious symbolism can be seen at the opening of the film when the small, lone figure of Tom Joad is shown walking toward a crossroads and later when he becomes a disciple and convert to Casey's philosophy of life.

Another strong symbolic image centers upon Ford's use of hands grasping for soil. The **62–70**
symbol recurs throughout the movie. In one scene, Muley squats down to pick up a handful of dirt and utters his plaintive cry that the land belongs to the ones who were born, lived, and

died on it. In another scene at John's farm, Grandpa grasps a handful of soil as he also reaffirms his dedication to the land he is losing. "This is my dirt," he says. "It's no good, but it's mine, all mine." Perhaps the most effective use of this symbol occurs as Grandpa is dying. His last action is to grasp a handful of dirt in a final attempt to hold onto his "land." All of this symbolism serves to re-emphasize the thematic qualities of courage and determination in the face of loss and despair by illustrating the characters' unwillingness to give up the only possession they feel they have left.

49–61 As with its use of symbolism, *The Grapes of Wrath* utilizes characterization to communicate some of the major truths of the film. And, in fact, the characterization truly makes the film come alive in many respects. Jane Darwell's Ma Joad was a brilliant portrayal of a woman who, while already a strong figure, develops into the sole anchor and strength of her family. Darwell's size and plain but expressive features helped her portrayal significantly, but Ma Joad really came alive on screen through a combination of Darwell's acting skills and the marvelous dialogue she had to work with in the majority of her scenes.

49–61 Examples of the artistry of the Ma Joad characterization abound in the film. At the start of the film, we see a tired and almost beaten woman burn her mementos and refuse to look back at the home she is forced to leave. But as the story progresses, Ma gradually makes more and more of the decisions as Pa gradually relinquishes his role as head of the family. Ma herself recognizes this fact when she tells Tom, "Your Pa's lost his place. He ain't the head no more." The often poor grammar and vocabulary used by the character make her seem more believable as an uneducated farm wife, but what she says and the power with which she says it reveal the true nature of her strong and noble character. Even small traits, such as the care with which she puts her hat on before she goes outside into the dirt and squalor, reveal her resolve not to let circumstances break down the last vestiges of the traditions she clings to so desperately.

49–61 Tom Joad, the other main character in *The Grapes of Wrath*, also shows development throughout the film. Starting as a somewhat hardened ex-convict who just wants to be left alone to tend to himself and his family, Henry Fonda's Tom comes to the conclusion that "a fella ain't got a soul of his own, just a little piece of a big soul." Ford develops Tom from a rather calm and controlled man with a chip on his shoulder to a man whose inner rage finally results in his taking action to try and change the injustices he can no longer tolerate.

49–61 That penchant for violence is carefully developed through what becomes a leitmotif for Tom—his punctuating of strong statements with exclamation marks of "violent action."
282–287 That violent undercurrent and the tension within Tom are constantly present as Fonda tenses his jaw muscles as though trying to control his inner rebellion. It finally erupts in scenes such as the one where he slams the door of the truck and tells the driver he was imprisoned for homicide. Another instance where he can no longer control his anger occurs when he smashes a whiskey bottle against a rock after telling Casey he "killed a guy in a dance hall." Finally, his anger in response to Casey's death explodes with his killing of Casey's murderer. By the end of the film, the preceding events have made him see that the only chance for the common folk is to work together to try and right things for everyone. As in the case of Darwell, Fonda was an excellent choice for the role he played. His tall, lanky build and his slow-moving, slow-talking manner, which seemed to mask an inner fire, makes Tom Joad come alive on the screen.

292 All of the characters were excellently cast and portrayed flawlessly down to the smallest bit part. Perhaps the most effective supporting player emerged with John Qualen's excellent portrayal of Muley Graves. In a classic example of name typing, Ford managed to use the name Muley to help convey the character's stubborn refusal to give up his land. Using Graves as the last name reinforced the "graveyard ghost" image of the character. Qualen's large, staring eyes and almost manic expressions added to the characterization of Muley as a dramatic foil to the Joads. Unlike the Joads, with their stoic acceptance of change and resolve to deal with it, Muley comes across as a man unable to deal with the realities of his situation. He is virtually destroyed by change. 53–57

The individual characters are interesting in themselves, but the conflicts involving them and revolving around them are what make the characters of importance to the viewer. The constant striving to maintain human dignity and family values against a system and against circumstances that seem bent on destroying those qualities is what gives *The Grapes of Wrath* its drama and power. That conflict and its implied resolution for each of the main characters is the very essence of the film itself. Each character's individual battle against the hardship and injustices foisted upon the family and the joint effort to survive as a family unit brings the viewer a sense of kinship with the people on the screen. The very fact that not all of the characters survive the conflict just adds to the film's realism. Without the Joads' constant battle to survive amid the forces of nature and society, *The Grapes of Wrath* would not have emerged as the classic it is but would have joined countless unimportant films that have not survived the test of time. 47–49

In considering time, it is also necessary to view the setting for *The Grapes of Wrath*. The time period in which the story takes place is obviously crucial to the theme and message of the film. Set in a time when countless numbers of people were out of work and faced with poverty and a loss of hope, *The Grapes of Wrath* explores a universal problem even though its focus is mainly on the plight of one family. The social structures and economic factors at work during the Depression of the 1930s led to a lot of questioning on the part of society itself, and individuals with ideas of social reform similar to the views held by Casey and Tom were making themselves heard by a larger number of citizens than ever before in society. The contrasting attitudes evinced by the camp guards and establishment figures in the film are also indicative of the times and add even more realism to the film. 88–98

With land and the loss of land an integral part of the story, the physical location of *The Grapes of Wrath* also proves important to the film's overall message. The rural roots of the Joads in the Oklahoma Dust Bowl region were obviously important in shaping their values and character. Although Ford relies mostly on dialogue and Muley Graves's narration of events to illustrate the ravaging of the Oklahoma farmland, the Joads' small, bleak farmhouse and the old, dilapidated truck adequately convey the poverty of their environment. In later scenes, as the Joads travel west, the setting of the camps also contributes to the realization of what they are up against in their struggle. The dirt and shabbiness of the first camps parallel one of the lowest points in the family's journey, and the clean and well-run government camp proves a better setting for the new sense of optimism emerging at the end of the film. 88–98

Ford has been criticized for setting so much of the film indoors and on studio sets rather than in a more visually appealing and realistic outdoor background; but his use of tents, small rooms, and the cab of the Joads' truck helps define the trapped and confined atmosphere of the Joads' world at that time. The sometimes artificial settings also help define the Joads as being more important than their surroundings. 88–98 87–88

One other dramatic element worth noting in *The Grapes of Wrath* is the use of irony. Throughout much of the film, the Joads continually refer to California as the land of milk 70–74

and honey, a place where they will be able to regain much of what has been taken from them.
As the story progresses, however, the viewer sees that the Joads are in for a rude awakening.
Part of the family is lost on the way; their first view of the land shows a dusty, barren desert
as bleak as the land they left; and the jobs they thought would be in plentiful supply are few
and far between. Indeed, the "grapes" that Grandpa wanted so badly have turned into a
harvest of injustice, poverty and unrest—truly "grapes of wrath."

111–112 Irony and all of the other dramatic and fictional elements utilized by Ford in the
production of his film classic are made even more effective by their combination with the
119–124 visual elements that are essential to the film medium. In *The Grapes of Wrath*, Ford manages
to keep a continuous flow of starkly dramatic and powerful images before the viewer, using a
very tight and controlled cinematic composition. As mentioned previously in the discussion
of setting, Ford placed most of the film's scenes in limited spaces. There are very few long
shots in the film. A long shot of Tom at the film's beginning as he walks toward the crossroads
is followed for the most part by scenes that are either tightly framed, set in small, cramped
areas, or shot so that darkness cuts off the outer edges of the visual image. Even the long shot
of Casey and Tom walking toward the Joad farm and the one of Tom walking up the hill at
the end have a closed feeling to them. The contrast between the dark, solid ground against
the "wall" of sky once again adds a studiolike look to the scenery and prevents the viewer
from perceiving any sense of spaciousness or freedom.

119–124 Unlike the typical modern film, *The Grapes of Wrath* purposely avoids movement and
physical action. Most of the dialogue is delivered by relatively still figures in an atmosphere of
oppressive silence. This static composition focuses our attention on the most dramatic points
in the film: tableau images of the characters, who are seemingly frozen by their inability to
173–175 understand or cope with the events that are turning their lives upside-down. Ford seems to
be trying to focus the viewer's attention on the family members and their personal reactions
to the problems surrounding them rather than on the problems themselves. The only real
sense of movement in the film is imparted through its montage sequences where the Joads
do momentarily become more a part of the overall surroundings. The montage shots are
used to portray the passage of time as the Joads travel across the country. Road signs and
glimpses of long lines of vehicles trailing down the road do give the viewer a sense of the
Joads as part of a larger world. Another montage showing the big "cats" ripping up farmland
compresses the torturous destruction of the farmers' lives into a brief but effective shot. The
137–139 constant background droning of the heavy engines and the superimposed low-angle image
of the treads almost make viewers feel that they are being run over by the massive, devouring
machines, which keep coming rapidly one after the other. This scene also symbolizes the
Okies' helplessness to halt the "progress" that threatens to annihilate them.

For the most part, however, the editing of the film is geared toward emphasizing the
family unit and not the social and physical environment. Slow fade-ins and fade-outs provide
154, 161–162 smooth visual transitions, adding to the overall mood and highlighting the dramatic tensions
within the separate scenes. There is an uncharacteristically jarring note resulting from the
editing of the film. Noah, the brother who begins the journey with the rest of the family, just
disappears somewhere along the way with no mention made of what happened to him.
Readers of Steinbeck's novel know that Noah is retarded, and although this condition is
clearly shown in the film, it is sometimes missed by viewers. In the novel, Noah believes
himself to be a burden to his family and simply walks off after the bathing scene, never to
return. This scene did not appear in the finished film.

On the whole, however, Ford utilized excellent cinematic compression to avoid filming **380–381**
unnecessary scenes from the book. In Grandpa's burial scene, the camera moves in for a close-up shot of Tom adding an "s" to the word "funeral" in the letter he has written. With the simple addition of this letter, Ford manages to foreshadow Grandma's death and imply that she also will receive the standard burial. Thus, he does not have to use additional film time to show the burial.

Another very important visual element that adds to the dramatic effect of *The Grapes of* **101–105**
Wrath is the lighting. The majority of scenes in the film take place at night or in very low-key lighting and fit in naturally with the dark and bleak future that seems to be awaiting the Joads. Casey and Tom meet at dusk; Muley's story is told in a darkened house lit only by a candle; most of the Joads' departures occur at night; the Keene ranch scenes take place mostly in the cabin, where low-key lighting provides a dim setting; and the fight scene is played out not only in the dark but amid the mist and fog hovering over the dark water. Tom and Ma's parting also is a night scene, but from there the film moves into sunlight as an accompaniment to the Joads' more optimistic departure from the government camp.

The contrast in lighting within individual scenes also creates some vivid effects. Most of **101–105**
the light that does exist in the various scenes comes from candles, lanterns, or flashlights
and results in the characters' faces taking on an unreal quality. The scene with Muley in the **154, 161–162**
Joads' deserted farmhouse is especially illustrative of Ford's mastery of low-key lighting. As Tom and Casey enter the deserted house, they and the viewer are met with a complete darkness that is broken only when Muley suddenly appears like a ghost, eerily illuminated in the flickering light of a candle. The viewer, along with Tom and Casey, senses the mysteriousness of the scene and wonders about the fate of the Joads. Muley even refers to himself as an "ol' graveyard ghost," and indeed, that is what he resembles in the dark and deserted farmhouse. The characters' pale faces and darkly expressive eyes give an added emphasis to their dialogue. Casey's final speech to Tom in the tent prior to his death is made with the light from a coal-oil lamp illuminating his face, and once again his Christ-like resemblance is emphasized. The low-key lighting here and throughout the film provides an intensity to the characters and scenes that would not exist in brightly lit conditions. Even in the few instances of high-key lighting included in *The Grapes of Wrath*, shadows are employed to add a dark overtone to the overall mood. When Muley squats in the dust following the destruction of his home, his shadow is diminished into a flat, one-dimensional figure, and we are made to see that Muley has become only the empty shell of a man. The high-angle camera shot also serves to diminish his importance.

One other visually effective tool employed by Ford in *The Grapes of Wrath* is his use of **134–136**
reflection to increase the dramatic depth of a scene. Ma's sad look back at her youth and happiness when she goes through her mementos is made even more dramatic when she holds up the dangling earrings and observes herself in a dusty mirror. For a moment, in the dust and gloom, the lines and wrinkles imposed by age and suffering are softened, and we can almost picture a younger and happier woman. The other highly effective use of reflection occurs in the scene of Pa, Tom, and Al in the cab of the truck. The cramped, tightly framed night scene acquires an added layer of depth when we see the panoramic desert scene unfolding before their ghostlike faces reflected on the dusty windshield.

Ford's composition throughout the film creates a very objective point of view. The **112–119**
viewer more or less observes the film through a "window" with an almost stage-like quality imparted to the scenes viewed through the camera's eye. This in turn makes the viewer

extremely conscious of the dramatic aspects of the film. There is really only one point in the film where Ford employs a sustained subjective point of view. As the Joads drive into the first camp, we see the camp through their eyes as though we were in the truck with them. Ford seems to be trying to make the viewer share the Joads' first jarring realization that their future may not be as promising as they had been led to believe. For a brief, uncomfortable moment, we "become" the Joads and feel like unwanted newcomers entering a hostile twilight zone of poverty and despair. The eyes of the camp residents are not only on the Joads; they are also viewing us with suspicion and hostility. On the whole, however, the scenes of *The Grapes of Wrath* are viewed as one might view a stage play, and once again we are made to focus on the Joads as opposed to the ongoing action around them.

243 Although point of view and visual elements are essential parts of any cinematic film, the use of sound can greatly enhance the dramatic message. In *The Grapes of Wrath*, it is often the silence or absence of sound that provides the emotional intensity emanating from the film. As mentioned earlier, most of the dialogue is delivered in an otherwise silent setting. This makes the viewer concentrate on each word and every nuance of meaning. In the scene where the Joads enter the first camp and see the dirt and despair around them, the silence broken only by the barking of stray dogs further increases the oppressiveness of the camp.

238 The lonely sound of howling wind is also used effectively to punctuate the dramatic movement within the film. Ford uses the sound at appropriate moments such as the scene where Muley tells why the Joads have to move. The sound of the duster and the visual signs of a blowing wind serve as narrative transitions between the present and the past as Muley relates his story. The wind also comes up to howl and blow debris around the farmyard as the Joads leave Uncle John's house. This gives an even more deserted look and feel to the abandoned farm.

249–259 Another aspect of the film related to sound is the use of music as a background for the unfolding events. In *The Grapes of Wrath*, the background music is limited like the rest of the sound. In fact, the dominant theme music heard throughout the film is the folk song "Red River Valley." The haunting refrains of this song are used sparingly to highlight the major emotional scenes such as the one of Ma reviewing her life's souvenirs and the final goodbye between Ma and Tom. It is also used to convey deep sadness as the Joads pull away from the abandoned farm. A flapping door is the only other accompaniment as papers and dust swirl around the abandoned farmhouse, increasing the sense of desertion and the ending of one phase of the Joads' lives. As the truck turns onto the main highway heading west, the music changes instantly into an optimistic and heroic hymn of hope. "Red River Valley" is also employed effectively at the dance, this time with words: When Tom starts singing the lines of the song while dancing with Ma, we see the frightened and sad look on her face as she listens to the part of the song signifying farewell. As Tom sings, "Come and sit by my side if you love me. Do not hasten to bid me adieu," we see the expression on Ma's face change from one of happiness to one of worry and fear. Ford uses this to foreshadow the final parting of Ma and Tom. The lyrics "Just remember the Red River Valley and the boy that has loved you so true" add to that foreshadowing and also re-emphasize the Okies' departure from Oklahoma (the Red River Valley). The song that Connie plays and sings on the store porch at one of the camps, "Goin' Down the Road Feelin' Bad," summarizes his feelings about the journey west and foreshadows his subsequent desertion of the family.

Throughout the previous discussion of sound, visual elements, and dramatic and fic- 309–314
tional elements, it has been clear that this film was strongly influenced by the director's style. A director who believed in the simplicity of visual statement, Ford was sparing in his use of camera movement, dialogue, and background sound, and this style is clearly evident in *The Grapes of Wrath*. Ford was also known as a director who shared an empathy with the common people but also imposed a rather strict and traditional moral code on their actions. He believed in an adherence to traditional values, and the Joads' fight to maintain their values fits in concisely with that style.

Ford's intention with *The Grapes of Wrath* was to film a strong, compelling story of a 349
family's struggle to survive and to maintain a level of human dignity, and in this he succeeded.
All of the elements described in the earlier part of this analysis were used to further Ford's 66–68
sense of what his film was meant to communicate. At times Ford and the film itself have been criticized for not following the aims of the original novel. Critics have said that the socialistic themes of the book and the implied suggestion of the common people banding together to combat the forces of established power and authority were lost in Ford's cinematic version of the Joad saga, and, in a very real sense, those critics are correct. Ford subordinated concern for the family of man to concern for one man's family. At the same time, however, he projected a sense of universality. The Joads may not have meshed as much as they might have with the surrounding families, but they served as a sharply delineated representation of an individual family's response to the forces around it. And in many ways, this imparted a sense of realism to the film. Most families, when their very existence is threatened, are much more concerned with their individual survival than they are with the survival of society as a whole. This viewpoint is clearly conveyed several times during the film. When Joe Davis's boy comes to bulldoze Muley's farm and is asked why he is doing this, he replies, ". . . for three dollars a day. That's what I'm doing it for. My wife and my three kids and my wife's mother got to eat." This same idea is repeated in the dialogue between Casey and Tom. When Casey wants Tom and the others to join the strike, Tom says, "I know what Pa'd say. We ate tonight. Not good, but we ate, and that's all Pa cares about." Even when Tom comes to share some of Casey's conclusions that "A fella ain't got a soul of his own, just a little piece of a big soul," he still implies that his concern is with making life better for his family by finding out what's wrong and trying to do something about it. He also voices the concern that if he stays, he will endanger the family he and Ma have been trying to save.

After an analysis of all of these various elements, I can truly say that I found *The Grapes* 351
of Wrath a strong and compelling film that more than deserves its reputation as a "classic." Ford's artistry in conveying his film's message through the use of clear and precise visual images and understated yet deep emotional content made the film reach out to me as a viewer. The perfect casting of such superb actors as Henry Fonda, Jane Darwell, and John Carradine added to the film's believability, as did Nunnally Johnson's well-structured screenplay and Gregg Toland's expressive photography. The parts of the film that perhaps can be termed as overly sentimental and optimistic somehow seemed to fit in with the overall theme. Even Ma's final speech ("They can't wipe us out. They can't lick us. We'll go on forever, Pa, 'cause we're the people.") has an honest ring to it despite the sentimental overtones

Although *The Grapes of Wrath* may not have been a completely realistic look at the plight of migrant workers from the nation's Dust Bowl, it wasn't meant to be a documentary. It succeeded as it was meant to succeed, as a haunting and evocative image of a specific era of American history and of the type of people that lived through it and endured.

Sample Student Paper: Analysis of Selected Film Elements

Instead of analyzing a whole film, you may be asked to write a brief paper focusing on the four or five elements you consider crucial to the film's overall impact. This kind of paper can be limited to four or five typed pages and can be designed to fit a simple but very workable organizational pattern. The marginal notes in the sample below describe how the paper is structured. The numbers in the margin indicate pages in the textbook used as a basis for the paper.

Assignment

1. Study the assigned film by watching it several times on a VCR, focusing on answering the questions on the basic approach to analysis of the whole film on page 366.
2. After watching the film, choose four or five elements that contribute significantly to the film's overall effect, and analyze in some detail the contributions of each. Use technical terms and concepts discussed in the text when they are pertinent to your analysis.
3. Use your analyses of the individual film elements as the body of your paper; then add an introductory paragraph, transitions, and a conclusion to shape the paper into a complete essay. The sample paper on *Taxi Driver* demonstrates how one student handled the assignment.

Martin Scorsese's *Taxi Driver*

—Kira Carollo

11–26 *The introductory paragraph accomplishes three goals:*

1. It provides necessary information on the film, in this case by placing it in historical context. The introduction could instead provide other kinds of information, such as awards won by the film, critical and popular response, or its relationship to other films by the same director. Any background information provided here should be both general and brief.

2. It identifies the elements to be analyzed in the body of the paper, and it attempts to relate each element to theme.

3. It attempts to state, as clearly as possible, the film's theme or central concern.

Martin Scorsese's powerful film *Taxi Driver* is one that delves into serious moral, social, and political issues of its time, issues that are still highly relevant today. Made in 1976, it surfaced at a time in American history during which there was much social and political unrest. Our country was divided on many issues of the day—the aftermath of the Vietnam War, political chaos resulting from our growing distrust of the government after the Watergate scandal, and increasing crime rates in our cities. Because many veterans returning from combat duty in Vietnam had serious difficulties coping with "normal" life, Paul Schrader's script for *Taxi Driver* embodies our nation's frustration, rage, and confusion in the character of Travis Bickle, a troubled young ex-marine. The film succeeds for a number of reasons. Robert De Niro's excellent portrayal of Travis gives the character meaning and significance in several ways. Scorsese's use of voice-over narration in the film is an element which adds impact to Bickle's struggle to make sense of his world. The use of ambient sound, music, and powerful visual elements is also instrumental in conveying the film's theme: one man's lonely struggle for some form of identity and human dignity, as well as some understanding of his place in the world as an individual.

One of the most important elements in *Taxi Driver* is the characterization of the title character, achieved through name typing, dialogue, and appearance. The names of characters in film are usually carefully chosen, often to suggest some important qualities of the character himself. Travis Bickle is a name that is easily remembered—it seems to stick in the viewer's mind. The name "Bickle" is simple and direct; "Travis" has a more melodic flow. The two together seem to fit the character's contradiction. He is methodical and steady as suggested by the fluent name. Yet he can also be direct and harsh, as evident in the abrupt name "Bickle." The nature of his dialogue also gives the viewer insight into Bickle's character—not only what is said, but how it is said. His frequent use of "rough" language, his lapse into poor grammar, his name-calling and stereotyping of the people in the streets, and his violent thought processes reveal much about his social, economic, and educational background. Travis's appearance adds even more clues to his character. He continually wears a dirty army jacket (collar turned up), his hair is greasy and ungroomed, and he always has a dark "five o'clock shadow." De Niro's portrayal of his constant worried expression, his obvious nervousness, and his social ineptness completes the picture and proves De Niro a wise casting choice. He is completely believable in the role.

In the first sentence of the body of the paper, the writer informs us of the subject of the first section (characterization) and names the various aspects to be discussed (name typing, dialogue, and appearance). She then proceeds to discuss each of these aspects in the order named. **49–61**

Another element used in this film that adds strength to its theme is voice-over narration, the use of a human voice off-screen that can have a variety of functions. Scorsese uses it to add a sense of authenticity and to tell the viewer what cannot satisfactorily be conveyed by cinematic means. Originating from Travis's reading of entries in his journal, the voice-over narration in *Taxi Driver* gives clear insight into Bickle's innermost thoughts and feelings, insight that is essential to understanding the real forces that drive the action of the film. Travis's sense of angst about his environment and his place in it, and his overwhelming desire for "a real rain to come and wash all this scum off the streets," are expressed only in voice-over. The soft, understated tone and unhurried rhythmic pace provide a chilling "verbal essence" to De Niro's narration, in ironic contrast to the anger and violence simmering inside the character. The sound of De Niro's voice combined with the environmental noises of the city enhances the dichotomy seen within the character of Bickle. The contrast between his calm, soft monotone and the chaotic, noisy, fast-paced street sounds helps to create another level of tension in the film.

In the second paragraph of the **282–286**
body, the writer provides transi- **269–270**
tion ("Another element"), intro- **239–243**
duces that element ("voice-over narration"), and then proceeds with her description of its effective use in the film. The writer scores points here for her clear and sensitive description of the special qualities of the voice-over and for the well-chosen quotation.

From the opening scene to the final scene, the background music also plays an important role. The rhythmic drumbeats in opposition to the melodic harp and orchestral sounds create a haunting cadence echoed throughout the film, evoking strong emotional responses. The drumbeats are pounding and heavy as op-

The third element to be analyzed, background music, is introduced in this paragraph's first sentence. The transitional "also" signals the new subject. Although **249–251**

music is hard to describe and the writer is sensitive to its overall effects, she loses points by simply generalizing the term "orchestral." What style of music is being used? Do certain kinds of instruments (such as strings, brass, or
137–145 *woodwinds) dominate the "orchestral" score?*

203 *The fourth element, unusual visual images, is introduced by the first sentence of this paragraph, with the transitional "also" again signaling a new subject. In this same sentence, the writer provides a breakdown of the topics to be covered: slow motion, unique camera angles, and color. She then proceeds to discuss the topics in the order named.*

The concluding paragraph in this simple pattern has two definite requirements:

1. It should remind the reader of the main points covered in the paper (the elements analyzed and the film's theme).

2. It should make "ending noises," giving the reader a sense that the paper is finished.

The brief conclusion provided here meets both of those requirements.

posed to the light, melodic sounds of the orchestra. We can feel our hearts beating in time with these beats while we breathe a sigh of relief with the orchestral sounds. The use of the harp during the final shootout is also especially effective, casting an eerie, surreal feeling over that portion of the film.

Unusual visual images also contribute significantly to the overall effect of *Taxi Driver*, especially Scorsese's use of slow motion, unique camera angles, and color. Slow motion, a technique often used to "stretch the moment" in order to intensify its emotional quality, is used in the final battle scene in the hallway. The shootout takes only a brief moment of time yet seems painfully long and brutal when viewed in slow motion. An exceptionally high camera angle is used at the ending of this scene. The camera seemingly retreats into the ceiling, drawn up and above the action, to create an almost ethereal mood. This unusual overhead view creates a strangely mixed reaction, enhancing the emotional impact of the scene by drawing the viewer into the action and away from it at the same time. This same scene is made potent by the use of contrast in color. As Bickle travels the staircase, the lighting is dim with a yellow cast, giving a cold eerie feel to the scene. The last quiet scene in the hotel room displays stark reds, which echo the brutality and violence of the earlier scene and send the audience into aftershock. These powerful visual images add greatly to the intensity of our emotional response to the film.

The skillful use of characterization, music and sound effects, voice-over narration, and unusual visual techniques helps to make *Taxi Driver* a striking and dynamic film. Through Martin Scorsese's masterful direction, Travis Bickle's poignant struggle for identity and human dignity becomes an unforgettable film experience.

Sample Student Paper: Analysis for Study

Here is another sample review. Use the margins to make your own annotations about the important points in this analysis.

Honor Versus Passion: May and Ellen as Dramatic Foils in *The Age of Innocence*

—CAROLYN DENISE TOMLINSON

New York in the 1870s paid homage to the Victorian age of England. Bound by excessive rules of etiquette and by a society dominated by the "right" bloodlines, the narrator of Martin Scorsese's *The Age of Innocence* explains, "this was a world balanced so precariously that its harmony could be shattered by a whisper." Scorsese's film shows us this world through the eyes of Newland Archer, a wealthy young lawyer from one of the acceptable families. Based on Edith Wharton's novel, the film uses the cinematic technique of dramatic foils to illustrate Archer's battle between honor and passion.

Engaged to May Welland, one of the gems of New York society, Newland Archer is tempted by the arrival of the beautiful Countess Olenska. The countess has escaped from a disastrous marriage to a Polish count and has returned home to her family. Her arrival scandalizes the proper society, and she feels the backlash for her unacceptable behavior soon after she arrives. Archer, however, feels honor-bound to protect his fiancée's cousin and uses his family connections to ensure her admittance to society. Throughout the film, May Welland, Archer's fiancée, and Ellen, Countess Olenska, are established as dramatic foils. By using this technique in casting, costuming, setting, and characterization, Scorsese is able to communicate the vast differences between the characters as well as to establish their opposing positions in the society of New York.

The casting of May and Ellen provides one of the most obvious elements of the dramatic foil. May is portrayed by Winona Ryder, Ellen by Michelle Pfeiffer. The actresses' physical characteristics are the first indication of the dramatic foil device: Ryder is a waifish brunette, whereas Pfeiffer is a willowy blonde. The age difference between May and Ellen is also easily distinguished through casting. Ryder gives a subtle but powerful performance as the twenty-two-year-old May; Pfeiffer, as the older worldly-wise Ellen, invests her character with a mystery that is essential to the role. By casting actresses with contrasting physical attributes and ages, Scorsese provides an immediate sense of their characters' opposing personalities.

Another example of how May and Ellen are dramatic foils in the film is the way in which they are costumed. When we first see the two ladies, sitting together in the balcony of the opera house, May is dressed in pale pink with white gloves and fresh flowers for adornment, while Ellen is wearing a turquoise gown and lavish jewelry. During dinner at the Van der Luydens, May and Ellen are also costumed very differently. As the narrator, Joanne Woodward, explains, "Dining with the Van der Luydens was at best no light matter. Dining there with a duke who was their cousin was almost a religious solemnity." Not only does the countess arrive late, but she does so wearing a bright red gown. May, on the other hand, is attired in a pale, almost white, gown, which we learn is the appropriate choice when Mrs. Van der Luyden mentions how lovely she looks and tells us that the duke thinks May "the handsomest woman in the room."

The actresses are also given very different hair and makeup styles. May's hair always appears smooth and shiny, and her makeup emphasizes her youth with pinks and pale tones. Ellen, however, is frequently seen in unflattering, harsher makeup tones, and her hair is often frizzy and rumpled. Through these physical characterizations, we are encouraged further to see the characters as opposites.

In addition, Scorsese uses setting to establish May and Ellen as dramatic foils. Although May and Ellen both live in New York, May lives in a lavishly decorated mansion, whereas Ellen lives in an "odd little house" in the wrong part of town. In one scene, Archer and Ellen are visiting at the Beauford farm. They are surrounded by ice and snow and are huddled beneath mounds of clothing. Immediately following this scene, we see May in a beautiful garden in Florida, surrounded by fresh flowers and flooded in sunlight.

Flowers are likewise important in another setting that establishes the foil between May and Ellen. Archer sends his fiancée the accustomed daily bouquet of lilies of the valley and notices a brilliant display of yellow roses, which he sends to Ellen. The audience sees Ellen lovingly arranging her flowers that evening in her home, dressed in a white gown with her hair down. The next scene shows us Archer and May, walking through a conservatory the next morning. May, dressed in navy, thanks Archer for her flowers and mentions her surprise over Ellen's reaction to receiving flowers. "She was so very delighted. Don't people send flowers in Europe?" At this point the audience truly begins to see May differently, as Scorsese, through setting, shows Ellen in the soft light of a fire and May in the bright morning sun.

Even as they are represented as visual opposites, they are also developed as character opposites. May is shown as quiet, demure, and very proper. She is the honorable choice for Archer, and, as the narrator tells us, "Archer's fiancée was innocent of all these intrigues and of much else. May Welland represented for Archer all that was best in their world, all that he honored, and she anchored him to it." Ellen, however, is shown as a free-spirited woman who is not afraid to speak her mind. Having lived abroad since her marriage, Ellen operates under a European set of norms and commits several faux pas in the first few minutes on-screen. One of these errors occurs when Ellen holds out her hand to Archer at their introduction. His reaction shows us that her behavior is not appropriate, but instead of embarrassing her, he bows over her hand in welcome. The narrator tells us that Ellen has always been eccentric and "was even allowed to wear black satin at her coming out."

The final element of the dramatic foil is created in Archer's relationships with May and Ellen. Although he is charmed by May's "inexpressive girlishness," he wonders if he will be challenged by her. The narrator expresses Archer's feelings and thoughts: "It was wonderful, he thought, how such depths of feeling could coexist with such an absence of imagination." Archer knows that choosing May will ensure him a place in New York society, but he begins to see that he wants more than just a proper wife: "The taste of the usual was like cinders in his mouth, and there were moments when he felt as if he were being buried alive under his future."

In contrast, Ellen challenges Archer to think about things he's never considered and to look at the world in a way he has never imagined. As the narrator observes, "Archer enjoyed such challenges to convention. He questioned conformity in private, but in public he upheld family and tradition." However, Archer panics when he realizes the depths of his feelings for Ellen and marries May. Although he tries to carry on his relationship with Ellen, it soon becomes impossible. Ellen refuses to hurt her cousin and eventually returns to her husband. In one of their final scenes together, Archer tells her, "You gave me my first glimpse of a real life and then you told me to carry on with a false one. No one can endure that." She replies, "I'm enduring it."

Archer tries to leave his wife but is thwarted when he learns that she is pregnant. Accepting his fate, the narrator tells us, "Archer embraced his new marriage even as he reverted to his old inherited ideas about matrimony. It was less trouble to conform with tradition. There was no use trying to emancipate a wife who hadn't the dimmest notion that she was not free."

Martin Scorsese masterfully uses the dramatic foil technique in *The Age of Innocence* to establish May, Archer's innocent and proper fiancée, and Ellen, his witty, exotic love, as opposites. By using this technique in casting, costuming, setting, and characterization, Scorsese is able to compare the two worlds between which Archer must choose. May versus Ellen must be thought of as "Honor" versus "Passion" in *The Age of Innocence.* And, although honor wins in the end, Archer, and the entangled path he follows, is clearly shown by the filmmaker's use of dramatic foils.

Notes

Chapter 1

1. Ernest Lindgrin, *The Art of the Film* (New York: Macmillan, 1963), pp. 204–205.
2. Aldous Huxley, *Brave New World* (New York: Harper, 1946), p. 23.
3. Richard Dyer MacCann, ed., *Film: A Montage of Theories* (New York: Dutton, 1966), p. 56.

Chapter 2

1. Sidney Lumet, *Making Movies* (New York: Knopf, 1995), p. 10.

Chapter 3

1. Cesare Zavattini, "Some Ideas on the Cinema," *Sight and Sound* (October 1953), p. 64.
2. Neil Simon, quoted in John Brady, *The Craft of the Screenwriter* (New York: Simon & Schuster, 1981), p. 318.
3. Ernest Lehman, quoted in Brady, pp. 203–204.
4. Danny De Vito, quoted in Robert Seidenberg, "Funny as Hell," *American Film* (September 1989), p. 47.
5. Griffin Dunne, quoted in Anna McDonnell, "Happily Ever After," *American Film* (January–February 1987), p. 44.
6. Robert Penn Warren, "Why Do We Read Fiction?" in *An Approach to Literature*, edited by Cleanth Brooks et al. (New York: Appleton-Century-Crofts, 1964), p. 866.
7. Frank Capra, quoted in *Directing the Film: Film Directors on Their Art*, edited by Eric Sherman (Los Angeles: Acrobat Books, 1976), pp. 308–309.
8. Paul Schrader, quoted in Brady, pp. 298–299.
9. Robert Towne, quoted in Brady, p. 394.
10. Tennessee Williams, *Suddenly, Last Summer.* Copyright © 1958 by Tennessee Williams. All rights reserved. All quotations reprinted by permission of New Directions Publishing Corporation.
11. Ernest Lehman, quoted in Brady, pp. 199–200.

Chapter 4

1. Peter Bogdanovich, quoted in *Film Makers Speak: Voices of Film Experience*, edited by Jay Leyda (New York: DaCapo Press, 1984), p. 145.
2. Nestor Almendros, quoted ibid., p. 40.
3. Nestor Almendros, *A Man With a Camera*, translated by Rachel Phillips Belash (Boston: Faber and Faber, 1984), p. 15.
4. Ibid., pp. 12–13.
5. Bart Mills, "The Brave New World of Production Design," *American Film* (January–February 1982), p. 40.
6. Paul Sylbert, quoted in Vincent LoBrutto, *By Design: Interviews With Production Designers* (Westport, CN: Praeger, 1992), p. 85.
7. Patricia Von Brandenstein, quoted ibid., p. 186.
8. Paul Sylbert, quoted ibid., p. 82.
9. John Box, quoted in *Film Makers Speak*, p. 45.
10. Charles Rosher, quoted ibid., p. 404.
11. Tennessee Williams, *Suddenly, Last Summer.* Copyright © 1958 by Tennessee Williams. All rights reserved. Reprinted by permission of New Directions Publishing Corporation.

12. Chuck Rosen, quoted in Linda Gross, "On Golde River," *Los Angeles Times Calendar* (November 13, 1983), p. 22.
13. Kristi Zea, quoted in LoBrutto, p. 248.
14. Robert Boyle, quoted ibid., p. 16.
15. Mills, p. 45.
16. Edith Head, quoted in *Film Makers on Film Making: The American Film Institute Seminars on Motion Pictures and Television*, vol. 2, edited by Joseph McBride (Los Angeles: J. P. Tarcher), p. 166.
17. Edith Head, quoted ibid., p. 167.
18. Edith Head, quoted ibid., p. 169.
19. Mary Astor, quoted in *Film Makers Speak*, p. 17.
20. Todd Rainsberger, *James Wong Howe: Cinematographer* (New York: A. S. Barnes, 1981), p. 75.
21. "Zsigmond," *American Film* (September 1982), p. 55.
22. "Almendros," *American Film* (December 1981), p. 19.

Chapter 5

1. Vilmos Zsigmond, "Dialogue on Film," *American Film* (June 1979), p. 41.
2. Alfred Hitchcock, quoted in Richard Dyer MacCann, ed., *Film: A Montage of Theories* (New York: Dutton, 1966), p. 57. From "Direction" by Alfred Hitchcock, in *Footnotes to the Film*, edited by Charles Davy; reprinted by permission of Peter Davies Ltd., publishers.
3. Alfred Hitchcock, quoted in *Directing the Film: Film Directors on Their Art*, edited by Eric Sherman (Los Angeles: Acrobat Books, 1976), pp. 254–255.
4. Nestor Almendros, *Man With a Camera*, translated by Rachel Phillips Belash (Boston: Faber and Faber, 1984), p. 14.
5. Alan Dwan, quoted in *Directing the Film*, p. 108.
6. Frank Brady, *Citizen Welles: A Biography of Orson Welles* (New York: Doubleday, 1989), p. 257.
7. Lily Tomlin, as told to Jane Wagner, "Memoirs of an Usherette," *The Movies* (July 1983), pp. 41–42.
8. The American Film Institute, *Visions of Light: The Art of Cinematography*, written and directed by Todd McCarthy, 1993.

Chapter 6

1. V. I. Pudovkin, *Film Technique and Film Acting* (New York: Grove Press, 1976), p. 24.

d Hitchcock, quoted in Richard Dyer
nn, ed., *Film: A Montage of Theories* (New
tton, 1966), p. 56.
Praan, quoted in Vincent LoBrutto, *Selected*
4. Tom *litors on Film Editing* (Westport, CN:
5. Ralph W p. 144.
6. Richard Ma ibid., p. 90.
7. Alfred Hitchc ted ibid., p. 44.
d ibid., pp. 181–182.
Directors and The d in *Directing the Film: Film*
Angeles: Acrobat Bo ted by Eric Sherman (Los
8. Elia Kazan, *A Life* (Nev 6), p. 107.
p. 380. Doubleday, 1989),
9. Ephraim Katz, *The Film Ency*
by Fred Klein and Ronald Dean, 3rd ed., revised
HarperPerennial, 1998), p. 718. n (New York:
10. Sergei Eisenstein, *The Film Sense*, tran
Leyda (New York: Harcourt, Brace and d by Jay
1947), pp. 30–31. ld,
11. Peter Biskind, quoted in "Jungle Fever," *Prem*
(July 1993), p. 67.
12. David Ansen, quoted in David Ehrenstein, "One From the Art," *Film Comment* (January–February 1993), p. 30.
13. Anne Bancroft, quoted in "AFI's 100 Years . . . 100 Movies," *CBS Television* (June 16, 1998).
14. Richard Edlund, quoted in Vision Films/Smithsonian Video (DVD), *The Art of Illusion: One Hundred Years of Hollywood Special Effects*, 1990, rev. 1995.

Chapter 7

1. Lewis Jacobs, "The Mobility of Color," in *The Movies as Medium*, ed. Lewis Jacobs (New York: Farrar, Straus, and Giroux, 1970), p. 196.
2. Weldon Blake, *Creative Color: A Practical Guide for Oil Painters* (New York: Watson-Guptill, 1972), p. 14.
3. Robert Boyle, quoted in Vincent LoBrutto, *By Design: Interviews With Film Production Designers* (Westport, CN: Praeger, 1992), p. 7.
4. Mark Rydell, quoted in Judith Crist, *Take 22: Moviemakers on Moviemaking*, new expanded ed. (New York: Continuum, 1991), p. 180.
5. Jonathan Baumbach, "From A to Antonioni," in *Great Film Directors: A Critical Anthology*, edited

by Leo Brandy and Morris Dickstein (New York: Oxford University Press, 1978), p. 29.

6. Gerald Mast, *A Short History of the Movies* (Ind... olis: Bobbs-Merrill, 1981), p. 295.
7. Paul Schrader, quoted in John Brady, *The ... the Screenwriter* (New York: Simon & S... 1981), p. 302.
8. Michael Pye and Lynda Myles, *Th... s: How the Film Generation Took Over H...* ...ew York: Holt, Rinehart and Winston ...213.
9. Richard Corliss, "Extra! D... s Tops," *Time,* June 18, 1990, p. 76.
10. John Huston, *John H... Open Book* (New York: Knopf, 1980), p. 2...
11. Laszlo Kovacs, "...ue on Film," *American Film* (June 1979), ...
12. John Schle... r, "Dialogue on Film," *American Film* (N... er 1987), p. 15.
13. Gilbe... ates, quoted in Susan Linfield, "The Color of M... ey," *American Film* (January–February 1987), p... 2.
14. Steven Spielberg, quoted in Rogert Ebert and Gene Siskel, *The Future of the Movies: Interviews With Martin Scorsese, Steven Spielberg, and George Lucas* (Kansas City: Andrews and McMeel, 1991), p. 58.
15. John Huston, "Dialogue on Film," *American Film* (January–February 1984), p. 22.
16. "Almendros," *American Film* (December 1981), p. 19.
17. Editors of the Eastman Kodak Company, *More Joy of Photography,* rev. ed. (Reading, MA: Addison-Wesley, 1988), p. 50.
18. Martin Scorsese, quoted in Mary Pat Kelly, *Martin Scorsese: A Journey* (New York: Thunder's Mouth Press, 1991), p. 125.
19. Robert Edmond Jones, "The Problem of Color," in *The Emergence of Film Art,* 2nd ed., edited by Lewis Jacobs (New York: Norton, 1970), pp. 207–208.
20. Martin Scorsese, quoted in "State of the Art," *Dateline NBC* (June 28, 1998).

Chapter 8

1. Leonard Bernstein, *The Joy of Music* (New York: Simon & Schuster, 1959), p. 66.

...rner, quoted in Vincent LoBrutto, *Sound-on-... nterviews With Creators of Film Sound* (West... t, CN: Praeger, 1994), p. 36.

3. Ray Sawhill, "Pumping Up the Volume: Movie Sound Has Been Getting Better—and Louder," *Newsweek* (July 6, 1998), p. 66.
4. Skip Lievsay, quoted in LoBrutto, *Sound-on-Film,* p. 264.
5. Steven Spielberg, quoted in Judith Crist, *Take 22: Moviemakers on Moviemaking,* new expanded ed. (New York: Continuum, 1991), p. 369.
6. Mark Mangini, quoted in LoBrutto, *Sound-on-Film,* p. 279.
7. Skip Lievsay, quoted ibid., p. 264.
8. Roger Ebert, "The Opposite of Sex," *Chicago Sun-Times* (June 19, 1998), *http://www.suntimes.com/ebert/.*

Chapter 9

1. Muir Mathieson, quoted in Roger Manvell and John Huntley, *The Technique of Film Music* (London: Focal Press, 1957), p. 210.
2. Quincy Jones, quoted in Fred Baker with Ross Firestone, "Quincy Jones—On the Composer," in *Movie People: At Work in the Business of Film* (New York: Lancer Books, 1973), p. 191.
3. Jerry Bruckheimer, quoted in Ray Sawhill, "Pumping Up the Volume," *Newsweek* (July 6, 1998), p. 66.
4. Martin Scorsese, quoted in "About Elmer Bernstein," *The Age of Innocence,* soundtrack compact disk notes, Epic Soundtrax, 1993.
5. Jerry Goldsmith, quoted in *Filmmakers on Filmmaking: The American Film Institute Seminars on Motion Pictures and Television,* vol. 2, ed. Joseph McBride (Los Angeles: J. P. Tarcher, 1983), pp. 136–137.
6. Frank Brady, *Citizen Welles: A Biography of Orson Welles* (New York: Doubleday, 1989), pp. 264–265.
7. Jonathan Demme, quoted in Roger Catlin (*Hartford Courant*), "The Perfect Soundtrack Is Music to a Director's Ears," *The* [Fort Wayne] *Journal Gazette* (April 11, 1998), p. 2D.
8. "Peter Weir, Reflecting on the Score for *The Truman Show,*" *The Truman Show,* soundtrack compact disk notes, Milan Entertainment Inc., 1998.
9. Brady, p. 264.

10. John Badham, quoted in Judith Crist, *Take 22: Moviemakers on Moviemaking*, new expanded ed. (New York: Continuum, 1991), pp. 420–421.
11. Terry Atkinson, "Scoring With Synthesizers," *American Film* (September 1982), p. 70.
12. Ibid., p. 68.
13. David Shire, quoted in Tony Thomas, *Music for the Movies*, 2nd ed. (Los Angeles: Silman-James Press, 1997), pp. 309–310, 311–312. Tony Thomas has also created (as writer and coproducer) the indispensable American Film Classics documentary *The Hollywood Soundtrack Story* (1995). Hosted by composer Randy Newman, the film discusses and illustrates the careers of many noteworthy film composers, including the following: Elmer Bernstein (*The Ten Commandments, The Magnificent Seven*), Danny Elfman (*Batman, Edward Scissorhands, Men in Black*), Jerry Goldsmith (*Patton, Air Force One*), Bernard Herrmann (*Citizen Kane, Psycho*), Maurice Jarre (*Lawrence of Arabia, Doctor Zhivago*), Erich Wolfgang Korngold (*The Adventures of Robin Hood*), Henry Mancini (*The Pink Panther, Breakfast at Tiffany's*), Alan Menken (*The Little Mermaid, Beauty and the Beast*), Alex North (*A Streetcar Named Desire, Who's Afraid of Virginia Woolf?*), Basil Poledouris (*Conan the Barbarian*), Rachel Portman (*Benny & Joon, Emma*), David Raksin (*Laura*), Leonard Rosenman (*East of Eden*), Miklos Rozsa (*The Last Weekend, Spellbound*), Marc Shaiman (*City Slickers, Sleepless in Seattle*), Max Steiner (*King Kong, Gone With the Wind, The Treasure of the Sierra Madre*), Dimitri Tiomkin (*High Noon*), Franz Waxman (*Sunset Boulevard, A Place in the Sun*), and John Williams (*Star Wars, E.T. The ExtraTerrestrial, Schindler's List*).

    Another very helpful and enjoyable video source about film music is the documentary/performance work *John Barry: Moviola*, which was first broadcast on the PBS series *Great Performances* in 1993 (Big Shot Films). Barry, the prolific composer of many of the James Bond film scores, is perhaps best known for the lyrical works in the films *Born Free, Midnight Cowboy, Somewhere in Time, Body Heat, Out of Africa, Dances With Wolves*, and *Chaplin*. In the documentary sections of this film, the extraordinary relationships between Barry and his movies' directors are examined through interviews with Kevin Costner, Sir Richard Attenborough, and Sydney Pollack.
14. Randy Newman, quoted in "Movie Music: Coupla White Guys Sitting Around Talking," *Premiere* (June 1989), p. 139.
15. Sidney Lumet, *Making Movies* (New York: Knopf, 1995), pp. 176, 178.

Chapter 10

1. Mark Rydell, quoted in "Dialogue on Film," *American Film* (June 1982), p. 23.
2. George R. Kernodle, *An Invitation to the Theatre* (New York: Harcourt, Brace and World, 1967), p. 259.
3. Alfred Hitchcock, quoted in Richard Dyer MacCann, ed., *Film: A Montage of Theories* (New York: Dutton, 1966), p. 57.
4. Rydell, "Dialogue on Film," p. 23.
5. Michael Caine, qoted in Judith Crist, *Take 22: Moviemakers on Moviemaking*, new expanded ed. (New York: Continuum, 1991), p. 446.
6. Edward James Olmos, quoted in Linda Seger and Edward Jay Whetmore, *From Script to Screen: The Collaborative Art of Filmmaking* (New York: Henry Holt, 1994), p. 161.
7. Cliff Robertson, quoted in Crist, pp. 106–107.
8. Joanne Woodward, quoted ibid., p. 60.
9. Michael Caine, *Acting in Film: An Actor's Take on Movie Making*, revised expanded ed. (New York: Applause Theatre Books, 1997), pp. 88–89.
10. Elia Kazan, *A Life* (New York: Doubleday, 1989), p. 530.
11. Henry Fonda, as told to Howard Teichman, *Fonda: My Life* (New York: New American Library, 1981), p. 104.
12. Robert Shaw, quoted in "Ask Them Yourself," *Family Weekly* (June 11, 1972).
13. Julian Fast, *Body Language* (New York: M. Evans, 1970), p. 185.
14. Jack Kroll, "Robert De Niro," in *The National Society of Film Critics on the Movie Star*, edited by Elisabeth Weiss (New York: Viking Press, 1981), p. 198.
15. Béla Balázs, *Theory of the Film: Character and Growth of a New Art*, translated by Edith Bone (New York: Dover, 1970), p. 168.

16. Michael Caine, quoted in Crist, p. 445.
17. V. I. Pudovkin, *Film Technique and Film Acting*, memorial edition, translated and edited by Ivor Montagu (New York: Grove Press, 1958), p. 168.
18. Sergio Leone, quoted in David Morrison, "Leonesque," *American Film* (September 1989), p. 31.
19. Edward A. Wright and Lenthiel H. Downs, *A Primer for Playgoers* (Englewood Cliffs, NJ: Prentice-Hall, 1969), pp. 217–220.
20. Steven Spielberg, quoted in Crist, p. 371.
21. Sidney Lumet, *Making Movies* (New York: Knopf, 1995), p. 67.
22. Steven Spielberg, quoted in Crist, p. 377.
23. Billy Wilder, quoted in Tom Wood, *The Bright Side of Billy Wilder, Primarily* (New York: Doubleday, 1970), p. 140.
24. Gary Busey, quoted in Thomas Wiener, "Carny: Bozo Meets Girl," *American Film* (March 1980), p. 28.
25. Paul Newman, quoted in Crist, p. 64.
26. Gene Hackman, quoted in Robert Ward, "I'm Not a Movie Star; I'm an Actor!" *American Film* (March 1983), p. 42.
27. Kazan, p. 525.
28. Paul Mazursky, quoted in Stephen Farber, "Who Is She This Time?" *American Film* (May 1983), pp. 32–33.
29. Dustin Hoffman, quoted in "Dialogue on Film," *American Film* (April 1983), p. 27.
30. Emma Thompson, *The "Sense and Sensibility" Screenplay & Diaries: Bringing Jane Austen's Novel to Film* (New York: Newmarket Press, 1995), pp. 266–267.
31. Hal Ashby, quoted in "Dialogue on Film," *American Film* (May 1980), p. 55.
32. Meryl Streep, quoted in Richard Schickel, "A Tissue of Implications," *Time* (December 19, 1983), p. 73.
33. Lily Tomlin, as told to Jane Wagner, "Memoirs of an Usherette," *The Movies* (July 1983), p. 37.
34. Schickel.
35. Sidney Lumet, quoted in Fred Baker with Ross Firestone, "Sidney Lumet—On the Director," in *Movie People: At Work in the Business of Film* (New York: Lancer Books, 1973), p. 58.

Chapter 11

1. Peter Bogdanovich, *Who the Devil Made It* (New York: Knopf, 1997), pp. 40–41.
2. Sidney Lumet, *Making Movies* (New York: Knopf, 1995), pp. 26–27.
3. Steven Spielberg, quoted in Rogert Ebert and Gene Siskel, *The Future of the Movies: Interviews With Martin Scorsese, Steven Spielberg, and George Lucas* (Kansas City: Andrews and McMeel, 1991), p. 71.
4. William Goldman, quoted in John Brady, *The Craft of the Screenwriter* (New York: Simon & Schuster, 1981), p. 168.
5. Sydney Pollack, quoted in Judith Crist, *Take 22: Moviemakers on Moviemaking*, new expanded ed. (New York: Continuum, 1991), pp. 213–214.
6. David Lynch, quoted in *Reel Conversations: Candid Interviews With Film's Foremost Directors and Critics*, edited by George Hickenlooper (New York: Carol Publishing Group, 1991), p. 103.
7. Orson Welles and Peter Bogdanovich, *This Is Orson Welles* (New York: HarperCollins, 1992), pp. 314–315.
8. Lumet, pp. 46–47.
9. Emma Thompson, *The "Sense and Sensibility" Screenplay & Diaries* (New York: Newmarket Press, 1995), pp. 236, 240.
10. Steven Spielberg, quoted in Crist, p. 362.
11. Billy Frolick, *What I Really Want to Do Is DIRECT: Seven Film School Graduates Go to Hollywood* (New York: Dutton, 1996), p. 347.

Chapter 12

1. "Rex Reed at the Movies: From Blood and Guts to Guts and Blood," *Holiday Magazine*, vol. 47, no. 4 (April 1970), p. 24. Permission to reprint granted by Travel Magazine, Inc., Floral Park, New York 11001.
2. "Low-Down Hoedown," *Time* (August 25, 1967), p. 78. Copyright 1967 Time Inc. All rights reserved. Reprinted with permission from *Time*.
3. John McCarten, "Up the Cattlemen," *The New Yorker* (May 2, 1953). From a review in *The New Yorker*. Reprinted by permission; © 1953, 1981 The New Yorker Magazine, Inc.

4. "The Shock of Freedom in Films," *Time* (December 8, 1967), p. 73.
5. William Goldman, quoted in John Brady, *The Craft of the Screenwriter* (New York: Simon & Schuster, 1981), pp. 124–125.
6. Dwight Macdonald, *On Movies* (New York: Berkley Medallion Books, 1971), p. 15. Reprinted by permission of Dwight Macdonald. Copyright © 1969 by Dwight Macdonald.
7. Renata Adler, *A Year in the Dark* (New York: Berkley Medallion Books, 1971), p. 330.
8. Vincent Canby, "Hitchcock: The Agony Is Exquisite," *New York Times* (July 2, 1972). © 1972 The New York Times. Reprinted by permission.
9. Macdonald, pp. 9–12. Reprinted by permission of Dwight Macdonald. Copyright © 1969 by Dwight Macdonald.

Chapter 13

1. Updike was speaking at a conference on religion in the arts, sponsored by the Center for the Study of Religion and American Culture at Indiana University–Purdue University at Indianapolis, April 3, 1994.
2. Randall Stewart and Dorothy Bethurum, *Modern American Narration* (Chicago: Scott, Foresman, 1954), pp. 66–67.
3. Reprinted from "The Battler" by Ernest Hemingway with the permission of Charles Scribner's Sons.
4. William Faulkner, "Spotted Horses," from *The Faulkner Reader* (New York: Random House, 1959).
5. From "The Rocking-Horse Winner," *The Complete Short Stories of D. H. Lawrence*, vol. 3. Copyright 1933 by The Estate of D. H. Lawrence, © 1961 by Angelo Ravagli and C. M. Weekley, Executors of the Estate of Frieda Lawrence Ravagli.
6. Copyright 1920 by Alfred A. Knopf, Inc., and renewed 1948 by John Middleton Murry. Reprinted from *The Short Stories of Katherine Mansfield* by permission of the publisher.
7. Reprinted from "The Killers" by Ernest Hemingway with the permission of Charles Scribner's Sons.
8. Reprinted by permission of Random House, Inc., from William Faulkner, *The Sound and the Fury*. Copyright 1929 by William Faulkner. Copyright renewed 1956 by William Faulkner.
9. George Bluestone, *Novels Into Film* (Berkeley: University of California Press, 1957), pp. 47–48.
10. J. D. Salinger, *The Catcher in the Rye* (New York: Bantam Books, 1951), p. 2.
11. William Goldman, quoted in John Brady, *The Craft of the Screenwriter* (New York: Simon & Schuster, 1981), p. 163.
12. Excerpted from *All the King's Men*, copyright 1946, 1974 by Robert Penn Warren. Reprinted by permission of Harcourt Brace Jovanovich, Inc. Excerpt appears on pp. 128–129 of the Bantam Books (1974) edition.
13. Excerpted from *All the King's Men*, copyright 1946, 1974 by Robert Penn Warren. Reprinted by permission of Harcourt Brace Jovanovich, Inc. Excerpt appears on pp. 313–314 of the Bantam Books (1974) edition.
14. Excerpted from *The Last Picture Show* by Larry McMurtry (New York: Dell, 1966), pp. 8–9.
15. Excerpted from *All the King's Men*, copyright 1946, 1974 by Robert Penn Warren. Reprinted by permission of Harcourt Brace Jovanovich, Inc. Excerpt appears on pp. 308–309 of the Bantam Books (1974) edition.
16. Elia Kazan, *A Life* (New York: Doubleday, 1989), p. 381.
17. Renata Adler, *A Year in the Dark* (New York: Berkley Medallion Books, 1971), p. 302.
18. Neil Simon, quoted in Brady, p. 342.
19. Sidney Lumet, *Making Movies* (New York: Knopf, 1995), pp. 15–16.
20. Nicholas Ray, quoted in *Directing the Film: Film Directors on Their Art*, edited by Eric Sherman (Los Angeles: Acrobat Books, 1976), p. 279.
21. Adler, p. 287.
22. Neil Simon, quoted in Brady, p. 341.
23. Richard Corliss, "Fire This Time," *Time* (January 9, 1989), pp. 57–58.
24. David Halberstam, "*Mississippi Burning*," *Premiere* (February 1989), pp. 97–98.
25. John Horn (Associated Press), "Redford Fudges Facts to Make Story Spicier," *The* [Fort Wayne] *Journal-Gazette* (October 7, 1994), p. 1D.

26. Jack Nicholson, quoted in Linda Seger and Edward Jay Whetmore, *From Script to Screen: The Collaborative Art of Filmmaking* (New York: Henry Holt, 1994), p. 159.
27. Leonard Maltin, *Movie & Video Guide* (New York: Signet, 1997), p. 409.

Chapter 14

1. "Rex Reed at the Movies: From Blood and Guts to Guts and Blood," *Holiday Magazine*, vol. 47, no. 4 (April 1970), p. 24. Permission to reprint granted by Travel Magazine, Inc., Floral Park, New York 11001.
2. Stephen Schiff, quoted in "Preface" of Richard Jameson, ed., *They Went* Thataway: *Redefining Film Genres* (San Francisco: Mercury House, 1994), p. xiv.
3. Ibid., pp. xviii–xix.
4. Ibid., pp. xv.
5. Ibid., p. 6.
6. Tom Ryall, "Genre and Hollywood," in John Hill and Pamela Church Gibson, eds., *The Oxford Guide to Film Studies* (New York: Oxford University Press, 1998), p. 337.
7. Foster Hirsch, *Film Noir: The Dark Side of the Screen* (New York: Da Capo Press, 1981), p. 21.
8. Eddie Muller, *Dark City: The Lost World of Film Noir* (New York: St. Martin's, 1998), p. 10.
9. See, for example, Jim Shephard's "'Chinatown': Jolting Noir With a Shot of Nihilism," in *The New York Times* (February 7, 1989); *www.nytimes.com/yr/mo/day/artsleisure/chinatown.film.html.*
10. James Naremore, *More Than Night: Film Noir in Its Contexts* (Berkeley: University of California Press, 1998), p. 275.
11. Paul Schrader, "Notes on Film Noir," in Barry Keith Grant, ed., *Film Genre Reader II* (Austin: University of Texas Press, 1995), p. 225.
12. Schrader is quoted in Jonathan Rosenbaum's *"Touch of Evil* Retouched," *Premiere* (September 1998), p. 81.
13. See Louis Menard, "Jerry Don't Surf," *The New York Review of Books* (September 24, 1998), p. 7.
14. Anthony Lane, *The New Yorker* (August 10, 1998), p. 78.
15. Ibid.
16. Bruce Kawin, quoted in Leo Braudy and Marshall Cohen, eds., *Film Theory and Criticism*, 5th ed. (New York: Oxford University Press, 1999), p. 610.
17. J. P. Telotte, *Replications: A Robotic History of the Science Fiction Film* (Urbana: University of Illinois Press, 1995), p. 195.
18. Ed Sikov, *Screwball: Hollywood's Madcap Romantic Comedies* (New York: Crown, 1989), p. 32.
19. Rick Altman, *The American Film Musical* (Bloomington: Indiana University Press, 1987), p. ix.
20. Jane Feuer, *The Hollywood Musical*, 2nd ed. (New York: Macmillan, 1993), p. ix.
21. Altman, pp. 371–378.
22. Kevin Brownlow, *Hollywood: The Pioneers* (London: Collins, 1979), p. 129.
23. Quoted in David Ansen, "'Psycho' Analysis," *Newsweek* (December 7, 1998), pp. 70–71.
24. Quoted in Stephen Rebello, "Cat People: Paul Schrader Changes His Spots," *American Film* (April 1982), pp. 40–43.
25. Leo Braudy, quoted in "Afterword" in Andrew Horton and Stuart Y. McDougal, eds., *Play It Again, Sam: Retakes on Remakes* (Berkeley: University of California Press, 1998), p. 331.
26. Betsy Sharkey, "The Return of the Summer Sequels," *American Film* (June 1989), p. 4.

Chapter 15

1. Renata Adler, *A Year in the Dark* (New York: Berkley Medallion Books, 1971), p. 167.
2. Ibid., pp. 158–159.
3. David A. Cook, *A History of Narrative Film*, 3rd ed. (New York: Norton, 1996), pp. 96–97.
4. Béla Balázs, *Theory of the Film: Character and Growth of a New Art*, translated by Edith Bone (New York: Dover, 1970), p. 40.
5. Alfred Hitchcock, quoted in *Directing the Film: Film Directors on Their Art*, edited by Eric Sherman (Los Angeles: Acrobat Books, 1976), pp. 202–203.
6. Desmond MacCarthy, quoted in Richard D. Altick, *Lives and Letters: A History of Literary Biography in England and America* (New York: Knopf, 1965), p. 15.
7. John Grierson, quoted in A. William Bluem, *Documentary in American Television: Form, Function, Method* (New York: Hastings House, 1965), p. 207.

8. Erik Barnouw, *Documentary: A History of the Non-Fiction Film*, 2nd rev. ed. (New York: Oxford University Press, 1993), p. 348.
9. Roger Ebert, *Roger Ebert's Video Companion, 1998 Edition* (Kansas City: Andrews and McMeel, 1997), p. 23.
10. Barnouw, pp. 251–253.
11. Susan Hayward, *Key Concepts in Cinema Studies* (London: Routledge, 1996), p. 39.
12. Ebert, p. 896.
13. Ian Christie, "Kings of Shadows," *Times Literary Supplement* (August 15, 1997), p. 19.
14. Nicca Ray, "A Rebel Because . . . ," *Icon* (December 1997), p. 109.
15. For a detailed account of the urgency of Cameron's photographic visit to the *Titanic*'s burial ground, see the early chapters of Paula Parisi's *"Titanic" and the Making of James Cameron* (New York: Newmarket Press, 1998).
16. *Baseline's Encyclopedia of Film*, "Animation," Microsoft Cinemania 97 (CD-ROM).
17. Roger Ebert, *www.suntimes.com/ebert/old_movies/pinocchio.html.* See also Leonard Maltin, *Of Mice and Magic: A History of American Animated Cartoons*, rev. ed. (New York: Plume: 1987), p. 59.
18. Nick Park, quoted in Kevin Macdonald, "A Lot Can Happen in a Second," *Projections 5: Film-makers on Film-making*, edited by John Boorman and Walter Donahue (London: Faber and Faber, 1996), p. 91.
19. Jeffrey Katzenberg, quoted in "No Dancing Teapots in 'Prince of Egypt,'" *New York Times* (December 14, 1998). *www.nytimes.com/yr/mo/day/news/arts/prince-egypt-katzenberg/html.*
20. Richard Corliss, "Can a Prince Be a Movie King?" *Time* (December 14, 1998), p. 92.
21. Roger Ebert, *www.suntimes.com/output/ebert1/18prin.html.*
22. Dwight Macdonald, *On Movies* (New York: Berkley Medallion Books, 1971), p. 18. Reprinted by permission of Dwight Macdonald. Copyright © 1969 by Dwight Macdonald.
23. Ibid., p. 20.

Chapter 16

1. Fred Baker with Ross Firestone, "Rod Steiger—On the Actor," in *Movie People: At Work in the Business of Film* (New York: Lancer Books, 1973), p. 146.
2. Budd Schulberg, *Waterfront* (New York: Random House, 1955), pp. 307–309.
3. Charles Champlin, *The Movies Grow Up, 1940–1980* (Chicago: Swallow Press, 1981), p. 46.
4. Stephen Farber, *The Movie Rating Game* (Washington, DC: Public Affairs Press, 1972), p. 117.
5. Ibid.
6. "What G, PG, R, and X Really Mean," *TV Guide* (October 4, 1980), p. 44.
7. Neil LaBute, quoted in "Rebel Yells: Vanguard Roundtable," *Premiere* (October 1998), p. 90. For a fascinating, illustrative discussion of the composition of a typical ratings board group, see "I Know It When I See It," *60 Minutes*, CBS television (October 28, 1990).
8. Charles Lyons, in Francis G. Covares, ed., *Movie Censorship and American Culture* (Washington, DC: Smithsonian Institution Press, 1996), pp. 309–311.

Appendix A

1. Roger Ebert and Gene Siskel, *The Future of the Movies: Interviews With Martin Scorsese, Steven Spielberg, and George Lucas* (Kansas City: Andrews and McMeel, 1991), pp. x, 16.
2. Michael Meyer, "HDTV Is Finally Here! Well, Almost," *Newsweek* (August 17, 1998), p. 45.
3. Richard Dreyfuss, quoted in Judith Crist, *Take 22: Moviemakers on Moviemaking*, new expanded ed. (New York: Continuum, 1991), p. 413.
4. Roger Director, "Video Confidential: Cable Days and Sleepless Nights," *The Movies* (September 1983), p. 16.
5. Martin Scorsese, quoted in Ebert and Siskel, pp. 24–25.
6. John Badham, quoted in Crist, p. 415.
7. Barry Diller, quoted in Patrick McGilligan, "Movies Are Better Than Ever—On Television," *American Film* (March 1980), p. 52.

Glossary

action acting The kind of acting seen in action/adventure films. It demands skill in facial reactions and body language, physical strength, and coordination but little subtlety or depth in communicating emotions or thoughts.

advancing colors Colors that, when given high intensity and dark value, seem to advance toward the foreground and make objects seem larger and closer to the camera: red, orange, yellow, and lavender.

allegory A story in which every object, event, and person has an immediately discernible abstract or metaphorical meaning.

ambient sounds Off-screen sounds natural to any film scene's environment, such as telephones ringing in a busy office building or birds chirping in a forest.

analogous harmony The effect created by colors adjacent to each other on the integrated color wheel, such as red, red orange, and orange. Such combinations result in a soft image with little harsh contrast.

atmospheric color Color that is influenced by the various colors and light sources in a color-rich environment.

auteur Literally, the "author" of the film. *Auteur* film criticism holds that certain directors provide the controlling vision for their films, conceiving the idea for the story, writing the script, producing, directing, and closely supervising most other steps in the filmmaking process.

blue-screen process A special visual effects film technique by which actors who are photographed in front of a blue screen can later be inserted into various movie environments; a kind of **matte shot.**

caricature The exaggeration or distortion of one or more personality traits; a technique common in cartooning.

cinematic point of view. *See* **point of view, cinematic.**

cinéma vérité "The term means 'camera truth' in French and applies to . . . documentary films which strive for immediacy, spontaneity, and authenticity through the use of portable and unobtrusive equipment and the avoidance of any preconceived narrative line or concepts concerning the material. . . . A distinctive technique . . . is the filmmaker questioning and probing those interviewed." (Ira Konigsberg, *The Complete Film Dictionary*, 2nd ed. [New York: Penguin, 1997], p. 57.) *See also* **direct cinema.**

climax The point at which the **complication** reaches its maximum tension and the forces in opposition confront each other at a peak of physical or emotional action.

close-up A close shot of a person or object; a close-up of a person generally focuses on the face only.

color A purely human perception of a radiant energy creating a visual quality distinct from light and shade.

colorization The computerized coloring of older black-and-white films for use on television and for sale and rental on videocassette.

color palette A limited number of specific colors used or emphasized throughout a film to subtly communicate various aspects of character and story.

color wheel A standard reference device that artists use to clarify the relationships that exist between primary and secondary hues.

commentators *See* **interpreters.**

complementary harmony The effect created by colors directly opposite each other on the integrated color wheel. Such colors react most vividly with each other, as in the case of red and green.

complication The section of a story in which a conflict begins and grows in clarity, intensity, and importance.

computer-generated images (CGI) Visual images that are created exclusively by computer commands rather than by standard live photography or **stop-motion animation.** This method has been widely used in many types of films, but only during the 1990s did entire CGI features such as *Toy Story* and *A Bug's Life* appear.

cool colors Colors that seem to convey or suggest a cool temperature: blues, greens, and beiges.

dailies Unedited footage of a day's shooting that the director evaluates for possible inclusion in the final version of a film.

dead screen A frame in which there is little or no dramatically or aesthetically interesting visual information. *See also* **live screen.**

dead track The complete absence of sound on the soundtrack.

deep focus Special lenses that allow the camera to focus simultaneously and with equal clarity on objects anywhere from two feet to several hundred feet away.

dénouement A brief period of calm following the **climax,** in which a state of relative equilibrium returns.

desaturated color A color of lowered intensity or value. A color is desaturated by being made lighter or darker than its normal value.

developing or dynamic characters Characters who are deeply affected by the action of the plot and who undergo some important change in personality, attitude, or outlook on life as a result of the action of the film. *See also* **static characters.**

digital sound Vastly improved quality sound reproduction in movie theaters that utilizes processes (such as Dolby and DTS) that convert standard optical sound to binary digital information.

direct cinema "A type of documentary that developed in America during the 1960s and was given this name by filmmaker Albert Maysles to suggest its direct, immediate, and authentic approach to the subject matter. A planned narrative and approach are avoided. . . . Events seem recorded exactly as they happened without rehearsal and with minimal editing. People are allowed to speak without guidance or interruption. . . . The zoom lens focuses directly on subjects, waiting for them to expose themselves. . . . Direct Cinema and ***cinéma vérité,*** which developed in France at the same time and employs many of the same techniques and . . . equipment, have been confused . . . , but ***cinéma vérité*** is quite distinct, with the filmmaker's voice intruding into the film, interviewing and probing the subject with questions in order to elicit the truth and create the dramatic exposure and situation" (Konigsberg, p. 96).

director's cut A special version of a motion picture that differs from its theatrical-release form. It most often appears on videocassette, laserdisc, or DVD under the personal supervision of its director, whose right of final edit may originally have been superseded by the film's producers or studio.

director's interpretive point of view *See* **point of view, cinematic.**

dissolve The gradual merging of the end of one shot with the beginning of the next, produced by superimposing a fade-out onto a fade-in of equal length or by imposing one scene over another.

Dolby-Surround Sound A multitrack stereophonic system for theaters that employs an encoding process to achieve a 360-degree sound field—thus creating the effect of more speakers than are actually present.

dramatic acting Acting that requires emotional and psychological depth, usually involving sustained, intense dialogue without physical action.

dramatic point of view *See* **point of view, literary.**

editing patterns *See* **inside/out editing; outside/in editing.**

ensemble acting A performance by a group of actors whose roles are of equal importance.

establishing shot A beginning shot of a new scene that shows an overall view of the new setting and the relative position of the actors in that setting.

exposition The part of a story that introduces the characters, shows some of their interrelationships, and places them within a believable time and place.

expressionism A dramatic or cinematic technique that attempts to present the inner reality of a character. In film, there is usually a distortion or exaggeration of normal perception to let the audience know that it is experiencing a character's innermost feelings.

external conflict A personal and individual struggle between the central character and another character or between the central character and some nonhuman force such as fate, society, or nature.

extrinsic metaphor *See* **metaphor, visual.**

eye-line shot A shot that shows us what a character is seeing.

fade-out/fade-in A transitional device in which the last image of one scene fades to black as the first image of the next scene is gradually illuminated.

fast motion The frantic, herky-jerky movement that results when a scene is filmed at less-than-normal speed (24 frames per second) and then projected at normal speed.

film noir "A term coined by French critics to describe a type of film that is characterized by its dark, somber tone and cynical, pessimistic mood. Literally meaning 'dark (or "black") film,' the term . . . was coined to describe those Hollywood films of the 40s and early 50s which portrayed the dark and gloomy underworld of crime and corruption. . . . The *film noir* characteristically abounds with night scenes, both interior and exterior, with sets that suggest dingy realism, and with lighting that emphasizes deep shadows and accents the mood of fatalism" (Ephraim Katz, *The Film Encyclopedia*, 3rd ed. [New York: HarperPerennial, 1998], p. 456). **Neo-*film noir*** refers to any film made after the mid-1960s that attempts to replicate many of these characteristics.

final cut A film in its finished form. A guarantee of final cut assures the filmmaker or producer that the film will not be tampered with after he or she approves it.

first-person point of view *See* **point of view, literary.**

fish-eye lens A special type of extreme wide-angle lens that bends both horizontal and vertical planes and distorts depth relationships.

flashback A filmed sequence that goes back in time to provide expository material—either when it is most dramatically appropriate and powerful or when it most effectively illuminates the theme. *See also* **flash-forward.**

flash cuts Fragmented bursts of images used to compress action.

flash-forward A filmed sequence that moves forward in time—the visual scene jumps from the present into the future.

flat characters Two-dimensional, predictable characters who lack the complexity and unique qualities associated with psychological depth. *See also* **round characters.**

flip frame A transitional device in which the entire frame seems to flip over to reveal a new scene—an effect very similar to turning a page.

foils Contrasting characters whose behavior, attitudes, opinions, lifestyle, physical appearance, and so on are opposites and thus serve clearly to define their personalities.

Foley artist A film sound technician who is responsible for adding **visible sounds** (such as walking, fighting, or falling) to enhance a soundtrack after the primary production has been completed.

forced perspective A production design technique that physically distorts certain aspects of the set and diminishes the size of objects and people in the background to create the illusion of greater foreground-to-background distance.

form cut A transition accomplished by framing objects or images of similar contour in two successive shots, so that the first image flows smoothly into the second.

freeze frame An effect, achieved in the laboratory after the film is shot, whereby a frame is reprinted so many times on the film strip that when the film is shown, the motion seems to stop as though frozen. *See also* **thawed frame.**

generalized score A musical score that attempts to capture the overall emotional atmosphere of a sequence and the film as a whole, usually by using rhythmic and emotive variations on only a few recurring motifs or themes. Also called *implicit score.*

genre film A motion picture (such as a western, a gangster film, a musical, or a *film noir*) most often based on a formula that plays on the expectation of the audience regarding formulaic plot structures, characters, setting, and so on. More broadly, the terms *genre* and *subgenre* are used to refer to various film types.

glancing rhythms The built-in sense of excitement or boredom created by fast or slow editing. Slow editing simulates the glancing rhythms of a tranquil observer; quick cutting simulates the glancing rhythms of a highly excited observer.

glass shot A cinematic technique that involves photographing live action through a scene painted on glass. In such celebrated films as *Gone With the Wind* and *Ben-Hur*, **glass shots** have often been used to integrate characters and stories into landscapes that would have been either impossible or too costly to construct in three-dimensional form. Increasingly, **CGI** techniques are being used to enhance or replace glass shots in contemporary filmmaking.

high-angle shot A shot made with the camera above eye level, thereby dwarfing the subject and diminishing its importance. *See also* **low-angle shot.**

high-key lighting Lighting that results in more light areas than shadows; subjects are seen in middle grays and highlights, with little contrast. *See also* **low-key lighting.**

hue A synonym for color.

impersonators Actors who have the talent to leave their real identity and personality behind and assume the personality and characteristics of a character with whom they may have little in common.

implicit score *See* **generalized score.**

indirect-subjective point of view *See* **point of view, cinematic.**

in medias res A Latin phrase meaning "in the middle of things" that refers to a method of beginning a story with an exciting incident that, chronologically, occurs after the complication has developed.

inside/out editing A dynamic editing pattern in which the editor takes us suddenly from a line of action that we understand to a close-up of a detail in a new setting. Because this detail is not shown in the context of a setting, we don't know where we are or what is happening. Then, in a series of related shots, the editor backs us off from the close-up to reveal the detail in relationship to its surroundings.

internal conflict A psychological conflict within the central character. The primary struggle is between different aspects of a single personality.

interpreters Actors who play characters that closely resemble themselves in personality and physical appearance and who interpret these parts dramatically without wholly losing their own identity. Also called *commentators.*

intrinsic metaphor *See* **metaphor, visual.**

invisible sound Sound emanating from a source *not* on the screen. *See also* **visible sound.**

irony A literary, dramatic, and cinematic technique involving the juxtaposition or linking of opposites.

jump cut The elimination of a strip of insignificant or unnecessary action from a continuous shot. The term also refers to a disconcerting joining of two shots that do not match in action and continuity.

leitmotif The repetition of a single phrase or idea by a character until it becomes almost a trademark for that character. In music, the repetition of a single musical theme to announce the reappearance of a certain character.

literary point of view *See* **point of view, literary.**

live screen A frame packed with dramatically or aesthetically interesting visual information, usually with some form of motion incorporated into the composition. *See also* **dead screen.**

local color Color seen in isolation from other colors in a totally white environment illuminated by a perfectly white light.

long shot A shot, taken from some distance, that usually shows the subject as well as its surroundings.

long take A continuous film shot that lasts for several minutes. Some directors (following the famous sustained opening movement in Orson Welles's *Touch of Evil*) have made a kind of game of creating such shots in their films. Notable examples include Martin Scorsese in *GoodFellas* (and other films), Paul Thomas Anderson in *Boogie Nights*, Brian De Palma in *The Bonfire of the Vanities*, and

Robert Altman in *The Player* (in an opening scene that both parodies and competes with Welles's work in *Touch of Evil*).

look of outward regard An objective shot that shows a character looking off-screen and thereby cues us to wonder what the character is looking at.

low-angle shot A shot made with the camera below eye level, thereby exaggerating the size and importance of the subject. *See also* **high-angle shot.**

low-key lighting Lighting that puts most of the set in shadow and uses just a few highlights to define the subject. *See also* **high-key lighting.**

matte shot Any special visual effects technique that uses some type of visual mask to allow more than one image to be photographed on a single film frame.

metaphor, visual A brief comparison that helps us understand or perceive one image better because of its similarity to another image, usually achieved through the editorial juxtaposition of two images in two successive shots. Two types of visual metaphors are commonly used in films:

> **extrinsic** A metaphor that has no place within the context of the scene itself but is imposed artificially into the scene by the director.
>
> **intrinsic** A metaphor found within the natural context of the scene itself.

Mickey Mousing The exact, calculated dovetailing of music and action that precisely matches the rhythm of the music with the natural rhythms of the objects moving on the screen.

microcosm Meaning "the world in little," a special type of isolated, self-contained setting in which the human activity is actually representative of human behavior or the human condition in the world as a whole.

mise-en-scène "A French term meaning 'putting into the scene' that was originally used to describe the staging of a theater director, the way he or she arranged all the visual components on the stage. The term has become fashionable in film criticism and has taken on new meanings and connotations from its filmic context. *Mise-en-scène*, in discussions of film, refers to the composition of the individual frame—the relation of objects, people, and masses; the interplay of light and dark; the pattern of color; the camera's position and angle of view—as well as the movement within the frame" (Konigsberg, p. 240). "Andre Bazin, and subsequently other theoreticians and critics, have used [the term] to describe a style of film directing basically distinct from that known as montage. Whereas montage derives its meaning from the relationship between one frame to the next through editing, *mise-en-scène* emphasizes the content of the individual frame. Its proponents see montage as disruptive to the psychological unity of man with his environment and cite such films as Orson Welles's *Citizen Kane* with its **deep-focus** compositions . . . as examples to support their argument. The schism between *mise-en-scène* and montage is deeper in theory than in practice; most filmmakers employ both in directing their films" (Katz, p. 956). *See also* **montage.**

monochromatic harmony The effect created by variations in the value and intensity of a single color.

montage A series of images and sounds that derive their meaning from complex internal relationships to form a kind of visual poem in miniature. "The term . . . as it is generally understood today is associated with the work and theory of [Russian filmmaker] Sergei Eisenstein, in which it came to represent the rhetorical arrangement of shots in juxtaposition so that the clash between two adjoining images suggests a third, independent entity and creates a whole new meaning. Eisenstein's ideas of montage were inspired by the editing techniques of [pioneer American filmmaker] D. W. Griffith" (Katz, p. 965). *See also* **mise-en-scène.**

motifs Images, patterns, or ideas that are repeated throughout the film and are variations or aspects of the film's theme.

muted color *See* **desaturated color.**

name typing The use of names possessing appropriate qualities of sound, meaning, or connotation to help describe a character.

objective camera A camera that views the action as a remote spectator. *See also* **point of view, cinematic, objective.**

objective point of view *See* **point of view, cinematic.**

omniscient-narrator point of view *See* **point of view, literary.**

opticals Effects created in the lab during the printing of the film. The primary image is superimposed on another image, and the two are composited onto one strip of film by an optical printer. Modern optical printers are guided by computer, affording precise matching of a tremendous number of different images.

outside/in editing The traditional editing pattern in which the editor begins with an establishing shot of the new setting—to help the audience get its bearings—and then follows with shots that gradually take us farther into the setting. Only after we are completely familiar with our surroundings does the editor focus our attention on details.

painterly effects The effects created by filmmakers who are consciously trying to imitate certain looks achieved by painters.

Panavision *See* **wide screen.**

panning Moving the camera's line of sight in a horizontal plane to the right and left.

panning and scanning A technique used to transfer films shot in **wide screen** to a format that will fill a traditional television screen. The lateral movement of the reproducing camera that allows this process to occur also generally ruins the original composition and pacing created by directors and cinematographers.

parallel cuts Shots that quickly alternate back and forth between two actions taking place at separate locations, creating the impression that the two actions are occurring simultaneously and will possibly converge.

period piece A film that takes place not in the present but in some earlier period of history.

personality actors Actors whose primary talent is to be themselves. Although personality actors generally possess some dynamic and magnetic mass appeal, they are incapable of assuming any variety in the roles they play, for they cannot project sincerity and naturalness when they attempt to move outside their own basic personality.

Peter-and-the-Wolfing Musical scoring in which certain musical instruments represent and signal the presence of certain characters.

point of view, cinematic Essentially, there are four points of view that may be employed in a film:

director's interpretive Using the special techniques of the medium, the director manipulates us so that we see the action or the character in the way the director interprets them.

indirect-subjective A viewpoint that brings us close to the action and increases our involvement. It provides us with the feeling and sense of immediacy of participating in the action without showing the action through a participant's eyes.

objective The viewpoint of a sideline observer, which suggests an emotional distance between camera and subject. The camera seems simply to be recording, as straightforwardly as possible, the characters and the actions of the story.

subjective The viewpoint of a character participating in the action. *See also* **point of view, literary.**

point of view, literary There are five viewpoints employed in literature:

dramatic or objective A viewpoint wherein we are not conscious of a narrator, for the author does not comment on the action but simply describes the scene, telling us what happens and what the characters say, so we get a feeling of being there, observing the scene as we would in a play.

first person An eyewitness gives a firsthand account of what happened as well as his or her response to it.

omniscient narrator, third person An all-seeing, all-knowing narrator, capable of reading the thoughts of all the characters and capable of being in several places at once if need be, tells the story.

stream of consciousness or interior monologue A third-person narrative that seems to incorporate the first-person form, although the participant in the action is not consciously telling the story. It is a unique inner view, as though a microphone and movie camera in the character's mind were recording every thought, image, and impression that passes through, without the conscious acts of organization, selectivity, or narration.

third-person selective or limited The narrator is omniscient except for the fact that his or her powers of mind reading are limited to or at least focused on a single character, who becomes the central figure through whom we view the action.

point-of-view character A film character with whom we emotionally or intellectually identify and through whom we experience the film. **Voice-over narration,** editing, and camera position may be employed for this effect.

rack focus Changing the focus setting on the camera during a continuous shot so that audience attention is directed deeper and deeper into the frame as viewers follow the plane of clearest focus. The technique can also be reversed so that the plane of clearest focus moves closer and closer to the camera.

reaction shot A shot that shows a character reacting rather than acting. The reaction shot is usually a close-up of the emotional reaction registered on the face of the person most affected by the dialogue or action.

receding colors Colors that seem to recede into the background, making objects appear smaller and more distant from the camera: green, pale blue, and beige.

Rembrandt effect The use of a subtle, light-diffusing filter to soften focus slightly and subdue the colors so that the whole film has the quality of a Rembrandt painting.

rough-grain film stock Film stock that produces a rough, grainy-textured image with harsh contrasts between blacks and whites and almost no subtle differences in contrast. *See also* **smooth-grain film stock.**

round characters Unique, individualistic characters who have some degree of complexity and ambiguity and who cannot easily be categorized. Also called *three-dimensional characters. See also* **flat characters.**

rushes. *See* **dailies.**

saturated color A strong, unadulterated, pure color. A saturated red cannot be made any redder.

scene A series of shots joined so that they communicate a unified action taking place at one time and place.

sequence A series of scenes joined in such a way that they constitute a significant part of a film's dramatic structure, like an act in a play.

setting The time and place in which the film's story takes place, including all of the complex factors that come packaged with a given time and place: climate, terrain, population density, social structures and economic factors, customs, moral attitudes, and codes of behavior.

shade Any color darker than its normal value. Maroon is a shade of red.

shot A strip of film produced by a single continuous running of the camera. After the editing and printing processes, a shot becomes the segment of film between cuts or optical transitions.

Skycam A small, computerized, remote-controlled camera that flies on wires at speeds of up to twenty miles per hour and can go practically anywhere that cables can be strung.

slow motion The effect of slowed action created by exposing frames in the camera at greater-than-normal speed and then projecting that footage at normal speed (24 frames per second).

smooth-grain film stock Film stock capable of reproducing an image that is extremely smooth or slick, registering a wide range of subtle differences between light and dark, and creating fine tones, artistic shadows, and contrasts. *See also* **rough-grain film stock.**

soft focus A slight blurring of focus for effect.

sound link A bridge between scenes or sequences created through the use of similar or identical sounds in both.

standard screen A screen whose width is 1.33 times its height.

star system An approach to filmmaking that capitalizes on the mass appeal of certain actors to increase the likelihood that a film will be a financial success.

static characters Characters who remain essentially the same throughout the film, either because the action does not have an important effect on their lives or because they are insensitive to the meaning of the action. *See also* **developing or dynamic characters.**

Steadicam A portable, one-person camera with a built-in gyroscope that prevents any sudden jerkiness and provides a smooth, rock-steady image.

stereotypes Characters who fit into preconceived patterns of behavior common to or representative of a large number of people (at least a large number of fictional people), allowing the director to economize greatly in treating them.

stills Photographs in which the image itself does not move. A sense of movement is imparted to the images by the camera zooming in or out or simply moving over their surface.

stock characters Minor characters whose actions are completely predictable or typical of their job or profession.

stop-motion animation A variation on drawn-animation techniques that uses puppets or other three-dimensional objects. To give the appearance of life on film when projected at the normal 24-frames-per-second speed, subjects are moved minimally between shots as they are being photographed.

stream of consciousness *See* **point of view, literary.**

subjective camera A camera that views the scene from the visual or emotional point of view of a participant in the action. *See also* **point of view, cinematic, subjective.**

subjective point of view *See* **point of view, cinematic.**

subtitling The method of providing visible words at the bottom of frames to translate the dialogue of films from one language into another. *See also* **voice dubbing.**

surrealism A dramatic or cinematic technique that uses fantastic imagery in an attempt to portray the workings of the subconscious. Surrealistic images have an oddly dreamlike or unreal quality.

symbol A literal element (such as an object, name, or gesture) in art, literature, and film that also stands for an abstract idea. This representation is established by triggering previously associated areas in the mind of the perceiver.

tableau A technique, used in melodrama, in which actors held dramatic postures for a few seconds before the curtain fell in order to etch the scene in the audience's memory.

take Variations of the same shot. In the cutting room, the editor assembles the film from the best take of each shot.

telephoto lens A lens that, like a telescope, draws objects closer but also diminishes the illusion of depth.

thawed frame An effect opposite to that of a **freeze frame**—the scene begins with a frozen image that thaws and comes to life.

theme The central concern around which a literary work or film is structured, its unifying focus. In film, theme can be broken down into five categories: plot, emotional effect or mood, character, style or texture, and ideas.

third-person limited point of view *See* **point of view, literary.**

three-dimensional characters *See* **round characters.**

tilting Moving the camera's line of sight in a vertical plane, up and down.

time-lapse photography An extreme form of fast motion in which a single frame is exposed at regular intervals (from a second to an hour or even longer) and then projected at normal speed (24 frames per second), thus compressing an action that usually takes hours or weeks into a few seconds on the screen.

tint Any color lighter than its normal value. Pink is a tint of red.

tinting The chemical coloring of film stock before the image is printed on it. When printed, the white portions of the image retain the color of the tint, resulting in an image composed of two colors—black and the color of the tint.

toning Adding dyes to the film emulsion so that the lines and tones of the image itself are colored.

traveling music Music that is employed almost as a formula to give the impression of various means of transportation.

triad harmony The effect created by the use of three colors equidistant from each other on the color wheel, such as the primary colors: red, yellow, and blue.

typecasting The tendency of major studios and some directors to lock certain actors into a narrow range of almost identical roles.

value The proportion of light or dark present in a given color.

visible sound Sound that would naturally and realistically emanate from the images on the screen. *See also* **invisible sound**

voice dubbing The replacement of the dialogue soundtrack in a foreign language with an English language soundtrack. Voices in English are recorded to correspond to the mouth and lip movements of the foreign actors. *See also* **subtitling.**

voice-over narration A voice off-screen that conveys necessary background information or fills in gaps for continuity.

warm colors Colors that seem to convey or suggest a warm temperature: red, orange, yellow, and lavender.

wide-angle lens A lens that takes in a broad area and increases the illusion of depth but sometimes distorts the edges of the image.

wide screen Known by many trade names such as Cinemascope, Panavision, and Vistavision, a screen whose width varies from 1.66 to 1.85 to 2.35 to 2.55 times its height (as compared with the standard 1.33 times).

wipe A transitional device in which a new image is separated from the previous image by means of a horizontal, vertical, or diagonal line that moves across the screen to wipe the old image away.

zoom lens A complex series of lenses that keep the image constantly in focus and, by magnifying the subject, give the camera the apparent power to vary movement toward or away from the subject without requiring any movement of the camera.

Selected Bibliography and Study Materials

Reference

Arany, Lynne, Tom Dyja, and Gary Goldsmith. *The Reel List: An Irreverent Guide Arranged by Uncommon Categories*. New York: Delta, 1995.

Foley, Catherine, and Milos Stehlik, eds. *Facets Movie Lovers Video Guide*. Chicago: Facets Multi-Media, 1998.

Hayward, Susan. *Key Concepts in Cinema Studies*. London: Routledge, 1996.

Hill, John, and Pamela Church Gibson, eds. *The Oxford Guide to Film Studies*. New York: Oxford University Press, 1998.

Kael, Pauline. *5001 Nights at the Movies*, expanded for the '90s with 800 new reviews. New York: Henry Holt, 1991.

Katz, Ephraim. *The Film Encyclopedia*, 3rd ed., revised by Fred Klein and Ronald Dean Nolan. New York: HarperPerennial, 1998.

Konigsberg, Ira. *The Complete Film Dictionary*, 2nd ed. New York: Penguin, 1997.

Maltin, Leonard. *Leonard Maltin's 1999 Movie & Video Guide*. New York: Signet, 1998.

Naughton, John. *Movies: A Crash Course*. New York: Watson Guptill Publications, 1998.

Silver, Alain, and Elizabeth Ward, eds. *Film Noir: An Encyclopedic Reference to the American Style*, 3rd revised and expanded ed. Woodstock, NY: Overlook Press, 1992.

Taub, Eric. *Gaffers, Grips, and Best Boys: A Behind-the-Scenes Look at Who Does What in the Making of a Motion Picture*. New York: St. Martin's, 1987.

Film History and Culture

Barnouw, Erik. *Documentary: A History of the Non-Fiction Film*, 2nd revised edition. New York: Oxford University Press, 1993.

Belton, John. *American Cinema/American Culture*. New York: McGraw-Hill, 1994.

Biskind, Peter. *Easy Riders, Raging Bulls: How the Sex–Drugs–and–Rock'n Roll Generation Saved Hollywood*. New York: Simon & Schuster, 1998.

Bogle, Donald. *Toms, Coons, Mulattoes, Mammies, and Bucks: An Interpretative History of Blacks in American Films*, 3rd ed. New York: Continuum, 1997.

Bohn, Thomas W., and Richard L. Stromgren. *Light and Shadows: A History of Motion Pictures*, 3rd ed. Mountain View, CA: Mayfield, 1987.

Bouzereau, Laurent. *Cutting Room Floor: Movie Scenes Which Never Made It to the Screen*. New York: Citadel, 1994.

Cagin, Seth, and Philip Dray. *Born to Be Wild: Hollywood and the Sixties Generation*. Boca Raton, FL: Coyote, 1994.

Champlin, Charles. *The Movies Grow Up, 1940–1980*. Chicago: Swallow Press, 1981.

Collins, Peter, and John E. O'Connor, eds. *Hollywood's Indian: The Portrayal of the Native American in Film*. Lexington: University of Kentucky Press, 1998.

Cook, David A. *A History of Narrative Film*, 3rd ed. New York: Norton, 1996.

Fregoso, Rosa Linda. *The Bronze Screen: Chicana and Chicano Film Culture*. St. Paul: University of Minnesota Press, 1993.

Friedrich, Otto. *City of Nets: A Portrait of Hollywood in the 1940's.* New York: Harper & Row, 1986.

Gabler, Neal. *An Empire of Their Own: How the Jews Invented Hollywood.* New York: Crown, 1988.

Haskell, Molly. *From Reverence to Rape: The Treatment of Women in the Movies.* Chicago: University of Chicago Press, 1987.

——. *Holding My Own in No Man's Land: Women and Men and Film and Feminists.* New York: Oxford University Press, 1997.

hooks, bell. *Reel to Real: Race, Sex, and Class at the Movies.* London: Routledge, 1996.

Kaplan, E. Ann. *Women and Film: Both Sides of the Camera.* New York: Methuen, 1983.

Knight, Arthur. *The Liveliest Art: A Panoramic History of the Movies,* revised ed. New York: Mentor Books, 1978.

MacCann, Richard Dyer, ed. *Film and Society.* New York: Scribner's, 1964.

Maltin, Leonard. *Of Mice and Magic: A History of American Animated Cartoons,* revised ed. New York: New American Library, 1990.

Mast, Gerald, and Bruce F. Kawin. *A Short History of the Movies,* 6th ed. New York: Prentice-Hall, 1996.

Mico, Ted, John Miller-Monzon, and David Rubel, eds. *Past Imperfect: History According to the Movies.* New York: Henry Holt, 1995.

Mordden, Ethan. *The Hollywood Studios: Their Unique Styles During the Golden Age of Movies.* New York: Simon & Schuster, 1988.

Robinson, W. R. *Man and the Movies.* Baton Rouge: Louisiana State University Press, 1967.

Rosen, Marjorie. *Popcorn Venus: Women, Movies and the American Dream.* New York: Avon, 1973.

Russo, Vito. *The Celluloid Closet: Homosexuality in the Movies,* revised ed. New York: HarperCollins, 1987.

Schatz, Thomas. *The Genius of the System: Hollywood Filmmaking in the Studio Era.* New York: Henry Holt, 1988.

Sklar, Robert. *Movie-Made America: A Cultural History of American Movies,* revised and updated. New York: Vintage, 1994.

Smith, Scott. *The Film 100: A Ranking of the Most Influential People in the History of the Movies.* Seacaucus, NJ: Citadel, 1998.

Sperling, Cass Warner, and Cork Millner, with Jack Warner, Jr. *Hollywood Be Thy Name: The Warner Brothers Story.* Rocklin, CA: Prima, 1994.

Telotte, J. P. *Replications: A Robotic History of the Science Fiction Film.* Urbana: University of Illinois Press, 1995.

Vidal, Gore. *Screening History.* Cambridge, MA: Harvard University Press, 1992.

Silent Film

Brownlow, Kevin, and John Kobal. *Hollywood: The Pioneers.* New York: Knopf, 1979.

Dardis, Tom. *Keaton: The Man Who Wouldn't Lie Down.* New York: Scribner's, 1979.

Everson, William K. *American Silent Film.* New York: Oxford University Press, 1978.

Geduld, Harry M., ed. *Focus on D. W. Griffith.* Englewood Cliffs, NJ: Prentice-Hall, 1971.

Henderson, Robert M. *D. W. Griffith, His Life and Work.* New York: Oxford University Press, 1972.

Mast, Gerald. *The Comic Mind.* Indianapolis: Bobbs-Merrill, 1973.

McCabe, John. *Charlie Chaplin.* New York: Doubleday, 1978.

Milton, Joyce. *Tramp: The Life of Charlie Chaplin.* New York: HarperCollins, 1996.

Robinson, David. *From Peepshow to Palace: The Birth of American Film.* New York: Columbia University Press, 1997.

Schickel, Richard. *D. W. Griffith: An American Life.* New York: Simon & Schuster, 1984.

Silva, Fred, ed. *Focus on* The Birth of a Nation. Englewood Cliffs, NJ: Prentice-Hall, 1973.

Swanson, Gloria. *Swanson on Swanson: An Autobiography.* New York: Random House, 1980.

Directors

Bogdanovich, Peter. *John Ford.* Berkeley: University of California Press, 1968.

——. *Who the Devil Made It.* New York: Knopf, 1997.

Brady, Frank. *Citizen Welles: A Biography of Orson Welles.* New York: Doubleday, 1989.

Braudy, Leo, and Morris Dickstein, eds. *Great Film Directors: A Critical Anthology*. New York: Oxford University Press, 1978.

Callow, Simon. *Orson Welles: The Road to Xanadu*. New York: Viking, 1996.

Capra, Frank. *The Name Above the Title*. New York: Bantam, 1971.

Coursodon, Jean-Pierre, with Pierra Sauvage. *American Directors*, Vols. 1 and 2. New York: McGraw-Hill, 1983.

Fellini, Federico. *Fellini on Fellini*. Translated by Isabel Quigley. New York: Delacorte, 1976.

Frolick, Billy. *What I Really Want to Do Is DIRECT: Seven Film School Graduates Go to Hollywood*. New York: Dutton, 1996.

Gelmis, Joseph. *The Film Director as Superstar*. Garden City, NY: Anchor, 1970.

Giannetti, Louis. *Masters of the American Cinema*. Englewood Cliffs, NJ: Prentice-Hall, 1981.

Gottesman, Ronald, ed. *Focus on Orson Welles*. Englewood Cliffs, NJ: Prentice-Hall, 1976.

Hayman, Ronald. *Fassbinder: Film Maker*. New York: Simon & Schuster, 1984.

Huston, John. *John Huston: An Open Book*. New York: Knopf, 1980.

Kazan, Elia. *A Life*. New York: Doubleday, 1989.

Kelly, Mary Pat. *Martin Scorsese: A Journey*. New York: Thunder's Mouth, 1991.

Koszarski, Richard, ed. *Great American Film Directors in Photographs*. New York: Dover, 1984.

Leaming, Barbara. *Orson Welles: A Biography*. New York: Viking Penguin, 1985.

LoBrutto, Vincent. *Stanley Kubrick: A Biography*. New York: Penguin, 1997.

Oliver, Roger W., ed. *Ingmar Bergman: An Artist's Journey on Stage, on Screen, in Print*. New York: Arcade, 1995.

Parisi, Paula. *"Titanic" and the Making of James Cameron*. New York: Newmarket, 1998.

Pye, Michael, and Lynda Myles. *The Movie Brats: How the Film Generation Took Over Hollywood*. New York: Holt, Rinehart & Winston, 1979.

Sarris, Andrew. *The American Cinema: Directors and Directions, 1929–1968*. New York: Dutton, 1968.

Sherman, Eric, ed. *Directing the Film: Film Directors on Their Art*. Los Angeles: Acrobat, 1976.

Simon, John. *Ingmar Bergman Directs*. New York: Harcourt Brace Jovanovich, 1972.

Spoto, Donald. *The Art of Alfred Hitchcock: Fifty Years of His Motion Pictures*. New York: Hopkinson and Blake, 1976.

——. *The Dark Side of Genius: The Life of Alfred Hitchcock*. New York: Ballantine, 1983.

Thomas, Bob, ed. *Directors in Action*. Indianapolis: Bobbs-Merrill, 1973.

Walker, Alexander. *Stanley Kubrick Directs*. New York: Harcourt Brace Jovanovich, 1972.

Welles, Orson, and Peter Bogdanovich. *This Is Orson Welles*. New York: HarperCollins, 1992.

Wood, Tom. *The Bright Side of Billy Wilder, Primarily*. New York: Doubleday, 1970.

Film Types and Topics

Almendros, Nestor. *A Man With a Camera*. Translated by Rachel Phillips Belash. Boston: Faber and Faber, 1984.

Altman, Rick. *The American Film Musical*. Bloomington: Indiana University Press, 1987.

Baker, Fred, with Ross Firestone. *Movie People: At Work in the Business of Film*. New York: Lancer, 1973.

Bluem, A. William. *Documentary in American Television: Form, Function, Method*. New York: Hastings House, 1965.

Bluestone, George. *Novels Into Film: The Metamorphosis of Fiction Into Cinema*. Baltimore: Johns Hopkins University Press, 1957.

Boorman, John, and Walter Donahue, eds. *Projections 5: Film-makers on Film-making*. London: Faber and Faber, 1996. (Includes a four-essay section on feature animation.)

Boyum, Joy Gould. *Double Exposure: Fiction Into Film*. New York: Mentor, 1985.

Brady, John. *The Craft of the Screenwriter: Interviews with Six Celebrated Screenwriters*. New York: Simon & Schuster, 1981.

Brando, Marlon, with Robert Lindsey. *Brando: Songs My Mother Taught Me*. New York: Random House, 1994.

Caine, Michael. *Acting in Film: An Actor's Take on Movie Making*, revised expanded ed. New York: Applause Theatre Books, 1997.

Christopher, Nicholas. *Somewhere in the Night: Film Noir and the American City.* New York: Henry Holt, 1997.

Corrigan, Timothy. *Film and Literature: An Introduction and Reader.* Upper Saddle River, NJ: Prentice-Hall, 1999.

Couvares, Francis G., ed. *Movie Censorship and American Culture.* Washington, DC: Smithsonian Institution Press, 1996.

Farber, Stephen. *The Movie Rating Game.* Washington, DC: Public Affairs Press, 1972.

Feuer, Jane. *The Hollywood Musical*, 2nd ed. London: Macmillan, 1993.

Fonda, Henry, as told to Howard Teichman. *Fonda: My Life.* New York: New American Library, 1981.

Goldman, William. *Adventures in the Screen Trade: A Personal View of Hollywood and Screenwriting.* New York: Warner, 1983.

Grant, Barry Keith, ed. *Film Genre Reader II.* Austin: University of Texas Press, 1995.

Harvey, James. *Romantic Comedy in Hollywood From Lubitsch to Sturges.* New York: Knopf, 1987; reissued, Da Capo, 1998.

Hirsch, Foster. *Film Noir: The Dark Side of the Screen.* New York: Da Capo, 1981.

Horton, Andrew, and Stuart Y. McDougal, eds. *Play It Again, Sam: Retakes on Remakes.* Berkeley: University of California Press, 1998.

Inglis, Ruth A. *Freedom of the Movies.* Chicago: University of Chicago Press, 1947.

Jameson, Richard T. *They Went* Thataway: *Redefining Film Genres.* San Francisco: Mercury House, 1994.

Kalinak, Kathryn. *Settling the Score: Music and the Classical Hollywood Film.* Madison: University of Wisconsin Press, 1992.

Kaminsky, Stuart. *American Film Genres.* New York: Nelson-Hall, 1984.

Klein, Michael, and Gillian Parker, eds. *The English Novel and the Movies.* New York: Frederick Ungar, 1981.

Koerner, Julie. *Hollywood Musicals.* New York: Friedman/Fairfax, 1997.

Litwak, Mark. *Reel Power: The Struggle for Influence and Success in the New Hollywood.* Los Angeles: Silman-James, 1986.

LoBrutto, Vincent. *By Design: Interviews With Film Production Designers.* Westport, CT: Praeger, 1992.

——. *Selected Takes: Film Editors on Film Editing.* Westport, CT: Praeger, 1991.

——. *Sound-on-Film: Interviews With Creators of Film Sound.* Westport, CT: Praeger, 1994.

Lumet, Sidney. *Making Movies.* New York: Knopf, 1995.

Lupack, Barbara Tepa, ed. *Take Two: Adapting the Contemporary American Novel to Film.* Bowling Green, OH: Bowling Green State University Popular Press, 1994.

Manvell, Roger, and John Huntley. *The Technique of Film Music*, revised ed. New York: Hastings House, 1975.

Muller, Eddie. *Dark City: The Lost World of Film Noir.* New York: St. Martin's, 1998.

Naremore, James. *More Than Night: Film Noir in Its Contexts.* Berkeley: University of California Press, 1998.

Obst, Lynda. *Hello, He Lied and Other Truths From the Hollywood Trenches.* Boston: Little, Brown, 1996.

Peary, Gerald, and Roger Shatzkin. *The Modern American Novel and the Movies.* New York: Frederick Ungar, 1978.

Pierson, John. *Spike, Mike, Slackers, & Dykes: A Guided Tour Across a Decade of American Independent Cinema.* New York: Hyperion, 1995.

Prendergast, Roy M. *Film Music: A Neglected Art.* New York: Norton, 1977.

Rainsberger, Todd. *James Wong Howe: Cinematographer.* New York: A. S. Barnes, 1981.

Reisz, Karel, and Gavin Millar. *The Technique of Film Editing*, revised ed. New York: Hastings House, 1968.

Rosenblum, Ralph, and Robert Karen. *When the Shooting Stops . . . The Cutting Begins: A Film Editor's Story.* New York: Da Capo, 1979.

Schatz, Thomas. *Hollywood Genre: Formulas, Filmmaking, and the Studio System.* New York: Random House, 1981.

Seger, Linda. *The Art of Adaptation: Turning Fact and Fiction Into Film.* New York: Henry Holt, 1992.

——. *When Women Call the Shots: The Developing Power and Influence of Women in Television and Film.* New York: Henry Holt, 1996.

Seger, Linda, and Edward Jay Whetmore. *From Script to Screen: The Collaborative Art of Filmmaking.* New York: Henry Holt, 1994.

Sikov, Ed. *Screwball: Hollywood's Madcap Romantic Comedies.* New York: Crown, 1989.

Skal, David J. *Screams of Reason: Mad Science and Modern Culture.* New York: Norton, 1998.

Solomon, Stanley J. *Beyond Formula: American Film Genres.* New York: Harcourt Brace Jovanovich, 1976.

Thomas, Tony. *Music for the Movies,* 2nd ed. Los Angeles: Silman-James, 1997.

Weales, Gerald. *Canned Goods as Caviar: American Film Comedies of the 1930s.* Chicago: University of Chicago Press, 1985.

Weis, Elisabeth, ed. *The National Society of Film Critics on the Movie Star.* New York: Viking, 1981.

Specific Films

Biskind, Peter. The Godfather *Companion.* New York: HarperCollins, 1990.

Carringer, Robert L. *The Making of* Citizen Kane, revised and updated ed. University of California Press, 1996.

French, Warren. *Filmguide to* The Grapes of Wrath. Bloomington: Indiana University Press, 1973.

Gottesman, Ronald, ed. *Focus on* Citizen Kane. Englewood Cliffs, NJ: Prentice-Hall, 1971.

Harmetz, Aljean. *The Making of* The Wizard of Oz: *Movie Magic and Studio Power in the Prime of MGM—and the Miracle of Production #1060.* New York: Delta, 1977, 1989.

——. *Round Up the Usual Suspects: The Making of* Casablanca—*Bogart, Bergman, and World War II.* New York: Hyperion, 1992.

Kael, Pauline, ed. *The* Citizen Kane *Book.* Boston: Atlantic Monthly, 1972.

Lebo, Harlan. Casablanca: *Behind the Scenes.* New York: Simon & Schuster, 1992.

——. The Godfather *Legacy: The Untold Story of the Making of the Classic* Godfather Trilogy. New York: Fireside, 1997.

Naremore, James R. *Filmguide to* Psycho. Bloomington: Indiana University Press, 1973.

Salamon, Julie. *The Devil's Candy:* The Bonfire of the Vanities *Goes to Hollywood.* New York: Delta, 1991.

Steene, Birgitta, ed. *Focus on* The Seventh Seal. Englewood Cliffs, NJ: Prentice-Hall, 1968.

Thompson, Emma. *The "Sense and Sensibility" Screenplay & Diaries: Bringing Jane Austen's Novel to Film.* New York: Newmarket, 1995.

Collections of Reviews, Essays, and Interviews

Adler, Renata. *A Year in the Dark.* New York: Random House, 1969.

Agee, James. *Agee on Film, Vol. 1, Reviews and Comments.* Boston: Beacon, 1964.

Brantley, Will, ed. *Conversations With Pauline Kael.* Jackson: University Press of Mississippi, 1996.

Crist, Judith. *The Private Eye, the Cowboy, and the Very Naked Girl.* New York: Holt, Rinehart & Winston, 1968.

——. *Take 22: Moviemakers on Moviemaking,* new expanded ed. New York: Continuum, 1991.

Denby, David, ed. *Awake in the Dark: An Anthology of American Film Criticism, 1915 to the Present.* New York: Vintage, 1977.

Ebert Roger. *Roger Ebert's Book of Film: From Tolstoy to Tarantino, the Finest Writing From a Century of Film.* New York: Norton, 1997.

——. *Roger Ebert's Movie Yearbook 1999.* Kansas City: Andrews and McMeel, 1998.

——. *Roger Ebert's Video Companion, 1998 Edition.* Kansas City: Andrews and McMeel, 1997.

Ebert, Roger, and Gene Siskel. *The Future of the Movies: Interviews With Martin Scorsese, Steven Spielberg, and George Lucas.* Kansas City: Andrews and McMeel, 1991.

Gallagher, John Andrew, ed. *Film Directors on Film Directing.* New York: Praeger, 1989.

Hickenlooper, George, ed. *Reel Conversations: Candid Interviews With Film's Foremost Directors and Critics.* New York: Carol, 1991.

Hunter, Stephen. *Violent Screen: A Critic's Thirteen Years on the Front Lines of Movie Mayhem.* New York: Delta, 1995.

Kael, Pauline. *For Keeps: 30 Years at the Movies.* New York: Dutton, 1994.

——. *Reeling*. Boston: Atlantic Monthly, 1976.

Kauffmann, Stanley, and Bruce Henstell, eds. *American Film Criticism: From the Beginnings to* Citizen Kane. New York: Liveright, 1972.

Kirschner, Allen, and Linda Kirschner. *Film: Readings in the Mass Media*. New York: Odyssey, 1971.

Leyda, Jay, ed. *Film Makers Speak: Voices of Film Experience*. New York: Da Capo, 1977.

Macdonald, Dwight. *On Movies*. New York: Berkley, 1969.

McBride, Joseph, ed. *Filmmakers on Filmmaking: The American Film Institute Seminars on Motion Pictures and Television, Vol. 2*. Los Angeles: J. P. Tarcher, 1983.

Plimpton, George, ed. *The Best American Movie Writing 1998*. New York: St. Martin's, 1998.

Simon, John. *Movies Into Films: Film Criticism, 1967–70*. New York: Dial, 1971.

Solomon, Stanley J. *The Classic Cinema: Essays in Criticism*. New York: Harcourt Brace Jovanovich, 1973.

Film Aesthetics and Theory

Andrew, J. Dudley. *The Major Film Theories*. New York: Oxford University Press, 1976.

Arnheim, Rudolph. *Film as Art*. Berkeley: University of California Press, 1957.

Balázs, Béla. *Theory of the Film: Character and Growth of a New Art*. Translated by Edith Bone. New York: Dover, 1970.

Braudy, Leo, and Marshall Cohen, eds. *Film Theory and Criticism: Introductory Readings*, 5th ed. New York: Oxford University Press, 1999.

Eisenstein, Sergei. *The Film Sense*. Translated by Jay Leyda. New York: Harcourt, Brace and World, 1947.

Jacobs, Lewis, ed. *The Emergence of Film Art*, 2nd ed. New York: Norton, 1979.

——, ed. *The Movies as Medium*. New York: Farrar, Straus & Giroux, 1970.

Lindgrin, Ernest. *The Art of the Film*. New York: Macmillan, 1963.

MacCann, Richard Dyer, ed. *Film: A Montage of Theories*. New York: Dutton, 1966.

Pudovkin, V. I. *Film Technique and Film Acting*. Translated and edited by Ivor Montagu. New York: Grove, 1958.

Zettl, Herbert. *Sight-Sound-Motion: Applied Media Aesthetics*. Belmont, CA: Wadsworth, 1990.

Film Periodicals

Cahiers du Cinéma
Cineaste
Cinefantastique
Cinefex. The Journal of Cinematic Illusions
Cinema Journal
Film Comment
Film Criticism
Film Quarterly
Journal of Popular Film and Television
Jump Cut
Literature/Film Quarterly
Premiere
Quarterly Review of Film Studies
Screen
Sight and Sound
Wide Angle

Multimedia Sources

The American Film Institute. *Visions of Light: The Art of Cinematography* (laserdisc). Written and directed by Todd McCarthy, 1993.

American Movie Classics. *The Hollywood Soundtrack Story* (videotape). 1995.

Big Shot Films. *John Barry: Moviola* (videotape). 1993.

Blackhawk Films. *Landmarks of Early Film* (DVD). 1994.

CBS Television. "I Know It When I See It." *Sixty Minutes* segment about MPAA film rating system, narrated by Harry Reasoner (videotape). October 28, 1990.

Fox Lorber. *Classified X*, written by and starring Melvin Van Peebles (DVD). 1998. (An analysis of African Americans in American film.)

——. *Lumiere & Company: Forty Intriguing Films From the World's Leading Directors*, directed by Sarah Moon (DVD). 1995.

Lumivision Corporation. *Animation Legend: Winsor McCay* (DVD). 1993.

Microsoft. *Cinemania 97: The Best-Selling Interactive Guide to Movies and the Moviemakers* (CD-ROM).

1996. (According to Roger Ebert, whose work appears in this now-defunct series, the Cinemania franchise now has new owners and will resume production.)

PolyGram Video. *Short Cinema Journal, I: 1* (DVD). 1997. (Includes *Some Folks Call It a Sling Blade* by Billy Bob Thornton.)

——. *Short Cinema Journal, I: 2* (DVD). 1997. (Includes *La Jetée* by Chris Marker.)

——. *Short Cinema Journal, I: 3* (DVD). 1998. (Includes *Night & Fog* by Alain Resnais.)

Public Broadcasting Service. *The American Experience: The Battle Over* Kane (videotape). January 1996.

——. *Nova: Special Effects:* Titanic *and Beyond* (videotape). November 1998. (800. 255. 9424)

Turner Classic Movies. *Glorious Technicolor* (videotape). 1998. (Written and directed by Peter Jones.)

Vision Films/Smithsonian Video. *The Art of Illusion: One Hundred Years of Hollywood Special Effects* (DVD). 1990, revised 1995.

Internet Sites

Each listing is to be preceded by *http://www.*

afionline.org (American Film Institute)

chireader.com/movies (reviews by *The Chicago Reader's* Jonathan Rosenbaum and others)

cinemachine.com ("The Movie Review Search Engine")

filmmusic.com

filmsite.org ("The Great Movies" by Tim Dirks)

filmtracks.com (music soundtracks)

imdb.com (Internet Movie Database)

mdle.com/ClassicFilms ("The Silents Majority")

movie-reviews.colossus.net (reviews by James Berardinelli)

mpaa.org/movieratings/content.htm (Motion Picture Association of America)

mrqe.com ("Movie Review Query Engine")

pbs.org/wgbh/nova/specialfx2 (*Special Effects:* Titanic *and Beyond*)

suntimes.com/ebert (reviews by Roger Ebert)

tcm.turner.com (Turner Classic Movies)

tvplex.com/BuenaVista/SiskelAndEbert (TV reviews by Roger Ebert and Gene Siskel)

Credits

Text

Chapter 2 p. 11, From *Making Movies* by Sidney Lumet. Copyright © 1995 by Sidney Lumet. Reprinted by permission of Alfred A. Knopf, Inc. **Chapter 3** pp. 43, 44, 60, Reprinted with permission of Simon & Schuster, Inc. from *The Craft of the Screenwriter* by John Brady. Copyright © 1981 by John Brady. p. 49, From *Directing the Film: Film Directors on their Art*, edited by Eric Sherman. Reprinted by permission from Little, Brown and Company. pp. 66, 67, From Tennessee Williams, *Suddenly, Last Summer.* Copyright © 1958 by Tennessee Williams. All rights reserved. All quotations reprinted by permission of New Directions Publishing Corporation. **Chapter 4** p. 87, From *By Design: Interviews with Production Designers*, Vincent LoBrutto, Praeger, 1992. Reproduced with permission of Greenwood Publishing Group, Inc., Westport, CT. **Chapter 5** p. 117, From *Directing the Film: Film Directors on their Art*, edited by Eric Sherman. Reprinted by permission from Little, Brown and Company. **Chapter 6** pp. 152-154, 165, From *Selected Takes: Film Editors on Film Editing* by Vincent LoBrutto. Praeger, 1991. Reproduced with permission of Greenwood Publishing Group, Inc. p. 165, From *Directing the Film: Film Directors on their Art*, edited by Eric Sherman. Reprinted by permission from Little, Brown and Company. **Chapter 7** p. 195, From *By Design: Interviews with Production Designers*, Vincent LoBrutto, Praeger, 1992. Reproduced with permission of Greenwood Publishing Group, Inc., Westport, CT; p. 195, From Judith Crist, *Take 22: Moviemakers on Moviemaking*, Continuum, 1991. Reprinted with permission from the author. p. 203, Reprinted with permission of Simon & Schuster, Inc. from *The Craft of the Screenwriter* by John Brady. Copyright © 1981 by John Brady. **Chapter 8** pp. 227, 237, From *Sound-on-Film: Interviews with Creators of Film Sound* by Vincent LoBrutto, Praeger, 1994. Reproduced with permission of Greenwood Publishing Group, Inc., Westport, CT. **Chapter 9** p. 261, From Judith Crist, *Take 22: Moviemakers on Moviemaking*, Continuum, 1991. Reprinted with permission from the author. p. 265 From *Making Movies* by Sidney Lumet. Copyright © 1995 by Sidney Lumet. Reprinted by permission of Alfred A. Knopf, Inc. **Chapter 10** pp. 270, 271, 276, 289, From Judith Crist, *Take 22: Moviemakers on Moviemaking*, Continuum, 1991. Reprinted with permission from the author. pp. 282, 301, From *Making Movies* by Sidney Lumet. Copyright © 1995 by Sidney Lumet. Reprinted by permission of Alfred A. Knopf, Inc. **Chapter 11** pp. 307, 319, From *Making Movies* by Sidney Lumet. Copyright © 1995 by Sidney Lumet. Reprinted by permission of Alfred A. Knopf, Inc. p. 312, Reprinted with permission of Simon & Schuster, Inc. from *The Craft of the Screenwriter* by John Brady. Copyright © 1981 by John Brady; From Judith Crist, *Take 22: Moviemakers on Moviemaking*, Continuum, 1991. Reprinted with permission from the author. **Chapter 12** p. 339, From "Rex Reed at the Movies: From Blood and Guts to Guts and Blood," *Holiday Magazine*, vol. 47, no. 4, April 1970, p. 24. Permission to reprint granted by Travel Magazine, Inc., Floral Park, New York 11001. P. 345, From "Low-Down Hoedown," *Time*, August 25, 1967, p. 78. Copyright © 1967 Time Inc. Reprinted by permission. P. 346, From John McCarten, "Up the Cattlemen," *The New Yorker*, May 2, 1953. Originally in *The New Yorker.* Copyright © 1953 The New Yorker. Reprinted by permission of the publisher. All rights reserved. P. 347, From "The Shock of Freedom in Films," *Time*, December 8, 1967, p. 73. Copyright © 1967 Time, Inc. Reprinted by permission; Reprinted with permission of Simon & Schuster, Inc. from *The Craft of the Screenwriter* by John Brady. Copyright © 1981 by John Brady. Pp. 349, 364, From Dwight Macdonald, *On Movies*, Berkeley Medallion Books, 1971, p. 15. Copyright © 1969 by Dwight Macdonald. Reprinted by permission of the author. P. 359, From Vincent Canby, "Hitchcock: The Agony is Exquisite," *The New York Times*, July 2, 1972. Copyright © 1972 The New York Times. Reprinted by permission. **Chapter 13** pp. 380, 390, 396, Reprinted with permission of Simon & Schuster, Inc. from *The Craft of the Screenwriter* by John Brady. Copyright © 1981 by John Brady. P. 381-383, 385, From *All the King's Men* by Robert Penn Warren. Copyright © 1946, 1974 by Robert Penn Warren. Reprinted by permission of Harcourt Brace Jovanovich, Inc. p. 391, From *Making Movies* by Sidney Lumet. Copyright © 1995 by Sidney Lumet. Reprinted by permission of Alfred A. Knopf, Inc. p. 393, From *Directing the Film: Film Directors on their Art*, edited by Eric Sherman. Reprinted by permission from Little, Brown and Company. p. 399, From Richard Corliss, "Fire This Time," *Time*, January 9, 1989. Copyright © 1989 Time, Inc. Reprinted by permission. p. 400, From John Horn, "Redford Fudges Facts to Make Story Spicier." Reprinted with permission from Associated Press. **Chapter 15** pp. 459, 475, From *Directing the Film: Film Directors on their Art*, edited by Eric Sherman. Reprinted by permission from Little, Brown and Company. **Appendix A** p. 511, From Judith Crist, *Take 22: Moviemakers on Moviemaking*, Continuum, 1991. Reprinted with permission from the author.

Photos

p. 5B, Photofest; p. 13BR, Photofest; p. 22MR, Everett Collection; p. 23L, Everett Collection; p. 124R, Photofest; p. 178, Kobal Collection; p. 187, Kobal Collection; p. 193TL, Kobal Collection; p. 193BL, Everett Collection; p. 193BR, Everett Collection; p. 199, Kobal Collection; p. 205B, Everett Collection; p. 209BR, Everett Collection; p. 211, Kobal Collection; p. 283, Everett Collection; p. 306, © Corbis/AFP; p. 311, © Corbis/AFP; p. 320, Everett Collection; p. 322TL, Kobal Collection; p. 323B, © Archive Photos; p. 402R, Kobal Collection; p. 421R, Kobal Collection; p. 423TR, Everett Collection; p. 431R, Kobal Collection; p. 447BR, Photofest; p. 446, Kobal Collection; p. 466, Kobal Collection; p. 473B, Kobal Collection; p. 470, Photofest

Index

Abbott, Bud, 434
ABC, 512
The Abyss, 182, 184, 324
Academy Awards, 460
Academy of Motion Picture Arts and Sciences, 213, 342
Acting
- action, 278–79
- becoming the character, 270–72
- differences between film and stage, 272–79
- director's influence on, 317
- dramatic, 278–79
- ensemble, 284
- "facial," 276
- goal of, 269–70
- importance of, 269
- inside approach, 271
- outside approach, 271–72
- sustained expression, 276

Action, 37–38
- acting, 278–79
- characterization through, 52–53
- choreographed, music as base for, 260–62
- cutting, 165
- films, 12
- internal, 38, 53
- and reaction, 155

Act of Violence, 100
Actors
- extras, 293–97
- supporting players, 292–93
- types of, 279–80

Adams, Ansel, 213
Adaptation
- change in creative artists, 370–72
- change in medium, 370
- cinematic potential of the original work, 373–74
- problems of, 370–74

Adaptation, of novels, 375–88
- cinematic compression of time versus novelistic summary, 385–86
- literary past tense versus cinematic present tense, 386–87
- literary versus cinematic points of view, 375–78
- other factors influencing, 387–88
- philosophical reflections, 381
- problem of length and depth, 380–81
- problems created by the viewer, 374
- summarizing of a character's past, 383–85

Adaptation, of plays, 389–98
- film language versus stage language, 393–94
- other changes, 396–97
- sense of space, 390–93
- stage conventions versus cinema conventions, 394–95
- structural divisions, 390

Adler, Renata, 350, 372, 393, 447, 448, 449
Advancing colors, 194
The African Queen, 466
After Hours, 46
The Age of Innocence, 11, 240, 252, 311
Aimée, Anouk, 230
Airplane!, 419
Airport '77, 162
Aladdin, 468
Alambrista!, 137
Alamo Bay, 322
Albee, William, 374
Alda, Alan, 54
Alexander, Jane, 289, 291
Alexie, Sherman, 475
Alfie, 491, 492
Ali, Muhammad, 464
Alice in Wonderland, 467
Aliens, 92, 178, 422
Allegory, 60–61, 61
Allen, Ray, 290
Allen, Woody, 72, 283, 509
- *Annie Hall*, 210
- *Antz*, 472
- and Diane Keaton, 284
- experimentation and growth, 321
- *Manhattan*, 130, 265
- seriousness of films, 152
- standard character, 49, 322
- use of color versus black and white, 216
- use of test audiences, 46
- *Wild Man Blues*, 465, 466
- *Zelig*, 182, 183

All Quiet on the Western Front, 431
All That Jazz, 231, 287, 425
All the King's Men, 43
All the King's Men (Warren), 381–83, 385–86
All the President's Men, 264
Allyson, June, 284, 285
Almendros, Nestor, 81–82, 105, 119–20, 214
Almodóvar, Pedro, 453
Altered States, 179, 180, 181
Altman, Rick, 425
Altman, Robert, 204, 236, 257, 321
Always, 251, 292
Amadeus, 87, 506
Amarcord, 335
Ambient sound, 236, 449
American, 347
American Cinematographer, 110
American Dream, 462, 466
American Film Institute, 217
American Gigolo, 263
American Graffiti, 22, 254
An American in Paris, 425
American Movie Classics, 217
The American Short Story, 381
An American Werewolf in London, 13, 179, 180, 181
Amistad, 19, 311
"Amos 'n' Andy," 43
Amplified sound, 235, 236
Anachronism, 92
Anaconda, 179
Analogous harmony, 196
Anamorphic lenses, 83
Anchors Away, 470
Anders, Allison, 323
Andrews, Julie, 398
"Andy Griffith Show," 54
Anima, 358
Animal House, 498, 499
Animated feature films, 466–74
Animation, stop-motion, 467, 470
Anna and the King of Siam, 431
Annie, 425
Annie Hall, 49, 152, 210, 216, 318, 321, 322
"Another Brick in the Wall," 262
Antonelli, Laura, 448
Antonioni, Michelangelo, 200, 237
Antz, 472, 473
Apocalypse Now, 69, 240, 241, 324
The Apostle, 356
Appearance, characterization through, 50, 51
Apted, Michael, 463
Archer, Anne, 71
Archetypes, 358
Argento, Dario, 204
Aristotle, 33
Armageddon, 252
Aronofsky, Darren, 424
Arrangement of people and objects, 122, 123
Arsenal, 364
Art direction, 85–98
Art director, 85
Arthur, 55
Arthur, Jean, 140, 281
Artificial light, 105
Arzner, Dorothy, 323
As Good As It Gets, 275
Ashby, Hal, 300, 370
Astaire, Fred, 56, 425
Astor, Mary, 100
Atlantic City, 322
Atmosphere, 42
Atmospheric color, 190, 191
Audience reactions, influence on viewing experience, 343
Auteur, 308, 321, 357
Auteur approach, to film analysis, 353, 359, 361
Avalon, 148
Avery, Tex, 467
Avildsen, John G., 400, 401

Babe, 179, 180, 471

Babe: Pig in the City, 211, 471
Background in motion, 122, 130
Background music, 249
Back lighting, 103
Back to the Future, sequel, 435
Badham, John, 261, 511
Badlands, 242, 325
The Bad News Bears, 262
The Bad Seed, 398
Bahr, Fax, 465
Bailey, John, 148
Baker, Dylan, 502
Baker, George, 455
Baker, Rick, 177, 181
Balanced lighting, 104
Balázs, Béla, 274, 446, 456
Balk, Fairuza, 22
Ballhaus, Michael, 96
Bananas, 321
Bancroft, Anne, 184
Bang the Drum Slowly, 144, 288–89
The Barber of Seville, 258
Barnouw, Erik, 462, 463
Barry Lyndon, 330
Barrymore, Drew, 423
Bartkowaik, Andrzej, 105
Basic Instinct, 501
Basinger, Kim, 420
Bates, Alan, 122, 128
Bates, Kathy, 398
Bates, Norman, 93
Batman, 36, 86, 204, 206, 207, 436
Batman and Robin, 436, 437
Batman Forever, 436, 437
Batman Returns, 436, 437
"The Battler" (Hemingway), 374
Beatty, Warren, 155, 207, 234, 236, 286, 301, 346
Beauty and the Beast, 468
Beginnings, 318
Being There, 370
Beloved, 253
Ben-Hur, 154, 190, 430
Benson, Lucille, 292
Berenger, Tom, 433
Berenson, Marisa, 167
Bergman, Ingmar, 23, 48, 101, 202, 308, 313
Bergman, Ingrid, 26, 212–13
Bernstein, Elmer, 252
Bernstein, Leonard, 221
Beron, David, 513
Bethurum, Dorothy, 373
Beverly Hills Cop, 13, 263
The Big Chill, 254, 284
Bigelow, Kathryn, 162, 211
Billy Bathgate, 289
Billy Budd, 55
Biloxi Blues, 208, 209
Bingo Long, 511
"The Bionic Women," 144
Bird, 466
The Birth of a Nation, 307, 313, 399, 501
Biskind, Peter, 181–82
Bitzer, Billy, 313
Black, Karen, 70, 99, 257
Black and white, versus color, 80–81, 213–17
Black (color), 188, 189
Black Rain, 153
Black Stallion, 293
Blade Runner, 422
  director's cut, 324
  set design, 86, 92, 97–98, 181, 183
  synthesizer score, 263
  voice-over narration, 240
Blank, Les, 465
Blazing Saddles, 419
"Bliss" (Mansfield), 377
The Blood of a Poet, 475
Blow Out, 237
Blowup, 237
Blue (color), 195
The Blue Danube Waltz, 251
The Blue Lagoon, 430
Blue-screen process, 177
Blue Sky, 361
Bluestone, George, 378
Blue tinting, 455
Blue Velvet, 197, 288
Bob & Carol & Ted & Alice, 451
Body and Soul, 428, 475
Body Heat, 56, 237, 361, 418, 420
Body language, 274, 275, 278
Body Language (Fast), 274
Bogart, Humphrey, 26, 49, 54, 133, 182, 183, 275
Bogdanovich, Peter, 81, 307, 373
Bolger, Ray, 198
Bonnie and Clyde, 342, 346, 417
  action and reaction editing sequence, 155–60
  amplification of sound, 235
  close-up violence, 118
  critical views of, 347
  French critics on, 453
  new standard of violence, 502
  sense of past, 386
  silence as sound effect, 243
  supporting characters, 292
  title music, 260
Boogie Nights, 21
Boop, Betty, 467
Boorman, John, 140, 211
Bottin, Rob, 180
Bottoms, Sam, 384
Box, John, 87–88, 89
Boyle, Danny, 476
Boyle, Robert, 96, 195
Boy on a Dolphin, 283
Brady, Frank, 131, 259
Bram Stoker's Dracula, 5, 179, 180, 183, 430
Branagh, Kenneth, 371, 394
The Branding Iron, 428
Brando, Marlon, 286, 514
  Apocalypse Now, 69, 241, 287
  On the Waterfront, 19, 230, 297, 298
  The Wild One, 275
Braudy, Leo, 431
Brave New World (Huxley), 3
Breaking Away, 106, 258, 292, 319
Breaking the Waves, 23
Breathless, 431
Bretherton, David, 167
Bride of Frankenstein, 432
The Bridge over the River Kwai, 249
The Bridges of Madison County, 42, 279, 381
A Brief History of Time, 464
Bringing Up Baby, 426
Broken Blossoms, 364, 455
Brooks, Mel, 184, 434
The Brothers McMullen, 325
Browning, Tod, 430
Brownlow, Kevin, 128, 425, 455, 456
Bruckheimer, Jerry, 252
Buffalo Bill and the Indians, 321
Bugs Bunny, 467
A Bug's Life, 472, 473
Bullets Over Broadway, 321
Bullitt, 505
Bulworth, 301
Bunker, Archie, 60
Burbank Studios, 97
Burden of Dreams, 465
Burghoff, Gary, 54
The Burning Bed, 512
Burton, Richard, 285
Burton, Tim, 471
Buscemi, Steve, 292, 293
Busey, Gary, 289
Butch Cassidy and the Sundance Kid, 99, 146, 147, 263, 292, 386, 433
Butch Cassidy and the Sundance Kid: The Early Days, 433
The Butcher Boy, 252, 293, 294
Butler, Bill, 138
Bwana Devil, 136

Cabaret, 89, 167, 239, 257, 425, 427
The Cabinet of Dr. Caligari, 396, 397, 475
Cage, Nicolas, 241, 497
Caine, Michael, 270, 272
Caligari, 364
"The Call of the Faraway Hills," 253
Camera
  fixed, 314
  hand-held, 137
  mobile, 128–29, 163, 314
  objective, 313
  placement, 112–19
  static, 113, 163, 314
  subjective, 313–14, 379
  technique, 154
  as window, 113
Camera angle, 137–40
  changing, 139
  objective, 137
Camera movement
  apparent, 131
  and depth, 130–31
Cameron, James, 184, *324*, 466
Campion, Jane, 323
Canby, Vincent, review of Hitchcock's *Frenzy*, 359
Cannery Row, 85, 240, 318

Cannes Film Festival, 70, 342
Cape Fear, 279, 430
Capra, Frank, 46, 50, 223, 281
Caravaggio, 105
Cardiff, Jack, 85
Caricature, 54
Carmen, 262
Carollo, Kira, 524
Carpenter, John, 236, 422
Carradine, Keith, 257
Carrey, Jim, 59, 286, 437
Carter, Rick, 182
Casablanca, 26, 54, 133, 212
Casting, 50, 282–86, 316–17
  problems, 286–87
  typecasting, 287–92
Cat Ballou, 260
Catch-22, 56, 216
The Catcher in the Rye (Salinger), 379–80
Categorical rejection, 339–41
Cates, Gilbert, 213
Cat People, 179, 263–64, 429
Caulfield, Holden, 379
CBS/Fox Video, 212
Celebrity, 215, 321
Censorship, 430, 483–84
  1930–1960, 484–90
  1948–1968, 490
  and made-for-television films, 511
  by religious leaders and their supporters, 498–501
  and televised films, 498
Central idea, 14–23
  coming of age/loss of innocence/growing awareness, 20–21
  complexity of human relationships, 19–20
  moral or philosophical riddle, 21, 23
  moral statements, 17
  social problems, 18
  struggle for human dignity, 18–19
  truth of human nature, 17–18
Chamberlain, Richard, 371
Chandler, Helen, 430
Chaney, Lon Jr., 179, 181
Change in creative artists, 370–72
Chaplin, Charlie, 456, 457, 459
Chapman, Michael, 203
Characterization, 49–50
  through appearance, 50, 51
  through caricature and leitmotif, 54–56
  through choice of name, 57
  through contrast, 54
  through dialogue, 50–52
  through external action, 52–53
  through internal action, 53
  through reactions of other characters, 53–54
Characters, 13–14
  developing, 58
  flat, 60–61
  irony of, 72
  point-of-view, 318
  round, 60–61
  static, 59–60
  stereotypes, 58
  stock, 57–58
  varieties of, 57–61
Character series, 434, 436
Chariots of Fire, 142–43, 143, 144, 147, 263
Charly, 271
Chase scenes
  in gangster films, 416–17
  on horseback, 414
Chasing Amy, 21, 284
Chayefsky, Paddy, 94
The Cheat, 425
Chemistry, he/she, 284–85
Chicago *Tribune*, 347
Children of Paradise, 364
Child stars, 292–93
Chinatown, 418
Cholodenko, Lisa, 323
Choreographed action, music as base for, 260–62
Christie, Ian, 465
Christie, Julie, 122, 147, 394
Christopher, Dennis, 258
Chronological (linear) structure, 44
Cinderella, 425, 467
Cinema Paradiso, 293
Cinemascope, 82, 83, 84, 148, 491
Cinematic composition, 119–36
Cinematic film, 111–12
Cinematic points of view, 112–13, 112–19, 389
  director's interpretation, 118–19
  indirect subjective, 116–18
  objective, 113
  subjective, 114–16
Cinematic tension, 393
Cinematographers, 80, 86
Cinematography, 111, 137–48, 313–14
Cinéma vérité, 463, 465
Cinemax, 510
Cinerama, 3, 136, 148, 491
Citizen Kane
  breakfast montage, 255
  cinematography, 313
  dead screen technique in, 234
  deep focus, 131, 133
  as a fictionalized biography, 403
  high-angle shot, 139
  make-up in, 100, 101
  music, 256, 259
  narrative structure, 317
  realistic dialogue, 223
  reflections, 135–36
  "rosebud" symbol, 65
  "snow picture" sequence, 259
  sound, 223, 225, 234, 239
  static character, 60
  thawed frame, 147
  three-dimensional sound, 223–24
City Lights, 456, 457
City of Angels, 13
City Slickers, 278
Clarity, of sound, 223, 224
Clark, Joe, 400, 401
Clash of the Titans, 470
Classic film, 24–26
Claustrophobic set, 88, 89
Clear and Present Danger, 12
Clerks, 106, 325
Cliché, 69
Clift, Montgomery, 286, 301, 302
Climax, 43, 44
A Clockwork Orange, 145, 260, 263, 330, 496
Clooney, George, 436
Close, Glenn, 44, 46, 71, 205, 282
Close Encounters of the Third Kind, 178, 310, 324, 332, 424
A Close Shave, 470
Close-up, 117, 122, 129, 273
  extreme, 122
  power of, 389
  reaction shot, 53, 116
  and standard screen, 82
Clouseau, Jacques, 436
Coal Miner's Daughter, 288
Cocteau, Jean, 475
Coherence, 154, 162
Cold colors, 211
Coleridge, Samuel Taylor, 36
Colorization, 212–13
Color palette, 81, 87, 98
The Color Purple, 332
Colors, 124, 188
  advancing, 194
  atmospheric, 190
  versus black and white, 80–81, 213–17
  cold, 211
  comic book, 206
  comic strip, 207
  cool, 195, 196
  desaturated (muted), 189–90, 216
  effects of impression of temperature, 195
  effects of on three-dimensionality, 194
  effects on the viewer, 192–97
  to enhance mood, 205
  expressionistic use of, 200–202
  functioning together, 195–96
  intermediate, 189
  ironic use of, 210
  leitmotifs in, 204
  local, 190
  painterly effects, 208–9
  primary, 189
  receding, 194
  recorded, 190–92
  saturated, 189, 193
  secondary, 189
  in silent films, 454–56
  special effects, 210–11, 216
  surrealistic use of, 203
  as symbol, 202
  as a transitional device, 197–200
  transitions in, 205
  value of, 188, 194, 195
  warm, 195, 196
Color Systems Technology, 212
Color wheel, 188, 189, 196
Come Back to the Five and Dime, Jimmy Dean, Jimmy Dean, 321
Comic book color, 206

Comic strip color, 207
Coming Home, 254, 300
Coming of age film, 20–21, 22
Comingore, Dorothy, 234
Commentators, 280
Commercial breaks, 508–10, 511
Communication
  face as medium of, 274
  nonverbal, 274
Complementary harmony, 195–96
Complexity, 40–41
Complication, of film structure, 43, 44, 45
Composition, 120, 154, 313
Computer-generated animation, 467, 572
Computer-generated digital imaging (CGI), 177, 179, 181–83, 184
Con Air, 252
Conan the Barbarian, 179
Concealed point of view, 377
Confession specialist, 415
Conflict, 47–49
  external, 48
  internal, 49–50
  symbolic values in, 68, 69
Connelly, Jennifer, 295
Connery, Sean, 307, 436
Constructed documentaries, 464
Contact, 177, 424
Context, and creation of symbolism, 65
Continuity, 154
The Conversation, 138, 229, 237, 264
The Cook, The Thief, His Wife, & Her Lawyer, 202
Cookie's Fortune, 321
Cool colors, 195, 196
Cool Hand Luke, 292
Coolidge, Martha, 323
Cooper, Gary, 61, 281
Cooper, Merian C., 177
Coppola, Eleanor, 465
Coppola, Francis Ford
  Apocalypse Now, 241, 324, 465
  Bram Stoker's Dracula, 183, 430
  The Conversation, 138, 229, 237
  The Godfather, 168
  Life with Zoe, 321
Copyright, 212, 213
Corliss, Richard, 399, 474
Cornwell, Lisa, 516
Cort, Bud, 55
Cosmic irony, 74
Costello, Lou, 434
Costner, Kevin, 412
Costume, 98–101
Costumer, 80, 86
Courage Under Fire, 290
Cousins, Mark, 465
Cowboy hero (western hero), 411–12
Coyote, Peter, 123
Craven, Wes, 422
Crawford, Broderick, 382
Credibility, of story, 33–37
Credits, 509
Crichton, Michael, 181
Cries and Whispers, 202
Crimes and Misdemeanors, 292, 321
Crist, Judith, 325
Cronyn, Hume, 356
Crosby, Bing, 434
Cross, as symbol, 63
Crothers, Scatman, 292
Crowther, Bosley, 347
Crumb, 325, 463, 464
The Crying Game, 361
Culkin, Macauley, 292
Cultural differences, 450–52
Cultural prejudice, 453
Curtis, Jamie Lee, 123
Curtis, Ken, 54–55
Curved lines, 119
Curved-screen projection, 3
Cuts, editorial, 161, 314–15
Cutting, of films on television, 509, 510
Cyrano de Bergerac, 256

Dafoe, Willem, 191, 401, 500
Dahl, Roald, 471
Dailies (rushes), 153
Daily News, 347
Daisy Miller, 373
Dallwitz, Burkhard, 257
Damon, Matt, 402
Dance-hall girl, 412
Dances With Wolves, 409, 412
Danish films, 453
Danson, Ted, 56, 513
Dante, Joe, 184, 495
Darby, Kim, 52
Dark City, 86, 422
Dark Passage, 182
Darwell, Jane, 147
Das Boot, 224–25, 449, 506
Dash, Julie, 323
Dave, 35
Daviau, Allen, 148
David and Lisa, 431
David Copperfield, 56
Davis, Bette, 100
Davis, Geena, 59
The Day After, 513
Day-for-night shooting, 455
Day of the Locust, 210
Days of Heaven, 94, 105, 242, 243, 380
The Day the Earth Stood Still, 36, 424
"The Dead" (Joyce), 381
Dead Man Walking, 136, 361
Dead Men Don't Wear Plaid, 182, 183, 419
Dead Poets Society, 143, 286
Dead screen, 126, 130, 234
Dead track, 243
Dean, James, 286, 465
Deconstructing Harry, 321
"Deep Night," 132, 260
The Deer Hunter, 111, 289
de Havilland, Olivia, 476
Deliverance, 18, 211
DeMille, Cecil B., 105
Demme, Jonathan, 256, 423
De Niro, Robert, 282
  Bang the Drum Slowly, 144, 288–89
  dramatic acting, 278–79
  Jacknife, 45
  Once Upon a Time in America, 295
  Raging Bull, 200, 222, 234
  Taxi Driver, 57, 58, 203
Denis, Claire, 323
Dennis, Sandy, 283
Dénouement, 43, 44, 46
De Palma, Brian, 237, 496
Depth. *See* Three-dimensionality
Dern, Bruce, 70
Desaturated (muted) color, 189–90, 216
Developing characters, 58
DeVito, Danny, 46, 437
DeWilde, Brandon, 53, 104
Diagonal lines, 119
Diagonal movement, 125
Dialects, 50
Dialogue, 45, 221, 316, 393–94
  and characterization, 50–52
  film versus stage, 222–23
  links, 239
  musical accompaniment of, 252
  mute, 457
  overlaps, 315
  poetic, 393
  rhythmic qualities of, 245
  stage, 393–94, 395
  transitions, 239
The Diary of Anne Frank, 431
Diaz, Cameron, 426
DiCaprio, Leonardo, 253
Dickens, Charles, 56
Dickerson, Ernest, 148
Dick Tracy, 207
Die Hard, 99
Dietrich, Marlene, 465
Diffused lighting, 104
Digital recording, 222, 225
Digital video disc (DVD), 6, 473, 507
Diller, Barry, 512
Direct cinéma, 463
"Direction" (Hitchcock), 114–15
Direct lighting, 104
Director, Roger, 508
Director of photography (DP), 148
Directors, 80, 86
  and actors' performance, 317
  amount of control, 308
  as *auteurs*, 308, 309
  camera movement, 314
  casting, 316–17
  choice of setting, 315
  choice of subject matter, 309–12
  cinematic style, 313–14
  editorial style, 314–15
  evolving style, 321–22
  experimental, 321–22
  intention, 349, 350
  interpretive point of view, 118, 119
  lighting choices, 314
  and narrative structure, 317–19

role of, 307
and screenplay, 319–20
style, 308–9
treatment of color, 314
use of musical score, 316
use of soundtrack, 315–16
women, 323
Director's cut, 324
Director's Guild of America, 213, 323
DIRECTV, 507
Disaster films, 177
Disbelief, suspension of, 36
Disney, 473
Disney, Walt, 467, 468
Dissolve, 161, 178
Dissonance, 254–55
"Do, Re, Mi," 390
D.O.A., 199
Doctor Zhivago, 147
Documentary: A History of the Non-Fiction Film (Barnouw), 462
Documentary films, 137, 325, 460–66
constructed, 464
thesis, 462
Dog Day Afternoon, 265, 307
Dolby Pro Logic, 507
Dolby stereo, 224–25, 236
Dolby-Surround Sound, 224
The Dollmaker, 143, 512
Dolly, 131
Domination, stage acting as, 273
Dooley, Paul, 292
Do the Right Thing, 19, 148, 237
Double features, 344
Double Indemnity, 418, 420
Double-viewing, 349
Douglas, Melvyn, 104
Douglas, Michael, 21, 44, 46, 71
Downs, Lenthiel H., 279–80
Dr. Death, 464
Dr. Strangelove, 73, 216, 251, 255, 292, 331
Doctor Zhivago, 92, 342
Dracula/Bram Stoker's Dracula, 5, 179, 180, 183, 430
Dragonslayer, 179, 180
Dramatic acting, 278–79
Dramatic arrangement of people and objects, 122, 123
Dramatic cutting. *See* Editorial cuts
Dramatic foils, 54, 55, 292, 413
Dramatic interest, 45
Dramatic irony, 70–71, 318
Dramatic (literary) point of view, 375–78
Dramatic structure, 43–47
Dramatic tension, 392
Drawn animation, 467, 469
Dreams, 229
Dreamworks, 472, 473
Dreyfuss, Richard, 236, 287, 324, 508
Driving Miss Daisy, 34
Drugstore Cowboy, 429
Duel, 512
Dullea, Keir, 191
Dumbo, 467
Dunaway, Faye, 155, 346
Dunne, Griffin, 46
Dunst, Kirsten, 100
Duvall, Robert, 282, 289, 291, 514
The Apostle, 356
The Great Santini, 56
To Kill a Mockingbird, 42
True Grit, 499
Wrestling Ernest Hemingway, 50
Duvall, Shelley, 204
Dwan, Allan, 131
Dye transfer, 217
Dykstra, John, 177

E. T. The Extra-Terrestrial, 36, 123, 148, 178, 183, 293, 333, 424
An Early Frost, 512
Earthquake!, 177, 224
Eastman Color, 192
Eastman Kodak, 196
East of Eden, 286, 512
Eastwood, Clint, 56, 278–79, 388, 465
Easy Rider, 24, 25, 46, 451
Ebert, Roger, 243, 462, 463, 469, 474, 506
Eclectic approach, to film analysis, 359, 361, 362
Economy, in musical score, 264–65
Edison, the Man, 437
Editing, 152–53, 163, 314–15
action and reaction sequence, 155
coherence, continuity, and rhythm, 154
expansion and compression of time, 166–67
ironic montage, 168–76
and movement, 129
outside/in, 162
rhythms, tempo, and time control, 162–66
selectivity, 153–54
sequence from *The Grapes of Wrath*, 175–76
and special visual effects, 151–86
transitions, 154–62
Editorial cuts, 161, 165, 314–15
Editorial juxtapositions, 315
Edlund, Richard, 177, 184
Edtv, 174
Edwards, Blake, 436
Edward Scissorhands, 36
Ed Wood, 292, 293
Effaced point of view, 377
The Effect of Gamma Rays on Man-in-the-Moon Marigolds, 271
8 1/2, 334, 349
Eisenstein, Sergei, 68, 69, 161, 174, 364, 454, 456
Elements, of cinematic composition, 119
The Elephant Man, 100, 215
Elizabeth, 209
El Mariachi, 325
Emotional approach, to film analysis, 354, 361
Emotional atmosphere, and setting, 92, 93
Emotional restraint, 41–42
The Empire Strikes Back, 178, 180, 437
Endings, 318
The English Patient, 16, 289
Enright, Don, 402
Ensemble acting, 284
Enterprise, 178
Environment, 90
Episodic plots, 33
Equus, 396, 397
Erasmus, 73
Escapist film, 40, 41
Establishing shot, 116, 162
Evaluation, subjective, 351
Ever After, 205
Everett, Rupert, 46
Everybody's All-American, 292
"Everybody's Talkin' at Me," 260
Excalibur, 140, 178
Executive Action, 404
The Exorcist, 236
Experimental directors, 321–22
Exposition, 43, 44, 45
Expression, sustained, 276
Expressionism, 200–202
External conflict, 48
Extras, 293–97
Extreme close-ups, 122
Extrinsic metaphors, 68–69
Eye-line shot, 116
Eyre, Chris, 475

Facial acting, 274, 276, 277, 457
Fade-out/fade-in, 161
Fairy tale musical, 425
"The Fall of the House of Usher," 91
Family Plot, 70, 99
Fantasia, 467, 468
Fantasia 2000, 468
Fantastic Voyage, 180
Fantasy films, 92, 211, 422, 424
Fantasy worlds, and production design, 97
Fargo, 51, 292, 293
The Farmer Takes a Wife, 273
Farrelly Brothers, 426
Farrow, Mia, 284
Fast, Cheap & Out of Control, 464
Fast, Julian, 274
Fast motion, 145
Fatal Attraction, 44, 46, 71
Faulkner, William, 57, 375–76, 378
Fawcett, Farrah, 402, 512
Fellini, Federico, 48, 349
Feminist approach, to film analysis, 356–57
Feuer, Jane, 425
F for Fake, 465
Fiber optics, 507
Field, Sally, 261
Field of Dreams, 371
Fields, Adam, 399
Fiennes, Ralph, 162, 290
The Fifth Element, 92
Film
naturalistic, 41, 68
slasher, 137, 180, 422
stop-action, 471
Film: A Montage of Theories (MacCann), 8
Film analysis
of *The Age of Innocence*, 526

Film analysis *(continued)*
auteur approach, 353, 359, 361
basic approach, 348–51
developing personal criteria, 364–65
difficulties of, 3–6
eclectic approach, 359, 361, 362
emotional approach, 354
feminist approach, 356–57
genre approach, 355
of *The Grapes of Wrath*, 516–23
humanistic approach, 353–54
level of ambition, 350
and literary analysis, 32
Marxist approach, 355–56
and objective evaluation, 350–51
personality cult approach, 352–53
psychoanalytical approach, 357–58
and relationship of the parts to the whole, 349–50
subjective evaluation, 351
of *Taxi Driver*, 524–26
and theme and filmmakers' intention, 349
value of, 6–9
viewer-centered challenges to, 339–41
writing, 515–29
Film Comment, 409
The Film Encyclopedia, 167
Film noir, 200, 206, 418–21, 420
Films
acting differences from stage, 272–79
affinity with music, 248–49
auteur approach, 353, 359, 361
as both industry and art form, 2
classic, 24–26
coming of age, 20–21, 22
complexity, 40–41
as conventionalized form, 355
distortions of reality, 399–400
emotional or sensual experience of, 354
escapist, 40, 41
four major elements of, 11
as gender statement, 356–57
historically important, 474–75
horror, 264
as insight to the mind, 357–58
international, 450–54
Italian, 452
length of, 40
level of ambition, 350
made for cable, 514
made-for-television, 509, 510–14
moral, philosophical, or social statement of, 353–54
narrative, 8
on network television, 343–44
objective evaluation of, 350–51
period, 96, 100, 236
as political statement, 355
portrayal of physical conflict in, 393
realism, 3
science fiction, 92, 178, 422, 424
as showcase for actor, 352–53
social problem, 18, 19, 24, 476–77
Swedish, 453
technical achievement, 352, 430
time in, 166
uniqueness among media, 2
unlimited range in subject matter and treatment, 2–3
watching on television, 505–14
Film stock, 82–85, 96
rough-grain, 82, 85
smooth-grain, 82, 85
Filters, 140
Final cut, 299
Firefox, 178
First-person point of view, 239, 375, 379–80
omniscient, 378
Firth, Peter, 397
Fischer, Gunnar, 313
Fish-eye lens, 141, 142
Fisk, Jack, 94
F.I.S.T., 208
Fitzcarraldo, 286, 465
Fixed camera, 314
Fixed frame, 129
and depth, 130
movement, 124
Flag, as symbol, 63
Flaherty, Robert, 461
Flashback, 239, 386, 395–96
functions of, 45
memory images, 167
montage, 175
visual, 229
Flash cut, 166–67
fragmented, 315
Flash-forward, 45
Flat characters, 60–61
Fleischer, Max, 467
Fleming, Victor, 273
Fletcher, Louise, 47
The Flim Flam Man, 293
Flip frame, 161
The Fly, 179
Flying-vehicle effects, 178
Focal planes, change of, 131
Focus
deep, 131–33, 132
rack, 131, 132
sharpness of, 121
soft, 229
"Foggy Mountain Breakdown," 258–59
Foil, 54, 55, 292, 413
Foley artist, 221
Folk musical, 425
Fonda, Henry, 59, 147, 175, 273, 281, 307
Fonda, Jane, 143, 300, 512, 514
Fonda, Peter, 167
Forced perspective, 88
Ford, Harrison, 38, 95, 98
Ford, John, 80, 175, 307, 338
and genre films, 411
The Grapes of Wrath, 105, 174, 175, 232, 477
The Informer, 372
"philosophy of camera," 113, 114
preference for black and white, 80
use of star system, 281
Foreground framing, 122, 123, 133–34
Foreign language films, 447–50, 460
Foreman, George, 464
Foreshadowing (tension-building) music, 254–55
Forman, Milos, 322, 506
Form cut, 161
Formulas, of genre films
gangster film formula, 414–17
stretching and breaking of, 417–18
western formula, 411–14
Forrest Gump, 5, 356
computer-generated imagery, 183, 184
nostalgic music, 254
repetition, 243, 244
supporting players, 293, 294
voice-over narration, 243, 318
Fosse, Bob, 89, 167, 231, 287, 296–97, 425, 427
Foster, Jodie, 20, 282, 424
Fox, Michael J., 435
The Fox, 195
Foxes, 263
Fragmented flash cut, 315
Frame, 81–82
Frankenstein, 73, 422, 430, 432
Frankenstein Meets the Wolf Man, 432
Frankie and Johnny, 398
Freeman, Morgan, 296, 311, 401
Freeze frame, 145–47, 243
Freleng, Fritz, 467
The French Connection, 120, 432
The French Connection II, 432
Freud, Sigmund, 70
Freudian criticism, 357
Friday the 13th, Part 3, 136
Friedkin, Billy, 236
Friendly Fire, 512
Frolick, Billy, 325
From Here to Eternity, 302, 431
Front lighting, 103
The Front Page, 298
The Fugitive Kind, 320
The Full Monty, 14
Furst, Anton, 86, 206
Future General Company, 177
F/x. *See* Special effects

Gable, Clark, 191
Gance, Abel, 128, 455, 456, 458
Gandhi, 124
Gangster films, 414–17, 421
dress, 416
hero, 415, 416
women, 415
Gardner, Ava, 252
Garland, Judy, 198, 292
Garofalo, Janeane, 284
Gary, Lorraine, 433, 435
Gates of Heaven, 463
Geer, Will, 54
Geffen, David, 472
Gel filters, 140
Gender approach, to film analysis, 361

The General, 456
Generalized (implicit) score, 251
Genre approach, to film analysis, 355, 361
Genre-based satire, 419
Genre films, 355, 409–10
fantasy films, 422, 424
film noir, 418–21
gangster films, 414–17
horror films, 422
musicals, 425
and reinforcement of values, 410
science fiction, 422, 424
screwball comedies, 424–25
strengths of, 410–11
stretching and breaking of formulas, 417–18
war films, 421–22
westerns, 411–14
Gertie the Dinosaur, 467
Gestures, 457
The Getaway, 429
Giannini, Giancarlo, 123, 452
Gibson, Mel, 69, 216, 296, 371
Gielgud, John, 55
Gilliatt, Penelope, 347
"Gilligan's Island," 94
Ginsburg v. *New York*, 492
Gish, Lillian, 459
Glancing rhythms, 165
Glass, Philip, 145, 257, 463
The Glass Menagerie, 239
Glory, 296, 402
The Go-Between, 122
The Godfather, 59, 167, 168–73, 210, 432
The Godfather Part II, 432
Godzilla, 178
The Golden Hour, 205
Goldman, William, 312, 347, 380
The Gold Rush, 456
Goldsmith, Jerry, 256
Goldwyn, Samuel, 490
Gone with the Wind, 177, 191, 192, 217, 292, 380, 502
GoodFellas, 96
Goodman, John, 261, 292
Good Morning, Vietnam, 73
Good Will Hunting, 43, 429
Goosen, Stephen, 86
Gordon, Ruth, 55
Gore effects, 180
Goris, Marleen, 323
Gossett, Lou Jr., 510
The Graduate, 49, 140, 141, 239, 260, 281, 289, 298
Graham, Martha, 272
A Grand Day Out, 470
Grand Illusion, 421, 451
Grant, Cary, 426
Grant, Lee, 323
The Grapes of Wrath, 5, 450–51
ironic juxtaposition of sound and image in, 234
lighting, 105
mechanical sounds in, 232
as social problem film, 477
special lighting effects, 147, 148
Tom Joad, 59
universal theme, 24
use of montage, 174–75
use of reflections, 135
G rating, 493–94, 495
Great Balls of Fire, 399
Great Mother, 358
The Great Santini, 15, 56
The Great Train Robbery, 456
Greed, 456
Greenaway, Peter, 202
Greene, Graham, 412
Greer, Jane, 420
Gremlins, 184, 494, 495
Grierson, John, 460, 461
Griffith, Andy, 54
Griffith, D. W., 40, 177, 307, 399, 455
Groundhog Day, 11
Guinness, Alec, 282–83
Gun moll, 415
"Gunsmoke," 54, 56
A Guy Named Joe/Always, 430
Gyrosphere shots, 129

Hackman, Gene, 287, 289, 290, 291, 292
The Conversation, 229, 237, 238
Mississippi Burning, 191, 401
Unforgiven, 413
Hair, 322, 425
Hairdressing, 99, 101
Halberstam, David, 399–400, 402
Hall, Cecilia, 222
Hall, Conrad, 210
Hall, Hanna R., 294
Hallmark Hall of Fame, 512
Halloween, 422
Halloween 13, 123
Hamilton, Murray, 433
Hamlet, 215, 216, 371, 394
Hand-held camera, 137, 314
Hanks, Tom, 184, 244, 311, 402
Hannah and Her Sisters, 321
Hanson, Curtis, 418, 420
Happiness, 502
Hardcore, 87, 135, 136
Hard lighting, 104, 105
Harlan County, U.S.A., 85, 462, 466
Harlow, Jean, 284
Harmony, color, 195–96
Harold and Maude, 55
Harper, Jessica, 127
Harris, Barbara, 257
Harris, Ed, 45, 257
Harris, Richard, 50
Harryhausen, Ray, 179, 470
Harsh lighting, 104
Hauser, Arnold, 8
Hawke, Ethan, 284
Hawking, Stephen, 464
Hawks, Howard, 105, 409, 426
Hayden, Sterling, 292
Hays, Will B., 484
Hays Office, 484, 485
HBO, 510, 514
Head, Edith, 98, 99, 100
Hearst, William Randolph, 403
The Heartbreak Kid, 323
Hearts of Darkness: A Filmmaker's Apocalypse, 465
Heaven Can Wait, 429
Heckerling, Amy, 323
Heffner, Richard D., 497
Heflin, Van, 235, 393
He Got Game, 290
Hemingway, Ernest, 373, 374, 377
Henchmen, 415
Henry, John, 48
Henry, O., 72
Henry & June, 494
Henry V, 215, 394
Hepburn, Audrey, 286, 288, 398
Hepburn, Katherine, 65, 91, 284, 285, 391, 426
Here Comes Mr. Jordan, 429
Hero
gangster, 415, 416
initiate, 413
western (cowboy), 411–12
Heroine, western, 412
Herrmann, Bernard, 256, 259
Herzog, Werner, 286, 465
He/she chemistry, 284–85
Heston, Charlton, 99, 431
Hickenlooper, George, 465
Hi-fi VCRs, 507
High-angle shot, 138–39
High contrast, 124
High-definition television (HDTV), 506–7
High-key lighting, 102
High Noon, 61, 94, 260, 317, 417
High Society, 430
Hill, George Roy, 99
Hill, Walter, 233
The Hill, 306
Hilter, Adolf, 462
Hiroshima, Mon Amour, 61, 491
Hirsch, Foster, 418
Historical accuracy, 402
Historically important films, 474–75
Hitchcock, Alfred, 11, 31, 312, 324, 359
as an *auteur* director, 310
on editing, 152
involvement in costume design, 99
philosophy of direction, 114, 115, 117
on the pictorial simplicity of silent film, 458–59
Psycho, 423
on role of actors, 269, 297
and terror/suspense film, 309
use of musical imagery to describe editing rhythm, 165–66
The Hitch Hiker, 323
Hoffa, 100, 403
Hoffa, Jimmy, 403
Hoffman, Dustin, 49, 140, 270, 282, 289, 298–99
Holden, William, 286
Holland, Agnieszka, 92, 323

Hollywood: The Pioneers (Brownlow), 425
Home Box Office (HBO), 510, 514
Homer, 45, 71
Honor Thy Father and Mother: The Menendez Killings, 513
Hoop Dreams, 460, 461
Hope, Bob, 434
Hopkins, Anthony, 39, 311, 423
Hopper, Dennis, 288
Hopper, Edward, 208
Hopscotch, 261
Horror films, 82, 92, 137, 180, 264, 422
Horse-and-buggy music, 258
Hoskins, Bob, 470
Hospital, 94
Houses, as indicators of character, 90
Howards End, 299
Howe, James Wong, 101, 104
The Howling, 179, 181
Huckleberry Finn (Twain), 379
Hud, 53–54, 60, 104, 216
Hudson, Rock, 142, 425
Hudson Hawk, 99
Hue. *See* Colors
Hughes, Howard, 484
Hughes Electronics Corporation, 507
Humanistic approach, to film analysis, 353–54, 359
Hummer, Jody, 296
Humor, repetition for, 244
Humphreys, Michael Conner, 294
"Humpty Dumpty," 43
Hunt, Helen, 275
Hunter, Holly, 513
Hunter, Jeffrey, 500
Hurt, John, 100
Husbands and Wives, 321
Hussey, Olivia, 394
Huston, John, 208, 213, 214, 240, 369, 381, 466, 509
Huxley, Aldous, 3

The Ice Storm, 322, 451
Iliad (Homer), 45
Image
  importance of, 111
  ironic juxtaposition with sound, 234
  memory, 167
  projected, 84
  secondary, 68
  size, change in, 165–66
Imaginary Crimes, 22
Imagining Reality: The Faber Book of the Documentary, 465
IMAX, 3, 468
Impersonators, 280
Implicit (generalized) score, 251
In Cold Blood, 431
Independence Day, 12, 177
In-depth movement, 125
Indiana Jones and the Last Crusade, 436
Indiana Jones and the Temple of Doom, 436, 494–95, 495, 505
Indirect-subjective point of view, 116–18, 119
Industrial Light and Magic, 177
The Informer, 372
Initiate hero, 413
In medias res, 45, 318
Inside approach, to acting, 271
Inside/out editing, 162, 193
Instrumentation, 255–56, 316
Intensity, of color, 189, 194
Intent
  of artist, 213
  of director, 349, 350
Intercutting (parallel cuts), 167, 315
Intercutting (parallel cutting), 167, 315
Interior monologue, 377–78
Interiors, 152, 321, 322, 324
Interior sets, 96–97
Intermediate colors, 189
Internal action, 38, 53
Internal conflict, 49–50
Internal truth, 34–35, 50
International films, 450–54
Interpreters, 280
Interstate v. *Dallas*, 492
Interview With the Vampire, 100
In the Company of Men, 19, 497
In the Line of Fire, 279
Intolerance, 40, 177, 364, 455, 456
Intrinsic metaphors, 69
Introductory paragraph, 524
Invasion of the Body Snatchers, 430
Invisible sounds, 226–28
An Invitation to the Theatre (Kernodle), 269
Ironic montage, 168–73
Irons, Jeremy, 502
Irony, 70–74, 312
  of character, 72
  cosmic, 74
  dramatic, 70–71, 318
  in juxtaposition of sound and image, 234
  of setting, 72
  of situation, 72
  of tone, 72–74
  in use of color, 210
Irving, John, 372
Italian films, 452
It Happened One Night, 425
Ivan the Terrible, 364

Jackie Brown, 356
Jacknife, 45
Jacobs, Lewis, 188
Jacobs, Rust, 295
Jacoby, Derek, 394
Jagger, Mick, 286
James, Henry, 373, 374
James, Steve, 460
James and the Giant Peach, 471
Jaws, 236, 281, 433, 435
Jaws 2, 433, 434, 435
Jaws 3-D, 136, 435
The Jazz Singer, 425
Jefferson in Paris, 403
Jerry Maguire, 293
JFK, 324, 403–4
Johnson, Ben, 292
Johnson, Georgann, 513
Jones, Chuck, 467
Jones, James, 421
Jones, James Earl, 370
Jones, Quincy, 247, 249
Jones, Robert Edmond, 187, 217
Jones, Tommy Lee, 437, 514
Jordan, Neil, 252, 294
Joyce, James, 381
Ju Dou, 192
Jump cut, 167
Jungian criticism, 358
Junior, 279
Jurassic Park, 38, 181, 225
Jurassic Park (Crichton), 181

Kael, Pauline, 325, 347
Kafka, 236–37
Kalmus, Herbert, 190
Kane, Carol, 231, 232
Kane, Charles Foster, 100, 135–36, 139
Kapur, Shekhar, 209
Kasdan, Lawrence, 418, 420
Katt, William, 433
Katz, Ephraim, 167
Katzenberg, Jeffrey, 472
Kaufman, Boris, 297
Kawin, Bruce, 422
Kazan, Elia, 166, 230, 272, 297, 298, 389, 485, 490
Keaton, Buster, 456
Keaton, Diane, 130, 210, 284, 323
Keaton, Michael, 177, 436
Keitel, Harvey, 22
Kelly, Gene, 427, 469
Kelly, Nancy, 398
Kernodle, George, 269
Kerr, Deborah, 284
Kidder, Margot, 179
Kilbride, Percy, 436
"The Killers" (Hemingway), 377
Kilmer, Val, 436
Kinetic, 251
King, Henry, 456
The King and I, 431
King Kong, 36, 101, 177, 179, 180, 430, 470
King of Kings, 500
Kingsley, Ben, 124, 289, 291
Kinsella, H. P., 371
Kinski, Klaus, 286
Knotts, Don, 54
Kopple, Barbara, 85, 462, 465, 466
Kosinski, Jerzy, 370
Kovacs, Laszlo, 208
Koyaanisqatsi, 145, 463
Kramer vs. Kramer, 105
Kroll, Jack, 274
Kubrick, 511
Kubrick, Stanley, 92, 145, 161, 216, 250, 321, 502
Kuleshov, Lev, 277–78
Kundun, 193, 311
Kurosawa, Akira, 220

Kurys, Diane, 323

L. A. Confidential, 83, 418–19, 420
LaBute, Neil, 497
La Cava, Gregory, 426
Ladd, Alan, 235, 283, 393
La Dolce Vita, 334, 491
Lady and the Tramp, 467
The Lady From Shanghai, 136
Lady in the Lake, 115
La Fetée, 147
Lamarr, Hedy, 284
Lancaster, Burt, 283
Landau, Martin, 292, 293
Lane, Anthony, 422
Lang, Fritz, 177
Lange, Dorothea, 105
Language, in silent films, 456–60
Lantz, Walter, 467
Laserdisc players, 6, 507
Lasseter, John, 471, 472, 473
The Last Days of Disco, 254
The Last Emperor, 193
The Last of the Mohicans, 38
The Last Picture Show, 34, 81, 92, 254, 292, 307, 384
The Last Picture Show (McMurtry), 383–84
La Strada, 335
Last Tango in Paris, 496, 502
The Last Temptation of Christ, 498, 500
Last Year at Marienbad, 46
Lateral movement, 125, 130
Laughton, Charles, 135
Lawman, 415
Lawrence, D. H., 195, 376
Lawrence of Arabia, 92, 324
Leach, Archibald (Cary Grant), 57
Leacock, Stephen, 463
Lean, David, 92, 312, 324, 496
Lean on Me, 400, 401, 402
Leaving Las Vegas, 476
Lee, Ang, 299, 320, 322
Lee, Spike, 148, 227, 356
Legends of the Fall, 21, 92
Lehman, Ernest, 44, 70, 372, 390–91
Leigh, Janet, 118, 139, 421
Leigh, Vivian, 191
Leitmotifs, 56, 256
Lelouche, Claude, 205, 230
Lemmon, Jack, 54, 162
Lenses, special, 140–41
Leone, Sergio, 278–79, 324, 417
Levinson, Barry, 148, 208
Lewis, Jerry, 453
Lewis, Jerry Lee, 399
Liddel, Eric, 144
Lievsay, Skip, 227, 237
Life Is Beautiful, 240
Life Lessons, 321
Lifetime, 514
Life With Zoe, 321
Lighting, 101–5, 123, 124, 154
  back, 103
  balanced, 104
  character of, 104
  for depth, 134–35
  direct, 104
  as expression of directorial style, 314
  hard, 104, 105
  high-key, 102
  low-key, 102
  medium, 104
  mood, 455
  natural, 105
  overhead, 102, 103
  painterly effects, 105
  side, 103
  special effects, 147–48
  studio, 94
Lightman, Herbert A., 110
Linear (chronological) structure, 44
Links
  dialogue, 239
  sound, 238–39
The Lion King, 468, 469
Lip synchronization, 448
Literary point of view, 375–78
Little Big Man, 239, 258
Little Caesar, 417
The Little Mermaid, 468
A Little Night Music, 431
Little Women, 100
Live screen, 129–30
Living spaces, 96–97
Lloyd, Christopher, 435
Lloyd, Harold, 456
Local color, 190
Location vs. studio shooting, 94–96
Lockwood, Gary, 191
Lolita, 491, 502
Lombard, Carole, 426
"Lone Ranger," 250
Lone-rider music, 258
Lone Wolf McQuade, 496, 497
Long, Huey, 43
A Long Day's Journey Into Night, 126, 391
The Longest Day, 339, 421
The Long Riders, 233
Long shot, 129
  with close-up, 165
Looking for Richard, 465
Look of outward regard, 116
Lord of the Flies, 18, 61, 94, 138
Loren, Sophia, 283
Lorre, Peter, 227, 292
The Lost Boys, 196
Lost Horizon, 86, 430
The Lost Weekend, 476
The Lost World, 181
Lottman, Evan, 152–53
Love Finds Andy Hardy, 4, 5
The Lovers, 491
Lovesick, 283
Love! Valour! Compassion!, 46
Low-angle shot, 118, 137–38, 139
Low-budget films, 105–6
Low-key lighting, 102
Lucas, George, 177, 436
Lugosi, Bela, 430
Lumet, Sidney, 265, 306
  Equus, 396
  Long Day's Journey Into Night, 126, 391–92
  Making Movies, 307, 320
  on Montgomery Clift, 301
  on screenwriting, 319
  on the star system, 282
  on theme of film, 11
  The Verdict, 105
Lupino, Ida, 323
Lynch, David, 197, 314–15
Lyne, Adrian, 502
Lynn, Vera, 73
Lyons, Charles, 500–501

M, 227
MacArthur, 25
MacCarthy, Desmond, 460
Macdonald, Dwight, 349, 364–65, 475
MacDonald, Kevin, 465
MacDowell, Andie, 287
Maclachlan, Kyle, 197
MacLaine, Shirley, 275
Madden, John, 209
Made-for-cable film, 514
Made-for-television film, 509, 510–14
The Magnificent Seven, 431
Main, Marjorie, 436
Makeup design, 98, 100–101, 180
Making Movies (Lumet), 307, 320
Malcolm X, 148
Malden, Karl, 231
Malick, Terrence, 94, 242, 421
Malle, Louis, 322, 463
The Maltese Falcon, 292
Maltin, Leonard, 404
Mamoulian, Rouben, 79
A Man and a Woman, 11, 140, 205, 230
A Man for All Seasons, 87, 89, 493
Mangini, Mark, 236–37
Manhattan, 38, 40, 49, 130, 152, 215, 321
  audience acceptance, 322
  musical score, 265
  use of black and white in, 216
Manhattan Murder Mystery, 321
Mankiewicz, Joseph L., 99, 100
Mansfield, Katherine, 377
The Man With the Golden Arm, 476
Manz, Linda, 242, 243
Marienbad, 364
Marker, Chris, 147
Marks, Richard, 165
Marlene, 465
Marshall, Penny, 323
Martin, Steve, 182, 183, 286, 426
Martin, Strother, 292, 293
Marvin's Room, 356
Marxist approach, 355–56
Mary Poppins, 36, 398
Mary Shelley's Frankenstein, 430
*M*A*S*H*, 54, 56, 257, 321, 339, 409
Mask, 307
The Mask of Zorro, 193

Mass audience, 410, 428, 456
Mastroianni, Marcello, 448, 449
Mathieson, Muir, 248
Mattes, 177, 207
Matthau, Walter, 54, 261
May, Elaine, 323
Mayles, Arthur, 463
Mazursky, Paul, 298
McCabe & Mrs. Miller, 92, 140, 236, 321
McCarten, John, 345
McCay, Winsor, 467
McCormack, Patty, 398
McDormand, Frances, 51
McDowell, Malcolm, 145
McDowell, Roddy, 100
McGovern, Elizabeth, 283, 295
McGregor, Ewan, 476
McMurray, Fred, 420
McMurtry, Larry, 383, 384
McQueen, Butterfly, 292
McQueen, Steve, 286
Mechanical sound, 232–33
Medavoy, Mike, 300
Medium, change in, 370
Medium lighting, 104
Meet Me in St. Louis, 425
Melato, Mariangela, 452
Mèliés, Georges, 177
Melville, Herman, 55
Memory images, 167
Memphis Belle, 182
Menacing frame, 123
Men in Black, 36
Merchant-Ivory team, 403
Metaphors, 53, 68–69, 87
Metropolis, 86, 177
Michelangelo, 79
Mickey Mousing, 251
Microcosm, setting as, 93–94
Midler, Bette, 514
Midnight Cowboy, 20, 210, 260, 270, 289, 318, 385, 496
Midnight Express, 17, 138, 263, 287
Midnight in the Garden of Good and Evil, 388, 466
Midway, 224
Mighty Aphrodite, 283, 321
Mighty Joe Young, 431, 470
Milcheaux, Oscar, 475
Miller, George, 211, 471
Miller, Henry, 380
Miniaturization, 177, 178
Minnelli, Liza, 427
The Mirror Has Two Faces, 35
Mise-en-scène, 174
Misery, 398
Mishima, 148
Mississippi Burning, 191, 399–400, 401, 402
Mister Roberts, 65
Mitchell, Thomas, 292
Mitchum, Robert, 135, 138, 255, 420, 514
Mitty, Walter, 53
Moana, 461
Mobile camera, 128–29, 163, 314
"A Modest Proposal" (Swift), 73
Monaural sound, 224
Monochromatic harmony, 195
Monologue, interior, 377–78
Monomyth, 358
Monroe, Marilyn, 255
Montage, 173–76, 315, 318
  breakfast, in *Citizen Kane*, 255
  flashback, 175
  in gangster films, 417
  ironic, 168–73
Montgomery, Elizabeth, 433
Montgomery, Robert, 115
Mood, 11–13, 92, 102
Mood lighting, 455
Moore, Dudley, 55, 283
Moore, Mary Tyler, 283, 286
Moore, Michael, 462, 465
Moral/philosophical approach, to film analysis, 361
Moral statement films, 17
More, Thomas, 88, 89
More Than Night: Film Noir *in its Contexts* (Moreman), 419
Morgenstern, Joseph, 341
Moroder, Giorgio, 263
Morris, Errol, 463, 464
Morrison, Marion. *See* Wayne, John
Moss, Elizabeth, 22
Motifs, 24
Motion, 112, 122
  background in, 122
  fast, 145
  keeping image in, 124–30
  slow, 141–44
"Motion control," 177
Motion Picture Association of America (MPAA)
  Code and Rating Appeals Board, 203, 496, 497
  Movie Rating System, 398, 492–97
  Production Code Administration, 484–85, 490, 491–92
Motion Picture Association of America (MPAA)
  Code and Rating Administration, 496, 497
Motion Picture Producers and Distributors of America, Inc. (Hayes office), 484, 485
Motion Picture Production Code, 410, 496
  1930–1960, 484–90
  1948–1968, 490–92
Moulin Rouge, 208
Movement. *See* Motion
The Movies, 508
Movie & Video Guide (Maltin), 404
Moving camera, 115
Mr. Deeds Goes to Town, 223
Mr. Smith Goes to Washington, 35, 48, 140, 174, 223, 292
Mrs. Dalloway, 167
Mrs. Sundance, 433
Mrs. Sundance Rides Again, 433
Mrs. Venable, 91
Much Ado About Nothing, 394
"Mugging," 273
Mulan, 468
Muller, Eddie, 418
Muller, Ray, 462
Mulroney, Dermot, 46
Multiplicity, 177
Muni, Paul, 416
Murder on the Orient Express, 129, 265, 307
Murnau, F. W., 88, 430, 458
Murphy, Eddie, 177
Murphy, Mary, 275
Music
  background, 249
  horse-and-buggy, 258
  lone-rider, 258
  nostalgic, 254
  saloon, 253
  stagecoach, 258
  title, 259–60
  traveling, 258–59
Musical codes, 257–58
Musicals, 257, 425, 427
Musical score, 42, 53, 66, 112, 221, 315–16
  to accompany titles, 259–60
  to add levels of meaning, 255
  affinity with film, 248–49
  as base for choreographed action, 260–62
  characterization through, 255–57
  to cover weaknesses in film, 251–52
  economy in, 264–65
  and emotional responses, 250
  to evoke nostalgic feelings, 254
  to foreshadow or build tension, 254–55
  functions of, 249–52
  generalized (implicit), 251
  to heighten dramatic effect of dialogue, 252
  importance of, 248–49
  as interior monologue, 260
  irony in, 73–74
  Mickey Mouse, 251
  Peter-and-the-Wolfing, 255–56
  to provide important transitions, 259
  to provide sense of time and place, 253–54
  and sense of structural rhythm, 249
  special functions of, 251–62
  synthesizer, 262–64
  to tell inner story, 252–53
  triggering conditioned responses, 257–58
Muted (desaturated) color, 189–90, 216
Mute dialogue, 457
My Best Friend's Wedding, 46, 425
My Fair Lady, 398, 431
My Man Godfrey, 426
My Own Private Idaho, 429

Nabokov, Vladimir, 502
Nair, Mira, 323
The Naked Gun, 419
Name typing, 57
Nanook of the North, 461
Napoleon, 128, 455, 456, 458
Naremore, James, 418–19
Narration, voice-over, 239–43, 318

Narrative films, 8
Narrator, 378
  essence, 379
  point of view, 377
Nashville, 236, 257, 321, 347–48, 425
National Film Preservation Board, 213
National Film Registry, 213
Native Americans, in western films, 413
The Natural, 205, 208, 265
Naturalistic film, 41, 68
Naturalistic interpretation, of setting, 90
Natural light, 105
Natural symbols, 63
The Navigator: A Medieval Odyssey, 199
NC-17 rating, 494, 495, 497, 500
Neal, Patricia, 104
Near Dark, 211
Neeson, Liam, 311
Nell, 20
Neo-*noir* films, 418
Neorealism, 37
Newman, 433
Newman, Paul, 53, 60, 104, 272, 283, 286–87, 289, 307
Newsweek, 341, 347
The New Yorker, 345–47, 347, 422
New York Film Critics, 342
New York Stories, 321
New York Times, 347, 359
The New York Times Book Review, 460
Nichols, Mike, 181, 183, 209, 216, 298, 321, 372, 391
Nicholson, Jack, 47, 100, 181, 183, 204, 206, 275, 286, 403
Night Falls on Manhattan, 265
The Nightmare Before Christmas, 471
'Night Mother, 398
The Night of the Hunter, 135, 138
Nixon, 403–4
Nonlinear structure, 45–46
Nonverbal communication, 274
Norris, Chuck, 497
North by Northwest, 70, 336
Norton, Edward, 244
Nosferatu, 430
Nothing Sacred, 425
Novels, adaptations of, 375–88
Novels Into Film (Bluestone), 378
Novelty effects, 182, 183
The Nutty Professor, 177
Nykvist, Sven, 313

Oates, Warren, 286
Objective camera, 313
Objective point of view, 113, 114, 115–16, 119, 228–30
The Object of My Affection, 356
O'Brien, Willis, 177, 470
Observable truths, 33–34, 50
October, 364
The Odd Couple, 20, 54
Odyssey (Homer), 45, 71
Oedipus Rex, 71, 72
Oedipus the King, 395–96
Oedipus Wrecks, 321
Offices, set design of, 96–97
Off-screen sound, 227
Of Human Bondage, 255
Of Mice and Men, 431
Oklahoma!, 425
Oldman, Gary, 430
Oliver!, 430
Oliver Twist, 430
Olivier, Sir Laurence, 215, 286, 371, 394–95
Olmos, Edward James, 271
Olympia, 364, 462
Omniscient, first person, 378
On Approval, 364
Once Upon a Time in America, 293, 295, 324, 417
One Flew Over the Cuckoo's Nest, 47, 292, 322
O'Neill, Eugene, 392
On Movies (Macdonald), 364–65
On the Beach, 252–53
On the Waterfront, 56, 287, 485
  internalized sound in, 230
  invisible sound in, 221, 226
  Marlon Brando's self-direction in, 297, 298
  struggle for human dignity in, 19
  universal theme, 24
Opera, 252
The Opposite of Sex, 241, 242, 243, 356, 380
Optical printers, 177, 178
Opticals, 154
Orchestration, 165–66
Ordinary People, 148, 286, 287
Ormond, Julia, 21
Orpheus, 364
Oscar and Lucinda, 289
O'Toole, Peter, 137
Our Daily Bread, 261
The Outlaw, 484
Out of Africa, 92
Out of Sight, 318
Out of the Past, 418, 420
Outside approach, to acting, 271–72
Outside/in and inside/out editing sequence, 163–64
Outside/in editing, 162, 163
Overhead lighting, 102, 103
Owens, Eamonn, 294
The Oz, 429

Pachelbel's Canon, 261
Pacino, Al, 59, 168, 210, 307, 416, 465, 499
Packed screen, 129
Painterly effects, 455
  in color, 208–9
Painting, 119
Paint Your Wagon, 496
Pakula, Alan J., 264
Pal, George, 470
Palance, Jack, 50, 54, 278
Panavision, 82, 83, 84, 506
Panning, 82, 125–26, 129
  and scanning, 505–6
Pantomime, 456
Paper Moon, 307
"The Paradox of Protest" (Lyons), 500
Parallel cutting (intercutting), 167, 315
Parenthood, 286
Park, Nick, 470
Parker, 400
Parker, Alan, 261, 287, 321, 322, 399–400, 401
Parker, Charlie, 466
Parody/sequel, 432, 434
Parsons, Estelle, 235, 292
Past tense, literary, 386
Patton, 25, 174, 256, 339, 409
Paull, Lawrence G., 97, 98
The Pawnbroker, 265, 491, 492
Peck, Gregory, 25, 42, 252
Peck, Richard E., 505
Penn, Arthur, 235, 341
Penn, Robert, 386
Penn, Sean, 136
Pennies From Heaven, 161, 286, 427
People, 148
The People Under the Stairs, 422
The People Vs. Larry Flynt, 322
Period films, 96, 100, 236
Perkins, Anthony, 93, 122, 423
Permanent Midnight, 476
Persona, 23, 361
Personality actors, 280
Personality cult approach, to film analysis, 352–53, 359
Peter-and-the-Wolfing scoring, 255–56
Peter Pan, 467
Peters, Bernadette, 427
Pfeiffer, Michelle, 398, 437
PG rating, 493–94, 495
PG-13 rating, 494, 495
The Phantom Menace, 178, 437
Phantom of the Opera, 190
Philadelphia, 256
The Philadelphia Story, 430
Pi, 424
The Piano, 11, 13, 293
Pickens, Slim, 292
The Pilgrim, 459
Pink Floyd, 261
Pink Floyd: The Wall, 261–62
Pink Panther series, 436
Pinocchio, 467, 468, 469
Pitt, Brad, 21, 60
Pixar, 471, 472, 473
Planet of the Apes, 100, 437
Planner, Franz, 307
The Player, 236, 257, 321
Play It Again Sam, 49
Plays, adaptations of, 389–98
Pleasantville, 199
Plot, 11
  rhythms, 112
  unity, 33
Plummer, Christopher, 307
Poe, Edgar Allan, 38, 40, 91
Poetic justice, 35
Point of view, cinematic
  director's interpretive, 118, 119

Point of view, cinematic *(continued)*
  indirect-subjective, 116–18, 119
  objective, 113, 114, 115–16, 119, 228–30
  subjective, 114–16, 119, 162, 228–30
Point of view, literary, 375–78
  concealed, 377
  dramatic or objective, 377, 378
  effaced, 377
  first-person, 239, 375, 379–80
  novelistic, 378
  omniscient, 378
  stream of consciousness, 377–78
  subjective, 379
  third-person limited, 376–77
  third-person omniscient, 375–76
Point-of-view character, 318
Polanski, Roman, 418
Polish films, 448
Pollack, Sydney, 299, 312
Pollard, Michael J., 155, 292
Poltergeist, 36, 496, 497
Ponette, 293
Popeye, 292, 321
Porgy and Bess, 425
Porky Pig, 467
Porter, Edwin S., 456
Portman, Rachel, 253
The Portrait of a Lady, 373
Poseidon Adventure, 347
Postlethwaite, Pete, 124
The Postman Always Rings Twice, 430
Potemkin, 161, 364, 454, 456
Potter, Dennis, 427
Powell, William, 426
Powers, Mala, 256
The Praise of Folly (Erasmus), 73
A Prayer for Owen Meany (Irving), 372
Preconceptions, 344–50
Preminger, Otto, 476, 509
Present tense, cinematic, 386
Pretty Baby, 322
Previn, Soon-Yi, 465
Primal Fear, 244
Primary colors, 189
A Primer for Playgoers (Wright and Downs), 279–80
The Prince of Egypt, 182, 472, 473, 474
"The Problem of Color" (Jones), 73
Producers, 319
Production design/art direction, 80, 85–98
  and fantasy worlds, 97
  and living quarters or offices, 96
  and location shooting, 94–95
  and period pieces, 96
  and the script, 87–88
  and setting, 88–94
  and studio shooting, 94
Projected image, 84
Propaganda, 462
Proyas, Alex, 422
Psycho, 93, 117, 118, 166, 336, 423, 429
Psychoanalytical approach, to film analysis, 357–58, 361
Psycho II, 93, 122
Public Housing, 463
Publicity, 347
Pudovkin, V. I., 152, 277–78
Pulp Fiction, 11, 46, 191, 317, 356
Punchline, 261
Pygmalion, 431
Pyle, Gomer, 57

Quaid, Dennis, 200
The Quiet Man, 80
Quinn, Aidan, 512
Quinn, Anthony, 19, 128
Quiz Show, 289, 290, 400, 401, 402

Rachel, Rachel, 271
Racial issues, 356
Rack focus, 132
  and depth, 131
Radio Days, 208
Raft, George, 292
Raging Bull, 15, 200, 215, 221, 222, 224, 289, 310
Ragtime, 265
Raiders of the Lost Ark, 95, 224, 225, 436
"Raindrops Keep Fallin' on My Head," 263
Rain Man, 34, 289, 356
Rainsberger, Todd, 101–2
Raise the Red Lantern, 192
Raising Arizona, 241
Rambo III, 10
Rampling, Charlotte, 307
Ranchers' daughters, 412
"The Ransom of Red Chief" (O. Henry), 72
Ratings, 398, 492–97
Ray, Nicca, 465
Ray, Nicholas, 393, 465, 500
RCA DSS (Digital Satellite System), 507
Reaction shots, 53
Ready to Wear, 321
Reality, distortions of, 401
Reality Bites, 284
Rear Window, 293, 337, 431
Rebel Without a Cause, 465
Receding color, 194
Recorded color, 190–92
Red (color), 189, 194
  saturated, 193, 195, 202
Red Desert, 200
Redford, Robert, 148, 283, 286, 400, 401, 402, 433
Redgrave, Vanessa, 307
Reds, 234, 301, 318, 342
Reed, Rex, 339, 409
Reeve, Christopher, 179
Reflection mapping, 182
Reflections, and depth, 135–36
Reflections in a Golden Eye, 208
The Remains of the Day, 38, 39
Remakes, 425, 428–31
  of international films, 431
  musical versions, 430–31
  TV versions, 431
Rembrandt effect, 105, 140, 386
Remington, Frederick, 105
Rennie, Michael, 424
Renoir, Jean, 421, 450
Repetition, 63
  for humor, 244
Replications: A Robotic History of the Science Fiction Film (Telotte), 422
Requiem for a Heavyweight, 19
Reservoir Dogs, 46, 417
Resnais, Alain, 46, 61
The Return of Martin Guerre, 431
Return of the Jedi, 178, 437
Return of the Secaucus Seven, 106
Reverberation, 223, 224, 229
Reviews, 344–47, 350, 362
  evaluating, 362–64
Rhythmic qualities, of sound and dialogue, 245
Rhythms, 112, 154, 162, 164–65
Ricci, Christina, 241, 242, 243
Richardson, Ralph, 391
Riefenstahl, Leni, 462
The Right Stuff, 132, 284
Rio Bravo, 105
Risky Business, 22
Ritter, Thelma, 292, 293
The River, 95, 296
A River Runs Through It, 60
The Road Warrior, 38, 51, 69, 92
Robards, Jason, 286, 391, 513
The Robe, 224
Roberts, Julia, 46
Robertson, Cliff, 271
Robeson, Paul, 475
Robinson, Edward G., 268
Robinson, W. R., 482
Robocop, 12
"The Rocking-Horse Winner" (Lawrence), 376
Rockwell, Norman, 209
Rocky, 174, 347, 434
Rocky IV, 193
Rocky V, 434
Roe vs. Wade, 513
Roger & Me, 462, 465
Rogers, Will, 453
Rolf, Tom, 153
Romeo and Juliet, 393, 394
A Room with a View, 194, 205
Rooney, Mickey, 292
The Ropin' Fool, 453
Rosebud, 65
Rose Marie, 425
Rosemary's Baby, 36
Rosen, Chuck, 95
Rosenblum, Ralph, 151, 152
Rosenthal, Elliott, 252
Rosher, Charles, 88
Ross, Herbert, 427
Ross, Katharine, 140, 433
Rossellini, Isabella, 197, 288
Rossen, Robert, 382
Rouch, Jean, 463
Rough-grain film stock, 82
Round (three-dimensional) characters, 60–61

R rating, 494, 495, 496
Rule, Ann, 403
Rule, Janice, 204
The Rules of the Game, 450
Rush, Richard, 137, 421
Rushes (dailies), 153
Russell, Jane, 484
Ryan, Robert, 55
Ryan's Daughter, 92, 496
Rydell, Mark, 195, 269, 270
Ryder, Winona, 284, 430

"The Sabre Dance," 261
Safety Last, 456
Saint, Eva Marie, 231
Salinger, J. D., 371, 379
Saloon music, 253
Sarandon, Susan, 59, 136, 297–98
Sartov, Hendrik, 455
Satire, genre-based, 419
Saturated color, 189, 193
Saturday Night Fever, 163, 261, 496, 498
Saving Private Ryan, 311, 402, 421
Savoca, Nancy, 323
Scarecrow, 325
Scarface, 416, 496, 497, 502
Scene, 153
Scenic backings, 97
Schaffner, Frank, 256
Schelder, Roy, 231, 243, 287, 300, 433, 435
Schell, Maximilan, 465
Schickel, Richard, 300
Schiff, Stephen, 409
Schindler's List, 214–15, 289, 290, 311, 333, 454, 509
Schlesinger, Arthur M. Jr., 408
Schlesinger, John, 210
Schoolmarm, 412
Schrader, Paul, 10, 57, 136, 148, 203, 419, 421, 429
Schulberg, Budd, 490
Schutzman, Scott, 295
Schwarzenegger, Arnold, 184, 279, 437
Science fiction films, 92, 178, 422, 424
Scofield, Paul, 89, 493
Score. *See* Musical score
Scorsese, Martin
  on color, 217
  The Last Temptation of Christ, 498, 500
  on music in film, 252
  Raging Bull, 200, 215, 234, 252, 321, 498
  subject matter, 309–10
Scott, George C., 25, 135, 136, 293
Scott, Ridley, 97, 98, 324
Scream, 41, 84, 422, 423
Scream 2, 422
Screen format, 81–82, 83, 84
Screenplay, 32, 80
Screen width, 83
Screenwriters, 319
Screwball comedies, 424–25, 426
Script, 87–88
The Seagull, 306
Sea of Love, 292
Secondary colors, 189
Secondary image, 68
Seconds, 142
The Secret Garden, 92
"The Secret Life of Walter Mitty" (Thurber), 48
Seduction, 273
Selick, Henry, 470, 471
Sellers, Peter, 283, 434, 436
Sense and Sensibility, 43, 277, 299, 320, 322
Sensurround, 224
Sentimentality, 41
Sequels, 425, 428–29, 432–37
  character series, 434, 436
Sequence, 153
Sergeant York, 15
Serpico, 498, 499
Setting, 88–90, 315, 397
  to create emotional atmosphere, 92
  as determiner of character, 90
  four aspects of, 90
  interior, 96–97
  irony of, 72, 73
  as microcosm, 93–94
  naturalistic interpretation, 90
  as reflection of character, 90–91
  for sheer visual impact, 92
  as symbol, 92–93
  for verisimilitude, 91–92
Seven Beauties, 123
7 Plus 7, 463
The Seven Samurai, 431
The Seventh Seal, 4, 5, 61, 313, 491
Sex, 341–42
  changing standards of, 502
sex, lies, & videotape, 106, 284, 287
Shade, 188
Shadow of a Doubt, 225
Shadows, three-dimensional, 135
Shaffer, Peter, 396
Shakespeare in Love, 208, 209
Shane, 92
  acting, 278
  break from formula, 417, 501
  characterization, 50, 54
  cinematic tension, 393
  color, 216
  music, 253
  narrative structure, 317
Sharif, Omar, 147
Sharkey, Betsy, 432
Sharpness of focus, 121
Shaw, Robert, 273
Sheen, Martin, 69, 240, 241
Shepherd, Cybill, 373
Sherlock, Jr., 456
The Shining, 13, 92, 292, 331, 431
Ship of Fools, 94
Shire, David, 264
Shire, Talia, 168
Shoeless Joe, 370
Shooting
  day-for-night, 455
Shootouts, 414, 415
Short Cuts, 236, 257, 321
Short story, 38
Shot, 120, 153
  establishing, 116, 162
  eye-line, 116
  high-angle, 138–39
  long, 129
  long, with close-up, 165
  low-angle, 118, 137–38, 139
Shots
  reaction, 53, 276, 277
Show Boat, 425
Show musical, 425
Showtime, 510
Sick: The Life & Death of Bob Flanagan, Supermasochist, 462
Sidekick, 413
Side lighting, 103
Sikov, Ed, 424–25
Silence, as sound effect, 243
The Silence of the Lambs, 256, 423
Silent films, 248, 454
  color in, 454–56
  language in, 456–60
  scores, 256
Silkwood, 300–301
Silver Streak, 292
Simon, Neil, 42–43, 396
Simon Birch, 372
Singin' in the Rain, 257, 425, 427
Sinise, Gary, 184
Siskel, Gene, 325
"Six Million Dollar Man," 144
Six Weeks, 283
Size and closeness of the object, 121
Skycam, 128–29
Slasher film, 137, 180, 422
Slaughterhouse Five, 292, 317
Sleeper, 321
Sleepless in Seattle, 293
Sling Blade, 244, 276, 356
Slow motion, 141–44
Slow-motion sound, 233–34
Small Sacrifices, 402–3
Small Sacrifices (Rule), 403
Smiles of a Summer Night, 431
"Smoke Gets in Your Eyes," 251
Smoke Signals, 475
Smooth-grain film stock, 82
Snake Eyes, 497
The Snake Pit, 476
Snow, Mark, 264
Snow White and the Seven Dwarfs, 467, 468
Social problem films, 18, 19, 24, 476–77
Social values, 483
Soft focus, 140, 229, 455
Soft lighting, 104
Solondz, Todd, 502
Somebody Up There Likes Me, 287
Something About Amelia, 513
Sommersby, 431
Sons and Lovers, 85
Sophie's Choice, 152, 200
Sorcerer, 263

Sorvino, Mira, 283
Sound, 66, 220–45, 315–16
  ambient, 236
  amplified, 235, 236
  distorted, 232
  invisible, 226–28
  ironic juxtaposition with image, 234
  links, 238–39
  mechanical, 232
  and modern film, 221–22
  monaural, 224
  musical, as part of score, 260
  off-screen, 227
  as a plot device, 237, 238
  point of view, 228–30
  points of view in, 228–30
  quality, 223, 224, 229
  rhythmic qualities of, 245
  silence as effect, 243
  special uses of, 230–37
  stereophonic, 224
  to suggest subjective states, 231–32
  to tell an inner story, 230–31
  as a transitional element, 238–39
  unusual emphasis on, 234–36
  visible, 226
The Sound and the Fury (Faulkner), 378
The Sound of Music, 390–91
"The Sounds of Silence," 260
Sound stages, 94
Soundtrack, 161
Southern lady, 412
The Spacehunter, 136
Spacek, Sissy, 204, 288, 398
Spader, James, 287
Special effects (f/x), 177–84
  camera angles, 137–40
  in color, 140, 210–11, 216
  diffusion and soft focus, 140
  fast motion, 145
  freeze frame, 145–47
  hand-held camera, 137
  lighting, 147–48
  slow motion, 141–44
  special lenses, 140–41
  stills, 147
  thawed frame, 147
Speed, 12
Spence, Bruce, 51
Spheeris, Penelope, 323
Spielberg, Steven, 472, 509, 512
  appeal to change the R rating on *Poltergeist*, 496
  on casting, 281, 282
  on colorization, 213
  E. T., 148
  Indiana Jones and the Temple of Doom, 495
  Saving Private Ryan, 421
  Schindler's List, 214–15, 454
  science fiction, 424
  on Special Edition of *Close Encounters*, 324–25
  subject matter, 310–11
The Spoils of Poynton (James), 374
"Spotted Horses" (Faulkner), 375–76
Stage acting, differences from film, 272–79
Stagecoach, 292, 430
Stagecoach music, 258
Stage convention, 394–95
Stage dialogue, 393–94, 395
Stage sets, 396
Stage Struck, 307
Stallone, Sylvester, 19
Stamp, Terence, 55
Standards, of acceptability, 501–2
Standard screen, 82, 83, 84
Standards for Production, 494
Stanislavski method (inside approach), 271
Stanley, Kim, 239
Stanwyck, Barbara, 281, 420
Stardust Memories, 215, 321
A Star is Born, 429, 430
Starship Troopers, 179
Star system, 280–82
Star Trek, 178
Star Trek: The Wrath of Khan, 180–81
Star Trek III: The Search for Spock, 177
Star Wars, 38, 178, 182, 436
Static camera, 113, 163, 314
Static characters, 59–60
"Stayin' Alive," 163, 261
Steadicam, 128
Steamboat Willie, 467
Steele, Bob, 412
Steenburgen, Mary, 289, 291
Steiger, Rod, 297, 298, 485, 492
Steinbeck, John, 85, 477
Stereophonic sound, 224, 491
Stereotypes, 58
Stevens, George, 83
Stewart, James, 48, 140, 281, 284, 285, 293
Stewart, Randall, 373
Stiers, David Ogden, 56
Stiller, Ben, 426
Still of the Night, 243, 300
Still photography, 119, 120
Stills, 147
The Sting, 99, 161
Stock characters, 57–58
Stockwell, Dean, 85, 391
Stone, Oliver, 324, 403
Stop-action film, 471
Stop-motion animation, 467, 470
Storaro, Vittorio, 207
Stormare, Peter, 293
Story
  credibility, 33–37
  interest, 37–38
  simplicity and complexity, 38–41
  unified plot, 33
Strange Days, 162
Stream of consciousness, 377–78, 378
Streep, Meryl, 243, 282, 300–301
Streisand, Barbra, 323
Strike, 68, 69
Structure, dramatic, 43–47
Structured films, 8
Studio system, 319, 410
Studio vs. location shooting, 94–96
The Stunt Man, 41, 137, 421
Style (texture), 14, 16
  director's, 308–9
  in film, 87
Subjective camera, 313–14, 379
Subjective evaluation, 351
Subjective point of view, 114–16, 119, 162, 228–30
Subject matter, 309–12
Subtitles, 449–50, 506
Sudden Impact, 56
Suddenly, Last Summer, 66–68, 91, 92, 130
Suddenly, Last Summer (Williams), 65, 374
Summer of '42, 22, 140, 147, 239–40, 386
Sunrise, 88, 458
Sunset Boulevard, 101, 286
Sun Times, 347
Superman, 71, 72, 144, 178, 179, 180, 182, 434
Superman II, 179
Superman III, 179
Supporting players, 292–93
Surprise ending, 40
Surrealism, 203
Surrealistic color, 203
Suspense, 37, 82, 126, 155
Suspiria, 204
Sutherland, Kiefer, 196
Swain, Dominique, 502
Swanson, Gloria, 101
Swedish films, 453
Swept Away, 61, 451, 452
Swift, 73
The Sword and the Sorcerer, 179
Sylbert, Paul, 87
Symbolic conflict, 68–69
Symbolic patterns, 66
Symbols, 62–70
  color as, 202
  creating, 63–66
  overreading, 70
  setting as, 92–93
  universal and natural, 62–63
Synthesizer scoring, 262–64

"The Tables Turned" (Wordsworth), 7
Takes, 153
Take the Money and Run, 321
Taking Off, 322
"Talking pictures," 226
The Taming of the Shrew, 105, 106, 140, 208, 209, 297, 386, 394
Tarantino, Quentin, 46, 356
Tarzan, the Ape Man, 502
Taxi Driver, 57, 58, 203, 281, 325, 380
Taylor, Dub, 155, 292
Taylor, Elizabeth, 67, 106, 130, 285
Technicolor, 196
Technicolor Corporation, 190, 192
The Technique of Film Music (Mathieson), 248
Teenage Mutant Ninja Turtle films, 409
Telephoto lens, 141
Television, 214, 215, 319
  censorship of films, 498

commercial breaks, 508–10
conventions and habits of watching movies on, 508
movies, 431
ratings symbols, 498
viewing environment, 505–8
Telotte, J. P., 422
The Tempest, 298
Temple, Shirley, 292
Tempo, 165, 248
Tension, dramatic, 126, 155, 392
Terminator 2: Judgment Day, 84, 182
Terms of Endearment, 275, 361
Tesich, Steve, 372
Test-marketing, 46
Thawed frame, 147
Thelma & Louise, 59
Theme, 349
in the context of film analysis, 11
evaluating, 24–26
identifying, 23–24
universal, 24, 26
Theremin, 464
There's Something About Mary, 13, 425, 426
Thesis documentary, 462
Thesis statement, 515, 524
They Shoot Horses, Don't They?, 46, 385
The Thief, 22, 263
The Thin Blue Line, 463, 464
The Thing, 180, 183, 430
The Thin Red Line, 242, 421
The Third Man, 249
Third-person limited point of view, 376, 378
Third-person omniscient point of view, 375
Third Reich, 462
This Is Cinerama, 3, 224
This Man Stands Alone, 510
Thomas, Betty, 323
Thomas, Henry, 123, 424
Thompson, Emma, 39, 277, 299, 320
Thompson, Lea, 435
Thornton, Billy Bob, 244, 276
3-D, 3, 136, 435, 491
Three-dimensionality, 125, 130, 132
in arrangement of people and objects, 133
of characters, 60
creating an illusion of, 112, 130–36
and fixed-frame movement, 125
and zoom lens, 131
360-degree pan, 126
3 Women, 204, 321
Thurber, James, 48
Thurman, Uma, 437
Thus Spake Zarathustra, 250
Tilting, 126, 129
Time
control, 165–66
expansion and compression of, 166–67
Time, 347
Time After Time, 182
Time Bandits, 178
Time-lapse photography, 145
Time magazine
review of *Bonnie and Clyde*, 341, 345
Tint, 188
Tinting, 454–55
Tiomkin, Dimitri, 248, 256
Titanic, 5, 184, 253, 466, 502
Titicut Follies, 463
Title
music, 259–60
significance of, 42–43
To Die For, 429
To Kill a Mockingbird, 42, 239–40, 380, 386
Tol'able David, 456
Toland, Gregg, 105, 131, 133, 139, 224, 313
Tomlin, Lily, 136, 301
Tomlinson, Carolyn Denise, 526
Tonal qualities, 223, 224
Tone, irony of, 72–74
Toning, 455–56
Tootsie, 289, 299
Top Gun, 222
Top Hat, 425
Tora! Tora! Tora!, 177, 450
Touch of Evil, 139, 421
Toulouse-Lautrec, 208
Tourneur, Jacques, 418, 420
Towne, Robert, 60, 418
Toy Story, 265, 471–72
Tracy, Dick, 57
Tracy, Spencer, 284, 285
The Trail of the Pink Panther, 436
Trainspotting, 476
Transitions, 516, 525
color as, 197–200, 205
dialogue as, 239
freeze frames, 147
provided by musical score, 259
sound, 238–39
sound as device for, 238–39
Traveling music, 258–59
Travolta, John, 163, 191
The Treasure of Sierra Madre, 213
Triad harmony, 196
A Trip to the Moon, 177
Triumph of the Will, 462
Tropic of Cancer (Miller), 380
True Grit, 52, 92, 292, 499
True Lies, 184, 279
Truffaut, François, 324, 421
The Truman Show, 59, 257, 286
Trumbull, Douglas, 177
Truths
artistic semblance of, 35–37
externally observable, 33–34, 50
internal, 34–35
"Try a Little Tenderness," 255
Tucker, 292
Turner, Kathleen, 21, 420
Turner, Lana, 284
Turner Broadcasting System, 212
Turner Productions, 514
The Turn of the Screw, 373
Turturro, John, 401
Twain, Mark, 379
Twelve Angry Men, 265
Twelve Monkeys, 147
21, 463
Twins, 279
2001: A Space Odyssey, 5, 161, 191, 251, 281, 511
Typecasting, 287–92

U. S. v. Paramount Pictures, 490
Ulee's Gold, 167
Ultrawide screens, 82, 83, 84
Understatement, 42
Unforgiven, 279, 409, 413
Universal Pictures, 500
Universal symbols, 62–63
Universal themes, 24, 26
Unstructured films, 8
28 Up, 463
35 Up, 463
Ure, Mary, 85
Ustinov, Peter, 55
The Usual Suspects, 124

Value, 63, 65
of color, 188, 194, 195
Vance, Marilyn, 99
The Vanishing, 131
Van Sant, Gus, 429
Varda, Agnes, 323
Venus flytrap, 65, 66
The Verdict, 105, 307
Vernon, Texas, 464
Vertical lines, 119
Vertigo, 337
Vicario, Marco, 448
Videocassette recorders (VCRs), 6
Vidor, King, 261
Viewer-centered challenges
great expectations, 342
influence of external factors, 343–44
mistaking the part for the whole, 341
Viewer-centered challenges, to film analysis
excess of expertise, 342–43
Villain, western, 412–13
Vincent & Theo, 257, 321
Violence, 41, 341–42
changing standards of, 501–2
Violet, 195
The Virgin Spring, 491
Virtual reality, 3
Visible sounds, 226
Visions of Light: The Art of Cinematography, 140
Vistavision, 82
Visual design, 42
color versus black and white, 80–81
costume and makeup design, 98–101
effect of budget on, 105–6
film stock, 82–85
lighting, 101–5
production design/art direction, 85–98
screen format, 81–82
Visual emphasis, 65–66
Visual metaphors, 68–69, 87
Voice dubbing, 447–49, 506

Voice-over narration, 239–43, 318, 378, 386
as ironic counterpart, 241
as structural glue, 241
Voight, Jon, 300
Volume, 223, 224, 229, 235
Von Brandenstein, Patrizia, 87
von Sternberg, Joseph, 1
von Stroheim, Eric, 456
von Trier, Lars, 23

Waking Ned Devine, 174
Walk, in silent films, 458
Walking Tall, 403
Wallace, Dee, 123
Walt Disney productions, 467–69
"The Waltons," 54
Wanted: The Sundance Woman, 433
War and Peace, 448
Ward, Vincent, 199, 208, 209
War films, 421–22
Warlock, Billy, 513
Warm colors, 195, 196
Warner, Frank, 221, 222
Warner Brothers, 467, 491
The War of the Roses, 21
Warren, Robert Penn, 47, 381–83
Washington, Denzel, 290, 296, 402
Washington Square, 373
Waterfront (Schulberg), 490
Wayne, John, 52, 57, 72, 255, 281, 283, 425, 499
Weaver, Dennis, 54
A Wedding, 321
Weill, Claudia, 323
Weir, Peter, 143, 257
Welcome to the Dollhouse, 17
Welles, Orson
as *auteur*, 308, 313
F for Fake, 465
A Man for All Seasons, 89, 493
opposition to colorization, 212
on role of director, 307
technique for rehearsing actors, 317
Touch of Evil, 139, 421
use of reflections, 136
See also Citizen Kane
"We'll Meet Again Some Sunny Day," 73
Wells, H. G., 182
Wepper, Fritz, 167
Wertmuller, Lina, 123, 323, 451
Western formula, 411–14
Western hero (cowboy hero), 411–12
Western heroine, 412
Western villain, 412–13
West Side Story, 356, 393, 425
Whale, James, 432
"What a Wonderful World," 73
What Dreams May Come, 208, 209
What I Really Want to Do Is DIRECT (Frolick), 325
What's Eating Gilbert Grape, 356
What's Up Doc?, 307
When a Stranger Calls, 231–32
"When I Heard the Learn'd Astronomer" (Whitman), 7
"When Johnny Comes Marching Home," 251
When We Were Kings, 464
When Worlds Collide, 470
White (color), 188, 189
White Hunter; Black Heart, 466
Whiting, Leonard, 394
Whitman, Walt, 7
Who Framed Roger Rabbit, 470, 471
Who's Afraid of Virginia Woolf?, 283, 372, 391, 392, 491
Who the Devil Made It (Bogdanovich), 307
"Why Do We Read Fiction?" (Warren), 47
Wide-angle lens, 140–41
Wide screen, 3, 82, 83, 84
Wide-screen-format television, 507
Wiene, Robert, 397
Wifemistress, 448–49, 452
Wilder, Billy, 286, 298, 418, 420, 476
Wilder, Gene, 292
Wild in the Streets, 24, 25
Wild Man Blues, 465, 466
Williams, John, 236
Williams, Robin, 59, 201, 208, 286
Williams, Tennessee, 65, 68, 92, 374
Williamson, Nicol, 371
William Tell Overture, 145, 250
Willis, Bruce, 99
Wilson, Woodrow, 399
The Wind, 459
The Wings of the Dove, 373
Winslet, Kate, 253, 277
Winters, Ralph, 154
Wipe, 161, 178
Wise, Robert, 391, 424
Wiseman, Frederick, 463
Witness, 38, 72, 257, 293
The Wizard of Oz, 36, 197–99, 425, 429
Wolf, 179, 181, 183
The Wolf Man, 179, 181, 422
Wolsey, Cardinal, 87–88, 89, 493
Woman in the Dunes, 61
Women on the Verge of a Nervous Breakdown, 453
The Wonderful, Horrible Life of Leni Riefenstahl, 462
Woo, John, 205
Wood, Natalie, 356
Woodpecker, Woody, 467
Woods, James, 295
Woodstock, 425
Woodward, Joanne, 514
Word-of-mouth (WOM), 46
Wordsworth, William, 7
The World According to Garp, 59–60, 146, 286, 318, 342, 372, 388
Wray, Fay, 101
Wrestling Ernest Hemingway, 50
Wright, Edward, 279–80
The Wrong Trousers, 470

The X-Files, 264
X-rating, 494

The Year of Living Dangerously, 257
Year of the Dragon, 501
Yellow (color), 195
Yentl, 425
Yoda, 178, 180
York, Michael, 167
Young, Robert, 137
Young Frankenstein, 432, 434
Young Tom Edison, 437
Your Friends & Neighbors, 497, 502

Zahn, Steve, 284
Zal, Roxana, 513
Zavattini, Cesare, 37
Zea, Kristi, 96
Zeffirelli, Franco, 105, 106, 140, 208, 209, 216, 297, 393, 394
Zelig, 182, 183, 321
Zemeckis, Robert, 177, 424, 435
Zero de Conduite, 364
Zhang Yimou, 192
Zinneman, Fred, 88
Zoom, 163
Zoom lens, 126–28, 129, 131, 314
Zorba the Greek, 128
Zsigmond, Vilmos, 104–5, 105, 111, 211
Zwick, Edward, 296
Zwigoff, Terry, 463